TURING
Problem Solving
and
Program Design

ELLIOT B. KOFFMAN
TEMPLE UNIVERSITY

RIC HOLT
UNIVERSITY OF TORONTO

CHRYSANNE DIMARCO
UNIVERSITY OF WATERLOO

ADDISON-WESLEY PUBLISHERS LIMITED

Don Mills, Ontario • Reading, Massachusetts • Menlo Park, California
New York • Wokingham, England • Amsterdam • Bonn
Sydney • Singapore • Tokyo • Madrid • San Juan

PUBLISHER: Ron Doleman
MANAGING EDITOR: Linda Scott
DESIGN: Brant Cowie/ArtPlus Limited
PAGE MAKEUP: Heather Brunton/ArtPlus Limited
REPRO OUTPUT: TypeLine Express Limited

The author and publisher have taken care in the preparation of this book, but make no expressed or implied warranty of any kind and assume no responsibility for errors or omissions. No liability is assumed for incidental or consequential damages in connection with or arising out of the use of the information contained herein.

Canadian Cataloguing in Publication Data

Koffman, Elliot B.
  Turing : problem solving and program design

Includes index.
ISBN 0-201-42640-4

1. Turing (Computer program language).   2. Turing (Computer program language) – Problems, exercises, etc.   I. Holt, Richard C., 1941–   .   II. DiMarco, Chrysanne. III. Title.

QA76.73.T85K6   1995   005.13'3   C94-931155-3

ISBN 0-201-42640-4

  B C D E   VG   98 97 96

Contents

Preface

This is a textbook for a first course in problem solving and program design using the Turing programming language. It assumes no prior knowledge of computers or programming. High school algebra is sufficient mathematics background for most of the material in this book. A limited knowledge of discrete mathematics, however, is desirable for certain sections.

This book is based directly on Elliot Koffman's highly successful textbook that uses the Pascal language. The reason for using the Turing programming language in this book is that it allows a course to cover more material, because Turing eliminates many of the syntactic difficulties in Pascal.

Problem Solving

The connection between good problem-solving skills and effective software development is established early in Chapter 1 with a section that discusses the art and science of problem solving. Chapter 1 also introduces a methodology for software development based on the systems approach to problem solving consisting of five phases: specify the problem, analyze the problem, design the solution, implement the solution, test the solution. The software development method is used in Chapter 2 to solve the first case study and is applied consistently to all the case studies in the text.

Chapter 3 continues the emphasis on problem solving by discussing top-down design, divide-and-conquer, solution by analogy, and generalizing a solution. An important section of this chapter demonstrates how a Turing program can be derived by editing the documentation that results from systematically following the software development method.

Software Engineering

Many aspects of software engineering are covered in the book. Program style issues are discussed throughout in special displays. The concept of a program as a sequence of control structures is introduced early in Chapter 3. There are sections in several chapters that discuss algorithm tracing, program debugging, and testing.

Chapter 10 concentrates on software engineering. This chapter discusses the system/software life cycle (SLC), prototyping, and programming teams. There is in-depth coverage of all phases of the SLC, including more discussion of informal techniques for program testing (e.g., glass-box versus black-box testing, integration testing, structured walkthroughs) and formal methods for program verification, including a discussion of assertions and loop invariants. This chapter also reviews procedural abstraction and introduces data abstraction. It concludes with a discussion of professional ethics.

Procedural Abstraction

Although there is no universal agreement on when to introduce procedures and procedure parameters, most educators agree on the following points: procedures should be introduced as early as feasible, procedures should generally avoid accessing global data, and procedure parameters are difficult for students to understand. The approach taken in the text is to discuss the importance of program modularization and reusability in Chapter 3 by introducing structure charts, procedures without parameters, and the standard functions of Turing. Sections 3.5 and 3.6 motivate the use of procedures as program-building blocks by showing some applications of procedures without parameters (for example, displaying long lists of user instructions, drawing diagrams). Section 3.7 discusses the need for parameters and the limitations of procedures without parameters, thereby providing a foundation for the later study of parameters. Section 3.8 shows how to use Turing's predefined functions.

Chapter 6, which introduces computer graphics, is an addition that was not present in the Pascal version of the book. This material has the advantages of motivating students (they are intrigued by graphical output) and of providing the basis of many interesting programming examples. The graphics procedures of Turing are particularly easy to teach. In a course that does not introduce graphics, this chapter can be skipped, as the following chapters do not depend on it.

Chapter 7 completes the study of procedures and functions, covering all aspects of parameters lists. The chapter begins by discussing procedures with only value parameters, then user-defined functions with value parameters, and, finally, procedures with both value and variable parameters. An optional section at the end of the chapter introduces recursion.

Some instructors prefer to cover procedures with and without parameters together. You can easily rearrange the sequence of topic coverage to do this. If you want to wait until Chapter 7 to cover procedures with and without parameters, you can defer sections 3.5-3.7 until then. Conversely, if you want to cover procedure parameters earlier, you can cover section 7.1 (value parameters) right after Chapter 3. You can cover sections 7.2-7.4 (user-defined functions, variable parameters, syntax of parameter lists) after completing the first two sections of Chapter 4 (Boolean expressions and the `if` statement).

Pedagogical Features

We employ several pedagogical features to enhance the usefulness of this book as a teaching tool. Some of these features are discussed below.

END-OF-SECTION EXERCISES: Most sections end with a number of self-check exercises. These include exercises that require analysis of program fragments as well as short programming exercises. Answers to selected self-check exercises appear at the back of the book.

END-OF-CHAPTER EXERCISES: Each chapter ends with a set of quick-check exercises with answers.

END-OF-CHAPTER PROJECTS: Most chapters have one or two special programming project pairs where the second project in the pair requires a modification to the solution of the first project in the pair.

EXAMPLES AND CASE STUDIES: The book contains a large number and variety of programming examples. Whenever possible, examples contain complete programs or procedures rather than incomplete program fragments. Each chapter contains one or more substantial case studies that are solved following the software development method.

SYNTAX DISPLAY BOXES: The syntax displays describe the syntax and semantics of each new Turing feature and provide examples.

PROGRAM STYLE DISPLAYS: The program-style displays discuss issues of good programming style.

ERROR DISCUSSIONS AND CHAPTER REVIEW: Each chapter ends with a section that discusses common programming errors. A chapter review includes a table of new Turing constructs.

The material in this book is suitable for a one-semester or a one-quarter course on introductory programming. Drafts of this book have been used for the last two years in such courses at the University of Waterloo by one of the authors (DiMarco).

The Turing Language

At the time of the writing of this book, the Turing language has enjoyed significant acceptance as a language for teaching concepts. This acceptance is most notable in Ontario, where approximately half the high schools and universities use it instead of Pascal or BASIC. On the larger stage, in the United States and in the other countries of the world, Pascal remains the most taught language for introductory programming courses in colleges and universities. However, many have questioned whether Pascal remains the best language choice for teaching.

One of the shortcomings of Pascal is that its syntax demands more attention from students than it deserves — what teacher would not rather dispense with the teaching of syntax and concentrate rather on concepts? With Pascal, the teacher is required to try to explicate the use of semi-colons, dangling else's, loop priming, etc., even though these ideas have little to do with the principles of programming. It is here that Turing is particularly helpful, in that it effectively eliminates such topics through careful language design. In teaching at the University of Toronto, it has been observed that about two more weeks' materials can be covered in one semester using Turing rather than Pascal due to its simpler structure.

Turing is available for the most common platforms used for introductory programming, including IBM PC compatibles, Macintoshes, and Unix systems. A newer version of Turing called OOT (Object-Oriented Turing), which supports object-oriented programming, concurrency, and systems programming features, is also available. Persons interested in the Turing software should contact:

Distribution Manager
Holt Software Associates Inc.
203 College Street, Suite 305
Toronto, Canada M5T 1P9
E-Mail: distrib@csri.toronto.edu
USA phone: 1-800-361-8324
International phone: (416) 978-8363

Acknowledgements

This book evolved out of the need for more and better material to teach computing concepts using the Turing language. Some years ago, Ron Baecker urged that we consider using material such as Koffman's highly successful textbooks.

The impetus to start this project came from the University of Waterloo, where Turing was being used in some programming courses and Pascal in others. The instructors there particularly liked Koffman's text, but the book was available for Pascal and not for Turing. One of the authors (Holt) approached Elliot Koffman about the possibility of a Turing version of the book. He welcomed the project and encouraged us to proceed. In the end, any success that this book may enjoy is due primarily to his carefully collected, well-organized, and well-presented materials, which are the backbone of this book.

Working at the University of Waterloo, one of the authors (DiMarco) produced a Turing version of Arnie Dyck's excellent Pascal teaching materials, which she used in teaching with drafts of the present book. For the last two years, Waterloo students in DiMarco's course have provided input to help improve these drafts.

Ron Doleman, our editor at Addison-Wesley, was consistently helpful and encouraged us in this endeavor, which was sometimes more challenging that we had expected.

We are particularly happy to acknowledge the help our reviewers provided in pointing inconsistencies and errors in our drafts and in helping make this a better book. These people were:

John Carter
Toronto Board of Education, Ontario

Gary Jaye
Stuyvesant High School, New York

Bill Atwood
Concordia University, Quebec

Mary MacCollum
Queen's University, Kingston, Ontario

Mike Bauer
University of Western Ontario, London, Ontario

Jeremy Sills
University of Toronto, Ontario

N. Graham
York University, Downsview, Ontario

Introduction to Computers and Programming

From the 1940s until today—a period of over 50 years—the computer's development has spurred the growth of technology into realms only dreamed of at the start of the century. The computer has also changed the way we live and how we do business. Today we depend on computers to send rockets into space, design and build cars and machines of all types, control chemical plant and nuclear reactors, and help us do our shopping and banking. The computer program's role in this technology is essential; without a list of instructions to follow, the computer is virtually useless. Programming languages allow us to write those programs, and thus to communicate with computers.

In this chapter, we introduce you to the computer and its components. We review the history of computers and describe the different categories of computers. We also describe the major categories of programming languages.

1.1 Electronic Computers Then and Now

It is difficult to live in today's society without having some contact with computers. However, it wasn't always this way. Just a short time ago, computers were fairly mysterious devices that only a small percentage of our population knew much about. Computer "know-how" turned around when advances in solid-state electronics led to large reductions in the size and cost of electronic computers. Today, a personal computer (see Fig. 1.1), which costs less than $2000 and sits on a desk, has as much computational power as one that 10 years ago would have cost more than $100,000 and would have filled a 9-by-12-foot room. This price reduction is even more remarkable when we consider the effects of inflation over the last decade.

Brief History of Computers

If we take the literal definition for a computer as a device for counting or computing, then the abacus might be considered the first computer. Table 1.1 lists some of the important milestones along the path from the abacus to modern-day computers and programming languages. The entries before 1890 list some of the earlier attempts to develop mechanical computing devices.

The first computer that used electronic switching circuits was designed in the late 1930s by Dr. John Atanasoff at Iowa State University. Atanasoff's computer enabled graduate students to perform the calculations necessary for their research in nuclear physics.

The first large-scale, general-purpose electronic digital computer, called the ENIAC, was built in 1946 at the University of Pennsylvania with funding supplied by the U.S. Army. The ENIAC was used for computing ballistics tables, for weather prediction, and for atomic energy calculations. The ENIAC weighed 30 tons and occupied a 30-by-50-foot space (see Fig. 1.2).

FIGURE 1.1   IBM Personal Computer with Mouse

(Photo Courtesy of IBM Canada Ltd.)

FIGURE 1.2   The ENIAC Computer

(Photo Courtesy of Unisys Corporation)

We often use the term "first generation" to refer to electronic computers that used vacuum tubes (1939–1958) as their switching component. The second generation began in 1958 with the changeover to transistors. The third generation began in 1964 with the introduction of integrated circuits. The fourth generation began in 1975 with the advent of large-scale integration. Each generation of computers has been faster, smaller, and less expensive than the generation that preceded it.

A number of milestones in the development of programming languages are also listed in Table 1.1. Fortran (1957) was the first high-level programming language.

Categories of Computers

Computers are classified according to their size and speed. The four categories of computers are microcomputers, minicomputers, mainframes, and supercomputers.

Many of you have seen or used *microcomputers* such as the IBM Personal Computer (see Fig. 1.1). Microcomputers are also called *personal computers* or *desktop computers* because they are used by one person at a time and are small enough to fit on a desk. The largest microcomputers, called *workstations* (see Fig. 1.3), are commonly used by engineers to produce engineering drawings and to assist in the design and development of new products.

Minicomputers are the next largest variety of computers. They generally operate at faster speeds than microcomputers and can store larger quantities of information. Minicomputers can serve several different users simultaneously. A small- or medium-size company might use a minicomputer to perform payroll computations and to keep track of its inventory. Engineers often use minicomputers to control a chemical plant or a production process.

The largest computers are called *mainframes* and *supercomputers*. A large company would have one or more mainframes at its central computing facility. Mainframes are often used as "number crunchers" to generate solutions to systems of equations that characterize an engineering or scientific problem. A mainframe can solve in seconds equations that might take hours to solve on a minicomputer or even days on a microcomputer.

A supercomputer has the computing power of several mainframes and can be used to solve the most complex systems of equations. One example would be using a supercomputer to solve the equations describing the motion of atomic particles. Because supercomputers are too expensive for individual companies or universities to purchase, a number of supercomputer centers have been established in the United States to make supercomputers more accessible to those who need their computational power.

TABLE 1.1	Milestones in Computer Development

2000 BC	The abacus is first used for computations.
1642 AD	Blaise Pascal creates a mechanical adding machine for tax computations. This machine is unreliable.
1670	Gottfried von Leibniz creates a more reliable adding machine, which adds, subtracts, multiplies, divides, and calculates square roots.
1842	Charles Babbage designs an analytical engine to perform general calculations automatically. Ada Augusta (a.k.a. Lady Lovelace) is a programmer for this machine.
1890	Herman Hollerith designs a system to record census data. The information is stored as holes on cards which are interpreted by machines with electrical sensors. Hollerith starts a company that will eventually become IBM.
1939	John Atanasoff, with graduate student Clifford Berry, designs and builds the first electronic digital computer. His project was funded by a grant for $650.
1946	J. Presper Eckert and John Mauchly design and build the ENIAC computer. The ENIAC used 18,000 vacuum tubes and cost $500,000 to build.
1946	John von Neumann proposes that a program be stored in a computer in the same way that data are stored. His proposal (called "von Neumann architecture") is the basis of modern computers.
1951	Eckert and Mauchly build the first general-purpose commercial computer, the UNIVAC 1.
1957	John Backus and his team at IBM complete the first Fortran compiler.
1958	The first computer series to use the transistor as a switching device, the IBM 7090, is introduced.
1958	Seymour Cray builds the first fully transistorized computer, the CDC 1604, for Control Data Corporation.
1964	The first computer using integrated circuits, the IBM 360, is announced.
1975	The first commercial personal computer, the Altair, is introduced.
1975	The first supercomputer, the Cray-1, is announced.
1977	Steve Wozniak and Steve Jobs found Apple Computer.
1981	IBM introduces the IBM PC.
1984	Apple Macintosh is introduced.

FIGURE 1.3   SUN Microsystems SPARCstation 10

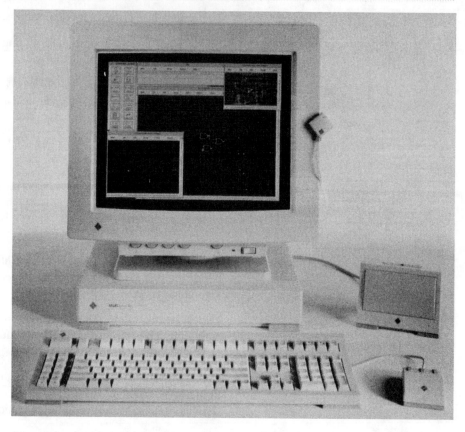

(Photo Courtesy of Sun Microsystems)

The boundary lines between computer categories are constantly shifting. In the late 1950s, mainframe computers could perform only 50 instructions per second. Now, there are much smaller workstations that can perform over 20 million instructions per second. Obviously, there have been tremendous changes in the speed and size of computers in a relatively short time.

1.2   Components of a Computer

Despite large variations in cost, size, and capabilities, modern computers are remarkably similar in a number of ways. Basically, a computer consists of the components shown in Fig. 1.4. The arrows connecting the components show the direction of information flow.

All information that is to be processed by a computer must first be entered into the computer's main memory via an input device. The information in main memory is manipulated by the central processor, and the results of this manipulation are stored in main memory. Information in main memory can be displayed through an output device. Secondary memory is often used for storing large quantities of information in a semi-permanent form. These components and their interaction are described in more detail in the following sections.

FIGURE 1.4   ## Components of a Computer

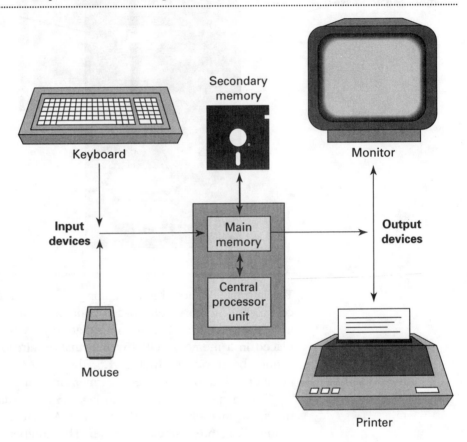

Main Memory

Main memory is used for storing information and programs. All types of information—numbers, names, lists, and even pictures—may be represented and stored in main memory.

Picture the memory of a computer as an ordered sequence of storage locations called memory cells. To be able to store and retrieve (access) information, we must have some way to identify the individual memory cells. To accomplish this, each memory cell has associated with it a unique address that indicates its relative position in memory. Figure 1.5 shows a computer memory consisting of 1000 memory cells with addresses 0 through 999. Almost all large-scale computers have memories consisting of millions of individual cells. Most personal computers have less than one million memory cells.

FIGURE 1.5 A Computer Memory with 1000 Cells

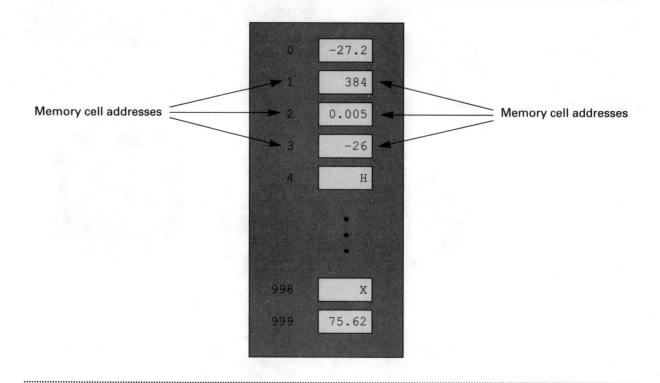

The information stored in a memory cell is called the contents of a memory cell. Every memory cell always contains some information, although we may have no idea what that information is. Whenever new information is placed in a memory cell, any information already there is destroyed and cannot be retrieved. In Fig. 1.5, the contents of memory cell 3 is the number –26, and the contents of memory cell 4 is the letter H.

The memory cells shown in Fig. 1.5 are actually aggregates, or collections, of smaller units called *bytes*. A byte is the amount of storage required to store a single character. The number of bytes in a memory cell varies from computer to computer. A byte is an aggregate of even smaller units of storage called *bits*, which are single binary digits (0 or 1). There are generally eight bits to a byte.

Each value is represented by a particular pattern of zeros and ones. To store a value, the computer sets each bit of a selected memory cell to 0 or 1, thereby destroying what was previously in that bit. To retrieve a value from a memory cell, the computer copies the pattern of zeros and ones stored in that cell to another storage area, the memory buffer register, where the bit pattern can be processed. The copy operation does not destroy the bit pattern currently in that memory cell.

The process just described is the same regardless of the kind of information—character, number, or program instruction—stored in a memory cell.

Central Processor Unit

The *central processor unit* (CPU) performs the actual processing or manipulation of information stored in memory. The CPU can retrieve information from memory. This information may be either data or instructions for manipulating data. It can also store the results of these manipulations back in memory for later use.

The CPU control unit coordinates all activities of the computer. It determines which operations should be carried out and in what order; it then transmits coordinating control signals to the computer components.

The CPU also performs a variety of arithmetic operations, including addition, subtraction, multiplication, and division. These arithmetic operations are performed on data that are stored in main memory; the computational results are then saved in memory. A typical CPU can perform an arithmetic operation in about a millionth of a second. The CPU also consists of electronic circuitry to compare information and to make decisions based on the results of the comparison.

Input and Output Devices

Input and output (I/O) *devices* enable us to communicate with the computer. Specifically, I/O devices provide us with the means to enter data for a computation and to observe the results of that computation.

A common I/O device used with large computers is the computer terminal. A *computer terminal* is both an input and an output device. A terminal consists of a keyboard (used for entering information) and a *monitor* (used for displaying information). If you are using a microcomputer, you will also use a keyboard and monitor (screen) as I/O devices. The keyboard and monitor may be built into the computer or connected to it by cables.

A computer keyboard resembles a typewriter keyboard except that it has some extra keys for performing special functions. On the IBM PC/AT keyboard shown in Fig. 1.6, the 12 keys in the top row labeled F1 through F12 are function keys. The function performed by pressing one of these keys depends on the program that is executing. Other keys highlighted in Fig. 1.6 are used to delete characters, to move the cursor (an electronic pointer displayed on the screen), or to "Enter" a line of data typed at the keyboard.

Another common input device is a mouse (see Fig. 1.1). A mouse is used to move the cursor around the display screen. You can select an operation by moving the cursor to the picture on the screen (called an *icon*) that represents that operation and then pressing a mouse button.

The information displayed on a monitor screen is lost when new information appears on the screen. If you want *hard-copy* or printed output, then you have to send your computational results to an output device called a *printer*.

FIGURE 1.6   Keyboard for the IBM PC/AT

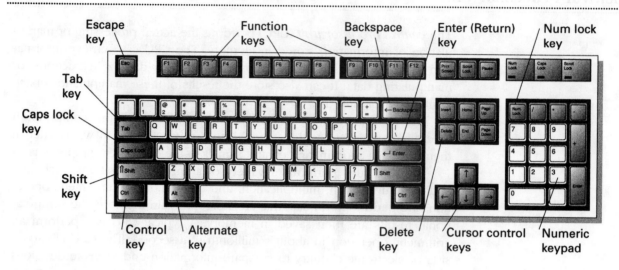

Secondary Memory

Most computers have a limited amount of main memory. Consequently, *secondary memory* provides additional data-storage capability on most computer systems. For example, a disk drive, which stores data on a disk, is a common secondary storage device for today's personal computers.

There are two kinds of disks: *hard disks* and *floppy disks*. A computer may have one or more drives of each kind. A hard disk normally cannot be removed from its drive, so the storage area on a hard disk is often shared by all the users of a computer. However, each computer user may have his or her own floppy disks that can be inserted into a disk drive as needed (see Fig. 1.7). Hard disks can store much more data than can floppy disks and operate much more quickly, but they are also much more expensive.

Many different kinds of information, such as a computer program, payroll data from a business, or data from earthquake seismic readings taken by a research center, can be stored on a disk. Each of these collections of information is called a file. You must give a file a unique name when you first store it on a disk, so that the computer can retrieve it at a later date.

Comparison of Main and Secondary Memory

Main memory is much faster and more expensive than secondary memory. The CPU can manipulate only data that are in main memory; therefore, data in secondary memory must be transferred to main memory before processing. Data in main memory are volatile and disappear when you switch off the computer. Data in secondary memory are permanent and do not disappear when the computer is switched off.

FIGURE 1.7   Inserting a Floppy Disk into a Disk Drive

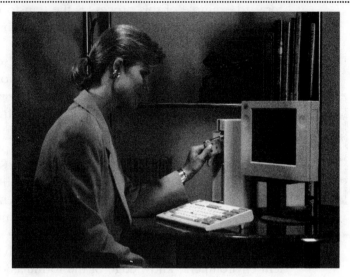

(Photo Courtesy of IBM Canada Ltd.)

Exercises for Section 1.2

Self-Check

1. What are the contents of memory cells 0 and 999 in Fig. 1.5? What memory cells contain the letter X and the fraction 0.005?
2. Explain the purpose of main memory, the central processor, and the disk drive and disk. What input and output devices will be used with your computer?

1.3 Problem Solving and Programming

We mentioned earlier that a computer cannot think; therefore, to do any useful work, a computer must be provided with a *program*, that is, a list of instructions. Programming a computer is a lot more involved than simply writing a list of instructions. Problem solving is a crucial component of programming. Before we can write a program to solve a particular problem, we must consider carefully all aspects of the problem and then develop and organize its solution.

The Art and Science of Problem Solving

To succeed in academics or in the real world, you must be able to solve problems. Problem-solving ability is a combination of art and science. The art of problem solving is the transforming of a description of a problem into a form that permits a mechanical solution. A relatively straightforward example of this process is the transformation of an algebra word problem into a set of algebraic equations, which can then be solved for one or more unknowns.

In the real world, this process is more difficult because problem descriptions are often incomplete, imprecise, or ambiguous. The successful problem solver must be able to ask the right questions to clarify the problem and obtain any information missing from the problem statement. Next, the problem solver must analyze the problem and extract its essential features, identifying what is provided (the problem inputs) and what is required (the problem outputs). The problem solver must also be able to determine whether any constraints or simplifying assumptions can be applied to facilitate the problem solution. Often we cannot solve the most general case of a problem; we must make some realistic assumptions that limit or constrain the problem so that it can be solved.

The science part of problem solving involves knowledge of the problem environment, knowledge of the formulas or equations that characterize the environment, and the ability to apply and manipulate those formulas. Using this knowledge, the problem solver develops a series of steps whose successful completion will lead to the problem solution. Once the solution is obtained, the problem solver must verify its accuracy by comparing the computed results with observed results.

Planning and Checking Your Programs

Like most programming students, at first you will probably spend a great deal of time in the computer laboratory entering your programs. You will spend more time later removing the errors that inevitably will crop up in your programs.

It is tempting to rush to the computer laboratory and start entering your program as soon as you have some idea of how to write it. Resist this temptation. Instead, think carefully about the problem and its solution before you write any program instructions. When you have a potential solution in mind, plan it out beforehand (using either paper and pencil or a word processor) and modify it if necessary before you write the program.

Once you have written the program out, *desk check* your solution by carefully performing each instruction much as the computer would. To desk check a program, simulate the result of each program instruction using sample data that are easy to manipulate (for example, small whole numbers). Compare these results with the expected results and make any necessary corrections to your program. Only then should you go to the computer laboratory and enter your program.

In this text, we stress a methodology for program solving and programming that has proved useful in helping students learn to program. This technique is described next.

1.4 The Software Development Method

Students in many subject areas receive instruction in specific problem-solving methods. For example, business students are encouraged to follow a *systems approach* to problem solving; engineering and science students are encouraged to follow the *engineering and scientific method*. Although these problem-solving methods are associated with very different fields of study, their essential ingredients are quite similar.

Software engineers are involved with the design and implementation of reliable software systems. The title emphasizes that programmers, like engineers, are concerned with developing practical, reliable solutions to problems. However, the programmer's product is a software system rather than a physical system. Software engineers and software developers use the following *software development method* for solving programming problems.

1. **Requirements specification.** State the problem and gain a clear understanding of what is required for its solution. This sounds easy, but it can be the most critical part of problem solving. A good problem solver must be able to recognize and define the problem precisely. If the problem is not totally defined, you must study the problem carefully, eliminating the aspects that are unimportant and zeroing in on the root problem.
2. **Analysis.** Identify problem inputs, desired outputs, and any additional requirements or constraints. Identify what information is supplied as problem data and what results should be computed and displayed. Also, determine the required form and units in which the results should be displayed (for example, as a table with specific column headings).
3. **Design.** Develop a list of steps (called an *algorithm*) to solve the problem, then verify that the algorithm solves the problem as intended. Writing the algorithm is often the most difficult part of the problem-solving process. Once you have the algorithm, you should verify that it is correct before proceeding further.
4. **Implementation.** Implement the algorithm as a program, which requires knowledge of a particular programming language. Each algorithm step must be converted into a statement in that programming language.
5. **Testing and verification.** Test the completed program and verify that it works as expected. Don't rely on just one test case – run the program several times using different sets of data.

The first three steps in the software development method are critical; if they are not done properly, you will either solve the wrong problem or produce an awkward, inefficient solution. To perform these steps successfully, you must read the problem statement carefully before you attempt to solve the problem. You may need to read each problem statement two or three times. The first time, you should get a general idea of what is being asked. The second time you should try to answer these questions: What information should the solution provide? What data do I have to work with? The answer to the first question will tell you the desired results, or the *problem outputs*. The answer to the second question will tell you the data provided, or the *problem inputs*. It may be helpful to underline the phrases in the problem statement that identify the inputs and outputs.

As already indicated, the design phase is often the most difficult part of the problem-solving process. When you write an algorithm, you should first list the major steps of the problem that need to be solved (the *subproblems*). Don't try to list each and every step imaginable; instead, concentrate on the overall strategy. Once you have a list of the subproblems, you can attack each one individually, in this way adding detail, or *refining the algorithm*. The process of solving a problem by breaking it up into its smaller subproblems is called *divide and conquer* and is a basic strategy for all kinds of problem-solving activities.

The software development method can be used with any programming language; indeed, only the implementation phase really requires detailed knowledge of a language or a particular computer. In industry, the testing phase is often carried out by individuals who do not specialize in programming but are experts in developing good tests of programs.

1.5 Programming Languages

Programming languages fall into three broad categories: machine, assembly, and high-level languages. *High-level languages* are more popular with programmers than the other two language categories. One reason for their popularity is that they are much easier to use than machine and assembly languages. Another reason is that a high-level language program is *portable*, which means that it can be used without modification on many different types of computers. An assembly language or a machine language program, on the other hand, can be used on only one type of computer.

Some common high-level languages are FORTRAN, BASIC, COBOL, Pascal, C, Ada, and Turing. Each language was designed with a specific purpose in mind. FORTRAN is an acronym for FORmula TRANslation and its principal users have been engineers and scientists. BASIC (Beginners All-purpose Symbolic Instructional Code) was designed to be a language that could be easily learned and used by students. COBOL (COmmon Business Oriented Language) is used primarily for business data-processing operations. Pascal was designed as a language for teaching structured programming techniques. C is a high-level language that is very powerful and flexible; programmers often use the C language to write system software. Ada is a language developed by the USA Department of Defense for use by their contractors. An example application would be an Ada program for controlling a missile. Turing is a language that is designed for teaching programming and is used as well for advanced software development.

An important feature of high-level languages is that they allow us to write program statements that resemble everyday language. We can reference data that are stored in memory using descriptive names (e.g., `Name`, `Rate`, `Radius`, `Weight`) rather than numeric memory-cell addresses. We can also describe operations that we would like performed using familiar symbols. For example, in several high-level languages, the statement

```
Price := Cost + Profit
```

means add `Cost` to `Profit` and store the result in `Price`.

Machine language is the native tongue of a computer. Each machine language instruction is a binary string (string of zeros and ones) that specifies an operation and the memory cells involved in the operation. The high-level language statement above might be written as

```
0010 0000 0000 0100
0100 0000 0000 0101
0011 0000 0000 0110
```

in a machine language. Obviously, what is easiest for a computer to understand is most difficult for a person and vice versa.

A computer can execute only programs that are in machine language. Consequently, a high-level language program must first be translated into machine language. This process is described in the next section.

Exercises for Section 1.5

Self-Check

1. What do you think the high-level language statements below mean?

```
X := A + B + C
X := Y / Z
D := C - B + A
X := X + 1
```

2. Which high-level languages were designed for teaching programming? Which was designed for business applications? Which was designed for translating scientific formulas?
3. Which type of language has instructions that are binary numbers?

1.6 Processing a High-Level Language Program

Before the computer can process a high-level language program, you must enter it at the terminal. The program will be stored in secondary memory (on disk). Recall that information stored on disk is organized into separate entities called files. A file that contains a program is called a *source file*. The programmer uses a program called an *editor* to enter the program and to save it as a source file. The editor program is part of the system software.

A Sample Turing Program

Before beginning our in-depth study of Turing, we will examine a short program. Don't worry about understanding the details of this program yet; they will all be explained later.

EXAMPLE 1.1
Figure 1.8 contains a Turing program followed by a sample execution of that program. The information entered by the program user is in **boldface** in the sample execution.

The program user enters the cross-sectional area (value is 25.5) and length (value is 65.0) of a steel beam, and the program computes the beam's volume (volume = area × length) and weight (weight = volume × density). The density of steel is assumed to be 0.28 pounds per cubic inch. The beam's volume and weight are displayed in the last two lines of Fig. 1.8.

FIGURE 1.8   Sample Turing Program

```
% The "beam" program
const Density := 0.28
var Area, Length, Volume, Weight : real
put "Enter cross-sectional area in square inches"
get Area
put "Enter beam length in inches"
get Length
Volume := Area * Length
Weight := Volume * Density
put "Volume in cubic inches is ", Volume
put "Weight in pounds is ", Weight
```

```
Enter cross-sectional area in square inches
25.5
Enter beam length in inches
65.0
Volume in cubic inches is 1657.5
Weight in pounds is 464.1
```

Preparing a Program for Execution

Once the source file has been entered into the computer, it needs to be translated into machine language (see Fig. 1.9). A compiler program processes the source file and attempts to translate each statement. Often, one or more statements in the source file will contain a *syntax error*. This means that these statements do not correspond exactly to the syntax (grammar) of the high-level language. In this case, the compiler will cause some error messages to be displayed.

FIGURE 1.9 Preparing a Program for Execution

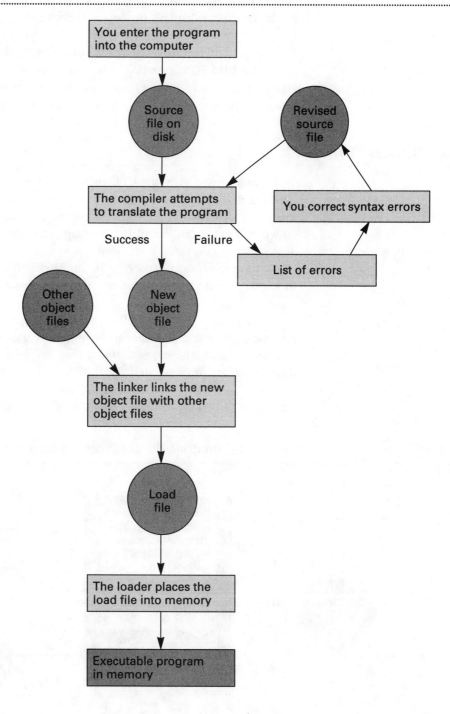

At this point, you can make changes to your source file and have the compiler process it again. If there are no more errors, the compiler will create an *object file*, which is your program translated into machine language. The object file is commonly stored in secondary memory. The *linker program* combines the object file with any additional object files (for example, programs for input and output) that may be needed into a *load file*. Finally, the *loader* program places the load file into main memory, ready for execution. This process is shown in Fig. 1.9. The editor, compiler, linker, and loader programs are part of the system software.

In special *programming environments*, such as the Turing environments for IBM PC compatibles, Macintoshes, and Unix, all these programs are integrated and the steps are carried out automatically for you when you give the command to run your source program.

Executing a Program

To execute a program, the CPU must examine each program instruction in main memory and send out the command signals required to carry out the instruction. Normally, the instructions are executed in sequence; however, as we will see later, the CPU may skip over some instructions or execute some instructions more than once.

During execution, data may be entered into memory and manipulated in some specified way. Then, the result of this data manipulation will be displayed.

Figure 1.10 shows the effect of executing the program shown earlier for computing the volume and weight of a steel beam. The first step requires entering the cross-sectional area and length of the beam. In step 2, these data are manipulated by the central processor as directed by the program, and the results of computations are stored in memory. In the final step, the computational results are displayed on the screen.

FIGURE 1.10   Flow of Information during Program Execution

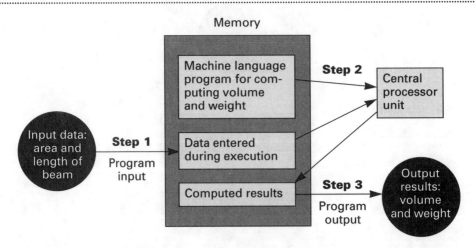

Exercises for Section 1.6

Self-Check

1. What is the role of the compiler? What is a syntax error? Which file can contain syntax errors?
2. What is the source file? An object file? A load file? Which do you create and which does the compiler create? Which does the linker create and which is processed by the loader? What do the linker and loader do?

1.7 Using the Computer

After you write a program, you must type it into the computer using a keyboard. We discussed the process of entering and executing a program in the last section. The mechanics of doing this differ on each computer system; we will provide a general description of the process in this section.

Operating Systems

Some of you will be using a *timeshared* computer. Universities often use timeshared computers for instructional purposes. In a timeshared environment, many users are connected by terminals to one central computer, and all users share the central facilities. Many of you will be using a personal computer, which is a smaller, desktop computer used by one individual at a time. Regardless of what type of computer you use, you will need to interact with a supervisory program, called the *operating system*, within the computer. In timeshared computers, the operating system allocates the central resources among many users. Some operating system tasks are as follows:

- validating user identification and account number (timeshared system)
- making the editor, compiler, linker, or loader programs available
- allocating memory and processor time
- providing input and output facilities
- retrieving needed files
- saving new files

In smaller personal computers, the operating system must perform all but the first task.

Each computer has its own special *control language* for communicating with its operating system. We cannot really provide the details here, but we will discuss the general process next. Your instructor will provide the specific commands for your system.

Booting or Logging-On

Before you can use a personal computer, you first need to *boot* the computer. Booting a personal computer may involve inserting a floppy disk containing the operating system into disk drive A and switching on the computer. On computers with a hard disk, you only need to switch on the computer. Once booted, the operating system displays a prompt (for example, A>) to indicate that it is ready to accept commands. Figure 1.11 demonstrates booting an IBM Personal Computer using MS-DOS®; the computer user enters the characters that are in **boldface**; the other characters are those that the operating system displays.

FIGURE 1.11 Booting a Personal Computer

```
MS-DOS Version 3.3

Current date is Wed 03-02-1994
Enter new date (mm-dd-yy):

Current time is 0:01:43.53
Enter new time: 10:30

A>
```

Before you can use a timeshared computer, you must log on, or connect, to the computer. To log on, you enter your account name and password (given to you by your instructor). For security reasons, your password is not displayed. Figure 1.12 demonstrates this process for the Digital Equipment Corporation™ VAX computer. The computer user enters the characters that are in **boldface**; the other characters are those that the operating system displays. The timeshared operating system shown (named VMS Version 5.1) displays the symbol $ as a prompt.

FIGURE 1.12 Logging on to a Timeshared Computer

```
Username: Koffman
Password: Madaket

CIS Department Vax-11/780 VMS V5.1

Last interactive login on Friday,
        28-April-1994 10:20

$
```

Creating a Source File

Once you have booted your personal computer or logged on to a time-shared computer, you can begin to create your program. In many cases, you will use a special program called an *editor* to enter your Turing program and save it in main memory. If you want a record of the program once it is entered, you must save it as a permanent file on disk; otherwise, your program disappears when your session with the editor is over.

In an integrated programming environment, once you have your source program in the editor, you have only to give a simple command, such as pressing the Control key and the R key (R for run). Your program will be compiled, and if it has no syntax errors, it will be run.

In the older and more traditional approach to programming, you would first use an editor to create your program and separately use a compiler to translate your program. Once you have logged on to a time-shared computer or booted up a personal computer, you would carry out these steps to create and save a program file:

1. Access the editor program.
2. Indicate that you are creating a new file.
3. Enter each line of the program file.
4. Name your file (if not named in step 2) and save it as a permanent file in secondary memory.
5. Exit from the editor.

Make sure you remember to perform step 5. The file created by the editor program is stored in main memory. Unless you save your editor file in secondary memory, it will be lost when you exit from the editor program.

Running the Program

Once you have created your program and you are satisfied that each line is entered correctly, you can attempt to compile, link, load, and execute it.

If your program will not compile because it contains syntax errors, you must edit, or correct, the program. When using older systems without a programming environment, you would have to follow these steps to correct and re-execute a program file:

1. Reaccess the editor program.
2. Access your program file.
3. Correct the statements containing syntax errors.
4. Save your edited program file.
5. Compile, link, load, and execute the new program file.

Exercises for Section 1.7

Self-Check

1. Will you be using a personal computer or a time-shared computer? What model computer? What operating system? What operating system command(s) will you use to edit and run Turing programs?

Programming

1. Try to enter and save the program shown in Fig. 1.8 as a source file on your computer system. Press the Enter or Return key after you type in each line. After you save the program on disk, attempt to run it.

Chapter Review

We introduced the basic components of a computer. They are main memory and secondary memory, the central processor, and the input and output devices. Remember these important facts about computers.

- A memory cell is never empty, but its initial contents may be meaningless to your program.
- The current contents of a memory cell are destroyed whenever new information is placed in that cell.
- Programs must first be placed in the memory of the computer before they can be executed.
- Data cannot be manipulated by the computer until they are first stored in memory.
- A computer cannot think for itself; you must instruct it how to perform a task by writing a program.
- Programming a computer can be fun—if you are patient, organized, and careful.

We reviewed the history of computing and discussed the four generations of computers. We also described the different categories of computers: microcomputers, minicomputers, mainframes, and supercomputers. Larger computers are generally faster and more powerful than smaller computers.

We also described the differences between high-level languages and machine language. We showed an example of a source program in one high-level language, Turing. We described how a source program is translated into a machine language object file by a compiler, linked with other object files by a linker, and finally loaded into memory, ready for execution, by a loader. We discussed how to use a computer and its operating system to accomplish the tasks of entering a new program and running it on a computer.

In the remainder of the text, we will introduce you to features of the Turing language and provide rules for using these features. You must remember throughout that, unlike the rules of English, the rules of Turing are precise and allow no exceptions. The compiler will be unable to translate Turing instructions that violate these rules.

Quick-Check Exercises

1. The _____ translates a(n) _____ program into
   _____.
2. After a program is executed, all program results are automatically displayed. True or false?
3. Specify the correct order for these four operations: execution, linking, translation, loading.
4. A high-level language program is saved on disk as a(n) _____ file.
5. The _____ finds syntax errors in the _____ file.
6. A machine language program is saved on disk as a(n) _____ file.
7. The _____ is used to create and save the source file.
8. The _____ creates the load file.
9. The _____ places the _____ file into memory.
10. Computers are becoming (more/less) expensive and (bigger/smaller) in size.
11. The _____ was the first large-scale, general-purpose electronic computer. It (was/was not) a stored-program computer.
12. Indicate whether each characteristic that follows applies to secondary memory or main memory: provides permanent storage of files; used by the editor program for temporary storage of a new file; provides storage of data and program results during program execution; provides relatively inexpensive storage; quantity of storage is limited; accessed by the CPU during program execution.

Answers to Quick-Check Exercises
1. Compiler, high-level language, machine language
2. False
3. Translation, linking, loading, execution
4. Source
5. Compiler, source
6. Object
7. Editor
8. Linker
9. Loader, load
10. Less expensive, smaller
11. ENIAC, was not
12. Secondary, main, main, secondary, main, main

Review Questions

1. List at least three kinds of information stored in a computer.
2. List two functions of the CPU.
3. List two input devices, two output devices, and two secondary storage devices.
4. A computer can think. True or false?
5. List three categories of programming languages.
6. Give three advantages of programming in a high-level language such as Turing.
7. Differentiate between systems software and applications software.
8. What processes are needed to transform a Turing program into a machine-language program ready for execution?
9. Describe the purpose of the following computer components: main memory, secondary memory, central processor.
10. Which memory component provides permanent storage for program files? Which is less expensive? Which is limited in size?

CHAPTER 2

Problem Solving
and Turing

Programming is a problem-solving activity. This means that if you are a good problem solver, you are likely to become a good programmer. Therefore, one important goal of this book is to help you improve your problem solving ability. We believe that it is beneficial to approach each programming problem in a systematic and consistent way. This chapter shows how to apply the software development method to solve programming problems.

This chapter also introduces Turing, which is a high-level, general-purpose programming language that was developed in 1982 by Ric Holt and Jim Cordy at the University of Toronto in Canada. (A general-purpose programming language is one that can be put to many different applications.) Turing is a good programming language for teaching programming concepts partly because its syntax is easy to learn. One reason for Turing's popularity is the fact that Turing compilers are available for many personal computers and workstations.

Turing facilitates writing *structured programs*—programs that are relatively easy to read, understand, and keep in good working order—which is now accepted as standard programming practice.

To ensure that a Turing program written on one computer will also execute on another, there is a *language standard* which describes all Turing language constructs and specifies their syntax.

This chapter describes Turing statements for performing computations and statements for entering data and displaying results.

Besides introducing problem solving and Turing, the chapter describes how to run Turing programs interactively and in batch mode. In interactive programming, the program user enters data during program execution; in batch mode, the program user must prepare a data file before program execution begins.

2.1 Applying the Software Development Method

In this textbook, we will provide case solutions for a number of programming problems, following the software development method outlined in Section 1.4. We begin each case study with a statement of the problem. As part of the problem analysis, we will identify the data requirements for the problem, indicating the problem inputs and desired outputs. Next, we will develop and refine the initial algorithm. Finally, we will implement this algorithm as a Turing program. We will provide a sample run of the program, and perform a more complete test of the program.

We walk you through a sample case study next. In this example, we provide a running commentary on the process being followed so that you will be able to apply it to other situations.

✖ Case Study:

Converting Units of Measurement

1. Problem

You work in a store that imports fabric. Most of the fabric you receive is measured in square meters; however, the store's customers want to know the equivalent amount in square yards. You need to write a program that performs this conversion.

2. Analysis

The first step in understanding this problem is to determine what you are being asked to do. It should be clear that you must convert from one system of measurement to another, but are you supposed to convert from square meters to square yards, or vice-versa? The problem states that you receive fabric measured in square meters, so the problem input is *fabric size in square meters*. Your customers want to know the *equivalent amount in square yards*, which must be your problem output. To write the program, we need to know the relationship between square meters and square yards. By examining a metric table, we find that one square meter equals 1.196 square yards.

We summarize the data requirements and relevant formulas below. As shown below, we will use the name `SqMeters` to identify the memory cell that will contain the problem input and the name `SqYards` to identify the memory cell that will contain the program result or the problem output.

DATA REQUIREMENTS AND FORMULAS

Problem inputs

```
SqMeters        % The fabric size in square meters
```

Problem outputs

```
SqYards         % The fabric size in square yards
```

RELEVANT FORMULAS
1 square meter equals 1.196 square yards

3. Design

Next, we try to formulate the algorithm that we must follow to solve the problem. We begin by listing the three major steps, or subproblems, of the algorithm.

ALGORITHM
1. Read the fabric size in square meters.
2. Convert the fabric size to square yards.
3. Display the fabric size in square yards.

Next, we decide whether any steps of the algorithm need further refinement or whether they are perfectly clear as stated. Step 1 (reading data) and step 3 (displaying a value) are basic steps and require no further refinement. Step 2 is fairly straightforward, but it might help to add some detail. The refinement of step 2 follows.

Step 2 Refinement
    2.1   The fabric size in square yards is 1.196 times the fabric size in square meters.

The complete algorithm with refinements is shown below. The algorithm resembles an outline for a paper. The refinement of step 2 is numbered as step 2.1 and is indented under step 2. We list the complete algorithm with refinements below to show you how it all fits together.

ALGORITHM WITH REFINEMENTS
1. Read the fabric size in square meters.
2. Convert the fabric size to square yards.
    2.1   The fabric size in square yards is 1.196 times the fabric size in square meters.
3. Display the fabric size in square yards.

4. Implementation

To implement the solution, we must write the algorithm as a Turing program. To do this, we must first tell the Turing compiler about the problem data requirements; that is, what memory cell names we are using and what kind of data will be stored in each memory cell. Next, we convert each algorithm step into one or more Turing statements. If an algorithm step has been refined, we convert its refinements into Turing statements. You will be able to do this yourself as you learn more about Turing.

    Figure 2.1 shows the Turing program along with a sample execution (the last three lines of the figure). Don't worry about understanding the details of this program yet. We will give an overview of the main points of the program here and go into more detail later in the chapter.

FIGURE 2.1

Metric Conversion Program

```
% The "Metric" conversion program
% Convert square meters to square yards

const MetersToYards := 1.196  % conversion constant

var SqMeters : real    % Input - fabric size in meters
var SqYards : real     % Output - fabric size in yards

% Read the fabric size in square meters.
put "Enter the fabric size in square meters >"
get SqMeters

% Convert the fabric size to square yards.
SqYards := MetersToYards * SqMeters
```

```
% Display the fabric size in square yards.
put "The fabric size in square yards is ", SqYards
```

```
Enter the fabric size in square meters >
2.00
The fabric size in square yards is 2.392
```

One thing you might notice in Fig. 2.1 is that a number of lines of text begin with a percent sign % such as

```
% Convert square meters to square yards
```

In Turing, a percent sign denotes a program comment. A program *comment* is like a parenthetical remark in a sentence; its purpose is to provide supplementary information to the person reading the program. Program comments are ignored by the Turing compiler and are not translated into machine language.

The program consists of *declarations* and *statements.* A declaration tells the compiler that a memory cell is needed in the program; the declarations are based on the problem data requirements identified earlier during the problem analysis. Memory cells are needed for storing the variables SqMeters and SqYards, and for storing the conversion constant MetersToYards (value is 1.196).

The Turing statements are translated into machine language and later executed. Each statement that begins with the word put causes a line of program output to be displayed. The first such line

```
put "Enter the fabric size in square meters >"
```

displays the first output line in the sample execution, which asks the user to type in a value in meters. The next line

```
get SqMeters
```

reads the data value typed by the program user (2.00) into the memory cell named SqMeters. The program statement

```
SqYards := MetersToYards * SqMeters
```

computes the equivalent fabric size in square yards by multiplying the size in square meters by 1.196; the product is stored in memory cell SqYards.

Finally, the program statement

```
put "The fabric size in square yards is ", SqYards
```

displays a message string and the value of SqYards. The value of SqYards is displayed as a real number (2.392).

5. Testing

The last three lines of Fig. 2.1 show one sample run of this program, but how do we know that the program result is correct? You should always examine program results carefully to make sure that they make sense. In this run, a fabric size of 2.00 square meters is converted to 2.392 square yards as it should be. To verify that the program works properly, we should enter a few more test values of square meters. We really don't need to try more than a few test cases to verify that a simple program like this is correct. ✖

Exercises for Section 2.1

Self-Check

1. List the five steps of the Software Development Method.
2. What would the data requirements and formulas look like for a computer program that converts a weight in pounds to a weight in kilograms?

2.2 An Overview of Turing

The rest of this chapter provides a description of some basic features of the Turing programming language. We will base our discussion on the program in Fig. 2.1 and the program in the next example.

EXAMPLE 2.1
Figure 2.2 contains a Turing program and a sample execution of that program (the last four lines of the figure). The program displays a personalized message to the program user.

FIGURE 2.2   Printing a Welcoming Message

```
% The "Hello" program
% Display the user's first and last names.

var FirstName, LastName : string
% a person's first and last names

put "Enter first and last names and press return >"
get FirstName, LastName
put "Hello ", FirstName, " ", LastName, "."
put "We hope you enjoy studying Turing!"
```

```
Enter first and last names and press return >
Bob Jones
Hello Bob Jones.
We hope you enjoy studying Turing!
```

The line starting with `var` identifies the two memory cells (`FirstName` and `LastName`) that will be used to store the person's name. The program instruction

```
get FirstName, LastName
```

reads the two words `Bob` and `Jones` (typed by the program user) into the two memory cells listed, with one string of letters per cell. The next line

```
put "Hello ", FirstName, " ", LastName, "."
```

displays `Bob Jones` after the message string `"Hello "`. The string `" "` causes a blank to be printed between `Bob` and `Jones`, and the string `"."` causes a period to be printed after `Jones`.

One of the nicest things about Turing is that it lets us write programs that resemble English. At this point, you probably can read and understand the two sample programs, even though you do not know how to write your own programs. In the following sections, you'll learn more details about the Turing programs we've looked at so far.

Keywords and Identifiers

Each line of the programs above satisfies the syntax rules for the Turing language. Each line contains a number of different elements such as keywords, standard identifiers, special symbols, and names for memory cells. Let's look at the first three categories. The keywords all appear in lowercase; they have special meaning in Turing and cannot be used for other purposes. The reserved words appearing in Figs. 2.1 and 2.2 follow.

```
const, var, put, get, real, string
```

Standard identifiers also have special meaning and they cannot be used by the programmer for other purposes. For example, the standard identifier `sqrt` (square root) is used for taking square roots and cannot be used to name a memory cell.

Some symbols (e.g., `=`, `*`, `:=`) have special meaning in Turing. The other identifiers, such as `LastName`, appearing in the programs in Figs. 2.1 and 2.2 are described in more detail next.

Exercises for Section 2.2

Self-Check

1. Can we use standard identifiers as names of memory cells in a program? Can we use reserved words instead?
2. Do you think that you could write a program that used `get` as the name of a memory cell for storing a data value and `put` as the name of a memory cell for storing a program result?

PROGRAM
STYLE

> **USE OF UPPERCASE AND LOWERCASE IN TURING PROGRAMS**
> Throughout the text, issues of good programming style will be discussed in displays such as this one. Programming style displays will provide guidelines for improving the appearance and readability of programs. Most programs will be examined or studied by someone else. A program that follows some consistent style conventions will be easier to read and understand than one that is sloppy or inconsistent. Although these conventions make it easier for humans to understand programs, they have no effect whatsoever on the computer.
>
> Reserved words will always appear in lowercase in programs in this text, and identifiers will be in mixed uppercase and lowercase. The first letter of each identifier will be capitalized. If an identifier consists of two or more words pushed together (e.g., `FirstName`), the first letter of each word will be capitalized. We recommend that you follow this convention in your programs so that it will be easy to distinguish reserved words from other identifiers.
>
> The compiler differentiates between uppercase and lowercase. This means that you can use `Get` for the name of a memory cell, but you can not use the reserved word `get`. However, we recommend that you avoid identifiers such as `Get`, which are easily confused with reserved words.

2.3 Declarations in Turing Programs

We tell the Turing compiler the names of memory cells used in a program through constant and variable declarations. The *constant declaration*

```
const MetersToYards := 1.196
```

specifies that the identifier `MetersToYards` will be used as the name of the memory cell that always contains the number `1.196`; the identifier `MetersToYards` is called a *constant*. Only data values that never change (e.g., the number of square yards in a square meter is always `1.196`) should be associated with an identifier that is a constant. Instructions that attempt to change the value of a constant cannot appear in a Turing program.

The memory cells used for storing a program's input data and its computational results are called *variables* because the value stored in a variable may change (and usually does) as the program executes. The *variable declaration*

```
var FirstName, LastName : string
```

in Fig. 2.2 gives the names of two memory cells used for storing strings of characters. The variable declarations

```
var SqMeters: real     % Input - fabric size in meters
var SqYards : real     % Output - fabric size in yards
```

in Fig. 2.1 gives the names of two memory cells used to store real numbers (for example, `30.0`, `562.57`). The variable names listed above are also identifiers.

In a variable declaration, the keyword (for example, `real`, `int`, `string`) appearing to the right of the symbol : tells the Turing compiler the *data type* (for example, a real number, an integer, or a string of characters) of the information stored in a particular variable. A variable that is used for storing an integer value (a number without a decimal point) has data type `int`. Data types will be discussed in more detail in Section 2.6.

You have quite a bit of freedom in selecting identifiers that you use in a program. The syntactic rules are:

1. An identifier must always begin with a letter.
2. An identifier must consist only of letters, digits and the underscore character _.
3. You cannot use a Turing keyword or standard indentifier as an identifer.

Some valid and invalid identifiers are listed below.

Valid identifiers

```
Letter2, Inches, Cent, CentPerInch, Hello,
FirstName, Cent_Per_Inch
```

Invalid identifiers

```
1Letter, const, var, Two*Four, Joe's
```

You can use an identifier of any length up to 50 characters. The Turing compiler uses all the letters in each identifier when trying to match one identifier to another. Although the identifier

```
Cent_Per_Inch
```

is valid, we prefer the style that eliminates underscores and just uses upper case letters, as in `CentPerInch`.

Turing requires a declaration for every identifier used in a program unless that identifier is a standard identifier. Identifiers that are not standard identifiers are called *user-defined identifers*. Each keyword and identifier used in Figures 2.1 and 2.2, along with the standard identifier `sqrt`, is shown in Table 2.1 under its appropriate category.

TABLE 2.1

Keywords and Identifiers in Figures 2.1 and 2.2

Keywords	Standard Identifiers	User-defined Identifiers
var, const, string, real, get, put	sqrt	MetersToYards, SqMeters, SqYards, FirstName, LastName

Syntax Displays for Declarations

This section introduced constant and variable declarations; the syntactic form of each Turing language element is summarized in the syntax displays below. Each display describes the syntactic form of a language element and provides an example.

CONSTANT DECLARATION

Form: `const constant := value`

Example: `const Pi := 3.14159`

Interpretation: The specified *value* is associated with the identifier *constant*. The *value* associated with *constant* cannot be changed.

Note: The constant declarations do not need to come first in a Turing program, but they must appear before they are used.

VARIABLE DECLARATION

Form: `var variable list : type`

Examples: `var X, Y : real`

                `var Me, You : int`

Interpretation: A memory cell is allocated for each variable (an identifier) in the variable list. The type of data (`real`, `int`, etc.) to be stored in each variable is specified after the colon. Commas are used to separate the identifiers in the variable list.

PROGRAM STYLE

CHOOSING IDENTIFIER NAMES

It is very important to pick meaningful names for identifiers; meaningful identifiers make it easier to understand their use. For example, the identifier `Salary` would be a good name for a variable used to store a person's salary; the identifiers `S` and `Bagel` would be bad choices.

As we mentioned above, Turing allows identifiers to be quite long (up to 50 characters). However, it is difficult to form meaningful names using fewer than three letters. On the other hand, typing errors become more likely when identifiers are too long. As a reasonable rule of thumb, use names that are between three and ten characters in length.

If you mistype an identifier, the compiler will usually detect this as a syntax error and display an error message during program translation saying the identifier has not been declared. Sometimes mistyped identifiers resemble other identifiers, so it is best to avoid picking names that are very similar to each other. You should avoid choosing two names that are identical except for their use of case because people will too easily confuse them.

Exercises for Section 2.3

Self-Check

1. Why should the value of `Pi` (`3.14159`) be stored in a constant?
2. Indicate which of the identifiers below are Turing keywords, standard identifiers, valid identifiers, and invalid identifiers.

```
put    Bill   Sue's   Rate   Start
const   XYZ123   123XYZ   ThisIsALongOne   Y=Z
Prog#2   "MaxScores"
```

Programming

1. Write a program with constant and variable declarations for variables `Radius`, `Area`, and `Circumf` (all type `real`) and a constant `Pi` (`3.14159`).

2.4   Executable Statements

One of the main functions of a computer is to perform arithmetic computations and display the results of computations. These operations are specified by the *executable statements* appearing in the program body. Each executable statement is translated by the Turing compiler into one or more machine language instructions, which are copied to the object file and later executed. The declarations, on the other hand, describe the meaning and purpose of each user-defined identifier to the Turing compiler; they are not translated into machine language instructions and do not appear in the object file.

Programs in Memory

Before examining each kind of executable statement in detail, let's see what computer memory looks like after a program is loaded into memory and after that program executes. Figure 2.3 shows the metric conversion program loaded into memory and the program memory area before and after execution of the program body. The question mark in memory cells `SqMeters` and `SqYards` indicates that these variables are undefined (value unknown) before program execution begins. During program execution, the data value `2.00` is read into variable `SqYards`. After the statement

```
SqYards := MetersToYards * SqMeters
```

executes, the variables are defined as shown in Fig. 2.3b.

FIGURE 2.3   Memory Before and After Execution of a Program

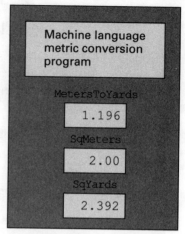

a. Memory before Execution   b. Memory after Execution

Assignment Statements

The *assignment statement* is used in Turing to perform computations. The assignment statement

```
SqYards := MetersToYards * SqMeters
```

in Fig. 2.1 assigns a value to the variable SqYards. In this case, SqYards is being assigned the result of the multiplication (* means multiply) of the constant MetersToYards by the variable SqMeters. Valid information must be stored in both MetersToYards and SqMeters before the assignment statement is executed. As shown in Fig. 2.4, only the value of SqYards is affected by the assignment statement; MetersToYards and SqMeters retain their original values.

FIGURE 2.4   Effect of SqYards : = MetersToYards * SqMeters

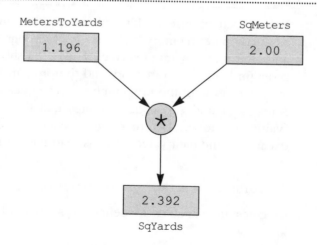

The symbol := is the assignment operator in Turing and should be pronounced "becomes" or "gets" or "takes the value of" rather than "equals". The : and = must be adjacent characters with no intervening space. The general form of the assignment statement is shown in the next display.

ASSIGNMENT STATEMENT (ARITHMETIC)
Form: *result := expression*
Example: X := Y + Z + 2.0

Interpretation: The variable specified by *result* is assigned the value of *expression*. The previous value of *result* is destroyed. The *expression* can be a single variable, a single constant, or involve variables, constants, and the arithmetic operators listed in Table 2.2. The *expression* must be assignment compatible (described below) with the variable specified by *result*.

TABLE 2.2   Some Arithmetic Operators

Arithmetic Operator	Meaning
+	addition
−	subtraction
*	multiplication
/	real division

The real division operator / always yields a real number as its result. Later we will introduce the div division operator that yields an integer as its result.

An expression is *assignment compatible* with a result variable if both are the same data type, or the expression is type int and the *result* variable is type real. This means that a type real expression can only be assigned to a type real variable, but a type int expression can be assigned to either a type int or a type real variable.

EXAMPLE 2.2

In Turing, you can write assignment statements of the form

```
Sum := Sum + Item
```

where the variable Sum is used on both sides of the assignment operator. This is obviously not an algebraic equation, but it illustrates a common programming practice. This statement instructs the computer to add the current value of the variable Sum to the value of Item; the result is saved temporarily and then stored back into Sum. The previous value of Sum is destroyed in the process, as illustrated in Fig. 2.5; however, the value of Item is unchanged.

FIGURE 2.5   Effect of Sum : = Sum + Item

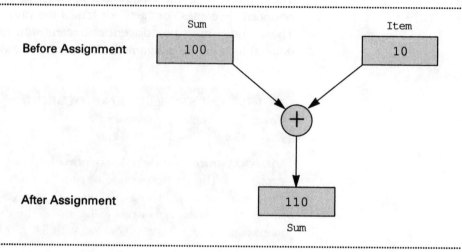

EXAMPLE 2.3

In Turing, you can also write assignment statements with an expression part that consists of a single variable or constant. The statement

    NewX := X

instructs the computer to copy the value of X into NewX. The statement

    NewX := -X

instructs the computer to get the value of X, negate this value, and store the result in NewX. For example, If X is 3.5, NewX is −3.5. Neither of the assignment statements above changes the value of X.

Input/Output Operations

Data can be stored in memory in three different ways: associate it with a constant, assign it to a variable, or read it into a variable. We have already discussed the first two methods. The third method, reading data into a variable, is necessary if you want the program to manipulate different data each time it executes. Reading data into memory is called an *input operation*.

As it executes, a program performs computations and assigns new values to variables. These program results can be displayed to the program user by an *output operation*.

All input/output operations in Turing are performed by executing special program units called *input/output statements*. The input/output statements are supplied as part of the Turing compiler and their names are keywords. In this section, we will discuss how to use the input statement named get and the output statement named put.

The Get Statement

You have seen examples of Turing's input/output statements in the examples you have seen. In Fig. 2.1, the `get` statement

    get SqMeters

reads data into the variable SqMeters. Where does the `get` statement find the data that it stores in variable SqMeters? It reads it from the *standard input device*. In most cases, the standard input device is the keyboard. Consequently, the computer attempts to store in SqMeters whatever information is typed at the keyboard by the program user. Since SqMeters is declared as type `real`, the input operation will proceed without error only if the program user types in a number. The program user should press the key labeled Return or Enter after typing the number. The effect of the `get` statement is shown in Fig. 2.6.

FIGURE 2.6   Effect of Get SqMeters

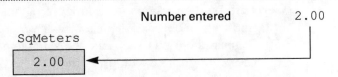

Example 2.1 reads a person's two names. Each person using the program may have names so the input statement

    get FirstName, lastName

calls the `get` statement to enter data into each of the two variables listed above. Since these variables are declared as type `string`, a string of characters will be stored in each variable. The string Bob is read into the FirstName variable, then the blank after Bob is skipped and then the string Jones is read into the LastName variable. Again, the program user should press the Return key after typing in the two words. Figure 2.7 shows the effect of this statement when Bob Jones is entered.

FIGURE 2.7   Effect of Get FirstName, LastName

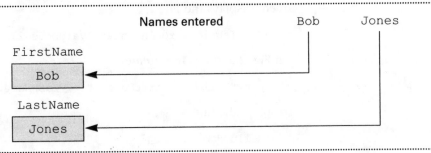

The number of characters read by the get statement depends on the type of the variable in which the data will be stored. Characters are read into a string variable until a blank or the end of the line is encountered. Any preceding blanks are skipped. For a type real variable, the program continues to read characters until it reaches a character that cannot be part of the number (usually indicated by entering the blank character) or the Return key is pressed.

How do we know when to enter the input data and what data to enter? Your program should print a prompting message as a signal that informs you what data to enter and when. (Prompting messages are discussed in more detail in the next section.) Each character entered by the program user is *echoed* on the screen.

THE GET STATEMENT

Form: get *input list*

Example: get Age, FirstInitial

Interpretation: The get statement reads into memory data typed at the keyboard by the program user during program execution. The program user must enter one data item for each variable specified in the *input list*. Commas are used to separate the variable names in the *input list*.

The order of the data must correspond to the order of the variables in the input list. Insert one or more blank characters between numeric data items. Do not insert any blanks within the characters being read into a string variable. Press the Return key after entering all data items.

The Put Statement

In order to see the results of a program execution, we must have some way of specifying what variable values should be displayed. In Fig. 2.1, the put statement

```
put "The fabric size in square yards is ", SqYards
```

displays a line of program output containing two items: the string literal "The fabric ... is " and the value of SqYards. A *string literal* is a sequence of characters enclosed in quotation marks (double quotes); the characters inside the quotes are printed but not the quotes. The put statement displays the line

```
The fabric size in square yards is 2.392
```

In Fig. 2.2, the put statement

```
put "Hello ", FirstName, " ", LastName, "."
```

displays the line

```
Hello Bob Jones.
```

In this case, two variable values are printed along with the strings `"Hello "`, `" "` (a single blank character) and the final period.

Finally, the statements

```
put "Enter the fabric size in square meters >"
put "Enter first and last names and press return >"
```

display prompts or prompting messages in Figs. 2.1 and 2.2, respectively. You should always display a prompting message just before a call to a `get` statement to remind the program user to enter data. The prompt may also describe the format of the data expected. It is very important to precede each `get` operation with a `put` that prints a prompt; otherwise, the program user may have no idea that the program is waiting for data or what data to enter.

The *cursor* is a moving place marker that indicates the next position on the screen where information will be displayed. After the `put` statement is executed, the cursor is advanced to the start of the next line on the screen.

Using the Put Statement to Write Blank Lines

The statements

```
put "The fabric size in square yards is ", SqYards
put ""
put "Metric conversion completed"
```

display the lines

```
The fabric size in square yards is 2.392

Metric conversion completed
```

The second `put` uses the *empty string* (a string with no characters) which is written as `""`, and causes the blank line in the middle of the program output. Execution of this `put` causes the cursor to be advanced to the next line.

We can avoid the second `put` statement by using the `skip` feature to cause a blank line to be output, as is shown here:

```
put "The fabric size in square yards is ", SqYards
put skip, "Metric conversion completed"
```

This produces exactly the same output as before.

> **THE PUT STATEMENT**
>
> **Form:**   put *output list*
>
> **Example:**   put "My height in inches is ", Height
>
> **Interpretation:** The put statement displays the value of each variable or constant in the order in which it appears in output list and then advances the cursor to the next line. A string is printed without the quotes. To cause a blank line to appear, you can use the empty string "" as the output list. You can use the keyword skip as an output item; this causes the current output line to be completed and starts a new line.

The Put Statement with Double Dot

Turing provides a special form of the put statement in which the cursor is not advanced to the start of the next line after put is finished executing. This form ends with a double dot (. .). If we use the put and get statements below for data entry

```
put "Enter the fabric size in square meters >" ..
get SqYards
```

the put statement will display the prompt and advance the cursor to the screen position just after the symbol >. Then, the program user can type in the data value at the end of that line:

```
Enter the fabric size in square meters >2.00
```

The statement pair

```
put "The fabric size in square yards is " ..
put SqYards
```

would display the same output line as the single statement

```
put "The fabric size in square yards is ", SqYards
```

It is generally more convenient to use the latter form.

> **PUT STATEMENT WITH DOUBLE DOT**
>
> **Form:**   put *output list* ..
>
> **Example:**   put "My height in inches is ", Height, " and my " ..
>
> **Interpretation:** The value of each variable or constant in the *output list* is printed. Any string in the *output list* is printed without the quotes. The cursor does not advance to the next line after the output is displayed.

Exercises for Section 2.4

Self-Check

1. Show the output displayed by the program lines below when the data entered are 5 and 7.

```
var M, N : int
put "Enter two integers:"
get M, N
M := M + 5
N := 3 * N
put "M = ", M
put "N = ", N
```

2. Show the contents of memory before and after the execution of the program lines shown in exercise 1.

3. Show the output displayed by the lines below.

```
put "My name is: " ..
put "Doe, Jane"
put ""
put "I live in " ..
put "Waterloo, Ontario " ..
put "and my postal code is: "
put "N2L 3G1"
```

Programming

1. Write statements that ask the user to type three numbers and read the three user responses into First, Second, and Third.

2. Write a statement that displays the value of X as indicated in the line below.

```
The value of X is _____
```

3. Write a program that will ask the user to enter the radius of a circle and will compute and display the circle's area and circumference. Use the formulas

   Area = Pi * Radius * Radius
   Circumference = 2 * Pi * Radius

   where *Pi* is the constant 3.14159.

2.5 General Form of Turing Programs

To summarize what we have learned so far, the programs shown earlier have the general form described in Fig. 2.8. A program is a list of inter-mixed declarations and statements. The statements we have looked at so far consist of statements that perform computations and input/output operations.

Every identifier used in a program must be declared, unless it is a standard identifier, before it is used in a statement. The reserved words `const` and `var` signal the beginning of a declaration. You can have several constant and variable declarations in any order, but each identifier can be declared only once.

FIGURE 2.8   General Form of a Turing Program

```
declaration or statement
declaration or statement

      .
      .
      .

declaration or statement
```

Each declaration or statement can extend over more than one line. For example, here is a variable declaration that starts on one line and finishes on the next.

```
var FirstName,          % Person's first name
    LastName : string   % Person's last name
```

A statement or declaration that extends over more than one line cannot be split in the middle of an identifier, a reserved word, a number, or a string.

Also, we can write more than one statement on a line. For example, the line

```
put "Enter two names >"   get Name1, Name2
```

contains a statement that displays a prompt message and a statement that reads the data requested. We recommend that you place only one state-ment on a line.

PROGRAM STYLE

USE OF BLANK SPACE

The consistent and careful use of blank spaces can significantly enhance the style of a program. A blank space is required between any two words in a program line (for instance, between `get` and `SqMeters` in Fig. 2.1).

The compiler ignores extra blanks between words and symbols. You may insert space to improve the style and appearance of a program. As shown in Fig. 2.1, you should always leave a blank space after a comma and before and after operators such as `*, -, :=`.

It helps make the program easier to read if you leave a blank line between the declarations and the statements, as shown in Fig. 2.2.

We take all of these measures for the sole purpose of improving the style—and hence the clarity—of our programs. Stylistic issues have no effect whatever on the meaning of the program as far as the computer is concerned; however, they can make it easier for people to read and understand the program.

Be careful not to insert blank spaces where they do not belong. For example, there cannot be a space between the characters `:` and `=` when they form the assignment operator `:=`. Also, the identifier `StartSalary` cannot be written as `Start Salary`.

Comments in Programs

The programs in Figs. 2.1 and 2.2 contain some English phrases, preceded by percent signs, that are program comments. Programmers use comments to make the program easier to understand by describing the purpose of the program (see the second comment line in Figs. 2.1 and 2.2), the use of identifiers (see the comments in the variable declarations), and the purpose of each program step (see the comments with the statements). Comments are an important part of the *documentation* of a program because they help others read and understand the program. The compiler, however, ignores comments and they are not translated into machine language.

As shown in Fig. 2.1, a comment can appear by itself on a program line or at the end of a line after a declaration or statement; each comment starts with `%` and continues to the end of the line. In the variable declaration below, the first comment is embedded in the declaration, and the second one follows it.

```
var SqMeters,      % input - fabric size in meters
    SqYards : real   % output - fabric size in yards
```

We will document the use of most variables in this way. The next displays describe the syntax and use of comments.

COMMENTS
Form: *% comment*
Alternate Form: */* comment */*
Examples: `% This is a comment`
                     `/* This a very long comment`
                     `   that does not fit on one line */`

Interpretation: A percent sign indicates the start of a *comment*, the end of the line indicates the end of the comment. Alternately, the symbol pair /* may be used to mark the beginning of a comment that is terminated by the symbol pair */. This alternate form of comment allows you to have a single comment that extends for several lines. Comments are listed with the program, but are otherwise ignored by the Turing compiler. **Note:** It is not permissable to place one /* ... */ comment inside another.

PROGRAM
STYLE

USING COMMENTS

Comments make a program more readable by describing the purpose of the program and by describing the use of each identifier. For example, the comment shown in this declaration

```
var SqMeters : real % Input - fabric size in meters
```

describes the use of the variable SqMeters.

You should also place comments with the statements in the program to describe the purpose of each section of the program. Generally, you will include one comment for each major algorithm step. The comment should describe what the step does rather than simply restate the step in English. For example, the comment

```
% Convert the fabric size to square yards
SqYards := MetersToYards * SqMeters
```

is more descriptive and, hence, preferable to

```
% Multiply MetersToYards by SqMeters and
% save the result in SqYards.
SqYards := MetersToYards * SqMeters
```

Before you implement each step in the initial algorithm, you should write a comment that summarizes the purpose of the algorithm step.

Each program should begin with a header section that consists of a series of comments specifying:

• the name of the program
• the programmer's name
• the date of the current version
• a brief description of what the program does

If you write the program for a class assignment, you should also list the class identification and your instructor's name as is shown next.

```
% The "FirstAsgn" program
% Programmer: William Bell
% Date completed: May 9, 1993
% This program reads a value in square meters and
% converts it to square yards.
```

Exercises for Section 2.5

Self-Check

1. Explain what is wrong with the comments below.

```
/* This is a comment?
/* How about this /*seems like a comment*/ is it? */
```

2. What is the purpose of including comments in a computer program?
3. Correct the syntax errors in the program below and rewrite it so that it follows our style conventions. What does each statement of your corrected program do? What values are printed?

```
VAR X, Y, X , real:
Y = 15.0,
Z:= -Y + 3.5 Y + z =: x
put x; Y; z
```

<table>
<tr><td>2.6</td><td></td></tr>
</table>

Data Types and Expressions

An *abstraction* is a model or simplification of a physical object. We frequently use abstractions in problem solving and programming. For example, in problem solving we sometimes make simplifying assumptions that enable us to solve a limited version of a more general problem. In programming, *abstraction* is the process of focusing on what we need to know, ignoring irrelevant details.

Real Data Type

A *data type* is a set of values and a set of operations on those values. A *standard data type* in Turing is a data type that is predefined (for example, `real`, `int`, `string`). In Turing, we use the standard data type `real` as an abstraction for the real numbers (in the mathematical sense). The data type `real` is an abstraction because it does not include all real numbers. Some real numbers are too large or too small, and some real numbers cannot be represented precisely because of the finite size of a memory cell (more on this in Chapter 8). However, we can certainly represent enough of the real numbers in Turing to carry out most of the computations we wish to perform with sufficient accuracy.

The basic four arithmetic operators (+, -, *, /) for real numbers can be performed on type `real` objects in Turing where * means multiply. Turing also has the exponentiation operator, for example, one and a half squared or 1.5^2 is written in Turing as `1.5 ** 2`. The assignment operator (`:=`) is another operator that can be used with type `real` objects. We can also use the input/output statements `get` and `put` with type `real` objects.

Objects of a data type may be variables, constants, or literals where a *literal* is a value that appears directly in a program. A type `real` literal is a number that consists of a sequence of digits including a decimal point) (e.g., `0.112`, `456.0`, `123.456`, `17.`, `.5`). A type `real` literal may have a scale factor, which is the capital letter E followed by an optional sign and an integer (e.g., `0.112E3`, `456.0E-2`). The scale factor may also follow a string of digits without a decimal point (e.g., `123E6` and `123.0E6` are equivalent `real` literals). A scale factor means multiply the number before the letter E by 10 raised to the power appearing after the letter E (e.g., `0.112E3` is `112.0`, `456.0E-2` is `4.56`). The letter E can be written in lower case, as in `0.112e3`. A `real` literal may be preceded by a + or - sign. Table 2.3 shows examples of valid and invalid `real` literals.

TABLE 2.3 Valid and Invalid Real Literals

Valid Real Literals		Invalid Real Literals
3.14159		150 (no decimal point)
0.005		12.5E.3(.3 invalid exponent)
.12345		-15E-0.3(0.3 invalid exponent)
12345.0		
16.		
15.0E-04	(value is 0.0015)	
2.345E2	(value is 234.5)	
12E+6	(value is 12000000)	
.123E3	(value is 123.)	
1.15E-3	(value is 0.00115)	

The last valid literal in the table, `1.15E-3`, has the same value as 1.15×10^{-3} in normal scientific notation, where the exponent -3 causes the decimal point to be moved left 3 digits. A positive exponent causes the decimal point to be moved to the right; the + sign may be omitted when the exponent is positive.

Integer Data Type

Another standard data type (or data abstraction) in Turing is type `int` which is used to represent the integer numbers (for example, -77, 0, 999, +999). Because of the finite size of a memory cell, not all integers can be represented. The largest possible integer that you can use in Turing is 214783647, which is $2^{31} -1$. This value is called `maxint`. The smallest integer is `-maxint`.

`Real` and `int` data types differ in one basic way: type `real` objects represent numbers with a decimal point or a fractional part; whereas, type `int` objects represent only whole numbers. For this reason, type `int` objects are more restricted in their use. We often use them to represent a count of items (for example, the number of children in a family) because a count must always be a whole number.

The data type of the object stored in a particular memory cell determines how the bit pattern (or *binary string*) in that cell is interpreted. For example, a bit pattern that represents a type `real` object is interpreted differently from a bit pattern that represents a type `int` object. But this is a detail that we do not need to be concerned with in order to use these data types in Turing.

We can use the arithmetic operators listed earlier and the assignment operator with type `int` operands. There are two additional operators, `div` (integer division operator) and `mod` (*modulus* operator), that produce type `int` results. We will discuss these operators in the next subsection.

Operators Div and Mod

The integer division operator, `div`, computes the integral part of the result of dividing its first operand by its second. For example, the value of `7/2` is `3.5`, and the value of `7 div 2` is the integral part of this result, or `3`. Similarly, the value of `299/100` is `2.99`, and the value of `299 div 100` is the integral part of this result, or `2`. The `div` operation is undefined when the divisor (the second operand) is `0`. Table 2.4 shows some examples of the `div` operator.

TABLE 2.4	The Div Operator

3 div 15 = 0	3 div −15 = 0
15 div 3 = 5	15 div −3 = −5
16 div 3 = 5	16 div −3 = −5
17 div 3 = 5	−17 div 3 = −5
18 div 3 = 6	−18 div −3 = 6

It is interesting to compare the value of the expressions `6/2` and `6 div 2`. The value of `6/2` is the real number `3.0`, whereas the value of `6 div 2` is the integer `3`. Although these two results are equivalent in a mathematical sense, they are not the same in Turing and are stored in memory as different binary strings.

The modulus operator, `mod`, returns the *integer remainder* of the result of dividing its first operand by its second. For example, the value of `7 mod 2` is `1` because the integer remainder is `1`. The top diagram on page 50 shows the effect of dividing `7` by `2`; that is, we get a quotient of `3` (`7 div 2`) and a remainder of `1` (`7 mod 2`). The bottom diagram shows that `299 mod 100` is `99` because we get a remainder of `99` when we divide `299` by `100`.

```
        3    ◄─────────── 7 div 2 = 3
     2 ) 7
        6
        1    ◄─────────── 7 mod 2 = 1


          2    ◄─────────── 299 div 100 = 2
    100 ) 299
        200
         99    ◄─────────── 299 mod 100 = 99
```

The magnitude of M mod N must always be less than the divisor N, so if M is positive, the value of M mod 100 must be between 0 and 99.

The mod operation is undefined when N is zero. Table 2.5 shows some examples of the mod operator.

TABLE 2.5
The Mod Operator

3 mod 5 = 3	5 mod 3 = 2
4 mod 5 = 4	5 mod 4 = 1
5 mod 5 = 0	15 mod 5 = 0
6 mod 5 = 1	15 mod 6 = 3
7 mod 5 = 2	15 mod 7 = 1
8 mod 5 = 3	15 mod 8 = 7

The formula

```
M = (M div N) * N + (M mod N)
```

defines the relationship between the operators div and mod when dividend M and divisor N are both positive. It is recommended that you avoid using mod when either M or N is negative. We can see that this formula holds for the two examples discussed earlier by plugging in values for M, N, M div N, and M mod N. In the first example below, M is 7 and N is 2; in the second example below, M is 299 and N is 100.

```
  7 = (7 div 2) * 2 + (7 mod 2)
    = 3 * 2 + 1 = 7

299 = (299 div 100) * 100 + (299 mod 100)
    = 2 * 100 + 99
    = 299
```

Using Integer Objects

The following case study gives an example of manipulating type int objects in Turing.

❖ Case Study:

Finding the Value of a Coin Collection

1. Problem   Your little sister has been saving nickels and pennies for quite a while. Because she is getting tired of lugging her piggy bank with her whenever she goes to the store, she would like to trade in her collection for bills and some change. In order to do this, she would like to know the value of her coin collection in dollars and cents.

2. Analysis   In order to solve this problem, we must be given the count of nickels and the count of pennies in the collection. The first step is to determine the total value of the collection in cents. Once we have this figure, we can do an integer division using 100 as the divisor to get the dollar value; the remainder of this division will be the loose change that she should receive. In the data requirements below, we list the total value in cents (TotalCents) as a *program variable* because it is needed as part of the computation process, but is not a required problem output.

DATA REQUIREMENTS

Problem Inputs
```
    Nickels : int      % the count of nickels
    Pennies : int      % the count of pennies
```

Problem Outputs
```
    Dollars : int      % the number of dollars she should
                       % receive
    Change : int       % the loose change she should receive
```

Additional Program Variables
```
    TotalCents : int   % the total number of cents
```

RELEVANT FORMULAS
1 dollar equals 100 pennies
1 nickel equals 5 pennies

3. Design   The algorithm is straightforward and is displayed next.

INITIAL ALGORITHM
1. Read in the count of nickels and pennies
2. Compute the total value in cents
3. Find the value in dollars and loose change
4. Display the value in dollars and loose change

Steps 2 and 3 may need refinement. Their refinements follow.

Step 2 Refinement

    2.1   `TotalCents` is 5 times `Nickels` plus `Pennies`

Step 3 Refinement

    3.1   `Dollars` is the integer quotient of `TotalCents` and `100`

    3.2   `Change` is the integer remainder of `TotalCents` and `100`

4. Implementation

The program is shown in Fig. 2.9. The statement

```
TotalCents := 5 * Nickels + Pennies
```

implements algorithm step 2.1. The statements

```
Dollars := TotalCents div 100
Change := TotalCents mod 100
```

use the `mod` and `div` operators to implement algorithm steps 3.1 and 3.2.

FIGURE 2.9   Value of a Coin Collection

```
% The "Coins" program
% Determine the value of a coin collection

var Pennies : int        % Input - count of pennies
var Nickels : int        % Input - count of nickels
var Dollars : int        % Output - number of dollars
var Change : int         % Output - loose change
var TotalCents : int     % Total cents

% Read in the count of nickels and pennies
put "Number of nickels >"
get Nickels
put "Number of pennies >"
get Pennies

% Compute the total value in cents
TotalCents := 5 * Nickels + Pennies

% Find the value in dollars and change.
Dollars := TotalCents div 100
Change := TotalCents mod 100

% Display the value in dollars and change.
put ""
put "Your collection is worth ",
    Dollars, " dollars" ..
put " and ", Change, " cents."
```

```
Number of nickels >30
Number of pennies >77

Your collection is worth 2 dollars and 27 cents.
```

---

5. Testing   To test this program, try running it with a combination of nickels and pennies that yields an exact dollar amount with no change leftover. For example, 35 nickels and 25 pennies should yield a value of 2 dollars and no cents. Then increase and decrease the number of pennies by one (26 and 24 pennies) to make sure that these cases are also handled properly.   ✖

Type of an Expression

The data type of each variable must be specified in its declaration, but how does Turing determine the data type of an expression? The data type of an expression depends on the type of its operands. For example, the expression

```
Ace + Bandage
```

is type `int` if both `Ace` and `Bandage` are type `int`; otherwise, it is type `real`. The expression

```
Ace / Bandage
```

is type `real` because the `real` division operator, `/`, always generates a type `real` result. The type of

```
Ace div Bandage
```

is type `int` because the integer division operator `div` always generates an `int` result.

A Turing expression combined by `+`, `-` or `*` is type `int` only if both its operands are type `int`. The expression is type `real` if either of its operands is type `real`. We say an expression is *mixed-mode* if it contains both `int` and `real` operands.

Mixed-Type Assignment Statement

When an assignment statement is executed, the expression is first evaluated and then the result is assigned to the variable listed to the left of the assignment operator (`:=`). Either a type `real` or type `int` expression may be assigned to a type `real` variable so if M and N are type `int` and X and Y are type `real`, all assignment statements below are valid.

```
M := 3
N := 2
X := M / N        % Assigns 1.5 to X
Y := M div N      % Assigns 1.0 to Y
```

In the last statement above, the expression M div N evaluates to the integer 1. This value is converted to type `real` (`1.0`) before it is stored in Y.

Turing does not allow a type `real` expression to be assigned to a type `int` variable because the fractional part of the expression cannot be represented and will be lost. This means that each of the assignment statements below is invalid if `Count` is a type `int` variable.

```
Count := 3.5              % Invalid assignment of a
                          %    real number to int
Count := Count + 1.0      % Invalid 1.0 is real,
                          %    so result is real
Count := Count / 2        % Invalid result of
                          %    division is real
```

Expressions with Multiple Operators

In our programs so far, most expressions have involved a single operator; however, expressions with multiple operators are common in Turing. To understand and write expressions with multiple operators, we must know the Turing rules for evaluating expressions. For example, in the expression X + Y / Z, is + performed before /, or vice-versa? Is the expression X / Y * Z evaluated as (X / Y) * Z or X / (Y * Z)? Verify for yourself that the order of evaluation does make a difference by substituting some simple values for X, Y, and Z. In both these expressions, the / operator is evaluated first; the reasons for this are explained in the Turing rules for expression evaluation which follow. These rules are based on standard algebraic rules.

Rules for Expression Evaluation

a. All parenthesized subexpressions must be evaluated separately. Nested parenthesized subexpressions must be evaluated inside out, with the innermost subexpression evaluated first.
b. *The operator precedence rule.* Operators in the same subexpression are evaluated in the following order: first ** (exponentiation); then *, /, div, and mod; finally + and −.
c. *The left associative rule.* Operators in the same subexpression and at the same precedence level (such as + and −) are evaluated left to right.

Knowledge of the above rules will help you understand how Turing evaluates expressions. Use parentheses as needed to specify the order of evaluation. Often it is a good idea to use extra parentheses to clearly document the order of operator evaluation in complicated expressions. For example, the expression

```
X * Y * Z + A / B - C * D
```

can be written in a more readable form using parentheses:

```
(X * Y * Z) + (A / B) - (C * D)
```

EXAMPLE 2.4

The formula for the area of a circle, $a = \pi\, r^2$ may be written in Turing as

```
Area := Pi * Radius * Radius
```

where `Pi` is the constant `3.14159`. Figure 2.10 shows the *evaluation tree* for this formula. In this tree, the arrows connect each operand with its operator. The order of operator evaluation is shown by the number to the left of each operator; the letter *c* to the right of the operator indicates which evaluation rule applies. Another way of writing this formula in Turing is this:

```
Area := Pi * Radius ** 2
```

In this version we have used Turing's exponentiation operator in writing *Radius²*. Since exponentiation is evaluated before multiplication (rule *b*), the evaluation tree for this version would show `Radius ** 2` being combined first and then its result multiplied by `Pi`.

FIGURE 2.10   Evaluation Tree for Area := Pi * Radius * Radius

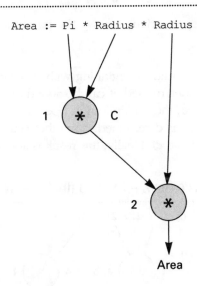

EXAMPLE 2.5

The formula for the average velocity, v, of a particle travelling on a line between points p_1 and p_2 in time t_1 to t_2 is

$$v = \frac{p_1 - p_2}{t_1 - t_2}$$

This formula can be written and evaluated in Turing as shown in Fig. 2.11.

FIGURE 2.11   Evaluation Tree for V : = (P2 – P1) / (T2 – T1)

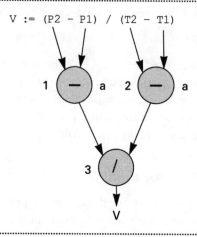

EXAMPLE 2.6

Consider the expression

```
Z - (A + B div 2) + W * Y
```

containing integer variables only. The parenthesized subexpression

```
(A+B div 2)
```

is evaluated first (rule a) beginning with `B div 2` (rule *b*). Once the value of `B div 2` is determined, it can be added to A to obtain the value of (A + B div 2). Next, the multiplication operation is performed (rule *b*) and the value for W * Y is determined. Then the value of (A + B div 2) is subtracted from Z (rule *c*). Finally, this result is added to W * Y. (See Fig. 2.12.)

FIGURE 2.12   Evaluation Tree for Z – (A + B div 2) + W * Y

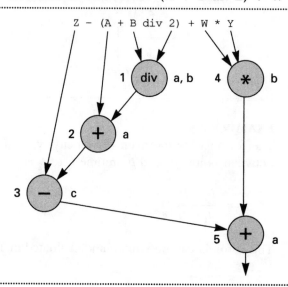

Writing Mathematical Formulas in Turing

There are two problem areas in writing a mathematical formula in Turing: one concerns multiplication and the other concerns division. Multiplication can often be implied in a mathematical formula by writing the two items to be multiplied next to each other; for example, a = bc. In Turing, however, you must always use the * operator to indicate multiplication, as in:

```
A := B * C
```

The other difficulty arises in formulas involving division. We normally write the numerator and denominator on separate lines:

$$m = \frac{y - b}{x - a}$$

In Turing, all assignment statements must be written in a linear form. Consequently, parentheses are often needed to separate the numerator from the denominator, and to clearly indicate the order of evaluation of the operators in the expression. The formula above would be written in Turing as

```
M := (Y - B) / (X - A)
```

EXAMPLE 2.7
This example illustrates how several mathematical formulas can be written in Turing.

Mathematical Formula	Turing Expression
1. $b^2 - 4ac$	B ** 2 - 4 * A * C
2. $a + b - c$	A + B - C
3. $\dfrac{a + b}{c + d}$	(A + B) / (C + D)
4. $\dfrac{1}{1 + x^2}$	1 / (1 + X ** 2)
5. $a \times - (b + c)$	A * (-(B + C))

The points illustrated are summarized as follows:

- Always specify multiplication explicitly by using the operator * where needed (1).
- Write exponentiation using ** (1, 4).
- Use parentheses when required to control the order of operator evaluation (3, 4).
- Avoid writing two arithmetic operators in succession; you can separate them using an open parenthesis (5).

Unary Minus

Formula 5 in Example 2.7 uses a unary minus to negate the value of (B + C) before performing the multiplication. The *unary minus* has only one operand and has the same precedence as the subtraction operator.

String Data Type

The third standard data type in Turing is type `string`. We have already seen (Fig. 2.2) that type `string` variables can be used to store strings (sequences) of characters. A type `string` literal must be enclosed in double quotes (e.g., `"Bob"`); however, you don't need to use quotes when you enter string data at a terminal.

The empty string, which contains no characters, is written as `""`. It may seem strange to have a string containing no characters, but this is a useful concept, just as the number 0, which is essentially the "empty number", is quite useful.

The `get` statement reads data into a type `string` variable in the following way. First it skips any *white space* : blanks, ends of lines, tab characters, etc. Then it collects characters until it finds more white space. For example, in Fig. 2.2, the letters in `Bob` were collected and placed in the variable called `FirstName`, then the blank was skipped and then the letters in Jones were collected and placed in the variable called `LastName`.

If you need blanks in a string value that is being input by a `get` statement, you must enclose the value in quotes. For example, if `"Mary Joe"` is considered to be a first name, it can be input in double quotes and all eight characters, including the blank, would be input into `FirstName`.

EXAMPLE 2.8

The program in Fig. 2.13 first reads and echoes two words entered at the keyboard. Next, it prints them in reverse order enclosed in asterisks. Each word is stored in a variable of type `string`; the string value `"*"` is associated with the constant `Border`.

The line

```
put Second, First
```

displays the two words in reverse order. As shown in the program output, the string values are output together, without a blank between them. To place a blank between them, we could explicitly output the literal string `" "`.

FIGURE 2.13   Program for Example 2.8

```
% The "Reverse" program
% Read 2 words and display them in reverse order

const Border := "*"    % Encloses 2 words

var First, Second : string
                          % Input/output - 2 words

put "Enter 2 words >"
get First, Second
put Border, Second, First, Border
```

```
Enter 2 words >Elliot Koffman
*KoffmanElliot*
```

In Fig. 2.13, the string literal "Enter 2 words > " is displayed as a prompt. In this example and in other earlier examples, we use strings as prompts and to clarify program output. We can also store them in `string` variables.

Boolean Data Type

The fourth standard data type in Turing is type `boolean` (named after the mathematician George Boole). `True` and `false` are the only two values associated with this data type. The identifier `Cloudy` is declared a type `boolean` variable by the declaration

```
var Cloudy : boolean
```

The assignment statement

```
Cloudy := true
```

assigns the `boolean` value `true` to `Cloudy`. We will see how to use `boolean` expressions (expressions that evaluate to `true` or `false`) in Chapter 4.

Exercises for Section 2.6

Self-Check

1. Indicate which of these literal values are legal in Turing and which are not. Identify the data type of each valid literal value.

```
15    "XYZ"    "*"    $   25.123   15.   -999   .123   "x"
'x'   "9"   "-5'"    true    "true"
```

2. a. Evaluate the following expressions with 7 and 22 as operands.

    22 div 7   7 div 22   22 mod 7   7 mod 22

   Repeat this exercise for the pairs of integers:

   b. 15, 16   c. 3, 23   d. −4, 16

3. Given the declarations

   ```
   const Pi   :=   3.14159
   const MaxI :=   1000
   var X, Y : real
   var A, B, I : int
   ```

   indicate which statements below are valid and find the result assigned
   in each valid statement. Also indicate which are invalid and why.
   Assume that A is 3, B is 4, and Y is −1.0.

   a. I := A mod B
   b. I := (990 − MaxI) div A
   c. I := A mod Y
   d. X := Pi * Y
   e. I := A / B
   f. X := A / B
   g. X := A mod (A / B)
   h. I := B div 0
   i. I := A mod (990 − MaxI)
   j. I := (MaxI − 990) div A
   k. X := A / Y
   l. I := Pi * A
   m. X := Pi div Y
   n. X := A div B
   o. I := (MaxI − 990) mod A
   p. I := A mod 0
   q. I := A mod (MaxI − 990)

4. Draw the evaluation trees for the expressions below.

   ```
   1.8 * Celsius + 32.0
   (Salary − 5000.00) * 0.20 + 1425.00
   ```

5. What values are assigned by the legal statements in Exercise 3 above,
   assuming A is 5, B is 2, and Y is 2.0?

6. Assume that you have the following variable declarations:

   ```
   var Color, Larry, Straw, Yanis, Ralph, Oman : int
   var Blair, Wally, Gary, Bill, Paul, Crayon : real
   ```

   Evaluate each of the statements below given the values: Color is 2,
   Blair is 2.5, Crayon is −1.3, Straw is 1, Ralph is 3, Paul is
   0.3E+1.

a. `Wally := Color * 2.5 / Paul`
b. `Gary := Color / Paul`
c. `Oman := Color div Ralph`
d. `Bill := (Color + Straw) / (Crayon + 0.3)`
e. `Larry := Ralph div Color + Ralph mod Color`
f. `Paul := Straw / Ralph * Color`

7. Let A, B, C, and X be the names of four type `real` variables and let I, J, and K be the names of three type `int` variables. Each of the statements below contains a violation of the rules for forming arithmetic expressions. Rewrite each statement so that it is consistent with these rules.

a. `X := 4.0 A * C`   d. `K := 3(I + J)`
b. `A := AC`   e. `X := 5A / BC`
c. `I := 2 - * J`   f. `I := 5J3`

Programming

1. Write an assignment statement that might be used to implement the equation below in Turing.

$$q = \frac{kA(T_1 - T_2)}{L}$$

2. Write a program that stores the values "X", "0", 1.345E10, and `true` in separate memory cells. Your program should read the first three values as data items; use an assignment statement to store the last value.
3. Extend the program in Fig. 2.9 to handle dimes and quarters as well as nickels and pennies.

2.7 Formatting Program Output

In the sample program output shown so far, the form of the output for all numbers was determined by defaults in Turing. Consequently, we had little control over the appearance or format of each output line. In this section we will learn how to specify the format of an output item.

Formatting Integer Values

It is fairly easy to specify the format of integer values displayed by a Turing program. All that we need to do is add the symbols :n to an integer output list item where n specifies the number of digits to be displayed (*field width*). For example, the lines

```
put "Your collection is worth ", Dollars : 1, "dollars" ..
put " and ", Change : 2, " cents."
```

indicate that one digit will be used to display the value of `Dollars` and two digits will be used to display the value of `Change` (a number between 0 and 99). If `Dollars` is 7 and `Change` is 8, the program output would be:

```
Your collection is worth 7 dollars and  8 cents.
```

In this line, note that there is an extra space before the value of `Change` (8). The reason is that the format specification `:2` allows space for two digits to be printed. If the value of `Change` is between 0 and 9, a single digit is displayed *right justified*, preceded by one blank space. We can use the format symbols `:2` to display any output value between -9 and 99. For negative numbers, the minus sign is included in the count of digits displayed.

Table 2.6 shows how two integer values are printed using different format specifications. The character • represents a blank character. The next to last line shows that the width specification may be a variable (or even an expression) that has an integer value. The last two lines show that when a width of 1 is used, the number is printed with no blanks preceeding it, and the number of print columns used varies with the size of the number (i.e., the display field expands as needed).

TABLE 2.6　　　　　　　　　Printing 234 and -234 Using Different Formats

Value	Format	Printed Output
234	:4	•234
234	:5	••234
234	:6	•••234
-234	:4	-234
-234	:5	•-234
-234	:6	••-234
234	:Len	•••234 (if Len is 6)
234	:1	234
-234	:1	-234

Formatting Real Values

To describe the format specification for a real value, we can indicate both the total field width needed and the desired number of decimal places. The total field width should be large enough to accommodate all digits before and after the decimal point. We should also leave a display column for the decimal point and, for negative numbers, a minus sign.

If X is a type real variable whose value will be between -99.9 and 999.9, we could use the output list item X `:5:1` to display the value of

X accurate to one decimal place. Table 2.7 shows different values of X displayed using this format specification. The values displayed in Table 2.7 are rounded to one decimal place, and all values are displayed right-justified in 5 columns.

TABLE 2.7 Displaying X Using Format Specification :5:1

Value of X	Output Displayed
−99.42	−99.4
0.123	••0.1
−9.53	•−9.5
−25.55	−25.6
99.999	00.0
999.43	999.4

Table 2.8 shows some real values that were printed using other format specifications. As shown in the table, it is possible to use a format specification of the form *:n* for real values. In this case, the real value is printed using at least *n* print positions.

TABLE 2.8 Formatting Real Values

Value	Format	Printed Output
3.14159	:5:2	•3.14
3.14159	:4:2	3.14
3.14159	:3:2	3.14
3.14159	:5:1	••3.1
3.14159	:5:3	3.142
3.14159	:8:5	•3.14159
3.14159	:9	••3.14159
0.1234	:4:2	0.12
−0.006	:4:2	−0.01
−0.006	:9	•••−0.006
−0.006	:8:5	−0.00600
−0.006	:8:3	••−0.006

In Turing you can use a third formatting field to give the number of digits in the scale factor; for example, the value 7.213E−05 with the format :7:2:1 produces the output 7.21E−5.

PROGRAM
STYLE

> **ELIMINATING LEADING BLANKS**
>
> As shown in Tables 2.6 through 2.8, a number that requires fewer display columns than are specified by the format field width is displayed with leading blanks. To eliminate extra leading blanks, choose a format that will display the smallest value expected without leading blanks. If the actual value requires more display columns, the field width will expand to accommodate it. Therefore, a format of :1 displays any integer value without leading blanks (for example, 29397 :1 is displayed as 29397). A format of :3:1 displays any real number accurate to one decimal place without leading blanks (for example, 99397.567 :3:1 is displayed as 99397.6); similarly, a format of :4:2 displays any real number accurate to two decimal places without leading blanks. By default, when you use no explicit format, Turing eliminates leading blanks and uses the minimum number of output columns.

Formatting Strings

A string value is always printed *left justified* in its field. Therefore, blank spaces will follow a string if the field in which it is printed is bigger than the string. If *field width* is too small to accommodate a string value, only the field will be expanded to accommodate it.

TABLE 2.9 Printing String Values Using Formats

String	Format	Printed Output
"*"	:1	*
"*"	:2	*•
"*"	:3	*••
"ACES"	:1	ACES
"ACES"	:2	ACES
"ACES"	:3	ACES
"ACES"	:4	ACES
"ACES"	:5	ACES•

Exercises for Section 2.7

Self-Check

1. Show the output lines for the following statements.

```
put -99 :4 ..
put "Bottles" :8
put "-99" :4, -99 :8:2
```

2. Correct the statement below.

```
put "Joe's salary is ", Salary :2:10
```

3. Show how the value -15.564 (stored in X) would be printed using the formats:

```
X :8:4   X :8:3   X :8:2   X :8:1   X :8:0   X :8
```

4. Assume X (type `real`) is `12.335` and I (type `int`) is `100`, show the output lines for the following statements. For clarity, use the symbol • to denote a blank space.

```
put "X is " :10, X :6:2, "I is " :4, I :5
put "I is " :10, I :1 ..
put "X is " :10, X :2:1
```

Programming

1. If the variables A, B, and C are `504`, `302.558`, and `-12.31`, respectively, write a statement that will display the line below (for clarity, a • denotes a blank space).

```
••504•••••302.56••••-12.3
```

2. Write a series of statements that will display a three-line heading consisting of your name, your school, and its city and state. Each line should be approximately centered on the computer screen or printed page.

2.8 Interactive Mode, Batch Mode, and Data Files

There are two basic modes of computer operation: batch and interactive. The programs that we have written so far are intended to be run in *interactive mode*. In this mode, the program user can interact with the program and enter data while the program is executing.

In batch mode, all data must be supplied beforehand as the program user cannot interact with the program while it is executing. Batch mode is an option on most computers.

If you use batch mode, then you must prepare a batch data file before executing your program. On a timeshared or personal computer, a batch data file is created and saved in the same way as a program or source file.

Input Redirection

Figures 2.14 and 2.15 show two versions of the metric conversion program rewritten as a batch program. In Fig. 2.14, we assume that the standard input file is associated with a batch data file instead of the keyboard. In most systems this can be done relatively easily through *input-output redirection* using the programming environment or the operating system commands. For example, Turing programming environments on IBM PC compatible systems, on Macintoshes, and under Unix® have facilities for doing this redirection.

In the Unix® and MS-DOS® operating systems, you can instruct your program to take its input from file `MyData` instead of the keyboard by placing the symbols `<MyData` at the end of the command line that causes your compiled and linked program to execute.

FIGURE 2.14 **Batch Version of Metric Conversion Program**

```
% The "Metric" conversion program
% Convert square meters to square yards

const MetersToYards := 1.196  % conversion constant

var SqMeters : real      % Input - fabric size in meters
var SqYards : real       % Output - fabric size in yards

% Read the fabric size in square meters.
get SqMeters
put "The fabric size in square meters is ", SqMeters :3:1

% Convert the fabric size to square yards.
SqYards := MetersToYards * SqMeters

% Display the fabric size in square yards.
put "The fabric size in square yards is ", SqYards :4:2
```

```
The fabric size in square meters is 2.0
The fabric size in square yards is 2.39
```

Output Redirection

You can redirect program output to a disk file instead of the screen. Then you can send the output file to the printer (using an operating system command) to obtain a hard-copy of the program output. There are facilities in Turing programming environments to do this redirection. In Unix® or MS-DOS®, the symbols `>MyOutput` are used to redirect output from the screen to file `MyOutput`. These symbols are placed on the command line that causes your program to execute. Unfortunately, it is difficult to interact with the running program because all program output, including any prompting messages, will be sent to the output file.

PROGRAM
STYLE

ECHO PRINTS VERSUS PROMPTS

In Fig. 2.14, the statement

```
get SqMeters
```

reads the value of SqMeters from the first (and only) line of the data file. Because the program input comes from a data file, there is no need to precede this statement with a prompting message. Instead we follow the get with the statement

```
put "Fabric size in square meters is ", SqMeters :3:1
```

which *echo prints* or displays the value just read into SqMeters. This statement provides a record of the data manipulated by the program. Without it, we would have no easy way of knowing what value was read.

Whenever you convert an interactive program to a batch program, make sure you replace each prompt with an echo print that follows the get statement.

Preview of Text Files (Optional)

This section previews the use of text files as data files in Turing. A complete treatment of this topic is discussed in Chapter 9. You should skip this section if you will not be using data files until then.

A batch program reads its data from a data file that is created and saved beforehand using an editor program. The process used to create a text file is the same as that used to create a program file (steps 1 through 5 in *Creating a Source File* in Section 1.7). The metric conversion program in Fig. 2.15 reads its data from data file InData instead of from the standard input file.

FIGURE 2.15   Metric Conversion Program Using File InData

```
% The "Metric" conversion program
% Convert square meters to square yards

const MetersToYards := 1.196  % conversion constant

var SqMeters : real       % Input - fabric size in meters
var SqYards : real        % Output - fabric size in yards
var fileNumber : int      % Input - data file

% Read the fabric size in square meters.
open : fileNumber, "InData", get
get : fileNumber, SqMeters
```

```
put "The fabric size in square meters is ", SqMeters :3:1

% Convert the fabric size to square yards.
SqYards := MetersToYards * SqMeters

% Display the fabric size in square yards.
put "The fabric size in square yards is ", SqYards :4:2
```

```
The fabric size in square meters is 2.0
The fabric size in square yards is 2.39
```

In Fig. 2.15, the declaration

```
var FileNumber : int
```

creates a variable that will be used to hold the connection number to the file InData. The statement

```
open : FileNumber, "InData", get
```

determines the connection number and places it in the FileNumber variable. Finally, the statement

```
get : FileNumber, SqMeters
```

reads a data value from the first (and only) line of file InData. The sample output shown in Fig. 2.15 is generated when file InData contains the line

```
2.00
```

Exercises for Section 2.8

Self-Check

1. Explain the difference in placement of put statements used to display prompts and put statements used to echo data. Which are used in interactive programs and which are used in batch programs?
2. How is input data provided to an interactive program? How is input data provided to a batch program?

Programming

1. Rewrite the program in Fig. 2.9 as a batch program. Assume data are read from file InData.
2. Redo programming exercise 1, this time assuming that the data are read from the file MyData.

2.9 Common Programming Errors

One of the first things you will discover in writing programs is that a program very rarely runs correctly the first time that it is submitted. Murphy's Law, "If something can go wrong, it will," seems to be written with the computer programmer or programming student in mind. In fact, errors are so common that they have their own special name—*bugs*—and the process of correcting them is called *debugging a program*. To alert you to potential problems, we will provide a section on common errors at the end of each chapter.

When the compiler detects an error, the computer will display an *error message* indicating that you have made a mistake and what the cause of the error might be. Unfortunately, error messages are often difficult to interpret and are sometimes misleading. However, as you gain some experience you will become more proficient at understanding them.

Two basic categories of error messages will occur: syntax error messages and run-time error messages. *Syntax errors* or *compile-time errors* are detected and displayed by the compiler as it attempts to translate your program. If a statement has a syntax error, then it cannot be translated and your program will not be executed.

Run-time errors are detected by the computer and are displayed during execution of a program. A run-time error occurs as a result of the user directing the computer to perform an illegal operation, such as dividing a number by zero or manipulating undefined or invalid data. When a run-time error occurs, the computer will stop executing your program and will print a diagnostic message that indicates the line where the error occurred.

Syntax Errors

Figure 2.16 shows a *compiler listing* of the metric conversion program which is a listing printed by the compiler during program translation that shows each line of the source program (preceded by a line number) and also displays any syntax errors detected by the compiler. The errors are indicated by lines in the program listing that begin with five asterisks and are summarized at the bottom of the compiler listing. The program contains the following syntax errors.

- use of : instead of := in the constant declaration (line 4)
- assignment statement with transposed variable and expression part (line 13)
- missing declaration for variable SqYards (lines 13 and 16)

FIGURE 2.16   Compiler Listing of a Program with Syntax Errors

```
     1  % The "Metric" conversion program
     2  % Convert square meters to square yards.
     3
     4  const MetersToYards : 1.196
     5
     6  var SqMeters : real     % Input - size in meters
*****    ^^^
     7
     8  % Read the fabric size in square meters.
     9  put "Enter fabric size in square meters >"
    10  get SqMeters
    11
    12  % Convert the fabric size to square yards.
    13  MetersToYards * SqMeters := SqYards
*****    ^^^^^^^^^^^^^
    14  % Display the fabric size in square yards.
    15  put "The fabric size in square yards is ",
    16          SqYards
*****            ^^^^^^^
```

```
Line  6:  Syntax error at 'var'
Line 13:  'MetersToYards' is not a procedure
Line 16:  'SqYards' has not been declared
```

The actual format of the listing and error messages produced by your compiler will differ from Fig. 2.16. In this listing, whenever an error is detected, the compiler prints a line starting with five asterisks, with caret symbols (^) marking the detected error.

As an example of how this works, look at the first error in the program, which was detected after the keyword const in line 4 was processed by the compiler. At this point the compiler recognized that the symbol := was missing and tried to find it. The compiler looked as far as line 6 before giving up and producing the error message "Syntax error at 'var'", for the following line (line 6).

The transposed assignment statement in line 13 is detected as an ill-formed procedure call (we have not yet introduced Turing's procedure calls) and results in the syntax error message "'MetersToYards' is not a procedure". The compiler recovers from this error, by skipping over the rest of the line, and as a result does not notice that SqYards on this line does not have a declaration.

Finally, the compiler gets to line 16 and detects that SqYards has not been declared. A missing declaration is a very common source of syntax errors. This can happen because the programmer forgot the declaration or mistyped the name of the identifier.

One syntax error often leads to the generation of multiple error messages. For example, forgetting to declare variable `FirstName` may cause an error message to be printed each time `FirstName` is used in the program. For this reason, it is often a good idea to initially concentrate on correcting the errors in the declaration part of a program and then recompile rather than attempt to fix all the errors at once. Many later errors will disappear once the declarations are correct.

Syntax errors are often caused by the improper use of quote marks with strings. Make sure that you always use a double quote or quotation mark to begin and end a string. A string must begin and end on the same line.

Another common syntax error is a missing or extra double quote in a string. If the double quote at the end is missing, the compiler will assume that whatever follows is part of the string.

The string below contains an extra quote.

```
put "Pedro says, "Hello"
```

The compiler will assume that the quote mark just before `Hello` is terminating the string. This string must be entered as

```
put "Pedro says, \"Hello\""
```

where `\"` is needed to indicate a single double quote inside a string. This put statement produces the output:

```
Pedro says, "Hello"
```

When using comments, you must be very careful to insert the symbols `%` or `/* ... */` where required. If the percent sign `%` is missing, the compiler will not recognize the beginning of the comment and will attempt to process the comment as a Turing statement. This should cause a syntax error. If the closing `*/` is missing from a `/* ... */` comment, the comment will simply be extended to include the program statements that follow it. If the comment is not terminated, the rest of the program will be included in the comment and a syntax error such as `"Comment ends at end of file"` will be printed.

Run-time Errors

Figure 2.17 shows an example of a run-time error. The program compiles successfully, but contains no statement assigning a value to variable `X` before the assignment statement

```
Z := X + Y
```

is executed. The error message shown after the program listing indicates the cause of the error (`"Variable has no value"`) and the location (line 6) of the error.

FIGURE 2.17   A Program with a Run-time Error

```
1  % The "Testerr" program
2
3  var X, Y, Z : real
4
5  Y := 5.0
6  Z := X + Y
7  put X, Y, Z
```

Line 6: Variable has no value.

Another common run-time error is "Division by zero," which occurs if the program attempts to divide one variable by another that has a value of zero. Another common error, "Arithmetic overflow," is detected when a program attempts to store a number that is too large in a variable.

As we indicated earlier, debugging a program can be very time-consuming. The best approach is to plan your program carefully and desk check it to eliminate bugs before running the program. If you are not sure of the syntax for a particular statement, look it up. If you follow this approach, you will save yourself much time and trouble.

Chapter Review

In this chapter you saw how to use the Turing programming language to perform some very fundamental operations. You learned how to instruct the computer to read information into memory, perform some simple computations, and print the results of the computation. All of this was done using symbols (punctuation marks, variable names, and special operators such as *, −, and +) that are familiar, easy to remember, and easy to use. You do not have to know very much about your computer in order to understand and use Turing.

The remainder of this text introduces more features of the Turing language and provides rules for using these features. You must remember throughout that, unlike the rules of English, the rules of Turing are precise and allow no exceptions. The compiler will be unable to translate Turing instructions that violate these rules. Remember to declare every identifier used as a variable or constant and to separate program statements with semicolons.

New Turing Constructs in Chapter 2

Table 2.10 describes the new Turing constructs introduced in this chapter.

TABLE 2.10 Summary of New Turing Constructs

Construct	Effect

Constant Declaration
`const Tax := 25.00`
`const Star := "*"`
	Associates the constant `Tax` with the real value `25.00` and the constant `Star` with the type string value `"*"`.

Variable Declaration
`var X, Y, Z : real`
`var Me, It : int`
	Allocates memory cells named `X`, `Y`, and `Z` for storage of real numbers and `Me` and `It` for storage of integers.

Assignment Statement `Area := Width * Height`	Assigns the product of `Width` and `Height` as the value of `Area`.
Get Statement `get Hours, Rate`	Enters data into the variable `Hours` and `Rate`.
Put Statement `put X, Y`	Displays the values of `X` and `Y` and advances the cursor to the next line.
Put Statement with Dot-Dot `put "X = ", X :4:2 ..`	Displays the string `"X = "` followed by the value of `X` printed in a field of four or more columns and rounded to two decimal places.
Open Statement (Optional) `open :n, "InData", get`	Prepares file `InData` for reading.
Get with File (Optional) `get :n, X, Y`	Reads values of `X` and `Y` from a line of the file.

Quick-Check Exercises

1. What value is assigned to X by the following statement?

   ```
   X := 25.0 * 3.0 / 2.5
   ```

2. What value is assigned to X by the statement below, assuming X is initially `10.0`?

   ```
   X := X - 20.0
   ```

3. Show the exact form of the output line displayed when X is 3.456.

```
put "Three values of X are ", X :4:1, "*",
          X :5:2, "*", X :6:3
```

4. Show the exact form of the output line when N is 345.

```
put "Three values of N are ", N :4, "*",
          N :5, "*", N :1
```

5. Give the appropriate data type to represent the following items: number of children at school, a letter grade on an exam, the average number of school days absent each year.
6. In which step of the software development method are the problem inputs and outputs identified?
7. How does put without dot-dot differ in its effect from put with dot-dot?
8. If a get statement is reading two numbers, what character is typed after the first number? What is typed after the second number?
9. How does the computer determine how many data values to enter when a get statement is performed?
10. How does the program user determine how many data values to enter when a get statement is performed?
11. The compiler listing shows what kind of errors (syntax or run-time)?

Answers to Quick-Check Exercises

1. 30.0
2. -10.0
3. Three values of X are 3.5* 3.46* 3.456
4. Three values of N are 345* 345*345
5. int, string, real
6. Analysis
7. Put without dot-dot causes subsequent output to be displayed on a new line.
8. A blank, Return key
9. It depends on the number of variables in the input list.
10. From reading the prompt
11. Syntax errors

Review Questions

1. What type of information should be specified in the program header section comments?
2. Check the variables that are syntactically correct.

Income	___	Two Fold	___
1time	___	C3PO	___
const	___	Income#1	___
Tom's	___	item	___

3. What is illegal about the declarations and statement below?

```
const Pi := 3.14159
var C, R : real
Pi := C / (2 * R * R)
```

4. What computer action is required by the statement below?

```
var Cell : real
```

5. If the average size of a family is `2.8` and this value is stored in the variable `FamilySize`, provide the Turing statement to display this fact in a readable way (leave the cursor on the same line).

6. Write the data requirements, necessary formulas, and algorithm for programming project 6.

7. List the four standard data types of Turing.

8. Convert the program statements below to read and echo data in batch mode.

```
put "Enter three numbers separated by spaces " ..
get X, Y, Z
put "Enter two words"
get Word1, Word2
```

9. Write an algorithm that allows for the input of an integer value, doubles it, subtracts 10, and displays the result.

Programming Projects

1. Write a program to convert a temperature in degrees Fahrenheit to degrees Celsius.

   Problem input
   ```
   Fahrenheit : int      % Fahrenheit temperature
   ```

   Problem output
   ```
   Celsius : real        % Celsius temperature
   ```

   RELEVANT FORMULA
   ```
   Celsius = (5/9) * (Fahrenheit - 32)
   ```

2. Write a program to read two data items and print their sum, difference, product and quotient.

   Problem inputs
   ```
   X, Y : int     % two items
   ```

   Problem outputs
   ```
   Sum : int             % Sum of X and Y
   Difference : int      % Difference of X and Y
   Product : int         % Product of X and Y
   Quotient : real       % Quotient of X divided by Y
   ```

3. Write a program to read in the weight (in pounds) of an object and to compute and print its weight in kilograms and grams. Hint: one pound is equal to 0.453592 kilograms or 453.59237 grams.

4. Write a program that prints your first initial as a block letter. Hint: Use a 6 x 6 grid for the letter and print six strings. Each string should consist of asterisks (*) interspersed with blanks.

5. If a human heart beats on the average of once a second, how many times does the heart beat in a lifetime of 78 years? (Use 365.25 for days in a year.) Rerun your program for a heart rate of 75 beats per minute.

6. Write a program that reads in the length and width of a rectangular yard and the length and width of a rectangular house situated in the yard. Your program should compute the time required to cut the grass at the rate of 2 square meters a second.

7. Write a program that reads in the numerators and denominators of two fractions. Your program should print the numerator and denominator of the fraction that represents the product of the two fractions. Also, print the percent equivalent of the resulting product.

8. Redo project 7, only this time compute the sum of the two fractions.

9. The Pythagorean theorem states that the sum of the squares of the sides of a right triangle is equal to the square of the hypotenuse. For example, if two sides of a right triangle have lengths 3 and 4, then the hypotenuse must have a length of 5. The integers 3, 4, and 5 together form a Pythagorean triple. There is an infinite number of such triples. Given two positive integers, m and n, where $m > n$, a Pythagorean triple can be generated by the following formulas:

```
side1 = m² - n²
side2 = 2mn
hypotenuse = m² + n²
```

Write a program that reads in values for m and n and prints the values of the Pythagorean triple generated by the formulas above.

CHAPTER 3

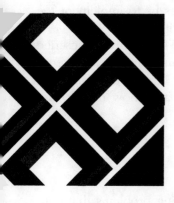

Top-Down Design with Procedures and Functions

In this chapter, we continue our discussion of problem solving. We will introduce top-down design and show how to develop a program starting from its system documentation. We will also show how to solve a new problem by extending the solution to a problem that has already been solved.

We discuss the importance of structured programming and why it is practiced. We describe the three types of control structures used in structured programming.

Next, we show how to represent the relationship between a problem and its subproblems using a structure chart. We will introduce an important system structure, the procedure, which enables us to implement the solution to a subproblem as a separate program entity.

Finally we discuss another system structure, the function, and describe how the use of functions and procedures enables us to more easily reuse code that has already been tested and debugged in new programs. We also introduce the predefined functions of Turing and show how to use them to perform mathematical computations.

3.1 Top-Down Design and Program Development

We will follow an approach to solving programming problems that consists of five separate phases:

1. Problem statement (or requirements specification)
2. Analysis
3. Design
4. Coding
5. Testing

During the requirements specification phase, we determine precisely what problem we are expected to solve and what the program solution is supposed to do. This may require further clarification from your instructor or the person posing the problem.

During the analysis phase, we study the completed problem specification and attempt to identify the problem inputs and desired outputs. We also list any formulas or relationships that might be relevant to the problem solution.

During the design phase, we write an algorithm that lists the major subproblems. Using a process called "divide and conquer", we solve these subproblems separately. We add solution details or refinements to the initial algorithm as required to clarify the solution.

During the coding phase, we implement the refined algorithm in Turing. The data requirements identified in the analysis phase form the basis of the declaration part of the program; the refined algorithm forms the basis for the program body. Finally we·test and debug the program. After all obvious errors are removed, we run the program several times with a variety of test data to ensure that the program works properly. We check the program results against computations that are done by hand or using a calculator.

The approach to algorithm development followed in the design phase is called *top-down design*. This means that we start with the most abstract formulation of a problem and work down to more detailed subproblems. In this chapter, we will show several ways to facilitate and enhance the top-down approach to programming. We begin by showing one way to move more efficiently from the analysis and design phase to the coding phase.

Developing a Program from Its System Documentation

If we carefully follow the software development method, we will produce important system documentation before we code the program. This *system documentation* summarizes our intentions and thought process as we develop the program data requirements and algorithm.

We also provide program documentation inside the program itself in the form of comments. We use comments to describe the purpose of each program variable. We also precede each major algorithm step in the program body with a comment that describes its implementation.

If you follow the software development method, you can use the system documentation developed as a starting point in coding your program. For example, you can begin by duplicating the problem data requirements (part of the analysis phase) in the program declaration part (see Fig. 3.1). Then you can edit these lines to conform to the Turing syntax for constant and variable declarations, thereby, writing the declaration part of the program (see Fig. 3.2).

To develop the program body, use the initial algorithm written as a list of comments as a framework for the program. Then, move each algorithm refinement under the algorithm step that it refines. Figure 3.3 shows the situation after this step occurs; note that the constant `MetersToYards` has been added to the declaration part. After the refinements are in place in the program body, you can begin to write actual Turing statements. Place the Turing code for a step that is not refined directly under that step. For a step that is refined, either edit the refinement to change it from English to Turing or replace it with Turing code (see Fig. 3.4). We will illustrate this process in the next case study.

FIGURE 3.1	**Program with Unedited Declaration Part**

```
% The "Metric" program
% Convert square meters to square yards


Problem inputs
    SqMeters      % Fabric size in square meters


Problem outputs
    SqYards       % Fabric size in square yards
```

FIGURE 3.2   Declaration Part After Editing

```
% The "Metric" program
% Convert square meters to square yards

var SqMeters : real    % Input - fabric size in square meters
var SqYards : real     % Output - fabric size in square yards
```

FIGURE 3.3   Using the Refined Algorithm as the Program's Framework

```
% The "Metric" program
% Convert square meters to square yards

const MetersToYards := 1.196  % conversion constant

var SqMeters : real    % Input - fabric size in square meters
var SqYards : real     % Output - fabric size in square yards

% 1. Read the fabric size in square meters

% 2. Convert the fabric size to square yards.
%    2.1  The fabric size in square yards is 1.196
%             times the fabric size in square meters

% 3. Display the fabric size in square yards
```

FIGURE 3.4   Final Edited Program

```
% The "Metric" program
% Convert square meters to square yards

const MetersToYards := 1.196  % conversion constant

var SqMeters : real    % Input - fabric size in square meters
var SqYards : real     % Output - fabric size in square yards

% Read the fabric size in square meters
put "Enter the fabric size in square meters >"
get SqMeters

% Convert the fabric size to square yards
SqYards := MetersToYards * SqMeters

% Display the fabric size in square yards
put "The fabric size in square yards is ", SqYards
```

Case Study:

Finding the Area and Circumference of a Circle

1. Problem

Read in the radius of a circle and compute and print its area and circumference.

2. Analysis

Clearly the problem input is the circle radius. There are two outputs requested: the circle area and circumference. These variables should be type `real` because the inputs and outputs may contain fractional parts.

From our knowledge of geometry, we know the relationship between a circle's radius and its area and circumference; these formulas are listed below along with the data requirements. Note that we have written the English description of each variable as a Turing comment to make it easier to produce the declaration part of our solution program.

DATA REQUIREMENTS

Problem constant

```
Pi = 3.14159
```

Problem inputs

```
Radius : real     % Radius of a circle
```

Problem outputs

```
Area : real       % Area of a circle
Circum : real     % Circumference of a circle
```

RELEVANT FORMULAS

area of a circle = $\pi \times \text{radius}^2$

circumference of a circle = $2\pi \times \text{radius}$

3. Design

Once you know the problem inputs and outputs, you should list the steps necessary to solve the problem. It is important that you pay close attention to the order of the steps. The initial algorithm follows.

INITIAL ALGORITHM

1. Read the circle radius.
2. Find the area.
3. Find the circumference.
4. Print the area and circumference.

ALGORITHM REFINEMENTS

Next, we should refine any steps that do not have an obvious solution (for instance, steps 2 and 3).

Step 2 refinement
    2.1 Assign Pi * Radius^2 to Area

Step 3 refinement
    3.1 Assign 2 * Pi * Radius to Circum

4. Implementation

Figure 3.5 shows the Turing program so far. The program body consists of the initial algorithm with its refinements.

FIGURE 3.5

Outline of Program Circle

```
% The "Circle" program
% Find and print the area and circumference of a circle

const Pi := 3.14159

var Radius : real    % Input - radius of a circle
var Area : real      % Output - area of a circle
var Circum : real    % Output - circumference

% 1. Read the circle radius

% 2. Find the area
%      2.1  Assign Pi * Radius ** 2 to Area

% 3. Find the circumference
%      3.1  Assign 2 * Pi * Radius to Circum

% 4. Print the area and circumference
```

To write the final program, we must convert the refinements (steps 2.1 and 3.1) to Turing, write Turing code for the unrefined steps (steps 1 and 4), and delete the step numbers from the comments. Figure 3.6 shows the final program.

FIGURE 3.6

Finding the Area and Circumference of a Circle

```
% The "Circle" program
% Find and print the area and circumference of a circle

const Pi := 3.14159

var Radius : real  % Input   - radius of a circle
var Area   : real  % Output  - area of a circle
var Circum : real  % Output  - circumference

% Read the circle radius
put "Enter radius >"
get Radius
```

```
% Find the area
Area := Pi * Radius * Radius

% Find the circumference
Circum := 2.0 * Pi * Radius

% Print the area and circumference
put "The area is ", Area :4:2
put "The circumference is ", Circum :4:2
```

```
Enter radius >5.0
The area is 78.54
The circumference is 31.42
```

5. Testing

The sample output shown in Fig. 3.6 provides a good test of the solution because it is relatively easy to compute the area and circumference by hand for a radius value of 5.0. The radius squared is 25.0 so the value of the area appears correct. The circumference should be ten times Pi which is also an easy number to compute by hand.   ✖

Exercises for Section 3.1

Self-Check

1. Describe the problem inputs and outputs and algorithm for computing an employee's gross salary given the hours worked and hourly rate.
2. Write a program outline from the algorithm you developed in exercise 1. Use Fig. 3.5 as a model for your outline.

Programming

1. Add statement refinements to the program outline shown below and write the final Turing program.

```
% The "Sumavg" program
% Find and print the sum and average of two numbers

var One, Two : real   % Input  - numbers to process
var Sum       : real   % Output - sum of One and Two
var Average : real   % Output - average of One, Two

% 1. Read two numbers
% 2. Compute sum of numbers
% 3. Compute average of numbers
% 4. Print sum and average
```

2. Write a complete Turing program for Self-Check exercise 1.

3.2 Extending a Problem Solution

Quite often the solution of one problem turns out to be the basis for the solution to another problem. For example, we can solve the next problem by building on the solution to the previous problem.

Case Study:

Finding the Most Pizza for Your Money

1. Problem

You and your college roommates frequently order a late-night pizza snack. There are many pizzerias in the area that deliver to dormitories. Since you are on a tight budget, you would like to know which pizza is the best value.

2. Analysis

To find which pizza is the best value, we must be able to do a meaningful comparison of pizza costs. One way to do this is to compute the unit price of each pizza. The *unit price* of an item is obtained by dividing the total price of that item by a measure of its quantity. A good measure of quantity is the pizza weight, but pizzas are not sold by weight — they are sold by size (diameter) measured in inches. Consequently, the best that we can do is to use some meaningful measure of quantity based on the pizza diameter. One such measure is the pizza area. So, for our purposes we will define the unit price of a pizza as its price divided by its area.

The data requirements below list the pizza size and price as problem inputs. Although the problem statement does not ask us to display the pizza area, we are listing it as a problem output because the pizza area will give us some idea of how many friends we can invite to share our pizza. The radius (one-half of the diameter) is listed as a program variable because we need it to compute the pizza area, but it is not a problem input or output.

DATA REQUIREMENTS

Problem constant

```
Pi = 3.14159
```

Problem inputs

```
Size : real           % Diameter of a pizza
Price : real          % Price of a pizza
```

Problem outputs

```
UnitPrice : real      % Unit cost of a pizza
Area : real           % Area of a pizza
```

Program variables

```
Radius : real         % Radius of a pizza
```

RELEVANT FORMULAS
area of a circle = $\pi \times radius^2$
radius of a circle = diameter / 2
unit price = total price / area

3. Design

We mentioned earlier that we are basing the problem solution on the solution to the case study in Section 3.1 (Finding the area and circumference of a circle). The initial algorithm is similar to the one shown earlier. The step that computes the circle circumference (Step 3) has been replaced with one that computes the pizza unit price.

INITIAL ALGORITHM
1. Read in the pizza diameter and price.
2. Compute the pizza area.
3. Compute the pizza unit price.
4. Display the unit price and area.

The algorithm refinements follow. The refinement of step 2 shows that we must compute the pizza radius before we can compute its area.

Step 2 Refinement
2.1   Assign `Diameter / 2` to `Radius`
2.2   Assign `Pi * Radius * Radius` to `Area`

Step 3 Refinement
3.1   Assign `Price / Area` to `UnitPrice`

4. Implementation

Figure 3.7 shows the Turing program. We will write this program the same way as before: by editing the data requirements to develop the declarations and by using the initial algorithm with refinements as a starting point for the program body.

FIGURE 3.7   Pizza Program

```
% The "Pizza" program
% Compute the unit price of a pizza
const Pi := 3.14159

var Diameter  : real    % Input - diameter of a pizza
var Price     : real    % Input - price of a pizza
var UnitPrice : real    % Output - unit cost of pizza
var Area      : real    % Output - area of a pizza
var Radius    : real    % Radius of a pizza

% Read in the pizza diameter and price
put "Diameter of pizza in inches >" ..
get Diameter
```

```
        put "Price of pizza $" ..
        get Price

        % Compute the pizza area
        Radius := Diameter / 2
        Area := Pi * Radius * Radius

        % Compute the pizza unit price
        UnitPrice := Price / Area

        % Display the area and unit price
        put skip, "The pizza unit price is $",
              UnitPrice :4:2, " per square inch"
        put "The pizza area is ", Area :3:1,
              " square inches"
```

```
Diameter of pizza in inches >9.0
Price of pizza $7.45

The pizza unit price is $0.12 per square inch
The pizza area is 63.6 square inches
```

5. Testing   To test this program, run it with a few different pizza sizes. You can verify that the program is working correctly by multiplying the unit price and area. This product should equal the price of the pizza.   ✖

Exercises for Section 3.2

Self-Check

1. What changes are required to extend the payroll algorithm described in Section 3.1 (Self-Check exercise 1), to allow for overtime hours to be paid at 1.5 times the employee's normal hourly rate when computing his or her gross salary? Assume that overtime hours are entered separately.

Programming

1. Write a complete Turing program for the revised payroll algorithm developed in Self-Check exercise 1.

3.3 Structured Programming and Control Structures

In this textbook we teach *structured programming*, which is a disciplined approach to programming that results in programs that are easy to read and understand, and are less likely to contain errors. The emphasis is on following accepted program style guidelines (such as using meaningful names for identifiers) to write code that is adequately documented with comments and is clear and readable. Obscure tricks and programming shortcuts are strongly discouraged. Government organizations and industry are strong advocates of structured programming because structured programs are much more cost effective in the long term.

Program maintenance involves modifying a program to remove previously undetected bugs and to keep it up-to-date as government regulations or company policies change. It is not uncommon to maintain a program for five years or more, often after the programmers who originally coded it have left the company or moved on to other positions.

FIGURE 3.8   A Program as a Sequence of Three Control Structures

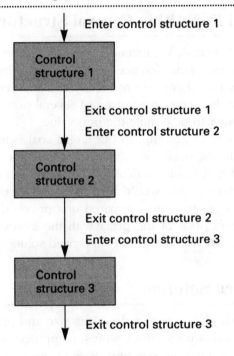

Control Structures

Structured programming utilizes *control structures* to control the flow of statement execution in a program. We can write a program as a sequence of control structures rather than as a sequence of individual statements (see Fig. 3.8).

Statement Sequences

There are three categories of control structures: sequence, selection, and iteration. So far, we have illustrated sequential control using sequences of Turing statements, as in:

$$statement_1$$
$$statement_2$$
$$\bullet$$
$$\bullet$$
$$\bullet$$
$$statement_n$$

Control flows from $statement_1$ to $statement_2$, and so on. The statements of a program form such a sequence. Later in this chapter, we will introduce two system structures, procedures and functions, that also contain sequences of statements. We will describe the control structures for selection in Chapter 4 and the control structures for repetition in Chapter 5.

Motivation for Selection and Repetition Control Structures

In the last section, we extended the solution for one problem (Find a circle radius and circumference) into a second related problem (Find the unit price of a pizza). We are not really finished yet because our goal was to be able to do a cost comparison of several pizzas with different prices and sizes in order to determine the best value.

One way to accomplish our larger goal is to run this program several different times, once for each pizza, and record the results. Then we can scan the list of results to determine which pizza has the lowest unit price.

A better solution would be to write a program that repeated the computation steps and also compared unit prices, displaying as its final result the size and price of the pizza with the lowest unit price. Let's write an algorithm that will give us this improved solution.

Initial Algorithm for Improved Solution

1. For each pizza, read in the pizza size and price and compute unit cost. Compare the unit cost just computed with the previous unit costs and save the size and price of the pizza whose unit cost is the smallest so far.
2. Display the size and price of the pizza with the smallest unit cost.

The purpose of step 1 of the algorithm is to perform the cost computation for each individual pizza and somehow save the size and price of the pizza whose unit cost was the smallest. After all costs are computed, step 2 displays the size and price of the pizza which is the best buy.

We don't know how to do step 1 yet in Turing because it involves the use of repetition and selection control structures. However, we can write a refinement of this step that will give you some idea of where we are heading in the next few chapters.

Step 1 refinement

 1.1 Repeat the following steps for each pizza:
 1.2 Read in the next pizza size and price.
 1.3 Compute the unit price.
 1.4 If the new unit price is the smallest one so far, then save this pizza's size, price, and unit price.

Step 1.1 above specifies the *repetition* of a group of steps: step 1.2 (read the data), step 1.3 (compute new price), step 1.4 (compare new price with smallest so far). We will repeat these steps as many times as necessary until all unit prices are computed and compared. Each time we compute a new unit price, step 1.4 compares it to the others, and the current pizza's size and price are saved if its unit price is smaller than any others computed so far. If the unit price is not the smallest so far, the current pizza's size and price are not saved. Step 1.4 is a *selection step* because it selects between the two possible outcomes: a) save the pizza's data b) do not save the pizza's data.

Exercises for Section 3.3

Self-Check

1. When would a repetition step be used in an algorithm?
2. Show how the pizza algorithm and problem inputs described in Section 3.2 could be modified to allow the computation of the unit price of either a single circular pizza or a single square (rectangular) pizza.

3.4   Structure Charts

As we mentioned earlier, one of the fundamental ideas in problem solving is dividing a problem into subproblems and solving each subproblem independently of the others. In attempting to solve a subproblem at one level, we often introduce new subproblems at a lower level. The splitting of a problem into its related subproblems is analogous to the process of refining an algorithm. Each time we refine an algorithm step (subproblem), we generate new refinements (subproblems) at a lower level. In this section, we introduce a documentation tool that will enable you to keep track of the relationships between subproblems. We do this by examining a case study.

�֎ Case Study:

Drawing Simple Diagrams

1. Problem   You would like to be able to draw some simple diagrams or figures on your printer or screen. Two examples are the diagram for a house and the stick figure of a girl in Fig. 3.9.

2. Analysis   The figure on the left of Fig. 3.9 consists of a triangle without its base on top of a rectangle. The figure on the right consists of a shape that resembles a circle, a triangle, and a triangle without its base. We should be able to draw both diagrams using the four basic graphical components below.

- a circle
- a base line
- parallel lines
- intersecting lines

FIGURE 3.9   House and Stick Figure

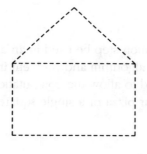 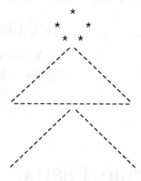

3. Design   Let's focus on the stick figure of a girl. We can divide the problem of drawing this figure into the three problems below.

INITIAL ALGORITHM
1. Draw a circle.
2. Draw a triangle.
3. Draw intersecting lines.

ALGORITHM REFINEMENTS
Since a triangle is not one of our basic components, we must refine step 2.

Step 2 Refinement
    2.1   Draw intersecting lines.
    2.2   Draw a base.

We can use a diagram called a *structure chart* to show the relationship between the original problem and its subproblems. The structure chart corresponding to the initial algorithm above is shown in Fig. 3.10.

FIGURE 3.10   Structure Chart for Drawing Stick Figure

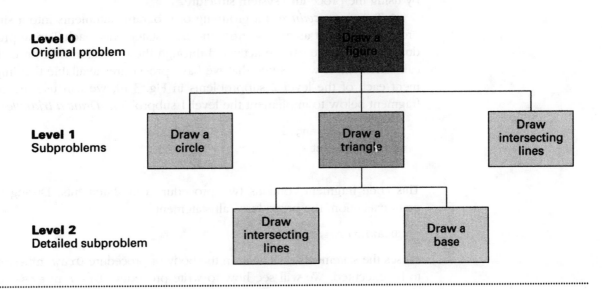

Level 0
Original problem

Level 1
Subproblems

Level 2
Detailed subproblem

As we trace down this diagram, we go from an abstract problem to a more detailed subproblem. The original problem is shown at the top, or level 0, of the structure chart. The major subproblems appear at level 1. The different subproblems resulting from the refinement of a level 1 step are shown at level 2, and are connected to their level 1 subproblem. The structure chart shows that the subproblem *Draw a triangle* (level 1) is dependent on the solutions to the subproblems *Draw intersecting lines* and *Draw a base* (both level 2). Since the subproblem *Draw a circle* is not refined further, no level 2 subproblems are connected to it.

Structure charts are intended to show the structural relationship between subproblems. The algorithm (not the structure chart) shows the order in which we must carry out each step to solve the problem.   ✖

Exercise for Section 3.4

Self-Check

1. Draw the structure chart for the pizza case study in Section 3.2.
2. Draw the structure chart for the problem of drawing the house shown in Fig. 3.9.
3. Draw the structure chart for the problem of drawing a triangle and a rectangle with a circle between them.

3.5 Procedures

The structure chart proceeds from the original problem at the top level down to its detailed subproblems at the bottom level. We would like to follow this *top-down* approach when we code a program. We can do this by using the procedure system structure.

A Turing *procedure* is a grouping of program statements into a single program unit. Just as we use get and put statements, each Turing procedure that we write can be activated through the execution of a procedure call statement. If we assume that we have procedures available that implement each of the level 2 subproblems in Fig. 3.10, we can use the code fragment below to implement the level 1 subproblem *Draw a triangle*.

```
% Draw a triangle
DrawIntersect
DrawBase
```

This code fragment contains two procedure call statements. During program execution, the procedure call statement

```
DrawIntersect
```

causes the statements contained in the body of procedure DrawIntersect to be executed. We will see how to write procedure DrawIntersect in the next section.

Figure 3.11 shows the body of the program that draws a stick figure, assuming that the solution to each subproblem in Fig. 3.10 is implemented as a separate procedure. The program body (called the *main program*) implements our original algorithm. The program body begins with the code for step 1 (Draw a circle) which consists of a call to procedure DrawCircle. The code for step 2 (Draw a triangle) consists of the two procedure call statements above. The code for step 3 (Draw intersecting lines) consists of a second call to procedure DrawIntersect.

FIGURE 3.11 Program for Drawing a Stick Figure

```
% StickFigure

% Draw a circle
DrawCircle

% Draw a triangle
DrawIntersect
DrawBase

% Draw intersecting lines
DrawIntersect
```

PROCEDURE CALL STATEMENT
Form: *pname*
Example: `DrawCircle`

Interpretation: The procedure call statement initiates the execution of procedure *pname*. After *pname* has finished executing, the program statement that follows the procedure call will be executed.

Declaring Procedures

Just like other identifiers in Turing, a procedure must be declared before it can be referenced in a program body. Figure 3.12 shows the declaration for procedure `DrawCircle`.

FIGURE 3.12   Procedure DrawCircle

```
% Draw a circle
procedure DrawCircle
    put "    *   "
    put " *     *"
    put "  * *  "
end DrawCircle
```

A procedure declaration begins with a *procedure heading,* which consists of the word `procedure` followed by the procedure name (an identifier). We will always place a comment before the header, describing the purpose of the procedure, although this is not required by Turing. Following the header comes the *procedure body.* The procedure body ends with `end` and the procedure's name. In Fig. 3.12, the procedure body contains the three `put` statements that cause the computer to draw a shape that resembles a circle. The procedure call statement

```
DrawCircle
```

causes these `put` statements to execute.

Each procedure declaration may contain declarations for its own constants and variables. These identifiers are considered *local* to the procedure; in other words, they can only be referenced within the procedure (more on this later).

PROCEDURE DECLARATION
Form: procedure *pname*
                            declarations and statements
                    end pname

Example:
```
% Skip three lines
procedure SkipThree
    put ""
    put ""
    put ""
end SkipThree
```

Interpretation: The procedure *pname* is declared. Any identifiers that are declared in the *local-declarations* are defined only during the execution of the procedure and can only be referenced within the procedure. The *procedure body* describes the data manipulation to be performed by the procedure.

The SkipThree procedure given as an example of a procedure declaration displays three blank lines using three copies of this statement:

```
put ""
```

Another way to display three blank lines is by using this single statement:

```
put skip, skip    % Display three blank lines
```

Each skip finishes a line and the end of the put statement itself finishes another line; the result is the display of three blank lines.

Placement of Procedure Declarations in a Program

The three procedures called in Fig. 3.11 must appear in the first part of the program. It makes no difference which procedure is declared first; their order of execution is determined by the order of procedure call statements in the program body. Figure 3.13 shows the complete program with its procedures.

The DrawIntersect procedure in Fig. 3.13 displays the right intersecting line using the back slash character \. As you may recall from Chapter 2, this character is used for special purposes inside string literals, for example, it is used to allow us to place a quote character in the middle of a string literal. When we want to use a back slash as an actual character in a string, and not for special purposes, we must write two copies of it. For example, this occurs in the DrawIntersect procedure in the statement:

```
put " / \\ "
```

When we write \\ this way, it is interpreted to mean a single back slash character.

FIGURE 3.13   Program to Draw a Stick Figure

```
% The "Stickfig" program
% Display a stick figure

% Draw a circle
procedure DrawCircle
    put "   *   "
    put "  *   *"
    put "   * *  "
end DrawCircle

% Draw intersecting lines
procedure DrawIntersect
    % Each double \ produces only one \
    put "  / \\"
    put " /  \\"
end DrawIntersect

% Draw a base
procedure DrawBase
    put "———"
end DrawBase

% StickFigure

% Draw a circle
DrawCircle

% Draw a triangle
DrawIntersect
DrawBase

% Draw intersecting lines
DrawIntersect
```

PROGRAM
STYLE

USE OF COMMENTS IN A PROGRAM WITH PROCEDURES
Figure 3.13 includes several comments. Each procedure is immediately preceded by a comment that describes its purpose.

Relative Order of Execution of Procedures and the Main Program

In the stick figure problem, we wrote the main program body as a sequence of procedure call statements before we specified the details of all procedures. The next step is to provide the missing procedure declarations.

When we actually put the separate procedures and main program body together, the procedures appear in the beginning of the program, preceding their use in the main program body. The compiler must translate the procedure declarations before it translates the main program body. When it reaches the end of each procedure body, the compiler inserts a statement that causes a *transfer of control* back from the procedure to the calling statement. In the main program body, the compiler translates a procedure call statement as a transfer of control to the procedure.

Figure 3.14 shows the main program body and procedure DrawCircle of the stick figure program in separate areas of memory. Although the Turing statements are shown in Fig. 3.14, the object code corresponding to each statement is actually stored in memory.

FIGURE 3.14   Flow of Control Between the Main Program and a Procedure

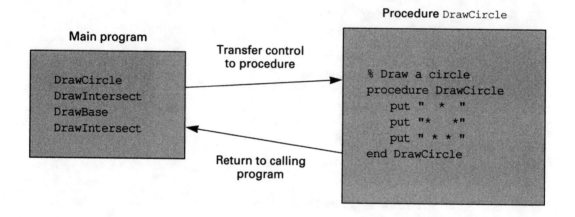

When we run the program, the first statement in the main program body is the first statement executed (the call to DrawCircle in Fig. 3.14). When the computer executes a procedure call statement, it transfers control to the procedure that is referenced. The computer allocates any memory that may be needed for the procedure's local data, and then performs the statements in the procedure body. After the last statement in the procedure body is executed, control returns to the main program and the computer releases any memory that was allocated to the procedure. After the return to the main program, the next statement will be executed (the first call to DrawIntersect in Fig. 3.14).

Procedural Abstraction

One important advantage of procedures is that their use allows us to remove from the main program the code that provides the detailed solution to a subproblem. Since these details are provided separately in the procedures and not in the main program, we can write the main program as soon as we have specified the initial algorithm. We should delay writing the procedure for an algorithm step until we have finished refining that step. This approach to program design is called *procedural abstraction.* Procedural abstraction enables us to defer implementation details to later and to write our program in logically independent sections in the same way that we develop the solution algorithm.

Reuse of Procedures

Another advantage of using procedures is that procedures may be executed more than once in a program. For example, procedure `DrawIntersect` is called twice in Fig. 3.13. Each time `DrawIntersect` is called, the list of output statements shown in Fig. 3.13 is executed and a pair of intersecting lines is drawn. If we were not using procedures, the `put` statements that draw the lines would have to be listed twice in the program body, thereby increasing the main program's length and the chance of an error.

Finally, once you have written and tested a procedure, you may use it in other programs or other procedures. For example, the procedures we created for the `Stickfig` program in Fig. 3.13 could easily be used in programs that draw other diagrams. We will discuss reuse of code in section 3.8.

EXAMPLE 3.1
Many diagrams contain triangles and rectangles. We can use procedures `DrawIntersect`, `DrawParallel`, and `DrawBase` to define two new procedures, `DrawTriangle` and `DrawRectangle` as shown in Fig. 3.15. The comment in Fig. 3.15 reminds us that we must precede our two new procedures with declarations for the three procedures that they call.

FIGURE 3.15   Procedures DrawTriangle and DrawRectangle

```
% Insert procedures DrawIntersect, DrawParallel,
% and DrawBase

% Draw a triangle
procedure DrawTriangle
    DrawIntersect
    DrawBase
end DrawTriangle

% Draw a rectangle
procedure DrawRectangle
    DrawBase
    DrawParallel
    DrawBase
end DrawRectangle
```

Local Declarations in Procedures

Identifiers declared within a procedure are called *local identifiers* because they can only be referenced within the procedure. Figure 3.16 shows another version of procedure DrawCircle with a local constant named OutSymbol. The put statements in the procedure body display OutSymbol at various locations in order to draw a shape that resembles a circle. The advantage of using this local constant is that we can easily change the appearance of the circle being displayed just by changing the line that defines the value of OutSymbol. The circle displayed by this new procedure follows.

FIGURE 3.16   Procedure DrawCircle with a Local Constant

```
% Draw a circle
procedure DrawCircle
    const OutSymbol := "@"

    put " ", OutSymbol
    put OutSymbol, " ", OutSymbol
    put " ", OutSymbol, " ", OutSymbol
end DrawCircle
```

Exercises for Section 3.5

Self-Check

1. Assume that you have procedures PrintH, PrintI, PrintM, and PrintO each of which draws a large block letter (for example, PrintO draws a block letter "O"). What is the effect of executing the main program body below?

   ```
   PrintH
   PrintI
   put skip, skip
   PrintM
   PrintO
   PrintM
   ```

Programming

1. Write a procedure named Skip5 that skips five blank lines.

2. Write procedure `DrawParallel`.
3. Write a main program to print `"HI HO"` in block letters using three procedures. First, provide a structure chart for this problem.
4. Write procedures `PrintH`, `PrintI`, `PrintM`, and `PrintO`.

3.6 Displaying User Instructions

Our use of procedures will be limited for the time being because we do not yet know how to pass information into or out of a procedure that we declare. (We will discuss this further in Section 3.7 and Chapter 7.) Until we have this ability, we will only use procedures to display multiple lines of program output such as instructions to a program user or a title page or a special message that precedes a program's results.

EXAMPLE 3.2

The procedure `Instruct` in Fig. 3.17 displays instructions to a user of our earlier program that computes the area and circumference of a circle (see Fig. 3.6). If procedure `Instruct` is placed in the declaration part of the original program, the new program body can begin with the procedure call statement

    Instruct

The rest of the program body will consist of the executable statements shown earlier. Figure 3.18 shows the output lines displayed by calling procedure `Instruct`. The rest of the program output will be the same as the output shown earlier.

FIGURE 3.17   Procedure Instruct

```
% Display instructions to a user of program "Circle"
procedure Instruct
    put "This program computes the area"
    put "and circumference of a circle."
    put skip, "To use this program, enter the radius"
    put "of the circle after the prompt:"
    put "    Enter radius >", skip
    put "The circumference will be computed in the"
    put "same units of measurement as the radius."
    put "The area will be computed in the same units"
    put "squared.", skip
end Instruct
```

FIGURE 3.18   Output Lines Displayed by Procedure Instruct

```
This program computes the area
and circumference of a circle.

To use this program, enter the radius
of the circle after the prompt:
    Enter radius >

The circumference will be computed in the
same units of measurement as the radius.
The area will be computed in the same units
squared.
```

Exercises for Section 3.6

Self-Check

1. Why is it better to place the user instructions in a procedure, rather than to insert the put statements in the program body itself?

Programming

1. Write a procedure similar to Instruct for the pizza program shown in Fig. 3.7.
2. Rewrite the metric conversion program shown in Fig. 3.4 so that it includes a procedure that displays instructions to its user.
3. Show the revised program Circle with a call to Instruct.

3.7   Procedures as Program Building Blocks

Programmers use procedures as building blocks to construct large programs. When you were very young, you probably used alphabet blocks to demonstrate your potential as a budding architect. These blocks were big so that they would be difficult to swallow. Two sides were smooth and two sides had "ribs" to enable you to build towers of blocks. Unfortunately, you could not place very many blocks on a tower without having the tower topple over. As you grew older, many of you started to play with Lego blocks (see Fig. 3.19). Instead of ribs, each Lego block has one surface with little protrusions and one surface with little cups. By placing the protrusions in the cups, you can build rather elaborate Lego structures.

What does all this have to do with programming? Well, procedures DrawCircle and DrawParallel are like alphabet blocks. You can write some cute little programs with these procedures, but they are not particularly useful. In order to be able to construct interesting programs, we must provide procedures with protrusions and cups so that they can be easily interconnected.

FIGURE 3.19   Lego Blocks

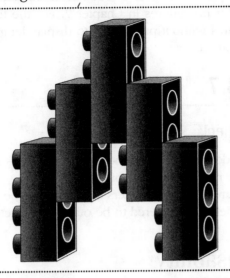

The parameters of a procedure fulfill this purpose. The put statement

```
put "The area is ", Area
```

consists of two parts: the name of the statement, put, and a parameter list. The parameter list contains two parameters (a string and a variable name) which are separated by commas. Because it has a parameter list, procedure put is more useful than a procedure such as PrintM, which can only print the the block letter M. The put statement can display whatever we want it to.

Procedures can have lists of parameters, much in the way that put has parameters. The parameters of a procedure are used to receive information passed into the procedure from the main program (or another procedure) or to return results computed by the procedure back to the main program (or another procedure). Parameters that receive information from the main program are called *input parameters;* parameters that return results to the main program are called *output parameters*. Figure 3.20 is a diagram of a procedure with inputs and outputs.

FIGURE 3.20   Procedure with Inputs and Outputs

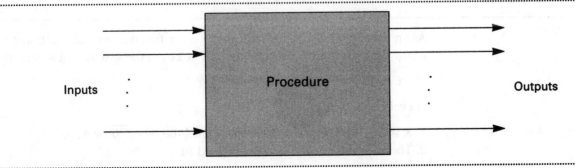

We provide a complete discussion of input parameters and output parameters for procedures in Chapter 7. For the time being, we will only use procedures without parameters to display lengthy messages or instructions to program users.

Exercises for Section 3.7

Self-Check

1. How does the use of procedure parameters make it possible to write larger, more interesting programs?
2. Why are put's parameters considered to be input parameters and get's parameters considered to be output parameters?

▨ 3.8 Functions and Reusability

Turing provides another system structure, called a *function*, that is similar to a procedure and that can also be used as a program building block. Unlike procedures, all function parameters should be input parameters. A function has a single result, which is returned directly to the main program without the use of an output parameter. Figure 3.21 is a diagram of a function showing its inputs and its single output.

FIGURE 3.21   Function with Multiple Inputs and Single Output

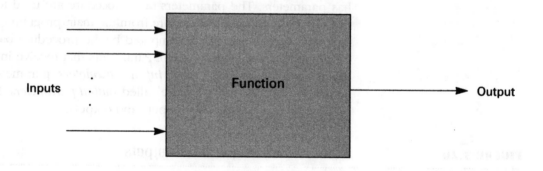

As an example, let's see how we might use a function named sqrt that performs the square root computation. If X is 16.0, the assignment statement

```
Y := sqrt(X)
```

is evaluated as follows:

1. X is 16.0 so function sqrt computes the $\sqrt{16.0}$ or 4.0.
2. The function result, 4.0, is assigned to Y.

The expression part of the assignment statement above is known as a *function designator* consisting of the function name, sqrt, followed by the function *argument*, X, enclosed in parentheses.

A function can be thought of as a "black-box" that is passed one or more input values and automatically returns a single output value. Figure 3.22 illustrates this for the call to function square root above. The value of X (16.0) is the function input and the function result or output is the square root of 16.0 (result is 4.0).

FIGURE 3.22   Function Sqrt as a "Black Box"

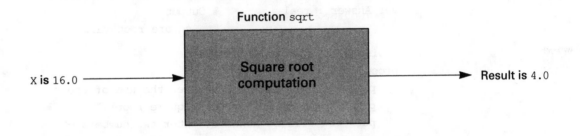

Functions are called into execution by a function designator that is written in an expression. After the function executes, its result is substituted for the function designator. If W is 9.0, the assignment statement

    Z := 5.7 + sqrt(W)

is evaluated as follows:

1. W is 9.0 so function sqrt computes the $\sqrt{9.0}$ or 3.0.
2. The value of 5.7 and 3.0 are added together.
3. The sum, 8.7, is stored in Z.

The two calls to function sqrt discussed so far have different arguments (X and W). We will illustrate this capability of functions again in the next example.

EXAMPLE 3.3
The program in Fig. 3.23 displays the square root of two numbers that are provided as input data (First and Second) and also displays the square root of their sum. To accomplish this, it must call the Turing function sqrt three times:

    Answer := sqrt(First)
    Answer := sqrt(Second)
    Answer := sqrt(First + Second)

For the first two calls, the function arguments are variables (`First` and `Second`). The third call shows that a function argument may also be an expression (`First + Second`). For all three calls, the result returned by function `sqrt` is assigned to variable `Answer`. The program begins with a call to procedure `Instruct`, which displays some user instructions.

FIGURE 3.23   ### Program to Compute Square Roots

```
% The "Sqrts" program
% Perform three square root computations

var First, Second : real   % Input - two data values
var Answer : real          % Output -
                           % a square root value

% Display user instructions
procedure Instruct
    put "This program demonstrates the use of the "
    put "Turing function sqrt (square root)."
    put "You will be asked to enter two numbers —"
    put "the program will display the square root"
    put "of each number and the square root of their"
    put "sum.", skip
end Instruct

% SquareRoots

% Display instructions
Instruct

% Get first number and display its square root
put "Enter the first number >" ..
get First
Answer := sqrt(First)
put "The square root of the first number is ",
            Answer :4:2

% Get second number and display its square root
put "Enter the second number >" ..
get Second
Answer := sqrt(Second)
put "The square root of the second number is ",
            Answer :4:2

% Display square root of the sum of both numbers
Answer := sqrt(First + Second)
put "The square root of the sum of both numbers is ",
            Answer :4:2
```

```
This program demonstrates the use of the
Turing function sqrt (square root).
You will be asked to enter two numbers —
the program will display the square root
of each number and the square root of their
sum.

Enter the first number >9.0
The square root of the first number is 3.00
Enter the second number >16.0
The square root of the second number is 4.00
The square root of the sum of both numbers is 5.00
```

In Fig. 3.23, we have used the Turing function `sqrt` three times. We have been using `sqrt` as a building block to construct our program.

Predefined Functions and Reusability

A primary goal of software engineering is to write error-free code. One way to accomplish this goal is to reuse code that has already been written and tested whenever this is possible. In software engineering, this is called *reusability*. Stated more simply, "Why reinvent the wheel?"

Turing promotes reusability by providing many predefined functions like `sqrt` which can be used to perform complicated mathematical computations. Table 3.1 provides the names and descriptions of some of these.

TABLE 3.1   Some Mathematical Functions

Function	Purpose	Argument	Result
abs(X)	Returns the absolute value of its argument.	real/int	Same as argument
arctan(X)	Returns the angle y in radians satisfying $X = \tan(y)$ where $-\pi/2 < y < \pi/2$.	real/int	real (radians)
cos(X)	Returns the cosine of angle X.	real/int	real (radians)
exp(X)	Returns e^X where e = 2.71828...	real/int	real
ln(X)	Returns the natural logarithm of X for X > 0.0.	real/int	real
round(X)	Returns the closest integer value to its argument.	real/int	int
sin(X)	Returns the sine of angle X.	real/int	real (radians)
sqrt(X)	Returns the positive square root of X for $X \geq 0.0$.	real/int	real
floor(X)	Returns the closest integer that is less than or equal to X.	real/int	int

Except for `abs`, `round`, and `floor`, each of the functions listed in Table 3.1 returns (computes) a `real` value regardless of its argument type (`real` or `int`). The type of the result computed by a reference to `abs` is the same as the type of its argument.

The functions `round` and `floor` always return integer values. These functions determine the integral part of a real-valued expression. Consequently the expressions

```
floor(1.5 * Gross)
round(Cents / 100)
```

have `int` values and may be assigned to `int` variables. When argument X is positive, `floor` *truncates*, or removes, the fractional part of its argument. Function `round` rounds its argument to the nearest whole number. For example, `floor(17.6)` is 17, while `round(17.6)` is 18. In the general case, when X can be negative, `floor` returns the closest integer that is less than or equal to argument X. For example, `floor(-3.8)` is -4, and `round(-3.8)` is -4.

Most of the functions in Table 3.1 perform common mathematical computations. The arguments for `ln` and `sqrt` must be positive. The arguments for `sin` and `cos` must be expressed in radians, not degrees. `Arctan` expresses its result in radians. If you want to use degrees instead of radians, you can use functions called `sind`, `cosd`, and `arctand`.

EXAMPLE 3.4

We can use the Turing function `sqrt` to compute the roots of a quadratic equation in X of the form

$$AX^2 + BX + C = 0$$

The two roots are defined as

$$\text{Root}_1 = \frac{-B + \sqrt{B^2 - 4AC}}{2A} \qquad \text{Root}_2 = \frac{-B - \sqrt{B^2 - 4AC}}{2A}$$

when the *discriminant* $(B^2 - 4AC)$ is greater than zero. If we assume that this is the case, we can use the assignment statements below to assign values to `Root1` and `Root2`.

```
% Compute two roots, Root1 and Root2
% for discriminant > 0.0
Disc := B**2 - 4 * A * C
Root1 := (-B + sqrt(Disc)) / (2 * A)
Root2 := (-B - sqrt(Disc)) / (2 * A)
```

Before using these statements we would have to declare `Disc`, `Root1`, and `Root2` to be real variables.

EXAMPLE 3.5

If we know the length of two sides (B and C) of a triangle (see Fig. 3.24) and the angle between them in degrees (*Alpha*), we can compute the length of the third side (A) using the formula

$$A^2 = B^2 + C^2 - 2BC \cos (Alpha)$$

If you want to use degrees instead of radians, change cos to cosd in this formula. Assuming the angle Alpha is in degrees, the Turing assignment statement below computes the unknown side length.

```
A := sqrt(B**2 + C**2 - 2 * B * C * cosd(Alpha))
```

FIGURE 3.24   Triangle with Unknown Side A

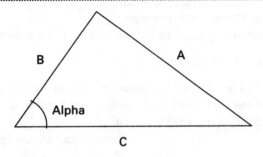

EXAMPLE 3.6

In some programming languages, such as Pascal and C, there is no exponentiation operator. In these languages, it is not possible to write u^v directly. But it is possible, using the theory of logarithms, to compute exponentials, and it is common for programmers to write their own *exp* functions when using those languages.

In Turing, you can compute exponentials directly using the notation u**v. Although this notation does not have the appearance of a function such as sqrt, the ** operator is a function; it takes two arguments (u and v) and it returns one result. In a similar way, operators such as + and * are actually functions, but they are written using special notation that is supported directly by the programming language.

A Look at Where We Are Heading

Turing allows us to write our own functions. Let's assume that we have already written these two functions:

- *Function* FindArea(R), which returns the area of a circle with radius R
- *Function* FindCircum(R), which returns the circumference of a circle with radius R

We can reuse these functions in the two programs shown earlier in this chapter (see Figs. 3.6 and 3.7). For example, Fig. 3.6 shows a program that displays the area and circumference of a circle whose radius is provided as input data. Figure 3.25 shows a revised program that uses our two functions. This program contains the two assignment statements

```
Area   := FindArea(Radius)
Circum := FindCircum(Radius)
```

The expression part of each assignment statement above is a function designator with argument Radius (the circle radius). The result returned by each function execution is stored in an output variable (Area or Circum).

FIGURE 3.25   **Finding Area and Circumference with Functions**

```
% The "Areacirc" program
% Find and print the area and circumference of a circle

const Pi := 3.14159

var Radius : real % Input - radius of a circle
var Area   : real % Output - area of a circle
var Circum : real % Output -
                  % circumference of a circle

% Insert functions FindArea and FindCircum here

% AreaAndCircum

% Read the circle radius
put "Enter radius >" ..
get Radius

% Find the area
Area := FindArea(Radius)

% Find the circumference
Circum := FindCircum(Radius)

% Print the area and circumference
put "The area is ", Area :4:2
put "The circumference is ", Circum :4:2
```

```
Enter radius >5.0
The area is 78.54
The circumference is 31.42
```

The declarations in Fig. 3.25 contains the comment

```
% Insert functions FindArea and FindCircum here
```

which reminds us to insert the functions that we are assuming have been written and tested. In Chapter 7, we will see how to write our own functions.

Besides the advantage of reusing "tried and true" code, the use of these two functions frees us from having to be concerned with the details of computing a circle's area or circumference when we write the main program. This is one of the ways that we can manage and reduce the complexity of writing programs.

Exercises for Section 3.8

Self-Check

1. Rewrite the following mathematical expressions using Turing functions.

   a. $\sqrt{U + V} \times W^2$

   b. $\log_n (X^Y)$

   c. $\sqrt{(X - Y)^2}$

   d. $| XY - W/Z |$

2. Evaluate the following.

   a. `floor(-15.8)`
   b. `round(-15.8)`
   c. `round(6.8) * 3**2`
   d. `sqrt(abs(round(-15.8)))`
   e. `round(3.5)`

Programming

1. Write statements that compute and display the absolute difference of two variables X, Y. If X > Y then the absolute difference is (X - Y); if Y > X then the absolute difference is (Y - X).
2. Using the `round` function, write a Turing statement to round any real value X to the nearest two decimal places. **Hint:** You will have to multiply by `100.0` before rounding.
3. Write a complete Turing program that prompts the user for the Cartesian coordinates of two points (X1, Y1) and (X2, Y2) and displays the distance between them computed using this formula:

   $$distance = \sqrt{(X1 - X2)^2 + (Y1 - Y2)^2}$$

3.9   Common Programming Errors

Remember to declare each procedure used in a program. The procedure declaration must precede the procedure call.

For the time being, use procedures only to display messages. Syntax or run-time errors may occur when you use Turing's predefined functions. For example, if the argument for function sqrt or ln is negative, a run-time error will occur.

Chapter Review

The first part of this chapter discussed more aspects of problem solving. We reviewed the top-down approach to solving problems and showed how to use the system documentation created by following the software development method as the framework for the final program. We also showed how we could extend a solution to one problem to form the basis of the solution for another problem. We also discussed how structure charts are used to show relationship between different levels of subproblems or between algorithm steps and their refinements.

We discussed the importance of using structured programming techniques to write programs that are easy to read, understand, and maintain. We explained that structured programs are constructed of three kinds of control structures: sequence, selection, and iteration. Statement sequences in Turing provide one of these three types of control structures.

We showed how to use a system structure, the procedure, to implement the solution to a subproblem as a separate program module. We also introduced Turing's built-in functions, and we discussed how functions enable us to reuse code that has been previously written and tested.

TABLE 3.2   Summary of New Turing Constructs

Construct	Effect
Procedure Declaration	

```% Print 3 lines```
 ```procedure Display```
 ```   const Star := "*"```
 ```   put Star```
 ```   put Star```
 ```   put Star```
 ```end Display```
	Procedure Display is declared and may be called to print three lines of asterisks. The local constant Star is defined only when Display is executing.

Procedure Call Statement	
Display	Calls procedure Display and causes it to begin execution.
Function Designator	
sqrt(X + Y)	Calls function sqrt to compute the square root of expression X + Y.

Quick-Check Exercises

1. The principle of reusability states that every procedure in your program must be used more than once. True or false?
2. Developing a program from its documentation means that every statement in the program has a comment. True or false?
3. Are put's parameters input parameters or output parameters?
4. Each procedure is executed in the order in which it is declared in the main program. True or false?
5. How is a procedure executed in a program?
6. What is a procedure parameter?
7. Explain how a structure chart differs from an algorithm.
8. Write this equation as a Turing statement

    $$y = (e^{a \ln b})^2$$

9. What does the procedure below do?

```
procedure Nonsense
    put "*****"
    put "*    *"
    put "*****"
end Nonsense
```

10. If the program contains the procedure in exercise 10, what does this program body do?

```
Nonsense
Nonsense
Nonsense
```

Answers to Quick-Check Exercises

1. False
2. False
3. Input
4. False
5. It is called into execution by a procedure call statement.
6. Parameters are used to receive information from the caller or to pass results back to the caller.
7. A structure chart shows the relationship between subproblems; an algorithm lists the sequence in which subproblems are performed.
8. `Y := exp(A * ln(B))**2`
9. It displays a rectangle.
10. It displays three rectangles on top of each other.

Review Questions

1. Describe what it means to extend a problem solution.
2. The diagram that shows the algorithm steps and their interdependencies is called a _____.
3. What are three advantages of using procedures?
4. When is a procedure executed and where must it appear in the main program?
5. Is the use of procedures a more efficient use of the programmer's time or the computer's time? Explain your answer.
6. How do functions differ from procedures?
7. Write a program that prompts the user for two legs of a right triangle and makes use of the sqrt functions to compute the length of the hypotenuse using the Pythagorean Theorem.
8. Write a program that draws a rectangle made up of asterisks. Use two procedures: DrawSides and DrawLine.
9. Draw a structure chart for the program described in review exercise 8.

Programming Projects

1. Write a procedure that displays a triangle and one that displays a square. Use these procedures to write a complete Turing program from the outline below.

   ```
   % The "Twohouse" program
   % 1. Draw triangle
   % 2. Draw rectangle
   % 3. Print 2 blank lines
   % 4. Draw triangle
   % 5. Draw rectangle
   ```

2. Write procedures that display each of your initials in block letter form. Use these procedures to display your initials.
3. Write a computer program that computes the duration of a projectile's flight and its height above ground when it reaches the target. As part of your solution, write and call a procedure that displays instructions to the program user.

   Problem constant
   ```
   G = 32.17          % Gravitational constant
   ```

   Problem input
   ```
   Theta    : real    % Input - angle (radians)
                      % of elevation
   Distance : real    % Input - distance (ft)
                      % to target
   ```

```
        Velocity : real     % Input - projectile
                            % velocity (ft/sec)
```

Problem output
```
    Time      : real    % Output - time (sec)
                        % of flight
    Height    : real    % Output - height at
                        % impact
```

RELEVANT FORMULAS
time = distance / (velocity * cos(Theta))
height = velocity * time – (g * time^2) / 2

4. Four track stars entered the mile race at the Penn Relays. Write a program that will read in the race time in minutes (Minutes) and seconds (Seconds) for a runner, and compute and print the speed in feet per second (FPS) and in meters per second (MPS). Hint : there are 5,280 feet in one mile and 3,282 feet in one kilometer. Test your program on each of the times below.

Minutes	Seconds
3	52.83
3	59.83
4	00.03
4	16.22

   Write and call a procedure that displays instructions to the program user.

5. A cyclist coasting on a level road slows from a speed of 16 km/hr. to 4 km/hr. in one minute. Write a computer program that calculates the cyclist's constant rate of acceleration and determines how long it will take the cyclist to come to rest, given an initial speed of 16 km/hr. Hint: Use the equation

$$a = (v_f - v_i) / t$$

   where a is acceleration, t is time interval, v_i is initial velocity, and v_f is the final velocity. Write and call a procedure that displays instructions to the program user.

6. In shopping for a new house, you must consider several factors. In this problem the initial cost of the house, estimated annual fuel costs, and annual tax rate are available. Write a program that will determine the total cost after a five-year period for each set of house data below. You should be able to inspect your program output to determine the "best buy."

Initial house cost	Annual fuel cost	Tax rate
$134,000	$4,600	0.025
$124,000	$5,000	0.025
$150,000	$3,700	0.020

To calculate the house cost, add the initial cost to the fuel cost for five years, then add the taxes for five years. Taxes for one year are computed by multiplying the tax rate by the initial cost. Write and call a procedure that displays instructions to the program user.

7. A manufacturer wishes to determine the cost of producing an open-top cylindrical container. The surface area of the container is the sum of the area of the base (π times the radius squared) plus the area of the side (2 π times the height of the container). Write a program to read in the radius (Radius) of the base, the height (Height) of the container, the cost per square centimeter of the material (Cost), and the number of containers to be produced (Quantity). Calculate the cost of each container and the total cost of producing all the containers. Write and call a procedure that displays instructions to the user.

CHAPTER 4

Selection Structures:
If and Case Statements

Thhis chapter shows how to write algorithms and programs with steps that select from several alternative courses of action. We will see two ways to do this in Turing. The first technique is to use a Turing if statement with a Boolean expression; the second approach is to use the case statement. The chapter provides many examples of the use of if and case statements. It also introduces syntax diagrams and shows how to use them to check the syntax of a Turing construct.

We continue our study of problem solving, and introduce one more problem-solving strategy: solution by analogy. We describe how to use data flow information in structure charts to provide additional system documentation. We also show how to hand-check or trace the execution of an algorithm or program to ensure that it does what we expect it to.

4.1 Boolean Expressions

In all the algorithms illustrated so far, we executed each algorithm step exactly once in the order in which it appears. Often we are faced with situations in which we must provide alternative steps that may or may not be executed, depending on the input data. For example, the percentage tax rate assessed by the U.S. Internal Revenue Service (IRS) depends on an individual's salary. Single persons who earn less than $18,550 pay a tax rate of 15% while those who earn between $18,550 and $44,900 pay a tax rate of 15% on the first $18,550 and a tax rate of 28% on the rest. Consequently, an accountant's income tax program must be able to select the correct tax rate to use in a tax computation.

To accomplish this goal, a program must be able to determine whether the correct answer to the question "Is annual income less than $18,550?" is Yes or No. In Turing, this is accomplished by evaluating a Boolean expression. Assuming that the taxable income is stored in the real variable Income, the Boolean expression corresponding to the above question is

```
Income < 18500.00
```

There are only two possible values for a Boolean expression: true or false. If Income is less than 18500.00, the Boolean expression above evaluates to true; if Income is not less than 18500.00, the expression evaluates to false.

Most Boolean expressions or *conditions* that we use will have one of the forms:

> *variable relational-operator variable*
> *variable relational-operator constant*

Relational operators are the symbols < (less than), <= (less than or equal to), > (greater than), >= (greater than or equal to), = (equal to), or not= (not equal to). An alternative way to write not= is ~=. The two operands of the relational operator must be the same data type (both type `boolean`, `string`, `int`, or `real`), or one may be type `real` and the other type `int`. A *constant* may be a *literal constant* (for example, `3`, `4.5`, `"X"`) or a constant identifier.

EXAMPLE 4.1

Table 4.1 shows the relational operators and some sample conditions. Each condition is evaluated assuming the variable values below.

X	Power	MaxPow	Y	Item	MinItem
-5	1024	1024	7	1.5	-999.0

MomOrDad	Num	Sentinel
"M"	999	999

TABLE 4.1 Turing Relational Operators and Sample Conditions

Operator	Condition	English meaning	Value
<=	X <= 0	X less than or equal to 0	true
<	Power < MaxPow	Power less than MaxPow	false
>=	X >= Y	X greater than or equal to Y	false
>	Item > MinItem	Item greater than MinItem	true
=	MomOrDad = "M"	MomOrDad equal to "M"	true
not=	Num not= Sentinel	Num not equal to Sentinel	false

Boolean Variables and Constants

The simplest Boolean expression is a Boolean variable or constant which can be set to either of the Boolean values, `true` or `false`. The statement

```
const Debug := true
```

specifies that the `boolean` constant `Debug` has the value `true`; the statement

```
var Switch, Flag : boolean
```

declares `Switch` and `Flag` to be `boolean` variables — variables that may be assigned only the values `true` and `false`. Given these declarations, the assignment statements below are all valid.

```
Switch := Debug      % Switch gets true
Flag := false        % Flag gets false
Switch := Flag       % Switch gets value of Flag
```

After executing these statements, both `Flag` and `Switch` will have the value `false`.

Boolean Operators

A Boolean variable or constant is the simplest form of a Boolean expression (for example, `Switch`). As we discussed earlier, we can use the relational operators ($<$, $=$, $>$, and so on) to form simple Boolean expressions or conditions, for example, `Income < 18500.00`.

We can use Boolean operators to form more complicated Boolean expressions. There are three basic Boolean operators: and, or, not. An alternative way to write not is $\sim$, and an alternative way to write and is &. These operators require type `boolean` operands. Some Boolean expressions formed with these operators are:

```
Salary < MinSal or NumDepend > 5
Temp > 90.0 and Humidity > 0.90
WinningRecord and not Probation
```

The first Boolean expression determines whether an employee is eligible for special scholarship funds. It evaluates to `true` if either condition is `true`. The second Boolean expression describes an unbearable summer day, with temperature and humidity both in the nineties (Fahrenheit). The expression evaluates to `true` only when both conditions are `true`. The third Boolean expression manipulates two Boolean variables (`WinningRecord`, `Probation`). A college team for which this expression is true may be eligible for the postseason tournament.

The Boolean operators, which can be used with Boolean expressions only, are described in Tables 4.2, 4.3, and 4.4.

TABLE 4.2 The And Operator

operand1	operand2	operand1 and operand2
true	true	true
true	false	false
false	true	false
false	false	false

TABLE 4.3 The Or Operator

operand1	operand2	operand1 or operand2
true	true	true
true	false	true
false	true	true
false	false	false

TABLE 4.4	The Not Operator

operand	not **operand**
true	false
false	true

Table 4.2 shows that the and operator yields a true result only when both its operands are true; Table 4.3 shows that the or operator yields a false result only when both its operands are false. The not operator has a single operand. Table 4.4 shows that the not operator yields the *logical complement,* or negation, of its operand (that is, if Switch is true, not Switch is false and vice-versa).

The precedence of an operator determines its order of evaluation. Table 4.5 shows the precedence of the operators in Turing that we have encountered, including the relational operators.

TABLE 4.5	Operator Precedence

Operator	**Precedence**
**	Highest (evaluated first)
+, - (positive, negative)	
*, /, **div**, **mod**	
+, - (plus, minus)	
<, <=, =, **not**=, >=, >	
not	
and	
or	Lowest (evaluated last)

As you can see, the exponentiation operator ($**$) has the highest precedence, followed by + and – (as used to give the sign of a number), the multiplicative operators (*, /, div, mod), the additive operators (+ , –), the relational operators, the not operator, the and operator, and finally the or operator.

EXAMPLE 4.2
The expression

    X < Minimum + Maximum

involving the variables X, Minimum, and Maximum is interpreted correctly as

    X < (Minimum + Maximum)

because < has lower precedence than +. The expression

    Minimum <= X and X <= Maximum

is interpreted correctly as

```
(Minimum <= X) and (X <= Maximum)
```

because and has lower precedence than <=.

If you are in doubt about the order of precedence, you can use parentheses just to be sure. Some programming languages such as Pascal require more parentheses than are needed in Turing. This is because the precedence levels in Pascal are different from those in mathematics.

Testing for a Range of Values

Expressions similar to the one above are quite common in programming. If Minimum represents the lower bound of a range of values and Maximum represents the upper bound (Minimum is less than Maximum), this expression tests whether X lies within the range Minimum through Maximum inclusive. In Fig. 4.1, this range of values is shaded. The expression is true if X lies within this range, and is false if X is outside this range.

FIGURE 4.1   Range of X for True Values of Minimum < = X and X < = Maximum

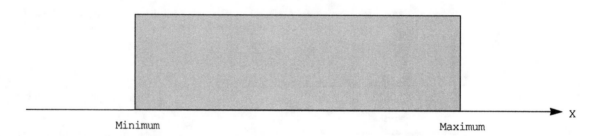

More Boolean Expressions

EXAMPLE 4.3

The following are all legal Boolean expressions if X, Y, and Z are type real and Flag is type boolean. The value of each expression, shown in brackets, assumes that X is 3.0, Y is 4.0, Z is 2.0, and Flag is false.

1.	(X > Z) and (Y > Z)	[true]
2.	(X + Y / Z) <= 3.5	[false]
3.	(Z > X) or (Z > Y)	[false]
4.	not Flag	[true]
5.	(X = 1.0) or (X = 3.0)	[true]
6.	(Z < X) and (X < Y)	[true]
7.	(X <= Z) or (X >= Y)	[false]
8.	not Flag or ((Y + Z) >= (X - Z))	[true]
9.	not (Flag or ((Y + Z) >= (X - Z)))	[false]

All of the parentheses with one exception in these nine lines can be removed without changing the meaning of the expressions. The exception is in line 9 in which the outermost pair of parentheses is used to make not apply to all of the rest of the line instead of just to Flag.

Expression 6 is the Turing form of the relationship $Z < X < Y$, i.e., "X is in the range Z(2.0) to Y(4.0)." The boundary values, 2.0 and 4.0, are excluded from the range of X values that yield a true result.

Expression 7 is true if the value of X lies outside the range bounded by Z and Y. In Fig. 4.2, the shaded areas represent the values of X that yield a true result. Both Y and Z are included in the set of values that yield a true result.

FIGURE 4.2

Range of X for True Values of X < = Z or X > = Y

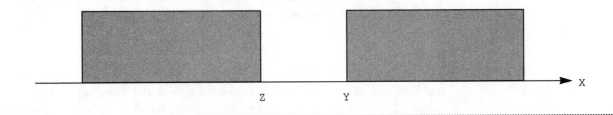

Finally, expression 8 is evaluated in Fig. 4.3; the values given at the beginning of Example 4.1 are shown above the expression.

FIGURE 4.3

Evaluation Tree for: not Flag or ((Y + Z) > = (X − Z))

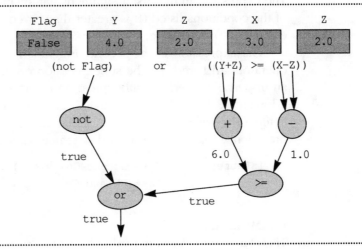

The expression in Fig. 4.3 is rewritten below with parentheses enclosing the term not Flag. Although these parentheses are not required, they do clarify the meaning of the expression and we recommend their use.

```
(not Flag) or ((Y + Z) >= (X - Z))
```

Boolean Assignment

We can write assignment statements that assign a Boolean value to a Boolean variable. If Same is type `boolean`, the statement

```
Same := true
```

assigns the value `true` to Same. Since assignment statements have the general form

variable := *expression*

we can use the statement

```
Same := (X = Y)
```

to assign the value of the Boolean expression `(X = Y)` to Same. The value of Same will be `true` when X and Y are equal; otherwise, Same will be `false`. The parentheses are optional in this statement.

EXAMPLE 4.4

The statements below assign values to two Boolean variables, InRange and IsLetter. InRange is assigned `true` if the value of N is in the range −10 through 10; IsLetter is assigned `true` if Ch is an uppercase or lowercase letter.

```
InRange := -10 <= N and N <= 10
IsLetter := "A" <= Ch and Ch <= "Z" or
            "a" <= Ch and Ch <= "z"
```

The expression in the first assignment statement is `true` if N satisfies both of the conditions listed (N is greater than or equal to −10 and less than or equal to 10); otherwise, the expression is `false`.

The expression in the second assignment statement uses the Boolean operators and andor. The subexpression on its first line is `true` if Ch is an uppercase letter; the subexpression on its second line is `true` if Ch is a lowercase letter. Consequently, IsLetter is assigned `true` if Ch is a letter; otherwise, IsLetter is assigned `false`. Since and has higher precedence than or, the second statement is equivalent to

```
IsLetter := ("A" <= Ch and Ch <= "Z") or
            ("a" <= Ch and Ch <= "z")
```

EXAMPLE 4.5

This statement assigns the value `true` to Even (type `boolean`) if N is an even number.

```
Even := (N mod 2) = 0
```

The expression on the right assigns a value of `true` to Even when the remainder of N divided by 2 is zero. (All even numbers are divisible by 2.)

Reading and Writing Boolean Values

As we will see in the next section, Boolean expressions appear primarily in control structures, where they are used to determine the sequence in which Turing statements are executed. We do not usually process Boolean data in the same way that we process numerical data. Consequently, we hardly ever read Boolean values as input data or display Boolean values as program results. There is no direct way to input or display the value of a Boolean variable using get and put statements. We will show how this can be done using subprograms in Chapter 7.

Exercises for Section 4.1

Self-Check

1. Assuming X is 15.0 and Y is 25.0, what are the values of the following conditions?

   X not= Y   X < X X >= (Y - X)   X = (Y + X - Y)

2. Evaluate each expression below when A is 5, B is 10, C is 15, and Flag is true.

   a. (C = (A + B)) or not Flag
   b. (A not= 7) and (C >= 6) or Flag
   c. not (B <= 12) and (A mod 2 = 0)
   d. not ((A > 5) or (C < (A + B)))

3. Draw the evaluation tree for expression 9 of Example 4.3.

Programming

1. Write a Boolean expression for each relationship described below.
   a. X is in the range -1.5 to 3.2, inclusive.
   b. A is in the range 17 to 23, inclusive.
   c. Y is greater than X and less than Z.
   d. W is equal to 6 or not greater than 3.
2. Write the following Boolean assignment statements:
   a. Assign a value of true to Between, if N is in the range -K and +K, inclusive; otherwise assign a value of false.
   b. Assign a value of true to Uppercase, if Ch is an uppercase letter; otherwise assign a value of false.
   c. Assign a value of true to Divisor, if M is a divisor of N; otherwise assign a value of false.

4.2 Introduction to the If Statement

A Turing programmer can use the `if` statement to select among several alternatives. An `if` statement always contains a Boolean expression. For example, the `if` statement

```
if Gross > 100.00 then
   Net := Gross - Tax
else
   Net := Gross
end if
```

selects one of the two assignment statements listed. It selects the statement following `then` if the Boolean expression is `true` (i.e., Gross is greater than `100.00`); it selects the statement following `else` if the Boolean expression is `false` (i.e., Gross is not greater than `100.00`).

Figure 4.4 is a graphical description, called a *flowchart*, of the `if` statement above. Figure 4.4 shows that the condition (Gross > 100.00) enclosed in the diamond-shaped box is evaluated first. If the condition is `true`, the arrow labeled `true` is followed, and the assignment statement in the rectangle on the right is executed. If the condition is `false`, the arrow labeled `false` is followed, and the assignment statement in the rectangle on the left is executed.

FIGURE 4.4   Flowchart of If Statement With Two Alternatives

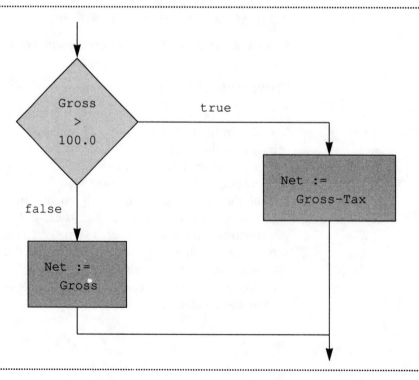

More If Statement Examples

The if statement above has two alternatives, but only one will be executed for a given value of Gross. Example 4.6 illustrates that an if statement can also have a single alternative that is executed only when the condition is true.

EXAMPLE 4.6
The if statement below has one alternative, which is executed only when X is not equal to zero. It causes Product to be multiplied by X; the new value is saved in Product, replacing the old value. If X is equal to zero, the multiplication is not performed. Figure 4.5 is a flowchart of this if statement.

```
% Multiply Product by a nonzero X only
if X not= 0.0 then
   Product := Product * X
end if
```

FIGURE 4.5   Flowchart of If Statement With One Alternative

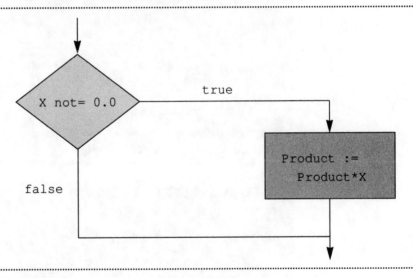

EXAMPLE 4.7
The if statement below has two alternatives. It displays either "Hi Mom" or "Hi Dad" depending on the character stored in variable MomOrDad (type string).

```
if MomOrDad = "M" then
   put "Hi Mom"
else
   put "Hi Dad"
end if
```

EXAMPLE 4.8

The if statement below has one alternative; it displays the message "Hi Mom" only when MomOrDad has the value "M". Regardless of whether or not "Hi Mom" is displayed, the message "Hi Dad" is always displayed. The "end if" terminates the if statement and is needed to separate the if statement from the second put statement.

```
if MomOrDad = "M" then
  put "Hi Mom"
end if
put "Hi Dad"
```

Syntax Displays for If Statement

The following display summarizes the forms of the if statement we have used so far. The next section illustrates the use of if statements and decision steps in solving problems.

IF STATEMENT (ONE ALTERNATIVE)

Form:
```
if condition then
    statement_T
end if
```

Example:
```
if X > 0.0 then
    PosProd := PosProd * X
end if
```

Interpretation: If the *condition* evaluates to true, then *statement$_T$* is executed; otherwise, it is skipped.

IF STATEMENT (TWO ALTERNATIVES)

Form:
```
if condition then
    statement_T
else
    statement_F
end if
```

Example:
```
if X >= 0.0 then
    put "Positive"
else
    put "Negative"
end if
```

Interpretation: If the *condition* evaluates to true, then *statement$_T$* is executed and *statement$_F$* is skipped; otherwise, *statement$_T$* is skipped and *statement$_F$* is executed.

PROGRAM
STYLE

> **FORMAT OF THE IF STATEMENT**
>
> In all the `if` statement examples, *statement_T* and *statement_F* are indented. If you use the word `else`, enter it on a separate line, aligned with the word `if`. The final `end if` should align with the initial `if`. The format of the `if` statement makes its meaning clear to the reader. We use indentation solely to improve program readability; the format used makes no difference to the compiler.
>
> Most Turing systems have an automatic *paragrapher* that will move these words to align them when you request this action.

Exercises for Section 4.2

Self-Check

1. What do the following statements display?

```
a. if 12 < 12 then
       put "Never"
   else
       put "Always"
   end if
b. Var1 := 15.0
   Var2 := 25.12
   if 2 * Var1 >= Var2 then
       put "O.K."
   else
       put "Not O.K."
   end if
```

2. What value is assigned to X for each segment below when Y is `15.0`?

```
a. X := 25.0
   if Y not= (X - 10.0) then
       X := X - 10.0
   else
       X := X / 2.0
   end if
b. if Y < 15.0 and Y >= 0.0 then
       X := 5 * Y
   else
       X := 2 * Y
   end if
```

Programming

1. Write Turing statements to carry out the following steps.

a. If `Item` is nonzero, then multiply `Product` by `Item` and save the result in `Product`; otherwise, skip the multiplication. In either case, print the value of `Product`.
b. Store the absolute difference of `X` and `Y` in `Z`, where the absolute difference is `(X - Y)` or `(Y - X)`, whichever is positive. Do not use the `abs` function in your solution.
c. If `X` is zero, add `1` to `ZeroCount`. If `X` is negative, add `X` to `MinusSum`. If `X` is greater than zero, add `X` to `PlusSum`.

4.3 Syntax Diagrams

Until now we have used syntax displays to describe each new Turing construct. The complete syntax of Turing can also be described using special *syntax diagrams*. Syntax diagrams are sometimes called railroad diagrams because they resemble diagrams that show the track layout for a model railroad. We introduce syntax diagrams at this point because they enable us to describe the syntax of Turing control structures in a very succinct format.

As an example, let's study the syntax diagrams in Fig. 4.6 that describe a Turing program and a list of statements and declarations. Each diagram consists of syntactic elements connected by arrows.

FIGURE 4.6 Syntax Diagram for program and statementsAndDeclarations

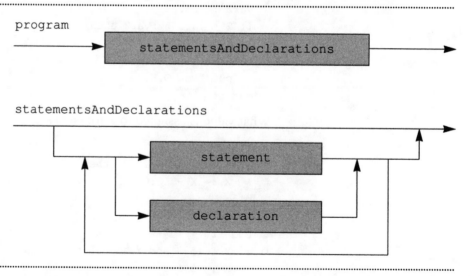

If we trace through the top diagram in Fig. 4.6 following the arrows, we see that a Turing program is defined by a syntactic element called

    statementsAndDeclarations

If we trace through the arrows for this element (in the second diagram), we find that it represents a sequence of statements and declarations. In other words, the diagrams in Fig. 4.6 tell us in a precise way that a Turing program consists of a sequence of statements and declarations.

You may have noticed that these diagrams allow a program that consists of no statements and no declarations, in other words, a null program. Although a null program is useless, it can be run and when it runs it does nothing, as might be expected.

You may have noticed that these diagrams allow declarations to come after statements. For the time being, we will place all declarations before statements, but later we will explain when it is meaningful to precede declarations by statements.

The syntax diagram for *identifier* (see Fig. 4.7) shows that an *identifier* may be a single *letter* (A-Z, a-z). We determine this by tracing the horizontal arrow at the top of the diagram from left to right. By tracing through the loops in the diagram, we see that the initial *letter* may be followed by one or more *letter*, *digit* (0-9), or underscore (_) characters (for example, R2D2, First). This corresponds to our earlier definition of *identifier* in Section 2.3.

FIGURE 4.7   Syntax Diagram

identifier

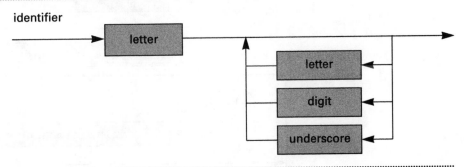

You can use syntax diagrams to verify that a program statement has correct syntax before you enter it. If a syntax error occurs during debugging, you can refer to the appropriate syntax diagram to determine the correct form of the element that is incorrect.

Exercises for Section 4.3

Self-Check

1. Which of the identifiers

    Ace   R2D2   R245   A23B   A1c   B34d5c   A23cd

satisfy the syntax diagram below?

2. Draw a syntax diagram that might be used to describe `real`-like numeric literals that begin with a digit, end with a digit, and contain a single decimal point somewhere in between.

4.4 If Statements Containing Multiple Statements

Figure 4.8 shows the syntax diagram for `if` statements as we have discussed them up to this point. There are two paths that lead from the leftmost arrow to the final (bottom right) arrow. We define an `if` statement with one alternative by tracing the vertical path past the `else` part. We define an `if` statement with two alternatives by tracing the path that leads down and through the reserved word `else`.

FIGURE 4.8   Syntax Diagram for If Statement

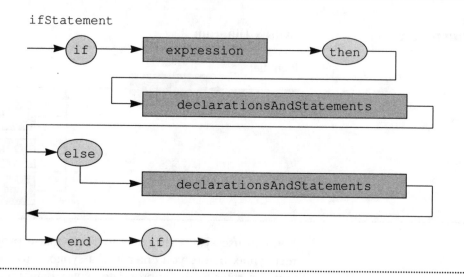

In the common case, the *statementsAndDeclarations* following the word `then` or `else` will be one or more statements such as assignment statements, `procedure` call statements, or other `if` statements. As will be explained later, you can place declarations inside an `if` statement.

More If Statement Examples

This section provides examples of `if` statements with multiple statements following `then` or `else`.

EXAMPLE 4.9

Suppose you are the manager of a clothing boutique and are planning a spring sale. You could use the `if` statement below to compute the discounted price of an item. The statement first determines the discount by multiplying the item price and the discount rate (a fraction); next, it deducts the discount. The statements inside the `if` statement are not executed when the discount rate is zero.

```
if DiscRate not= 0.0 then
    % Compute discount amount
    Discount := Price * DiscRate
    % Deduct discount from price
    Price := Price - Discount
end if
```

EXAMPLE 4.10

In later chapters we will see that it is useful to be able to order a pair of data values in memory so that the smaller value is stored in one variable (say X) and the larger value in another (say Y). The `if` statement in Fig. 4.9 rearranges any two values stored in X and Y so that the smaller number will be in X and the larger number will be in Y. If the two numbers are already in the proper order, the statements inside the `if` statement will not be executed.

FIGURE 4.9

If Statement to Order X and Y

```
if X > Y then
    Temp := X          % Store old X in Temp
    X := Y             % Store old Y in X
    Y := Temp          % Store old X in Y
end if
```

The variables X, Y, and Temp should all be the same data type. Although the values of X and Y are being switched, an additional variable, Temp, is needed for storage of a copy of one of these values. Table 4.6 is a step-by-step simulation of the execution of the if statement when X is 12.5 and Y is 5.0. The table shows that Temp is initially undefined (indicated by ?). Each line of the table shows the part of the if statement that is being executed, followed by its effect. If any variable gets a new value, its new value is shown on that line. The last value stored in X is 5.0 and the last value stored in Y is 12.5.

TABLE 4.6

Step-by-Step Simulation of If Statement

Statement	X	Y	Temp	Effect
	12.5	5.0	?	
if X > Y then				12.5 > 5.0 is true
Temp := X			12.5	Store old X in Temp
X := Y	5.0			Store old Y in X
Y := Temp		12.5		Store old X in Y
end if				

EXAMPLE 4.11

As manager of a clothing boutique, you may want to keep records of your checking transactions. In the `if` statement below, the `true` task processes a transaction (`TransAmount`) that represents a check you wrote as payment for goods received (in which case, `TransType` is `"C"`); the `false` task processes a deposit made into your checking account. In either case, an appropriate message is printed and the account balance (`Balance`) is updated. There are multiple statements following both `then` and `else`.

```
if TransType = "C" then
    % Deduct check amount
    put "Check for $", TransAmount :4:2
    Balance := Balance - TransAmount
else
    % Add deposit amount
    put "Deposit of $", TransAmount :4:2
    Balance := Balance + TransAmount
end if
```

Exercises for Section 4.4

Self-Check

1. Indent to improve readability.

```
if X > Y then
X := X + 10.0
put "X Bigger"
else
put "X Smaller"
put "Y is ", Y
end if
```

2. What would be the effect of removing the `else` in exercise 1?
3. What would be the effect of placing `end if` one line higher in exercise 1?
4. Correct the following `if` statement.

```
if Num1 < 0 then
    Product := Num1 * Num2 * Num3
    put "Product is ", Product : 1
else
    Sum := Num1 + Num2 + Num3
    put "Sum is ", Sum :1
```

5. What syntax diagrams would be used to validate the following `if` statement? Provide the label of every syntax diagram that describes an element of this statement.

```
if X > 0 then
    X := 25.0
    put "Positive"
end if
```

Programming

1. Write an `if` statement that might be used to compute the average of a set of N numbers whose sum is `Total` when N is greater than 0 and that prints an error message when N is not greater than 0. The average should be computed by dividing `Total` by N.
2. Write an interactive program that contains an `if` statement and may be used to compute the area of a square (area = side^2) or triangle (area = 1/2 * base * height) after prompting the user to type the first character of the figure name (S or T).

4.5   Decision Steps in Algorithms

In the problem that follows, we will see how to write a payroll program that can be used to compute an employee's gross pay and net pay after deductions.

✖ Case Study:

Payroll Problem

1. Problem   Write a payroll program that computes an employee's gross pay. The program should also compute net pay using the following criterion to determine the amount to be deducted from the employee's gross salary for social security tax: if an employee earns more than $100.00 in a week, deduct a tax of $25.00; otherwise, deduct no tax.

2. Analysis   To compute gross pay, we must know the hours worked and the hourly rate (the problem inputs). After reading these data, we can compute gross pay by finding their product. Next, we can compute the employee's net pay by subtracting any tax deduction from gross pay. The problem data requirements and relevant formulas follow.

DATA REQUIREMENTS

Problem constants
```
TaxBracket = 100.00        % Maximum salary without a
                           % tax deduction

Tax = 25.00                % Amount of tax withheld
```

Problem inputs

```
    Hours : real              % Hours worked
    Rate  : real              % Hourly rate
```

Problem outputs

```
    Gross : real              % Gross pay
    Net   : real              % Net pay
```

RELEVANT FORMULAS
gross pay = hourly rate x hours worked
net pay = gross pay - deductions

3. Design

The initial algorithm follows and the structure chart is shown in Fig. 4.10. We have added *data flow* information to the structure chart, which shows the inputs and outputs of each individual algorithm step. The structure chart shows that the step "Enter data" provides values for Hours and Rate as its outputs (data flow arrow points up). Similarly, the step "Compute gross pay" uses Hours and Rate as its inputs (data flow arrow points down) and provides Gross as its output. We will discuss the relevance of the data flow information after we complete the problem solution.

INITIAL ALGORITHM
1. Display user instructions.
2. Enter hours worked and hourly rate.
3. Compute gross pay.
4. Compute net pay.
5. Print gross pay and net pay.

FIGURE 4.10 Structure Chart for Modified Payroll Problem

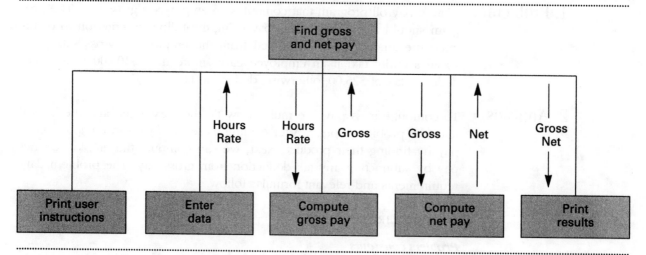

ALGORITHM REFINEMENTS
Now let's write the refinement of algorithm step 4 as a *decision step*.

Step 4 refinement

```
4.1  if Gross > TaxBracket then
          Deduct a tax of $25
     else
          Deduct no tax
     end if
```

The decision step above is expressed in *pseudocode* which is a mixture of English and Turing used to describe algorithm steps. In the pseudocode for a decision step, we use indentation and if, then, else, and end if to show the logical structure of the decision step. The decision step condition may be written in English or Turing; similarly, the true and false tasks may be written in English or Turing.

4. Implementation

The program is shown in Fig. 4.11. It begins with a multiple-line comment explaining the program purpose.

FIGURE 4.11

Program for Payroll Problem

```
% The "Payroll" program

% Compute and print gross pay and net pay given
% an hourly rate and number of hours worked.
% Deduct a tax of $25 if gross salary exceeds
% $100; otherwise, deduct no tax.

const TaxBracket := 100.00
              % Maximum salary for no deduction
const Tax := 25.00 % tax amount

var Hours, Rate : real
        % Input (hours worked, hourly rate)
var Gross, Net : real
        % Outputs (gross pay, net pay)

procedure InstructPay
    % Display user instructions
    put "This program computes gross and net salary."
    put "An amount of $", Tax :4:2, " is deducted"
    put "for an employee who earns more than $",
                    TaxBracket :4:2
    put ""
    put "Enter hours worked and hourly rate"
    put "on separate lines after the prompts."
    put "Press <return> after typing each number."
    put ""
end InstructPay

InstructPay          % Display user instructions
```

```
% Enter Hours and Rate
put "Hours worked> " ..
get Hours
put "Hourly rate> " ..
get Rate

% Compute gross salary
Gross := Hours * Rate

% Compute net salary
if Gross > TaxBracket then
    Net := Gross - Tax     % Deduct a tax amount
else
    Net := Gross           % Deduct no tax
end if

% Print Gross and Net
put "Gross salary is $", Gross :4:2
put "Net salary is $", Net :4:2
```

```
This program computes gross and net salary.
An amount of $25.00 is deducted
for an employee who earns more than $100.00

Enter hours worked and hourly rate
on separate lines after the prompts.
Press <return> after typing each number.

Hours worked> 40.0
Hourly rate> 5.0
Gross salary is $200.00
Net salary is $175.00
```

The program begins by calling procedure InstructPay to display the user instructions (the first lines of program output). After the input data are read, the if statement

```
if Gross > TaxBracket then
    Net := Gross - Tax   % Deduct a tax amount
else
    Net := Gross         % Deduct no tax
end if
```

implements the decision step (step 4). The comments on the right are embedded in the if statement.

5. Testing

To test this program, you should run it with at least two sets of data. One data set should yield a gross salary greater than $100.00, and one should yield a gross salary less than $100.00. You should also test the program with a data set that yields a gross salary that is exactly $100.00.

PROGRAM STYLE

USING CONSTANTS TO ENHANCE READABILITY AND MAINTENANCE

The constants `TaxBracket` and `Tax` appear in the preceding `if` statement and in Fig. 4.11. We could just as easily have placed the constant values (`100.00` and `25.00`) directly in the `if` statement.

The result would be

```
if Gross > 100.00 then
   Net := Gross - 25.00         % Deduct a tax amount
else
   Net := Gross                 % Deduct no tax
end if
```

However, the use of constants rather than literal values provides two advantages. First, the original `if` statement is easier to understand because it uses the descriptive names `TaxBracket` and `Tax` rather than numbers, which have no intrinsic meaning. Second, a program written with constants is much easier to maintain than one written with constant values. For example, if we want to use different constant values in the `Payroll` program in Fig. 4.11, we need to change only the constant declaration. However, if we had inserted constant values directly in the `if` statement, we would have to change the `if` statement and any other statements that manipulate the constant values.

Note that the constants also appear in two `put` statements in procedure `InstructPay`. It is perfectly permissible to reference program constants in a procedure body.

Adding Data Flow Information to Structure Charts

In Fig. 4.10, we added data flow information to the structure chart showing the inputs and outputs of each individual algorithm step. The data flow information is an important part of the system documentation. It shows what program variables are processed by each step and the manner in which these variables are processed. If a step gives a new value to a variable, then the variable is considered an *output of the step*. If a step displays a variable's value or uses it in a computation without changing its value, the variable is considered an *input to the step*. For example, the step "Compute net pay" processes variables `Gross` and `Net`. This step uses the value of `Gross` (its input) to compute `Net` (its output).

Figure 4.10 shows that a variable may have different roles for different subproblems in the structure chart. When considered in the context of the original problem statement, `Hours` and `Rate` are problem inputs (data supplied by the program user). However, when considered in the context of the subproblem "Enter data", the subproblem's task is to deliver values for `Hours` and `Rate` to the main program, so they are considered outputs from this step. When considered in the context of the subproblem "Compute gross pay", the subproblem's task is to use `Hours` and `Rate` to compute a value of Gross, so they are considered inputs to this step. In the same way, the role of the variables Gross and Net changes as we go from step to step in the structure chart.

❖ Case Study:

Finding the First Letter

1. Problem

Read three letters. Find and display the one that comes first in the alphabet.

2. Analysis

From our prior experience with conditions and decision steps, we know how to compare two numbers to see which one is smaller using the relational operator <. In Turing, we can also use this operator to determine whether one letter precedes another in the alphabet. For example, the condition "A"< "F" is true because A precedes F in the alphabet. Since we have no direct way to compare three items, our strategy will be to do a sequence of pairwise comparisons. We will start by comparing the first two letters, finding the smaller of that pair. Next, we can compare this result to the third letter, finding the smaller of that pair. The result of the second comparison will be the smallest of all three letters.

DATA REQUIREMENTS
Problem inputs
```
% Three letters Ch1, Ch2, Ch3 : string
```

Problem outputs
```
% The alphabetically first letter AlphaFirst : string
```

3. Design

The initial algorithm follows. Figure 4.12 shows the structure chart corresponding to the algorithm.

INITIAL ALGORITHM
1. Read three letters into Ch1, Ch2, and Ch3.
2. Save the alphabetically first of Ch1, Ch2, and Ch3 in AlphaFirst.
3. Display the alphabetically first letter.

ALGORITHM REFINEMENTS
You can perform step 2 by first comparing Ch1 and Ch2 and saving the alphabetically first letter in AlphaFirst; this result can then be compared to Ch3. The refinements of step 2 follows. Figure 4.13 is a structure chart that shows the relationship between step 2 and its refinements.

Step 2 Refinement
2.1 Save the alphabetically first of Ch1 and Ch2 in AlphaFirst.
2.2 Save the alphabetically first of Ch3 and AlphaFirst in AlphaFirst.

FIGURE 4.12   Structure Chart for Finding Alphabetically First Letter

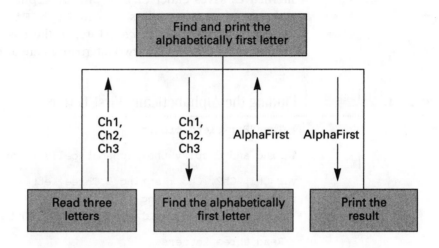

Step 2.1 Refinement
```
2.1.1  if Ch1 precedes Ch2 then
           2.1.2   AlphaFirst gets Ch1
       else
           2.1.3   AlphaFirst gets Ch2
       end if
```

Step 2.2 Refinement
```
2.2.1  if Ch3 precedes AlphaFirst then
           2.2.1   AlphaFirst gets Ch3
       end if
```

FIGURE 4.13   Structure Chart for Step 2 of First Letter Problem

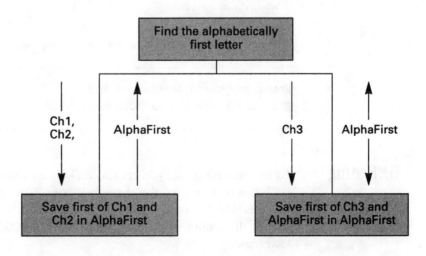

4. Implementation

Program `Firstlet` is shown in Fig. 4.14. The `if` statement with two alternatives saves either `Ch1` or `Ch2` in `AlphaFirst`. The `if` statement with one alternative stores `Ch3` in `AlphaFirst` if `Ch3` precedes the value already in `AlphaFirst`. Later in the chapter, we will see that `if` statements with more than two alternatives are also possible in Turing.

FIGURE 4.14

Finding the Alphabetically First Letter

```
% The "Firstlet" program

% Find and display the alphabetically first letter

var Ch1, Ch2, Ch3 : string % Three letters read
var AlphaFirst : string
                  % Alphabetically first letter

% Read three letters
put "Enter any three letters >" ..
get Ch1, Ch2, Ch3

% Save the alphabetically first of Ch1 and Ch2
% in AlphaFirst
if Ch1 < Ch2 then
    AlphaFirst := Ch1    % Ch1 comes before Ch2
else
    AlphaFirst := Ch2    % Ch2 comes before Ch1
end if

% Save the alphabetically first of Ch3 and
% AlphaFirst
if Ch3 < AlphaFirst then
    AlphaFirst := Ch3 % Ch3 comes before AlphaFirst
end if

% Display result
put AlphaFirst,
    " is the first letter alphabetically"
```

```
Enter any three letters >E B K
B is the first letter alphabetically
```

5. Testing

To test this program, you should make sure that it works when the smallest letter is in any of the three positions. The next section describes the four cases that should be tested. You should also see what happens when one of the letters is repeated, and when one or more of the letters is in lowercase. ✖

Using Functions in Programming

The program in Fig. 4.14 is an example of where we can use functions to improve the structured programming process by facilitating top-down design thereby generating more concise, readable code. Let's assume we have a function named `GetFirst` which returns the alphabetically first of its two type `string` arguments. Rather than use the `if` statements in the main program to compare `Ch1` and `Ch2` and then `Ch3` and `AlphaFirst`, we can call function `GetFirst` to do this:

```
% Save the alphabetically first of Ch1 and Ch2 in
% AlphaFirst
AlphaFirst := GetFirst(Ch1, Ch2)

% Save the alphabetically first of Ch3 and
% AlphaFirst
AlphaFirst := GetFirst(Ch3, AlphaFirst)
```

These two assignment statements would replace the two `if` statements appearing in Fig. 4.14 resulting in a much shorter and more readable program. The first call to `GetFirst` returns the smaller (alphabetically first) of `Ch1` and `Ch2` which is saved in `AlphaFirst`. The second call to `GetFirst` returns the smaller of `Ch3` and the current value of `AlphaFirst` which is also saved in `AlphaFirst`. After both statements execute, `AlphaFirst` contains the smallest of all three letters as required. Of course, function `GetFirst` must contain an `if` statement which compares its arguments, and `GetFirst` must be inserted in the program declaration part. We will write this function in Chapter 7.

Exercises for Section 4.5

Self-Check

1. Draw a structure chart for the pizza problem in Section 3.2 showing the relationship between the main program and its four subproblems. Add data flow information to this structure chart. Discuss how the role of the variable representing pizza area (a problem output) changes for each subproblem.

Programming

1. Modify the structure chart and program for the first letter problem to find the first of four letters.
2. Write a structure chart and program to find the alphabetically last of three letters.

4.6 Tracing an Algorithm

A critical step in the design of an algorithm or program is to verify that it is correct before you spend extensive time entering or debugging it. Often a few extra minutes spent in verifying the correctness of an algorithm will save hours of testing time later.

One important technique, a hand trace or desk check, consists of a careful, step-by-step simulation on paper of how the computer would execute the algorithm or program. The results of this simulation should show the effect of each step's execution using data that are relatively easy to process by hand. In Section 4.4, we simulated the execution of an `if` statement that switches the values of two variables. Next, we will simulate the execution of the refined algorithm for the smallest letter problem.

REFINED ALGORITHM

1. Read three letters into `Ch1`, `Ch2`, and `Ch3`.
2. Save the alphabetically first of `Ch1`, `Ch2`, and `Ch3` in `AlphaFirst`.

    2.1   Save the alphabetically first of `Ch1` and `Ch2` in `AlphaFirst`.
        2.1.1 `if Ch1 precedes Ch2 then`
               2.1.2 `AlphaFirst gets Ch1`
           `else`
               2.1.3 `AlphaFirst gets Ch2`
           `end if`
    2.2   Save the alphabetically first of `Ch3` and `AlphaFirst` in `AlphaFirst`.
        2.2.1 `if Ch3 precedes AlphaFirst then`
               2.2.1 `AlphaFirst gets Ch3`
           `end if`

3. Display the alphabetically first letter.

Table 4.7 shows a trace of the algorithm for this input data: `T H E`. Each step is listed at the left in order of its execution. If a program step changes the value of a variable, then the table shows the new value. The effect of each step is described at the far right. For example, the table shows that the statement

    `get Ch1, Ch2, Ch3`

stores the letters `T`, `H`, and `E` in the variables `Ch1`, `Ch2`, and `Ch3`.

The trace in Table 4.7 clearly shows that the alphabetically first letter, `E`, of the input string is stored in `AlphaFirst` and printed. In order to verify that the algorithm is correct, you would need to select other data that cause the two conditions to evaluate to different combinations of their values. Since there are two conditions and each has two possible values (`true` or `false`), there are 2 x 2, or 4, different combinations that should be tried. (What are they?) An exhaustive desk check of the algorithm would show that it works for all of these combinations.

TABLE 4.7   Trace of Program in Figure 4.14

Algorithm Step	Ch1 ?	Ch2 ?	Ch3 ?	AlphaFirst ?	Effect
1. Read three letters	T	H	E		Reads the data
2.1.1 if Ch1 precedes Ch2					Is "T" < "H"? Value is false
2.1.3 AlphaFirst gets Ch2				H	"H" is first so far
2.2.1 if Ch3 precedes AlphaFirst					Is "E"< "H"? Value is true
2.2.2 AlphaFirst gets Ch3				E	"E" is first
3. Display AlphaFirst					Prints E is the first letter...

Besides the four cases discussed above, you should verify that the algorithm works correctly for unusual data. For example, what would happen if all three letters or a pair of letters were the same? Would the algorithm still provide the correct result? To complete the desk check, you would need to show that the algorithm does indeed handle these special situations properly.

In tracing each case, you must be very careful to execute the algorithm exactly as the computer would execute it. Often programmers assume that a particular step will be executed without explicitly testing each condition and tracing each step; however, a trace performed in this way is of little value.

Exercises for Section 4.6

Self-Check

1. Provide sample data and traces for the remaining three cases of the alphabetically first letter problem.
    a. Case 1, both conditions are true.
    b. Case 2, first condition is true, second is false.
    c. Case 3, both conditions are false.
2. Consider two special cases of the alphabetically first letter problem. Determine the value of the conditions when:
    a. Two of the 3 letters are the same.
    b. All three letters are the same.
3. Trace the Payroll program in Fig. 4.11 when:
    a. Hours is 30.0 and Rate is 5.00.
    b. Hours is 20.0 and Rate is 4.00.

4.7 More Problem-Solving Strategies

Often what appears to be a new problem will turn out to be a variation of one that you already solved. Consequently, an important skill in problem solving is the ability to recognize that a problem is similar to one solved earlier. As you progress through this course, you will start to build up a *library* of programs and procedures. Whenever possible, you should try to adapt or reuse parts of successful programs.

Modifying a Problem Solution

An experienced programmer usually writes programs that can be easily changed or modified to fit other situations. For one reason, programmers (and program users) often wish to make slight improvements to a program after having used it. If the original program is designed carefully from the beginning, the programmer will be able to accommodate changing specifications with a minimum of effort. As you will find by working through the next problem, it may be possible to modify one or two control statements rather than rewrite the entire program.

❊ Case Study:

Computing Overtime Pay

1. Problem

We need to modify the payroll program so that employees who work more than 40 hours a week are paid double for all overtime hours worked.

2. Analysis

This problem is a modification of the payroll problem solved in Fig. 4.11. Employees who work more than forty hours should be paid one rate for the first forty hours and a higher rate for the extra hours over forty. Employees who work forty hours or less should be paid the same rate for all hours worked. We can solve this problem by replacing step 3 (compute gross pay) in the original algorithm with a decision step that selects either a straight pay computation or a computation with overtime pay.

DATA REQUIREMENTS

Problem constants

```
TaxBracket = 100.00      % Maximum salary without a
                         % tax deduction
Tax = 25.00              % Amount of tax withheld
MaxHours = 40.0          % Maximum hours without
                         % overtime pay
OvertimeRate = 2.0       % Double pay for overtime
```

Problem inputs

```
Hours : real     % Hours worked
Rate : real      % Hourly rate
```

Problem outputs

```
Gross : real     % Gross pay
Net : real       % Net pay
```

RELEVANT FORMULAS
regular pay = hourly rate * hours worked
overtime pay = hours over MaxHours **OvertimeRate*
                    * hourly rate
net pay = gross pay − deductions

3. Design

The critical change to the algorithm involves modifying step 3 of the algorithm. The algorithm is repeated below followed by a new refinement for step 3.

INITIAL ALGORITHM
1. Display user instructions.
2. Enter hours worked and hourly rate.
3. Compute gross salary including any overtime pay.
4. Compute net salary.
5. Print gross salary and net salary.

ALGORITHM REFINEMENTS
Step 3 Refinement
3.1   if no overtime hours were worked then
       3.2 Gross is assigned Hours * Rate
else
       3.3 Compute the gross salary for regular hours.
       3.4 Add the pay for overtime hours to gross pay.
end if

4. Implementation

To write the program, we should replace the assignment statement in Fig. 4.11 that computes gross salary

```
% Compute gross salary
Gross := Hours * Rate
```

with the if statement

```
% Compute gross salary including any overtime pay
if Hours <= MaxHours then
    Gross := Hours * Rate
else
    % Overtime
    Gross := MaxHours * Rate
    Gross := Gross + (Hours - MaxHours) *
                  OvertimeRate * Rate
end if
```

If the condition `Hours <= MaxHours` is `true`, there is no overtime pay so gross salary is computed as before; otherwise, `Gross` is computed in two steps. The first step computes the pay for the regular hours only; the second step adds the pay for any overtime hours (`Hours - MaxHours`) to the value just computed.   ✖

More Problem Solving: Solution by Analogy

Sometimes a new problem is simply an old one presented in a new guise. Each time you face a problem, you should try to determine whether you have solved a similar problem before and, if so, adapt the earlier solution. This problem-solving strategy requires a careful reading of the problem statement in order to detect requirements similar to those of earlier problems, but which may be worded differently.

✖ Case Study:
Computing Insurance Dividends

1. Problem

Each year an insurance company sends out dividend checks to its policyholders. The basic dividend rate is a fixed percentage (4.5%) of the policyholder's paid premium. If the policyholder has made no claims, the dividend rate for that policy is increased by a bonus rate (0.5%). Write a program to compute dividends.

2. Analysis

This problem is quite similar to the modified payroll problem discussed earlier. Just as there was a bonus pay rate for workers with overtime hours there is a bonus dividend for policyholders with no claims. We must first read in the input data (number of claims and premium). We then use a decision step to select either the basic dividend computation or the computation with a bonus dividend.

DATA REQUIREMENTS

Problem constants
```
    BasicRate = 0.045      % Basic rate of 4.5%
    BonusRate = 0.005      % Bonus rate of 0.5%
```

Problem inputs
```
    Premium : real         % Premium amount
    NumClaims : int        % Number of claims
```

Problem outputs
```
    Dividend : real        % Dividend amount
```

3. Design The initial algorithm and structure chart (see Fig. 4.15) follow.

INITIAL ALGORITHM
1. Display user instructions.
2. Enter premium amount and number of claims.
3. Compute dividend including a bonus dividend when earned.
4. Print total dividend.

FIGURE 4.15 Structure Chart for Insurance Dividend Problem

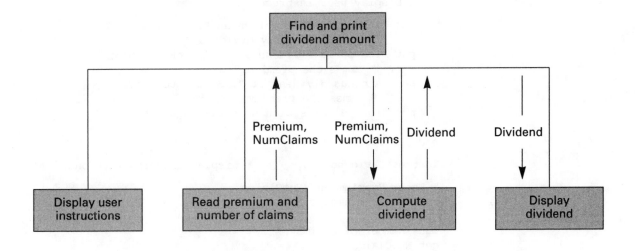

ALGORITHM REFINEMENTS
The refinement of step 3 in this problem is similar to the refinement of step 3 in the modified payroll problem.

Step 3 Refinement

3.1 if the basic dividend applies then
        3.2 Dividend gets Premium * BasicRate
    else
        3.3 Compute the basic dividend.
        3.4 Add the bonus dividend to the basic dividend.
    end if

4. Implementation The complete program is shown in Fig. 4.16. The basic dividend rate, 4.5%, is written as the decimal fraction 0.045 and the bonus rate, 0.5%, is written as the decimal fraction 0.005. Because Turing has no percent (%) operator, decimal fractions are required. The if statement at the end of the program displays an extra message to policyholders who receive a bonus dividend.

FIGURE 4.16   Insurance Company Dividend Program

```
% The "Compdiv" program

% Find and print the insurance dividend

const BasicRate := 0.045          % Basic rate 4.5%
const BonusRate := 0.005          % Bonus rate 0.5%

var NumClaims : int       % Input   - number of claims
var Premium   : real      % Input   - premium amount
var Dividend  : real      % Output  - dividend amount

procedure InstructDividend
    % Display user instructions

    put "This program displays an ",
            "insurance policy dividend."
    put "The basic dividend is ", BasicRate :5:3,
            " times the premium."
    put "A bonus dividend of ", BonusRate :5:3,
            " times the premium is paid"
    put "for policies with no claims against them."
    put ""
end InstructDividend

InstructDividend                % Display user instructions

% Enter Premium and NumClaims
put "Premium amount > $" ..
get Premium
put "Number of claims> " ..
get NumClaims

% Compute dividend using bonus rate when earned
if NumClaims not= 0 then
    Dividend := Premium * BasicRate
else
    Dividend := Premium * BasicRate % Basic dividend
    Dividend := Dividend + Premium * BonusRate
            % Plus bonus
end if

% Print total dividend
put "Total dividend is $", Dividend :4:2
if NumClaims = 0 then
    put "Includes a bonus dividend for zero claims!"
end if
```

```
This program displays an insurance policy dividend.
The basic dividend is 0.045 times the premium.
A bonus dividend of 0.005 times the premium is paid
for policies with no claims against them.

Premium amount > $1200.00
Number of claims> 0
Total dividend is $60.00
Includes a bonus dividend for zero claims!
```

Exercises for Section 4.7

Self-Check

1. Draw a structure chart for programming exercise 2 below, including data flow information.

Programming

1. Provide the complete program for the overtime pay problem.
2. Rewrite the pizza program from Section 3.2, so that the user may decide to compute the unit price of either a circular or rectangular pizza.

4.8 Nested If Statements and Multiple Alternative Decisions

Until now, we have used `if` statements to implement decisions involving up to two alternatives. In this section, we will see how the `if` statement can be used to implement decisions involving several alternatives.

A nested `if` statement occurs when the `true` or `false` statement of an `if` statement is itself an `if` statement. A nested `if` statement can be used to implement decisions with several alternatives as shown in the next examples.

EXAMPLE 4.12

The nested `if` statement below has three alternatives. It causes one of three variables (NumPos, NumNeg, or NumZero) to be increased by one depending on whether X is greater than zero, less than zero, or equal to zero, respectively.

```
% Increment NumPos, NumNeg or NumZero depending on X
if X > 0 then
    NumPos := NumPos + 1
else
    if X < 0 then
        NumNeg := NumNeg + 1
    else % X = 0
        NumZero := NumZero + 1
    end if
end if
```

The execution of this `if` statement proceeds as follows: the first condition (X > 0) is tested; if it is `true`, NumPos is incremented and the rest of the `if` statement is skipped. If the first condition is `false`, the second condition (X < 0) is tested; if it is `true`, NumNeg is incremented; otherwise, NumZero is incremented. It is important to realize that the second condition is tested only when the first condition is `false`.

Figure 4.17 is a flowchart that shows the execution of this statement. This diagram shows that one and only one of the statement sequences in a rectangular box will be executed. Table 4.8 traces the execution of this statement when X is −7.

FIGURE 4.17   Flowchart of Nested If Statement in Example 4.12

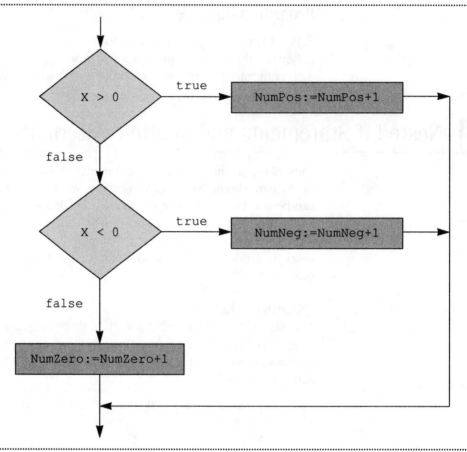

TABLE 4.8   Trace of If Statement in Example 4.12 for X = −7

Statement Part	Effect
if X > 0 then	−7 > 0 is false
else if X < 0 then	−7 < 0 is true
NumNeg := NumNeg + 1	Add 1 to NumNeg

PROGRAM
STYLE

NESTED IF STATEMENTS VERSUS A SEQUENCE OF IF STATEMENTS
Beginning programmers sometimes prefer to use a sequence of `if` statements rather than a single nested `if` statement. For example, the previous `if` statement is rewritten below as a sequence of `if` statements.

```
if X > 0 then
    NumPos := NumPos + 1
end if
if X < 0 then
    NumNeg := NumNeg + 1
end if
if X = 0 then
    NumZero := NumZero + 1
end if
```

Although the above sequence is logically equivalent to the original, it is not nearly as readable or as efficient. Unlike the nested `if`, the sequence does not show clearly that exactly one of the three assignment statements is executed for a particular X. With respect to efficiency, all three of the conditions are always tested. In the nested `if` statement, only the first condition is tested when X is positive.

Cascaded If Statements

Nested `if` statements may become quite complex. If there are more than three alternatives and indentation is not done consistently, the statements can be quite confusing. The Turing language provides another form of the `if` statements that should be used in this situation. This form is called the *cascaded* `if` statement because it allows you to cascade through (check one after another) a set of tests. As the syntax diagram shows in Fig. 4.18, you can use the keyword `elsif` (a contraction for `else if`) for the cascade of tests.

You may notice in the diagrams, and below in the syntax display for cascaded `if` statements, that each clause contains a sequence of statements and declarations. For the time being, we will only place statements in these clauses and will place all our declarations at the beginning of our programs. We will explain later that declarations in these clauses create variables and constants whose lifetime or *scope* is limited to the clause.

As you can see from the syntax diagram in Fig. 4.18, the cascaded `if` statement is a generalization of the basic `if` statement (see Fig. 4.8). We can always use the syntax diagram in Fig. 4.18 instead of the one in Fig. 4.8.

It is easier to write the nested `if` statement in Example 4.12 as a cascaded `if` statement, described in the next syntax display.

FIGURE 4.18 Syntax Diagram for Cascaded If Statement

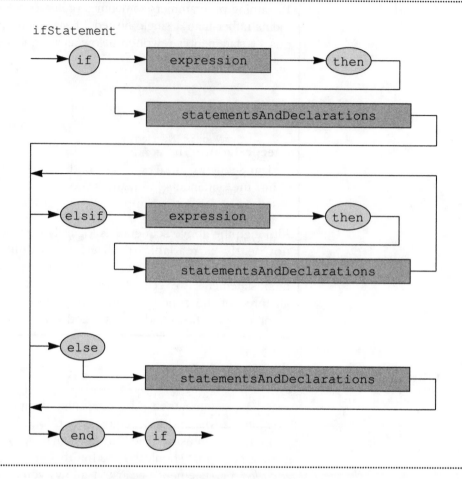

CASCADED IF STATEMENT

Form:
```
if condition₁ then
    statementsAndDeclarations₁
elsif condition₂ then
    statementsAndDeclarations₂

    .
    .
    .

elsif conditionₙ then
    statementsAndDeclarationsₙ
else
    statementsAndDeclarationsₑ
end if
```

Example:
```
% Increment NumPos, NumNeg, or NumZero
%      depending on X
if X > 0 then
    NumPos := NumPos + 1
elsif X < 0 then
    NumNeg := NumNeg + 1
else % X = 0
    NumZero := NumZero + 1
end if
```

Interpretation: The conditions in a cascaded if statement are evaluated in sequence until a true condition is reached. If a condition is true, the statements following it are executed and the rest of the cascaded if statement is skipped. If a condition is false, the statements and declarations following it are skipped and the next condition is tested. If all conditions are false, then $statement_e$ following the else is executed. The final else clause is optional. If it is omitted and none of the conditions is true, the whole cascaded if statement has no effect. Figure 4.18 is another way of defining the form of this statement.

Order of Conditions

Very often the conditions in a cascaded if statement are not *mutually exclusive;* in other words, more than one condition may be true for a given data value. If this is the case, then the order of the conditions becomes very important because only the statement sequence following the first true condition is executed.

EXAMPLE 4.13

Suppose you want to match exam scores to letter grades for a large class of students. The table below describes the assignment of grades based on each exam score.

Exam Score	Grade Assigned
90 and above	A
80 – 89	B
70 – 79	C
60 – 69	D
below 60	F

The cascaded if statement below prints the letter grade assigned according to this table. If you had an exam score of 85, the last three conditions would be true; however, a grade of B would be assigned because the first true condition is Score >= 80.

```
% Correct grade assignment
if Score >= 90 then
    put "A"
elsif Score >= 80 then
    put "B"
elsif Score >= 70 then
    put "C"
elsif Score >= 60 then
    put "D"
else
    put "F"
end if
```

The order of conditions can also have an effect on program efficiency. If we know that low exam scores are much more likely than high scores, it would be more efficient to test first for scores below 60, next for scores between 60 and 69, and so on (see Programming Exercise 1 at the end of this section).

It would be incorrect to write the decision as shown below. All passing exam scores (60 or above) would be incorrectly categorized as a grade of D because the first condition would be true and the rest would be skipped.

```
% Incorrect grade assignment
if Score >= 60 then
    put "D"
elsif Score >= 70 then
    put "C"
elsif Score >= 80 then
    put "B"
elsif Score >= 90 then
    put "A"
else
    put "F"
end if
```

EXAMPLE 4.14

You could use a cascaded `if` statement to implement a *decision table* that describes several alternatives. For instance, let's say you are an accountant setting up a payroll system for a small firm. Each line of Table 4.9 indicates an employee's salary range and a corresponding base tax amount and tax percentage. Given a salary, you can calculate the tax by adding the base tax for that salary range, and the product of the percentage of excess and the amount of salary over the minimum salary for that range.

For example, the second line of the table specifies that the tax due on a salary of $2000.00 is $225.00 plus 16% of the excess salary over $1,500.00 (i.e., 16% of $500.00, or $80.00). Therefore, the total tax due is $225.00 plus $80.00, or $305.00.

TABLE 4.9   Decision Table for Example 4.14

Range	Salary	Base Tax	% of Excess
1	0.00 – 1,499.99	0.00	15%
2	1,500.00 – 2,999.99	225.00	16%
3	3,000.00 – 4,999.99	465.00	18%
4	5,000.00 – 7,999.99	825.00	20%
5	8,000.00 – 15,000.00	1425.00	25%

The `if` statement in Fig. 4.19 implements the tax table. If the value of `Salary` is within the table range (0.00 to 15,000.00), exactly one of the statements assigning a value to `Tax` will be executed. A trace of the `if` statement for `Salary = 2,000.00` is shown in Table 4.10. You can see that the value assigned to `Tax`, `305.00`, is correct.

FIGURE 4.19   If Statement for Table 4.3

```
if Salary < 0.0 then
    put "Error! Negative salary $", Salary :10:2
elsif Salary < 1500.00 then            % First range
    Tax := 0.15 * Salary
elsif Salary < 3000.00 then            % Second range
    Tax := (Salary - 1500.00) * 0.16 + 225.00
elsif Salary < 5000.00 then            % Third range
    Tax := (Salary - 3000.00) * 0.18 + 465.00
elsif Salary < 8000.00 then            % Fourth range
    Tax := (Salary - 5000.00) * 0.20 + 825.00
elsif Salary <= 15000.00 then          % Fifth range
    Tax := (Salary - 8000.00) * 0.25 + 1425.00
else
    put "Error! Too large salary $", Salary :10:2
end if
```

TABLE 4.10   Trace of If Statement in Fig. 4.19 for Salary = $2000.00

Statement Part	Salary 2000.00	Tax ?	Effect
if Salary < 0.0			2000.0 < 0.0 is false
elsif Salary < 1500.00			2000.0 < 1500.0 is false
elsif Salary < 3000.00			2000.0 < 3000.0 is true
Tax := (Salary - 1500.00)			Evaluates to 500.00
* 0.16			Evaluates to 80.00
+ 225.00		305.00	Evaluates to 305.00

PROGRAM
STYLE

VALIDATING THE VALUE OF VARIABLES

It is important to validate the value of a variable before performing computations using invalid or meaningless data. Instead of computing an incorrect tax amount, the if statement in Fig. 4.19 prints an error message if the value of Salary is outside the range covered by the table (0.0 to 15,000.00). The first condition detects negative salaries; an error message is printed if Salary is less than zero. All conditions evaluate to false if Salary is greater than 15,000.00 and the alternative following else displays an error message.

Testing More than One Variable

The if statements seen so far have all involved testing the value of a single variable; consequently, we were able to write each nested if statement as a cascaded if statement. If several variables are involved in the decision, we will not always be able to use a cascaded if statement. The first example shows a situation in which we use a nested if statement as a "filter" to select out data which satisfy several different criteria.

EXAMPLE 4.15

The Department of Defense would like a program that identifies single males between the ages of 18 and 26 inclusive. One way to do this is to use a nested if statement that sets a Boolean variable AllMet to true if all criteria are satisfied. In the nested if below, we assume that all variables have initial values and the Boolean variable Single has been previously set to indicate whether the individual is single (Single is true) or not (Single is false).

```
% Set AllMet to true if all criteria are met
AllMet := false                    % Criteria not met yet
if Single then
   if Gender = "M" then
      if Age >= 18 then
         if Age <= 26 then
            AllMet := true         % Criteria are all met
         end if
      end if
   end if
end if
```

The Boolean flag AllMet is initialized to false. The assignment statement sets AllMet to true only when all of the conditions listed above it are true.

Another approach to solving this problem is to write a Boolean expression that represents the logical and of all the individual conditions that must be true. This expression appears on the right hand side of the Boolean assignment below. The if statement following the Boolean assignment displays an appropriate message based on the value assigned to AllMet.

```
% Set AllMet to true if all criteria are met
AllMet := Single and Gender = "M" and
                Age >= 18 and Age <= 26
% Display the result of the filtering operation
if AllMet then
    put "Current person satisfies the criteria"
else
    put "All criteria are not satisfied"
end if
```

EXAMPLE 4.16

You have just had a meeting with your parents to discuss your alternatives for next year. Your parents told you that you could apply to an Ivy League school if you could get your SAT scores above 1300 and earned more than $2000 over the summer. If your SAT scores are not over 1300 but you still earn over $2000 this summer, then your parents suggest you apply to a local university and live at the dorm. If you cannot earn the necessary $2000, your parents would like you to commute to a community college. The nested if statement below summarizes the decision process you should follow; the flowchart in Fig. 4.20 diagrams it.

```
if Earnings > 2000.00 then
    if SAT > 1300 then
        put "Apply to Ivy League"
    else
        put "Apply to Local University"
    end if
else
    put "Apply to Community College"
end if
```

To verify that the nested if statement above is correct, it would be necessary to trace its execution for all possible combinations of SAT scores and summer earnings. It is clear that the rightmost rectangle is entered only when both conditions are true. The leftmost rectangle is always entered when the condition involving Earnings is false. The rectangle in the middle is entered when the condition involving earnings is true, but the condition involving SAT scores is false.

FIGURE 4.20   Flowchart of College Decision Process

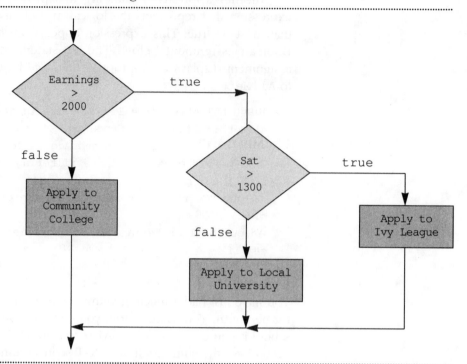

We could also use the cascaded `if` statement below to implement this decision structure.

```
if Earnings > 2000.00 and SAT > 1300 then
    put "Apply to Ivy League"
elsif Earnings > 2000.00 then
    put "Apply to Local University"
else
    put "Apply to Community College"
end if
```

The first condition is `true` if both summer earnings and SAT scores are high enough. The second condition is tested only when the first condition fails, so it can be `true` only when earnings are sufficient but SAT scores are too low. Note that it is not necessary to test the value of SAT in the condition following `elsif`. Finally, the `else` clause executes when summer earnings are too low.

Short Circuit Evaluation of Boolean Expressions

When evaluating Boolean expressions, we often employ a technique called *short-circuit evaluation*. This means that we can stop evaluating a Boolean expression as soon as its value can be determined. For example, if the value of `Single` is `false`, then the Boolean expression

```
        Single and Gender = "M" and
            Age >= 18 and Age <= 25
```

must be `false` regardless of the value of the other conditions (i.e., `false and (...)` must always be `false`). Consequently, there is no need for us to evaluate the other conditions when `Single` is `false`.

Turing always uses short-circuit evaluation. This means that it will not continue to evaluate a Boolean expression after its value is determined.

EXAMPLE 4.17
If X is zero, the `if` condition below

```
    if X not= 0.0 and Y / X > 5.0 then
```

is `false` because `X not= 0.0` is `false` so `false and (...)` must always be `false`. Consequently, there is no need to evaluate the subexpression `Y / X > 5.0` when X is zero. If this expression were evaluated, a "division by zero" run-time error will occur because the divisor X is zero.

In some languages such as Pascal this error can occur, but since Turing always uses short-circuit evaluation, this error will not occur.

Exercises for Section 4.8

Self-Check

1. Trace the execution of the nested `if` statement in Fig. 4.19 for `Salary = 13500.00`.
2. What would be the effect of reversing the order of the first two conditions in the `if` statement of Fig. 4.19?
3. Evaluate the expressions below, with and without short-circuit evaluation, if X = 6 and Y = 7.

   a. X > 5 and Y div X <= 10
   b. X <= 10 or X / (Y - 7) > 3

Programming

1. Rewrite the `if` statement for Example 4.13 using only the relational operator < in all conditions.
2. Implement the decision table below using a cascaded `if` statement. Assume that the grade point average is within the range 0.0 through 4.0.

Grade Point Average	Transcript Message
0.0 – 0.99	Failed semester – registration suspended
1.0 – 1.99	On probation for next semester
2.0 – 2.99	(No message)
3.0 – 3.49	Dean's list for semester
3.5 – 4.0	Highest honors for semester

3. Implement the decision table from programming exercise 2 without using a cascaded `if` statement.
4. Write a Turing program that reads a person's age, sex (a character), and a letter indicating the person's marital status. The program should display a message indicating whether the individual meets the criteria described in Example 4.15.

4.9 The Case Statement

The `case` statement can also be used in Turing to select one of several alternatives. It is especially useful when the selection is based on the value of a single variable or a simple expression (called the *case selector*). The case selector must be an integer. In Chapter 8 we will encounter other data types that may be used as case selectors.

EXAMPLE 4.18

This `case` statement

```
case Size of
    label 1, 2 : put "This is one or two"
    label 3, 4 : put "This is three or four"
end case
```

behaves the same way as the `if` statement below when the integer stored in `Size` is one of the four numbers listed (1, 2, 3, or 4).

```
if Size = 1 or Size = 2 then
    put "This is one or two"
elsif Size = 3 or Size = 4 then
    put "This is three or four"
end if
```

The message displayed by the `case` statement depends on the value of the case selector `Size`. If the case selector value is 1 or 2 the first message is displayed. If the *case selector* value is 3 or 4 the second message is displayed. The lists 1, 2 and 3, 4 are called *case labels*.

EXAMPLE 4.19

The `case` statement below computes the gross pay earned for a particular day where the value of `DayNumber` indicates whether the day is a Saturday (`DayNumber` is 7), a Sunday (`DayNumber` is 1), or a weekday (`DayNumber` is 2 through 6). The worker is paid time and a half during the weekend. Of course, the values of `DayNumber`, `DailyRate`, and `Hours` must be defined before the `case` statement executes.

```
% Compute gross pay for a particular day
case DayNumber of
    label 1, 7 :
        WeekendRate := 1.5 * DailyRate
        Gross := Hours * WeekendRate
    label 2, 3, 4, 5, 6 :
        Gross := Hours * DailyRate
end case
```

One common error is using a string such as `"Saturday"` or `"Sunday"` as a case label. This causes a syntax error such as `"Case expression must be an integer"`. (An advanced version of Turing, namely Object Oriented Turing, allows case labels to be character strings.)

The syntax display for the `case` statement follows; Figure 4.21 shows its syntax diagram.

FIGURE 4.21   Syntax Diagrams of a Case Statement and Case Labels

caseStatement

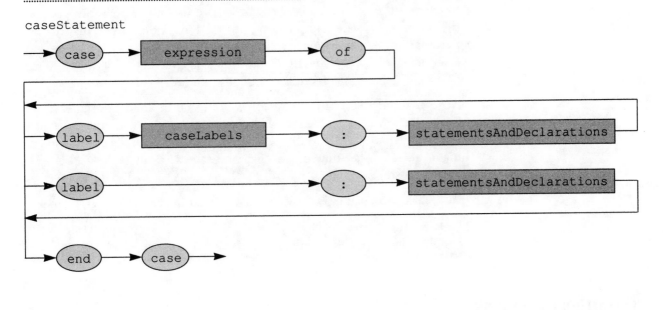

caseLabels

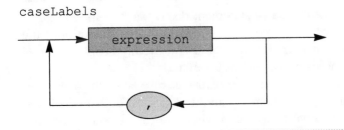

CASE STATEMENT

Form:
```
case selector of
    label label₁ : statementsAndDeclarations₁
    label label₂ : statementsAndDeclarations₂
            .
            .
            .
    label labelₙ : statementsAndDeclarationsn
    label : statementsAndDeclarationsₒ
end case
```

Example:
```
case N of
    label 1, 2 : put "Buckle my shoe"
    label 3, 4 : put "Shut the door"
    label 5, 6 : put "Pick up sticks"
end case
```

Interpretation: The *selector* expression is evaluated and compared to each of the `case` labels. Each $label_i$ is a list of one or more possible values for the selector, separated by commas. Only one $statementsAndDeclarations_i$ will be executed; if the selector value is listed in $label_i$, $statementsAndDeclarations_i$ is executed. Control is then passed to the first statement following the `end case`.

Note 1: If the value of the selector is not listed in any `case` label, the final *otherwise* alternative, $statementsAndDeclarations_o$ is executed. If the value is not listed and the otherwise alternative with its corresponding "`label :`" is omitted, an error message is printed and program execution stops.

Note 2: A particular selector value may appear in at most one case label.

Note 3: The type of each selector value must be an integer. (Later we will introduce enumerated types which can also be case labels.)

The Otherwise Clause

As indicated in Note 1 of the `case` statement display, a "`Case expression out of range`" error message is printed during execution if the selector value does not match any case label and the final (optional) *otherwise* alternative of the `case` statement is omitted.

If no action is to be performed for a particular case label, this is indicated by completely omitting the statements and declarations for that case label.

The *otherwise* alternative is activated when the case selector does not match any of the explicitly given case labels. In Fig. 4.22 the otherwise clause executes and displays an error message if the value of `DayNumber` does not match any of the case labels (values 1 through 7).

FIGURE 4.22   Case with Otherwise Clause

```
% Compute gross pay for a particular day
case DayNumber of
    label 1, 7 :
        WeekendRate := 1.5 * DailyRate
        Gross := Hours * WeekendRate
    label 2, 3, 4, 5, 6 :
        Gross := Hours * DailyRate
    label :
        put DayNumber, " is an invalid day number"
end case
```

Comparison of the Cascaded If Statement and the Case Statement

You can use cascaded if statements, which are more general than the case statement, to implement any multiple-alternative decision. The case statement, however, is more readable and should be used whenever practical. Case labels that contain type real values or strings are not permitted.

You should use the case statement when each case label contains a list of values of reasonable size (ten or less). However, if the number of values in a case selector is large or there are large gaps in those values, use a nested if statement.

Exercises for Section 4.9

Self-Check

1. Write a cascaded if statement that corresponds to this case statement

   ```
   case X of
   label 0 : put "X is zero"
   label 1 : put "X is one"
   label 2 : put "X is two"
   end case
   ```

2. Why can't we rewrite our nested if statement examples from Section 4.8 using case statements?
3. The Standard Version of the Pascal programming language does not have an otherwise clause in its case statement. What difficulty do you think this causes in programming?

Programming

1. Write a case statement that prints a message indicating whether Number (type int) is a square number less than 10 (0, 1, 4, 9), a square number from 10 to 19 (16), or a square from 20 to 29 (25). Your statement should print the category selected.

2. Write a cascaded `if` statement equivalent to the `case` statement described in programming exercise 1.

3. In the `case` statement in programming exercise 1, add an otherwise clause that displays the message "Not a square number less than 30".

4.10 Common Programming Errors

You can use the Boolean operators, `and`, `or`, and `not` only with Boolean expressions. In the expression

```
Flag and (X = Y)
```

the variable `Flag` must be type `boolean`.

When using a `case` statement, make sure the `case` selector and labels are integers. Remember that no value may appear in more than one `case` label. If the selector evaluates to a value not listed in any of the `case` labels, there must be an otherwise clause or an error diagnostic will occur and your program may stop. Don't forget to terminate an `if` statement with `end if` and a `case` statement with `end case`.

Chapter Review

In this chapter, we discussed how to represent decision steps in an algorithm (using pseudocode) and how to implement them in Turing using `if` and `case` statements. We also introduced the Boolean operators (`and`, `or`, `not`) and showed how to use them to write Boolean expressions. We learned how to describe the syntax of Turing using syntax diagrams. To avoid syntax errors, you should refer to the appropriate syntax diagrams if you are unsure of the form of a statement. If the compiler detects a syntax error that you do not understand, refer again to the syntax diagram to determine the cause of the error.

We continued our discussion of problem solving and showed how to solve a new problem by making an analogy to an earlier problem. We also showed how to add data flow information to structure charts to improve system documentation. We saw that a variable processed by a subproblem is classified as an input or an output based on how it is used by that subproblem, and the same variable may be an input to one subproblem and an output from another.

You also saw how to use traces to verify that an algorithm or program is correct. You can discover errors in logic by carefully tracing an algorithm or program. Tracing an algorithm or program before entering the program in the computer will save you time in the long run.

A second selection structure, the `case` statement, was introduced in this chapter as a convenient means of implementing decisions with several alternatives. We saw how to use the `case` statement to implement decisions that are based on the value of a variable or simple expression (the `case` selector). The `case` selector must be an integer.

New Turing Constructs in Chapter 4

The new Turing constructs introduced in this chapter are described in Table 4.11.

TABLE 4.11   Summary of New Turing Constructs

Construct	Effect
If Statement	

One Alternative
``turing
if X not= 0.0 then
    Product := Product * X
end if
``
	Multiply `Product` by X only if X is nonzero.

Two Alternatives
``turing
if X >= 0.0 then
    put X :12:2, " is positive"
else
    put X :12:2, " is negative"
end if
``
	If X is greater than or equal to zero, display " is positive" otherwise, display " is negative"

Several Alternatives
``turing
if X < 0.0 then
    put "negative"
    AbsX := -X
 	
elsif X = 0.0 then
    put "zero"
    AbsX := 0.0
else
    put "positive"
    AbsX := X
end if
``
	One of three messages is printed depending on whether X is negative, positive, or zero. `AbsX` is set to represent the absolute value or magnitude of X.

Case Statement	

``turing
case Ranking of
    label 10 :
        put "Excellent"
    label 8, 9 :
        put "Good"
    label 6, 7 :
        put "O.K."
    label :
        put "Poor, student is"
        put "on probation"
end case
``
	Prints one of four messages based on the value of `Ranking` (type `int`). If `Ranking` is anything other than 6, 7, 8, 9, or 10 the student is put on probation.

Quick-Check Exercises

1. An `if` statement implements _____ execution.
2. What is a cascaded `if` statement?
3. A `case` statement is often used instead of _____.
4. What values can a Boolean expression have?
5. The relational operator >= means _____.
6. A hand trace is used to verify that a(n) _____ is correct.
7. A(n) _____ is used to verify that a program statement is grammatically correct.
8. Correct the syntax error below.

```
if X > 25.0 then
    Y := X
else
Y := Z
```

9. What value is assigned to Fee by the `if` statement below when speed is 75?

```
if Speed > 35 then
   Fee := 20.0
elsif Speed > 50 then
   Fee := 40.00
elsif Speed > 75 then
   Fee := 60.00
end if
```

10. Answer question 9 for the `if` statement below. Which `if` statement is correct?

```
if Speed > 75 then
   Fee := 60.00
elsif Speed > 50 then
   Fee := 40.00
elsif Speed > 35 then
   Fee := 20.00
end if
```

11. What output line(s) are displayed by the statements below when Grade is 2? When Grade is 6? When Grade is 0?

```
case Grade of
    label 7 : Points := 4
    label 6 : Points := 3
    label 5 : Points := 2
    label 4 : Points := 1
    label 3, 2, 1 : Points := 0
end case
```

```
if 7 >= Grade and Grade >= 4 then
put "Passed, points earned = ", Points
else
put "Failed, no points earned"
end if
```

12. Explain the difference between the statements on the left and the statements on the right below. For each of them, what is the final value of X if the initial value of X is 0?

```
if X >= 0 then              if X >= 0 then
   X := X + 1                   X := X + 1
                            end if
elsif X >= 1 then           if X >= 1 then
   X := X + 2                   X := X + 2
end if                      end if
```

Answers to Quick-Check Exercises

1. Conditional
2. An `if` statement that contains `elsif` clauses
3. Nested `if` statements or a multiple alternative `if` statement
4. `true` and `false`
5. Greater than or equal
6. Algorithm
7. Syntax diagram
8. Add `end if` at the bottom
9. `20.00`, first condition is met
10. `40.00`, the one in exercise 10
11. When `Grade` is 2:

    ```
    Failed, no points earned
    ```

    when `Grade` is 6:

    ```
    Passed, points earned = 3
    ```

    when `Grade` is 0:

    ```
    a case selector out of range error occurs
    ```

12. A cascaded `if` statement is on the left; a sequence of `if` statements is on the right. X becomes 1 on the left; X becomes 3 on the right.

Review Questions

1. A decision in Turing is actually an evaluation of a(n) _____ expression.
2. How does a relational operator differ from a Boolean operator?
3. What is short-circuit Boolean evaluation?

4. Trace the following program fragment and indicate which procedure will be called if a data value of 27.34 is entered.

```
put "Enter a temperature >"
get Temp
if Temp > 32.0 then
    NotFreezing
else
    IceForming
end if
```

5. Write a nested if statement to display a message indicating the educational level of a student based on his or her number of years of schooling. (None, 1 < Elementary School <= 5, 6 <= Middle School <= 8, 9 <= High School <= 12, College > 12). Print a message to indicate bad data as well.

6. How can syntax diagrams aid a new user in becoming comfortable with an unfamiliar programming language?

7. Given the following syntax diagram, which of the words under the diagram that are valid.

Syntax Diagram for Words

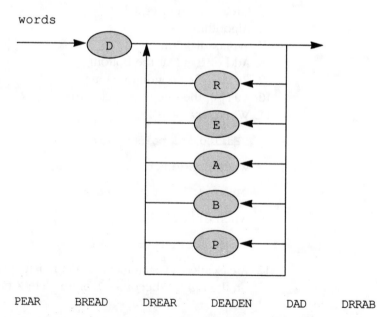

PEAR   BREAD   DREAR   DEADEN   DAD   DRRAB

8. Write an if statement to select an operation based on the value of Inventory. Increment TotalPaper by PaperOrder if Inventory is "B" or "C"; increment TotalRibbon if RibbonOrder is "E", "F", or "D"; increment TotalLabel by LabelOrder if Inventory is "A" or "X". Do nothing if Inventory is "M".

9. Write the six pairs of words that satisfy the syntax diagram for *thing*.

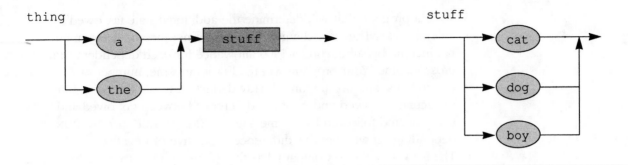

thing · · · stuff

10. In the syntax diagram for `case` statement (see Fig. 4.21), what syntactic element does `DayNumber` in Fig. 4.22 correspond to? Answer the same question for the symbols 1, 7 and the symbols 2, 3, 4, 5, 6.

Programming Projects

1. Write procedures to draw a square and a triangle. Write a program that reads a letter S or T and based on that letter draws either a square or a triangle.
2. Write a program to simulate a highway police radar gun. The program should read an automobile speed and print the message `"Speeding"` if the speed exceeds 100 km/hr.
3. While spending the summer as a surveyor's assistant, you decide to write a program that transforms compass headings in degrees (0 to 360) to compass bearings. A compass bearing consists of three items: the direction you face (north or south), an angle between 0 and 90 degrees, and the direction you turn before walking (east or west). For example, to get the bearing for a compass heading of 110.0 degrees, you would first face due south (180 degrees) and then turn 70.0 degrees east (180.0 – 110.0). Be sure to check the input for invalid compass headings.
4. Write a program that reads in a room number, its capacity, and the size of the class enrolled so far and prints an output line showing the classroom number, capacity, number of seats filled and available, and a message indicating whether the class is filled or not. Call a procedure to display the heading below before the output line.

Room   Capacity   Enrollment   Empty seats   Filled

Display each part of the output line under the appropriate column heading. Test your program with the following classroom data:

Room	Capacity	Enrollment
426	25	25
327	18	14
420	20	15
317	100	90

5. Write a program that will determine the additional state tax owed by an employee. The state charges a 4% tax on net income. Determine net income by subtracting a $500 allowance for each dependent from gross income. Your program will read gross income, number of dependents, and tax amount already deducted. It will then compute the actual tax owed and print the difference between tax owed and tax deducted followed by the message "SEND CHECK" or "REFUND" depending on whether this difference is positive or negative.

6. The New Telephone Company has the following rate structure for long-distance calls:

   1. Any call started after 6:00 P.M. (1800 hours) but before 8:00 A.M. (0800 hours) is discounted 50%.
   2. Any call started after 8:00 A.M. (0800 hours) but before 6:00 P.M. (1800 hours) is charged full price.
   3. All calls are subject to a 4% Federal tax.
   4. The regular rate for a call is $0.40 per minute.
   5. Any call longer than 60 minutes receives a 15% discount on its cost (after any other discount is subtracted before tax is added).

   Write a program that reads the start time for a call based on a 24-hour clock and the length of the call. The gross cost (before any discounts or tax) should be printed, followed by the net cost (after discounts are deducted and tax is added). Use a procedure to print instructions to the program user.

7. Write a program that will calculate and print out bills for the city water company. The water rates vary depending on whether the bill is for home use, commercial use, or industrial use.

   A code of H means home use, a code of C means commercial use, and a code of I means industrial use. Any other code should be treated as an error.

   The water rates are computed as follows:

Code H:	$5.00 plus $0.0005 per litre used
Code C:	$1,000.00 for the first 4 million litres used and $0.00025 for each additional litre
Code I:	$1,000.00 if usage does not exceed 4 million litres; $2,000.00 if usage is more than 4 million litres but does not exceed 10 million litres; and $3,000.00 if usage exceeds 10 million litres

   Your program should prompt the user to enter an integer account number, use code (type string), and the litres of water used expressed as a real number. Your program should echo the input data and print the amount due from the user.

Repetition:
Loop and For Statements

o far we have covered Turing control structures for sequence and selection. In this chapter, we will discuss Turing's control structures for repetition. You will see how to specify the repetition of a group of program statements (called a *loop*) using the `loop` and `for` statements.

We will discuss the relative advantages of various forms of these two statements and determine when it is best to use each form. We will also reexamine nested control structures, especially nested loops, and see how to use them.

5.1 Repetition in Programs: The Loop Statement

Just as the ability to make decisions is a very important programming tool, so is the ability to specify the repetition of a group of operations. For example, if a company has seven employees, we will want to perform the same gross pay and net pay computations for each of the employees. Rather than duplicate these steps seven times in a program, we can write them once and tell Turing to repeat them.

The repetition of steps in a program is called a *loop*. The *loop body* contains the steps to be repeated. Turing provides two control statements for specifying repetition, the `loop` statement and the `for` statement.

The Loop Statement with an Initial Test

The program shown in Fig. 5.1 computes and displays the weekly pay for each of seven employees assuming no overtime pay. The loop body (steps that are repeated) consists of those lines between the keyword `loop` and the phrase `end loop`.

The loop body begins with this line

```
exit when CountEmp = 7
```

This line is an `exit` statement. It contains a *test* to see if the loop body should be repeated or if the loop should be terminated. As you will learn, a `loop` statement can contain an `exit` statement in this initial position, or in the final position, just before `end loop`. These two forms of `loop` statements, with an *initial test* or a *final test*, are the most commonly used. Besides these two forms, you can also use `loop` statements with intermediate tests, many tests, or no tests at all.

The loop body in Fig. 5.1 reads an employee's payroll data, then computes and displays that employee's gross pay. After seven weekly pay amounts are displayed, the last statement in Fig. 5.1 uses a `put` statement to display the message `"All employees processed"`.

FIGURE 5.1   Loop to Process Seven Employees

```
% The "Pay7" program
% Compute the pay for seven employees

var CountEmp : int          % Current employee
var Hours    : real         % Hours worked
var Rate     : real         % Hourly rate
var Pay      : real         % Weekly pay

CountEmp := 0        % No employees processed yet
loop
    exit when CountEmp = 7      % Test value of CountEmp
    CountEmp := CountEmp + 1    % Increment CountEmp
    put "Hours> " ..
    get Hours
    put "Rate> $" ..
    get Rate
    Pay := Hours * Rate
    put "Weekly pay is $ ", Pay :4:2
end loop

put "All employees processed"
```

There are three lines in Fig. 5.1 that change or test the CountEmp variable. These three lines control the looping process. The first statement

```
CountEmp := 0          % No employees processed yet
```

stores an initial value of 0 in the variable CountEmp which represents the count of employees processed so far. The next line evaluates the boolean expression CountEmp = 7. If it is false, the compound statement representing the loop body is executed, causing a new pair of data values to be read and a new pay to be computed and displayed. The next statement in the loop body

```
CountEmp := CountEmp + 1      % Increment CountEmp
```

adds 1 to the value of CountEmp. After executing the last step in the loop body, control returns to the beginning of the loop, and the boolean expression is reevaluated for the next value of CountEmp.

The loop body will be executed once for each value of CountEmp from 0 to 7. Eventually CountEmp becomes 7, and the boolean expression will evaluate to true. When this happens the loop body is not executed, and control passes to the put statement that follows end loop.

The boolean expression in the exit statement is called the *exit condition*. The loop is repeated while this condition is false. We say that the *loop is exited* when this condition is true.

The flowchart of the loop in Fig. 5.2 summarizes what we have learned about this `loop` statement. It shows that the expression in the diamond shaped box is evaluated first. If it is `false`, the loop body is executed, and the process is repeated. The loop is exited when the expression becomes `true`.

FIGURE 5.2   Flowchart of a Loop with an Initial Test

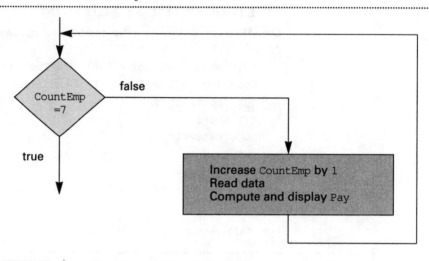

Make sure you understand the difference between the `loop` statement in Fig. 5.1 and the `if` statement below.

```
if CountEmp = 7 then
    ...
end if
```

The statements after the reserved word `then` execute at most one time. In a `loop` statement, the loop body may execute many times.

Syntax of the Loop Statement with an Initial Test

In Fig. 5.1, variable `CountEmp` is called the *loop control variable* because its value determines whether or not the loop body is repeated. Three critical steps involve the loop control variable `CountEmp`.

- `CountEmp` is set to an initial value of 0 (*initialized to 0*) before the `loop` statement is reached.
- `CountEmp` is tested before the start of each `loop` repetition (called an *iteration* or a *pass*).
- `CountEmp` is updated (its value increases by 1) during each iteration.

Steps similar to these three steps (initialization, test, and update) must be performed for every `loop` statement containing an exit test. If the first step is missing, the initial test of CountEmp will be meaningless. The last step ensures that we make progress towards the final goal (CountEmp = 7) during each repetition of the loop. If the last step is missing, the value of CountEmp cannot change, so the loop will execute "forever" (an *infinite loop*). The syntax display for the basic loop statement, as we have used it so far, follows; Figure 5.3 shows the syntax diagram.

THE LOOP STATEMENT WITH AN INITIAL TEST

Form:
```
loop
    exit when expression
    statementsAndDeclarations
end loop
```

Example:
```
% Display N asterisks
CountStar := 0
loop
    exit when CountStar = N
    put "*"
    CountStar := CountStar + 1
end loop
```

Interpretation: The *expression* (a condition to control the loop process) is tested and if it is false the statements and declarations are executed and the *expression* is retested. The loop body (the statements and declarations) is repeated as long as the *expression* is false. When the *expression* is tested and found to be true, the loop is exited and the next statement after end loop is executed.

Note: If the *expression* evaluates to true the first time it is tested, the loop body will not be executed.

Loop Statements without Exits

In some special circumstances it makes sense for a loop to keep on repeating with no possibility of exiting. For example, if the loop controls a traffic light, it would keep on turning the light red, then yellow, then green repeatedly, without quitting. Loops that never exit are called infinite loops. The loop in the following program is an infinite loop that repeatedly requests a radius and computes the area of the corresponding circle.

```
% The "Circarea" program
% Repeatedly read a radius and display circle's area

const Pi := 3.14159
var Radius : real
```

```
loop
    put "Enter radius of a circle> " ..
    get Radius
    put "Area of circle is ", Pi * Radius ** 2
end loop
```

This uses the formula for the area of a circle, which is p r^2. The constant *Pi* is declared to represent the value of p. In principle, an infinite loop such as the one in this example will execute forever. However, when you run this program on a particular computer, there will be a way for you to halt the program. For example, when running Turing on an IBM compatible personal computer, you can halt this program by holding down the Control key and pressing the Break key. On a Macintosh computer this is done by holding down the "Apple" key and typing a period. On Unix systems this is done by holding down the Control key and pressing the letter C key.

Figure 5.3 gives the syntax diagram for `loop` statements and `exit` statements. Most `loop` statements contain an `exit` statement. An `exit` statement can appear only inside a `loop` statement, or, as will be explained later, inside a `for` statement.

FIGURE 5.3   Syntax Diagram of Loop Statements and Exit Statements

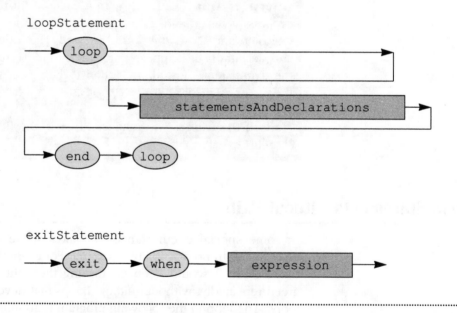

PROGRAM
STYLE

FORMATTING THE LOOP STATEMENT
For clarity, we indent the body within a `loop` statement. This is similar to the way we indent the parts of an `if` statement and the parts of a `case` statement.

Exercises for Section 5.1

Self-Check

1. How many times is the loop body below repeated? What is printed during each repetition of the loop body?

```
X := 3
Count := 0
loop
    exit when Count >= 3
    X := X * X
    put X
    Count := Count + 1
end loop
```

2. Answer exercise 1 if the last statement in the loop is

```
Count := Count + 2
```

3. Answer exercise 1 if the last statement in the loop body is omitted.

Programming

1. Write a loop that displays each integer from 1 to 5 on a separate line together with its square.
2. Write a loop that displays each integer from –2 to 3 on a separate line. Display the values in the sequence –2, –1, 0, and so on.

5.2 Accumulating a Sum or Product in a Loop

Often we use loops to accumulate a sum or a product by repeating an addition or multiplication operation. The next example uses a loop to accumulate a sum.

EXAMPLE 5.1

The program in Fig. 5.4 has a loop similar to the one in Fig. 5.1. Besides displaying each employee's weekly pay, it accumulates the total payroll (`TotalPay`) for a company. The assignment statement

```
TotalPay := TotalPay + Pay     % Add next pay
```

adds the current value of `Pay` to the sum being accumulated in `TotalPay`. Figure 5.5 traces the effect of repeating this statement for the three values of `Pay` shown in the sample run. In this program we have initialized the values of `CountEmp` and `TotalPay` as a part of the declarations of those variables.

FIGURE 5.4 Computing a Company Payroll

```
% The "Company" program
% Compute the payroll for a company

var NumberEmp : int              % Number of employees
var CountEmp  : int := 0         % Current employee
var Hours     : real             % Hours worked
var Rate      : real             % Hourly rate
var Pay       : real             % Weekly pay
var TotalPay  : real := 0.0      % Company payroll

% Enter number of employees
put "Enter number of employees> " ..
get NumberEmp

% Compute each employee's pay and add it to the payroll
loop
    exit when CountEmp = NumberEmp
    put "Hours> " ..
    get Hours
    put "Rate> $" ..
    get Rate
    Pay := Hours * Rate
    put "Pay is $", Pay :4:2
    put ""
    TotalPay := TotalPay + Pay   % Add next pay
    CountEmp := CountEmp + 1
end loop

put "All employees processed"
put "Total payroll is $", TotalPay :4:2
```

```
Enter number of employees> 3
Hours> 5
Rate> $4.00
Pay is $20.00

Hours> 6
Rate> $5.00
Pay is $30.00

Hours> 1.5
Rate> $10.00
Pay is $15.00

All employees processed
Total payroll is $65.00
```

FIGURE 5.5   Accumulating Partial Sums

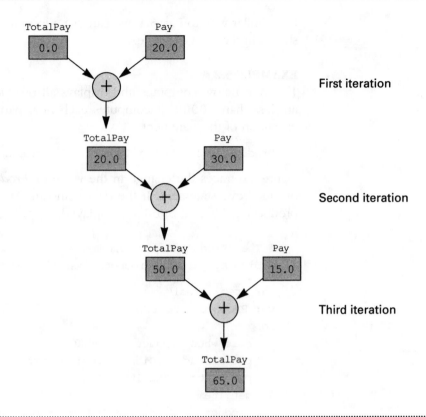

Prior to loop execution, the declaration

```
var TotalPay : real := 0.0    % Company payroll
```

initializes the value of `TotalPay` to zero. This initialization is critical. If it is omitted, the statement that increments `TotalPay`, namely

```
TotalPay := TotalPay + Pay    % Add next pay
```

will produce a run-time error when it tries to use the *uninitialized* value of `TotalPay`.

Generalizing a Loop

The first loop shown in Fig. 5.1 has a serious deficiency: it can only be used when the number of employees is exactly 7. The loop in Fig. 5.4 is much better because it can be used for any number of employees. This program begins by reading the total number of employees into variable `NumberEmp`. Before each execution of the loop body, the loop repetition condition compares the number of employees processed so far (`CountEmp`) to `NumberEmp`.

Accumulating Partial Products

In a similar way to Fig. 5.4, we can use a loop to accumulate a product as shown in the next example.

EXAMPLE 5.2

The loop below computes and displays all products of its data items that are less than `10000`. It computes each new partial product by repeated execution of the statement

```
Product := Product * Item    % Compute next product
```

Figure 5.6 traces the change in the value of *Product* with each execution of the above statement. If the data items are 10, 500, and 3, the partial products 1, 10, and 5000 are displayed.

```
% The "Products" program
% Display partial products less than 10000

var Item : real
var Product : real := 1
loop
    exit when Product >= 10000
    put Product % Display partial product
    put "Enter next item> " ..
    get Item
    Product := Product * Item % Compute next product
end loop
```

Loop exit occurs when the value of `Product` is greater than or equal to `10000`. Consequently, the last value assigned to `Product` (15000 in Fig. 5.6) is not displayed.

The loop in Fig. 5.6 differs from the other loops in this section. Its repetition condition involves a test of the variable `Product`. Besides controlling loop repetition, the variable `Product` also stores the result of the computation being performed in the loop. The other loops involve a test of a variable, `CountEmp`, that represents the count of loop repetitions. `CountEmp` is not directly involved in the computation being performed in the loop. We will discuss these differences further in the next section.

FIGURE 5.6   Accumulating Partial Products

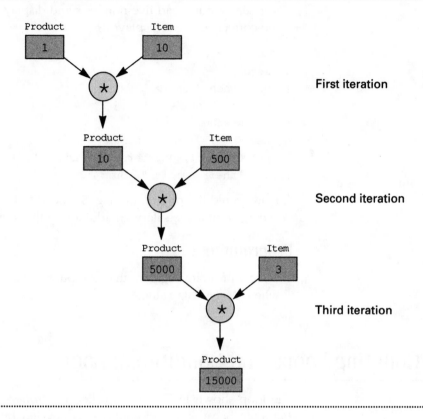

First iteration

Second iteration

Third iteration

Exercises for Section 5.2

Self-Check

1. What output values are displayed by the loop below for a data value of 5?

```
put "Enter an integer> " ..
get X
Product := X
Count := 0
loop
    exit when Count >= 4
    put Product
    Product := Product * X
    Count := Count + 1
end loop
```

2. What values are displayed if the put statement comes at the end of the loop instead of the beginning?

3. Insert the `end loop` where needed and correct the errors. The corrected segment should read five numbers and display their sum. What does the correct segment display?

```
Count := 0
loop
exit when Count > 5
put "Next number> " ..
get NextNum
NextNum := Sum + NextNum
put Count :1, "numbers were added;"
put "their sum is ", Sum:4:2
```

4. How would the program in Fig. 5.4 need to be modified to display the average employee salary, in addition to the total payroll amount?

Programming

1. Write a program segment that computes $1 + 2 + 3 + \ldots + (N-1) + N$ where N is a data value.

5.3 Counting Loops and Conditional Loops

The loop shown in Fig. 5.4 is called a *counter-controlled loop* (or *counting loop*) because its repetition is controlled by a variable whose value represents a count. The counter-controlled loop in Fig. 5.4 has this format.

```
Set counter variable to an initial value of 0
loop
    exit when counter variable = final value
    increase counter variable by 1

       ...
end loop
```

We use a counter-controlled loop when we can determine prior to loop execution exactly how many loop repetitions will be needed to solve our problem. This number should appear as the *final value* in the exit condition. Section 5.5 shows how to use the `for` statement to implement counter-controlled loops.

Conditional Loops

In many programming situations, we cannot determine the exact number of loop repetitions before loop execution begins. The number of repetitions may depend on some aspect of the data that is not known before the loop is entered, but usually can be stated by a condition. For example, we may want to continue writing checks as long as our bank balance is positive, as indicated by the pseudocode description below.

```
loop
    exit when the balance becomes negative
    Read in the next transaction
    Update and print the balance
end loop
```

The actual number of loop repetitions performed depends on the type of each transaction (deposit or withdrawal) and its amount.

EXAMPLE 5.3

The program in Fig. 5.7 traces the progress of a hungry worm approaching an apple. Each time it moves, the worm cuts the distance between itself and the apple by its own body length until the worm is close enough to enter the apple. A `loop` statement is the correct looping structure to use because we have no idea beforehand how many moves are required.

FIGURE 5.7

Worm Bites Apple

```
% The "Worm" program

% Print distances between a worm and an apple. With
% each move, the worm reduces the distance by its body
% length until it is close enough to enter the apple.

const WormLength := 3.5      % Worm body length in inches

var InitialDist : real       % Starting distance of worm
                             % from apple
var Distance : real          % Distance between worm and apple

put "Enter initial distance"
put "between worm and apple in inches> " ..
get InitialDist

% Reduce the distance between the worm and the apple
% by the worm's body length until the worm is close
% enough to enter the apple
Distance := InitialDist
loop
    exit when Distance < WormLength
    put "The distance is ", Distance :4:2
    Distance := Distance - WormLength % Reduce Distance
end loop

% Print final distance before entering the apple
put ""
```

```
put "The last distance before the worm enters"
put "the apple is ", Distance :3:1
```

....

```
Enter initial distance
between worm and apple in inches> 12.0
The distance is 12.00
The distance is 8.50
The distance is 5.00

The last distance before the worm enters
the apple is 1.5
```

....

Let's take a close look at the `loop` statement in Fig. 5.7. The assignment statement just before the loop initializes the variable `Distance` to the starting distance (12.0), which was previously read into `InitialDist`. Next, the `exit` statement is reached and the *loop exit condition*

```
Distance < WormLength
```

is evaluated. Since this condition is `false`, the loop body (down to `end loop`) is executed. The loop body displays the value of `Distance` and the statement

```
Distance := Distance - WormLength % Reduce Distance
```

reduces the value of `Distance`, thereby bringing the worm closer to the apple. The loop repetition condition is retested with the new value of `Distance` (`8.5`); since `8.5 < 3.5` is `false`, the loop body displays `Distance` again, and `Distance` becomes `5.0`. The loop repetition condition is tested a third time; since `5.0 < 3.5` is `false`, the loop body displays `Distance` again, and `Distance` becomes `1.5`. The loop repetition condition is tested again; since `1.5 < 3.5` is `true`, loop exit occurs, and the statements following the loop end are executed.

It is important to realize that the loop is not exited at the exact instant that `Distance` becomes `1.5`. If more statements appeared in the loop body after the assignment to `Distance`, they would be executed. Loop exit does not occur until the loop repetition condition is retested at the top of the loop and found to be true.

Just as counting loop shown earlier in Fig.5.4, there are three critical steps in Fig. 5.7 that involve the loop control variable `Distance`:

- `Distance` is initialized to `InitialDist` before the loop header is reached.
- `Distance` is tested before each execution of the loop body.
- `Distance` is updated (reduced by `3.5`) during each iteration.

Remember that steps similar to those above must appear in every loop that contains an exit.

Exercises for Section 5.3

Self-Check

1. What is the least number of times that the body of a `loop` statement may be executed?
2. a. What is displayed by the segment below?

   ```
   Sum := 0
   loop
   exit when Sum >= 100
   Sum := Sum + 5
   end loop
   put Sum : 1
   ```

   b. Rewrite the loop so that it prints all multiples of 5 from 0 through 100, inclusive.
3. a. What values are displayed if the data value in the sample run of the program in Fig. 5.7 is 9.45?
   b. What values would be displayed by this program if the order of the statements in the loop body were reversed?
4. a. How would you modify the loop in Fig. 5.7 so that it also determines the number of moves (`CountMoves`) made by the worm before entering the apple?
   b. In your modified loop, which is the loop control variable, `Distance` or `CountMoves`?

Programming

1. There are 9,870 people in a town whose population increases by 10% each year. Write a loop that determines how many years (`CountYears`) it takes for the population to go over 30,000.

5.4 Loop Design

It is one thing to be able to analyze the operation of a loop and another to design our own loops. We will attack this problem in two ways. One approach is to analyze the requirements for a new loop to determine what initialization, test, and update of the loop control variable are needed. A second approach is to develop templates for loop forms that frequently reoccur and to use the template as the basis for the new loop. We will discuss loop templates later in this section.

To gain some insight into the design of the loop needed for the worm and apple problem, we should study the comment in Fig. 5.7 that summarizes the goal of this loop.

```
% Reduce the distance between the worm and the apple
% by the worm's body length until the worm is close
% enough to enter the apple
```

In order to accomplish this goal, we must concern ourselves with loop control and loop processing. Loop control involves making sure that loop exit occurs when it is supposed to; loop processing involves making sure the loop body performs the required operations.

To help us formulate the necessary loop control and loop processing steps, it is useful to list what we know about the loop. In this example, if `Distance` is the distance of the worm from the apple, we can make the following observations.

1. `Distance` must be equal to `InitialDist` just before the loop begins.
2. `Distance` during pass i must be less than the value of `Distance` during pass *i-1* by the length of the worm.
3. `Distance` must be between zero and the worm's body length just after loop exit.

Statement (1) above simply indicates that `InitialDist` is the starting distance of the worm from the apple. Statement (2) says that the distance of the worm from the apple must be cut by the worm's body length during each iteration. Statement (3) derives from the fact that the worm must be close enough to enter the apple on its next move right after loop exit. Therefore, the worm's distance from the apple must be less than its body length. Because the worm has not yet entered the apple, the distance cannot be negative.

Statement (1) by itself tells us what initialization must be performed. Statement (2) tells us how to process `Distance` within the loop body (that is, subtract the length of the worm). Finally, statement (3) tells us when to exit the loop. Since `Distance` is decreasing, loop exit should occur when `Distance < WormLength` is `true`. These considerations give us the outline below, which is the basis for the loop shown in Fig. 5.7.

```
1. Initialize Distance to InitialDist
2. loop
     exit when Distance < WormLength
   3. Display Distance
   4. Reduce Distance by WormLength
end loop
```

Loop Statements with Zero Iterations

The body of a loop is not executed if the exit test passes (evaluates to `true`) when it is first reached. To verify that you have the initialization steps correct, you should make sure that a program still generates the correct results for zero iterations of the loop body. If `WormLength` is greater than the value read into `InitialDist` (say, 0.4), the loop body in Fig. 5.7 would not execute and the lines below would be correctly displayed.

```
Enter initial distance
between worm and apple in inches> 0.4

The last distance before the worm enters
the apple is 0.4
```

Displaying a Table of Values

The next example shows how to use a loop to display a table of values.

EXAMPLE 5.4

Your Physics professor wants you to write a program that displays the effect of gravity on a free-falling object. The table should show the height of an object dropped from a tower for every second that it is falling.

Assuming *t* is the time of free-fall, we can make the following observations about the height of an object dropped from a tower.

- At t = 0.0, the object height is the same as the tower height.
- While it is falling, the object height is the tower height minus the distance that it has travelled.
- Free-fall ends when the object height is <= 0.0.

These considerations form the basis for the `loop` statement shown in Fig. 5.8. The object height (`Height`) is initialized to the tower height (`Tower`). The exit condition

```
Height <= 0.0
```

ensures that loop exit occurs when the object hits the ground. Within the loop body, the assignment statement

```
Height := Tower - 0.5 * G * T ** 2
```

computes the object height where distance travelled is represented by the formula

```
distance = 1/2 × gt²
```

and g is the gravitational constant.

The number of lines in the table depends on the time interval between lines (`DeltaT`) and the tower height (`Tower`), both of which are data values. During each loop iteration, the current elapsed time, `T`, and the current object height, `Height`, are displayed and new values are assigned to these variables. The message following the table is displayed when the object hits the ground.

FIGURE 5.8   Dropping an Object from a Tower

```
% The "Freefall" program

% Display the height of an object dropped
% from a tower until it hits the ground

const G := 9.80665
          % Gravitational constant for metric units

var Height : real          % Height of object
var Tower  : real          % Height of tower
var T      : real := 0.0   % Elapsed time
var DeltaT : real          % Time interval

% Enter tower height and time interval
put "Tower height in meters> " ..
get Tower
put "Time in seconds between table lines> " ..
get DeltaT
put ""

% Display object height until it hits the ground
put "      Time", "      Height"
Height := Tower
loop
    exit when Height <= 0.0
    put T :10:2, Height :10:2
    T := T + DeltaT
    Height := Tower - 0.5 * G * T ** 2
end loop

% Object hits the ground
put ""
put "SPLATT!!!"
```

```
Tower height in meters> 100.0
Time in seconds between table lines> 1.0

         Time      Height
         0.00      100.00
         1.00       95.10
         2.00       80.39
         3.00       55.87
         4.00       21.55

SPLATT!!!
```

PROGRAM
STYLE

> **DISPLAYING A TABLE**
> The program in Fig. 5.8 displays a table of output values. Before the loop is reached, the statement
>
>   put "••••••Time", "••••Height"
>
> displays the two strings appearing in the table heading. Here we are using the symbol • to represent a blank character. We have preceded each label, such as Time, by enough blanks to force it to the right side of a field of width 10.
> Within the loop body, the statement
>
>   put T :10:2, Height :10:2
>
> displays a pair of output values each time it is executed. The rightmost digit of the first number appears in column 10, and the rightmost digit of the second number appears in column 20. Therefore, a table consisting of two columns of numbers is displayed, and each column is right-aligned with its respective heading. Make sure that the field width (10 in this case) is big enough to accommodate the largest value that will be printed.

Working Backwards to Determine Loop Initialization

It is not always so easy to come up with the initialization steps for a loop. In some cases, we must work backwards from the results that we know are required in the first pass to determine what initial values will produce these results.

EXAMPLE 5.5
Your little cousin is learning the binary number system and has asked you to write a program that displays all powers of two that are less than a certain value (say, 10,000). Assuming that each power of 2 is stored in the variable Power, we can make the following observations about the loop.

1. Power during pass i is 2 times Power during pass $i - 1$ (for $i > 1$).
2. Power must be between 10,000 and 20,000 just after loop exit.

Statement 1 derives from the fact that the powers of 2 are all multiples of 2; statement 2, that only powers less than 10,000 are displayed. From statement 1 we know that Power must be multiplied by 2 in the loop body. From statement 2 we know that the loop exit condition is Power >= 10,000. These considerations lead us to the outline below.

```
1. Initialize Power to ___
2. loop
      exit when Power >= 10000
   3. Display Power
   4. Multiply Power by 2
   end loop
```

One way to complete step 1 is to ask what value should be displayed during the first loop repetition. The value of N raised to the power 0 is 1 for any number N. Therefore, if we initialize Power to 1, the value displayed during the first loop repetition will be correct.

```
1. Initialize Power to 1
```

Sentinel-Controlled Loops and Intermediate Exits

Frequently, the number of data items to be handled by a program will not be known until the program begins to execute. This may happen because there are too many data items to count beforehand or because the number of data items provided may depend on how the computation proceeds.

One way to handle this situation is to instruct the user to enter a unique data value, called a *sentinel value*, as the last data item. The program would test each data item and terminate when this sentinel value is read. The *sentinel value* should be carefully chosen and must be a value that could not normally occur as data.

EXAMPLE 5.6

The statements 1 and 2 below must be true for a sentinel-controlled loop that accumulates the sum (in Sum) of a collection of exam scores where each score is read into the variable Score. The sentinel score must not be included in the sum.

1. Sum is the sum of all scores read so far.
2. Score contains the sentinel value just after loop exit.

From statement 1 we know that we must add each score to Sum in the loop body, and that Sum must initially be zero in order for its final value to be correct. From statement 2 we know that loop exit must occur after the sentinel value is read into Score. These considerations lead to the trial loop form below.

> ### Incorrect sentinel-controlled loop
> ```
> 1. Initialize Sum to zero
> 2. loop
>        exit when Score is the sentinel
>     3. Read the next score into Score
>     4. Add Score to Sum
>    end loop
> ```

Since Score has not been given an initial value, the exit condition in Step 2 cannot be evaluated when the loop is first reached. Another problem is that after step 3 reads the sentinel value, step 4 adds the sentinel to Sum before the exit occurs. One solution to these problems is to read the first score as the initial value of Score before the loop is reached, and to switch the order of the read and add steps in the loop body. The outline for this solution is shown below.

Correct sentinel-controlled loop with initial exit test

```
1. Initialize Sum to zero
2. Read the first score into Score
3. loop
       exit when Score is sentinel
   4. Add Score to Sum
   5. Read the next score into Score
   end loop
```

Step 2 reads in the first score, and step 4 adds this score to 0 (initial value of Sum). Step 5 reads all remaining scores, including the sentinel. Step 4 adds all scores except the sentinel to Sum.

The initial read before the loop (step 2) is often called the *priming read*. This is analogous to the process of priming a pump, which is done by pouring a cup of water into the pump chamber before the pump can be used to draw water out of a well.

Although priming works correctly, it is clumsy in that it requires us to repeat the statement that does the reading in Steps 2 and 5. We can avoid this problem by using an exit statement in the middle of the loop. We will use a loop with an *intermediate exit*, in other words, an exit that appears neither at the beginning nor the end of the loop body. The outline of this solution is shown below.

Correct sentinel-controlled loop with intermediate exit test

```
1. Initialize Sum to zero
2. loop
       3. Read the next score into Score
       exit when Score is sentinel
       4. Add Score to Sum
   end loop
```

This solution eliminates the need for priming by placing the first read statement at the beginning of the loop. Following this is the exit test to see if we have just read the sentinel. If so, we exit the loop and proceed to the statement following end loop. If not, we continue to Step 4 in which we increase Sum by Score.

If you study these two correct solutions, you will see that the order of executing the statements that do the reading, the testing, and the adding is exactly the same in the two. For example, when the two actually run, both start by reading a score and testing it. Then both exit the loop if the score is the sentinel. If it isn't the sentinel, both proceed to add the score to the sum, and so on.

Figure 5.9 shows a Turing program that codes the loop with the intermediate exit. The sentinel value used is −1 because all exam scores should be non-negative. The constant declaration

```
const Sentinel := -1      % Sentinel value
```

associates the constant Sentinel with the sentinel value.

FIGURE 5.9　　　　　A Sentinel-Controlled Loop with an Intermediate Exit

```
% The "Sumscore" program
% Accumulate the sum of exam scores

const Sentinel := -1        % Sentinel value

var Score : int             % Input - each exam score
var Sum : int := 0          % Output - sum of scores

put "When done, enter -1 to stop"
loop                        % Accumulate the sum
    put "Enter score> " ..
    get Score
    exit when Score = Sentinel
    Sum := Sum + Score
end loop

% Display the sum
put ""
put "Sum of exam scores is ", Sum :1
```

```
When done, enter -1 to stop
Enter the score> 55
Enter the score> 33
Enter the score> 77
Enter the score> -1

Sum of exam scores is 165
```

It is usually instructive (and often necessary) to question what happens when there are no data items to process. In this case, the sentinel value could be entered as the "first score." Loop exit would occur right after the first (and only) test of the loop repetition condition, so the loop body would not be executed (i.e., it is a loop with zero iterations). Sum would retain its initial value of zero, which would be correct.

Template for a Sentinel-Controlled Loop

Sentinel-controlled loops have this general form.

```
Initialization such as setting a sum to zero
loop
    Read value of input variable
    exit when input variable equals the sentinel
    Process the input variable
end loop
```

The sentinel value must be a value that would not be entered as a normal data item. For program readability, we usually give the sentinel value a name using a `const` declaration.

Loops Controlled by Boolean Flags

Boolean variables are often used as *program flags*, which signal whether or not a particular event occurs. The flag value should be `false` if the event has not occurred and true if it has occurred. A flag-controlled loop executes until the event being monitored occurs.

For example, let's assume we are reading various data characters entered at the keyboard and waiting for the first digit character that is entered. A `boolean` variable, say `DigitRead`, could be used as a flag to monitor whether a digit character has been entered.

Program variable

```
DigitRead : boolean    % Program flag - value is true
                       % after a digit character has
                       % been read; otherwise, value
                       % is false.
```

Because no characters have been read before the data entry loop executes, we should initialize `DigitRead` to `false`. The `loop` must continue to execute as long as `DigitRead` is `false` because this means that the event "digit character entered as data" has not yet occurred. Therefore, the loop repetition condition should be (`not DigitRead`), because this condition is `true` when `DigitRead` is `false`. Within the loop body, we will read each data item and set the value of `DigitRead` to `true` if that data item is a digit character. The loop follows.

```
var NextChar : string      % The input character
var DigitRead : boolean    % True when digit character
                           % has been read
DigitRead := false         % No digit character
                           % has been read yet
loop
    exit when DigitRead
    put "Enter another data character >"
    get NextChar
    DigitRead := ("0" <= NextChar) and (NextChar <= "9")
end loop
```

Inside the loop body, the assignment statement

```
DigitRead := ("0" <= NextChar) and (NextChar <= "9")
```

assigns a value of true to DigitRead if NextChar is a digit character (within the range "0"through "9"); otherwise, DigitRead remains false. If DigitRead becomes true, loop exit occurs; if DigitRead remains false, the loop continues to execute until a digit character is finally read.

A Loop Statement with a Final Exit Test

Since DigitRead is guaranteed to be false, at the first test in the exit statement in the preceding example, we can move this statement to the end of the loop. The resulting loop must have a *final test* ; in other words, its exit test is the last thing in the loop body. Since the operator precedence of <= is higher than and, we can omit the parentheses in the assignment to DigitRead. When we make these two changes, we get the following loop that works just like the preceding loop.

```
loop
    put "Enter another data character >"
    get NextChar
    DigitRead := "0" <= NextChar and NextChar <= "9"
    exit when DigitRead
end loop
```

Template for a Flag-Controlled Loop

Flag-controlled loops with a final exit have this general form.

```
Initialize flag to false
loop
    Take an action, such as reading a character
    Set flag to true if event being monitored occurs
    exit when flag is true
end loop
```

The last step in the loop body updates the flag value, setting it to true after the first occurrence of the event being monitored.

Exercises for Section 5.4

Self-Check

1. Describe how it would be possible to "work backwards" to determine the initial value of the loop variable required for programming exercise 3 of this section.

2. Why would it be incorrect to move the assignment statement in the sentinel-controlled loop of Fig. 5.9 to the beginning of the loop body?

Programming

1. Modify the counter-controlled loop in Fig. 5.4 so that it is a sentinel-controlled loop. Use a negative value of `Hours` as the sentinel.
2. Write a program segment that allows the user to enter values and prints out the number of positive and negative values entered. Use 0 as the sentinel value.
3. Write the loop that displays all powers of an integer, N, less than a specified value, `MaxPower`. On each line of a table, show the power (0, 1, 2, ...) and the value of the integer N raised to that power.
4. Write a loop that prints a table of angle measures along with their sine and cosine values. Assume that the initial and final angle measures (in degrees) are available in `InitDeg` and `FinalDeg` (type `real`), respectively, and that the change in angle measure between table entries is given by `StepDeg`. Note that the `sind` and `cosd` built-in functions implement sine and cosine for degrees.
5. Write a flag-controlled loop that continues to read pairs of integers until it reads a pair with the property that the first integer in the pair is evenly divisible by the second.

5.5 The For Statement

So far we have used the `loop` statement to implement repetition in programs. Recall from Section 5.2 that a counter variable controls the repetition of a counter-controlled loop. Such a loop that is repeated for values 1 up to the final value has the template shown below.

```
Set counter to 0
loop
    exit when counter = final value
    increment counter to its next value
    ...
end loop
```

Turing provides another loop form, the `for` statement, which is more convenient for implementing counter-controlled loops. The pseudo-code below describes a `for` statement that has the same behaviour as the `loop` statement above.

```
for counter : 1 .. final value
    ...
end for
```

All manipulation of the *counter* is specified in the `for` statement header. These three operations are:

1. Declare and initialize the *counter* to *initial value*.
2. Test if *counter <= final value*.
3. Increment *counter* to its next value before each test.

As will be explained in Example 5.7, the `for` statement also declares the counter variable.

EXAMPLE 5.7

The sets of statements on the left and right below behave in the same way. Both of them print *N* lines numbered 1 up to *N*.

```
var LineNo : int := 0           for LineNo := 1 .. N
loop                                put LineNo
    exit when LineNo = N        end for
    LineNo := LineNo + 1
    put LineNo
end loop
```

The `loop` statement implementation shown on the left is longer because it must explicitly initialize `LineNo` to zero and increment it by one in the loop body using this statement

```
LineNo := LineNo + 1
```

The declaration of `LineNo`, which is done by the line beginning with `var` on the left, is done by the line beginning `for` on the right.

The `for` statement does all of the following: it declares `LineNo`, initializes it, tests it and increments. You must not have another, preceding declaration of `LineNo`, such as

```
var LineNo : int
```

because this would result in two declarations of the same name, which Turing does not allow.

EXAMPLE 5.8

The `for` statement in Fig. 5.10 reads payroll data for seven employees and computes and displays each employee's weekly pay. This is just like the program in Fig. 5.1 except here we are using a `for` statement instead of a `loop` statement.

FIGURE 5.10   For Loop to Process Seven Employees

```
% The "Pay7b" program
% Compute the pay for seven employees

var Hours : real        % Hours worked
var Rate  : real        % Hourly rate
var Pay   : real        % Weekly pay
```

```
for CountEmp : 1 .. 7
    put "Hours> " ..
    get Hours
    put "Rate> $" ..
    get Rate
    Pay := Hours * Rate
    put "Weekly pay is $", Pay :4:2
end for

put "All employees processed"
```

You should read the first line of the `for` statement in Fig. 5.10 as "for each value of `CountEmp` from 1 to 7 do the following". There is no need to provide additional Turing statements to set `CountEmp` to an initial value or to update the value of `CountEmp`; these two operations are automatically performed in a `for` loop. Notice that in Fig. 5.1 there is an explicit declaration for `CountEmp`, but in Fig. 5.10 the `for` loop replaces this declaration.

In Chapter 7, when we talk about subprograms, you will see that some variables have a lifetime or `scope` that is limited to only a part of the program. In the case of the `for` statement, the scope of `CountEmp` is limited to the body of the statement. This means that `CountEmp` can be used inside the loop but not outside of it. If you want, you can have several `for` statements, one after the other, that use the same counter variable name. However, this case these are considered to be distinct from each other.

EXAMPLE 5.9
Figure 5.11 shows a procedure `PrintLetterI` that displays the letter I in block form. This procedure prints seven lines that contain asterisks in columns 4 and 5. A blank line is printed just before the return from the procedure.

FIGURE 5.11   Procedure PrintLetterI

```
procedure PrintLetterI
    % Print the block letter I
    for LineCounter : 1 .. 7
        put " **"
    put ""
end PrintLetterI
```

The `for` statement in Fig. 5.11 specifies that the counter variable `LineCounter` should take on each of the values in the range 1 to 7 during successive loop repetitions. This means that the value of `LineCounter` is 1 during the first loop repetition, 2 during the second loop repetition, and 7 during the last loop repetition.

The counter variable may also be referenced in the loop body, but its value cannot be changed. In the next example, you'll see a `for` statement for which the counter variable is referenced in the loop body.

EXAMPLE 5.10

The program in Fig. 5.12 uses a `for` loop to print a list of integer values and their squares and square roots. During each repetition of the loop body, the statements

```
Square := I ** 2
Root := sqrt (I)
```

compute the square and the square root of the counter variable I; then, the value of I and Square and Root are displayed. Table 5.1 traces the execution of the `for` loop.

FIGURE 5.12

Table of Integers, Squares, and Square Roots

```
% The "Squares" program
% Display a table of integers and their squares
% and square roots

const MaxI := 4         % Largest integer in table
var Square : int        % Output - square of I
var Root : real         % Output - square root of I

% Print a list of integers, their squares, and
% their square roots
put "          I", "      I ** 2":10, "      Square root"
for I : 1 .. MaxI
    Square := I ** 2
    Root := sqrt (I)
    put I :10, Square :10, Root :15:1
end for
```

```
     I      I ** 2    Square root
     1        1            1.0
     2        4            1.4
     3        9            1.7
     4       16            2.0
```

TABLE 5.1

Trace of For Statement in Figure 5.12

Statement	I	Square	Root	Effect
	?	?	?	
Initialize I	1			Initialize I to 1
Square := I ** 2		1		Assign 1 to Square

Root := Sqrt(I)		1.0	Assign 1.0 to Root
put ...			Print 1, 1, 1.0
Increment I	2		Assign 2 to I
Square := I ** 2	4		Assign 4 to Square
Root := Sqrt(I)		1.4	Assign 1.4 to Root
put ...			Print 2, 4, 1.4
Increment I	3		Assign 3 to I
Square := I ** 2	9		Assign 9 to Square
Root := Sqrt(I)		1.7	Assign 1.7 to Root
put...			Print 3, 9, 1.7
Increment I	4		Assign 4 to I
Square := I ** 2	16		Assign 16 to Square
Root := Sqrt(I)		2.0	Assign 2.0 to Root
put ...			Print 4, 16, 2.0

Exit from the for loop

The trace in Table 5.1 shows that the counter variable I is initialized to 1 when the for loop is reached. After the final pass through the loop, when I has its final value of 4, the loop is exited. After the exit from the loop, I can no longer be referenced.

Syntax of For Statement

The syntax display for a for statement follows; Figure 5.13 shows the syntax diagram.

THE FOR STATEMENT

Form: for *counter* : *initial* .. *final* by *stepsize*
                  statementsAndDeclarations
              end for

              for decreasing *counter* : *initial* .. *final* by *stepsize*
                  statementsAndDeclarations
              end for

Example: for I : 1 .. 5
                  get Indata, NextNum
                  Sum := Sum + NextNum
              end for

              for decreasing CountDown : 10 .. 0
                  put CountDown :2
              end for

Interpretation: The loop body is executed once for each value of the *counter* between *initial* and *final* inclusive. *Initial* and *final* must be constants, variables, or expressions that are integers.

The by *stepsize* clause of the for statement is optional. It is usually omitted. When it is present, for example, when it is "by 2" it causes the counter to be changed by 2 with each new iteration. The looping steps when the new counter value would exceed the *final* value.

Note 1: The value of *counter* cannot be modified in *statement*.

Note 2: The value of *final* is computed once, just before loop entry. If *final* is an expression, any change in the value of this expression will have no effect on the number of iterations performed.

Note 3: After loop exit, the *counter* is no longer defined. This counter can be referenced only in the loop body.

Note 4: The loop body is not executed if *initial* is greater than *final*. (In the decreasing form, the *statement* is not executed if *initial* is less than *final*.)

FIGURE 5.13   Syntax Diagram of For Statement

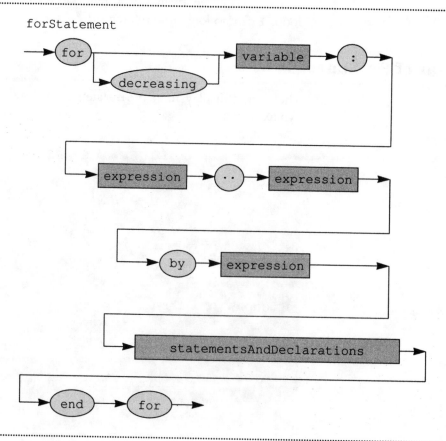

forStatement

Changing Variables in Final Expressions

The `for` statement below

```
get K
for I : 0 .. 3 * K - 1
    put I + K
end for
```

contains a variable K in its *final expression*. This expression is evaluated when the `for` statement is entered. If the value read into K is 3, the *final expression* value is 8, so the loop body executes for values of I between 0 and 8, inclusive, and the `for` statement displays the nine integers in the range 3 through 11.

What happens if we try to change the value of K in the loop body? In the `for` statement below

```
get K
for I := 0 .. 3 * K - 1
    put I + K
    K := K + 1
end for
```

the value of K increases each time the loop body executes. If the same value is read into K as before, does this change the number of loop repetitions or the values displayed by the loop? The answer to the first question is "No"; the *final expression* is evaluated only once and its value depends only on the initial value read into K. However, because the values of both I and K increase by one each time the loop body executes, the values displayed will change. If we read the value 3 into K again, the `for` loop will now display the nine odd integers in the range 3 through 19. Self-Check exercise 2 asks you to trace the loop execution for yourself to confirm this result.

Decreasing Counters

The examples seen so far increase the value of the counter variable after each loop repetition. If the reserved word *decreasing* is used, the value of the counter variable decreases after each loop repetition.

EXAMPLE 5.11

A student wants a fast way to compute and print the Fahrenheit temperature corresponding to each integer Celsius (C) temperature *decreasing* from 5 degrees C to –10 degrees C . She could use the `for` loop below.

```
var Fahrenheit : real
for decreasing Celsius : 5 .. -10
    Fahrenheit := 1.8 * Celsius + 32;
    put Celsius :10, Fahrenheit :15:1
end for
```

Exercises for Section 5.5

Self-Check

1. a. Trace the following program segment.

```
var J : int := 10
for I : 1 .. 5
    put I, " ", J
    J := J - 2
end for
```

   b. Rewrite the previous program segment so that it produces the same output, but uses 0 as the initial value of I.
2. Trace both `for` statements in the subsection "Changing Variables in Final Expressions".
3. Write `for` statement headers that process all values of `Celsius` (type integer) in the ranges indicated below.
   a. −10 through +10
   b. 100 through 1
   c. 15 through 50
   d. 50 through −75
4. Which of the built-in Turing data types may be used to declare `for` statement variables ?

Programming

1. Write a program segment containing a `for` statement that computes the sum of the odd integers in the range 0 to 100 inclusive.
2. Redo programming exercise 1 from section 5.2 using a `for` statement to compute the sum of the first N positive integers and compare this sum to the value computed using the formula

$$\frac{(N(N+1)}{2.0}$$

5.6 Kinds of Exit Tests

Most `loop` statements can contain an `exit` statement, which is used to stop the repeated execution of the loop body. The exit test can be placed in the initial, intermediate, or final position in the `loop` statement. Example 5.12 contrasts `loop` statements with initial and final tests. Example 5.13 gives a loop with a final exit test. Example 5.14 gives a loop with an intermediate exit test.

EXAMPLE 5.12

Both programs in Fig. 5.14 print the powers of two whose values lie between 1 and 1000. The left one has an initial exit test and the right one has a final exit test. As a rule, when you know that the entire loop body is always executed at least once, you should use a final exit test. This means that the loop on the right is the preferable style.

FIGURE 5.14   Initial and Final Exit Tests in Loop Statements

```
var Power : int := 1            var Power : int := 1
loop                           loop
    exit when Power>=1000          put Power :5
    put Power :5                   Power := Power * 2
    Power := Power * 2             exit when Power>=1000
end loop                       end loop
```

EXAMPLE 5.13

The program in Fig. 5.15 uses a `loop` statement to find the largest value in a sequence of data items. The variable `Item` is used to hold each data item and the variable `LargestSoFar` is used to save the largest data value encountered. Within the loop, the `if` statement

```
if Item > LargestSoFar then
    LargestSoFar := Item % Save new largest number
end if
```

redefines the value of `LargestSoFar` if the current data item is larger than all previous data values.

FIGURE 5.15   Finding the Largest Value

```
% The "Largest" program
% Find the largest number in a sequence of
% positive integers

const Sentinel := -1          % Not allowed as input
var Item : int                % Each data value
var LargestSoFar : int := 0   % Largest value so far

% Save the largest number encountered so far
put "Finding the largest value in a sequence"
put "of positive integers"
loop
    put "Enter a positive integer or ", Sentinel,
        " to stop> " ..
    get Item
```

```
        if Item > LargestSoFar then
            LargestSoFar := Item    % Save new largest number
        end if
        exit when Item = Sentinel
    end loop

    put "Largest positive value entered was ", LargestSoFar
```

....

```
Finding the largest value in a sequence
of positive integers
Enter a positiveinteger or -1 to stop> 99
Enter a positiveinteger or -1 to stop> 500
Enter a positiveinteger or -1 to stop> 116
Enter a positiveinteger or -1 to stop> -1
Largest positive value entered was 500
```

....

EXAMPLE 5.14

A `loop` statement with an `exit` in the middle of the loop body is often used to control a *menu-driven program* which prints a list of choices from which the program user selects a program operation. For example, the menu displayed for a statistics program might look like this:

```
1. Compute an average.
2. Compute a standard deviation.
3. Find the median.
4. Find the smallest and largest values.
5. Plot the data.
6. Exit the program.
```

The main control routine for such a program would follow the pseudocode below. In this pseudocode, `ExitChoice` represents the constant 6, which is the number of the menu item requesting an exit from the program.

```
loop
    Display the menu
    Read the user's choice
    exit when choice is ExitChoice
    Perform the user's choice
end loop
```

The program fragment below implements this loop in Turing. For each iteration, procedure `DisplayMenu` displays the menu and the user's choice is read. Procedure `DoChoice` is called with actual parameter `Choice` and the loop repeats if the user's choice was not `ExitChoice`.

FIGURE 5.16   Main Control Loop for Menu-Driven Program

```
loop
    DisplayMenu              % Display the menu choices
    put "Enter a number between 1 and ", ExitChoice
    get Choice
    exit when Choice = ExitChoice
    DoChoice (Choice)        % Perform the user's choice
end loop
```

Exits Using Case and If Statements

All of the exit statements that you have seen so far have had the form exit when *expression*. You can use an exit statement that consists of only the keyword exit without the "when *expression*" part. For example, the loop in Example 5.14 can be rewritten using a case statement this way.

```
loop
    DisplayMenu        % Display the menu choices
    put "Enter a number between 1 and ", ExitChoice
    get Choice
    case Choice of
        label 1 : Compute an average
        label 2 : Compute a standard deviation
        label 3 : Find the median
        label 4 : Find the smallest and largest values
        label 5 : Plot the data
        label 6 : exit
        label : put "Sorry, bad choice"
    end case
end loop
```

The exit statement in case alternative number 6 causes the loop to exit and causes control to continue with the statement following end loop. This example shows how to exit from a loop using an exit statement in a case statement. In a similar way, you can use an exit statement in an if statement to exit a loop.

Exiting from a For Statement

Just as you can use an exit statement in a loop statement, you can also use an exit statement in a for statement. Exiting from a for statement is usually not necessary, because the statement always exits when it has handled the last number in its range of values. The only reason to use an exit statement in a for statement is to exit conditionally from the loop before the full range of values has been covered. In this example, the purpose of the following `for` statement is to read scores until either ten scores have been read or the sum of the scores read so far exceeds 50.

```
var Sum : int := 0
var Score : int
for i : 1 .. 10
    put "Enter your score >"
    Sum := Sum + Score
    exit when Sum > 50
end for
```

Review of For and Loop Statements

Turing contains two kinds of `loop` statements: `for` and `loop`. You should use the `for` statement as a counting loop – a loop for which the number of iterations required can be determined at the beginning of loop execution. The loop control variable of a `for` loop must be an integer. This counter is declared by the `for` statement and its scope is limited to the body of the loop. You can use an `exit` statement in a `for` loop to cause it to exit before its full range of values has been covered.

A `loop` statement containing an `exit` statement is a conditional loop. The continued iteration depends on whether the value of a condition is `true` or `false`. The loop statement is repeated as long as its `exit` condition is `false`. The `exit` statement in a conditional loop can be an initial test, an intermediate test, or a final test. If there are circumstances in which the loop body may need to be entirely skipped, with no repetitions at all, the test should be in the initial position. If the loop body is always executed at least once, the final position is appropriate. If certain actions need to be taken before the exit test, such as reading in data values, the intermediate position is appropriate.

As an illustration of three forms of loops, a simple counting loop is written in Fig. 5.17. The dotted lines represent the loop body. The `for` loop is the best to use in this situation. The second form, with an initial exit test, is equivalent to the for statement, but is clumsier and requires the declaration of `Count`. The third form, with an intermediate exit test, always executes its loop body at least one time, even when `StartValue` is greater than `StopValue`.

FIGURE 5.17

Comparison of Three Counting Loops

```
for Count : StartValue .. StopValue
    ...
end for
```

```
var Count : int := StartValue - 1
loop
    exit when Count >= StopValue
    Count := Count + 1
    ...
end loop
var Count : int := StartValue
loop
    ...
    exit when Count >= StopValue
    Count := Count + 1
end loop
```

In Fig. 5.17, Count, StartValue, and StopValue must all be integers. The assignment statement

```
Count := Count + 1
```

is used in the last two loops to update the loop control variable Count (not required in the for statement). If StartValue is less than or equal to StopValue, Count will be equal to StopValue after these two loops are executed. If StartValue is greater than StopValue, Count will be equal to StartValue when these loops exit in their first iteration. The Count variable does not exist (is out of its scope) following the for loop version.

Exercises for Section 5.6

Self-Check

1. What does the loop statement below display? Rewrite it as a for statement.

   ```
   Num := 10
   loop
       exit when Num = 100
       put Num
       Num := Num + 10
   end loop
   ```

2. What does the for statement below display? Rewrite it as a loop statement.

   ```
   for N : 3 .. -1
       put N, "squared is", N ** 2
   end loop
   ```

3. When would you make use of a loop statement rather than a for statement in a program?

Programming

1. Write a program fragment that skips over a sequence of positive integer values read as data until it reaches a negative value.
2. Write a program fragment that could be used as the main control loop in a menu-driven program for updating an account balance (W = withdrawal, D = deposit, Q = quit). Assume that procedures ProcessWithdrawal and ProcessDeposit already exist and are called with the actual parameter Balance. Prompt the user for a transaction code (W, D, or Q) and call the appropriate procedure.

5.7 Nested Loops

This section examines nested control structures. You have seen examples of nested if statements in earlier programs. It is also possible to nest loops. Nested loops consist of an outer loop with one or more inner loops. Each time the outer loop is repeated, the inner loops are reentered, their loop control parameters are reevaluated, and all required iterations are performed.

EXAMPLE 5.15

Figure 5.18 shows a sample run of a program with two nested for loops. The outer loop is repeated three times (for I equals 1, 2, 3). Each time the outer loop is repeated, the statement

```
put "Outer ", I
```

displays Outer and the value of I (the outer loop control variable). Next, the inner loop is entered, and its loop control variable J is reset to 1. The number of times the inner loop is repeated depends on the current value of I. Each time the inner loop is repeated, the statement

```
put " Inner ", J
```

displays Inner and the value of J.

FIGURE 5.18 Nested For Loop Program

```
% The "Nestloop" program
% Illustrate a pair of nested for statements

put "         I J"              % Print heading
for I : 1 .. 3                  % Outer loop
   put "Outer      ", I
   for J : 1 .. I               % Inner loop
      put "     Inner      ", J
   end for
end for
```

```
                  I    J
Outer             1
    Inner              1
Outer             2
    Inner              1
    Inner              2
Outer             3
    Inner              1
    Inner              2
    Inner              3
```

A body of the outer `for` loop displays the value of the outer loop control variable `I` and then executes the inner `for` loop. The body of the inner `for` loop is a single statement displaying the value of the inner loop control variable `J`. This statement executes `I` times where `I` is the outer loop control variable.

The outer loop control variable `I` determines the number of repetitions of the inner loop. You cannot use the same variable as the loop control variable of both an outer and inner `for` loop in the same nest. In this example, a new variable, `J`, is used in the inner loop.

EXAMPLE 5.16

Program `Triangle` in Fig. 5.19 prints an isosceles triangle. The program contains an outer loop (loop control variable `Row`) and two inner loops. Each time the outer loop is repeated, two inner loops are executed. The first inner loop prints the leading blank spaces; the second inner loop prints one or more asterisks.

FIGURE 5.19

Isosceles Triangle Program

```
% The "Triangle" program
% Draw an isosceles triangle

const NumLines := 5        % Number of rows in triangle
const Blank := " "
const Star := "*"

for Row : 1 .. NumLines    % Draw each row
    for decreasing LeadBlanks : NumLines - Row .. 1
        put Blank ..           % Print leading blanks
    end for
    for CountStars : 1 .. 2 * Row - 1
        put Star ..            % Print asterisks
    end for
    put ""                    % Terminate line
end for
```

```
    *
   ***
  *****
 *******
*********
```

The outer loop is repeated five times; the number of repetitions performed by the inner loops is based on the value of Row. Table 5.2 lists the inner loop-control parameters for each value of Row. As shown in Table 5.2, four blanks and one asterisk are printed when Row is 1, three blanks and three asterisks are printed when Row is 2, etc. When Row is 5, the first inner loop is skipped and nine (2 * 5 - 1) asterisks are printed.

TABLE 5.2 **Inner Loop Control Parameters**

Row	LeadBlanks	CountStars	**Effect**
1	4 to 1	1 to 1	Displays 4 blanks and 1 star
2	3 to 1	1 to 3	Displays 3 blanks and 3 stars
3	2 to 1	1 to 5	Displays 2 blanks and 5 stars
4	1 to 1	1 to 7	Displays 1 blank and 7 stars
5	0 to 1	1 to 9	Displays 0 blanks and 9 stars

EXAMPLE 5.17

The program in Fig. 5.20 prints the addition table for integer values between 0 and 9. For example, the table line beginning with the digit 9 shows the result of adding to 9 each of the digits 0 through 9. The initial for loop prints the table heading, which is the operator + and the list of digits from 0 through 9.

The nested for loops are used to print the table body. The outer for loop (loop control variable Y) first prints the current value of Y. In the inner for loop, each value of X (0 through 9) is added to Y and the individual sums are printed. Each time the outer loop is repeated, ten additions are performed; 100 sums are printed.

FIGURE 5.20 Printing an Addition Table

```
% The "Addtable" program
% Print an addition table

const MaxDigit := 9      % Largest digit
var Sum : int            % Sum of addends

% Print the table heading
put "+" ..
for X : 0 .. MaxDigit
```

```
        put X: 3 ..              % Print each digit in heading
    end for
    put " "                      % Terminate heading

    % Print the table body
    for Y : 0 .. MaxDigit
        % Print each row of the table
        put Y ..                 % Identify first addend
        for X : 0 .. MaxDigit
            Sum := Y + X
            put Sum :3 ..         % Print sum of addends
        end for
        put " "                  % Terminate table row
    end for
```

```
+   0   1   2   3   4   5   6   7   8   9
0   0   1   2   3   4   5   6   7   8   9
1   1   2   3   4   5   6   7   8   9  10
2   2   3   4   5   6   7   8   9  10  11
3   3   4   5   6   7   8   9  10  11  12
4   4   5   6   7   8   9  10  11  12  13
5   5   6   7   8   9  10  11  12  13  14
6   6   7   8   9  10  11  12  13  14  15
7   7   8   9  10  11  12  13  14  15  16
8   8   9  10  11  12  13  14  15  16  17
9   9  10  11  12  13  14  15  16  17  18
```

Exercises for Section 5.7

Self-Check

1. What is displayed by the following program segments assuming M is 3
   and N is 5?
   a. ```
   for I : 1 .. N
       for J : 1 .. I
           put "*" ..
       end for
       put ""
   end for
   ```
   b. ```
   for decreasing I : N .. 1
       for decreasing J : M .. 1
           put "*" ..
       end for
       put ""
   end for
   ```

2. Show the output printed by the nested loops below.

```
for I : 1 .. 2
    put "Outer", I :3
    for J : 1 .. 3
        put "Inner", I :3, J :3
    end for
    for decreasing K : 2 .. 1
        put "Inner", I :3, K :3
    end for
end for
```

Programming

1. Write a program that prints the multiplication table.
2. Write a nest of loops that causes the output below to be printed.

```
1
1 2
1 2 3
1 2 3 4
1 2 3
1 2
1
```

5.8 Debugging and Testing Programs

In Section 2.9, we described the general categories of error messages that you are likely to see: syntax errors and run-time errors. It is also possible for a program to execute without generating any error messages, but still produce incorrect results. Sometimes the cause of a run-time error or the origin of incorrect results is apparent and the error can easily be fixed. However, very often the error is not obvious and may require considerable effort to locate.

The first step in attempting to find a hidden error is to examine the program output to determine which part of the program is generating incorrect results. Then you can focus on the statements in that section to determine which ones are at fault. To help you locate problem areas, you may need to insert extra debugging statements that display intermediate results at different points in your program. You may also want to insert extra put statements to trace the values of certain critical variables during program execution. For example, if the loop in Fig. 5.9 is not computing the correct sum, you might want to insert an extra diagnostic put statement containing the five stars in the loop below.

```
loop                            % Accumulate the sum
    put "Enter score> " ..
    get Score
    exit when Score = Sentinel
    Sum := Sum + Score
    put "***** score is ", Score, " sum is ", Sum
end loop
```

The diagnostic put statement will display each partial sum that is accumulated and the current value of Score. This put statement displays a string
of asterisks at the beginning of its output line. This makes it easier to
identify diagnostic output in the debugging runs and makes it easier to
locate the diagnostic put statements in the source program.

Once you have located an error, you will want to take out the extra
diagnostic statements. As a temporary measure, it is sometimes advisable
to make these diagnostic statements into comments by placing a percent
sign (%) before them. (We will see how to use a boolean constant to
turn diagnostic print statements off and on in the next chapter.) If these
errors crop up again in later testing, it is easier to remove the percent
signs than retype the diagnostic statements.

Off by One Errors

A fairly common error in programs with loops is a loop that executes one
more time, or one less time, than it is supposed to. If a sentinel-controlled
loop performs an extra repetition, it may erroneously process the sentinel
value along with the regular data.

If a loop statement performs a counting operation, make sure that
the initial and final values of the loop control variable are correct. For
example, the loop body below executes N + 1 times instead of N times.
If your intention is to execute the loop body N times, change the exit condition to Count = N (or to Count >= N).

```
Count := 0
loop
    exit when Count > N
    Sum := Sum + Count
    Count := Count + 1
end loop
```

Checking Loop Boundaries

You can get a good idea as to whether a loop is correct by checking what
happens at the *loop boundaries*, or at the initial and final values of the
loop control variable. In a for loop, you should carefully evaluate the

initial expression and *final expression* to make sure that these values make sense. Then substitute these values everywhere the counter variable appears in the loop body and verify that you get the expected result at the boundaries. As an example, in the for loop below

```
Sum := 0
for I : K .. N - K
    Sum := Sum + I ** 2
end for
```

check that the first value of the counter variable I is supposed to be K and that the last value is supposed to be N − K. Next, check that the assignment statement

```
Sum := Sum + I ** 2
```

is correct at these boundaries. When I is K, Sum gets the value of K squared. When I is N − K, the value of (N − K) squared is added to the previous Sum. As a final check, pick some small value of N and K (say 3 and 1) and trace the loop execution to see that it computes Sum correctly for this case.

Using Debugger Programs

Many computer systems have *debugger programs* available to help you debug your program. The debugger program lets you execute your program one statement at a time (*single-step execution*) so that you can see the effect of each statement. You can select several variables whose values will be automatically displayed after each statement executes. This allows you to trace the program's execution. Besides printing a diagnostic when a run-time error occurs, the debugger indicates the statement that caused the error and displays the values of the variables you selected.

You can also separate your program into segments by setting *breakpoints* at selected statements. A breakpoint is like a fence between two segments of a program. You can request the debugger to execute all statements from the last breakpoint up to the next breakpoint. When the program stops at a breakpoint, you can select variables to examine, in this way determining whether the program segment executed correctly. If a program segment executes correctly, you will want to execute through to the next breakpoint. If it does not, you may want to set more breakpoints in that segment or perhaps perform single-step execution through that segment.

Testing

After all errors have been corrected and the program appears to execute as expected, the program should be tested thoroughly to make sure that it works. In Section 4.6, we discussed tracing an algorithm and suggested that enough sets of test data be provided to ensure that all possible paths are traced. The same statement is true for the completed program. Try enough test runs to verify that the program works properly for representative samples of all possible data combinations.

Exercises for Section 5.8

Self-Check

1. For the `loop` statement in the subsection entitled "Off by One Errors", add debugging statements to show the value of the loop control variable at the start of each repetition. Also, add debugging statements to show the value of `Sum` at the end of each loop repetition.
2. Repeat exercise 1 for the loop in the subsection "Checking Loop Boundaries.

5.9 Common Programming Errors

Beginners sometimes confuse `if` and `loop` statements because both statements contain conditions. Make sure that you use an `if` statement to implement a decision step and a `loop` statement to implement a conditional loop.

Be very careful when using tests for inequality to control the repetition of a loop. For instance, the loop below is intended to process all transactions for a bank account while the balance is positive.

```
loop
    exit when Balance = 0.0
    UpDate (Balance)
end loop
```

If the bank balance goes from a positive to a negative amount without being exactly `0.0`, the loop will not terminate; it will become an infinite loop. The loop below would be safer.

```
loop
    exit when Balance <= 0.0
    UpDate (Balance)
end loop
```

You should verify that the exit condition for a `loop` statement will eventually become `true`. If you use a sentinel-controlled loop, remember to provide a prompt that tells the program user what value to enter as the sentinel. Make sure that the sentinel value cannot be confused with a normal data item.

Be sure to initialize a variable to zero if it is to be used for accumulating a sum by repeated addition, and to initialize a variable to 1 if it is to be used for accumulating a product by repeated multiplication. Omitting this step will lead to results that are incorrect or that are halted with an error message.

The value of the counter variable in a `for` statement either increases by 1 or decreases by 1 (`decreasing` form) after each repetition. If M is greater than N, the `put` statement below will not execute because the initial value that would be assigned to I is larger than its final value.

```
for I : M .. N
    put I, " ", M, " ", N
end for
```

Similarly, the `put` statement below will not execute because the initial value that would be assigned to I is smaller than its final value.

```
for decreasing I : N .. M
    put I, " ", M, " ", N
end for
```

A `loop` statement with its `exit` at the bottom always executes at least once. Use this kind of statement only if you are certain that there is no possibility of zero loop iterations.

Be sure to trace each nest of loops carefully, checking the inner loop and outer loop control variables. The loop control variable of a `for` statement cannot be changed inside the loop body. It is also illegal to use the same loop control variable for two `for` statements within the same nest. The loop variable can only be used in the loop body; its scope does not extend beyond the loop body.

Chapter Review

In this chapter, we examined `loop` statements that contain an `exit` statement in an initial, intermediate, or final position. We also examined `loop` statements with no exit; these are infinite loops. We learned how to implement counter-controlled loops, or loops where the number of repetitions required can be determined before the loop is entered. We also found the `loop` statement with an exit to be useful when we do not know the exact number of repetitions required before the loop begins. We use a `loop` statement with a final exit test when we know that the loop will always execute at least one time.

In designing a loop, we need to consider both the loop control and loop processing operations that must be performed. Separate Turing statements are needed for initializing and updating the loop control variable that is tested in the loop repetition condition.

We also discovered a common technique for controlling the repetition of a loop: using a special sentinel value to indicate that all required data have been processed. In this case, an input variable must appear in the loop exit condition. This variable is initialized in the first part of the loop body, where the first data value is read, and is updated when the next new data value is read. An intermediate exit test examines the data value to see if it is the sentinel, indicating that the loop should be exited. The last part of the loop body processes the non-sentinel data value.

We also introduced the `for` statement (`for` loop). We use the `for` statement to implement counting loops in which the exact number of loop iterations could be determined before loop repetition begins. The counter variable may increase in value or decrease in value (`decreasing` form) after each loop iteration. Remember that the final value expression for the counter variable is evaluated when the loop is first reached and cannot be changed during loop execution. An `exit` statement can be used in a `for` loop to cause exiting before the full range of values of the counting variable has been covered.

We also analyzed nested loops. Every inner loop of a nest is reentered and executed to completion each time an outer loop is repeated.

New Turing Constructs in Chapter 5

The new Turing constructs introduced in this chapter are described in Table 5.3.

TABLE 5.3   Summary of New Turing Constructs

Construct	Effect
Loop and Exit Statements	
```Sum := 0 loop exit when Sum > MaxSum put "Next integer> " .. get Next Sum := Sum + Next end loop```	A collection of input data items is read and their sum is accumulated in Sum. This process stops when the accumulated sum exceeds MaxSum.
For Statement	
```for CurMonth : 3 .. 9 get MonthSales YearSales := YearSales + MonthSales end for```	The loop body is repeated for each value of CurMonth from 3 to 9, inclusive. For each month, the value of MonthSales is read and added to YearSales

Quick-Check Exercises

1. A `loop` statement with an exit is called a _____ loop.
2. It is an error if a loop body never executes. (True/False)
3. How can the priming step for a loop with an initial exit test be avoided?
4. The sentinel value is always the last value added to a sum being accumulated in a sentinel-controlled loop. (True/False)
5. Which loop form (`for` statement, loop with initial test, loop with final test, loop with intermediate test)
   a. executes at least one time?
   b. should be used to implement a counting loop?
   c. should be used in a menu-driven program?
6. What does the following program display?

```
var Product : int := 1
var Counter : int := 2
loop
exit when Counter > 5
Product := Product * Counter
end loop
Counter := Counter + 1
put Product
```

7. What does the program in exercise 6 display if end `loop` is inserted where intended?
8. During the execution of the program below:

```
for I : 1 .. 10
    for J : 1 .. I
        put I * J :4 ..
    end for
    put ""
end for
```

   a. How many times does the first `put` statement execute?
   b. How many times does the second `put` statement execute?
   c. What is the last value displayed?

Answers to Quick-Check Exercises

1. Conditional
2. False
3. Use an intermediate exit test, preceded by reading the data value.
4. False, the sentinel should not be processed.
5. a. `loop` with final test
   b. `for` statement
   c. `loop` with intermediate test
6. Nothing, the loop executes "forever" (eventually the value of `Product` becomes too large and overflows causing a run-time error message).

7. The value of 1 * 2 * 3 * 4 * 5 or 120.
8. a. 1 + 2 + 3 + ... + 9 + 10 (or 55)
   b. 10
   c. 100

Review Questions

1. How does a sentinel value differ from a program flag as a means of loop control?
2. For a sentinel value to be used properly when reading in data, where should the input statements appear?
3. Write a program called Sum to add up and print a collection of payroll amounts entered at the terminal until a sentinel value of −1 is entered.
4. Hand trace the program below given the following data:

```
4 2 8 4    1 4 2 1    9 3 3 1    -22 10 8 2    3 3 4 5
```

```
% The "Slopes" program
const Sentinel := 0.0
var Slope, Y2, Y1, X2, X1 : real

put "Enter four numbers"
put "The last two numbers cannot be the same, but"
put "the program terminates if the first two are."
loop
    put "Enter four numbers> " ..
    get Y2, Y1, X2, X1
    Slope := (Y2 - Y1) / (X2 - X1)
    exit when Slope = Sentinel
    put "Slope is ", Slope :5:2
end loop
```

5. Rewrite the loop appearing in program Slopes as a flag-controlled loop.
6. Consider the program shown below

```
const N := 4
var Count : int := 0
var X : int
for I : 1 .. N
    get X
    if X = I then
        Count := Count + 1
    end if
    put Count
end for
```

Write an equivalent program that uses a loop statement instead of a for statement.

Programming Projects

1. Write a program that will find the smallest, largest, and average value in a collection of N numbers, where the value of N is the first data item read.

2. Modify programming project 1 to compute and display both the range of values in the data collection and the variance of the data collection. To compute the variance, accumulate the sum of the squares of the data values (SumSquares) in the main loop. After loop exit, use the formula

   $$variance = sum\text{-}of\text{-}squares - (sum\text{-}of\text{-}data)^2 / N$$

   Finally, compute the standard deviation, s, which is a measure of how much the data values deviate from the average value. Use the formula

   $$s^2 = variance / (N - 1)$$

3. Bunyan Lumber Co. needs to create a table of the engineering properties of its lumber. The dimensions of the wood are given as base and height in inches. Engineers need to know the following information about lumber:

cross sectional area:	*(base * height)*
moment of inertia:	*base * height³)/12*
section modulus:	*(base * height²)/6*

   The owner, Paul, makes lumber with base sizes 2, 4, 6, 8, 10, and 12 inches. The height sizes are 2, 4, 6, 8, and 10 inches. Produce a table with appropriate headings to show these values and the computed engineering properties. Do not duplicate a 2-by-6 with a 6-by-2 board.

4. Write a program to read a collection of integer data items and find and print the index of the first occurrence and the last occurrence of the number 12. Your program should print index values of 0 if the number 12 is not found. The index is the sequence number of the data item 12. For example, if the eighth data item is the only 12, then the index value 8 should be printed for the first and last occurrence.

5. a. Write a program to read in a collection of exam scores ranging in value from 1 to 100. Your program should count and print the number of outstanding scores (90–100), the number of satisfactory scores (60–89), and the number of unsatisfactory scores (1–59). It should also display the category of each score. Test your program on the following data:

63	75	72	72	78	67	80	63	75
90	89	43	59	99	82	12	100	

   b. Modify your program to display the average exam score (a real number) at the end of the run.

6. Write a program to process weekly employee time cards for all employees of an organization. Each employee will have three data items indicating an identification number, the hourly wage rate, and the number of hours worked during a given week. Each employee is to be paid time-and-a-half for all hours worked over 40. A tax amount of 3.625 percent of gross salary will be deducted. The program output should show the employee's number and net pay. Display the total payroll and average amount paid at the end of the run.

7. Suppose you own a bulk-food store that sells potato chips (ID number 1), pretzels (ID number 2), tortilla chips (ID number 3), and popcorn (ID number 4) by the case. Write a program to
   a. read in the case inventory for each type of snack for the start of the week;
   b. process all weekly sales and purchase records for each snack;
   c. print out the final inventory.
   Each transaction will consist of two data items. The first item will be the snack identification number (an integer). The second will be the amount purchased (a positive integer value) or the amount sold (a negative integer value). The weekly inventory for each snack (for the start of the week) will also consist of two items: the identification and initial inventory for that type of snack. For now, you may assume that you always have sufficient foresight to prevent depletion of your inventory for any snack. (**Hint:** Your data entry should begin with eight values representing the case inventory. These should be followed by the transaction values.)

8. Revise project 7 to make it a menu-driven program. The menu operations supported by the revised program should be (E)nter Inventory, (P)urchase Snack, (S)ell Snack, (D)isplay Inventory, and (Q)uit Program. Negative quantities should no longer be used to represent goods sold.

9. Write a menu-driven savings account transaction program that will process the following sets of data:

Group 1

I	1234	1054.07
W		25.00
D		243.35
W		254.55
Z		

Group 2

I	5723	2008.24
W		15.55
Z		

Group 3

```
I     2814      128.24
W               52.48
D               13.42
W               84.60
Z
```

Group 4

```
I     7234      7.77
Z
```

Group 5

```
I     9367      15.27
W               16.12
D               10.00
Z
```

Group 6

```
I     1134      12900.00
D                9270.00
Z
```

The first record in each group contains the code (I) along with the account number and its initial balance. All subsequent transaction records show the amount of each withdrawal (W) and deposit (D) made for that account, followed by a sentinel value (Z). Display the account number and its balance after processing each record in the group. If a balance becomes negative, print an appropriate message and take whatever corrective steps you deem proper. If there are no transactions for an account, print a message so stating. A transaction code (Q) should be used to allow the user to quit program execution.

CHAPTER **6**

Computer Graphics

Up to this point in this book, all output from programs has been produced by the put statement and has appeared as characters. In your programs, you had little control of where the characters appeared on the screen. They were always displayed sequentially, from left to right and from top to bottom. In this chapter, you will learn how to output characters directly to any location on the screen. You will also learn how to draw figures such as boxes and circles on the screen using dots.

This chapter introduces you to *computer graphics*, which means using computers to create graphical patterns. Sometimes these are simple patterns, for example, words in the center of the screen that flash the message "Season's Greetings!!". Sometimes the pattern can be more diagrammatic, such as a picture of a smiling face. We will also see how to use *animation*, which means making the figures on the screen move, and *interactive graphics*, in which the user can control the action on the screen.

Computer graphics, in advanced forms, is used extensively in many applications. It is most often used in movie scenes, such as in science fiction movies, and in advertisements. It is increasingly used in science to help people visualize concepts, and as a replacement for text in applications in which it is more natural to display information as diagrams rather than as words.

The first part of the chapter is concerned with *character graphics*, which means that the patterns are created with the use of characters. The second part of the chapter is concerned with *pixel graphics*, which means that the patterns are made of dots (called *picture elements* or *pixels*).

6.1 Output to Specific Locations on the Screen

You have seen computer screens used by people, such as airline reservation staff, to access information about a particular application. For example, the message, "This flight is overbooked" may be displayed in the center of the screen. Various messages appear at different places on the screen as the person makes inquiries about flights and available seats. In your programs you can make messages appear where you want on the screen using the locate statement.

Using the Locate Statement

A computer screen can be divided up into horizontal *rows* of characters, each of which contains characters. When the output is produced by the put statement, each character has the same width, so the characters line up in vertical *columns*.

As you can see in Fig. 6.1, the rows and columns are numbered from the top left corner, starting with row 1 and column 1. In the figure, the message "Hello Bob" has been displayed starting in row 3 and column 6. We could write a program to place this message on the screen using only put statements by first outputting two blank lines and then five blanks preceding "Hello Bob". Instead of doing that, we can use the locate statement, to place this message directly where we want it, as follows:

```
locate (3, 6)     % Locate to row 3 and column 6
put "Hello Bob"
```

The computer keeps track of where on the screen the next output from a put statement is to appear. By default, the output will start at the top of the screen and will continue across and down the screen. There is an *output cursor* that marks the place where the output will be displayed or the next input will be typed. The locate statement moves this cursor to a new position.

FIGURE 6.1   Rows and Columns on the Screen

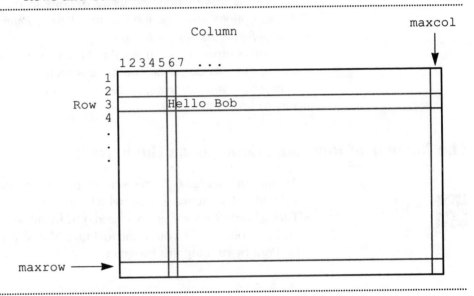

Setting the Mode of Your Screen

On older computer screens, it was not possible to relocate the output cursor. As new versions of screens were introduced, they had new *modes* that allowed more flexibility in using graphical features such as locate. On some computers, notably IBM PC compatibles, we must explicitly change the mode to allow the use of the locate statement. To change to the IBM *CGA* (Color Graphics Adapter) mode, which supports relocation of the output cursor, you should use this statement at the beginning of your program.

```
setscreen ("graphics")
```

Although this statement is in principle necessary, it can usually be omitted, because any time your program attempts to use locate, the Turing system automatically changes the screen to a graphics mode.

By now (the mid 1990s), most IBM compatible computers have a mode called VGA, which supports more graphical options than CGA, with the result that the CGA mode is becoming obsolete.

To use VGA mode in Turing on PCs, you should begin your program with this statement:

```
setscreen ("graphics:vga")
```

This command allows you to use the 16 colors of VGA. There is a newer, more flexible mode, called *SVGA*, which is becoming common. Most examples given in this chapter can be easily adapted to work in various modes. We will present examples so they work directly in VGA mode.

Turing systems support a wide range of screen modes. Your program can access these modes by using options in the `setscreen` procedure. These options are described in the *Turing Reference Manual (R.C. Holt, Holt Software Associates Inc.)*.

On computers such as the Macintosh, you do not need to use `setscreen` because the computer screen is in graphics mode by default. Similarly, if you are using an X-terminal on a Unix system, it is not necessary to use `setscreen`.

The Number of Rows and Columns on the Screen

As shown in Fig. 6.1, the screen has a limited number of rows and columns. The actual limits, which are called `maxrow` and `maxcol` in Turing, vary from screen to screen. On many screens, there to be 25 rows and 80 columns. If you want to know the size of your screen, you can find out by running this program:

```
% Find size of screen in terms of rows and columns
put "Number of rows: ", maxrow
put "Number of columns: ", maxcol
```

On a computer such as a Macintosh, the screen is divided into rectangular areas called *windows*. If you are using a screen with windows, `maxrow` and `maxcol` give the size of the *run-time* window, which displays the program's output. On such a system, you can use the setscreen command to change the size of your run-time window (see the *Turing Reference Manual* for details).

Using Random Numbers

We will develop a simple program that places stars (asterisk characters) at random locations on the screen, to produce a picture of a "snow storm" (see Fig. 6.2).

FIGURE 6.2   Stars Placed Randomly on the Screen

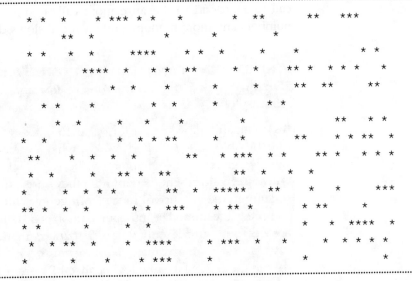

Before writing this program, we need to learn how to get the computer to pick random integers for us. This is done using the `randint` procedure. This procedure, which is predefined by (provided by) Turing, chooses an integer in a given range. For example, the statement:

```
randint (Row, 1, maxrow)
```

picks a number from the range 1 to maxrow and assigns the number to the Row variable. For example, if maxrow = 25, this might set the value of Row to be 17. In Fig. 6.3, there is a similar statement that picks a random column in the range 1 to maxcol, and assigns this number to the Column variable.

There is another predefined procedure, called `rand`, which is used for randomly picking real numbers in the range 0.0 to 1.0. For example:

```
rand (X)
```

will set real variable X to a value such as 0.739262.

The numbers picked using `randint` and `rand` are not truly random. We say the sequences produced by these procedures are *pseudo-random* (fake random). They are *generated* (picked) using an algorithm that produces a sequence of numbers that is very much like a truly random sequence, but with one important difference. The difference is that the sequence is the same each time you run a program.

To avoid this reproducibility, we use the `randomize` procedure. This procedure starts the sequence of pseudo-random numbers at an unpredictable point. We use `randomize` in much the same way that we shuffle a deck of cards before dealing out a hand of playing cards.

In order to produce a new pattern of output for each run of the `Stars` program in Fig. 6.2, we have used `randomize` before the call to the `RandomStars` procedure. Without `randomize`, each run of the program would output the same pattern of stars. A program should make only one call to randomize, because more calls to randomize do not make the numbers any more random, and each call slows down your program.

THE RANDINT, RAND, AND RANDOMIZE PROCEDURES

Form: randint *(integerVariable, first, last)*

Example:
```
% Roll a six-sided die from a pair of dice
var RollAmount : int
randint (RollAmount, 1, 6)
put "We rolled ", RollAmount
```

Interpretation: The randint procedure is used to pick a random integer in the (inclusive) range from *first* to *last*. Both *first* and *last* must be integer values. The number is assigned to the *integerVariable*. This procedure is useful only when *first* is less than *last*. The values picked by randint approximate a *uniform distribution*, meaning each number in the range has an equal chance of being picked.

Form: rand *(realVariable)*

Example:
```
% Location of a rain drop on a
% one meter long board
var Location : real
rand (Location)
put "The rain drop fell at ", Location
```

Interpretation: The rand procedure is used to pick a random real number in the range from 0.0 to 1.0. The number is assigned to the realVariable. The values picked by rand approximate a uniform distribution.

Form: randomize

Example:
```
% Flip a coin 10 times and count the heads
randomize
var Coin : int
var NumberOfHeads : int := 0
for i : 1 .. 10
    randint (Coin, 0, 1)
    % 0 = head, 1 = tail
    if Coin = 0 then
        NumberOfHeads := NumberOfHeads + 1
    end if
end for
put "Got ", NumberOfHeads, "heads in 10 flips"
```

Interpretation: The randomize procedure resets the sequence of pseudo-random numbers in an unpredictable fashion. This is done so that the random numbers generated by randint and rand will be different each time the program is run. Your program should make only one call to randomize.

FIGURE 6.3   Program to Place Stars Randomly on the Screen

```
% The "Stars" program
% Place stars at random locations on the screen

procedure RandomStars
    const NumberOfStars := 250
    var Row, Column : int
    for i : 1 .. NumberOfStars
        randint (Row, 1, maxrow)
        randint (Column, 1, maxcol)
        locate (Row, Column)
        put "*" ..
    end for
end RandomStars

randomize % Make pattern of stars unpredictable
RandomStars % Call the procedure
```

The program in Fig. 6.3 displays 250 stars at random locations on the screen. This number has been recorded in the constant NumberOfStars so we can easily change the program to produce more or fewer stars. The program contains a procedure named RandomStars, which is activated (called) by the last line in the program.

Using Dot-Dot in a Put Statement

The put statement in Fig. 6.3 uses dot-dot (..) in a special way. Without the dot-dot, the put statement would blank out the rest of the current output line, setting each location on the row to the right of the star to be blank.

With dot-dot present, the statement changes only that part of the screen that is explicitly output by the put statement. In this case, we want to output a star, but we do not want the right part of the line to be blanked, so we must use the version of put ending with dot-dot.

There is another reason why we use dot-dot with put when we are using locate. The reason is that put without dot-dot, when placing output on the last row of the screen, causes the screen to be *scrolled*. Everything on the screen is moved up one line, erasing the top line from the screen and making room for a new line at the bottom of the screen. When we are not creating graphical displays, scrolling is useful, but it is rarely what we want when we are explicitly locating output items on the screen.

Exercises for Section 6.1

Self-Check

1. In Fig. 6.3, what will the output on the screen look like if the dot-dot is removed from the `put` statement?
2. Change the program in Fig. 6.3 so it places copies of your name at random locations on the screen. Make sure you change the program so that your name will fit on the screen when a location near the right side is picked.
3. How can your program randomly generate a real number in range 0.0 to 1.0? How can your program use this number to create a random number in the range 0.0 to 20.0 or the range 20.0 to 40.0?

Programming

1. Write a program that outputs a pattern of asterisks, using `locate`, to draw the first initial of your last name.
2. Write a program that uses the `locate` statement in a for loop to draw a diagonal using only the character "x". The diagonal should start at the top left of the screen and continue down and to the right until it hits the bottom of the screen. When it hits the bottom, the program should output "Boom!!" at the point where the line hits the bottom.
3. Write a program that simulates tossing two dice 100 times. Each die of the two dice randomly lands with one of the sides numbered 1 to 6 facing up. Use `randint` twice in a loop body, once for each die. Compute and output the average total of the two dice for the 100 tosses.

6.2 Using Colors with Character Graphics

There are many kinds of computer screens. Just a short time ago, most of these were *monochrome*, meaning that they used only a *foreground* color, the color of the output, and a *background* color on which the output appeared. These screens are often called *black and white* in spite of the fact that the two colors may not necessarily be black and white.

On IBM PC compatibles, the default is that the background is black and the foreground is white. The Macintosh uses the opposite convention, with the background white and the foreground black. The advantage of the Macintosh convention is that it is like black ink on white paper, which is used in most writing, as, for example, in this book.

With the rapid decrease in the cost of hardware, it is now common that display screens support the use of colors. The first color screens allowed only a few colors, for example, only four colors including the background in the IBM PC CGA screen mode. Sixteen colors are now commonly available, and many more are available on newer or more expensive screens.

Because of this rapidly changing technology, it is possible that you may have to make slight adjustments in the programs that are shown in this chapter so they work well with your computer.

The Numbers and Names of Colors

There are sixteen colors that we will be concerned with in this chapter. Each has a number and a name. Figure 6.4 gives these for IBM PCs.

FIGURE 6.4   Color Numbers and Names

0	black	8	brightgray
1	blue	9	brightblue
2	green	10	brightgreen
3	cyan (light blue)	11	brightcyan
4	red	12	brightred
5	magenta	13	brightmagenta
6	brown	14	yellow
7	white	15	brightwhite

If you do not have a PC with VGA, it may be that the colors and their numbers may not be the same as those shown in Fig. 6.4. We will write a Turing program to display all the colors that the screen supports. Before doing this, we need to introduce Turing's `color` statement. This statement causes subsequent character output to be displayed in a specified color. For example, the following will cause "Stop lights are red" to be output in color number 4:

```
setscreen ("graphics:v16")    % Only for PCs
const red := 4                % Not needed on some systems
color (red)
put "Stop lights are red"
```

In the `color` statement, you can use a number, such as 4, instead of a name, such as `red`. The above `color` statement would work the same if written as:

```
color (4)
```

However, it is better programming style to use the names of the colors rather than their numbers.

In older versions of Turing, you had to supply your own declarations of the names of the colors, as in:

```
const red := 4
```

This is not needed (or allowed) in recent versions of Turing, in which the names of colors are predefined as a part of the language.

Although this book uses American spelling, the Turing language supports the British spelling of `colour` for the `color` statement. In general, any Turing keyword, such as `maxcolor`, can be spelled the British way, as `maxcolour`.

Displaying All Available Colors Using Maxcolor

We will now develop a program that displays all the colors that are available on the screen. On a VGA screen with the mode set to "`graphics:v16`", the program in Fig. 6.5 outputs the following:

```
Display of all colors
 0
 1 EXAMPLE OF COLOR
 2 EXAMPLE OF COLOR
 ...
15 EXAMPLE OF COLOR
```

Each number on the left is displayed in the foreground color and each line "EXAMPLE OF COLOR" is displayed in the color corresponding to that number.

You may be surprised that the line numbered zero (0) seems to be missing the phrase "EXAMPLE OF COLOR". The reason for this is that the phrase was displayed in color zero, which is, by convention, the background color. Technically speaking, the phrase was displayed, but since it was output in the background color, we cannot see it.

It is sometimes useful to output a message in the background color. In particular, we sometimes do this to erase a message from the screen, by locating to the beginning of the message and writing the message again, but now in the background color. Another way to erase the message is to write a sequence of N blanks on top of the message, where N is the length of the message.

FIGURE 6.5 Displaying All Available Colors

```
% The "Allcolor" program
% Output a line in each available color

const LeftColor := maxcolor

put "Display of all colors", skip

for ColorNumber : 0 .. maxcolor
    color (LeftColor)
    put ColorNumber : 2 ..
    color (ColorNumber)
    put " EXAMPLE OF COLOR"
end for
```

You can determine the number of colors that your screen supports in its current mode using these statements:

```
put "Largest available color number is: ", maxcolor
put "Total number of colors is: ", maxcolor + 1
```

In the VGA mode "graphics:v16", maxcolor is 15. The total number of colors available, including the background color (number zero), is maxcolor + 1.

In Fig. 6.5, it is tempting to change the counter variable in the for loop so it is called color, as in:

```
for color : 0 .. maxcolor     % Not legal in Turing
```

This would not be allowed in Turing because color is the name of a statement and therefore cannot also be used as a variable name. You could get around this problem using capitalizing the c in color, as in:

```
for Color : 0 .. maxcolor     % Legal, but poor style
```

Since Turing considers that Color with a capital C is distinct from color with a small c, this would be allowed in your program. However, this is not good style, because the reader can too easily confuse the two spellings, color and Color. It is better to pick a distinct name such as ColorNumber.

Flashing a Greeting in Colors

In the next example, we will use Turing's character graphics features to flash the message "Season's Greetings!!" in the middle of the screen (see Fig. 6.6). We will use the color statement, to display the message in various colors.

EXAMPLE 6.1

We want the greeting message to be centered from top to bottom, in the middle row, which we will call MidRow. We also want the message to be centered from left to right. To accomplish this centering, we will use the predefined values that give the number of rows and columns on the screen, namely, maxrow and maxcol.

In the program in Fig. 6.7, we define the middle row, MidRow, and the middle column, MidCol, in this way:

```
const MidRow := maxrow div 2
const MidCol := maxcol div 2
```

We have used the div operator instead of the / operator for division because div gives an integer result. We need an integer result because the locate statement will only accept integers, not real numbers. The div operator always truncates a fraction produced by the division. For example, if maxrow is 25, the above will calculate MidRow as 12.

FIGURE 6.6   Flashing a Greeting

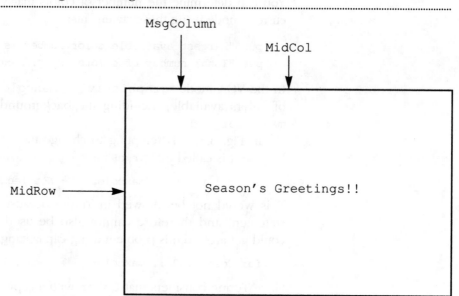

To calculate the location in which the message is to be started, the FlashGreeting procedure subtracts half the message's length from MidCol, as follows:

```
const Msg := "Season's Greetings!!"
const MsgLength := length (Msg)
const MsgColumn := MidCol - MsgLength div 2
```

The procedure uses MidRow and MsgColumn to position the message on the screen, in this way:

```
locate (MidRow, MsgColumn)
put Msg ..
```

The FlashGreeting procedure in Fig. 6.7 displays its message in a sequence of different colors, with each color shown for half a second and then blanked out for a tenth of a second. This repeated action causes the message to flash.

We will first explain how the color numbers are selected, so that all available colors are used, and then we will explain the delay statement that is used to slow down the speed of flashing.

Just before the locate and put statements, which place the message in the middle of the screen, the color statement is used to determine the color in which the message is to appear on the screen:

```
color (ColorNumber)
```

Variable ColorNumber is initially set to 1:

```
var ColorNumber : int := 1
```

Near the end of the loop body, the `ColorNumber` variable is incremented by one. If it becomes larger than the maximum color number, it is set back to 1. The result is that all non-background color numbers are used in order and then used again, and so on.

If the last available color number, `maxcolor`, is 15, the message will be displayed using color numbers in this order:

$$1 \quad 2 \quad 3 \quad \ldots \quad 13 \quad 14 \quad 15 \quad 1 \quad 2 \quad 3 \quad 4 \quad 5$$

Since `NumberOfFlashes` is 20, the loop stops after `ColorNumber` has become 5 for the second time. If `NumberOfFlashes` were increased, the loop would keep on cycling through the available colors until the given number of flashes had occurred.

If you are using a computer with a monochrome screen, the program in Fig. 6.7 will still work, so that it will still flash the message. However, the color number used will always be 1. In the final part of the loop body, `ColorNumber` will be incremented to 2 and then will immediately set back to 1 in the `if` statement. As a result, the final part of the loop body will not actually change `ColorNumber`.

FIGURE 6.7

Flashing a Greeting

```
% The "Greeting" program

procedure FlashGreeting
    % Flash a message in the middle of the screen

        const NumberOfFlashes := 20
        const MidRow := maxrow div 2
        const MidCol := maxcol div 2

        const Msg := "Season's Greetings!!"
        const MsgLength := length (Msg)
        const MsgColumn := MidCol - MsgLength div 2
        % BlankMsg has the same length as Msg
        const BlankMsg := "                    "

        var ColorNumber : int := 1

        for i : 1 .. NumberOfFlashes

            % Display the message, in a new color
            color (ColorNumber)
            locate (MidRow, MsgColumn)
            put Msg ..
            delay (500)    % Show message half a second

            % Erase the message
            locate (MidRow, MsgColumn)
            put BlankMsg ..
            delay (100)    % Leave blank for 0.1 second
```

```
                    % Cycle through the non-zero color numbers
                    ColorNumber := ColorNumber + 1
                    if ColorNumber > maxcolor then
                        ColorNumber := 1
                    end if

                end for
            end FlashGreeting

            FlashGreeting
```

Using the Mod Operator to Cycle Through a Range of Numbers

There is a better way to make ColorNumber cycle through the non-zero color numbers. This is done by replacing the statement that adds one to ColorNumber and the following if statement by this single statement:

```
    ColorNumber := ColorNumber mod maxcolor + 1
```

This statement uses the modulo operator mod, which returns the remainder of ColorNumber divided by maxcolor (see Table 2.5). Since mod has higher precedence than +, this statement computes the result of mod first and then adds 1 to this result.

When ColorNumber is less than maxcolor, the mod operation simply returns the value of ColorNumber. For example, if ColorNumber is 7 and maxcolor is 15, we have 7 mod 15 = 7. When ColorNumber becomes 15, the result becomes zero, as in 15 mod 15 = 0. So, when ColorNumber has reached the last value, maxcolor, the mod operator produces the result 0, which is added to 1, to cause us to start back with the first non-zero color number. In summary, this single statement neatly allows us to cycle through the non-zero color numbers. In the case of a monochrome screen, when maxcolor = 1, this statement has no effect, and will always set ColorNumber to 1.

The mod operator is commonly used to cycle through a range of numbers, so you should make sure that you understand this example.

Delaying Execution

The Greeting program in Fig. 6.7 has been slowed down so a person watching the screen can see the message in each color. This has been done using the delay statement. This statement is given a time in milliseconds. For example, when it receives the value 500, it causes the program to pause for 500 milliseconds, which is half of a second.

Our eyes can distinguish images only if the images do not change too quickly. For example, in a movie theater, when we watch an action scene, we do not notice that we are being shown, in rapid succession, a series of distinct pictures or *frames*. We perceive smooth motion, not the actual sequence of pictures. If we slow down the speed of a movie to about 10 to 20 frames per second, we start to notice jerkiness.

If the `Greeting` program runs too quickly, people will see a blur of color instead of the individual colors in which the message is being flashed. In the program, immediately after the message is displayed in color, the `delay (500)` statement is used to hold up the execution for half a second. Later, the execution is held up for a tenth of a second by the statement `delay (100)` while the message is blanked out.

Erasing a Message Using a Blank String

In the `Greeting` program, the message is erased by outputting a string of blanks on top of the message. For this to work, we must make sure that the string of blanks is the same length as (or longer than) the message. In the program, it is not easy to make sure that the blank message is the right length, except by carefully counting the number of blanks. Here is a better way create the blank message:

```
const BlankMsg := repeat (" ", MsgLength)
```

We can use this as a replacement for the declaration of `BlankMsg` in Fig. 6.7. This new declaration uses the `repeat` function, a predefined function in Turing, to make N copies of a string S. For example, in the declaration, N is `MsgLength` and S is a single blank. The result is a string of `MsgLength` blanks.

When we use `repeat`, we do not have to rely on manual counting of blanks, which is error prone. Instead, the computer automatically creates a blank string of the correct length.

There is another advantage to using `repeat` in this program. If we decide we want a new greeting, such as `"Happy New Year!!"`, all we have to do is change a single line, the line that declares Msg. The blank message will automatically be changed to the length of the new message.

Clearing the Screen Using the Cls Statement

Sometimes we need to blank out the entire screen. In the `Greeting` program, we erased the message to create a flashing effect. In that program, there was nothing else on the screen, so we could have blanked out the whole screen instead of just blanking out the message. This is done by the *clear screen* statement, which has this form:

```
cls              % Clear the whole screen
```

This could be used in place of these statements:

```
locate (MidRow, MsgColumn)
put BlankMsg ..
```

In this program, there is no particular advantage to either of these methods, except that `cls` is simpler and does not require the use of `BlankMsg`. However, `cls` cannot be used if there is other output on the screen besides the message that you want to keep.

Exercises for Section 6.2

Self-Check

1. How can you modify the `Stars` program in Fig. 6.3 to do the following? After it has placed stars on the screen, it waits three seconds, clears the screen, and starts placing stars on the screen again. This sequence of actions is repeated again and again.
2. What statements should you write to display the message `"Hello World"` using the largest available color number?
3. What statements should you write to place the letter `X` in the middle of the screen?
4. How can you change the `Stars` program in Fig. 6.3 so it will use a new color for each star, repeatedly cycling through the color numbers from 1 to `maxcolor`?
5. How can you change the `Stars` program in Fig. 6.3 so it will output colored stars, where the color number for each star is picked randomly from the range 1 to `maxcolor`?
6. What statement should you use if you want your program to pause for five seconds?

Programming

1. Write a program that outputs the following poem, with the first line in red, the second in green and the last in yellow.

   ```
   Stop at the red
   Go with the green
   Don't mess with Mr. In-Between
   ```

2. Change the program from exercise 1 so that it alternately displays the first line, the second line, and finally the third line.
3. Write a program that starts by outputting this line in the middle of the screen:

   ```
   Who is the greatest?
   ```

   Next, the program waits three seconds. Then it outputs a line of twenty > signs on the last line of the screen, with two tenths of a second delay between each `">"`. Finally, to the right of this line, it outputs your name in red.

6.3 Animation: Making Things Move on the Screen

You have seen video games in which figures move around on the screen. A video game uses a special purpose computer, with a good graphics screen, and very clever software that controls the screen and reacts to the user's actions, such as button presses. In this section, we will show how a program can make it appear that an item is moving on the screen.

EXAMPLE 6.2

When we create the impression of movement on the screen, we call this *animation*. One of the simplest cases of animation is a moving object such as a ball. We can draw a ball as a small letter "o". If we erase this ball and redraw it in a nearby location, it will appear as if the ball moves to the new location. The program in Fig. 6.8 makes a ball appear to move back and forth in row 5 from column 10 to column 11 and back repeatedly.

FIGURE 6.8   Moving a Ball Back and Forth

```
% The "Wiggle" program
% Make a ball move back and forth in row 5
% from column 10 to 11 to 10 etc.

const Ball := "o"
const Erase := " "
loop
    locate (5, 10)          % Draw ball at row 5 column 10
    put Ball ..
    delay (100)
    locate (5, 10)          % Erase ball at row 5 column 10
    put Erase ..

    locate (5, 11)          % Draw ball at row 5 column 11
    put Ball ..
    delay (100)
    locate (5, 11)          % Erase ball at row 5 column 11
    put Erase ..
end loop
```

Each time the ball is drawn, it is then erased using a blank character. Before erasing, the program is delayed a tenth of a second, so our eyes have time to see the ball.

EXAMPLE 6.3

We will now extend this idea of a moving ball so the ball moves along in diagonal directions and "bounces" off the edges of the screen. The ball will start at row 1 and column 1 and will trace the pattern shown in Fig. 6.9.

FIGURE 6.9 Bouncing Ball Pattern

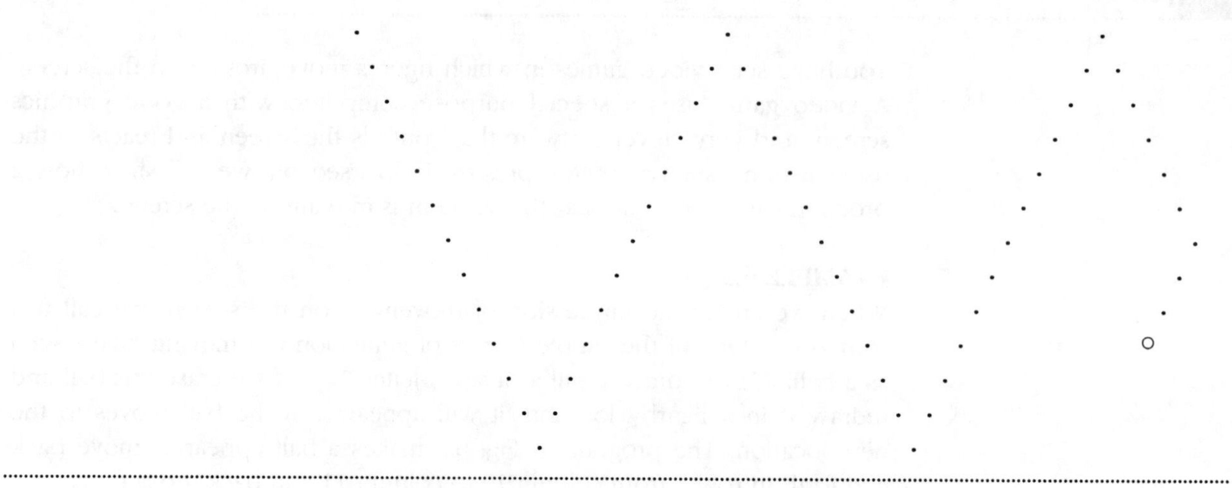

The program that draws this pattern is given in Fig. 6.10. When the program is running, the ball will appear to bounce off each edge of the screen, leaving a trail of dots behind it as it moves. In this program, we have used a constant to set the erasing character Erase to be a dot (a period). If we do not want the ball to leave a trail, we simply change this constant to a blank character.

Each time after the ball has been displayed on the screen and overwritten by the Erase character, the Row variable has the value RowMove added to it. While RowMove is 1, this causes the row in which the ball appears to increase by one with each iteration of the loop. As a result, the ball moves down the screen.

When the ball reaches the bottom of the screen, the sign of RowMove is reversed so that it becomes −1. Once this is done, each iteration causes the Row to decrease by 1, and the ball moves up the screen. This reversal of the sign of RowMove is done in this if statement:

```
% If reach top or bottom, make opposite move
if Row = 1 or Row = maxrow then
    RowMove := - RowMove
end if
```

This if statement assures that whenever the ball reaches either the top of the screen (Row = 1) or the bottom of the screen (Row = maxrow), the sign of RowMove will be reversed, to cause the ball to bounce either down or up. In a similar way, the final if statement in the program in Fig. 6.10 causes the ball to bounce when it reaches the left or the right column of the screen.

FIGURE 6.10   Program to Draw a Bouncing Ball

```
% The "Bounce" program
% This program shows a ball that starts at row 1
% and column 1 and travels in diagonal lines,
% bouncing off each edge of the screen

var Row, Col : int := 1
var RowMove, ColMove : int := 1
const Ball := "o"
const Erase := "."      % Leave a trail of dots
loop
    locate (Row, Col)
    put Ball ..     % Draw the ball
    delay (100)     % Pause a tenth of a second

    locate (Row, Col)
    put Erase ..    % Replace the ball with a dot

    Row := Row + RowMove       % Move vertically
    Col := Col + ColMove       % Move horizontally

    % If reach top or bottom, make opposite move
    if Row = 1 or Row = maxrow then
        RowMove := - RowMove
    end if

    % If reach left/right edge, make opposite move
    if Col = 1 or Col = maxcol then
        ColMove := - ColMove
    end if
end loop
```

Exercises for Section 6.3

Self-Check

1. Describe how to modify the Bounce program in Fig. 6.10 so that instead of a ball bouncing, your own name will bounce around the screen.
2. What do you think the screen will look like if you run the Bounce program with its delay statement removed?

Programming

1. Write a program in which a ball constantly circles the edge of the screen. The ball starts at the top left, runs down the left side, across the bottom to the right, then up the right side, across the top to the left and continues circling.

2. Change the program from exercise 1 so that the ball spirals inward. It leaves a track of dots (periods). When it circles, it never goes on top of its track of dots. Instead it always takes a new route right next to its track (or next to the edge of the screen). The program stops when the row it is on is equal to half of `maxrow`.

3. Write a program that outputs `"Be careful!!"` on the left and `"Don't crash!!"` on the right, both on the middle row of the screen. Make each of these phrases move toward the middle of the screen until they run into each other. When this happens, flash the phrase `"BOOM!!"` in the middle of the screen. You will need to use a `delay` statement so the phrases do not move too quickly.

6.4 Interactive Graphics

In the preceding section, we saw how a ball, which was actually the letter `"o"`, could be made to appear to bounce across the screen. While this is interesting to watch, it becomes more interesting if the motion can be controlled by the user. For example, the user might want to be able to bat the ball so it bounces before it gets to an edge.

We use the term it *interactive graphics* to describe the situation when the user interacts with computer graphics. A video game, which is based on a computer screen and various controlling devices such as a joy stick, is an obvious example of interactive graphics.

In this section, we will modify the `Bounce` program in Fig. 6.10 so that the user can press keys to control the motion of the ball. We will use the number keys to control the motion. The right side of many keyboards is laid out with this pattern of number keys:

```
7 8 9
4 5 6
1 2 3
```

Taking advantage of this arrangement, we will use this convention:

8 (middle top key) will bat the ball **upward**
2 (middle bottom key) will bat the ball **downward**
6 (middle right key) will bat the ball to the **right**
4 (middle left key) will bat the ball to the **left**

For example, if the ball is moving down and to the right, pressing the 8 key will make the ball start moving up and to the right, as if the ball had been batted in the upward direction. This action is illustrated in Fig. 6.11.

FIGURE 6.11   Batting the Bouncing Ball

Reading One Character at a Time

Each time the user presses an action key (8, 2, 6, or 4) during the game, the program is to carry out the batting action, without waiting for the user to press the Return key. If the program used the `get` statement to read these keys, this immediate interaction would not be possible, because `get` always waits until the Return key is pressed. To avoid this problem, we will use a set of Turing language features that allow a program to read a single character at a time, and to test to see if the user has pressed any keys.

The first of these is called `getch`, which is short for "get character". This reads a single character without waiting until Return is pressed. The second is called `hasch`, which is short for "has character". It is used to test to see if the user has typed a character that can be read.

Here is a simple example of the use of `getch`:

```
var KeyStroke : string (1) % Single character
getch (KeyStroke) % Wait for a key press
```

In this example, the program waits until the user presses a key. The character that the user types is stored in KeyStroke. As you can see in Fig. 6.12, these two statements are used in the beginning of the program to cause it to wait until the user signals that he or she is ready to play the game.

The `getch` procedure can only read a single character, and we must use a special form of the `string` type with it that allows only one character, namely the form `string(1)`. Since the KeyStroke is declared with this type, Turing will not allow any string containing more than one character to be stored in this variable.

Testing to See if Characters Are Available to be Read

We want the game to keep running when there have been no key strokes, but we want it to read a character when the user has typed one. To accomplish this, we will use `hasch` to test to see if there is a character that needs to be read by `getch`. We should not use `getch` without first making this test, because if we did, the game would come to a halt without moving the ball until the user presses another key.

A typical way to use `hasch` in a program, in combination with `getch`, is as follows:

```
% Read a key stroke if there is one
KeyStroke := "#"              % Use # to mean no input
if hasch then
    getch (KeyStroke)         % Read one character
end if
```

If a key has been pressed, this reads the character into the `KeyStroke` variable. If none has been pressed, the program avoids waiting. If there was no character to read, the `KeyStroke` variable is left containing the character #, which records the fact that a key has not been pressed by the user. There is nothing special about the character #, except that it is not an action key.

Disabling the Echoing of Characters

There is one more problem we need to solve before writing our game of batting the ball. When the user types a character such as 8, we want the ball to be batted, but we do not want the 8 to be displayed on the screen. To avoid this, we use this Turing statement:

```
setscreen ("noecho")      % Do not show the input
```

This statement changes the default action of the system so that the characters that the user types are not *echoed* on the screen.

We will introduce another option of the `setscreen` statement, which is used to turn off the cursor on the screen. Usually, the cursor, which marks the current position on the screen, is useful because it lets the user know where his or her typing will appear on the screen. However, in some situations, such as our game, the cursor simply gets in the way. With some computer screens, we need to turn off the cursor because it takes the system too long to draw it, and this slows down the program. To turn off the cursor, we use this statement:

```
setscreen ("nocursor")    % Hide the cursor
```

We can specify several options in `setscreen` at one time. For example, the following both turns off echoing and hides the cursor:

```
setscreen ("noecho,nocursor")
```

Similarly, we can use `setscreen` in the following way to turn echoing back on:

```
setscreen ("echo")          % Show input as it is typed
```

We can use the "cursor" option in `setscreen` to make the cursor visible.

EXAMPLE 6.4

We have introduced the Turing features that we needed to change the Bounce program in Fig. 6.10 into an interactive program in which the user can bat the ball. The new program is shown in Fig. 6.12. This program is like the Bounce program except that we have added new lines in two places. First, we added lines at the top to defined the action keys (8, 2, 6, and 4) and to display a start-up screen telling the user how to bat the ball using these keys. Second, we added lines just before the final end loop that check to see if an action key has been pressed, and if so, to cause the ball to be batted.

FIGURE 6.12

Program to Draw a Bouncing Ball

```
% The "Batball" program
% This program makes a ball bounce across the screen.
% The user can press keys to bat the ball up, down,
% right or left.

% Turn off key echoing and turn off cursor
setscreen ("noecho,nocursor")

% Key strokes that control the motion of ball
const UpKey := "8"
const DownKey := "2"
const RightKey := "6"
const LeftKey := "4"

put "GAME TO BAT A BALL AROUND THE SCREEN", skip

put "Press these keys to bat the ball", skip

put "    ", UpKey, "=up"
put "    ", DownKey, "=down"
put "    ", RightKey, "=right"
put "    ", LeftKey, "=left"

put skip, "Press any key to start"

var KeyStroke : string (1)   % Single character
getch (KeyStroke)            % Wait for a key press
cls        % Clear the screen and start the game

var Row, Col : int := 1
var RowMove, ColMove : int := 1
const ball := "o"
```

```
const Erase := "."        % Leave a trail of dots
loop
    locate (Row, Col)
    put ball ..           % Draw the ball
    delay (100)           % Pause a tenth of a second

    locate (Row, Col)
    put Erase ..          % Replace the ball with a dot

    Row := Row + RowMove     % Move ball vertically
    Col := Col + ColMove     % Move ball horizontally

    % If reach top or bottom, make opposite move
    if Row = 1 or Row = maxrow then
        RowMove := - RowMove
    end if

    % If reach left/right edge, make opposite move
    if Col = 1 or Col = maxcol then
        ColMove := - ColMove
    end if

    % Read a key stroke if there is one
    KeyStroke := "#"          % Use # to mean no input
    if hasch then
        getch (KeyStroke)     % Read one character
    end if

    % Bat the ball if an action key was pressed
    if KeyStroke = UpKey and Row > 1 then
        RowMove := -1         % Bat upwards
    elsif KeyStroke = DownKey and Row < maxrow then
        RowMove := 1          % Bat downwards
    elsif KeyStroke = LeftKey and Col > 1 then
        ColMove := -1         % Bat to left
    elsif KeyStroke = RightKey and Col < maxcol then
        ColMove := 1          % Bat to right
    else
        % Ignore other keys, including the # character
    end if

end loop
```

The `Batball` program in Fig 6.12 is a very simple game. It allows us to bat a ball around, but it is not a game that we can win and there is no score in the game. In the last section of this chapter, after we have introduced pixel graphics, we will develop another game that uses the idea of a bouncing ball, but the new game will be considerably more complicated, and it will keep track of a score for the user.

Exercises for Section 6.4

Self-Check

1. Describe the difference between reading a character using the `get` statement and reading it using `getch`.
2. What would happen in the `Batball` game if echoing were left enabled? What if the cursor were not hidden?
3. The 7, 9, 1, and 3 keys could be used to bat the ball as well as 8, 4, 6, and 2. Key 7 would bat up and to the left, 9 up and to the right, 1 down and to the left and 3 down and to the right. Explain how to modify the `Batball` program to support these four new action keys.

Programming

1. The `Batball` program is quite predictable in that the ball always moves in a straight line unless it is batted or it hits an edge of the screen. Modify and run the program so the ball has the following unpredictable motion. Each time through the loop, with a probability of 1 in 10, cause the ball to be randomly batted in one of the four directions (up, down, left, or right). Use the `randint` procedure to generate a number from 1 to 10 and if it is 1, the program should do the random batting. When the number is 1, use the `randint` procedure a second time to generate a number from 1 to 4, and use these four numbers in a `case` statement to select among the four directions of batting.
2. Change the `Batball` program so that two people can play the game. The second player uses these action keys: "e" for up, "s" for left, "d" for right and "x" for down. There are two independent bouncing balls: the original which is the letter `"o"` and a new one which is the "`*`" character. The trail of the new ball is the "`@`" character. The goal of each player is to cover as much of the screen as possible with his trail character.
3. There is a problem with the game described in exercise 2. The problem is that the Turing system records key strokes in a *buffer* and delivers these characters one at a time to the program. A problem is that if one player keeps typing characters, these will be stored up and given to the `getch` procedure each time through the loop of the program. To solve this problem, add a loop with `hasch` in its exit condition to discard all but the most recent character.

6.5 Pixel Graphics

You have seen how to use character graphics, in which you can output character strings in colors directly to any row or column on the screen. However, there has been no way to change anything on the screen that is smaller than a single character. This section introduces *pixel graphics*, in which you can change a much smaller unit. This unit is called a *picture element*, or *pixel*, for short. We sometimes call it simply a *dot*.

A computer screen is divided up into a large number of pixels, which are arranged as shown in Fig. 6.13. As the figure shows, each pixel is a small rectangle. The rectangles are numbered horizontally and vertically. The horizontal number is known as x and the vertical *number* is known as *y*. The bottom left pixel has these *x* and *y* values: $x = 0$ and $y = 0$. We call *x* and *y* the *coordinates* of the pixel. We write *(x,y)* to give the location of a particular pixel.

It is common in computer graphics to number the pixels in the vertical direction starting with *y* as zero on the top of the screen, with increasing values of *y* running downward. Turing does not use that approach for pixel graphics because it clashes with the standard mathematical convention in which increasing values of *y* locate higher positions.

FIGURE 6.13   Pixels on the Screen

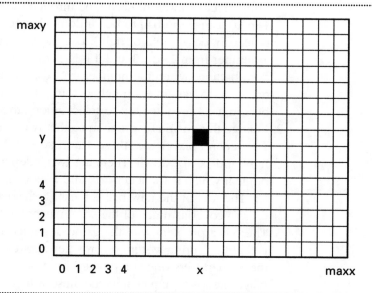

To be able to use pixel graphics on an IBM PC compatible, you must set the mode of the screen. It is recommended that you set the mode to the VGA graphics mode with 16 colors, using this statement:

```
setscreen ("graphics:v16")  % Needed on a PC
```

Once this statement is executed by your program, it can use Turing's graphics procedures to set the colors of pixels on the screen. This statement is not needed on some systems such as Macintoshes.

Drawing Dots on the Screen

In Turing, each pixel can be set to a specified color. For example, to set the pixel with x = 3 and y = 2 to color number 13, we use this statement:

```
drawdot (3, 2, 13) % Set pixel (3,2) to color 13
```

More generally, the `drawdot` procedure has this form:

```
drawdot (x, y, ColorNumber)
```

This sets pixel (x, y) on the screen to the specified color number.

There is a limit to the range of both x and y. In particular, `maxx` gives the screen's largest x position and `maxy` gives the largest y position. If you are using an IBM PC compatible and you have set the screen to VGA mode using:

```
setscreen ("graphics:v16")
```

the limits on x and y will be `maxx = 639` and `maxy = 199`. If you want to know the size of your screen, you can find out by running this program:

```
% Find size of screen in terms of pixels
put "Maximum x for a pixel: ", maxx
put "Maximum y for a pixel: ", maxy
```

The values of `maxx` and `maxy` depend on the screen you are using. *High resolution* screens have more, smaller, pixels, and *low resolution* screens have fewer, larger, pixels.

EXAMPLE 6.5

Figure 6.15 shows an example of a program that uses the `drawdot` procedure. The pattern drawn on the screen by this program is shown in Fig. 6.14.

FIGURE 6.14 Screen with Randomly Placed Dots

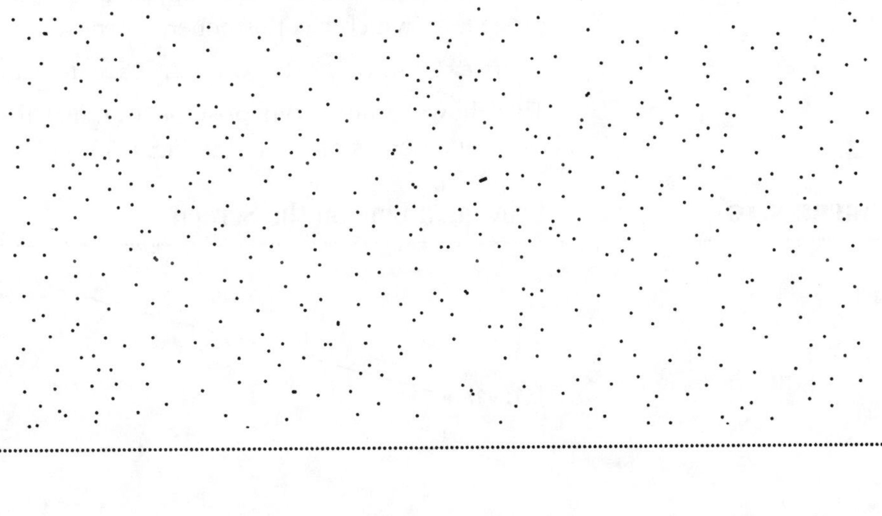

The Dots program in Fig 6.15 uses maxx and maxy to set the colors of pixels at random positions on the screen. This is similar to the Stars program in Fig. 6.3 in which asterisks were placed at random locations on the screen.

FIGURE 6.15 Program to Draw Dots at Random Locations in Random Colors

```
% The "Dots" program
% Place dots at random locations on the screen
procedure RandomDots
    const NumberOfDots := 1000
    var X, Y, ColorNumber : int
    for i : 1 .. NumberOfDots
        randint (X, 1, maxx)
        randint (Y, 1, maxy)
        randint (ColorNumber, 1, maxcolor)
        drawdot (X, Y, ColorNumber)
    end for
end RandomDots
RandomDots    % Call the procedure
```

Figures 6.3 and 6.15 illustrate two key differences between character graphics and pixel graphics. First, pixels are much smaller than characters. Second, in character graphics, a location is specified by giving a row and column, while in pixel graphics, the location is given by x and y.

You must be careful not to confuse these two methods of locating items on the screen. Character graphics gives the vertical position (row) first while pixel graphics gives the horizontal position (x) first. Character graphics uses increasing numbers (row numbers) to move down the screen while the pixel graphics uses increasing numbers (the value of y) to move up the screen.

Drawing Lines on the Screen

Instead of drawing a single dot (pixel) at a time, we can draw an entire line, which in turn is made up of dots. This is done by the drawline procedure, which has this general form:

    drawline (x1, y1, x2, y2, ColorNumber)

This draws a line from position ($x1$, $y1$) to position ($x2$, $y2$) using the color number, as illustrated in Fig. 6.16.

FIGURE 6.16 Drawing a Line on the Screen

EXAMPLE 6.6

Figure 6.17 gives a program that uses the drawline procedure. This program is much like the Dots program of Fig. 6.15, except that instead of drawing dots at random locations, it draws lines from the center of the screen to random pixel positions.

FIGURE 6.17 — The Explode Program

```
% The "Explode" program
% This draws lines from the center of
% the screen to random locations on the
% screen in random colors

var X, Y, ColorNumber : int
const MidX := maxx div 2
const MidY := maxy div 2

for I : 1 .. 500
    randint (X, 0 , maxx)
    randint (Y, 0, maxy)
    randint (ColorNumber, 1, maxcolor)
    drawline (MidX, MidY, X, Y, ColorNumber)
end for
```

The output of Fig. 6.17 is the "star burst" pattern shown in Fig. 6.18. Each line that the program draws is produced by the drawline procedure, which draws a line from the middle of the screen, which is (MidX, MidY), to the random point (X, Y).

FIGURE 6.18 — Screen Produced by the Explode Program

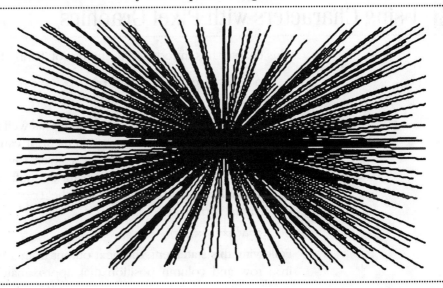

Exercises for Section 6.5

Self-Check

1. How would you set the pixel that is on the right edge of the screen and two pixels from the bottom so it becomes green?
2. How would you draw a triangle on the screen with corners at (20, 20), (120, 20) and (70, 120)?
3. How would you draw the triangle from question 1, but at a random location on the screen?

Programming

1. Using only a sequence of `drawline` statements, draw the initial of your first name on the screen.
2. Draw the trace of a gnat that moves randomly around the screen. The gnat is red and consists of a single pixel. Each move, it randomly goes up, down, left, or right by one pixel. Its trace is a single pixel that is colored brown. Stop your program when the gnat reaches the edge of the screen. Note: in science, the wiggling path the gnat makes is called *Brownian motion.*
3. On some computer screens the pixels are square, but on others they are rectangles that are somewhat higher than they are wide (or somewhat wider than they are high). Write a program that uses `drawdot` to completely fill in a rectangle in the middle of your screen that is 100 pixels on each size. Use a ruler to measure the width and height of this figure on the screen. From this, determine the width and height of each pixel and whether the pixels are square. **Note:** the ratio between the width and the height of a pixel is called the *aspect ratio.*

6.6 Using Characters with Pixel Graphics

This chapter has introduced a number of Turing features. These include:

```
locate     cls      maxrow     maxcol
maxcolor   color    put
```

You can use all of these in pixel graphics as well as in character graphics.

When you use the `locate` statement, it causes the next output from the `put` statement to be placed at a given row and column. Sometimes, instead of a row and column, we want the output to appear at an *x* and *y* position. When we want this we use the `locatexy` statement, which has this general form:

```
locatexy (x, y)
```

Following this statement, the next output from a `put` statement will appear in a row and column position that approximates the requested *x* and *y* position. The reason the position is approximate but not exact is that `locatexy` can only place the output cursor at a row and column position and not at an exact x and y location. For example, these statements:

```
locatexy (150, 100)
put "Surprise!"
```

will locate the left bottom corner of the message `"Surprise!"` close to x and y location (`150, 100`) on the screen.

EXAMPLE 6.7

As an example of the use of `locatexy`, we will show how to plot a simple graph from mathematics. We will plot the square root function. For each value of x starting with 0, we will draw a dot (pixel) whose height y is proportional to the square root of x. For example, when x is 25, y will be 5 and when x is 100, y will be 10. The plot is shown in Fig. 6.19.

FIGURE 6.19   Plotting a Function

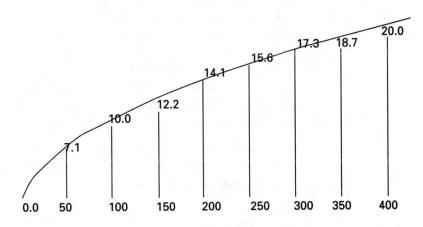

The program in Fig 6.20, which draws the plot in Fig. 6.19, uses two `locatexy` statements. The first one locates the x labels on the bottom of the screen, including `50`, `100`, and `150`. This `locatexy` statement and the following `put` are:

```
locatexy (X, 0)
put X ..
```

The second `locatexy` locates the y labels on the curve, including `7.1`, `10.0`, and `12.1`. This statement and the following `put` are:

```
locatexy (X,Y)
put SqrtRoot : 1 : 1 ..
```

The first 1 in the put statement nominally gives the width (number of characters) of the value. It has purposely been made smaller than the actual width. This reason this has been done is so that Turing will automatically pick the minimum width required to display the actual value. Turing does this when the specified width is too small. The second 1 determines the number of fractional digits. For example, in 17.3, there is one fractional digit, namely 3.

As can be seen in Fig. 6.19, the *y* labels, such as 17.3, 18.7, and 20.0 are not output at exactly the right height. They are output to a row and column position, which is close the right height, although not exact.

As you can see in Fig. 6.20, the value of *y* that is plotted is actually ten times the square root value. We have *scaled* the value of *y* by 10 so that the height of the curve is large enough to be easily inspected. Without this scaling, the final height of the curve would only be about 20 pixels, which is less that half the distance between the vertical lines. It is common to scale curves, in both the *x* and *y* dimensions, so the curve is easy to inspect.

FIGURE 6.20   Program to Plot the Square Root Function

```
% The "Plotsqrt" program
% Plot the graph of the square root of x
setscreen ("graphics:vga")
% Place title on the first row in center of screen
const Title := "Plot of the Square Root Function"
const MidCol := maxcol div 2
const TitleColumn := MidCol - length (Title) div 2
locate (1, TitleColumn)
put Title ..

% Set color of the dots and lines. If red and blue
% are not predefined in your system, you will have
% to change them to numbers to run this program

const DotColor := red
const LineColor := blue

% For each x position, leave 50 pixels on the
% right for outputting the sqrt value

for X : 0 .. maxx - 50
    const SqrtRoot := sqrt (X) % Find square root
    % Scale the vertical size by 10 so it is
    % large enough to make a nice plot
    const ScaleFactor := 10
    const Y := round (ScaleFactor * SqrtRoot)
    drawdot (X, Y, DotColor) % Plot the graph

    % Each 50 horizontal positions, draw vertical
    % line and output point's square root value
```

```
        if X mod 50 = 0 then % Is X is a multiple of 50
            % Draw vertical line
            drawline (X, 0, X, Y, LineColor)

            % Output X values at bottom of graph
            locatexy (X, 0)
            put X ..

            % Output sqrt values on the plot
            locatexy (X, Y)
            put SqrtRoot : 1 : 1 ..
        end if
    end for
```

Exercises for Section 6.6

Self-Check

1. In Fig. 6.19, there are numbers that run along the bottom of the screen. These are 0.0, 50, 100, 150, and so on. Explain why the first one has a fractional part (.0 following the initial 0) but the others do not.
2. The locatexy command does not locate the output cursor exactly to location (x, y). What does it actually do?
3. How would you change the program in Fig. 6.20 so the vertical lines it draws (see Fig. 6.19) go all the way to the top of the screen? How would you change the program so that all these lines stop at the same height, such that none of them runs into the letters that make up the title "Plot of the Square Root Function".

Programming

1. Change the program in Fig. 6.20 so that it plots the function x^2 instead of the square root of x. When you do this, you will want to change the scaling of the y value. Experiment with scaling factors such as 0.01, 0.1, and 10.0 until the plot fits nicely on the screen.
2. Change the program in Fig. 6.20 so that it labels the left margin of the plot with numbers that give the value of the function. For example, the labels running up the left side of the screen could be 5.0, 10.0, 15.0, and 15.0. Along with each of these labels, draw a horizontal line across the screen that corresponds to the labeled height.

6.7 Drawing Figures

We have seen how the pixel graphics commands drawdot and drawline allow us to draw dots and lines on the screen. This section will introduce Turing commands for drawing boxes, ovals, and arcs.

Drawing Boxes, Ovals, and Arcs

You may recall that in Section 3.4 of this book, we showed how very simple figures can be drawn using characters and the put statement. We will now see how figures can be drawn using pixels.

Turing's command for drawing a box has this form:

```
drawbox (x1, y1, x2, y2, ColorNumber)
```

One corner is located at (*x1, y1*) and the opposite corner is at (*x2, y2*).

FIGURE 6.21 Drawing a Box on the Screen

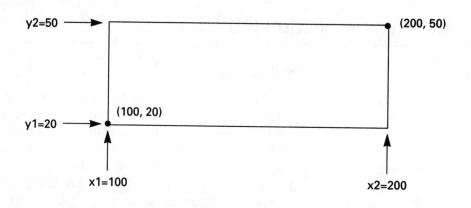

For example, if we want the bottom left hand corner of the box at (100, 20) and the top right corner at (200, 50), we use this command:

```
drawbox (100, 20, 200, 50, ColorNumber)
```

Fig. 6.21 shows how this box is drawn on the computer screen.

We commonly draw boxes with the first two arguments to drawbox, (*x1, y1*), as the bottom left corner, but we can as well make it be any other corner. For example, we can draw the same box as above with (*x1, y1*) as the top left corner using this command:

```
drawbox (100, 50, 200, 20, ColorNumber)
```

We can draw an oval on the screen by giving its center and its size. The oval's size is specified by its *x* radius and *y* radius, as shown in Fig. 6.22. The command to draw an oval has this general form.

```
drawoval (x, y, XRadius, YRadius, ColorNumber)
```

If the XRadius and YRadius are equal, this draws a circle.

FIGURE 6.22   Drawing an Oval on the Screen

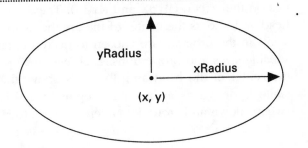

In a similar way, we can draw an arc on the screen. An arc is part of an oval, beginning with an initial angle and ending with a final angle, as illustrated in Fig. 6.23. The general form for drawing an arc is:

```
drawarc (x, y, XRadius, YRadius,
         InitialAngle, FinalAngle, ColorNumber)
```

The two angles are given in degrees. Zero degrees is at the right, at the "three o'clock" position. The angle increases counterclockwise, so 90 degrees is at the top at the "twelve o'clock" position.

FIGURE 6.23   Drawing an Arc on the Screen

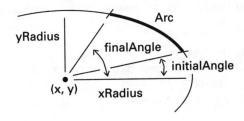

EXAMPLE 6.8
We will use the `drawoval` and `drawarc` commands to draw the happy face shown in Fig. 6.24. The program to draw this face is in Fig. 6.25.

FIGURE 6.24   Drawing of a Happy Face

The Happy program in Fig 6.25 starts by finding the middle x and y values on the screen (MidX and MidY). These are used as the center of the head and also as the center of the arc that is the mouth. The various constants in the program are chosen to make the face and its parts have reasonable sizes and proportions. Each eye is 20 pixels to the left or right of the center of the head and 30 pixels above the center of the head. The smile is drawn as an arc that begins at 180 degrees (on the left) and sweeps down and around counterclockwise to 360 degrees (on the right).

FIGURE 6.25 Happy Face as Drawn by Program

```
% The "Happy" program
% Draw a happy face on the screen
setscreen ("graphics:vga")
const MidX := maxx div 2
const MidY := maxy div 2
const HeadRadius := 100
const SmileRadius := 50
const EyeRadius := 10

const red    := 4    % This may not be required
const brown := 6    % This may not be required

% Draw the head in the center of the screen
drawoval (MidX, MidY, HeadRadius, HeadRadius, brown)

% Draw the two eyes
drawoval (MidX - 20, MidY + 30,
        EyeRadius, EyeRadius, brown)
drawoval (MidX + 20, MidY + 30,
        EyeRadius, EyeRadius, brown)

% Draw the smile
drawarc (MidX, MidY,
        SmileRadius, SmileRadius, 180, 360, red)
```

Filling in Figures

The figures that are drawn by the commands drawbox and drawoval consist of the lines that surround these figures. There are versions of these commands that completely fill in the figures. For example, this drawfillbox command

```
drawfillbox (10, 20, 100, 80, red)
```

will draw a box with corners at (10, 20) and (100, 80) that is completely filled in with the color red. (Older versions of Turing do not support these "fill" commands, but recent versions do.)

Corresponding to drawarc is the drawfillarc command. Although drawarc does not actually make a closed figure (the curved part is drawn, but not the two sides), drawfillarc fills in the "wedge of pie" defined by drawarc.

EXAMPLE 6.9

We will illustrate the use of drawfillarc by drawing a pie chart. A pie chart is drawn like a circular pie, in which the size of each slice of the pie represents the fraction used for a particular purpose. In the example, in Fig. 6.26, a student has spent a total of $100.00, with $25.00 spent on food, $15.00 on clothes, and so on. In the picture, one quarter of the pie (the top right piece) represents the amount spent on food. Continuing clockwise around the pie, the pieces represent the fraction of the money spent on clothes, entertainment, and transportation.

FIGURE 6.26 Pie Chart for Expenses

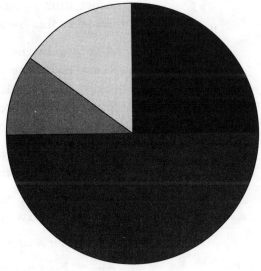

Pie chart for four types of expenses

Give your spending on:

Food	$25.00
Clothes	$15.00
Entertainment	$10.00
Transportation	$50.00

Each piece of the pie has been drawn using the drawfillarc command, in the program shown in Fig. 6.27. The beginning of the program consist of constants that determine the center of the pie and its radius, as well as the colors of the pieces. Next, the program reads in the amounts spent for each of the four categories (food, clothes, entertainment, and transportation). After summing up these amounts (as Sum), the program computes the fraction of the expenses that were due for each category. For example, the fraction due for food is computed by:

```
const FoodFraction := Food / Sum
```

This fraction is used to used to compute the final angle for the piece of the pie that represents the food expense, as follows:

```
const FoodAngle := round (FoodFraction * 360)
```

For example, the piece of the pie corresponding to food begins at zero degrees (on the right) and ends with FoodAngle degrees. The angle computed for each expense category gives the final angle for the piece of pie for that category. The final angle for the final category (for transportation) is 360 degrees, which is back to the beginning of the circle on the right.

FIGURE 6.27

Program to Draw a Pie Chart

```
% The "Piechart" program
% Read four expenses and draw the corresponding
% pie chart
setscreen("graphics:vga")
% Location and size of pie chart
const MidX := maxx div 2
const MidY := maxy div 2
const Radius := maxy div 3

% Colors in the pie chart for each expense
const FoodColor := 1
const ClothesColor := 2
const EntertainColor := 3
const TransportColor := 4

% Four expense items
var Food, Clothes, Entertain, Transport : real

put "Pie chart for four types of expenses "
put skip, "Give your spending on:", skip

const QueryWidth := 17 % Used to align the responses

put "  Food " : QueryWidth, "$" ..
get Food
put "  Clothes " : QueryWidth, "$" ..
get Clothes
put "  Entertainment " : QueryWidth, "$" ..
get Entertain
put "  Transportation " : QueryWidth, "$" ..
get Transport

const Sum := Food + Clothes + Entertain + Transport

% Determine fraction of sum spent for each item
const FoodFraction := Food / Sum
```

```
const ClothesFraction := Clothes / Sum
const EntertainFraction := Entertain / Sum
const TransportFraction := Transport / Sum

% Final angles for segments for each expense
const FoodAngle := round (FoodFraction * 360)
const ClothesAngle :=
    round ( (FoodFraction + ClothesFraction) * 360)
const EntertainAngle := round ( (FoodFraction
    + ClothesFraction + EntertainFraction) * 360)
const TransportAngle := 360

% Draw the four segments of the pie chart
drawfillarc (MidX, MidY, Radius, Radius,
    0, FoodAngle, FoodColor)
drawfillarc (MidX, MidY, Radius, Radius,
    FoodAngle, ClothesAngle, ClothesColor)
drawfillarc (MidX, MidY, Radius, Radius,
    ClothesAngle, EntertainAngle, EntertainColor)
drawfillarc (MidX, MidY, Radius, Radius,
    EntertainAngle, TransportAngle, TransportColor)
```

Exercises for Section 6.7

Self-Check

1. How would you draw a brown donut in the middle of the screen? You are to pick the size and thickness of the donut. Hint: use `drawfilloval` twice with the same center.
2. How can you draw an eye in the center of the screen? The eye should have a white almond shape, with a round blue pupil inside the almond and a black iris inside that. Hint: this can be done with multiple uses of `drawfilloval`.
3. How can you draw a box on the screen whose edge is three pixels thick, using `drawbox`? How can you do this using `drawfillbox`?
4. How would you change the `Happy` program in Fig. 6.25 so that it draws a sad face?

Programming

1. Modify the `Piechart` program so that it produces both a pie chart and a bar chart. The bar chart consists of four rectangles arranged horizontally, with the height of each proportional to the corresponding expense.
2. Using `drawarc` and `drawline`, draw a box with rounded corners with the name of your school in the middle of the box.

6.8 Animation Using Pixel Graphics (Optional)

In Section 6.3, we showed how to make a ball, which was actually the letter "o", appear to bounce around the screen. In this section, we will give examples of animation that involve pixel graphics.

EXAMPLE 6.10
The first example is a simplified picture of a face, such as you might have seen in an old video game. The face has a mouth that is repeatedly opening and closing (see Fig. 6.28). We will call this figure with its chewing action the "munching mouth".

FIGURE 6.28   The Munching Mouth

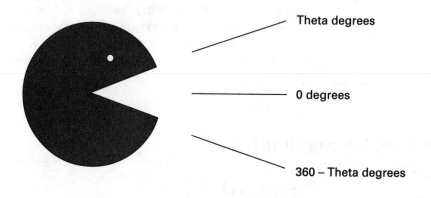

The head for the munching mouth is initially drawn as a filled circle, using drawfilloval. The eye is drawn in a similar way, using a smaller radius.

The mouth to made to open wider and wider by drawing filled arcs from Theta to Theta + DeltaTheta degrees (and from 360 – Theta – DeltaTheta to 360 – Theta degrees) for values of Theta increasing by DeltaTheta. This for loop from the Munch program (see Fig. 6.29) makes the mouth open.

```
% Open the mouth
for Theta : 0 .. OpenAngle by DeltaTheta
    % Draw mouth (erase part of head)
    drawfillarc (MidX, MidY, HeadRadius, HeadRadius,
        Theta, Theta + DeltaTheta, MouthColor)
    drawfillarc (MidX, MidY, HeadRadius, HeadRadius,
        360 - Theta - DeltaTheta, 360 - Theta, MouthColor)
    delay (DelayTime) % Slow down the munching
end for
```

The mouth (really the space seen behind the mouth) is drawn in the background color, which is color number 0. The result is that the mouth appears to open.

In this loop, the angle called `Theta` starts out as 0 and increases in steps of `DeltaTheta` degrees, which is 5 degrees, until it becomes `OpenAngle`, which is 30 degrees (see Fig. 6.28). The first `drawfillarc` command in the loop fills an arc from an initial angle of `Theta` (degrees above the horizontal) and a final angle of `Theta + DeltaTheta`. This opens the mouth on the top. The second `drawfillarc` similarly opens the mouth on the bottom.

FIGURE 6.29   **Program for Munching Mouth**

```
% The "Munch" program
% Show a face that seems to be chewing food
setscreen ("graphics:vga")
const Title := "The Munching Mouth"
% Write title in center of top line
locate (1, maxcol div 2 - length (Title) div 2)
put Title ..

% Constants for center of head
const MidX := maxx div 2
const MidY := maxy div 2

% Radius of head and radius of eye
const HeadRadius := 50
var EyeRadius := 3

const red := 4          % Maybe not needed
const brown := 6        % Maybe not needed

const EyeColor := red
const HeadColor := brown
const MouthColor := 0    % The background color

% Tenth second pause at each mouth position
const DelayTime := 100

% Degrees mouth opens/closes with each move
var DeltaTheta : int := 5

% Angle mouth opens (above and below horizontal)
const OpenAngle := 30

% Draw the head
drawfilloval (MidX, MidY, HeadRadius, HeadRadius, HeadColor)
```

```
% Draw the eye
drawfilloval (MidX + 20, MidY + 20,
                EyeRadius, EyeRadius, EyeColor)

loop    % Show the mouth opening and closing

    % Open the mouth
    for Theta : 0 .. OpenAngle by DeltaTheta
        % Draw mouth (erase part of head)
        drawfillarc (MidX, MidY, HeadRadius, HeadRadius,
            Theta, Theta + DeltaTheta, MouthColor)
        drawfillarc (MidX, MidY, HeadRadius, HeadRadius,
            360 - Theta - DeltaTheta, 360 - Theta, MouthColor)
        delay (DelayTime) % Slow down the munching
    end for

    % Close the mouth
    for decreasing Theta : OpenAngle .. 0 by DeltaTheta
        % Draw head (erase part of mouth)
        drawfillarc (MidX, MidY, HeadRadius, HeadRadius,
            Theta, Theta + DeltaTheta, HeadColor)
        drawfillarc (MidX, MidY, HeadRadius, HeadRadius,
            360 - Theta - DeltaTheta, 360 - Theta, HeadColor)
        delay (DelayTime) % Slow down the munching
    end for
end loop
```

The loop for closing the mouth is similar to the one for opening the mouth, but instead of drawing the mouth, it draws the head. Here is the loop:

```
    % Close the mouth
    for decreasing Theta : OpenAngle .. 0 by DeltaTheta
        % Draw head (erase part of mouth)
        drawfillarc (MidX, MidY, HeadRadius, HeadRadius,
            Theta, Theta + DeltaTheta, HeadColor)
        drawfillarc (MidX, MidY, HeadRadius, HeadRadius,
            360 - Theta - DeltaTheta, 360 - Theta, HeadColor)
        delay (DelayTime) % Slow down the munching
    end for
```

This repeatedly draws a filled arc from `Theta` to `Theta + DeltaTheta` degrees (and another arc from `360 - Theta - DeltaTheta` to `360 - Delta` degrees) in the head's color. The loop decreases the value of `Theta`, and this closes the mouth by filling arcs closer and closer to the horizontal line.

The Game of Scoot

In this section, we will give a case study involving animation based on pixel graphics. The program in the case study implements a game that supports user interaction. As a part of this case study, we will introduce the following new Turing feature that is needed to support interaction.

> whatdotcolor (x, y): This is used to find out the color of the pixel at location (x, y).

We will develop a very simple video game, called Scoot. We will now give an overview of the game. The game begins by displaying the start-up screen shown in Fig. 6.30. This screen gives basic instructions for the game. It tells the user that certain keys (8, 2, 6, 4, t, and q) are to used to control the progress of the game. When the user is finished reading this screen, he or she presses any key to start the game.

FIGURE 6.30 **Start-Up Screen for Scoot Game**

```
THE GAME OF SCOOT

Try to maximize the number of balls on the screen
You get only 10 crashes (hitting another item)

    8=up
    2=down
    6=right
    4=left
    t=trace (give current position and velocity)
    q=quit

Press any key to start
```

The game is based on the idea of a bouncing ball that starts in the middle of the screen (see Fig. 6.31). The ball moves down and to the right until it bounces off the edge of the screen, then keeps on moving and bouncing off the edges of the screen.

In the actual game, instead of having a single moving ball, new balls are drawn along the path of motion. Each ball is numbered, from 1 to 2 to 3, and so on.

If the center of a new ball lands on an old ball, there is a "crash". For example, in Fig. 6.31, ball number 8 has crashed into ball number 6 and ball number 9 has crashed into ball number 5. Each time there is a crash, a number of circles are drawn around the new ball involved in the crash.

The game keeps going until you have 10 crashes. The object of the game is to get as many balls on the screen as possible before it ends. As you can see in Fig. 6.31, the current score is 25. This is recorded in the top left corner, and it is also the number of the newest ball. So far there have been two crashes. This is recorded in the top left corner and also by the fact that two balls are surrounded by circles.

How the User Controls the Velocity

By pressing the number keys 8, 2, 6, and 4, the user can change the speed of the motion. Technically speaking, we should call it *velocity* instead of speed, because it is sometimes positive (when moving to the right or up) and sometimes negative (when moving to the left or down). Pressing 8 increases the velocity in the y direction (in the upward direction), while pressing 2 increases it in the negative y direction (in the downward direction). Pressing 6 increases the velocity in the x direction (to the right), while pressing 4 increases it in the negative x direction (to the left).

In Fig. 6.31, the user has pressed the 8 key to increase the upward speed while balls 14, 15 and 16 were being drawn. As a result, the path through those balls curves upwards. After that, the user presses no more keys and the motion continues on its own, but now with a positive y velocity (in the upward direction).

Just as ball 25 is drawn, the user pressed the "t" key ("t" for trace). As a result, the position and velocity of the ball are displayed. As you can see in Fig. 6.31, at that point, x is 139, y is 131. The velocity is 40 to the right, and 9 in the upwards direction.

FIGURE 6.31   Screen During Game of Scoot

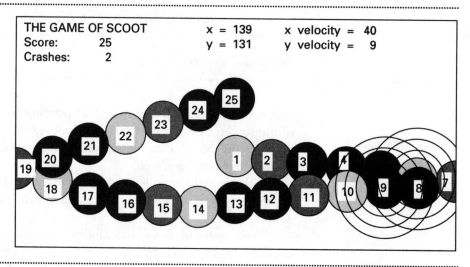

❇ Case Study:

The Game of Scoot

1. Problem

You are to write the computer program that allows a user to play the game of Scoot. The program gives the user instructions and then simulates the motion of the ball and responds to the user's action keys. The program displays the score, and it halts the game when there have been too many crashes.

2. Analysis

The program begins by displaying a start-up screen (Fig. 6.30) that gives a brief description of the game including a list of action keys for user commands. Once the user presses any key, the program starts the animation of the bouncing ball. The motion of the ball is determined by its velocity. When the ball reaches an edge, it is caused to bounce by reversing its x or y velocity. The main action keys cause the velocity to be increased or decreased in the x and y directions. There is also an action key to cause a trace, which outputs the current position and velocity, and an action key to halt the game.

DATA REQUIREMENTS
Problem Inputs

```
    KeyStroke : string (1)    % Latest key press, if any
```

Problem Outputs

```
    Score : int               % Number of balls on screen
    CountOfCrashes : int      % Hits of other balls
    X : int                   % Horizontal position
    Y : int                   % Vertical position
    XVelocity : int           % Horizontal velocity
    YVelocity : int           % Vertical velocity
```

Program Variable

```
    BallColor : int           % Color of ball
```

3. Design

The program begins by displaying the start-up screen and then repeats a loop body that draws each new ball. The structure chart for the design is given in Fig. 6.32.

ALGORITHM
1. Display the start-up screen and wait for a key stroke
2. loop % Run the actual game
    2.1 Draw the next ball
    2.2 Cycle to the next color for ball
    2.3 Slow down game for 0.3 seconds
    2.4 Increase the score (number of drawn balls)
    2.5 Output the score (on top of screen and on ball)

2.6 Stop game when there have been too many crashes

2.7 Carry out user's requested action

2.8 Handle bounce if edge is being hit

2.9 See if there is a crash, i.e., if the center of the ball lands
on a pixel that has already been colored

end loop

FIGURE 6.32 Structure Chart for Game of Scoot

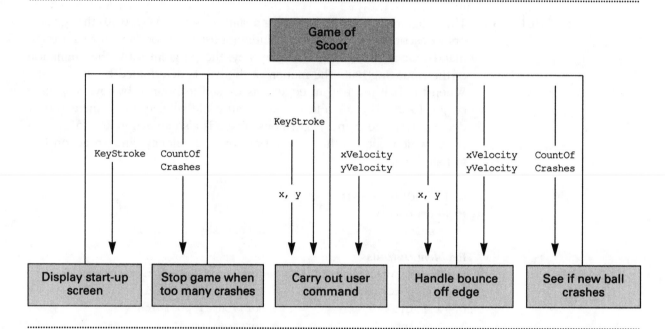

4. Implementation   The implementation for the game of Scoot is given in Fig. 6.33. The Batball program in Fig. 6.12 has a similar structure to this program, but it was done with character graphics instead of pixel graphics, and it did not keep track of the user's score.

Distance and Velocity in the Game

In the game of Scoot, the unit of distance is the pixel. As you can see in Fig. 6.31, ball 25 is 139 pixels from the left of the screen ($x = 139$) and 131 units from the bottom of the screen ($y = 131$). (Beware that Fig. 6.31 is not to scale.)

The basic unit of time in the program is three tenths of a second, because the main loop of the Scoot program delays for that length of time each time through its main loop.

The next ball to be drawn in Fig. 6.31, ball 26, will be drawn 40 pixels to the right of ball 25 (*x* velocity = 40) and 9 pixels above ball 25 (*y* velocity = 9). This change in the position from one ball to the next is determined by the following statements in the Scoot program:

```
X := X + XVelocity    % Move ball horizontally
Y := Y + YVelocity    % Move ball vertically
```

In the Batball program in Fig 6.12, the position of the ball was always increased or decreased by one, which means that the velocity in each direction was always 1 or -1. In the Scoot game, the *x* and *y* velocity are used to increase and decrease the *x* and *y* position, and the user's key stroke actions cause their velocities to change.

The following statements in the Scoot program cause the ball to bounce off the edges of the screen:

```
if X < Radius or X > maxx - Radius then
    % Bounce off left or right edge
    XVelocity := - XVelocity
end if

if Y < Radius or Y > maxy - Radius then
    % Bounce off top or bottom edge
    YVelocity := - YVelocity
end if
```

This is very similar to the part of the program in Fig. 6.12 that caused the bouncing of the letter "o". A difference in the Scoot program is that a bounce occurs whenever the center of the ball approaches within one radius of any edge. When a bounce occurs, the corresponding *x* or *y* velocity is negated. This causes the ball to start moving in the opposite direction.

Determining If a Ball Has Hit Another Ball

The final part of the main loop of the Scoot program checks to see if the new ball that is about to be drawn will crash into an old ball. This check is done using the whatdotcolor function, which inspects a pixel and determines the number of its color. If a pixel has not yet been set to a color, it will still have the background color, whose number is 0. The following line in the Scoot program checks to see if the center of the new ball has already been set to a color:

```
if whatdotcolor (X, Y) not= 0 then ...
```

If the color at position (*x, y*), which is the center of the new ball, has already been set to a non-zero (non-background) color, the program increases the count of crashes. It graphically indicates that there has been a crash by drawing circles around the new ball.

5. Testing

There are many situations in which a program such as Scoot can be wrong. Given the entire program, the first thing you should do is run it and see if the game seems to be working.

However, to see if the all parts of the program are working, you need to test it systematically. You should carefully read the start-up screen to verify that its explanation is reasonable and if it contains any misspellings.

It would probably be best to increase time in the game's delay statement, to slow down the speed of the game, and to modify the program so that every time through its main loop, it outputs the tracing information. With these changes, you can more easily verify that each individual action is working.

Observe the motion of the ball and make sure that the ball moves the correct amount each time through the loop, by looking at the trace. Observe a bounce off each edge and make sure that these bounces are working correctly, by studying the trace and observing the graphics. Try each action key, observe its action, and make sure each is working as expected.

FIGURE 6.33   Program for the Game of Scoot

```
% The "Scoot" program

% This is a very simple video game.
% A ball bounces around the screen.
% It leaves its "shadow" each time it moves.
% You get a point for each shadow.
% You crash each time you hit a shadow.
% The game is over after 10 crashes.
% You try to direct the motion of the ball to
% maximize your score.

% The game is designed for color screens but
% will work in monochrome

% This setscreen is used only on IBM PC compatibles
setscreen ("graphics:vga")

% This constant may not be needed on some systems.
const red := 1

% Turn off key echoing and turn off cursor
setscreen ("nocursor,noecho")

% Key strokes that control motion of ball
const UpKey      := "8"
const DownKey    := "2"
const RightKey   := "6"
const LeftKey    := "4"

const Title := "THE GAME OF SCOOT"
```

```
% Start-up screen

% Give introductory instructions
% Wait for a key press
% Then clear the screen and start the game

put Title, skip
put "Try to maximize number of balls on screen"
put "You get only 10 crashes (hitting any item)",
    skip

put "   ", UpKey,      "=up"
put "   ", DownKey,    "=down"
put "   ", RightKey,   "=right"
put "   ", LeftKey,    "=left"
put "   ", "t=trace (give position and velocity)"
put "   ", "q=quit"

put skip, "Press any key to start"

var KeyStroke : string (1)    % Latest key press,
                              % if any
getch (KeyStroke) % Wait for a key press
cls % Clear the screen for the game

put Title % Place the title back on the screen

% Position and velocity (speed) of ball

var X : int := maxx div 2 % Horizontal position
var Y : int := maxy div 2 % Vertical position

var XVelocity : int := 40 % Horizontal velocity
var YVelocity : int := -5 % Vertical velocity

const XBoost := 4    % Speed up in x velocity when
                     % left/right key pressed
const YBoost := 4    % Speed up in y velocity when
                     % up/down key pressed

const Radius := 20        % Size of ball
var BallColor : int := 1   % Color of ball

var CountOfCrashes : int := 0   % Hits of other balls
const MaxCrashes := 10
var Score : int := 0   % Number of balls on screen

loop
    % Draw the ball
    drawfilloval (X, Y, Radius, Radius, BallColor)

    % Cycle through all colors for the balls
    BallColor := BallColor mod maxcolor + 1
```

```
% Slow down game 0.3 second for each ball
delay (300)

% Increase the score (number of balls drawn)
Score := Score + 1

% Output the score in two places
locate (2, 1)              % Top left of screen
put "Score:   ", Score : 3 ..
locatexy (X, Y)            % On the new ball
put Score ..

% Stop game if there have been too many crashes
if CountOfCrashes = MaxCrashes then
    locate (4, 1)
    put "Sorry, too many crashes" ..
    exit
end if

% Read a key stroke if there is one
KeyStroke := "#" % This means no character read
if hasch then
    getch (KeyStroke)
end if

% Carry out requested action
if KeyStroke = UpKey then
    % Increase speed upward
    YVelocity := YVelocity + YBoost
elsif KeyStroke = DownKey then
    % Increase speed downward
    YVelocity := YVelocity - YBoost
elsif KeyStroke = RightKey then
    % Increase speed to right
    XVelocity := XVelocity + XBoost
elsif KeyStroke = LeftKey then
    % Increase speed to left
    XVelocity := XVelocity - XBoost
elsif KeyStroke = "t" then
    % Output current position and velocity
    locate (1, 30)
    put "X = ", X : 4,
        "   X velocity = ", XVelocity : 4 ..
    locate (2, 30)
    put "Y = ", Y : 4,
        "   Y velocity = ", YVelocity : 4 ..
elsif KeyStroke = "q" then
    locate (4, 1)
    put "Quitting game" ..
    exit % Stop the game
else
    % Ignore all other keys
end if
```

```
% Find position of new ball
X := X + XVelocity % Move ball horizontally
Y := Y + YVelocity % Move ball vertically

% Handle bounce if edge is being hit
if X < Radius or X > maxx - Radius then
    % Bounce off left or right edge
    XVelocity := - XVelocity
end if

if Y < Radius or Y > maxy - Radius then
    % Bounce off top or bottom edge
    YVelocity := - YVelocity
end if

% See if there is a crash, i.e., if the center
% of the ball is landing on a pixel that has
% already been colored.
if whatdotcolor (X, Y) not= 0 then

    % This is a crash
    CountOfCrashes := CountOfCrashes + 1
    locate (3, 1)
    put "Crashes: ", CountOfCrashes : 3 ..

    % Draw rings around a crashing ball
    for R: Radius .. Radius + 24 by 8
        drawoval (X, Y, R, R, red)
    end for

end if
end loop

locate (5, 1)
put "End of Game" ..
```

Exercises for Section 6.8

Self-Check

1. In the Scoot program, describe what would happen if the test to see if a ball should bounce off the left or right edge were changed to this:

   ```
   if X <= 0 or X >= maxx then
   ```

3. The 7, 9, 1, and 3 keys could be used to direct the ball as well as 8, 4, 6, and 2. Key 7 would accelerate the ball up and to the left, 9 up and to the right, 1 down and to the left and 3 down and to the right. Explain how to modify the Scoot program so it would support these four new action keys.

Programming

1. Modify the `Munch` program so that as the mouth opens and closes, it also moves from left to right across the screen. Place a string of candies (colored circles) in front of the mouth, which it will appear to eat as it moves across the screen.

2. Write a program that starts by displaying a happy face on the screen. Inside each eye is an iris (a little circle), that moves from left to right, so that the face appears to look to one side and then to the other. Make the face appear to be smiling when looking to the right and sad when looking to the left.

3. There is a problem with the `Scoot` game in that the Turing system records all key strokes and delivers them one by one to the `getch` command. If one player keeps pressing keys, all of the corresponding characters will be saved. They will be given to `getch`, one by one, each time through the outer loop of the program. You are to modify the game so that each time through the loop, only the most recent character is acted upon, and all the rest are ignored. You can do this using a loop that uses `getch` to read characters and exits when there are no more characters to be read.

4. Modify the `Scoot` program so it is less predictable. Randomly choose a place on the screen for the first ball and randomly pick its initial *x* and *y* velocities. When selecting these values, make sure you use a reasonable range for each random choice.

5. Modify the `Scoot` game so that after it has been played, it asks you if you want to play again. This continues until you indicate that you no longer want to play.

6.9 Common Programming Errors

When using the `put` statement in graphics, it is easy to forget to use the dot-dot at the end of the statement. Without the dot-dot, the end of the output line on the screen will be cleared to blanks, which is not usually desirable when doing graphics.

If you try to use `color` as the name of a variable or constant, the Turing system will mark this as a syntax error. This is because `color` is the name of the predefined subprogram that determines the color of the output produced by `put`. If this occurs, simply change the name of your variable.

If you are using animation, you must often slow down the action so that it occurs at a speed that is easy to follow. To do this, you should use the `delay` statement. If you forget to use `delay`, the motion may be so fast that you do not see anything on the screen except some flickering.

If you use `get` instead of `getch` in an action game, the system will require the user to press the Return key before any reading will be done.

If you want your program to wait for a key stroke only if a key has been pressed, you must remember to use `hasch` to see if the character is available before using `getch`.

If is easy to make mistakes when trying to write programs to do computer graphics. It is best to write little parts of your program at a time, and test the parts separately, to see if you are getting the effect that you intend. In the patterns you are drawing, it is sometimes helpful to add `delay` statements to your program temporarily, to allow you to see the effect of each individual statement that produces graphical output.

The screens of computers vary in their graphical capabilities. On an IBM PC compatible, you will need to use the statement:

```
setscreen ("graphics:v16")
```

in order to use the 16 colors we have described in this chapter. The number of rows and columns available on your screen can be determined by outputting the values of `maxrow` and `maxcol` using a `put` statement. Similarly, the maximum x and y pixel positions can be determined by outputting `maxx` and `maxy`.

When you are writing a program, be sure to remember that, in character graphics, rows are numbered starting from 1 at the top of the screen, but that in pixel graphics, y positions are numbered from 0 starting at the bottom of the screen.

Chapter Review

This chapter introduced character graphics and pixel graphics. In character graphics, you can place characters at any specified location on the screen and you can set the colors in which the characters are displayed.

The `locate` statement is used to set the row and column on the screen in which the next output from a `put` statement will appear.

The `color` statement determines the color in which the characters will appear. If you have a *monochrome* screen, you cannot use colors, because your screen has only a *background* color and a *foreground* color. It is common for screens to have 16 or more colors. If your PC has a VGA screen, this will allow you to use both the character graphics and the pixel graphics features of Turing. Although the number of colors varies from screen to screen, you can always determine the number on your screen using the predefined `maxcolor` function. The background is a color number of 0.

Sometimes a program is designed to use all the available colors in succession, for example, to flash a message in all available colors. The best way to cycle through all the available colors is to use the `mod` operator. For example, in this statement

```
ColorNumber := ColorNumber mod maxcolor + 1
```

the value of `ColorNumber` is increased by 1 to the next available color number or else is set back to 1.

If you are changing things on the screen rapidly, you may need to use the `delay` statement to slow down your program. This statement is given times in milliseconds. For example, a delay of 500 causes your program to pause for half of a second. If you want people to be able to see changes on the screen, you will need a delay of around a tenth of a second, or else people may see nothing but a flickering on the screen.

There are a number of ways that you can erase characters on the screen. If you want to erase the entire screen, you should use the cls (clear screen) statement. If you want to erase a particular message, you can reposition the *output cursor* to the beginning of the message. Then you can either write out a dummy message consisting of blanks, which is the same length as the real message, or you can write out the message with the color set to the background color (color number zero).

When figures on the screen seem to move, we call this *animation*. If the user can take actions to affect this motion, this becomes *interactive graphics*. A video game is an example of interactive graphics. If you are writing a program that supports interactive graphics in which the user presses keys to control the motion, you will need to use `getch` (get character). The `getch` statement reads a single character without waiting for the user to press the Return key. The variable read by `getch` must have the type `string (1)`. If no character has been typed by the user, `getch` waits until the user actually types one. The `hasch` (has character) function is used to test to see if the user has typed a character. Using `hasch`, the program can avoid using `getch` when there is nothing to be read.

In pixel graphics, your program can set the colors of the *picture elements*, called *pixels*, on the screen. These pixels are little rectangles that are considerably smaller than characters. Pixels are located using an x coordinate that starts at 0 on the left of the screen and increases to the right and a y coordinate that starts at 0 on the bottom and increases upwards. Although the number of pixels in the x and y directions varies from screen to screen, you can always determine the size of your screen using the predefined `maxx` and `maxy` functions. For example, no matter what screen you have, the middle x position is `maxx div 2`.

If you want to output characters to an (x, y) location, you should use the `locatexy` statement before using `put`. This will place the output characters in a row and column position that approximates the specified (x, y) location.

The `drawdot` procedure sets the color of a pixel at location (x, y). A line is drawn on the screen in a specified color using the `drawline` procedure. Similarly, `drawbox`, `drawoval`, and `drawarc` are used to draw boxes, ovals and arcs. If you want the interior of these figures to be colored, you use `drawfillbox`, `drawfilloval`, and `drawfillarc`. You can use the `whatdotcolor` function to the determine the color of the pixel at a specified (x, y) location.

New Turing Constructs in Chapter 6

The new Turing constructs introduced in this chapter are described in Table 6.1.

TABLE 6.1 Summary of New Turing Constructs

Construct	Effect
Character Graphics	
maxrow	Number of rows on screen
maxcol	Number of rows on screen
maxcolor	Largest color number
locate (Row, Column)	Next output goes in the row and column
color (ColorNumber)	Set color used by put statement
cls	Clear the screen
delay (Ms)	Delay for Ms milliseconds
length (Str)	Number of characters in string Str
repeat (Str, N)	Make a string consisting of N copies of the string Str
Pixel Graphics	
maxx	Maximum x (horizontal pixels)
maxy	Maximum y (vertical pixels)
setscreen ("graphics:vga")	Set PC to VGA
setscreen ("noecho")	Do not echo keystrokes
setscreen ("nocursor")	Do not show the cursor
hasch	See if character can be read
getch	Read one character immediately
string (1)	Type that holds only one character; used by getch
locatexy (x, y)	Next output goes near (x,y)
drawdot (x, y, c)	Set pixel (x,y) to color c
drawline (x1, y1, x2, y2, c)	Draw line from $(x1,y1)$ to $(x2,y2)$ in color c
drawbox (x1, y1, x2, y2, c)	Draw box with corners at $(x1,y1)$ and $(x2,y2)$ in color c
drawoval (x1, y1, XRadius, YRadius, c)	Draw oval with center at $(x1,y1)$ with x radius and y radius in color c
drawarc (x1, y1, XRadius, YRadius, InitialAngle, FinalAngle, c)	Like drawoval, but draw just an arc, from initial to final angle in color c
drawfillbox (...)	Like drawbox, but fill the box
drawfilloval (...)	Like drawoval, but fill the oval
drawfillarc (...)	Like drawarc, but fill the arc
whatdotcolor (x, y)	Return the color number of the pixel

Quick-Check Exercises

1. The `maxrow` function tells you how wide the screen is. (True/False)
2. It is an error if you attempt to `put` characters after you have used the `color` statement to set the color to the background color. (True/False)
3. How can you draw a circle that is completely filled with red?
4. What is an easy way to output a string of 50 asterisks?
5. What pattern does this produce on the screen

   ```
   drawbox (100, 100, 150, 150, green)
   drawoval (125, 125, 25, 25, green)
   ```

6. What is wrong with the following loop, which is suppose to draw a light that turns from red to yellow to green and back repeatedly?

   ```
   loop
       drawfilloval (100, 100, 20, 20, red)
       drawfilloval (100, 100, 20, 20, yellow)
       drawfilloval (100, 100, 20, 20, green)
       drawfilloval (100, 100, 20, 20, yellow)
   end loop
   ```

7. What do the terms `hasch` and `getch` stand for?
8. In `drawarc`, what angle corresponds to pointing downward?
9. What will the following `if` statement accomplish?

   ```
   if whatdotcolor (X, Y) = green then
       drawdot (X, Y, red)
   end if
   ```

Answers to Quick-Check Exercises

1. False
2. False
3. Use this statement:

   ```
   drawfilloval (X, Y, Radius, Radius, red)
   ```

4. Use this statement:

   ```
   put repeat ("*", 50)
   ```

5. It draws a box with corners at (100, 100) and (150, 150) with a circle drawn so that it just fits inside the box. The drawing is done in green.
6. There should be a `delay` statement following each `drawfilloval` to slow down the speed at which the light changes. Also, it would be better to name both the radius and the x and y positions as follows:

   ```
   const Radius := 20
   const X := 100
   const Y := 100
   ```

   These names should be used instead of 20 and 100 in the `drawfilloval` statements.

7. They stand for "has character" and "get character".
8. 270 degrees or –90 degrees.
9. If the pixel at location (*x*, *y*) is green, it will be changed to red.

Review Questions

1. What does the following program do? Give a much shorter and faster program that does the same thing.

```
for X : 50 .. 150
    for Y : 20 .. 90
        drawdot (X, Y, blue)
    end for
end for
```

2. Write a program that outputs the word `"tower"` written vertically in the middle of the screen.
3. Write a program that draws a white sign with a red border around it that says `"NO PARKING"` in the middle of the screen.
4. Modify the `Stars` program in Fig. 6.3 so that instead of putting stars on the screen, it outputs each most recently typed character. It should initially output stars, until the user has typed a character.
5. Write a program that draws a "worm" that crawls around the screen in the following fashion. The worm is draw using `drawline`. It starts in the middle of the screen. With each move, it randomly picks a new (*x, y*) position such that each of *x* and *y* are 0 to 10 pixels from the preceding position. Each new position is connected to the old one by a line. The program halts when the worm falls off the screen.
6. Write a program that repeatedly draws circles on the screen. Each circle is filled in with a color. The user can use these action keys to control the drawing of the circles. To control the color of the circle: r (red), b (blue), g (green). To control the position of the circle: x (move right by 5), X (move left by 5), y (move up by 5), Y (move down by 5). To control the radius of the circle: > (increase radius by 4), < (decrease radius by 4).

Programming Projects

1. Write a program called `Shades` that colors in a square that is 100 pixels on a side in the middle of the screen in the following way. First it asks the user to choose three numbers that add up to 100. These numbers are used to pick a shade of color that is made of red, blue, and yellow. The square is to be colored using pixels that are chosen according to the proportions among the numbers. For example, if the numbers

chosen are 25, 25, and 50, then 25% of the pixels should be red, 25% blue, and 50% yellow. Do this in the following way. First, randomly generate an (*x, y*) location in the box. Next pick a random number from 1 to 100. If this number is less or equal to the first number the user typed, color the pixel red. Otherwise, if it is less than or equal to the sum of the first two numbers typed, color the pixel blue. Otherwise, color the pixel yellow. Repeat this action in a loop. The program should stop when the user types the letter "q".

2. Write a program that makes the screen into a digital clock. Do this in the following way. When the program starts up, it should ask the user for the time of day, given in terms of the hour, the minutes after the hour and the number of seconds after the hour. For example, if the user gives the hour as 4 and the minutes as 16 and the seconds as 37, the program displays "4:16:37" in the middle of the screen. The program then uses the delay statement to wait for a second and changes the display to "4:16:38" and so on. The program must increase the minute time by one and set the second count back to zero when the second count would be incremented to 60. Similarly, the hour time must be incremented by one and the minute count must be set back to zero when the minute count would be set to sixty. Each time the hour would be set to 13, it is set back to 1. Allow the user to set the running clock as follows: s moves the time ahead a second and S moves it back; m moves the time ahead a minute and M moves it back; h moves the time ahead an hour and H moves it back.

3. Write a program that makes the screen into a analog clock. First, complete programming project 2, but place the digital clock display on the bottom line of the screen. An analog clock (a dial with a second hand, a minute hand and an hour hand) is to be drawn and updated as follows. Each hand can be draw using drawfillarc. The second hand is the longest (has the largest radius) and the thinnest (has a narrow range of degrees) among the three hands. The minute hand is shorter and thicker. The hour hand is the shortest and thickest. The angular position in degrees of the second hand can be computed as six times the current second count, because there six degrees for each second as the second had moves around the face of the clock. In a second, the minute hand moves a sixtieth as far as the second hand, and the hour hand moves a sixtieth as far as the minute hand. Be warned that drawfillarc measures angles starting at the 3 o'clock position and counts degrees in a counterclockwise direction; you will have to adjust for this in your program. To keep your program simple, you do not need to label the hour positions (1 o'clock, 2 o'clock, and so on) around the face of your clock.

4. You have been hired by the Washo Soap Company to create an advertisement for their new soap. The sales motto for the soap is, "Good for washing your clothes, and your face too." Your advertisement is to run on a computer screen. Use plenty of color and motion, as well as figures on the screen, to catch the user's attention. Show off the motto in

flashing colors. You are allowed to use any artistic or advertising tricks you can think of to make a good advertisement.

5. You are to write a program to show the motion of a "tumbling stick", which is a computer animation that will now be described. The stick consists of two balls attached by a stretchy cord. The two balls have their own positions and their own x and y velocities. The balls bounce when they hit the edge of the screen. A stick, which is really the stretchy cord, is drawn as the line between the two balls. The balls are not actually drawn. As the stick moves, draw it for 20 positions in one color, then use another color for 20 positions, and so on. Make the action more dramatic by reflecting the stick left-to-right and top-to-bottom. This gives you four sticks, as if there were mirrors held vertically along the middle y position and along the middle x position.

6. Modify the program in Fig. 6.20 so that it will plot the curve for a sine function. Use the Turing function `sind`, which takes degrees, instead of `sin`, which expects radians. You should remove the line in the program that computes the square root and replace it by a line that computes `sind`. You will need to change the scale factor so it is large enough to show the curve well.

7. Write a program that simulates a baseball being hit. The batter stands at home base, which is at the position $x = 0$, $y = 4$. The reason y starts off as 4 is to represent an initial height of 4 feet off the ground when the ball is hit. The user is asked to give the speed with which the ball leaves the bat, in feet per second. For example, if the ball is hit at a 45 degree angle, it would be hit at the same speed in the x and y directions, for example, at 50 feet per second in both the x and y directions. If the ball is goes straight up, the speed in the x direction is 0, but the speed in the upward (y) direction might be 60 feet per second. A "line drive" is a hit with little y velocity, for example, 10 feet per second, but a fast x velocity, for example, 100 feet per second. The position of the ball is plotted each tenth of a second. The program should contain a loop, which plots each position of the ball using `drawdot`. Each time through the loop the ball should move to the right by its x velocity multiplied by a tenth (corresponding the passage of a tenth of a second) and should move up by its y velocity multiplied by a tenth. Each time through the loop the y velocity should be decreased because of gravity. This decrease should be one tenth of the gravitational constant which is 32 (the units are feet per second per second). Eventually the y velocity will become negative and the baseball will start falling. When the ball reaches ground (y becomes zero or less), the loop should exit. After the loop exits, the program should print out how far the ball was hit (the final x value) and how high it went (the maximum value that y reached).

8. Make the program from project 7 into a game in which the player tries to "catch" the ball. Draw the player as a box on the screen that is 7 feet (pixels) on a side. The box sits on the bottom edge of the screen. The user can move this box from left to right as follows: j (move left 3 feet),

J (move left 20 feet), k (move right 3 feet), K (move right 20 feet). If the *x* position of the center of the box is within 5 feet of the ball when it hits the ground, the program announces that the player caught the ball. Otherwise it announces that the player did not catch the ball. Your program should begin with a start-up screen that explains the game to the user. The user should be able to hit many balls and try to catch them. The game should quit when the user types q.

CHAPTER 7

Subprograms

Chapter 3 introduced you to procedures; you learned how to use them to write separate program parts corresponding to the individual steps in a problem solution. We have not used procedures extensively because we have not yet discussed how to pass information between individual procedures, or between procedures and the main program. So far, our procedures can only manipulate data that are stored locally.

Chapter 3 also introduced you to functions. A function returns a single result. You saw how to write expressions that call Turing's predefined functions (for example, sqrt), and how functions could be used to facilitate structured design.

Procedures and functions taken together are called *subprograms*, which is the subject of this chapter.

This chapter introduces a very important concept in programming: the use of parameters. In this chapter you will see that parameters provide a convenient way to pass information to and from a subprogram. Parameters make procedures and functions more versatile because they enable a subprogram to manipulate different data each time that it is called. For example, sqrt(X) computes the value of its parameter X; whereas, sqrt(Y) computes the value of its parameter Y.

Our goal throughout this course will be to use procedures and functions as building blocks of larger program systems. As you progress through the course, your programming skills and own personal *library* of procedures and functions will grow. You should be able to reuse procedures and functions written for earlier applications in new programs.

7.1 Introduction to Parameter Lists

We can make an analogy between a carefully designed program that uses procedures and functions and a stereo system. Each stereo component is an independent device that performs a specific operation. The stereo receiver and compact disk (CD) player are "black boxes" that we connect together. We know the purpose of each component, but we have no idea what electronic parts are used inside each box or how they function, nor do we need to know this in order to use the stereo system.

Information in the form of electronic signals is sent back and forth between these components over wires. If you look at the rear of a stereo receiver, you will find that some connection points or plugs are marked as inputs and others are marked as outputs. The wires attached to the plugs marked inputs carry electronic signals into the receiver, where they are processed. (These signals may come from a cassette deck, tuner, or CD player). New electronic signals are generated by the receiver. These signals come out of the receiver from the plugs marked as outputs and go to the speakers or back to the cassette deck for recording.

Currently, we know how to design the separate components (procedures) of a programming system, but we don't know how to pass data between the main program and a procedure that we write. In this chapter, we will learn how to use *parameter lists* to provide communication paths between the main program and its subprograms (or between two subprograms).

Actual Parameter Lists

Each procedure call statement has two parts: a procedure name and an actual parameter list. Similarly, in the put statement

```
put X, Y
```

the *actual parameter list* is X, Y, so there are two *actual parameters*, X and Y, whose values are passed into procedure put. We know that put displays the values of X and Y.

In the get statement

```
get V, W
```

the actual parameters are V and W. In this case, the statement reads data values into these variables. The data type of each variable determines what kind of value is read.

The actual parameters are treated differently in these two statements. In the first call statement, the values of X and Y are passed into procedure put and the procedure displays these values. Since the procedure does not change the values of X and Y, they are considered *procedure inputs*. In the second statement, the execution of get changes the contents of V and W. Because get sends values back to the calling program, V and W are considered *procedure outputs*. Figure 7.1 is a block diagram of a procedure with input and output parameters.

FIGURE 7.1   Procedure with Inputs and Outputs

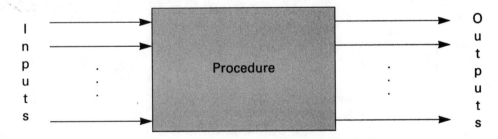

Formal Parameter Lists

The put and get statements differ from procedures that you will write in two important respects. For these two procedures, the number of actual parameters may vary from one call to the next, and the data type of a particular actual parameter (say the first) may also vary from one call to the next. For each procedure that we write, the number of actual parameters must be the same each time it is called, and the data type of a particular parameter must always be the same. Besides these differences, each procedure we write requires parentheses around the list of actual parameters, while get and put do not use parentheses.

How do we tell the Turing compiler the number of procedure parameters and the type of each parameter? The answer is through the formal parameter list.

Procedure ReportSumAve in Fig. 7.2 computes and displays the Sum and Average of two type real values that are passed into the procedure as procedure inputs. The *formal parameter list*

```
(Num1, Num2 : real)
```

tells the Turing compiler the number of parameters being processed (two), the data type of each parameter (both type real), and the names that we will use in place of the actual parameter names in the procedure body (Num1 for the first parameter and Num2 for the second). We use the *formal parameters*, Num1 and Num2, in the procedure body to describe what we want done to the actual parameters. The actual parameters are not known when the procedure is written but are determined when the procedure call statement executes.

FIGURE 7.2   Procedure to Display Sum and Average

```
procedure ReportSumAve (Num1, Num2 : real)

    % Compute and display the sum and average of Num1
    % and Num2.
    % Pre : Num1 and Num2 are defined.
    % Post: The sum and average value of Num1 and Num2
    %        are computed and displayed
    var Sum : real                  % Sum of Num1, Num2
    var Average : real              % Average of Num1, Num2
    Sum := Num1 + Num2
    Average := Sum / 2.0
    put "The sum is ", Sum :4:2
    put "The average is ", Average :4:2
end ReportSumAve
```

Parameter Correspondence

Procedure ReportSumAve begins with a lengthy comment that describes the procedure's operations. We will discuss this comment further at the end of this section.

There are two local variables declared in the procedure, Sum and Average. The statements

```
Sum := Num1 + Num2
Average := Sum / 2.0
```

assign values to these local variables as follows: the sum of the values passed into parameters Num1 and Num2 is stored in Sum and their average is stored in Average. For the procedure call statement ReportSumAve (6.5, 3.5) the formal parameter Num1 is passed the value 6.5 and the formal parameter Num2 is passed the value 3.5. The value assigned to Sum is 10.0 and the value assigned to Average is 5.0. These two values are displayed. The correspondence between the actual and formal parameters is shown next.

Actual Parameter	Formal Parameter
6.5	Num1
3.5	Num2

For the procedure call statement

```
ReportSumAve (X, Y)
```

the value of X is passed to formal parameter Num1 and the value of Y is passed to formal parameter Num2.

Actual Parameter	Formal Parameter
X	Num1
Y	Num2

Figure 7.3 shows the main program data area and the procedure data area after the procedure call statement above executes. The values 8.0 and 10.0 are passed into the formal parameters Num1 and Num2, respectively. The local procedure variables Sum and Average are initially undefined; the execution of the procedure body changes the values of these variables to 18.0 and 9.0, respectively.

FIGURE 7.3   Data Areas at Call of ReportSumAve (X, Y)

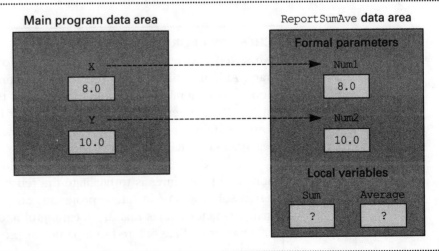

Procedure `ReportSumAve` can compute and display the sum and average of any pair of type `real` numbers. We can get the procedure to operate on a different pair of numbers by simply changing the parameter list. The procedure call statement

```
ReportSumAve (Y, X)
```

would generate the same results as the one above; however, in this case formal parameter `Num1` corresponds to actual parameter `Y` and formal parameter `Num2` corresponds to actual parameter `X`.

Actual Parameter	Formal Parameter
Y	Num1
X	Num2

The Procedure Data Area

Each time a procedure call statement is executed, an area of memory is allocated for storage of that procedure's data. Included in the procedure data area are storage cells for any local variables or constants that may be declared in the procedure. The procedure data area is erased when the procedure terminates; it is re-created empty (all values undefined) when the procedure is called again.

Illegal Parameter Substitution Errors

The data type of each actual parameter must be assignment compatible with the data type of its corresponding formal parameter; otherwise, a `"wrong parameter type"` syntax error occurs. How does the Turing compiler determine whether an actual parameter has a correct data type? The Turing compiler knows the required data type for each actual parameter because a procedure's declaration must precede its first call. The formal parameter list (in the procedure declaration) specifies the data type of each procedure parameter.

PROGRAM
STYLE

CHOOSING FORMAL PARAMETER NAMES

We stated above that the names used for formal parameters are arbitrary. Although this is true, you should continue to follow the convention of picking names that help to document the use of the formal parameter. Remember that the correspondence between an actual and a formal parameter is determined solely by position in the parameter lists, regardless of what names are used.

As we discussed earlier, one of the main reasons for having functions and procedures is to facilitate the reuse of previously written and tested subprograms in future programs. So you should try to pick formal parameter names that are meaningful and generic rather than specific names that are tailored to a particular program application.

Preconditions and Postconditions

The multiple-line comment at the beginning of procedure `ReportSumAve` documents its operation. The comment line

```
% Pre : Num1 and Num2 are defined.
```

describes the condition that must be true before the procedure is called; this condition is known as the *precondition*. The lines

```
% Post: The sum and average value of Num1 and Num2
%       are computed and displayed.
```

describe the condition that must be true after the procedure execution is completed; this condition is called the *postcondition*.

The use of explicit preconditions and postconditions provides valuable documentation to another programmer who might want to use the procedure. For example, the precondition tells the programmer what must be done before the procedure is called. In this case, two data values must be assigned or read into the actual procedure parameters prior to calling `ReportSumAve`. The postcondition tells the programmer the effect of the procedure's execution on its parameters. In this case, their sum and average are computed and displayed.

You might say that the preconditions and postconditions serve as an informal contract between the procedure and any program that uses it. The precondition indicates any expectations the procedure may have with respect to its parameters. The postcondition tells what the procedure does and what will happen to its parameters if the precondition is met. All bets are off if the precondition is not met, therefore, the calling program must check to make sure that all actual parameters satisfy the procedure preconditions before each call.

Exercises for Section 7.1

Self-Check

1. What is the primary purpose of procedure parameters?
2. Consider the procedure `Cube` shown below.

```
procedure Cube (N : int)
    put N, " cubed is " ..
    put N ** 3
end Cube
```

a. What is displayed when the procedure call statement

```
Cube (3)
```

executes?

b. If M is 5, what happens when the procedure call statement
    Cube (M)
executes?

c. What is the value of the actual parameter M after the procedure executes?

d. Where should M be declared and what should its data type be?

3. Write pre and post conditions for
    a. procedure Cube in self-check exercise 2 above.
    b. the procedure described in programming exercise 1 below.

Programming

1. Write a procedure that displays the positive difference of its two formal parameters, X and Y, i.e., if X is larger or the same, the positive difference is X – Y; if Y is larger, the positive difference is Y – X.

7.2 Functions: Subprograms that Return a Single Result

In Section 3.8, we introduced functions and discussed how functions return a single result to the program that calls them. We also showed how to call a function through a function designator in an expression. The expression part of the assignment statement below is a function designator that calls the predefined function sqrt.

```
Z := sqrt (X * Y)
```

Variable Z gets the function result after function exit occurs. Figure 7.4 is a block diagram of a function showing its inputs and its single output.

FIGURE 7.4   **Function with Multiple Inputs and a Single Output**

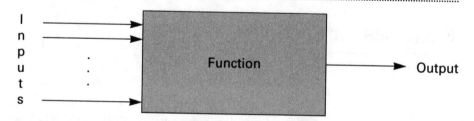

In Section 3.8 we discussed how we can simplify numeric computations by using Turing's built-in functions in writing arithmetic expressions. We also showed how to use two of these functions, exp and ln, to raise a value to a power. Because this is a relatively common operation, it would be useful to write our own library function that does this. Figure 7.5 shows function Exponent, which raises its first argument to the power indicated by its second argument.

FIGURE 7.5   Function Exponent

```
function Exponent (U, V : real) : real
    % Return first argument raised to the power
    % specified by its second argument
    % Pre : U and V are defined
    % Post: Return U raised to the power V
    if U = 0.0 then
        result 0.0
    elsif U > 0.0 then
        result exp(V * ln(U))
    else
        put "*** Error in first parameter of Exponent"
    end if
end Exponent
```

The function heading indicates that `Exponent` has two type `real` parameters (or arguments); the identifier following the colon tells us that `Exponent` returns a type `real` result. Turing defines a function result by using a `result` statement.

The `if` statement in the function body causes one of three statements to execute. If the value passed into `U` is zero, the `result` statement

```
result 0.0
```

sets the function result to zero. If the value passed into `U` is positive, the `result` statement

```
result exp(V * ln(U))
```

calls Turing's built-in functions `exp` and `ln` to calculate the desired result and assign it to `Exponent`. The logarithm of a negative number is not defined, so the `put` statement outputs an error message. If we have a main program with three type `real` variables, `X`, `Y`, and `Z`, the main program statement

```
Z := Exponent(X, Y)
```

calls `Exponent` to raise `X` to the power `Y`. Upon return from the function, the function result is substituted for the function designator above and is assigned to `Z`.

Figure 7.6 shows the main program and function data areas after the function call above but before the function body begins execution. For the particular values of `X` and `Y` shown (`3.0` and `2.5`), the function execution defines the function result as `15.59`. Figure 7.7 shows the program and function data areas after the function body finishes execution but before the function return. Notice that there is no connection between main program variable `Z` and the memory cell in `Exponent`'s data area that represents the function result. The fact that the function result will later be assigned to `Z` by the main program does not affect the function's execution.

FIGURE 7.6   Data Areas After Function Call

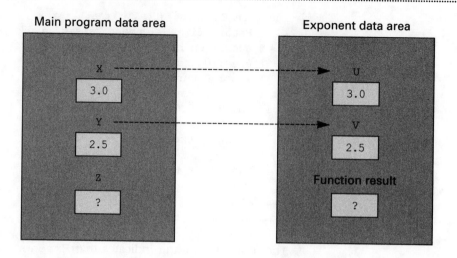

FIGURE 7.7   Data Areas After Function Execution

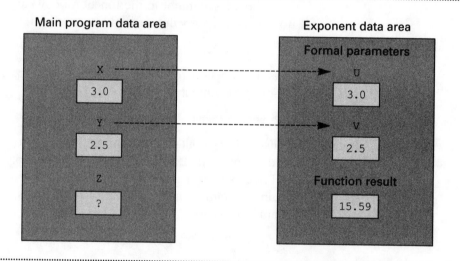

In the Turing language, you would not need to use the Exponent function because the ** operator can be used instead; for example, X ** Y computes X to the Y power. In some programming languages such as Pascal and the C language, there is no exponentiation operator. When using such a language, it is common to write an exponentiation function.

EXAMPLE 7.1

In Section 4.5 we discussed how we might use a function named GetFirst in a program that finds the alphabetically first letter in a sequence of three letters. Function GetFirst returns the alphabetically smallest of its two arguments and is shown in Fig. 7.8.

FIGURE 7.8   Function GetFirst

```
function GetFirst (Str1, Str2 : string) : string
   % Return the alphabetically smallest of its two
   % arguments
   % Pre : Str1 and Str2 are defined
   % Post: If Str1 < Str2, the result is Str1
   %       otherwise, the result is Str2

   if Str1 < Str2 then
      result Str1
   else
      result Str2
   end if
end GetFirst
```

The function heading tells us that GetFirst has two type string parameters (Str1 and Str2) and returns a type string result. The function body consists of an if statement that compares its parameter values. Each time the function is called, the if statement executes exactly one of the result statements below.

```
result Str1
result Str2
```

These statements determine the function result (either Str1 or Str2).

If St1, St2, and St3 are the main program variables being compared, we can call GetFirst using the assignment statement below

```
% Save the alphabetically first of St1 and St2 in
% AlphaFirst
AlphaFirst := GetFirst(St1, St2)
```

The actual parameters are St1 and St2, so the alphabetically first of St1 and St2 is returned and stored in AlphaFirst. In the next call to GetFirst

```
% Save the alphabetically first of St3 and
% AlphaFirst
AlphaFirst := GetFirst(St3, AlphaFirst)
```

the actual parameters are St3 and AlphaFirst, so the alphabetically first of St3 and the current value of AlphaFirst is returned and stored in AlphaFirst. The fact that the function result will be stored in AlphaFirst after the function return does not affect the function's execution. The final value of AlphaFirst will be the alphabetically first of St1, St2, and St3.

We will leave the trace of the first call to GetFirst as an exercise. The parameter correspondence for the second call, GetFirst (St3, AlphaFirst), follows:

Actual Parameter	Formal Parameter
St3	Str1
AlphaFirst	Str2

FIGURE 7.9   Data Areas for Main Program and GetFirst

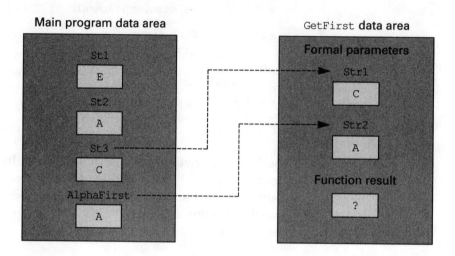

Figure 7.9 shows the main program data area and the function data area right after this function call assuming main program variables St3 and AlphaFirst contain C and A, respectively. Because C < A is false, function GetFirst executes the result statement

```
result Str2
```

which defines the function result as A. This result is returned and substituted for the function designator in the main program statement that called the function.

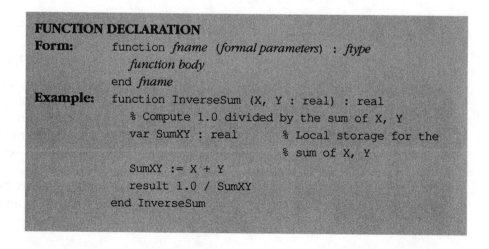

FUNCTION DECLARATION

Form: function *fname* (*formal parameters*) : *ftype*
          function body
          end *fname*

Example: function InverseSum (X, Y : real) : real
          % Compute 1.0 divided by the sum of X, Y
          var SumXY : real   % Local storage for the
                                  % sum of X, Y

          SumXY := X + Y
          result 1.0 / SumXY
          end InverseSum

Interpretation: The function *fname* is declared. The *formal parameters* are enclosed in parentheses. The identifiers that are declared in the *local declaration section* are local to the function and are defined only during the execution of the function. A formal parameter cannot be declared as a local identifier.

The *function body* describes the data manipulation to be performed by the function using the formal parameter names in the description. When a formal parameter is referenced during function execution, the value of the corresponding actual parameter is manipulated.

Function *fname* returns a single result of type *ftype* in the following way. Each time the function is called, a statement of the form

```
result expression
```

must execute. This statement causes the function to stop executing and to produce the expression's value as the function result.

Note 1: The identifier *ftype* must be the name of a standard data type (`int`, `real`, `boolean`, or `string`) or any of the other types that will be defined later.

Note 2: If there are no parameters, omit the *formal parameters* and the parentheses.

FUNCTION DESIGNATOR

Form: *fname* (*actual parameters*)
Example: `InverseSum(3.0, Z)`

Interpretation: The *actual parameters* are enclosed in parentheses. When function `fname` is called into execution, the first actual parameter corresponds to the first formal parameter, the second actual parameter corresponds to the second formal parameter, and so on. A function designator must always appear within an expression; after execution, the function result replaces the function designator in that expression.

Note: If there are no parameters, omit the *actual parameters* and the parentheses.

Writing a Driver Program to Test a Function

In the next example, we will write a function that computes income tax owed and a small program whose sole purpose is to call and test that function. A program that is used to test the operation of a function or procedure is called a *driver* program.

EXAMPLE 7.2

Figure 4.19 contains an `if` statement used by your tax accountant to determine the income tax due for a particular salary based on the tax table shown in Table 4.9. Since this table appears in many different programs, your accountant has decided to place it in function `FindTax` (see Fig. 7.10). The assignment statement

```
MyTax := FindTax (MySalary)
```

calls function `FindTax`, passing the value of `MySalary` into input parameter `Salary`. If the value passed into `Salary` is within the range of the table, the tax owed is computed and returned as the function result; otherwise, −1.0 is returned as the function result.

FIGURE 7.10 Driver Program with Function FindTax

```
% The "Driver" program
% Test function FindTax

var MySalary : real              % Input - salary
var MyTax    : real              % Output - tax

function FindTax (Salary : real) : real
    % Return tax amount owed for a salary < $15000
    % Pre : Salary is assigned a value
    % Post: If Salary is within range, return the tax
    %       owed; otherwise, return -1.0
    const MaxSalary := 15000.00    % Maximum salary for table
    const OutOfRange := -1.0       % "Tax" for an out-of-range
                                   % salary

    if Salary < 0.0 then
        result OutOfRange          % Salary too small
    elsif Salary < 1500.00 then    % First range
        result 0.15 * Salary
    elsif Salary < 3000.00 then    % Second range
        result (Salary - 1500.00)  * 0.16 + 225.00
    elsif Salary < 5000.00 then    % Third range
        result (Salary - 3000.00)  * 0.18 + 465.00
    elsif Salary < 8000.00 then    % Fourth range
        result (Salary - 5000.00)  * 0.20 + 825.00
    elsif Salary <= MaxSalary then % Fifth range
        result (Salary - 8000.00)  * 0.25 + 1425.00
    else
        result OutOfRange          % Salary too large
    end if
end FindTax

put "Enter a salary less than or equal to $15000.00> $"
```

```
get MySalary
MyTax := FindTax (MySalary)
if MyTax >= 0.0 then
    put "Tax on $", MySalary :4:2, " is $", MyTax :4:2
else
    put "Salary $", MySalary :4:2, "is out of table range"
end if
```

```
Enter a salary less than or equal to $15000.00> $6000.00
The tax on $6000.00 is $1025.00
```

VALIDATING INPUT PARAMETERS

The `if` statement in function `FindTax` tests for an invalid value of the input parameter `Salary` before performing the tax computation. You should make sure that all procedures validate their input parameters; there are no guarantees that the values passed to an input parameter will be meaningful.

COHESIVE SUBPROGRAMS

Function `FindTax` is concerned only with the tax computation. It neither reads in a value for `Salary` nor displays the computed result. The result is returned to the calling program, which may display it or pass it on to a procedure that prints results. Note that `FindTax` does not display an error message in the event that the value passed to `Salary` is out-of-range. It simply returns a special value (-1.0) to indicate this, and the calling program displays the error message.

Subprograms that perform a single operation are called *cohesive subprograms*. It is good programming style to write cohesive subprograms. This helps to keep each function or procedure relatively compact and easy to read, write, and debug.

WRITING DRIVER PROGRAMS TO TEST SUBPROGRAMS

The main program body in Fig. 7.10 consists of a statement for data entry, an assignment statement with a function designator in its expression part, and an `if` statement to display the function result. Its sole purpose is to test function `FindTax`. Such a program is called a *driver program.*

Experienced programmers often use driver programs to pretest functions and procedures. Generally, the small investment in time and effort required to write a short driver program will pay off by reducing the time spent debugging a large program system containing several subprograms.

Boolean Functions

We have seen examples of functions that return type `real` or type `string` results. We can also write functions that return type `int` or type `boolean` results (boolean functions). Boolean functions are sometimes used as conditions in `if` statements.

EXAMPLE 7.3

You have written an algorithm that contains the following decision step. For the purposes of this example, we have no interest in the details of the three procedures called in the `if` statement, but are just interested in making sure that the correct procedure is called.

```
if Ch is a letter then
    Call procedure ProcessLetter
elsif Ch is a digit character then
    Call procedure ProcessDigit
else
    Call procedure ProcessSpecial
end if
```

There are many ways to implement this decision. One would be to use a `case` statement with separate case labels for letters, for digits, and for special characters. Another approach is to write the `if` statement below which uses functions `IsLetter` and `IsDigit` to determine whether `Ch` is a letter or a digit.

```
if IsLetter(Ch) then
    ProcessLetter (Ch)
elsif IsDigit(Ch) then
    ProcessDigit (Ch)
else
    ProcessSpecial (Ch)
end if
```

The function designator `IsLetter` (Ch) is a boolean expression. It has value `true` if `Ch` is a letter, and it has value `false` if `Ch` is not a letter. Similarly, the `boolean` expression `IsDigit` (Ch) has value `true` if `Ch` is a digit character, and it has value `false` otherwise.

Figure 7.11 shows functions `IsLetter` and `IsDigit`. Each function contains a single statement whose result is the value of a boolean expression. (The function `IsLetter` will work correctly on any computer that supports the usual (ASCII) representation of letters. However, some computers, such as IBM mainframes, use another representation (EBCDIC), in which case a longer version of `IsLetter` (not shown here) should be used.)

FIGURE 7.11 Functions IsLetter and IsDigit

```
function IsLetter (Ch : string) : boolean
    % Return true when its argument is a letter
    % otherwise, return false
    result ("A" <= Ch and Ch <= "Z") or
            ("a" <= Ch and Ch <= "z")
end IsLetter

function IsDigit (Ch : string) : boolean
    % Return true when its argument is a digit character
    % otherwise, return false
    result "0" <= Ch and Ch <= "9"
end IsDigit
```

Exercises for Section 7.2

Self-Check

1. Why is the `if` statement currently in `FindTax` better than the one sketched below?

   ```
   if Salary < 0.0 then
       put Salary :4:2, " is out of range"
           % Salary too small
       ...
   else
       put (Salary :4:2, " is out of range"
           % Salary too large
   end if
   ```

2. What does the following function do?

   ```
   function Hypot (X, Y : real) : real
   result sqrt (X ** 2 + Y ** 2)
   end Hypot
   ```

   Write a statement that calls this function with arguments A and B and stores the function result in C.

3. Write pre and post conditions for function `Hypot` shown in exercise 2 above.

Programming

1. Write a driver program that tests function `FindTax` for all values of `Salary` from `-100.00` to `15,100.00` in increments of `500.00`.
2. Write a function that computes the absolute difference of its two arguments, where the absolute difference of A and B is A − B if A is greater than or equal to B and B − A if B is greater than A.

3. Write a function that raises a real number (X) to an integer power (N) by multiplying X by itself N times (use a `for` loop). Will your function work for negative values of X or N? **Hint:** To make your function work for negative values of N use `abs(N)` as the `final` expression in the for loop. Then use the fact that $X^N = 1.0 / X^{-N}$ to compute the correct result when N is negative.

7.3 Value Parameters and Variable Parameters

So far we know how to pass inputs into a procedure or a function and how to return a single result from a function. In this section, we will learn how to return one or more results from a procedure.

When a procedure call executes, the computer allocates memory space in the procedure data area for each formal parameter. The value of each actual parameter is stored in the memory cell(s) allocated to its corresponding formal parameter. The procedure body can manipulate this value. Next, we will discuss how a procedure returns outputs to the program (or procedure) that calls it.

Procedure `ComputeSumAve` in Fig. 7.12 is similar to `ReportSumAve`. The differences are that `ComputeSumAve` has four parameters: two for input (`Num1` and `Num2`) and two for output (`Sum` and `Average`). Procedure `ComputeSumAve` computes the sum and average of its inputs but does not display them. Instead, these values are assigned to formal parameters `Sum` and `Average` and returned as procedure results to the calling program.

FIGURE 7.12   Procedure to Compute Sum and Average

```
procedure ComputeSumAve (Num1, Num2 : real,
                              var Sum, Average : real)
   % Compute the sum and average of Num1 and Num2
   % Pre : Num1 and Num2 are assigned values
   % Post: The sum and average of Num1 and Num2 are
   %         computed and returned

   Sum := Num1 + Num2
   Average := Sum / 2.0
end ComputeSumAve
```

To see how this works, assume that the main program declares X, Y, Sum, and Mean as type `real` variables (values undefined). The procedure call statement

```
ComputeSumAve (X, Y, Sum, Mean)
```

sets up the parameter correspondence below.

Actual Parameter	Formal Parameter
X	Num1
Y	Num2
Sum	Sum
Mean	Average

The values of X and Y are determined by the main program and passed into the procedure when it is first called. These values are associated with formal parameters Num1 and Num2. The statement

```
Sum := Num1 + Num2
```

stores the sum of the procedure inputs in the main program variable Sum (the third actual parameter). The statement

```
Average := Sum / 2.0
```

divides the value stored in the main program variable Sum by 2.0 and stores the quotient in the main program variable Mean (the fourth actual parameter). Figure 7.13 shows the main program and procedure data areas just before the procedure body begins execution, and Fig. 7.14 shows these data areas just after the procedure body finishes execution. The procedure execution sets the values of main program variables Sum and Mean to 18.0 and 9.0, respectively.

FIGURE 7.13   Data Areas before Procedure Execution

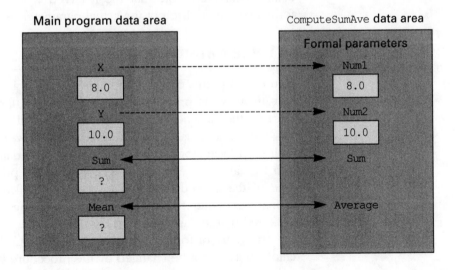

FIGURE 7.14   Data Areas after Procedure Execution

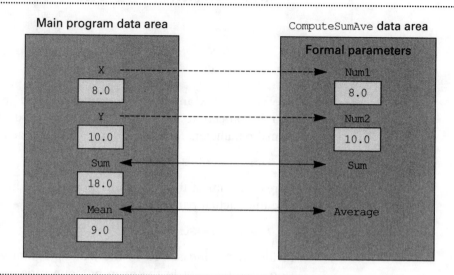

In Fig. 7.12, the reserved word `var` precedes the declaration of formal parameters `Sum` and `Average`. This tells the compiler to treat them as *variable parameters*. The compiler stores the memory address of the actual variable that corresponds to each variable parameter in the procedure data area. Through this address, the procedure can access the actual variable in the calling program and change its value, or use its value, in a computation. In Fig. 7.13, this relationship is shown by using a double headed arrow to connect each variable parameter with its corresponding actual parameter. Note that the reserved word `var` appears only in the formal parameter list, not the actual parameter list.

Protection Afforded by Value Parameters

Figure 7.13 points out an important difference between formal parameters that are used as procedure inputs and those used as procedure outputs. Because they are not preceded by the reserved word `var`, formal parameters `Num1` and `Num2` are considered *value parameters*. As such, they have their own local storage cells in the procedure data area. The value passed into formal parameter `Num1` is stored in the procedure data area at the time of the procedure call, and there is no further connection between formal parameter `Num1` and its corresponding actual parameter. This is indicated by the dashed line in Fig. 7.13.

The value of formal parameter `Num1` or `Num2` can be used in computations but cannot be changed by the procedure body. For example, if we add the statement

```
Num1 := -5.0
```

to the end of procedure `ComputeSumAve`, the compiler would produce an error message.

By making an input parameter a value parameter, we protect its value and prevent it from being changed by the procedure's execution. If we forget to declare an output parameter as a variable formal parameter, then its value (not address) will be stored locally.

PROGRAM
STYLE

> **WRITING FORMAL PARAMETER LISTS**
> In Fig. 7.12, the formal parameter list
>
> ```
> (Num1, Num2 : real,
>  var Sum, Average : real)
> ```
>
> is written on two lines to improve program readability. Generally, we will follow the practice shown here in writing formal parameter lists. Input parameters will be listed first and any output parameters will be listed last. The order of the actual parameters in the procedure call must correspond to the order of the formal parameters.

Passing Information between Procedures

So far you have seen two similar procedures, `ReportSumAve` and `ComputeSumAve`, and you have learned how to pass information between a main program and a procedure. Sometimes we need to pass information between procedures. For example, we might want to pass the results returned by `ComputeSumAve` to another procedure, say `Correlate`, for further processing.

Let's assume that the main program variables `X` and `Y` are passed into procedure `ComputeSumAve`. We can declare two more main program variables, say `TempSum` and `TempAve`, to hold the procedure results. The following procedure call statements

```
ComputeSumAve (X, Y, TempSum, TempAve)
Correlate (TempSum, TempAve)
```

pass the outputs of `ComputeSumAve` (`TempSum` and `TempAve`) to `Correlate` for further processing. Frequently, we will use main program variables to facilitate the exchange of information between procedures.

When to Use a Variable or a Value Parameter

You may be wondering how to decide when to use a variable parameter and when to use a value parameter. Some rules of thumb follow:

- If information is to be passed into a procedure and does not have to be returned, or passed out of the procedure, then the formal parameter representing that information should ordinarily be a value parameter (e.g. `Num1` and `Num2` in Figs. 7.2 and 7.12). A parameter used in this way is called an `input` parameter.

- If information is to be returned to the calling program from a procedure, then the formal parameter representing that information must be a variable parameter (e.g., Sum and Average in Fig. 7.12). A procedure used in this way is called an *output* parameter.
- If information is to be passed into a procedure, perhaps modified, and a new value returned, then the formal parameter representing that information must be a variable parameter. A parameter used in this way is called an *input/output* parameter.

Although we make a distinction between output parameters and input/output parameters, Turing treats them in the same way. Both kinds of parameters must be declared as variable parameters, so the address of the corresponding actual parameter is stored in the procedure data area when the procedure is called. For an input/output parameter, we assume there is some meaningful data in the actual parameter before the procedure executes; for an output parameter, we make no such assumption.

Passing Expressions to Value Parameters

You can use an assignment compatible expression (or variable, or constant) as an actual parameter corresponding to a value parameter. For example, the procedure call statement

```
ComputeSumAve (X + Y, 10, MySum, MyAve)
```

calls ComputeSumAve to compute the sum (returned in MySum) and the average (returned in MyAve) of the expression X + Y and the integer 10. However, only variables can correspond to variable parameters, so MySum and MyAve must be declared as type real variables in the calling program. This restriction is imposed because an actual parameter corresponding to a variable parameter may be modified when the procedure executes; it is illogical to allow a procedure to change the value of either a constant or an expression.

Writing Functions as Procedures

Now that we know how to return results from a procedure, we can write a function as a procedure with a single var parameter. Figure 7.15 shows function Exponent from Fig. 7.5 rewritten as procedure ProcExponent. ProcExponent returns a single result through the var parameter Exponent. If the main program declares X, Y, and Z as type real variables, you could use the procedure call statement

```
ProcExponent (X, Y, Z)
```

to save in Z the value of X raised to the power Y.

FIGURE 7.15   Procedure ProcExponent

```
procedure ProcExponent ( U, V : real,
                           var Exponent : real)
   % Return the value of U raised to the power V
   % through Exponent
   % Pre : U and V are defined
   % Post: Exponent has the value of U raised to the
   % power V
   if U = 0.0 then
      Exponent := 0.0
   elsif U > 0.0 then
      Exponent := exp(V * ln(U))
   else
      Exponent := 1.0 / exp(V * ln(-U))
   end if
end ProcExponent
```

In general, you should avoid doing this and use functions whenever a procedure computes and returns a single result. Use procedures for subprograms that return any other number of results. If a subprogram performs input/output operations, it should be implemented as a procedure even when it only returns a single result. The only exception would be a function that displayed an error message for invalid data and otherwise returned a single result.

Software Engineering and Function Side-effects

Until now, we have written all functions using value parameters. This allows us to use an expression as a function argument. You may be wondering about using variable parameters with functions. If a function has a variable parameter, it would be possible to modify this parameter, thereby returning a second result when the function executes. A result returned in this way is called a function *side-effect*. Function side-effects are very undesirable, and it is difficult to debug programs that have them because they are not expected. Therefore, we recommend all function parameters be value parameters to prevent the occurrence of a function side-effect.

Multiple Calls to a Procedure

In this section we will study two procedures that would generally be called more than once in a given program. Each procedure processes different data values each time it is called. The use of procedure parameters makes this possible.

EXAMPLE 7.4

Procedure MakeChange (see Fig. 7.16) can be used to determine the quantity of a particular denomination of bills or coins given as change. The input parameter ChangeDenom specifies the value of each change unit (for example, 10.00 for ten-dollar bills, 0.10 for dimes). The input/output parameter ChangeNeeded is passed the amount of change that must be made. The procedure determines how many units (NumUnits) of a particular change denomination should be dispensed. The value returned through ChangeNeeded is the amount of change remaining after the change is dispensed. For example, if the value passed into ChangeNeeded is 20.45 and ChangeDenom is 10.00, the value of floor(2.045), or 2, is returned through NumUnits and the value of (20.45 – 20.00) or 0.45 is returned through ChangeNeeded.

FIGURE 7.16

Procedure MakeChange

```
procedure MakeChange ( ChangeDenom : real,
                       var ChangeNeeded : real,
                       var NumUnits : int)
  % Determine the number of units (NumUnits) of
  % change of a particular denomination (ChangeDenom)
  % to dispense when making change for amount
  % ChangeNeeded. Also return the remaining amount
  % of change left to make in ChangeNeeded.
  % Post: NumUnits is the number of units of change
  %        to dispense and ChangeNeeded is reduced by
  %        the change amount given

  NumUnits := floor (ChangeNeeded/ChangeDenom)
  ChangeNeeded := ChangeNeeded - (NumUnits * ChangeDenom)
end MakeChange
```

If the main program declares Change as type real and NumTens as type int, the second statement below

```
Change := 20.45
MakeChange (10.00, Change, NumTens)
put "Number of tens is ", NumTens
put "Change left to dispense is ", Change :4:2
```

calls MakeChange to determine how many ten dollar bills to dispense in change and the amount of Change remaining. The put statements display the output lines

```
Number of tens dispensed is 2
Change left to dispense is 0.45
```

Figure 7.17 shows the main program and procedure data areas just after the procedure call; Figure 7.18 shows the main program and procedure data areas just before the return from procedure `MakeChange`. These figures show that the procedure execution updates the value of Change (from `20.45` to `0.45`) and defines the value of `NumTens` as 2.

FIGURE 7.17 Data Areas before Execution of MakeChange

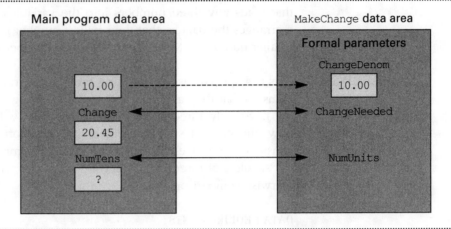

If the main program continues with the statements

```
MakeChange (0.10, Change, NumDimes)
put "Number of dimes is ", NumDimes
put "Change left to dispense is ", Change :3:2
```

where `NumDimes` is type `int`, the lines below would be displayed.

```
Number of dimes dispensed is 4
Change left to dispense is 0.05
```

FIGURE 7.18 Data Areas after Execution of MakeChange

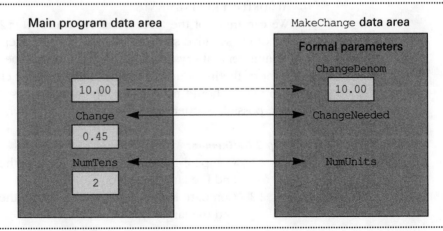

✖ Case Study:

Sorting Three Numbers

1. Problem

In many real-life and programming situations we wish to arrange a set of data so that it follows some numerical or alphabetical sequence. In programming, this is called the sorting problem. You won't be able to solve this problem for large data sets yet; however, you can write a program that reads any three numbers into the variables Num1, Num2, Num3 and rearranges the data so that the smallest number is stored in Num1, the next smaller number in Num2, and the largest number in Num3.

2. Analysis

This is a special case of a sorting problem: rearranging a collection of data items so that the values are either in increasing or decreasing order. Since we have only three items to be sorted, we will solve this special case now; the general sorting problem is a bit more complicated so we will consider it later. We will follow an approach similar to the one used to find the smallest of three letters (Section 4.5)—we will develop a sequence of pairwise comparisons.

DATA REQUIREMENTS

Problem Inputs
```
Num1, Num2, Num3 : real        % Three numbers
```

Problem Outputs
    The three numbers stored in increasing order in Num1, Num2, Num3

3. Design

INITIAL ALGORITHM
1. Read the three numbers into Num1, Num2, and Num3
2. Place the smallest number in Num1, the next smaller in Num2, and the largest number in Num3
3. Print Num1, Num2, and Num3

ALGORITHM REFINEMENTS
We can think of the three variables Num1, Num2, Num3 as representing a list of consecutive storage cells. To perform Step 2, we can compare pairs of numbers, always moving the smaller number in the pair closer to the front of the list (Num1) and the larger number closer to the end of the list (Num3). It should take three comparisons to sort the numbers in the list; one possible sequence of comparisons is shown here.

Step 2 Refinement
    2.1   Compare Num1 and Num2 and store the smaller number in Num1 and the larger number in Num2
    2.2   Compare Num1 and Num3 and store the smaller number in Num1 and the larger number in Num3

2.3   Compare Num2 and Num3 and store the smaller number in Num2 and the larger number in Num3

Table 7.1 traces this refinement for the input sequence: 8.0, 10.0, 6.0. The final order is correct.

TABLE 7.1   Trace of Step 2 Refinement for Data 8.0, 10.0, 6.0

Algorithm Step	Num1	Num2	Num3	Effect
	8.0	10.0	6.0	
2.1				Num1, Num2 are in order
2.2	6.0		8.0	Switch Num1 and Num3
2.3		8.0	10.0	Switch Num2 and Num3

The structure chart for step 2 of this algorithm is shown in Fig. 7.19. The data flow information for step 2.1 shows that Num1 and Num2 are used as both inputs and outputs. Since steps 2.1, 2.2, and 2.3 perform the same operation on different data, it would be a waste of time and effort to write a different procedure for each step. We will use one procedure, Order, to order any pair of numbers.

FIGURE 7.19   Structure Chart for Step 2 of Sorting Problem

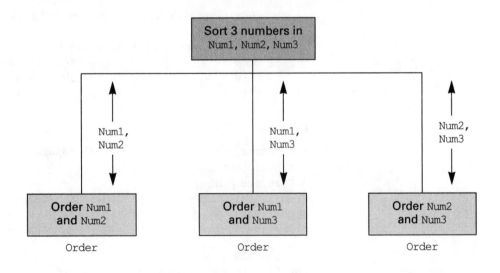

Implementation

The procedure call statement

```
Order (Num1, Num2)
```

can be used to perform Step 2.1 of the algorithm – store the smaller number in Num1 and the larger number in Num2. The complete program is shown in Fig. 7.20. The main program body contains three statements that call procedure `Order`:

```
Order (Num1, Num2)    % Order the data in Num1 and Num2
Order (Num1, Num3)    % Order the data in Num1 and Num3
Order (Num2, Num3)    % Order the data in Num2 and Num3
```

Since each of these statements contains a different actual parameter list, a different pair of variables will be manipulated each time the procedure is called.

FIGURE 7.20   **Program to Order Three Numbers**

```
% The "Sort3" program
% Read three numbers and sort them
% so that they are in increasing order

var Num1, Num2, Num3 : real % A list of three cells

procedure Order (var X, Y  : real)
    % Order a pair of numbers represented by X and
    % Y so that the smaller number is in X and the
    % larger number is in Y.
    % Pre : X and Y are assigned values.
    % Post: X is the smaller of the pair and Y is
    %       the larger.

    var Temp : real % Copy of number originally in X
    if X > Y then
        % Switch the values of X and Y
        Temp := X         % Store old X in Temp
        X := Y            % Store old Y in X
        Y := Temp         % Store old X in Y
    end if
end Order

put "Enter 3 numbers to be sorted separated by spaces> "
get Num1, Num2, Num3
% Sort the numbers
Order (Num1, Num2)        % Order the data in Num1 and Num2
Order (Num1, Num3)        % Order the data in Num1 and Num3
Order (Num2, Num3)        % Order the data in Num2 and Num3

% Print the results
put "The three numbers in order are:"
put Num1 :8:2, Num2 :8:2, Num3 :8:2


Enter 3 numbers to be sorted separated by spaces>
8.0 10.0 6.0
The three numbers in order are:
6.00    8.00    10.00
```

The body of procedure `Order` consists of the `if` statement from Fig. 4.9. The procedure heading contains the formal parameter list

```
(var X, Y : real)
```

which identifies `X` and `Y` as the formal parameters. `X` and `Y` are classified as input/output parameters because the procedure uses the current actual parameter values as inputs and may return new values.

The sequence of the actual parameters is most important. The first actual parameter is paired with the first formal parameter, the second actual parameter is paired with the second formal parameter, and so on. If the first procedure call statement in Fig. 7.20 were written as

```
Order (Num2, Num1)
```

the smaller number would be stored in `Num2` and the larger number in `Num1` instead of the other way around.   ✖

Exercises for Section 7.3

Self-Check

1. Trace the execution of procedure `MakeChange` when `ChangeNeeded` is `5.56` and `ChangeDenom` is `5.00`.
2. Show the output displayed by the program below in the form of a table of values for `X`, `Y`, and `Z`.

```
% The "Show" program

var W, X, Y, Z : int

procedure SumDiff (Num1, Num2 : int,
                       var Num3, Num4 : int)
    Num3 := Num1 + Num2
    Num4 := Num1 - Num2
end SumDiff

X := 5
Y := 3
Z := 7
W := 9
put "   X   Y   Z   W"
SumDiff (X, Y, Z, W)
put X :4, Y :4, Z :4, W :4
SumDiff (Y, X, Z, W)
put X :4, Y :4, Z :4, W :4
SumDiff (Z, W, Y, X)
put X :4, Y :4, Z :4, W :4
```

```
    SumDiff (Z, Z, X, Y)
    put X :4, Y :4, Z :4, W :4
    SumDiff (Y, Y, Y, W)
    put X :4, Y :4, Z :4, W :4
```

   a. Show the program output.
   b. Write the pre and post conditions for procedure SumDiff.
3. Trace the execution of the three procedure call statements

```
    Order (Num3, Num2)
    Order (Num3, Num1)
    Order (Num2, Num1)
```

   a. Trace the execution of the three procedure call statements
     for the data sets: 8.0, 10.0, 6.0 and 10.0, 8.0, 6.0.
   b. What is the effect of this sequence of procedure calls?
4. A procedure has four formal parameters: W, X, Y, and Z (all type real). During its execution the procedure stores the sum of W and X in Y and the product of W and X in Z. Which parameters are inputs and which are outputs?

Programming

1. Write a main program that reads in an amount of change to make and calls procedure MakeChange with different parameters to determine the number of twenties, tens, ones, quarters, dimes, and pennies to dispense as change.
2. Write a procedure that displays a table showing all powers of its first argument from zero through the power indicated by its second argument (a positive integer) without using the exponentiation operator **. The procedure should also return the sum of all values displayed. For example, if the first argument is 10 and the second argument is 3, the procedure should display 1, 10, 100, and 1000 and return 1111 as its result.
3. Write a procedure that raises its first parameter (type real) to the power indicated by its second parameter (a positive integer) without using the exponentiation operator **. Return the result through the third parameter.

7.4 Syntax Rules for Parameter Lists

This section formally presents the syntax rules for procedure declarations and procedure call statements with parameters. The displays that follow summarize these rules.

PROCEDURE DECLARATION (PROCEDURE WITH PARAMETERS)

Form: procedure *pname* (*formal parameters*)
                   procedure body
              end *pname*

Example: procedure Highlight (Ch : string,
                                    var NumStars : int)
                  % Display Ch between two asterisks and
                  % return the numbers of asterisks printed.
                  % Pre : Ch is defined
                  % Post: Return 3 in NumStars if Ch = Border
                  %   otherwise, return 2 in NumStars

                  const Border := "*"
                  put Border, Ch, Border
                  if Ch = Border then
                     NumStars := 3
                  else
                     NumStars := 2
                  end if
              end Highlight

Interpretation: The procedure pname is declared. The *formal parameters* are enclosed in parentheses. The identifiers that are declared in the procedure are local to the procedure and are defined only during the execution of the procedure. A formal parameter cannot be redeclared as a local identifier.

In this example, we could change the type of Ch to string(1) to emphasize that it is expected to receive a single character.

The *procedure body* describes the data manipulation to be performed by the procedure using the formal parameter names in the description. For a variable parameter, the procedure manipulates the corresponding actual parameter; for a value parameter, a local memory cell is initialized to the actual parameter's value, and the procedure is not allowed to alter this value.

PROCEDURE CALL STATEMENT (PROCEDURE WITH PARAMETERS)

Form: *pname (actual parameters)*

Example: Highlight ("A", NumAsterisks)

Interpretation: The *actual parameters* are enclosed in parentheses. When procedure pname is called into execution, the first actual parameter is associated with the first formal parameter, the second actual parameter with the second formal parameter, and so on. For a value parameter, the actual parameter's value is saved in the procedure. For a variable parameter, the actual parameter's address is saved in the procedure.

Notes: The actual parameters must satisfy the rules for parameter list correspondence discussed later in this section.

Certain rules must be followed when writing parameter lists, as illustrated by this syntax diagram for a formal parameter list.

Formal Parameter List

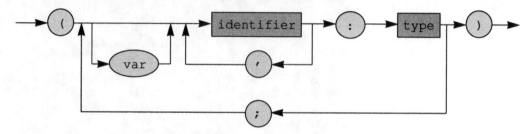

This diagram shows that a *formal parameter list* is always enclosed in parentheses. It consists of one or more lists of identifiers. Each list may be preceded by var. Identifiers and lists of identifiers are separated by commas, and each list must end with a colon followed by a data type name (e.g., real or string).

EXAMPLE 7.5
Two formal parameter lists are shown below. Each list is printed on two or more lines to improve readability.

```
(St3 : string,                (M, N, O : int,
var X, Y, Z : real)            var X, Y, Z : real,
                                    A, B, C : real)
```

In both lists above, X, Y, Z are declared to be type real variable parameters; St3 is a type string value parameter on the left; A, B, C are type real value parameters on the right; M, N, O are type int value parameters on the right.

This example points out a common error with formal parameter lists. In the list on the right, we indented A, B, and C. Students often think that the word var is implied by this indentation and that A, B, and C are also variable parameters. This is not correct! The word var must explicitly appear before each list of variable parameters.

The formal parameter list determines the form of any actual parameter list that may be used to call the procedure. This form is determined during the translation of the program when the compiler processes the procedure declaration.

Later, when it reaches a procedure call statement, the compiler checks the actual parameter list for consistency with the formal parameter list. An actual parameter list may be a list of expressions, variables, or constants separated by commas. An actual parameter list and its corresponding formal parameter list must agree in Number, Order, and Type (abbreviated as NOT) as described in the rules below.

1. Correspondence between actual and formal parameters is determined by position in their respective parameter lists. These lists must be the same size. The names of corresponding actual and formal parameters may be different.
2. For variable parameters, the types of corresponding actual and formal parameters must be identical. For value parameters, the types of corresponding actual and formal parameters must be assignment-compatible (see Section 8.7).
3. For variable parameters, an actual parameter must be a variable. For value parameters, an actual parameter may be a variable, constant, or expression.

EXAMPLE 7.6
The main program contains the following declarations:

```
var X, Y : real
var M : int
var Next : string
```

and

```
procedure Test (A, B : int,
                var C, D : real, var E : string)
```

where only the heading for procedure Test is shown. Procedure Test has two value parameters (A and B) and three variable parameters (C, D, and E). Any of the procedure call statements below would be syntactically correct in the main program.

```
Test (M + 3, 10, X, Y, Next)
Test (M, 10000, Y, X, Next)
Test (35, M * 10, Y, X, Next)
```

The correspondence specified by the first parameter list above is shown in Table 7.2.

TABLE 7.2   Parameter Correspondence for Test (M + 3, 10, X, Y, Next)

Actual Parameter	Formal Parameter	Description
M + 3	A	int, value
10	B	int, value
X	C	real, variable
Y	D	real, variable
Next	E	string, variable

The last column in Table 7.2 describes each formal parameter. Table 7.2 shows that an expression (M + 3) or a constant (10) may be associated with a value parameter. All the procedure call statements in Table 7.3 contain syntax errors as indicated.

TABLE 7.3 Invalid Procedure Call Statements

Procedure Call Statement	Error
Test (30, 10, M, X, Next)	Type of M is not `real`
Test (M, 19, X, Y)	Not enough actual parameters
Test (M, 10, 35, Y, "E")	Constants 35 and "E" cannot correspond to variable parameters
Test (M, 3.0, X, Y, Next)	Type of 3.0 is not an `integer`
Test (30, 10, X, X + Y, Next)	Expression X + Y cannot correspond to a variable parameter
Test (30, 10, C, D, E)	C, D, and E are not declared in the main program

The last procedure call statement above points out an error that is often made in using procedures. The actual parameter names (C, D, E) are the same as their corresponding formal parameter names. However, since these names are not declared in the main program, they cannot appear in an actual parameter list used in the main program.

When writing long parameter lists such as the ones above, you must be very careful not to transpose two actual parameters; that will result in a syntax error if it causes a violation of a parameter correspondence rule. If no syntax is violated, the procedure execution will probably generate incorrect results.

Exercises for Section 7.4

Self-Check

1. Provide a table similar to Table 7.2 for the other correct parameter lists shown in Example 7.6.
2. Correct the syntax errors in the formal parameter lists below.

   ```
   (var A, B : int, C : real)
   (value M : int, var Next : string)
   (var Account, real X + Y , real)
   ```

3. Assuming the declarations

   ```
   const BigInt := 32767
   var X, Y, Z : real
   var M, N : int
   procedure Massage (var A, B : real,
                          X : int)
   ```

which of the following are correct, which are incorrect, and if incorrect, why?

a. Massage (X, Y, Z)
b. Massage (X, Y, 8)
c. Massage (Y, X, N)
d. Massage (M, Y, N)
e. Massage (25.0, 15, X)
f. Massage (X, Y, M + N)
g. Massage (A, B, X)
h. Massage (Y, Z, M)
i. Massage (Y + Z, Y-Z, M)
j. Massage (Z, Y, X)
k. Massage (X, Y, M, 10)
l. Massage (Z, Y, BigInt)

7.5 Stepwise Design with Functions and Procedures

Now that we can pass data into and out of procedures, we can make more use of procedures and functions in our programming. Many of the level 1 subproblems shown in a structure chart will be implemented as separate procedures or functions. If the solution to a subproblem cannot be written easily using just a few Turing statements, it will be coded as a procedure or function. In this section, you will see how to practice stepwise design of programs using procedures and functions. We will do this by considering the problem outlined next.

❋ Case Study:

General Sum-and-Average Problem

1. Problem

We have written earlier program fragments that found the sum or product of a collection of data items. Accumulating a sum of data values is a problem that occurs again and again in programming. We would like to solve the general case of this problem by writing a program that finds and displays the sum and average of a list of real data values. We will use an approach that allows us to develop subprograms, which can be reused when this problem surfaces again.

2. Analysis

Figure 5.4 shows a loop that computes the total payroll for a company. We can adapt this approach to compute the sum of a collection of data values. To compute an average, we must divide a sum by the number of items considered. We must be careful not to perform this division if the number of items summed is zero.

DATA REQUIREMENTS

Problem Inputs

```
NumItems : int        % Number of data items to be summed
Item : real           % Each data item
```

Problem Outputs

```
Sum : real            % Sum of data items
Average : real        % Average of data
```

RELEVANT FORMULAS

average = sum of data / number of data items

3. Design

INITIAL ALGORITHM

1. Read the number of data items.
2. Compute the sum of the data.
3. Compute the average of the data.
4. Print the sum and the average.

The structure chart is drawn in Fig. 7.21. The data flow between subproblems is documented in this chart. We will implement each step that has a non-trivial solution as a separate subprogram. A label under a step denotes the name of the subprogram that implements the step. Each step except for the first is implemented in a separate subprogram.

FIGURE 7.21   Structure Chart with Data Flow Information

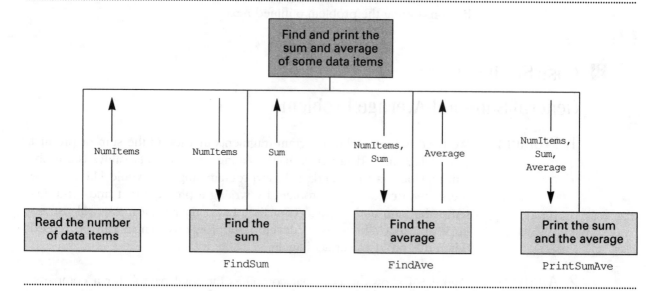

Figure 7.21 shows the data flow between the main program and each subprogram. Recall from Section 4.5 that all variables whose values are set by a subprogram are considered subprogram outputs (indicated by an arrow

pointing out of the subprogram). All variables whose values are used in a computation but are not changed by the subprogram are considered subprogram inputs (indicated by an arrow pointing into the subprogram). Since the step "Read the number of data items" defines the value of the variable NumItems, NumItems is an output of this step. Subprogram FindSum needs this value in order to know how many data items to read and sum; consequently, NumItems is an input to subprogram FindSum. The variable Sum is an output of subprogram FindSum. Sum must be provided as an input to subprograms FindAve and PrintSumAve. The variable Average is an output of subprogram FindAve and an input to subprogram PrintSumAve.

4. Implementation

Once the data flow information has been added to the structure chart, the main program can be written before we even refine the algorithm. We can follow the approach described in Section 3.1 to write the main program. We begin by transferring the data requirements above into the program declaration part. All the variables that appear in the structure chart should be declared in the main program because they are used to store data passed to a subprogram or results returned from a procedure. We will omit the declaration for variable Item because it does not appear in the structure chart; however, it must be declared later in subprogram FindSum. Next, we move the initial algorithm into the program body, writing each algorithm step as a comment (see Fig. 7.22).

FIGURE 7.22

Outline of Program for General Sum and Average

```
% The "Sumitems" program
% Find and print the sum and average of a list of
% data items

var NumItems : int        % Input - number of items to
                          % be added
var Sum: real             % Output - sum being accumulated
var Average : real        % Output - average of the data

% Insert declarations for procedures FindSum and
% PrintSumAve and function FindAve here
% Read the number of items
% Compute the sum of the data
% Compute the average of the data
% Print the sum and average
```

To complete the main program, we must implement each algorithm step *in-line* (as part of the main program code) or as a procedure or function call. We will implement the data entry step in-line because it consists of a simple put (for a prompt) and a get. The structure chart shows

FindSum and FindAve as subprograms that return a single result. We will implement FindAve as a function; however, we will implement FindSum as a procedure because FindSum must read each data item before including it in the sum. We will implement PrintSumAve as a procedure with three input parameters.

The data flow information in Fig. 7.21 tells us the actual parameters to use in each procedure or function call. In the case of a function, it also tells us the name of the main program variable that will hold the function result. For example, the assignment statement

```
Average := FindAve (NumItems, Sum)
```

should be used to call FindAve and set the value of Average. We can determine that the procedure call statement

```
FindSum (NumItems, Sum)
```

should be used to call FindSum (NumItems is an input parameter and Sum is an output parameter). The procedure call statement

```
PrintSumAve (NumItems, Sum, Average)
```

should be used to call PrintSumAve (all input parameters). The final main program is shown in Fig. 7.23.

FIGURE 7.23   Main Program for General Sum-and-Average Problem

```
% The "Sumitems" program
% Find and print the sum and the average of a list
% of data items

var NumItems : int      % Input - number of items to be
                        % added
var Sum : real          % Output - sum being accumulated
var Average : real      % Output - average of the data

% Insert declarations for procedures FindSum and
% PrintSumAve and function FindAve here

% Read the number of items
put "How many items will be added? "..
get NumItems

% Compute the sum of the data
FindSum (NumItems, Sum)

% Compute the average of the data
Average := FindAve(NumItems, Sum)

% Print the sum and average
PrintSumAve (NumItems, Sum, Average)
```

Procedure FindSum

Now that the main program is complete, we can concentrate on its individual subprograms. We will begin with FindSum. In specifying the data requirements for FindSum, we should list the procedure inputs and outputs. We also need a local variable for storing each data item (Item).

DATA REQUIREMENTS FOR FINDSUM

Procedure Inputs
```
    NumItems : int        % Number of data items to be summed
```

Procedure Outputs
```
    Sum : real            % The sum of the data items
```

Local Variables
```
    Item : real           % Each data item
```

In Section 5.2, we discussed accumulating a sum in a loop. We emphasized the need to initialize the sum to zero prior to loop entry. The loop control steps must ensure that the correct number of data items are read and included in the sum being accumulated. Since we know the number of items to sum beforehand (NumItems), we can use a counting loop. These considerations lead to the algorithm for FindSum shown below. The code for FindSum appears in Fig. 7.24.

ALGORITHM FOR FINDSUM

1. Read in the number of items to be summed
2. Initialize Sum to zero.
3. for each value of Count from 1 to NumItems
   4. Read in the next item.
   5. Add it to Sum
   end for

FIGURE 7.24

Procedure FindSum

```
procedure FindSum (NumItems : int,
                   var Sum : real)
% Compute the sum of a list of NumItems data items
% Pre : NumItems is assigned a value.
% Post: NumItems data items are read; their sum is
%       stored in Sum.

var Item : real % The next data item to be added

% Read each data item and add it to Sum
Sum := 0.0
for Count := 1 .. NumItems
      put "Next number to be added> "
      get Item
      Sum := Sum + Item
   end for
end FindSum
```

Figure 7.25 shows the parameter correspondence specified by the procedure call statement

```
FindSum (NumItems, Sum)
```

assuming the value 10 is read into NumItems just before the procedure call. The local variables, Count and Item, are undefined when the procedure is called. The procedure begins by initializing to zero the main program variable Sum, which corresponds to variable parameter Sum. The for loop reads each data item into the local variable Item and adds it to the main program variable Sum. The loop and procedure return will occur after 10 items are added.

FIGURE 7.25   Parameter Correspondence for FindSum (NumItems, Sum)

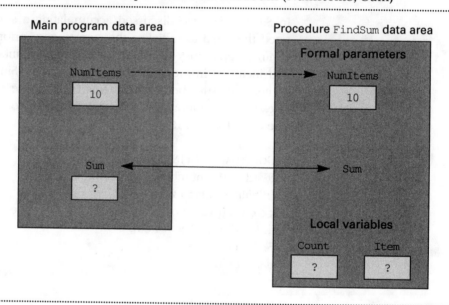

FUNCTION FINDAVE AND PROCEDURE PRINTSUMAVE
Both FindAve and PrintSumAve are relatively straightforward. We list their data requirements and algorithms next. Both algorithms include a test of NumItems. If NumItems is not positive, it makes no sense to compute or display the average of the data items. Figure 7.26 shows function FindAve and Fig. 7.27 shows procedure PrintSumAve.

DATA REQUIREMENTS FOR FINDAVE

Function Inputs

```
NumItems : int          % The number of data items
Sum : real              % The sum of all data
```

Function Output

```
The average of the data
```

INITIAL ALGORITHM FOR FINDAVE
1. if NumItems is positive then
      2. Set FindAve to Sum divided by NumItems
else
      3. Set FindAve to zero
end if

DATA REQUIREMENTS FOR PRINTSUMAVE

Procedure Inputs

NumItems : int	% The number of data items
Sum : real	% The sum of all data
Average : real	% The average of the data

INITIAL ALGORITHM FOR PRINTSUMAVE
1. If NumItems is positive then
      2. Display the sum and average of the data
      end if

FIGURE 7.26   Function FindAve

```
function FindAve (NumItems : int, Sum : real) : real
    % Return the average of NumItems data items with sum of Sum
    % Pre : NumItems and Sum are defined
    % Post: If NumItems is positive, return Sum / NumItems;
    %        otherwise, return zero

    % Compute the average of the data
    if NumItems > 0 then
        result Sum / NumItems
    else
        result 0.0
    end if
end FindAve
```

FIGURE 7.27   Procedure PrintSumAve

```
procedure PrintSumAve (NumItems : int,
                        Sum, Average : real)
    % Display the sum and average of NumItems data items
    % Pre : NumItems, Sum, and Average are defined
    % Post: Display Sum, also Average, if NumItems > 0

    if NumItems > 0 then
        put "The sum is ", Sum :4:2
        put "The average is ", Average :4:2
    else
        put "Sum and average are not defined"
    end if
end PrintSumAve
```

5. Testing

You must insert the function and procedure declarations in the declaration part of SumItems (after the variable declarations) before you can run it. In testing SumItems, you should make sure that the program displays the sum and average correctly when NumItems is positive and displays a diagnostic when NumItems is zero or negative. Figure 7.28 shows a sample run.

FIGURE 7.28   Sample Run of SumItems

```
How many numbers will be added? 3
Next number to be added> 5.0
Next number to be added> 6.0
Next number to be added> -7.0
The sum is 4.00
The average is 1.33
```

When to Use a Function or Procedure

The structure chart for the general sum-and-average program shown in Fig. 7.21 contains four steps, and all but the first are performed by separate subprograms. We used a procedure (FindSum) for step 2 because its algorithm was relatively complicated. Even though it was relatively easy to implement steps 3 and 4, we used a function (FindAve) for step 3 and a procedure (PrintSumAve) for step 4 because their implementation was rather lengthy. It was obvious that step one could be implemented using a put and get so that step was written directly in the main program. You should follow this line of reasoning in determining whether to implement a step as a separate subprogram. From this point on, your main program body will consist primarily of a sequence of procedure and function calls.

Multiple Declarations of Identifiers in a Program

The identifiers Sum and NumItems are declared as variables in the main program and as formal parameters in the three subprograms called by the main program. Each function or procedure call in the main program associates the main program variable Sum with formal parameter Sum, and the main program variable NumItems with formal parameter NumItems. You may be wondering if this violates any rules of Turing. It does not and the compiler is able to distinguish between the different uses of these two identifiers. We explain how this is done in Section 7.7.

Exercises for Section 7.5

Self-Check

1. Procedure `FindSum` returns a single value. Why do you think it was not implemented as a function?
2. Draw the main program and function data areas for the call to `FindAve` assuming that `Sum` is `100.0` and `NumItems` is `10`.
3. Draw the main program and procedure data areas for the call to `PrintSumAve`.

7.6 Positions of Declarations

In all the programs we've seen so far the declarations for the main program have come at the beginning of the program. There has been one exception and this has been counters in `for` loops, which are declared implicitly by the `for` statement. However, declarations are not required to be at the beginning of the program. They can occur any place a statement can occur. When you place a declaration at the beginning of a program, the declared item, say variable `I`, has a *scope* that lasts for the entire execution of the program. Other declarations, including the declaration of a `for` statement counter, are more limited and have a scope that consists of only a part of the program.

The general rule is that an identifier has a scope that lasts from its declaration to the end of whatever construct, such as the entire program or a `for` loop body, within which it is declared.

EXAMPLE 7.7
Figure 7.23 gives the main program for the general sum-and-average program. In that program, the declarations for the variables `NumItems`, `Sum`, and `Average` are given at the top of the main program. In Fig. 7.29 we have rewritten this program to move the declarations of each of theses variables as far down in the program as possible. For example, the declaration for `NumItems` now just precedes the statements that cause it to be read in, and the declaration for `Sum` just precedes the call to `FindSum` which computes the sum. The program works just as it did before, but each of these variables has a minimum scope in the program. For example, `NumItems` is created at its declaration, just before it is needed, and lasts until it is destroyed at the end of the program.

```
% The "Sumitems" program
% Find and print the sum and the average of a list
% of data items

% Insert declarations for procedures FindSum,
% PrintSumAve, and function FindAve here

% Read the number of items to be added
put "How many items will be added? "..
var NumItems : int
get NumItems

% Compute the sum of the data
var Sum : real
FindSum (NumItems, Sum)

% Compute the average of the data
var Average : real := FindAve(NumItems, Sum)

% Print the sum and average
PrintSumAve (NumItems, Sum, Average)
```

This example shows that declarations need not be given at the beginning of the program. The main advantage of moving the declarations down to the positions shown in Fig. 7.29 is that there is less chance that the variables will be accidentally used in some unintended way. The intention in this program is that the variables whose declarations we moved are only to be used in the last few statements of the program, and not by the subprograms. With the original placement, the subprograms could directly access these variables. This idea of placing declarations so that the declared items can be referenced only as intended is called *localization* of declarations. There is a second advantage to localization that you can see if you compare Fig. 7.23 and Fig. 7.29. In Fig. 7.23 we explained the purpose of a variable with its declaration and then later we repeated almost the same explanation when we used the variable. When the variable is localized, these two explanations may be combined into a shorter and clearer explanation.

Although localization of declarations is of help in making our programs easier to read, some people prefer a style, at least for small programs, that places all the declarations at the beginning of the program. They argue that this allows the reader to find the declarations more easily, at the beginning of the program. We will not take a stand on this issue, but will point out that in large programs, localization is generally accepted as good programming style.

As another example of localization, we will look at the Order procedure shown in Fig. 7.20. The purpose of this procedure is to inspect the two variable parameters and to swap them if necessary so the first is the smaller and the second is the larger. In this procedure, the placement of the declaration of `Temp` is a good example of localization, as it is placed inside the procedure rather than preceding the procedure (in which case the program would still work the same way).

We can go a step further, by moving the declaration inside the `if` statement as is shown in the following version of `Order`. In this case, we have also changed `Temp` from a variable to a constant, because we know that Temp in its very short existence (down to `end if`) will not have its value changed. As you can see, this shortens the program by combining the declaration of `Temp` with its initialization to X. A similar shortening with an accompanying localization occurred in Fig. 7.29 in the declaration of `Average`. Although we did not choose to do so, we could have declared `Average` to be a constant to emphasize the fact that once it was computed, it would not be changed again.

```
procedure Order (var X, Y : real)
    % Order a pair of numbers represented by X and
    % Y so that the smaller number is in X and the
    % larger number is in Y.
    % Pre : X and Y are assigned values.
    % Post: X is the smaller of the pair and Y is
    %       the larger.

    if X > Y then
        % Switch the values of X and Y
        const Temp := X     % Store old X in Temp
        X := Y          % Store old Y in X
        Y := Temp       % Store old X in Y
    end if
end Order
```

Exercises for Section 7.6

Self-Check

1. What are good reasons for moving a declaration from the beginning of a program down toward the end of the program?
2. What would be the disadvantage of declaring an item to be a constant rather than a variable?

Programming

1. Rewrite the procedure `FindSum` in Fig. 7.24 to localize the declaration for Item as much as possible. Can `Item` be declared as a constant? Why or why not?

2. Rewrite program Sort3 in Fig. 7.20 so that three calls to procedure Order in the main program are replaced by a single call to a procedure named Sort3Numbers. Write Sort3Numbers in a way that localizes declarations as much as possible.

7.7 Scope of Identifiers

Each declaration defines a new identifier (or new identifiers) that you can use in your program. The identifier represents an item, such as a variable, a constant, or a subprogram that can be referenced in your program.

Figure 7.30 shows the organization of a program that uses the Order procedure. The boxes in this figure show where in the program the various declared identifiers can be referenced. Turing's *scope rules* tell us where an identifier is *visible* and can be referenced.

FIGURE 7.30   Scopes of Variables in a Program

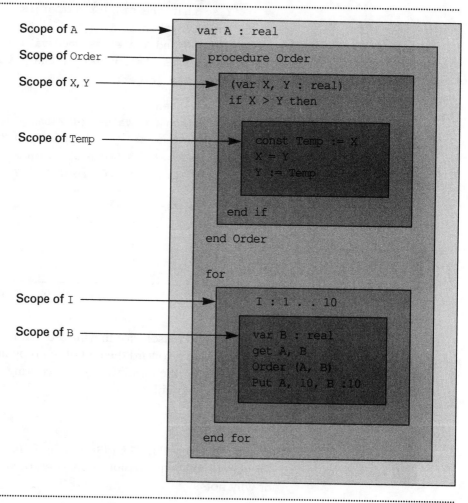

Turing Scope Rules

1. The scope (or lifetime) of an identifier lasts from its declaration to the end of the construct (main program, procedure, `if` statement, `for` statement, etc.) in which the declaration appears. The identifier is visible (can be referenced) only in its scope. Therefore, an identifier declared in procedure `P` can be referenced in procedure `P` but not outside of `P`.

2. If an identifier is already visible, it cannot be redeclared, except in the case in which the new declaration is in a subprogram and the old declaration is in the main program. In this case, inside the subprogram, the identifier represents the new declaration and not the old one.

From Rule 1, we know that the scopes of the parameter `X` and `Y` are limited to the body of procedure `Order`, and the scope of `Temp` lasts from its declaration to `end if` (see Fig 7.30). This means that `X` and `Y` are visible throughout the body of `Order`, but `Temp` is visible only from `const Temp := A` to `end if`. The `for` loop counter `I` has a scope that is limited to the body of the loop. Variable `B`'s scope lasts from its declaration down to `end for`.

The only global variable is `A`, whose scope is the entire program. This means that `A` could be referenced, for example, or assigned to, inside the `Order` procedure. Although global variables can be referenced in subprograms, this is a dangerous practice. If a procedure references a global variable, it is possible for the value of that variable to change when the procedure is executed (a phenomenon called a `side effect`). Often, no documentation exists to indicate that the procedure manipulates a global variable; consequently, it may be difficult to find a statement in a procedure that is responsible for assigning an incorrect or unexpected value to a global variable. If the statement

```
A := A + 3.5 % Example of a side-effect
```

appears in the procedure in Fig. 7.30, it will cause a side-effect (adding `3.5` to global variable `A`) whenever that procedure is called. We can avoid this possibility by moving the declaration for `A` down inside the `for` loop, with the declaration for `B`, thereby localizing `A`'s scope as much as possible. When this is done, there are no longer any global variables, so there is no possibility of side effects.

There is an advanced Turing feature, which has not yet been discussed, called the `module`, which provides the programmer with a method of limiting the scope of global identifiers. Modules are used to group subprograms together with the global variables that the subprograms manipulate. This is sometimes called *information hiding* because the global variables in a module are hidden from all subprograms except those that are intended to reference them.

The formal parameter list and local declarations for a procedure explicitly document the data that will be manipulated. We will continue to manipulate only identifiers (including formal parameters) that are declared locally in a subprogram. The only exceptions will be global constants and type identifiers (discussed in later chapters). Referencing a global constant cannot cause a side effect because Turing does not allow the value of a constant to be changed.

Table 7.4 shows the visibility of the identifiers in three parts of the program in Fig. 7.30. For example, in the body of the `if` statement in the `Order` procedure, it is possible to reference global variable A, formal parameters X and Y, and local variable Temp, as well as the `Order` procedure itself. (It may seem surprising that the identifier `Order` is visible inside the `Order` procedure; this visibility allows subprograms to be *recursive*, as discussed in Section 7.10.) In the body of the `for` statement, it is possible to reference `Order` (it is possible to call `Order`) as well as A, I, and B.

TABLE 7.4　　Visible Identifiers for Figure 7.30

Program Part	Visible Identifiers	Item Named by Identifier
Body of Order	Order	Procedure
	X, Y	Formal parameters to Order
Body of if statement	Order	Procedure
	A	Global variable
	X, Y	Formal parameters to Order
	Temp	Local to if statement body
Body of for statement	Order	Procedure
	A	Global variable
	I	For loop counter
	B	Local to for statement body

Multiple Declarations of Identifiers

Next, we will look at a program example in which particular identifiers are declared more than once. This example uses bad programming style in that identifier names are not meaningful. However, studying this example should help you master the Turing scope rules.

EXAMPLE 7.8

In Fig. 7.31 procedure Change is declared in the main program. There are declarations for variable W in both the procedure and the main program; X is declared as a variable in the main program and as a parameter in the procedure; Y is declared as a variable in the main program only.

FIGURE 7.31 Example of Scope Rules

```
% The "Scope" program
var W, X, Y : real

procedure Change (var X : real)
   var W, Z : real

   W := 35.0           % Change local W
   X := 6.0            % Change parameter X
   Y := Y + 1.0        % Side effect - change global Y
   Z := 3.0            % Change local Z
   put "    W      X      Y      Z"
   put W :5:1, X :5:1, Y :5:1, Z :5:1, " in Change"
end Change

W := 5.5               % Initialize global W
X := 2.0               % Initialize global X
Y := 3.0               % Initialize global Y
Change (W)             % Update global W
put W :5:1, X :5:1, Y :5:1, "          in main program"
```

```
    W      X      Y      Z
  35.0   6.0    4.0    3.0   in Change
   6.0   2.0    4.0           in main program
```

The main program begins by initializing global variables W, X, and Y. The initial values of the three main program variables are shown next.

```
    W      X      Y
   5.5    2.0    3.0
```

The procedure call statement

```
   Change (W)              % Update global W
```

calls procedure Change with main program variable W corresponding to formal parameter X. In Change, the assignment statement

```
   X := 6.0                % Change parameter X
```

stores 6.0 in the main program variable W, and the assignment statement

```
   Y := Y + 1.0            % Side effect - change global Y
```

increments main program variable Y (a side-effect). The other two assignment statements in Change affect its local variables W and Z only.

The second put statement in Change displays the values of its local identifiers (W, X, and Z) and global variable Y just before the procedure return. The put statement in the main program displays the values of the three main program variables after the return, as follows.

```
     W     X     Y
    6.0   2.0   4.0
```

Notice that main program variable X is unchanged and that the value of W is 6.0 (not 35.0). It is interesting to consider what happens if X or Y is used as the actual parameter instead of W. This question is left as an exercise.

One reason why the program in Fig. 7.31 is bad programming style is that it makes it difficult for the reader to keep track of the meaning of repeated identifiers such as X. However, there are some circumstances in which repeating identifiers is quite natural and is considered acceptable style. We will illustrate this in the following program.

```
procedure P (var X : real)
   ...
end P

procedure Q (var X : real)
   ...
end Q
...
for I : 1 .. 5
    ... use procedure P ...
end for
...
for I : 1 .. 5
    ... use procedure Q ...
end for
```

In this example the formal parameters of both procedures P and Q are called X. Since these parameters have *parallel* scopes, that is, scopes that do not overlap, there is no confusion when referencing them. If the two procedures carry out similar computations, such as computing tax, but using different methods, it is probably best to use the same identifiers for their parameters.

The for-loop bodies in this program are another set of parallel set of scopes. It is acceptable, and often desirable, to use the same name, such as I, for such counter variables, when they are used for similar purposes. You should keep in mind that the counters, both of which are called I, are not the same variable.

Exercises for Section 7.7

Self-Check

1. Explain why variable Temp declared in procedure Order cannot be referenced by the main program (see Fig. 7.30).

2. In Fig. 7.31 suppose that the body of the Change procedure were replaced by the following. When this new body has just finished executing and the procedure has not yet returned, what will be the values of global variables W, X, and Y?

```
X := 22.0
W := 13.0
Z := X + W
```

3. If the statement sequence above appeared in the main program, some of the assignment statements may be syntactically incorrect. Identify any incorrect statements.

4. Consider the program Scope shown in Fig. 7.31.
   a. What kind of an error would occur if the assignment statement

   ```
   Z := 15.0
   ```

   was inserted in the main program?
   b. Show the new values of W, X, and Y if X is the actual parameter in the call to procedure Change.
   c. What is the answer if Y is the actual parameter in the call to Change?
   d. What would be the effect of making formal parameter X a value parameter?

7.8 Problem Solving Illustrated

In this section, we demonstrate the top-down design process in solving a problem. The program solution will be implemented in a stepwise manner starting at the top of the structure chart, or with the main program. The problem solution makes extensive use of procedures with parameters.

✖ Case Study:

Balancing a Checkbook

1. Problem
You have just received a new personal computer and would like to write a program to help balance your checkbook. The program will read your initial checkbook balance and each transaction (check or deposit). It will print the new balance after each transaction and a warning message if the balance becomes negative. At the end of the session, the starting and final balance should be printed, along with a count of the number of checks and deposits processed.

2. Analysis
After the starting balance is read, each transaction will be read and processed separately. We can use a simple code ("C" or "D") to distinguish

between checks and deposits. The transaction amount will be a real number. We will display the result of each transaction as it occurs, flagging transactions that cause the account balance to become negative. We will terminate processing transactions when the user enters a special code (`"Q"`).

The starting balance must be available at the end, so we will save it in variable `StartBal`. We will use a different variable, `CurBal`, to keep track of the current balance; the final value of `CurBal` is a problem output. We must also enter and save the transaction data, including the type code and amount.

DATA REQUIREMENTS

Problem Inputs
```
StartBal : real        % Starting checkbook balance
TranType : string      % Type of transaction
Amount : real          % Amount of transaction
```

Problem Outputs
```
CurBal : real          % Current balance after
                       % each transaction
NumCheck : int         % Number of checks
NumDep : int           % Number of deposits
```

3. Design

INITIAL ALGORITHM
1. Display the instructions and read the starting balance.
2. For each transaction: read the transaction, update and print the current balance, and increment the count of checks or deposits.
3. Print the starting and final balance and the number of checks and deposits processed.

Figure 7.32 shows the structure chart for this algorithm. The level 1 subproblems will be written as procedures `Initiate`, `Process`, and `Report`, respectively. The data flow information shows that `StartBal` is read by `Initiate` and passed to `Process`. Procedure `Process` defines the program results (`CurBal`, `NumCheck`, `NumDep`); these results are passed to `Report` and printed.

The variables shown in the structure chart should be declared in the main program, because each variable must be declared at the highest level in which it appears in the structure chart. Variables that are passed between the main program and a level 1 procedure must be declared in the main program.

Notice that the variables that represent the transaction data do not appear in the structure chart. They will be manipulated only by procedure `Process` and its subordinate procedures, so they do not have to be visible in the main program and will be declared later as local variables in `Process`.

FIGURE 7.32   Structure Chart for Checkbook Problem

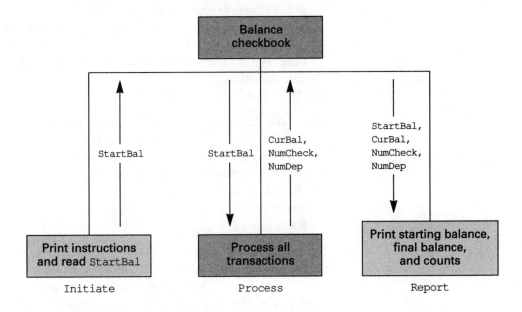

4. Implementation

CODING THE MAIN PROGRAM

The data flow information from Fig. 7.32 is used to write the parameter lists in the main program shown in Fig. 7.33. Procedures Initiate and Report consist of input/output statements only, so we write them now. Because procedure Process requires further refinement, we will write it as a *stub*. The main program body consists of calls to its three level-1 procedures.

FIGURE 7.33   Checkbook Balancing Program with Stub for Process

```
% The "Checkbook" program

% Read the starting balance for a checking account and
% process all transactions. Print the new balance
% after each transaction is processed. Also print a
% count of the total number of checks and deposits
% processed.

procedure Initiate (var StartBal : real)
    % Display the instructions and read the starting
    % balance
    % Pre : None
    % Post: User instructions are displayed and StartBal
    %        is read in
```

```
                    put "Balance your checking account!", skip
                    put "Enter C (Check), D (Deposit), or Q (Quit)"
                    put "after prompt C, D, or Q > ", skip
                    put "Enter a positive number after prompt Amount $",
                        skip
                    put "Begin by entering your starting balance $" ..
                    get StartBal
                 end Initiate

                 procedure Process (StartBal : real, var CurBal : real,
                                    var NumCheck, NumDep : int)
                    % This is the stub for the Process procedure
                    put "Procedure Process entered."
                    CurBal := 0.0
                    NumCheck := 0
                    NumDep := 0
                 end Process

                 procedure Report (StartBal, CurBal : real,
                                   NumCheck, NumDep : int)
                    % Print the starting and final balances and the
                    % count of checks and deposits
                    % Pre : StartBal, CurBal, NumCheck, and NumDep are
                    %          assigned values
                    % Post: Program results are displayed

                    put ""
                    put "Starting balance was $", StartBal :10:2
                    put "   Final balance is $", CurBal :10:2
                    put "Number of checks written: ", NumCheck :3
                    put "Number of deposits made : ", NumDep :3
                 end Report

                 % Variables for main program
                 var StartBal : real       % Input - starting balance
                 var CurBal   : real       % Output - current balance
                 var NumCheck : int        % Output - number of checks
                 var NumDep   : int        % Output - number of deposits

                 % Display user instructions and read StartBal
                 Initiate (StartBal)

                 % Process each transaction
                 Process (StartBal, CurBal, NumCheck, NumDep)

                 % Print starting and final balances and count of
                 % checks/deposits
                 Report (StartBal, CurBal, NumCheck, NumDep)
```

Coding the Process Procedure and Its Level 2 Procedures

Procedure `Process` performs step 2 of the algorithm, which is repeated below.

2. For each transaction: read the transaction, update and print the current balance, and increment the count of checks or deposits.

It is obvious that a loop is needed. Assuming that we do not know how many transactions will occur, we can use a sentinel-controlled loop that compares the transaction code to a sentinel value. The loop properties follow:

a. `CurBal` is `StartBal` plus all transactions that are deposits and minus all transactions that are checks.
b. `NumCheck` is the count of checks so far.
c. `NumDep` is the count of deposits so far.
d. The transaction code is the sentinel just after loop exit.

These statements suggest the refinement below.

ALGORITHM FOR PROCESS
1. Initialize `NumCheck` and `NumDep` to zero
2. Initialize `CurBal` to `StartBal`
3. `loop`
      4. Read transaction
         `exit` when transaction code is the sentinel
      5. Update `CurBal` and increment `NumCheck` or `NumDep`
      6. Display `CurBal` and the transaction
`end loop`

The structure chart for `Process` is shown in Fig. 7.34. Procedure `ReadTran` performs step 4 above, `UpDate` performs step 5, and `DisplayTran` performs step 6. Two new variables, `TranType` and `Amount` (the transaction data), should be declared as local variables in procedure `Process`. Variables passed only between a level-1 and level-2 procedure should be declared in the level-1 procedure. The identifiers `CurBal`, `NumCheck`, and `NumDep` are declared already as formal parameters of `Process`.

Local Variables for Process

```
TranType : string     % The transaction type
Amount : real         % The transaction amount
```

The three procedures that are subordinate to `Process` are fairly easy to write. One decision that we must make at the beginning is how to handle invalid transaction codes. If we take care of them in the beginning (that is, in procedure `ReadTran`), we will not have to be concerned about them in the remaining procedures. We will use a loop statement with a final exit test (step 1 of the algorithm below) to ensure that `ReadTran` ignores any invalid transaction types (not "C", "D", or "Q"). The data requirements for ReadTran follow.

FIGURE 7.34   Structure Chart for Procedure Process

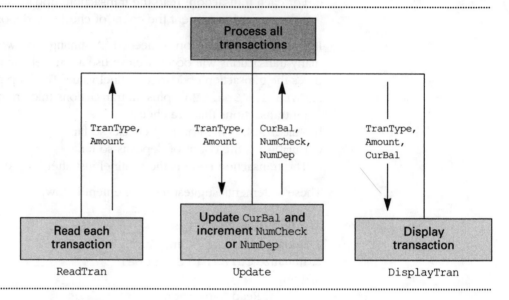

DATA REQUIREMENTS FOR READTRAN
Procedure Inputs
None

Procedure Outputs
```
TranType : string      % Transaction type
TranAmount : real      % Transaction amount
```

ALGORITHM FOR READTRAN
1. loop
     2. Read TranType
        exit when TranType is "C", "D", or "Q"
     end loop
3. if TranType is not "Q" then
     4. Read the transaction amount
     end if

Procedure Update must update the values of its three input/output parameters, CurBal, NumCheck, and NumDep using the strategy outlined in decision Table 7.5. We will implement this table using a cascaded if statement .

DATA REQUIREMENTS FOR UPDATE
Input Parameters
```
TranType : string      % Transaction type
TranAmount : real      % Transaction amount
```

Input/Output Parameters

```
CurBal    : real      % Current balance
NumCheck  : int       % Number of checks
NumDep    : int       % Number of deposits
```

TABLE 7.5 Decision Table for Update

Condition	Desired Action
TranType="D"	Increment NumDep, add Amount to CurBal
TranType="C"	Increment NumCheck, subtract Amount from CurBal

We will not discuss DisplayTran further, since its implementation is relatively straightforward. Because Process calls all three procedures, the declaration for Process must follow the declaration for its subordinate procedures. Figure 7.35 shows all four procedures; notice that we have added the line

```
% Uses: ReadTran, Update, and DisplayTran
```

to the documentation section for Process.

FIGURE 7.35 Procedures for the Checkbook Balancing Program

```
procedure ReadTran (var TranType : string,
                    var Amount : real)
   % Read each transaction.
   % Pre : None
   % Post: TranType and Amount are read in.
   %       Value returned through TranType is "C", "D",
   %       or "Q"

   put ""
   loop
       put "C, D, or Q >" ..
       get TranType
       exit when TranType = "C" or TranType = "D" or
           TranType = "Q"
   end loop
   if TranType not= "Q" then % Read amount
       put "Amount $" ..
       get Amount
   end if
end ReadTran

procedure UpDate (TranType : string, Amount : real,
                  var CurBal : real,
```

```
                        var NumCheck,
                            NumDep : int)
        % Update CurBal and increment NumCheck for a check
        % or NumDep for a deposit
        % Pre : TranType is "C", "D", or "Q"
        % Post: CurBal is increased (deposit) or decreased
        %         (check) by Amount. NumCheck or NumDep is
        %         increased by one.

        if TranType = "C" then
            CurBal := CurBal - Amount
            NumCheck := NumCheck + 1
        elsif TranType = "D" then
            CurBal := CurBal + Amount
            NumDep := NumDep + 1
        elsif TranType = "Q" then
            % Do nothing
        end if
    end UpDate

    procedure DisplayTran (TranType : string,
                            Amount, CurBal : real)
        % Display current transaction and balance
        % Pre : TranType is "C", "D", or "Q"
        % Post: Transaction data are displayed

        if TranType = "C" then
            put "Check for $", Amount: 12:2,
                "     Balance of $", CurBal :12:2
            if CurBal < 0.0 then
                put "Warning! Your account is overdrawn"
            end if
        elsif TranType = "D" then
            put "Depositing $", Amount :12:2,
                "     Balance of $", CurBal :12:2
        elsif TranType = "Q" then
            % Do nothing
        end if
    end DisplayTran

    procedure Process (StartBal : real, var CurBal : real,
                        var NumCheck, NumDep : int)
        % Process each transaction. Read each transaction,
        % update and print the current balance, and increment
        % the count of checks or deposits
        % Pre : StartBal is assigned a value
        % Post: CurBal is StartBal plus deposits and minus
        %         withdrawals
```

```
% NumCheck is the count of checks.
% NumDep is the count of deposits.
% Uses: ReadTran, Update, and DisplayTran

var TranType : string    % Transaction type (check or deposit)
var Amount : real        % Transaction amount

% Initialize counters to zero and CurBal to StartBal
NumCheck := 0
NumDep := 0
CurBal := StartBal

% Process each transaction until done
loop
    ReadTran (TranType, Amount)
    exit when TranType = "Q"
    UpDate (TranType, Amount, CurBal, NumCheck, NumDep)
    DisplayTran (TranType, Amount, CurBal)
end loop
end Process
```

Procedure `DisplayTran` contains an `if` statement that differentiates between checks and deposits. When `TranType` is "C" an `if` statement executes that detects an overdrawn account (`CurBal` is negative). Don't forget to include the `end if` for the `if` statements.

5. Testing

Before running this program, make sure you insert procedure `Process` and its subordinate procedures in the main program (in place of the stub for `Process`). A sample run of the checkbook-balancing program is shown in Fig. 7.36. When testing this program, you should provide invalid as well as valid transaction types. Also make sure that invalid transaction types are ignored.

FIGURE 7.36

Sample Run of Checkbook Balancing Program

```
Balance your checking account!

Enter C (Check), D (Deposit), or Q (Quit)
after prompt C, D, or Q >

Enter a positive number after prompt Amount $

Begin by entering your starting balance $1000.00

C, D, or Q >D
Amount $100.00
Depositing $        100.00      Balance of $      1100.00
```

```
C, D, or Q >C
Amount $1200.00
Check for$      1200.00      Balance of $      -100.00
Warning! Your account is overdrawn

C, D, or Q >X
C, D, or Q >Q

Starting balance was $    1000.00
   Final balance is $    -100.00
Number of checks written:  1
Number of deposits made :  1
```

Software Engineering: Stepwise Design

The program system for the checkbook problem is a good illustration of the stepwise design process. It uses procedures to implement each of the subproblems shown in the structure chart. Each of the procedures is clear and concise.

The main program at the bottom of Fig. 7.33 contains three procedure call statements. The second procedure call statement

```
Process (StartBal, CurBal, NumCheck, NumDep)
```

is used to process all transactions. Procedure Process calls procedures ReadTran, UpDate, and DisplayTran to perform the read, update, and display operations, respectively. These level-2 procedures must be declared before procedure Process.

The variables TranType and Amount are declared in Process (not the main program) since they are used only by Process and the level 2 procedures that Process calls. A variable should be declared in the highest level subprogram that uses it and no higher. Process passes these variables as actual parameters to the level-2 procedures.

PROGRAM
STYLE

REPEATED NAMES FOR PARAMETERS
The procedures written for the checkbook balancing program are a little different from others that we have written in that there is little likelihood that they will be reused in other programs. For this reason we have not attempted to use generic names to represent the formal parameters in these procedures. In cases like this, we recommend using the same formal parameter name to represent a particular data item in each subprogram, rather than choosing different names for that data item.

Exercises for Section 7.8

Self-Check

1. Write the data requirements and algorithm for procedure `DisplayTran`.
2. Write the algorithm for procedure `Update`.

Programming

1. Modify the checkbook program so that a penalty amount of $15.00 is deducted for each overdrawn check, and a count of overdrawn checks is maintained and printed next to each overdrawn check. Reset the count of overdrafts to zero whenever the balance becomes positive.

7.9 Debugging and Testing a Program

Top-Down and Bottom-Up Debugging and Testing

As the number of statements in a program system grows, the possibility of error also increases. If we keep each subprogram to a manageable size, the likelihood of error will increase much more slowly. It will also be easier to read and test each subprogram. Finally, passing global variables to procedures through parameter lists will minimize the chance of harmful side effects that are always difficult to locate.

In the last case study, we inserted a stub in the main program for a procedure (`Process`) that was not yet written. When a team of programmers is working on a problem, this is a common practice. Obviously not all subprograms will be ready at the same time. The use of stubs enables us to test and debug the main program flow and those subprograms that are available.

Each stub displays an identification message and assigns values to its output parameters to prevent execution errors caused by undefined values. We show the stub for procedure `Process` again in Fig. 7.37. If a program contains one or more stubs, the message printed by each stub when it is called provides a trace of the call sequence, and allows the programmer to determine whether the flow of control within the main program is correct. The process of testing a main program in this way is called *top-down* testing.

When a subprogram is completed, it can be substituted for its stub in the main program. However, often we perform a preliminary test of a new subprogram first because it is easier to locate and correct errors when dealing with a single subprogram rather than a complete program system. We can test a new subprogram by writing a short driver program similar to the driver program shown in Fig. 7.10 and used to test function `FindTax`.

FIGURE 7.37   Stub for Procedure Process

```
procedure Process (StartBal : real, var CurBal : real,
                        var NumCheck, NumDep : int)
    % This is the stub for the Process procedure
    put "Procedure Process entered."
    CurBal := 0.0
    NumCheck := 0
    NumDep := 0
end Process
```

Don't spend a lot of time creating an elegant driver program because you will discard it as soon as the new subprogram is tested. A driver program should contain only the declarations and executable statements necessary to perform a test of a single subprogram. A driver program should begin by reading or assigning values to all input parameters and to input/output parameters. Next comes the call to the subprogram being tested. After calling the subprogram, the driver program should display the subprogram results. The body of the driver program for function FindTax is repeated in Fig. 7.38.

FIGURE 7.38   Driver Program for Function FindTax

```
% The "Driver" program
% Test function FindTax

var MySalary : real      % Input - salary
var MyTax    : real      % Output - tax

% Insert function FindTax here

put "Enter a salary less than or equal to $15000.00> $"
get MySalary
MyTax := FindTax (MySalary)
if MyTax >= 0.0 then
    put "Tax on $", MySalary :4:2, " is $", MyTax :4:2
else
    put "Salary $", MySalary :4:2, "is out of table range"
end if
```

Once we are confident that a subprogram works properly, it can be substituted for its stub in the program system. The process of separately testing individual subprograms before inserting them in a program system is called *bottom-up testing*.

By following a combination of top-down and bottom-up testing, the programming team can be fairly confident that the complete program system will be relatively free of errors when it is finally put together. Consequently, the final debugging sessions should proceed quickly and smoothly.

Debugging Tips for Program Systems

1. Carefully document each subprogram parameter and local identifier using comments as you write the code. Also describe the subprogram operation using comments.
2. Leave a trace of execution by printing the subprogram name as you enter it.
3. Print the values of all input and input/output parameters upon entry to a subprogram. Check that these values make sense.
4. Print the values of all subprogram outputs after returning from a subprogram. Verify that these values are correct by hand-computation. For procedures, make sure that all input/output and output parameters are declared as variable parameters.
5. Make sure that a subprogram stub assigns a value to each of its outputs.

It is a good idea to plan for debugging as you write each subprogram rather than after the fact. Include the output statements required for Steps 2 through 4 above in the original Turing code for the subprogram. When you are satisfied that the subprogram works as desired, you can remove the debugging statements. One efficient way to remove them is to change them to comments by preceding them with the symbol %. If you have a problem later, you can remove these symbols, thereby changing the comments back to executable statements.

Another approach to turning debugging statements on and off is to use a `boolean` constant (say `Debug`) which is declared in the main program. The declaration

```
const Debug := true      % Turn debugging on
```

should be used during debugging runs, and the declaration

```
const Debug := false     % Turn debugging off
```

should be used during production runs. Within the main program body and its procedures, each diagnostic print statement should be part of an `if` statement with `Debug` as its condition. If procedure `Process` begins with the `if` statement below, the `put` statements will execute only during debugging runs (`Debug` is `true`) as desired.

```
if debug then
    put "Procedure Process entered"
    put "Input parameter StartBal has value ", StartBal :4:2
end if
```

7.10 Recursive Functions (Optional)

In the last section we stated that the Turing scope rules allow a function or procedure to reference (to call) itself. A subprogram that calls itself is a `recursive` subprogram. We will describe one recursive function in this section. Chapter 14 will discuss recursion in detail.

We will begin by describing a function that returns an integer value representing the factorial of its argument. The `factorial of N` is the product of all integers less than or equal to N and is written in mathematics as N!. Fiure 7.39 shows one version of the factorial function.

FIGURE 7.39   Function Factorial

```
function Factorial (N : int) : int
    % Return the product 1 * 2 * 3 *...* N when N is > 1
    % Return 1 when N is 0 or 1

    var ProductSoFar : int := 1  % Accumulated product

    % Perform the repeated multiplication for N > 1
    for I : 2 .. N
        ProductSoFar := ProductSoFar * I
    end for
    result ProductSoFar   % Define function result
end Factorial
```

The local variable `ProductSoFar` is used to accumulate the partial product and is initialized to 1. The `for` statement performs the repeated multiplication when N is greater than 1. If N is 0 or 1, the for statement does not execute so `ProductSoFar` remains 1. After loop exit, the last value of `ProductSoFar` is returned as the function result.

Figure 7.40 shows function `Factorial` rewritten as a recursive function. A `recursive function` is one that calls itself. In Fig. 7.40, the if statement implements the recursive definition of N! shown below.

$$N! = N * (N - 1)! \qquad \text{for } N > 1$$
$$N! = 1 \qquad \text{for } N = 0 \text{ or } 1$$

When N is greater than 1, instead of executing a loop to perform repeated multiplication as in Fig. 7.39, the statement

```
result N * Factorial(N-1)
```

executes, which is the Turing form of the first formula above. The expression part of this statement contains a valid function designator, `Factorial(N-1)`, which calls function `Factorial` with an argument that is one less than the current argument (called a `recursive call`). When N is less than or equal to 1, the statement

    result 1

executes, stopping the chain of recursive calls and returning a result of 1.

FIGURE 7.40   Recursive Function Factorial

```
function Factorial (N : int) : int
    % Return the product 1 * 2 * 3 * ... * N when N is > 1
    % Return 1 when N is 0 or 1

    if N <= 1 then
        result 1
    else
        result N * Factorial(N-1)
    end if
end Factorial
```

Each new call to Factorial creates a new copy of the value parameter N. If the argument in the initial call to `Factorial` is 3, the following chain of recursive calls occurs:

```
Factorial(3) Result is 3 * Factorial(2)
Factorial(2) Result is 2 * Factorial(1)
Factorial(1) Result is 1
```

In the first call, N has the value 3; in the second call, there is a new copy of N whose value is 2; in the last call, there is a third copy of N whose value is 1. The last call in the chain evaluates to 1, and the value of 3 * 2 * 1, or 6, is returned as the result of the original call.

Exercises for Section 7.10

Self-Check

1. Show the chain of recursive calls to function `Mystery` when M is 4 and N is 3. What do you think `Mystery` does?

```
function Mystery (M, N : int) : int
    if N = 1 then
        result M
    else
        result M * Mystery(M, N-1)
    end if
end Mystery
```

Programming

1. Write a function `C(N, R)` that returns the number of different ways R items can be selected from a group of N items. The mathematical formula for `C(N, R)` follows. Test `C(N, R)` using both the recursive and non-recursive versions of function `Factorial`.

$$C(N, R) = \frac{(N!}{R!(N-R)!)}$$

2. Write a recursive function that finds the greatest common divisor (GCD) of two integers. The GCD of two integers is the largest integer that divides them both. It is defined recursively as:

```
GCD(M, N) is GCD(N, M) for M < N
GCD(M, N) is N when N is a divisor of M
     (M mod N is zero)
GCD(M, N) is GCD(N, M mod N) when N is not a
     divisor of M
```

7.11 Common Programming Errors

There are many opportunities for error when using subprograms with parameter lists, so you must be extremely careful. The proper use of parameters is difficult for beginning programmers to master, but it is an essential skill. One obvious pitfall occurs in ensuring that the actual parameter list has the same number of parameters as the formal parameter list. A syntax error message such as `"too many parameters"` will indicate this problem.

Each actual parameter must be assignment compatible with its corresponding formal parameter (for a value parameter) or the same data type (for a variable parameter). You are not allowed to change the value of a value parameter. An actual parameter that corresponds to a variable formal parameter must be a variable. A violation of this rule will result in an error message such as `"expression passed to var formal"`.

A procedure result should be returned to the calling subprogram by assigning a value to a variable parameter. You are not allowed to assign a value (using `:=`) to a value parameter. If you try to do this you will get an error message such as `"left side of assignment is not a variable"`.

Remember to return all function results by using a `result` statement. It is a bad programming practice to return a function result through a variable parameter (function side-effect). It is also a bad programming practice to directly manipulate a global variable in a procedure or function; all non-local variables should be passed to a subprogram through its parameter list.

The Turing scope rules determine where an identifier is visible and can be referenced. If an identifier is referenced outside its scope, an `"identifier not declared"` syntax error will result.

Chapter Review

We discussed the use of parameters for passing data to and from functions and procedures. The parameter list provides a highly visible communication path between a subprogram and its calling program. By using parameters, we can cause different data to be manipulated by a subprogram each time we call it, making it easier to reuse the subprogram in another program.

There are two types of parameters: value and variable. A value parameter is used only for passing data into a subprogram. A variable parameter is used to return results. The actual parameter corresponding to a value parameter may be an expression or a constant; the actual parameter corresponding to a variable parameter must be a variable.

We discussed the scope of identifiers. An identifier is visible and can be referenced from the position of its declaration down to the end of the construct it is declared in. For example, an identifier declared in the main program has a scope that lasts from its declaration down to the end of the entire program. An identifier declared in a `loop` statement is (re)created each time its declaration is encountered in the loop body and is (re)destroyed at the end of the loop body. Ordinarily, redeclaring a visible identifier is not allowed. However, if the original declaration is in the main program and the redeclaration is in a subprogram, the new declaration is allowed and takes precedence over the original during the execution of the subprogram.

A global variable is one that is declared in the main program before the declaration of any subprograms. A local variable is one that is declared in a subprogram, `if` statement, `loop` statement, or other statement. The counter variable of a `for` statement is local to that statement. A local variable is defined only during the execution of its scope; its value is lost when the enclosing subprogram or statement is done.

In the optional section, we discussed writing a recursive function, which is a function that calls itself.

New Turing Constructs in Chapter 7

The new Turing constructs introduced in this chapter are described in Table 7.6.

TABLE 7.6   Summary of New Turing Constructs

Construct	Effect

Function Declaration

```
function Sign (X : real) : string
    if X > 0.0 then
        result "+"
    else
        result "-"
    end if
end Sign
```

Return a string value that indicates the sign ("+" or "-") of its type real argument X.

Procedure Declaration

```
procedure DoIt (X : real,
                Op : string,
                var Y : real ,
                var Sign : string)
    if Op = "+" then
        Y := X + X
    elsif Op = "*" then
        Y := X * X
    end if
    if X > 0.0 then
        Sign := "+"
    else
        Sign := "-"
    end if
end DoIt
```

If Op is "+", return X + X through Y; if Op is "*", return X * X through Y. Return a string value that indicates the sign "+" or "-" of X through Sign.

Procedure Call Statement

```
DoIt (-5.0, "*", Y, MySign)
```

Call procedure DoIt. -5.0 is passed into X, "*" into Op, 25.0 is returned to Y, and "-" is returned to MySign.

Quick-Check Exercises

1. The _____ parameters appear in the procedure call and the _____ parameters appear in the procedure declaration.
2. Constants and expressions can correspond to formal parameters that are _____ parameters.
3. Formal parameters that are variable parameters must have actual parameters that are _____.
4. Formal parameters that are variable parameters must have actual parameters that are the _____ data type.

5. The data types of corresponding value parameters must be _____.
6. Which of the following is used to test a procedure: a driver or a stub?
7. Which of the following is used to test main program flow: a driver or a stub?
8. A(n) _____ occurs when a function assigns a value to one of its variable parameters or when a procedure changes a global variable.
9. What are the values of main program variables X and Y after the program below executes?

```
% The "Silly1" program
var X, Y : real := 13.0
procedure Silly (X : real)
    var Y : real
    Y := 25.0
end Silly

Silly (X)
```

10. What are the values of main program variables X and Y after the program below executes?

```
% The "Silly2" program
var X, Y : real := 13.0

procedure Silly (var X : real)
    var Y : real
    Y := 25.0
    X := Y
end Silly

Silly (X)
```

11. Answer exercise 10 if the local declaration for Y is removed from Silly.
12. Answer exercise 10 if the procedure call statement is changed to Silly (Y).
13. How does a function return its value?

Answers to Quick-Check Exercises
1. Actual, formal
2. Value
3. Variables
4. Same
5. Assignment compatible
6. Driver
7. Stub
8. Side effect
9. Both are 13.0
10. X is 25.0, Y is 13.0

11. Both `25.0`
12. X is `13.0`, Y is `25.0`
13. A function returns its single value by giving the value as an expression in a `result` statement.

Review Questions

1. Write the procedure heading for a procedure called `Script` that accepts three parameters passed to it. The first parameter will be the number of spaces to print at the beginning of a line. The second parameter will be the character to print after the spaces, and the third parameter will be the number of times to print the second parameter on the same line.
2. Write a function called `LetterGrade` that has a parameter called `Grade`, and returns the appropriate letter grade using a straight scale (90–100 is an A, 80–89 is a B, and so on).
3. Why would you choose to make a formal parameter a value parameter rather than a variable parameter?
4. Explain the allocation of memory cells when a procedure is called.
5. Write the procedure heading for a procedure named `Pass` that will pass two integer parameters. The first parameter should be a value parameter and the second a variable parameter.
6. Explain the use of a stub in refining an algorithm.
7. List two reasons for implementing a subprogram as a procedure rather than as a function.

Programming Projects

1. The assessor in your town has estimated the market value of fourteen properties and would like you to write a program that determines the tax owed on each property and the total tax to be collected. The tax rate is 12.5 cents per dollar of assessed value. The assessed value of each property is 28% of its estimated market value. The market values are:

$50,000	$48,000	$45,500	$67,000	$37,600
$47,100	$65,000	$53,350	$28,000	$58,000
$52,250	$48,000	$56,500	$43,700	

You need to write procedures that correspond to the procedure headers shown below as part of your solution.

```
procedure PrintInstructions
    % Display instructions to the user

procedure ProcessProperties (var TotalTax : real)
    % Read market values and compute taxes on all
    % properties
```

```
function ComputeTax (Market : real) : real
    % Compute tax on a property with market value
    % of Market

procedure PrintSummary (TotalTax : real)
    % Displays value of TotalTax
```

2. Revise programming project 1 assuming a 5% surcharge for all properties with market value over $50,000. Also, grant a 10% discount for senior citizens. You will need to enter a second data item for each property indicating whether its owner is a senior citizen. Write a separate procedure that reads and returns the current property market value and sets a `boolean` parameter to `true` if the owner is a senior citizen.

3. The trustees of a small college are considering voting a pay raise for the 12 faculty members. They want to grant a 5.5% pay raise; however, before doing so, they want to know how much this will cost. Write a program that will print the pay raise for each faculty member and the total amount of the raises. Also, print the total faculty payroll before and after the raise. Test your program for the following salaries:

$32,500	$24,029.50	$36,000	$43,250
$35,500	$22,800	$30,000.50	$28,900
$43,780	$47,300	$44,120.25	$24,100

4. Revise programming project 3, assuming that faculty earning less than $30,000 receive a 7% raise, faculty earning more than $40,000 receive a 4% raise, and all others receive a 5.5% raise. Write a new function that determines the raise percentage. Also, for each faculty member, print the raise percentage as well as the amount.

5. Patients required to take many kinds of medication often have difficulty in remembering when to take their medicine. Given the following set of medications, write a program that prints an hourly table indicating what medication to take at any given hour. Use a counter variable `Clock` to go through a 24-hour day. Print the table based upon the following prescriptions:

Medication	Frequency
Iron pill	0800, 1200, 1800
Antibiotic	Every 4 hours starting at 0400
Vitamin	0800, 2100
Calcium	1100, 2000

6. A monthly magazine wants a program that will print out renewal notices to its subscribers and cancellation notices when appropriate. Using procedures when advisable, write a program that first reads in the current month number (1 through 12) and year. For each subscription processed, read in four data items: the account number, the month and year the subscription started, and the number of years paid for the subscription.

   Read in each set of subscription information and print a renewal notice if the current month is either the month prior to expiration or the month of expiration. A cancellation notice should be printed if the current month comes after the expiration month.

Sample input might be

```
10, 88              for a current month of October 1988
1364, 4, 85, 3      for account 1364 whose 3-year
                    subscription began in April 1985
```

7. The square root of a number N can be approximated by repeated calculation using the formula

```
NG = .5(LG + N / LG)
```

where NG stands for next guess and LG stands for last guess. Write a procedure that implements this process. The first parameter will be a positive real number, the second will be an initial guess of the square root, and the third will be the computed result.

The initial guess will be the starting value of LG. The procedure will compute a value for NG using the formula above. The difference between NG and LG is checked to see whether these two guesses are almost identical. If so, the procedure is exited and NG is the square root; otherwise, the new guess (NG) becomes the last guess (LG) and the process is repeated (i.e., another value is computed for NG, the difference is checked, and so forth).

For this program the loop should be repeated until the magnitude of the difference is less than 0.005 (Delta). Use an initial guess of 1.0 and test the program for the numbers 4, 120.5, 88, 36.01, and 10,000.

8. It was a dark and stormy night. Our secret agent (007), is behind enemy lines at a fuel depot. He walks over to a cylindrical fuel tank, which is 20 feet tall and 8 feet in diameter. He opens a 2-inch-diameter circular nozzle. He knows that the volume of the fuel leaving the tank is

*volume lost = velocity * area of the nozzle * time*

and that

velocity = 8.02 * $\sqrt{\text{height of fluid in the tank}}$

How long will it take to empty the tank?

Hint: Although this is really a calculus problem, we can simulate it with the computer and get a close answer. We can calculate the volume lost over a short period of time, say, 60 seconds, and assume that the loss of fluid is constant. We can then subtract the volume from the tank and determine the new height of the fluid inside the tank at the end of the minute. We can then calculate the loss for the next minute. This can be done over and over until the tank is dry. Print a table showing the elapsed time in seconds, the volume lost, and the height of the fluid. At the very end, convert the total elapsed seconds to minutes. The fluid height can be negative on the last line of the table.

CHAPTER **8**

Standard Data Types

So far in your programming experience you have used the four standard data types of Turing: int, real, string, and boolean. In this chapter we will take a closer look at these data types and introduce some new operators and operations that you can perform on them.

You'll also learn how to declare two new kinds of data types: enumerated types and subrange types. To make large programs more readable, you can declare new data types (called *enumerated types*) whose values you specify, depending on the problem domain. A *subrange type* is a limited range of values defined over integers or an enumerated type.

The int, real, and boolean types, as well as subrange types and enumerated types, are *simple* or *scalar* data types—that is, only a single value can be stored in each variable. A variable of type string is used to store a sequence of characters.

In an optional section at the end of the chapter, we will discuss how to evaluate a series and how to find a function root using iterative approximations. We will use Newton's method to solve the latter problem.

8.1 Constants

Let's begin by re-examining the syntax for constants in Turing. Each constant definition has the form

const *identifier* := *expression*

This form is illustrated in Fig. 8.1 as a syntax diagram.

FIGURE 8.1   Syntax Diagrams for Constant Declaration

Constant declaration

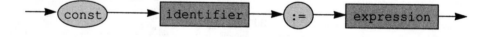

EXAMPLE 8.1

Here are some sample constant declarations:

```
const Maximum := 100
const Minimum := -Maximum
const SpeedOfLight := 2.998E+5
const Debug := true
const Name := "Alice"
const SideOfSquare := sqrt(Area)
        % Area is a variable
```

The constant declaration for `Minimum` uses the previously defined constant `Maximum`. Because `Maximum` has the value `100`, `Minimum` has the value `-100`. The constant `SpeedOfLight` is associated with a `real` value (`299800.0`) expressed in scientific notation. The `boolean` constant `Debug` is associated with the `boolean` value `true`. The constant `Name` is associated with the literal string `"Alice"`.

In languages such as Pascal, a constant is restricted to being a value, such as `2` or `"Alice"`, that is known before the program begins execution. Turing is more flexible and allows the value to be any expression—and the expression can be computed at run time. The value of `SideOfSquare` is computed using the `sqrt` function. The parameter to `sqrt`, which is `Area`, can be a variable. The value of `Area` could be determined, for example, by a `get` statement. Although we do not know the value of `SideOfSquare` before run time, we do know that once it has been computed, it cannot be changed.

As mentioned earlier, there are several reasons for using constants. One is that the name `SpeedOfLight` has more meaning to a reader of a program than the value 2.998E+5. Another is that if we change the value of a constant in its declaration, we also change the value of that constant wherever it is referenced in the program. A final reason is that it allows us to document the fact that an item, such as `SideOfSquare` in the above example, is not to be changed in this program.

Exercises for Section 8.1

Self-Check

1. Which of the constants declared below are valid and which are invalid?

   ```
   const MinInt := -100000
   const MaxLetter := "Z"
   const MinusZ := -MaxLetter
   const MaxSize := 50
   const MinSize := MaxSize - 10
   const Less := Less - 1
   ```

2. Why would you declare an identifier as a constant, rather than as a variable?

8.2 Numeric Data Types: Integer and Real

The data types `int` and `real` are used to represent numeric information. We have used `int` variables to represent data, such as exam scores, that were whole numbers. In most other instances, we used type `real` numeric data.

Differences Between Numeric Types

You may be wondering why it is necessary to have two numeric types. Can the data type `real` be used for all numbers? The answer is yes, but on many computers, operations involving integers are faster than those involving real numbers. Less storage space is needed to store integers. Also, operations with integers are always precise, whereas there may be some loss of accuracy when dealing with `real` numbers.

These differences result from the way real numbers and integers are represented internally in your computer's memory. All data are represented in memory as *binary strings*, strings of 0s and 1s. However, the binary string stored for the integer 13 is not the same as the binary string stored for the real number 13.0. The actual internal representation is computer-dependent, and real numbers often require more bytes of computer memory. Compare the sample int and real formats shown in Fig. 8.2.

FIGURE 8.2　　　　Integer and Real Formats

Integer format

Binary number

Real format

Mantissa	Exponent

Figure 8.2 shows that positive integers are represented by standard binary numbers. If you are familiar with the binary number system, you know that the integer 13 is represented as the binary number 01101.

Real format is analogous to scientific notation. The storage area occupied by a real number is divided into two sections: the *mantissa* and the *exponent*. The mantissa is a binary fraction between 0.5 and 1.0 for positive numbers (between −0.5 and −1.0 for negative numbers). The exponent is a power of two. The mantissa and exponent are chosen so that the formula below is correct.

real-number = mantissa × $2^{exponent}$

Because of the finite size of a memory cell, not all real numbers in the range of reals can be represented precisely. We will talk more about this later.

Besides the capability of storing fractions, the range of numbers that may be represented in real format is considerably larger than for integer format. For example, on an older computer, the Control Data Corporation Cyber, positive real numbers ranged in value from 10^{-294} (a very small fraction) to 10^{+322}, whereas the range of positive integers extended from 1 to approximately 10^{15}. In that computer, a real number required twice the storage space of an integer.

Numeric Literals

An item such as 21 or "Alice" that defines its own value is called a literal. The data type of a numeric literal is determined in the following way. If the literal has a decimal point, then it is considered type real. A type real literal may also have a decimal *scale factor*. For example, in the literal 2.998E+5, the scale factor is 10^5. A literal without a decimal point is considered type int unless it has a scale factor. For example, the literal 5E2 is considered type real (value is 500.0) because it has a scale factor.

Review of Integer Division

In Section 2.6, we introduced the div and mod operators. The operator div yields the integer quotient of its first operand divided by its second; the operator mod yields the integer remainder of its first operand divided by its second (for example, 7 div 2 is 3, and 7 mod 2 is 1). The next example illustrates the use of these operators.

EXAMPLE 8.2

Procedure PrintDigits in Fig. 8.3 prints each digit of its parameter Decimal in reverse order (e.g., if Decimal is 738, the digits printed are 8, 3, 7). This is accomplished by setting local variable Dec to Decimal and printing each remainder (0 through 9) of Dec divided by 10; the integer quotient of Dec divided by 10 becomes the new value of Dec.

FIGURE 8.3

Printing Decimal Digits

```
procedure PrintDigits (Decimal : int)
    % Print the digits of Decimal in reverse order
    % Pre : Decimal is strictly positive
    % Post: Each digit of Decimal is displayed,
    %        starting with the least significant one

    const Base := 10          % Number system base
    var Dec : int := Decimal   % Copy of Decimal
    var Digit : int            % Each digit

    % Print remainders of Dec divided by Base
    loop
        Digit := Dec mod Base  % Get next digit
        put Digit ..
        Dec := Dec div Base    % Get next quotient
        exit when Dec = 0
    end loop
    put ""
end PrintDigits
```

The Dec variable is the loop control variable. Within the loop, the mod operator assigns to Digit the rightmost digit of Dec. The div operator assigns the rest of the number to Dec. The loop is exited when Dec becomes 0. In this example, it would be tempting to eliminate the declaration of Dec and instead to use Decimal directly. This would not be allowed because Turing will not let you change Decimal because it is a value (non-var) parameter.

Table 8.1 shows a trace of the procedure execution for an actual parameter of 43. The digits 3 and 4 are displayed.

TABLE 8.1 Trace of Execution of PrintDigits (43)

Statement	Decimal	Digit	Effect
Digit := Dec mod Base		3	Next digit is 3.
put Digit ..			Print 3.
Dec := Dec div Base	4		Quotient is 4.
exit when Dec = 0			4 not= 0.
Digit := Dec mod Base		4	Next digit is 4.
put Digit ..			Print 4. Quotient is 0.
Dec := Dec div Base	0		0 = 0 so exit loop.

Numerical Inaccuracies

One of the problems in processing real numbers is that sometimes an error occurs in representing real data. Just as certain numbers cannot be represented exactly in the decimal number system (e.g., the fraction 1/3 is 0.333333...), so some numbers cannot be represented exactly in real format. The *representational error* will depend on the number of binary digits (bits) used in the mantissa: the more bits, the smaller the error.

The number 0.1 is an example of a real number that has a representational error. The effect of a small error is often magnified through repeated computations. Therefore, the result of adding 0.1 ten times is not exactly 1.0, so the loop below may fail to terminate on some computers.

```
Trial := 0.0
loop
    exit when Trial = 1.0

        ...

    Trial := Trial + 0.1
end loop
```

If the loop repetition test is changed to Trial >= 1.0, the loop may execute ten times on one computer and eleven times on another. For this reason, it is best to use integer variables whenever possible in loop repetition tests.

Other problems occur when manipulating very large and very small real numbers. In adding a large number and a small number, the larger number may "cancel out" the smaller number (resulting in a *cancellation error*). If X is much larger than Y, then X + Y may have the same value as X (e.g., 1000.0 + 0.0001234 is equal to 1000.0 on some computers).

If two very small numbers are multiplied, the result may be too small to be represented accurately, so it will be represented as zero. This phenomenon is called *arithmetic underflow*. Similarly, if two very large numbers are multiplied, the result may be too large to be represented. This phenomenon, called *arithmetic overflow*, is handled in different ways on various computers. (Arithmetic overflow can occur when processing very large int values as well.)

EXAMPLE 8.3

The program in Fig. 8.4 draws a sine curve. It uses the Turing function sind, which returns the trigonometric sine of its parameter, an angle expressed in degrees. As an illustration of the numerical inaccuracy that results in performing real computations, examine the sine value displayed for angles of 180 and 360 degrees. The real numbers as represented on the computer that ran this program have an accuracy of about one part in 1016. The actual sine should be zero for both 180 and 360 degrees; the sine value computed is quite small (approximately 10-16) in both cases – but it is not zero.

FIGURE 8.4   Plotting a Sine Curve

```
% The "Sinecurve" program
% Plot a sine curve

const Scale := 10              % Scale factor for plot
const MinAngle := 0            % Smallest angle
const MaxAngle := 360          % Largest angle
const StepAngle := 18          % Increment in degrees
var Theta : real := MinAngle   % Angle in degrees

put "Theta Sine"
loop
    exit when Theta > MaxAngle
    put Theta :4 ..                       % Print Theta
    const Sine := sind(Theta)
    put Sine :25:20 ..                     % Print Sine
    const ScaledSine := Scale * Sine
    const Indent := 1 + Scale + round(ScaledSine)
    put "": Indent, "*"                    % Indent and print *
    Theta := Theta + StepAngle             % Next angle
end loop
```

```
Theta  Sine
    0  0.0000000000000000000                           *
   18  0.30901699437494740685                           *
   36  0.58778525229247318151                             *
   54  0.80901699437494745126                              *
   72  0.95105651629515346457                               *
   90  1.0000000000000000000                               *
  108  0.95105651629515364220                               *
  126  0.80901699437494745126                              *
  144  0.58778525229247327033                             *
  162  0.30901699437494749567                           *
  180  0.00000000000000012246                         *
  198  -0.30901699437494727363                       *
  216  -0.58778525229247300388                     *
  234  -0.80901699437494727363                    *
  252  -0.95105651629515346457                  *
  270  -1.0000000000000000000                   *
  288  -0.95105651629515364220                  *
  306  -0.80901699437494762890                    *
  324  -0.58778525229247327033                     *
  342  -0.30901699437494762890                       *
  360  -0.00000000000000024493                         *
```

The loop in Fig. 8.4 executes for values of Theta equal to 0, 18, 36, ... , 360 degrees. The constant ScaledSine is set to a value in the range −10.0 to 10.0. It is used in computing the value of Indent which is in the range 1 (when Sine is −1.0) to 21 (when Sine is 1.0). The statement

```
    put "": Indent, "*"          % Indent and print *
```

causes Indent blanks to precede the star, by placing the null string in a field whose width is Indent. This in turn produces the plot of a sine-shaped curve.

PROGRAM STYLE

CHECKING BOUNDARY VALUES

The discussion for Example 8.3 states that the value of Indent ranges from 1 to 21 as the sine value goes from −1 to 1. It is always a good idea to check the accuracy of these assumptions; you can usually do so by checking the boundaries of the range, as shown below.

```
    Case 1: Sine = -1

        ScaledSine = Scale * Sine
                   = -10

            Indent = 1 + Scale + round(ScaledSine)
                   = 1 + 10 - 10
                   = 1
```

```
Case 2: Sine = +1

    ScaledSine = Scale * Sine
               = +10

        Indent = 1 + Scale + round(ScaledSine)
               = 1 + 10 + 10
               = 21
```

Exercises for Section 8.2

Self-Check

1. How does cancellation error differ from representational error?
2. Assume that the program shown in Fig. 8.4 has been modified to plot the Turing function `ln`. Determine the range of values for `Indent` using the assignment statement below as X goes from `0.1` to `5.0`.

```
Indent := 1 + Round(Scale * (1.0 + ln(X)))
```

Programming

1. Write a Turing program to determine the largest `int` and largest `real` number that can be used on your computer system.

8.3 Boolean Data Type

We have used `boolean` expressions as conditions in `if` and `exit` statements. In this section, we will discuss how to read a `boolean` value and how to complement a `boolean` expression.

Reading and Writing Boolean Values

The `get` and `put` statements cannot be used to read or write `boolean` values. Procedure `GetBool` (see Fig. 8.5) "reads" a `boolean` value. It does this by assigning a `boolean` value to output parameter `BoolVal` based on the next data character. The statement

```
BoolVal := NextCh = "T" or NextCh = "t"
```

assigns `true` to `BoolVal` if the data character read into `NextCh` is T or t; otherwise, it assigns `false` to `BoolVal`.

FIGURE 8.5   Procedures GetBool and PutBool

```
procedure GetBool (var BoolVal, Success : boolean)
    % Read a boolean value (represented by T or F)
    % into BoolVal and set the flag Success
    % Pre : None
    % Post: BoolVal is set to true if T or t is read
    %          otherwise, BoolVal is set to false.
    % Success is set to true only if one of the
    % four characters T, t, F, or f is read

    var NextCh : string        % A data character
    get NextCh
    BoolVal := NextCh = "T" or NextCh = "t"
    Success := BoolVal or NextCh = "F" or NextCh = "f"
end GetBool

procedure PutBool (BoolVal : boolean)
    % Print a boolean value (as T or F)
    % Pre: BoolVal is initialized
    % Post: BoolVal is displayed as T or F

    if BoolVal then
        put "T" ..
    else
        put "F" ..
    end if
end PutBool
```

Using a Boolean Parameter as a Flag

The second parameter of GetBool is used as a flag to signal whether a valid data character was read. In GetBool, the assignment statement

```
Success := BoolVal or NextCh = "F" or NextCh = "f"
```

assigns true to Success if the character read was T, t, F, or f.

If the value returned in Success is false, the calling program should call GetBool again. Assuming the calling program contains the variable declarations

```
var NextBool : boolean     % Input - next boolean value
var ReadDone : boolean     % Flag - True if read
                           % succeeds; otherwise, false
```

the loop statement below could be used to read a boolean value into NextBool.

```
var NextBool, ReadDone : boolean
loop
    put "Enter T or F> "
    GetBool (NextBool, ReadDone)
    exit when ReadDone
end loop
```

The `loop` statement executes until procedure `GetBool` sets `ReadDone` to `true`.

The `PutBool` procedure in Fig. 8.5 takes a `boolean` value (`true` or `false`) and displays *T* or *F*. The test to see if the `boolean` value is `true` is written as:

```
if BoolVal then
```

This line can be written using this longer form

```
if BoolVal = true then
```

Although beginners prefer the second form, experienced programmers prefer the first form which they read as "if `BoolVal` is true then ...". A particular `boolean` value, such as `NextBool`, can be printed using this call to `PutBool`

```
PutBool (NextBool)
```

This will cause the letter `T` or `F` to be displayed.

Complementing a Condition

Chapter 5 introduced the conditional loop. Figure 5.14 shows an `exit` statement with the exit condition `Power >= 1000`. The loop continuation condition is just the opposite of this, namely, `Power < 1000`. To convert from the exit condition to the continuation condition we need to know how to form the *complement* of a condition. We can complement a simple condition by changing the relational operator as shown below.

Operator	Operator in Complement
<	>=
<=	>
>	<=
>=	<
=	not=
not=	=

For example, the complement of X `<=` Y is X `>` Y. Also, if the expression begins with `not`, remove the `not` (e.g., the complement of `not Flag` is `Flag`).

DeMorgan's theorem explains how to complement a compound `boolean` expression: write the complement of each individual `boolean` expression and change each and to or and each or to and. Another way to complement a boolean expression is to precede the entire expression with not. Table 8.2 shows the complements of some Boolean expressions *E1* and *E2*.

DeMorgan's Theorem

not (*E1* and *E2*) = (not *E1*) or (not *E2*)
not (*E1* or *E2*) = (not *E1*) and (not *E2*)

TABLE 8.2   Complements of Boolean Expressions

Expression	Complement
X >= 1 and X <= 5	X < 1 or X > 5
(not Flag) or X <= Y	Flag and X > Y
Flag and not Switch	(not Flag) or Switch
N mod M = 0 and Flag	N mod M not= 0 or not Flag
Next = "A" or Next = "a"	Next not= "A" and Next not= "a"
Next = "A" or Next = "a"	not(Next = "A" or Next = "a")

In Table 8.2, Flag is a boolean variable, Next is type string and X, Y, M, and N are type int. In the complement of the expression on the first line, the relational operators are reversed (e.g., >= changed to <) and the operator and is changed to or. The last two lines show two complements of the same expression. In the last line, the expression is complemented by simply inserting the boolean operator not in front of the entire condition. Any boolean expression can be complemented in this way.

Exercises for Section 8.3

Self-Check

1. Write the complements of the conditions below.
   a. X <= Y and X not= 15
   b. X <= Y and X not= 15 or Z = 7.5
   c. X not= 15 or Z = 7.5 and X <= Y
   d. Flag or not X not= 15.7
   e. not Flag and X <= 8
2. Why does good programming style require GetBool be implemented as a procedure rather than as a function?

Programming

1. Write a loop controlled by a boolean flag that prompts the program user to enter an integer X in the range −K to +K inclusive. Loop termination occurs after the user enters an appropriate value of X.

2. Write a procedure that has two integer input parameters M and N, and one `boolean` output parameter that is set to `true` when the value of M is a divisor of N and `false` otherwise.

8.4 String Variables and Functions

Turing provides a `string` data type that can store and manipulate sequences of characters such as those that comprise a person's name, address, and other personal data. A type `string` literal consists of zero or more characters (letters, digits, punctuation marks, or the like) enclosed in quotation marks. A `string` value may be assigned to a `string` variable or associated with a constant identifier, as shown below.

```
const Star := "*"
var Scientist : string := "Einstein"
```

The `string` variable `Scientist` is assigned the value `"Einstein"` in its declaration. A `string` variable or value may appear on the right-hand side of an assignment statement. `String` values may also be compared, read, and printed. There are also operations to extract parts of a string, find the length of a string, and attach or *catenate* two strings into one longer string.

Comparing Strings for Equality

Assuming `Next` and `First` are variables of type `string`, the `boolean` expressions

```
Next = First
Next not= First
```

determine whether the two `string` variables have the same or different values. Uppercase letters are not considered to be equal to lowercase letters, so, for example, `"D"` is not equal to `"d"`. Two strings are considered to be equal if they have the same length and are equal character by character (or if they are both the null string, containing zero characters). For example, the following are equalities.

```
"Mr. Jones" = "Mr. Jones"
"$2.16" = "$2.16"
"" = ""        Two null strings
```

The following are inequalities.

```
"Him" not= "Her"
"Here" not= "Her"     Different lengths of strings
"ACME" not= "Acme"    Lower and uppercase are distinct
"$2.00" not= "$2"     The characters and not the amounts
                      are compared
```

Comparing Strings for Ordering

Order comparisons can also be performed on character variables using the relational operators < , <= , > , >= . To understand the result of an order comparison, it helps to know something about the way characters are represented internally within your computer. Each character has its own unique numeric code; the binary form of this code is stored in a memory cell that has a character value. These binary numbers are compared by the relational operators in the normal way.

The digit characters are an increasing sequence of consecutive characters. For example in ASCII (American Standard Code for Information Interchange), the digit characters "0" through "9" have code values of 48 through 57 (decimal). The order relationship below holds for the digit characters:

    "0"<"1"<"2"<"3"<"4"<"5"<"6"<"7"<"8"<"9"

The uppercase letters are also an increasing sequence of characters, but they are not necessarily consecutive. In ASCII, the uppercase letters have the consecutive decimal code values 65 through 90. The order relationship below holds for uppercase letters.

    "A"<"B"<"C"< ... <"X"<"Y"<"Z"

If the lowercase letters are included in the character set, they are also an increasing, but not necessarily consecutive, sequence of characters. In ASCII, the lowercase letters have the consecutive decimal code values 97 through 122 and the order relationship below holds.

    "a"<"b"<"c"< ... <"x"<"y"<"z"

In our examples and programs we will assume that both uppercase and lowercase letters are available, and that the letters have consecutive decimal codes for both uppercase and lowercase.

In ASCII, the *printable characters* have codes from 32 (code for a blank or space) to 126 (code for the symbol ~) . The other codes represent non-printable *control characters*. Sending a control character to an output device causes the device to perform a special operation such as returning the cursor to column one, advancing the cursor to the next line, or ringing a bell.

Ordering among strings, such as "Johnston" and "Jones" is determined by character by character comparison of individual characters. In the following example,

    "Johnston" < "Jones"

you can read this as *Johnston comes alphabetically before Jones.* In Turing, the ordering is determined by the fact that the first letters of both names, Jo, are identical, but the third letter of Johnston precedes the third letter of Jones: "h" < "n". If you have two strings, such as "Rock" and

"Rocky", which are identical except that one is shorter than the other, the shorter comes first:

```
"Rock" < "Rocky"
```

This method of ordering is called *lexicographical ordering*. It is the essentially the same as the alphabetic ordering using in dictionaries, except that, in Turing, uppercase precedes lowercase and Turing's ordering applies to special characters, such as blanks, periods, "+" and "?", and digits ("0", "1" up to "9") as well as letters.

The Ord, Chr, Succ, and Pred Functions

Turing provides a function called ord which returns the numerical code for a single character. For example:

```
ord ("A") = 65
```

For computers that support ASCII characters, the returned number is exactly the ASCII character code.

The name of the ord function comes from the more general concept of the *ordinal* position of the characters, as placed in one-to-one correspondence with the non-negative integers 0, 1, 2, ... ASCII defines this correspondence by giving the binary codes for each character.

The inverse of the ord function is the chr function, which takes a number and returns a character. For example:

```
chr (65) = "A"
```

In general, if C is a character, and N = chr (C) then ord (N) = C, which we can write more succinctly as:

```
C = chr (ord (C))
```

The succ (successor) function returns the character following a character; for example:

```
succ ("A") = "B"
```

The pred (predecessor) function returns the preceding character. For example:

```
pred ("y") = "x"
```

Instead of using the succ and pred functions, we could use ord, then add or subtract one and then use chr, as in the following,

```
succ (C) = chr (ord (C) + 1)
pred (C) = chr (ord (C) - 1)
```

However, direct use of succ and pred provides us with the preceding and following characters in a more direct fashion.

Each of ord, succ and pred require a parameter that is a single character. If you try to use one of these functions with a string of several characters, as in ord ("Judy"), you will get a Turing run-time error message such as "Parameter is not of length one."

EXAMPLE 8.4
Table 8.3 shows some results of the ord, succ, and pred functions for ASCII.

TABLE 8.3 Result of Ord, Succ, and Pred Functions for ASCII

Parameter	Ord	Succ	Pred
C	67	D	B
7	55	8	6
y	121	z	x
blank	32	!	unprintable

The table shows that the digit "7" has the ordinal number 55 in ASCII. Regardless of the character code used, the expression

    ord ("7") - ord ("0") = 7

will always be true because the digit characters must be in consecutive sequence.

Table 8.3 shows that the character "C" has the ordinal number 67 in ASCII. Since the character "D" is the successor of the character "C", it has an ordinal number of 68. Since the letters are in consecutive sequence in ASCII, the boolean expression

    ord("C") - ord("A") = 2

is true. In ASCII, the lowercase letters follow the uppercase letters, and the difference in code values for both cases of the same letter is 32 (e.g., ord("a") - ord("A") is 32).

EXAMPLE 8.5
Function LowerCase in Fig. 8.6 returns the lowercase form of an uppercase letter passed to its parameter Ch. If Ch does not contain an uppercase letter, LowerCase returns Ch as its result.

FIGURE 8.6   Function LowerCase

```
function LowerCase (Ch : string) : string
    % Return the lowercase form of the argument
    % Pre : Ch must be a single character
    % Post: Return the lowercase equivalent of Ch if
    %         Ch is an uppercase letter;
    %         otherwise return Ch

    if "A" <= Ch and Ch <= "Z" then
        result chr(ord(Ch) - ord("A") + ord("a"))
    else
        result Ch
    end if
end LowerCase
```

If Ch has the value "C" the boolean expression is true and the first result statement is evaluated as shown below (assuming the letters are consecutive characters).

```
result chr(ord("C") - ord("A") + ord("a"))
result chr(2 + ord("a"))
result chr(99) = "c"
```

EXAMPLE 8.6

A *collating sequence* is a sequence of characters arranged by ordinal number. The program in Fig. 8.7 prints part of the collating sequence. It lists the characters with ordinal numbers 32 through 90, inclusive. The sequence shown is for the ASCII code; the first character printed is a blank (ordinal number 32).

FIGURE 8.7   Printing Part of a Collating Sequence

```
% The "Collate" program
% Print part of a collating sequence
% Print characters chr(32) through chr(90)

const First := 32        % First ordinal number
const Last := 90         % Last ordinal number

for Ordinal : First .. Last
    put chr(Ordinal) ..   % Print Ordinal's character
end for
```

```
 !"#$%&'()*+,./0123456789:;<=>?@ABCDEFGHIJKLMNOPQRSTUVWXYZ
```

The functions introduced in this section are summarized in Table 8.4.

TABLE 8.4   The Chr, Ord, Pred, and Succ Functions

Function	Purpose	Argument	Result
chr (N)	Return the character whose ordinal number is N	An integer	A single character
ord (N)	Return the ordinal number of its argument	A single character	An integer
pred (N)	Returns the predecessor of its argument	A single character	A single character
succ (N)	Return the successor of its argument	A single character	A single character

Catenating Strings

In Turing, you can join or *catenate* character strings to form a longer character string. For example, "pine" can be catenated with "cone" to form "pinecone". We use + to mean catenation, so we write this as

```
"pine" + "cone" = "pinecone"
```

We will write a program that reads a person's first name, such as "Alicia" and last name, such as "Garcia", and produces the string "Garcia, Alicia", which is the usual way of giving names with last name first.

```
% The "Lastname" program
% Read in a first and a last name and form a string
% with the last name first
var FirstName, LastName : string
var LastNameFirst : string

put "Enter your first name> " ..
get FirstName
put "Enter your last name> " ..
get LastName
LastNameFirst := LastName + ", " + FirstName
put "Name with last name first is:"
put LastNameFirst
```

Here is the result of running the program with first and last names of "Alicia" and "Garcia".

```
Enter your first name> Alicia
Enter your last name> Garcia
Name with last name first is:
Garcia, Alicia
```

In this example we have catenated together three values: `Garcia`, a string containing a comma followed by a blank, and `Alicia`, using the statement

```
LastNameFirst := LastName + ", " + FirstName
```

Substrings

It is sometimes useful to be able to extract parts or `substrings` of strings. For example, we sometimes abbreviate words by taking their first three letters. If the variable `Word` has the value `"photon"`, we might abbreviate this to `"pho"`. In Turing we write `Word (1 .. 3)` to extract the first three letters of `Word`. Here is a program that reads words and outputs their abbreviations.

```
% The "Abbrev" program
% Read in words and display their abbreviations,
% which consist of their first three letters

put "Enter words and their abbreviations will"
put "be displayed."
put "Enter 'stop' to halt the program."

var Word, Abbreviation : string
loop
    put "Enter a word> " ..
    get Word
    exit when Word = "stop"
    Abbreviation := Word (1 .. 3)
    put "The abbreviation is ", Abbreviation
end loop
```

Here is the result of running the program with `"photon"`, `"electron"`, and `"neutron"` entered as words, followed by the word `"stop"`.

```
Enter words and their abbreviations will
be displayed.
Enter 'stop' to halt the program.
Enter a word> photon
The abbreviation is pho
Enter a word> electron
The abbreviation is ele
Enter a word> neutron
The abbreviation is neu
Enter a word> stop
```

In the above program we have assigned `Abbreviation` its value using this statement

```
Abbreviation := Word (1 .. 3)
```

If we wanted the abbreviation to consist of the first and last letters of the words, we would use a different form of substring. In particular, Word (1) extracts the first character and Word (*) extracts the last character. In this case we would replace the above statement with

```
Abbreviation := Word (1) + Word (*)
```

This catenates the first character Word (1) and the last character Word (*). The abbreviations for "photon", "electron", and "neutron" would now be printed as "pn", "en", and "nn".

Another possibility is to use the first two letters and the last letter for the abbreviation. This would be accomplished by this statement

```
Abbreviation := Word (1 .. 2) + Word (*)
```

The abbreviations for "photon", "electron", and "neutron" would now be "phn", "eln", and "nen".

A part of a string can be selected by a variable or an expression that evaluates to an integer. In the following example, a triangle pattern is displayed by printing the first N letters of the string "triangle" on line number N.

```
% The "Triangle" program
% Display a triangle pattern based on the word
% triangle.
const Pattern := "triangle"
for I : 1 .. 8
    put Pattern (1 .. I)
end for
```

When this program runs, it will produce the following output

```
t
tr
tri
tria
trian
triang
triangl
triangle
```

The Length of a String

Turing provides a function, length, that is used to determine the number of characters in a string. For example, length ("Trudeau") is equal to 7. Here is a program that reads in words, until stop is entered, and displays the length of each word. It also records and displays the length of the longest string it has read.

```
% The "Length" program
% Read words and output their lengths
% Stop when 'stop' is typed
% Finish by outputting the longest length

var Word : string
var Longest : int := 0     % Longest so far

put "Enter words and their lengths will be output"
put "Enter 'stop' to halt the program"

loop
    put "Enter a word> " ..
    get Word
    exit when Word = "stop"
    put "The length of ", Word, " is ", length (Word)
    if length (Word) > Longest then
        Longest := length (Word)
    end if
end loop
put "The longest word had ", Longest, " characters"
```

If you enter the words "music", "elephant", and "computer", followed by the word stop, this will be the output

```
Enter words and their lengths will be output
Enter 'stop' to halt the program
Enter a word> music
The length of music is 5
Enter a word> elephant
The length of elephant is 8
Enter a word> computer
The length of computer is 8
Enter a word> stop
The longest word had 8 characters
```

Exercises for Section 8.4

Self-Check

1. Evaluate the following assuming the letters are consecutive characters.

a. ord("D") - ord("A")

b. ord("d") - ord("a")

c. succ(pred("a"))

d. chr(ord("C"))

e. chr(ord("C") - ord("A") + ord("a"))

f. ord("7") - ord("6")

g. ord("9") - ord("0")

h. succ(succ(succ("d")))

i. chr(ord("A") + 5)

2. Write a `loop` statement equivalent to the `for` loop shown below

```
for OrdCh : ord("A") .. ord("Z")
    put chr(OrdCh), " ", OrdCh
end for
```

3. Which of the following string comparisons are true?

   a. `"Ralph" >= "Andy"`
   b. `"ABC" = "abc"`
   c. `"3+4" = "7"`
   d. `"Bob" < "Bobby"`
   e. `"12" > "1"`

4. What is displayed by the following program?

```
% The "Strtest" program
const P := "pinecone"
const R := "railroad"
var S : string
S := P (5 .. *)
put S
S := R + "s and " + P + "s"
put S
const T := P (1) + R (2 .. 4)
put T
put R (1) + R (* - 2 .. *)
put length (P)
```

Programming

1. Write a function `UpperCase` that returns as its value the uppercase equivalent of its character argument if one exists or the value of its argument if there is none.
2. Write a function `LowerCaseStr` that accepts a string of characters and returns the equivalent string in uppercase.

8.5 Subrange Types

One of the important features of Turing is that it permits the declaration of new data types. Many of these data types will be discussed in later chapters. In this section we focus on new data types that are subranges of the ordinal types where a *subrange* defines a subset of the integers. Subranges both make a program more readable and enable Turing to detect when a variable is given an unreasonable value.

EXAMPLE 8.7

Type declarations begin with the reserved word `type` and are used to declare a new data type. The Turing scope rules for identifiers (see Section 7.7) apply to names of data types. Two subrange types are declared below as well as a variable of each new type.

```
type DaysInWeek : 1..7
type DaysInMonth : 1..31

var WeekDay : DaysInWeek
var MonthDay : DaysInMonth
```

Any integer value from 1 to 7 inclusive may be stored in a variable of type `DaysInWeek`. The computer displays an error message and stops program execution if an attempt is made to store any other integer in a variable of type `DaysInWeek`. For example, the assignment statement

```
WeekDay := 13
```

will cause the run-time error `"value out of range"`, stopping program execution because the value 13 is not included in data type `DaysInWeek`.

DaysInMonth is also a subrange with base type `int`. A variable of type `DaysInMonth` may be used to keep track of the current date, a value between 1 and 31 inclusive. The statement

```
get MonthDay
```

reads a data value into `MonthDay` (type `DaysInMonth`). A `"value out of range"` run-time error occurs if the data value is less than 1 or greater than 31.

SUBRANGE TYPE DECLARATION

Form: type *subrange type* : *minvalue* .. *maxvalue*

Example: type LowCaseOrd : ord("a") .. ord("z")

Interpretation: A new data type named *subrange type* is defined. A variable of type *subrange type* may be assigned a value from minvalue through *maxvalue* inclusive. The values *minvalue* and *maxvalue* must both be integers and *minvalue* must be less than or equal to *maxvalue*.

Note: *Minvalue* and *maxvalue* may be expressions but it must be possible to determine their values at compile time.

The scope rules for a subrange type identifier are the same as for other Turing identifiers. The operations that may be performed on a variable whose type is an integer subrange are the same as for the integers.

PROGRAM
STYLE

> **MOTIVATION FOR USING SUBRANGES**
> You may be wondering why subranges are useful. They don't seem to provide any new capabilities. However, they do provide additional opportunity for your program to "bomb" because attempting to store an out-of-range value in a variable whose type is a subrange stops program execution. This should happen only as the result of an error by the programmer or program user. If MonthDay is type int (instead of DaysInMonth), then the program continues to execute regardless of what integer value is assigned to MonthDay. Assigning an overly large value (say 1000) to MonthDay may cause a later statement to fail or the program to generate incorrect results. In the former case, the program user may have difficulty finding the statement that was actually at fault (i.e., the statement that assigned the out-of-range value). In the latter case, the program user may not even be aware that an error occurred if program execution is completed in a normal manner. The use of subranges ensures the immediate detection of an out-of-range value.

Exercises for Section 8.5

Self-Check

1. Identify the illegal subranges below.

   a. 1 .. 10000
   b. "A" .. "Z"
   c. -15 .. 15
   d. "A" .. "z"
   e. -5.0 .. 5.0
   f. 0 .. "9"
   g. 15 .. -15
   h. "ACE" .. "KING"
   i. "a" .. "Z"
   j. 1000 - 25 .. 1000 + 25

2. Explain why using procedure GetInt (described in the programming exercise below) would be safer than using get as a means of reading int subrange values into a program.

Programming

1. Write a procedure GetInt that has input parameters Min and Max (type int) and output parameters N (type int) and Success (type boolean). Your procedure should prompt the user to enter a value for N and set Success to true if N is in the range Min to Max inclusive; Success should be set to false otherwise.

8.6 Type Equivalence and Assignability

Two data types are considered *equivalent* if they are the same type. For example, two variables both of whose types are string have equivalent types. If the types are subranges, their upper and lower values must be equal; for example, the types `Marks` and `Grades` are equivalent types:

```
type Marks : 1 .. 10
type Grades : 1 .. 10
```

The *root* type of these subranges is the `int` type. In the next section we will introduce enumerated types, which also have subranges; in this case, the root type of the subrange will be the enumerated type.

When used in an expression, values of a subrange type are considered to have their root type. For example, if `Mark` is declared to have type `Marks`, in the expression `Mark + 2`, the value of `Mark` is considered to be an integer. This implies that any variable whose type is a subrange can be used in an expression just like a variable declared using the root type. In the most common case, the subrange's root type is `int` so the variable can use integer operators such as +, −, and *.

Operands whose types or root types are equivalent may be manipulated by the same operator. For example

```
NextCh not= "3"
```

is syntactically correct as long as `NextCh` is type `string`. On the other hand, the expression

```
NextCh not= 3
```

causes a syntax error because `NextCh`'s type (`string`) is not equivalent to 3's type (`int`).

Any time you pass an actual parameter to a formal `var` parameter, the two types must be equivalent. This means you could pass a variable of type `Marks` to a `var` formal parameter of type `Grades`, but you could not pass an `int` variable to the same `var` formal parameter.

There is a special case that occurs when an integer value is used in an expression where a real number is required. In this case, the integer is implicitly converted to be a real number. This means that you can always use an integer in an expression when a real number is expected. However, an actual parameter being passed to a `var` formal parameter is not considered to be an expression. This means that an integer value cannot be passed to a `var real` formal parameter.

If a variable's type is equivalent to an expression's type, it is allowable to assign the expression to the variable. For example, if both `V` and `E` have the type `boolean`, the following is allowed.

```
V := E
```

In the general case, for an assignment to be allowed, the expression `E` must be *assignable* to variable `V`, as will now be explained. Expression `E` is assignable to variable `V` if their root types are equivalent or if `V`'s type is real and `E`'s root type is `int`.

You would be allowed to assign integer value 27 to a `real` variable, but you would not be allowed to assign `real` value 3.7 to an integer variable I. You could first convert 3.7 to be an integer, for example by rounding it as in `round (3.7)`, and then this assignment would be allowed.

```
I := round (3.7)
```

When you pass an actual parameter to a value (non-`var`) formal parameter, the actual parameter must be assignable to the type for the formal parameter. This means that if variable V were declared to have the type of the formal value parameter, the assignment statement

```
V := actual parameter
```

is allowed if and only if it is allowed to pass the actual parameter to the formal parameter.

When you are using subrange types, you can get a run-time error message due to an out-of-range assignment. For example, given these declarations

```
type LetterOrd : ord("A") .. ord("Z")
var NextCh : LetterOrd
```

the assignment statement

```
NextCh := ord("3")
```

is allowed by the Turing compiler, because the integer `ord ("3")` is assignable to type `int`. However, when this is executed it will cause the run-time error `"value to be assigned is out of bounds"`, because the value `ord("3")` is not in the range `ord("A")` to `ord("Z")`.

We will discuss more issues of type compatibility and assignment compatibility in later chapters.

Exercises for Section 8.6

Self-Check

1. Assuming that I is type 0 .. 10, J is type `int`, and R is type `real`, indicate whether each expression below is assignment compatible with the variable on the left and whether any constraints are necessary to avoid an out-of-range error.

```
a. K := 3 * I + J
b. I := 15
c. J := floor(R) + 2 * I
d. I := I div J
e. I := I / J
f. I := J mod 11
g. J := 2 * K + 3
```

2. Explain why the compiler cannot in general determine whether a `"value out of range"` error may or may not occur occur at run-time for an assignment statement.

Enumerated Types

This section introduces a feature of Turing that improves the readability of large programs. In many programming situations, the standard data types and their values are inadequate. For example, in a budget program you might want to distinguish among the following categories of expenditures: entertainment, rent, utilities, food, clothing, automobile, insurance, and miscellaneous. Although you could create an arbitrary code that associates entertainment with a character value of `"e"`, rent with a character value of `"r"`, and so on, Turing allows you to create *enumerated types*, each with its own set of meaningful values.

For example, the following enumerated type, Expenses, has eight possible values enclosed in parentheses.

```
type Expenses : enum (Entertainment, Rent,
                      Utilities, Food, Clothing,
                      Automobile, Insurance,
                      Miscellaneous)
   var ExpenseKind : Expenses
```

The variable ExpenseKind (type Expenses) can contain any of the eight values. The following `if` statement tests the value stored in ExpenseKind.

```
if ExpenseKind = Expenses.Entertainment then
    put "Postpone until after your payday"
elsif ExpenseKind = Expenses.Rent then
    put "Pay before the first of the month!"
end if
```

As you can see in this example, each value of an enumerated type is written as the type name, then a dot (period), and then the name of the value, as in `Expenses.Entertainment`.

EXAMPLE 8.8

The enumerated type Day declared below has the values Sunday, Monday, and so on.

```
type Day : enum (Sunday, Monday, Tuesday, Wednesday,
                 Thursday, Friday, Saturday)
```

The values associated with an enumerated type must be identifiers; they cannot be numeric, character, or string literals (e.g., `"Sunday"` cannot be a value for an enumerated type).

The scope rules for identifiers apply to the names of enumerated types. Each enumerated-type value, such as Day.Monday is treated as a constant. The type declaration must precede any variable declaration that references it.

ENUMERATED TYPE DECLARATION

Form: type *enumerated type* : enum (*identifier list*)

Example: type Class : enum (Freshman, Sophomore,
                                 Junior, Senior)

Interpretation: A new data type named *enumerated type* is declared. The values associated with this type are specified in the *identifier list*. Each value is defined as a constant. When an enumerated value is used in a program, it must be preceded by the type name and a dot (period), as in Class.Freshman.

Note: A particular identifier can appear in the *identifier list* of more than one enumerated type.

An identifier can appear in more than one enumerated-type declaration. If type Day is already declared, the type declaration

```
type TDay : enum (Tuesday, Thursday)
```

is valid. When used in the program, the values of this type would be written as TDay.Tuesday and TDay.Thursday. The two types, Day and TDay, are completely distinct (they are not equivalent). It is not legal to compare their values; for example, if you write Day.Thursday = TDay.Thursday in a program, the compiler would produce an error message.

Operators for Enumerated Types

Like the standard type int, each enumerated type has a fixed order relationship between its values. For type Day, the first value is Sunday, the next value is Monday, and so on. The only operators that apply to enumerated types are the relational and assignment operators. The following order relations are all true:

```
Day.Sunday < Day.Monday
Day.Wednesday not= Day.Tuesday
Day.Wednesday = Day.Wednesday
Day.Wednesday >= Day.Tuesday
Expenses.entertainment < Expenses.rent
```

The order relation

```
Expenses.Entertainment < Day.Wednesday
```

would cause a syntax error because the values shown are associated with two different enumerated types.

You can assign enumerated values to enumerated variables. The variable declaration

```
var Today: Day          % Current day of the week
var Tomorrow : Day      % Day after Today
```

specifies that Today and Tomorrow are type Day; therefore, they can be assigned any of the values listed in the declaration for type Day. Consequently, the assignment statements

```
Today := Day.Friday
Tomorrow := Day.Saturday
```

assign the value Friday to variable Today and Saturday to variable Tomorrow. After the assignments, the following order relations are all true.

```
Today = Day.Friday
Tomorrow = Day.Saturday
Today < Tomorrow
Today not= Day.Wednesday
Today >= Day.Sunday
```

We can use functions succ, pred, and ord (see Section 8.4) with enumerated types. The ordinal value of the first listed enumerated item in a list is 0, the next is 1, and so on. Some examples are given below, assuming that Today is Day.Friday and Tomorrow is Day.Saturday.

```
ord(Today) is 5
ord(Tomorrow) is 6
succ(Today) is Day.Saturday
pred(Today) is Day.Thursday
pred(succ(Today)) is Day.Friday
succ(Tomorrow) is undefined
pred(Tomorrow) is Day.Friday
```

The next-to-last example above is undefined because no value of type Day follows Saturday. Similarly, the value of pred(Day.Sunday) is undefined. Succ or pred operations leading to undefined results may cause a range error during program execution.

EXAMPLE 8.9
The following if statement assigns the value of Tomorrow based on the value of Today (both type Day).

```
if Today = Day.Saturday then
    Tomorrow := Day.Sunday
else
    Tomorrow := succ(Today)
end if
```

Because the days of a week are cyclical, `Tomorrow` is set to `Sunday` when `Today` is `Saturday`. The last value (`Saturday`) in the enumerated type `Day` is treated separately because `succ(Today)` is undefined when `Today` is `Saturday`.

We can use variables that belong to enumerated types as *counter* variables in `for` statements and as *case selectors* in `case` statements. This is illustrated in the next two examples.

EXAMPLE 8.10

The `for` loop in Fig. 8.8 reads the hours worked during each week day for an employee and accumulates the sum of the hours worked in `WeekHours`. Assuming that the counter variable `Today` is declared as the enumerated type `Day`, the `loop` executes for `Today` equal to `Monday` through `Friday`. During each iteration, the calls to `put` and `PutDay` display a prompt such as

```
Enter hours for Monday>
```

where `PutDay` (see programming exercise 3 at the end of this section) displays the day name (string `"Monday"`). Next, each value read into `DayHours` is added to `WeekHours`. After loop exit, the final value of `WeekHours` is displayed.

FIGURE 8.8　　　Accumulating Hours Worked

```
var WeekHours : real := 0.0
for Today : Day.Monday .. Day.Friday
    put "Enter hours for "
    PutDay (Today)
    put "> "
    get DayHours
    WeekHours := WeekHours + DayHours
end for

put "Total weekly hours are ", WeekHours :4:2
```

Reading and Writing Enumerated Type Values

The Turing `get` and `put` statements cannot read or write enumerated-type values. However, you can write your own procedures for this purpose.

EXAMPLE 8.11

Given the declarations

```
type Color : enum (Red, Green, Blue, Yellow)
var Eyes : Color
```

the statement

```
put ord(Eyes)
```

can be used for diagnostic printing during debugging. It does not print the value of Eyes, but it does display the ordinal number of the value that is an integer from 0 (for Red) to 3 (for Yellow).

Procedure PutColor in Fig. 8.9 prints a string that represents a value of type Color. If the value of Eyes is defined, the statement

```
PutColor (Eyes)
```

displays the value of Eyes as a string. Make sure you understand the difference between the string "Blue" and the enumerated value Color.Blue.

FIGURE 8.9   **Procedure to Print a Value of Type Color**

```
procedure PutColor (InColor : Color)
    % Display the value of InColor
    % Pre : InColor is assigned a value
    % Post: The value of InColor is displayed as a string

    case InColor of
        label Color.Red      : put "Red"
        label Color.Green    : put "Green"
        label Color.Blue     : put "Blue"
        label Color.Yellow   : put "Yellow"
    end case
end PutColor
```

We often use case statement such as the one in Fig. 8.9 whose case labels are values associated with an enumerated type. Be careful not to use a string such as "Red" as a case label. This causes a syntax error such as "case alternative is the wrong type." Remember that only integers and enumerated values may appear in case labels.

It is more difficult to read the value of an enumerated-type variable than it is to display it. The next example shows one method.

EXAMPLE 8.12

Procedure GetColor in Fig. 8.10 returns one value of type Color and one of type boolean. If Eyes has type Color and ValidColor has type boolean, the procedure call statement

```
GetColor (Eyes, ValidColor)
```

attempts to read the value of Eyes and sets ValidColor to indicate the success (ValidColor is true) or failure (ValidColor is false) of this operation. GetColor reads a single color value from each data line, ignoring all but the first letter on the line. If Black and Brown are added to the list of values for Color, it becomes necessary to read additional characters when the first letter read is B. We will leave this as an exercise (see programming exercise 2 at the end of this section).

FIGURE 8.10   Procedure GetColor

```
procedure GetColor (var ItemColor  : Color,
                    var ValidColor : boolean)
   % Assign value to ItemColor based on an input
   % character. Set ValidColor to indicate whether
   % the assignment was made.
   % Pre : None
   % Post: ItemColor is defined if the character read
   %       is "r", "g", "b", "y", or their uppercase
   %       forms. ValidColor is set to true if ItemColor
   %       is defined; otherwise, ValidColor is set to
   %       false.

   var ColorChar : string    % First letter of color name
   put "Enter first letter of color> " ..
   get ColorChar

   % Assign the color value
   ValidColor := true    % Start by assuming a valid color
   if ColorChar = "r" or ColorChar = "R" then
       ItemColor := Color.Red
   elsif ColorChar = "g" or ColorChar = "G" then
       ItemColor := Color.Green
   elsif ColorChar = "b" or ColorChar = "B" then
       ItemColor := Color.Blue
   elsif ColorChar = "y" or ColorChar = "Y" then
       ItemColor := Color.Yellow
   else
       ValidColor := false % Invalid color
   end if
end GetColor
```

Subranges of Enumerated Types

We can declare subranges of enumerated types. The following declarations specify that WeekDay (values Monday through Friday) is a subrange of type Day and variable SchoolDay is type WeekDay.

```
type Day : enum (Sunday, Monday, Tuesday, Wednesday,
                 Thursday, Friday, Saturday)
type WeekDay : Day.Monday .. Day.Friday
                 % Week days only
var SchoolDay : WeekDay
```

The assignment statement

```
SchoolDay := Day.Monday
```

is valid; however, the assignment statement

```
SchoolDay := Day.Sunday
```

causes an out-of-range syntax error.

Why Use Enumerated Types?

At this point you may have a legitimate concern: Is it worth using enumerated types, considering that it is so much trouble to read and write their values? Also, if we need to use a letter code to enter the value of an enumerated type variable, why not use that code throughout the program? The fact is that enumerated types in a program can make that program easier to read and understand.

EXAMPLE 8.13

The `if` statement

```
if DayNum = 1 then
    PayFactor = 2.0        % Double pay for Sunday
elsif DayNum = 7 then
    PayFactor := 1.5       % Time and a half for Saturday
else
    PayFactor := 1.0       % Regular pay
end if
```

might appear in a payroll program without enumerated types if `Sunday` and `Saturday` are "coded" as the integers 1 and 7, respectively. If we use the enumerated type `Day` and variable `Today` (type `Day`), we can write this statement as

```
if Today = Day.Sunday then
    PayFactor := 2.0
elsif Today = Day.Saturday then
    PayFactor := 1.5
else
    PayFactor := 1.0
end if
```

The latter form is more readable because, instead of an obscure codes (1 and 7), it uses values (`Saturday` and `Sunday`) that are meaningful to the problem. Consequently, the comments on the right in the original statement are not needed.

In a lengthy program, the extra overhead required to implement procedures for reading and writing the values associated with an enumerated type will be insignificant. If these procedures are placed in your own library of modules, it will be easy to reuse read and write procedures that you have already written.

Another advantage of using enumerated types is that the creation of an enumerated type automatically limits the range of values that can be assigned to a variable. If we use an integer code, any integer value may be assigned unless we take the trouble to declare a subrange type. When we declare an enumerated type, we explicitly declare the set of values that may be assigned to a variable of that type. In the example above, any integer value may be assigned to variable DayNum; however, only one of the seven values listed in the declaration for enumerated type Day may be assigned to variable Today.

Exercises for Section 8.7

Self-Check

1. Evaluate each of the following, assuming before each operation that Today (type Day) is Thursday.

   a. ord(Day.Monday)
   b. ord(Today)
   c. Today < Day.Tuesday
   d. succ(Day.Wednesday)
   e. pred(succ(Today))
   f. succ(Today)
   g. pred(Today)
   h. Today >= Day.Thursday
   i. pred(Day.Sunday)
   j. ord(succ(succ(Today)))

2. Indicate whether each type declaration below is valid or invalid. Explain what is wrong with each invalid type declaration.

   a. type Letters   : enum ("A", "B", "C")
   b. type Letters   : enum (A, B, C)
   c. type TwoLetters : enum (A .. B)
   d. type Letters   : enum ("A" .. "Z")
   e. type Boolean   : enum (true, false)
   f. type Day   : enum (Sun, Mon, Tue, Wed,
                                 Thu, Fri, Sat)
   g. type WeekDay   : Day.Mon .. Day.Fri
   h. type WeekEnd   : Day.Sat .. Day.Sun
   i. type TDay   : enum (Tue, Thu)

Programming

1. Declare an enumerated type Month and rewrite the if statement below assuming that CurMonth is type Month instead of type int. Also, write the equivalent case statement.

```
        if CurMonth = 1 then
            put "Happy new year"
        elsif CurMonth = 6 then
            put "Summer begins"
        elsif CurMonth = 9 then
            put "Back to school"
        elsif CurMonth = 12 then
            put "Happy Holidays"
        end if
```

2. Rewrite procedure `GetColor` (see Fig. 8.10), assuming that `Black` and `Brown` are also values for enumerated type `Color`.
3. Write procedure `PutDay` for enumerated type `Day`.

8.8 Iterative Approximations (Optional)

Numerical analysis is the field of study that is concerned with developing methods to use the computer to solve computational problems in mathematics. Some examples of numerical methods include: finding solutions to sets of equations, performing operations on matrices, finding roots of equations, and performing mathematical integration. This section contains two case studies that illustrate methods for iteratively approximating solutions to computational problems. You may wish to skip this material if you do not have the appropriate mathematical background.

✖ Case Study:

Approximating the Value of e

1. Problem

There are a number of mathematical quantities that can be represented using a series approximation where a series is represented by a summation of an infinite number of terms. We are interested in using this technique to compute *e* (value is 2.71828183), the base of the natural logarithms.

2. Analysis

We can get an approximation to the value of *e* by evaluating the series

$$1 + 1/1! + 1/2! + 1/3! + \ldots + 1/N! + \ldots$$

where N! is the factorial of N as defined in section 7.10 and repeated here.

```
N! = 1           For N = 0 or N = 1
N! = N * (N-1)!  For N > 1
```

We can approximate the series by adding up its first N terms. The larger the value of N we use, the more terms will be included in the series, resulting in increased accuracy. The value of N will be a problem input.

DATA REQUIREMENTS

Problem Inputs

```
N : int              % The number of terms, N, in the sum
```

Problem Outputs

```
E : real             % The approximate value of e
```

Program Variable

```
IthTerm : real   % The ith term of the series
```

3. Design

We can use a counting loop to implement the summation formula above.

INITIAL ALGORITHM
1. Read in the value of N
2. Initialize E to 1.0
3. Initialize the *i*th (the zero-th) term to 1.0
4. for each I from 1 to N
       5. Compute the *i*th term in the series
       6. Add the *i*th term to E
   end for
7. Print the value of E

4. Implementation

The program is shown in Fig. 8.11. Inside the for loop, the statement

```
IthTerm := IthTerm / I
```

computes the value of the *i*th term in the series by dividing the previous term by the loop control variable I. The formula below shows that this division does indeed produce the next term in the series.

$$\frac{1}{(I-1)!} \star \frac{1}{I} = \frac{1}{I \star (I-1)!} = \frac{1}{I!}$$

Because 0! is 1, IthTerm must be initialized to 1.0. The statement

```
E := E + IthTerm
```

adds the new value of IthTerm to the sum being accumulated in E. Trace the execution of this loop to satisfy yourself that IthTerm takes on the values 1/1!, 1/2!, 1/3!, and so on, during successive loop iterations.

FIGURE 8.11

Series Approximation to e

```
% The "Eseries" program
% Compute the value of e by a series approximation
```

```
var E : real := 1.0            % Value being approximated
var IthTerm : real := 1.0      % Ith term in series
var N : int                    % Number of terms in series

put "Enter the number of terms in the series> " ..
get N

% Compute each term and add it to the accumulating sum
for I : 1 .. N
    IthTerm := IthTerm / I
    E := E + IthTerm
end for

% Print the result
put "The approximate value of e is ", E :12:10
```

```
Enter the number of terms in the series> 15
The approximate value of e is 2.7182818285
```

---

5. Testing

To determine whether this algorithm works, it is sufficient to run the program for a particular value of N and compare the result with e which is 2.71828183. Obviously the value computed for N equals 15 is very close to the actual value. It would be interesting to see the effect of the value of N on the accuracy of the final computed result. Programming exercise 1 asks you to compute and display such a table. ✖

✖ Case Study:

Newton's Method for Finding Roots

1. Problem

Your calculus instructor would like you to write a program that uses Newton's method for finding a root of an equation, $y = f(x)$, where k is a root if $f(k)$ equals zero. Newton's method starts with an initial guess for a root, x_0, and then generates successive approximate roots x_1, x_2 ... , x_j, x_{j+1}, ... using the iterative formula

$$x_{j+1} = x_j - \frac{f(x_j)}{f'(x_j)}$$

where $f'(x_j)$ is the derivative of function f evaluated at $x = x_j$. The formula above generates a new guess, x_{j+1}, from a previous one, x_j. Newton's method terminates when successive guesses are sufficiently close in value, that is, when

$$|x_{j+1} - x_j| < epsilon$$

where *epsilon* is a very small constant (for example, 0.00001).

Sometimes Newton's method will fail to converge to a root. In this case, the program should terminate after a large number of trials (say 100).

2. Analysis

Figure 8.12 shows the geometric interpretation of Newton's method where x_0, x_1, and x_2 represent successive guesses for the root. At each point x_j, the derivative, $f'(x_j)$, is the tangent to the curve, $f(x)$. The next guess for the root, x_{j+1}, is the point where the tangent crosses the x axis.

FIGURE 8.12

Geometric Interpretation of Newton's Method

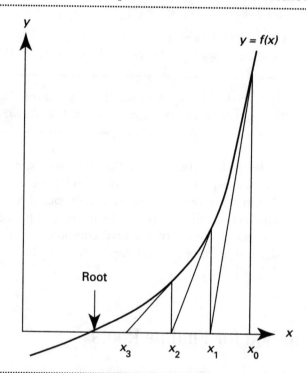

From geometry, we get the equation

$$\frac{y_{j+1} - y_j}{x_{j+1} - x_j} = m$$

where m is the slope of the line between points $(x_{j+1},\ y_{j+1})$ and $(x_j,\ y_j)$. From Fig. 8.12, if $(x_j,\ y_j)$ is a point on the curve, and $(x_{j+1},\ y_{j+1})$ is the next point on the x-axis, then y_{j+1} is zero, y_j is $f(x_j)$, and m is $f'(x_j)$. By substituting and rearranging terms, we get

$$-f(x_j) = f'(x_j) \times (x_{j+1} - x_j)$$

which leads to the formula shown at the beginning of the case study. In the data requirements that follow, XLast corresponds to x_j and XNext corresponds to x_{j+1}.

DATA REQUIREMENTS

Problem Constants

```
Epsilon = 0.00001      % The minimum distance between
                       % successive guesses
MaxGuess = 100         % The maximum number of guesses
```

Program Outputs

```
XNext : real           % The next guess for a root
NumGuess : int         % The count of guesses
```

Program Variables

```
XLast : real           % The last guess for a root
```

Functions

```
F(X)          % The function whose root is being determined
FPrime(X)     % The derivative of function F(X)
```

3. Design The initial guess for the root is read into XNext. Inside a loop, we compute the next guess for the root value, XNext, from the last guess, XLast. The loop must continue to execute until the difference between successive guesses is less than Epsilon. The algorithm follows.

ALGORITHM FOR NEWTON'S METHOD

1. Read the initial guess into XNext and set NumGuess to 1.
2. loop
     3. Set XLast to the last guess, which is stored in XNext.
     4. Compute the next guess, XNext, from XLast by evaluating
        f(XLast) and f'(XLast).
     5. Increment NumGuess.
     exit when abs(XNext - XLast) is less than Epsilon or
        NumGuess > MaxGuess
   end loop
6. if a root was found then
     7. Display the root and the function value at the root.
   end if
8. Display the number of guesses

4. Implementation The program must contain declarations for function F(X), the function whose root is being computed, and function FPrime(X), the derivative of F(X). The program in Fig. 8.13 computes the root for the function

$$f(x) = 5x^3 - 2x^2 + 3$$

with derivative

$$f'(x) = 15x^2 - 4x$$

FIGURE 8.13 Newton's Method

```
% The "Newton" program
% Find a root of an equation using Newton's method

const Epsilon := 0.00001        % Minimum distance
const MaxGuess := 100           % Maximum number of guesses

var XLast : real                % Last guess for a root
var XNext : real                % Next guess for a root
var NumGuess : int := 1         % Count of guesses

function F(X : real) : real
    % The function whose root is being found
    % Insert function here
    result 5 * X ** 3 - 2 * X ** 2 + 3
end F

function FPrime(X : real) : real % The derivative of F(X)
    % Insert function derivative here
    result 15 * X ** 2 - 4 * X
end FPrime

% Read the initial guess into XNext
put "Initial guess for a root> " ..
get XNext

% Compute successive guesses
loop
    NumGuess := NumGuess + 1
    XLast := XNext                  % XLast is last guess
    XNext := XLast - F(XLast) / FPrime(XLast)
    exit when abs(XNext - XLast) < Epsilon or
                NumGuess > MaxGuess
end loop

% Display the root and function value if root was found
if abs(XNext - XLast) < Epsilon then
    put "The approximate root is ", XNext
    put "The function value is ", F(XNext)
else
    put "Root not found"
end if

put NumGuess, " guesses made"
```

```
Initial guess for a root> 1.0
The approximate root is -0.729001
The function value is -6.302603e-11
9 guesses made
```

5. Testing   The function value in Fig. 8.13 is sufficiently close to zero that we can feel confident that we have found a root. To test Newton's method, run the program on several mathematical functions and with several different starting points for each function. In most cases, Newton's method should find a solution relatively quickly.

You may find there are situations in which Newton's method will not work, but will cycle until `MaxGuess` guesses are made. At other times Newton's method will fail because `FPrime(XLast)` becomes zero and a division by zero run-time error occurs. In these cases, you must try a different technique for finding function roots. One such technique (the bisection method) is described in project 6 at the end of this chapter. ✖

Exercises for Section 8.8

Self-Check

1. Determine the output from program `Newton` (Fig. 8.13) if the initial guess for the root is `0.0`, the value used for constant `Epsilon` is `0.00001`, and

$$f(x) = x^2 - 2x + 1$$
$$f'(x) = 2x - 2$$

Programming

1. Display a table showing e and N for values of N between 3 and 15.
2. The value of e^x is represented by the series

$$1 + x + x^2/2! + x^3/3! + \ldots + x^n/n! + \ldots$$

Write a program to compute and print the value of this series for any x and any positive n. Compare the result to `exp(x)` and print a message `"O.K."` or `"Not O.K."` depending on whether the difference between these results exceeds `0.0001`.

8.9 Common Programming Errors

You must take a good deal of care when working with complicated expressions. It is easy to inadvertently omit parentheses or operators. If an operator or a single parenthesis is omitted, a syntax error will be detected. If a pair of parentheses is omitted, the expression, although syntactically correct, will compute the wrong value.

Sometimes it is beneficial to break a complicated expression into subexpressions that are separately assigned to *temporary variables*, and then to manipulate these temporary variables. For example, it is easier to write correctly the three assignment statements below

```
Temp1 := sqrt(X + Y)
Temp2 := 1 + Temp1
Z := Temp1 / Temp2
```

than the single assignment statement

```
Z := sqrt(X + Y) / (1 + sqrt(X + Y))
```

which has the same effect. In this case, using three assignment statements is more efficient because the square root operation is performed only once; it is performed twice in the single assignment statement above.

You cannot directly combine `string` and numeric values. The `boolean` expression

```
6 + "3"                % Incompatible operands
```

is invalid because one of its operands is an integer and the other is a `string` value.

Make sure you use any required parentheses properly in compound `boolean` expressions.

Syntax or run-time errors may occur when using the built-in functions. The argument of the function `chr` must be type `int`; the argument of the functions `ord`, `succ`, and `pred` should be a single character or an enumerated value. The result of the functions `succ`, `pred`, and `chr` will be undefined for certain arguments.

Subranges can help you detect erroneous computations or data. If a value being assigned is outside the subrange, an `"out of range"` error occurs. The operations that can be performed on a variable with a subrange type are determined by the root type for that subrange. However, a variable whose type is a subrange type cannot correspond to a formal variable parameter whose type is the root type for that subrange.

When declaring enumerated types, remember that only identifiers can appear in the list of values for an enumerated type. Strings, characters, or numbers are not allowed. Remember that there are no standard procedures available to read or write the values of an enumerated type.

Chapter Review

This chapter presented the manipulation of standard data types, including the `boolean` and `string` types, along with programmer-defined subranges and enumerated types. We discussed the internal representation of standard types and discussed the differences between the numeric types, `int` and `real`. We explained that real arithmetic on a computer has inherent inaccuracies because not all real numbers can be represented exactly. We described other sources of numerical errors such as cancellation errors and arithmetic overflow and underflow.

We introduced DeMorgan's theorem which describes how to form the complement of a `boolean` expression.

We introduced the functions `pred`, `succ`, and `ord` for the manipulation of single characters and enumerated values. We used the function `chr`, the inverse of `ord`, to find the character corresponding to a given ordinal number.

We showed how subrange declarations provide additional documentation for ordinal variables that have a restricted range of values. We discussed how a run-time error may occur if such a variable is assigned an out-of-range value.

We also saw how to declare enumerated types with a list of values tailored to a particular application. The use of enumerated types makes large programs more readable.

Finally, we discussed numerical analysis, which is the branch of mathematics and computer science concerned with developing techniques for mathematical computation. We showed how to use iterative approximations to evaluate a series and to find the root of an equation.

New Turing Constructs in Chapter 8

The new Turing constructs introduced in this chapter are described in Table 8.5.

TABLE 8.5	Summary of New Turing Constructs
Construct	**Effect**
Subrange declaration `type Digit : 0 .. 9`	A subrange of the integers is declared. This subrange (named `Digit`) consists of the numbers 0 through 9.
Enumerated Type Declaration `type BColor : enum (Blue, Black, Brown)`	An enumerated type `BColor` is declared with values `Blue`, `Black`, and `Brown`.

String Comparisons
`"Angela" < "Beth"`
`"21.0" not= "21"`
	The string `Angela` comes before the string `Beth` because A comes before B. These two strings cannot be equal because their lengths differ.

String Catenation `"dist" + "rust" = "distrust"`	The strings `dist` and `rust` are catenated to form the the string `distrust`.

Substrings
`const Language := "Turing"`
`Language (1) = "T"`
`Language (*) = "g"`
`Language (3 .. *) = "ring"`
	`Language` is a constant string. Its first character is extracted by writing `Language (1)`.
	Its last character is extracted by `Language (*)`.
	Its third through last characters are extracted by `Language (3 .. *)`.

Quick-Check Exercises

1. a. Evaluate the `boolean` expression

   ```
   true and ((30 mod 10) <= 3)
   ```

   b. Is the outer pair of parentheses required?

   c. What about the inner pair?

   d. Write the complement of the `boolean` expression.

2. In ASCII, what is the value of

   a. `chr(ord("a"))`   b. `chr(ord("a") + 3)`

   c. `chr(ord("z") - 25)`   d. `chr(ord("z") - 32)`

3. What is the value of `ord("9") - ord("0")`. Is this answer the same for all Turing compilers? What about `ord("z") - ord("a")`?

4. a. Can a variable whose type is a subrange type correspond to a formal variable parameter whose type is the root type?

   b. Answer the same question if the formal parameter is a value parameter.

5. If two variables have equivalent types, can one always be assigned to the other?

6. Under what condition can one variable be assigned to another when they do not have equivalent types?

7. String variable S has the value `"Sodium"` and string variable C has the value `"Chloride"`. Give a Turing statement that uses C and S to assign the value `"Sodium Chloride"` to the string variable SC.

8. Give a statement that displays the number of characters in the string SC from question 7.

9. What is wrong with the following enumerated type declaration?

   ```
   type Prime : enum (2, 3, 5, 7, 9, 11, 13)
   ```

10. Consider the enumerated type declaration

    ```
    type Class : enum (Frosh, Soph, Jr, Sr)
    ```

    What is the value of

    a. `ord(succ(pred(Class.Soph)))`

    b. `pred(pred(Class.Jr))`

Answers to Quick-Check Exercises

1. a. `true`

   b. Outer not needed

   c. Inner not needed

   d. `false or not ((30 mod 10) <= 3)`

2. a. `"a"`

   b. `"d"`

   c. `"a"`

   d. `"Z"`

3. `9`, yes, `26` on ASCII and CDC character sets but not on EBCDIC

4. a. No

   b. Yes

5. Yes.
6. A variable whose type is int or a subrange type whose host type is int can be assigned to a type real variable. A variable whose root type is the same as the root type of another can be assigned to the other. If the variable being assigned to is a subrange type, a run-time error will occur if the value is not within that subrange.
7. SC := S + " " + C
8. put length (SC)
9. Integers cannot appear as enumerated type values.
10. a. 1
    b. Class.Frosh

Review Questions

1. What are the advantages of data type int over data type real?
2. List and explain three computational errors that may occur in type real expressions.
3. Write an enumerated type declaration for Fiscal as the months from July through June. Declare the subrange Winter as December through February.
4. Write procedures for reading and writing values for variables of enumerated type Season.

   ```
   type Season : enum (Winter, Spring, Summer, Fall)
   ```

5. Write a for loop that runs from ord("Z") to ord("A") and prints only the letters that are consonants.
6. Write a case statement that tests to see if Today is a working day. Print either the message "Workday" or "Weekend". Assume Today is type Day, an enumerated type that has days of the week as its values.
7. Write an if statement that will write out true or false according to the following conditions: either Flag is true or Color is Red, or both Money is Plenty and Time is Up.
8. Write the statement to assign a value of true to the boolean variable OverTime only if a worker's weekly Hours are greater than 40.
9. Write a boolean expression using the ord function that will determine whether the ordinal value for "a" is greater than the ordinal value for "Z".
10. Write the Turing statements necessary to enter an integer between 0 and 9 inclusive and convert it to an equivalent character value (e.g., 0 to "0" and 1 to "1") to be stored in a character variable Num.
11. Write a Turing function with int argument N and real argument X, which returns as its value the first N terms of the series shown below

$$x + 1/2\ x^2 + 1/3\ x^3 + 1/4\ x^4 + \dots + 1/n\ x^n$$

12. Write a Turing function that takes a string as an argument and returns two copies of the string catenated together.

13. Write a Turing function that takes a string with an odd number of characters as an argument and returns the middle character of the string.

14. Write a `boolean` function that takes a string as an argument and returns `true` if the string seems to be an adverb. The function should test to see if the last two letters of the string are `"ly"`.

Programming Projects

1. An integer N is divisible by 9 if the sum of its digits is divisible by 9. Recall how we used `mod` in procedure `PrintDigits` (Fig. 8.3) to print a number's digits one at a time. Develop a program to determine whether or not the following numbers are divisible by 9.

   N = 154368
   N = 621594
   N = 123456

2. Redo programming project 1 using a function that accepts an argument that is a string of digits that specify N. For example, if N = 154368, the actual parameter would be the string "154368" The function returns `true` if N is divisible by 9

3. A number is said to be *perfect* if the sum of its divisors (except for itself) is equal to itself. For example, 6 is a perfect number because the sum of its divisors (1 + 2 + 3) is 6. The number 8 is said to be *deficient* because the sum of its divisors (1 + 2 + 4) is only 7. The number 12 is said to be *abundant* because the sum of its divisors (1 + 2 + 3 + 4 + 6) is 16. Write a program that lists the factors of the numbers between 1 and 100 and classifies each number as perfect, deficient, or abundant.

4. Find out how to access the printer from a Turing program running on your computer system. Write a program for generating a bar graph on the printer summarizing the rainfall in the city of Bedrock for one year. Include the average monthly rainfall and the maximum monthly rainfall during the year as part of the program output.

   Prompt the user for the amount rainfall for a particular month and instruct the computer to send an appropriate output line to the printer. Assume that no single month will have more than 14 inches of rainfall. Your graph should resemble the following:

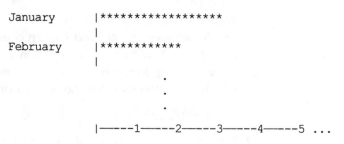

```
January      |******************
             |
February     |************
             |
                        .
                        .
                        .

             |-----1-----2-----3-----4-----5 ...

                          Inches of Rainfall
```

As a part of your program, write procedures corresponding to the procedure headers shown here.

```
procedure PutMonth (Month : int)
    % Write the string corresponding to the Month

procedure GetMonthlyTotal (Month : int
                                var Inches, MaxInches,
                                TotInches : real)
    % User is prompted for Inches of rainfall
    % during a Month. MaxInches and TotInches are
    % updated so that they contain the maximum and
    % the total inches of rainfall input so far.

procedure DrawBar (Month : int, Inches  : real)
    % Draw a bar whose length is computed from Inches
    % and whose label is determined by the value of
    % Month

procedure DrawScaleLine
    % Draw scale and label at bottom of graph
```

5. The interest paid on a savings account is compounded daily. This means that if you start with StartBal dollars in the bank, at the end of the first day you will have a balance of

   ```
   StartBal * (1 + Rate/365)
   ```

   dollars, where rate is the annual interest Rate (0.05 if the annual rate is 5 percent). At the end of the second day, you will have

   ```
   StartBal * (1 + Rate/365) * (1 + Rate/365)
   ```

   dollars, and at the end of N days you will have

   ```
   StartBal * (1 + Rate/365)N
   ```

   dollars. Write a program that processes a set of data records, each of which contains values for StartBal, rate, and N, and computes the final account balance.

6. The bisection method is another means of finding an approximate root for the equation $f(X) = 0$ on the interval XLeft to XRight inclusive (assuming the function is continuous on this interval). The interval endpoints (XLeft and XRight) and the tolerance for the approximation (Epsilon) are input from the user.

   The bisection method calls for the identification of an interval [XLeft, XRight] which is less than Epsilon in length over which $f(X)$ changes sign (from positive to negative or vice versa). The midpoint (XMid = (XLeft + XRight)/2.0)) of the interval will be an approximation to the root of the equation when $f(XMid)$ is very close to zero. Of course, if you find a value of XMid so that *f*(XMid*)* = 0 you have found a very good approximation of the root and the algorithm should stop.

One way to detect a sign change is to examine the value of the products *f*(XLeft*)* * *f*(XMid*)* and *f*(XMid*)* * *f*(XRight*)*. If one of the products is negative then a sign change has occurred over that interval either [XLeft, XMid] or [XMid, XRight]. If neither product is negative there is no root in the interval [Xleft, XRight]. If the sign change occurs in the interval [XLeft, XMid], let XRight = XMid and repeat the process. Similarly, if the sign change occurs in the interval [XMid, XRight], let XLeft = XMid and repeat the process. Figure 8.14 shows an example of a root in the interval [XLeft, XMid].

FIGURE 8.14   Root in Interval [XLeft, XMid]

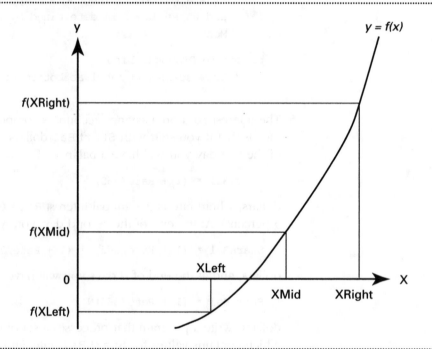

Write a program that uses the bisection method to determine an approximation to the solution of the equation

$$5x^3 - 2x^2 + 3 = 0$$

over the interval [–1, 1] using Epsilon = 0.001.

7. We can approximate the area under the curve described by a function *f*(*x*) by dividing the area into a number of rectangles and then accumulating the sum of all the rectangular areas. Figure 8.15 shows an example of the *midpoint method,* so named because the curve intersects each rectangle at its middle (as measured along the *x*-axis). The area of

each rectangle is w (its width) times the function value at its midpoint. The area of the rectangle with left endpoint x_1 is $w * f(x_1 + w/2)$. If the interval [a, b] is divided into n rectangles, the area under the curve is represented by the sum terms of the form

$$f(a + i \times w + w/2)$$

with i running from 0 to $n - 1$, where w is $(b - a) / n$. The first rectangle begins at $x = a$, the second at $x = a + w$, the third at $x = a + 2w$, and so on. Write a program that uses the midpoint approximation to find the area under the curve (the value of the definite integral) for the function

$$f(x) = -3x^2 + 2x + 4$$

over the interval [–2, 3]. Test your program using several different values of n. The larger n is, the better the approximation should be.

FIGURE 8.15 Midpoint Method

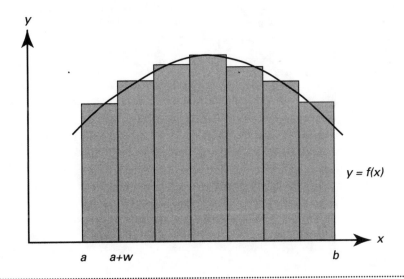

8. Experiments that are either too expensive, or dangerous, to perform are often simulated on a computer when the computer is able to provide a good representation of the experiment. Use Turing's procedure `rand` that generates random `real` numbers in the range 0 to 1. For example, if x is a real number, the statement `rand (x)` sets x to a number between 0 and 1 inclusive. Write a program which uses this random number generator to simulate the dropping of glass rods which break into three pieces. The purpose of the experiment is to estimate the probability that the lengths of the three pieces are such that they might form the sides of a triangle.

For the purposes of this experiment you may assume that the glass rod always breaks into three pieces. If you use the line segment 0 to 1 (on the real number line) as a mathematical model of the glass rod, a random number generator (function) can be used to generate two numbers between 0 and 1 that represent the coordinates of the breaks. The triangle inequality (the sum of the lengths of two sides of a triangle are always greater than the length of the third side) may be used to test the length of each piece against the lengths of the other two pieces.

To estimate the probability that the pieces of the rod form a triangle, you will need to repeat the experiment many times and count the number of times a triangle can be formed from the pieces. The probability estimate is the number of successes divided by the total number of rods dropped. Your program should prompt the user for the number of rods to drop and allow the experiment to be repeated. Use a sentinel value of −1 to halt execution of the program.

9. A *palindrome* is a word such as `deed` that is spelled the same way backwards and forwards. Write a program that reads in words and displays a message saying whether the word is a palindrome. Stop reading when the sentinel value `"quit"` is input. Use a function named `Palindrome` whose formal parameter is a `string` and whose result is a `boolean`.

CHAPTER 9

Input/Output
and Text Files

In your programming, you have seen how to use `get` statements to read values typed at the keyboard and `put` statements to write values onto the screen. In this chapter, we will review these two statements, give new ways of formatting input/output items using these statements, and show how to read and write files that contain text.

9.1 Formatting in Put Statements

This section discusses the format options that can be used to determine the form of output from a `put` statement.

The `put` statement prints items one after another, as in:

```
var Debt : int := 7
put "You owe me $", Debt
```

This prints `You owe me $7`. There is no extra blank printed before an item such as `7` (from `Debt`). In the following, the blank must be placed explicitly between `X` and `Y` to keep the numbers from being run together in the output.

```
var X : int := 7
var Y : int := 9
put "X and Y: ", X, " ", Y
```

This produces the output `X and Y: 7 9`.

Sometimes the simple, default form of output is not sufficient. For example, when you are printing columns of figures, you would like the numbers to be right-justified. This is illustrated in the program in Fig. 9.1 which produces a table of the squares and square roots of numbers from 1 to 10. The program uses format items, which optionally follow each expression in a `put` statement.

The first `put` statement in Fig. 9.1 prints the title of the table. It uses the `skip` output item to output a blank line. The `put` statement in the `for` loop uses explicit format items:

```
put N :2, N ** 2 : 5, sqrt (N) :10:3
```

For example, `N` is output right-justified in a field that is 2 characters wide. This is done so that `N`'s values 1 through 9 line up directly above the zero in 10 in the left column. In a similar way, `N` squared, written as `N**2`, is output right-justified in a field that is 5 characters wide. The square root of `N`, written as `sqrt(N)`, is written out in a field that is 10 characters wide. We have used an additional format item to specify that three fractional digits of the result are to be displayed.

There is an optional format item that is used for determining the number of digits of an exponent to display. For example, if we use the `put` item `sqrt(N):10:3:2` for the square root, the displayed result will have two exponent digits, as in `3.16e+00`. This format item is not very commonly used.

FIGURE 9.1   Print Table of Squares and Square Roots

```
% The "Squares" program
% Print a table of squares and square roots from 1 to 10

put "Table of Squares and Square Roots", skip
put "  n     n**2      sqrt(n)"
for N : 1 .. 10
    put N :2, N ** 2 : 5, sqrt (N) :10:3
end for
```

```
Table of Squares and Square Roots

put "  n     n**2      sqrt(n)"
   n       n**2       sqrt(n)
   1         1        1.000
   2         4        1.414
   3         9        1.732
   4        16        2.000
   5        25        2.236
   6        36        2.449
   7        49        2.646
   8        64        2.828
   9        81        3.000
  10       100        3.162
```

The general form of the put statement, with its format items, is summarized in the following syntax display. As you can see in the display, the put statement has an optional *fileNumber* that allows you to use this statement to write data values into a computer file. You can ignore this part of the description until the last part of this chapter, which discusses files.

Exercises for Section 9.1

Self-Check

1. Explain why the following statement displays two blank lines rather than just one.

    put skip

2. If MyMoney is a real variable representing a dollar amount, how would you print it to display dollars and cents, as in $7.13?

Programming

1. Rewrite the program in Fig. 9.1 so it displays the squares and square roots of numbers from 0.0 to 1.0 in steps of 0.1. Display all numbers with two fractional digits.

PUT STATEMENT

Form: put [: *fileNumber*,] { *putItem*, } *putItem* [..]

Examples: put "Alexander Graham Bell"

put : StreamNo, "X is ", X :8:3

Interpretation: A put statement contains an optional file number followed by one or more *putItems*. This statement is used to place output, as determined by the list of comma-separated *putItems*, on the screen or in a file. If the final dot-dot (..) is omitted, the put statement terminates the output line, and the next put statement produces output on the following line. When dot-dot is present, further output continues on the current line.

A *putItem*, which is optionally followed by formatting items, can have this form:

expression [: *width* [: *fractionWidth* [: *exponentWidth*]]]

The expression, such as variable X, is output in a field of *width* characters (*width* is 8 in the above example). This width will be automatically increased if it is not large enough for the value of the *putItem*. The optional *fractionWidth* determines the number of fractional digits for a number. For example, X:8:3 will produce an output such as ••72.546 where • represents a blank. The optional *exponentWidth* determines the number of exponent digits for a number. For example, the putItem X:8:1:2 will produce an output such as •7.3e+01 where • represents a blank.

In Turing, numbers are displayed right-justified but strings are displayed left-justified in the width of field given in the *width* format item.

A *putItem* can be the keyword skip, which is used to output a blank line. If the current output line has not yet been terminated, skip terminates it and further output will occur on the following line.

If the optional *fileNumber* is omitted, the output goes to the screen. If the *fileNumber* is present, it designates the file that is to receive the output. In most cases, the *fileNumber* is set by an open statement.

Note: The only types that can be output by a put statement are integers, real numbers, and strings.

9.2 Reading Tokens, Characters, and Lines

This section discusses the three forms of input supported by Turing's get statement.

Let's begin by considering a get statement that reads in the first and last names of a person.

```
var FirstName, LastName : string
get FirstName, LastName     % Token-oriented input
```

If you type `Mick` followed by a space and then `Jagger`, this will cause the string `Mick` to be assigned to `FirstName` and `Jagger` to `LastName`. Before reading `Mick`, any preceding white space characters (such as blanks, tab characters and end-of-line characters) are skipped. Similarly, following `Mick`, any white space characters preceding `Jagger` will be skipped. Strings such as `Mick` and `Jagger` that are read this way are called tokens, and this method of doing input is called *token-oriented*.

Token-oriented input is used in most small programs. It effectively reads a word at a time into the next variable. It can be used for numbers (integers and real numbers) as well as for strings.

If you want to read a string that contains blanks, such as "`Mick the Great`", you must surround it by quotation marks. As a result the entire string will be read as a single token.

Occasionally it is handy to read the input a single character at a time. This is done in the following program segment, which reads characters until encountering a star (`*`).

```
var ch : string
loop
    get ch : 1        % Character-oriented input
    exit when ch = "*"
end loop
```

This approach, which explicitly gives the number of characters to be read, is called *character-oriented* input. More generally, the format width, which is the number 1 in the above example, can specify any number of characters you want to read. In a language like Turing in which there are convenient facilities for string manipulation, such as substring operations, character-oriented input is not common when reading from the key board. However, it is very useful when reading from files of data that are arranged in fixed columns.

Besides token-oriented and character-oriented input, Turing supports *line-oriented* input, which allows you to read an entire line at a time. For example, the program in Fig 9.2 reads and counts lines until it reads a line that ends with a period.

FIGURE 9.2

Read and Count Lines Until a Line Ends with a Period

```
% The "Readline" program
% Read in lines until one ends with a period
% Print the number of lines read

put "Please type lines of text"
put "The final line should end with a period (.)"
var Line : string
var LineCount : int := 0
```

```
loop
    get Line : *        % Line-oriented input
    LineCount := LineCount + 1
    exit when length (Line) > 0 and Line (*) = "."
end loop
put "You typed ", LineCount, " lines"
```

In the program in Fig. 9.2, the `get` statement uses a star (`*`) as a format item. This item specifies that the entire line is to be read. The `exit` condition terminates the loop when the line ends with a period. Before testing for the period, it makes sure that the line contains at least one character. This test is necessary to avoid having the program halt with an error message if the person typed a line with no characters. This would occur if the Return key were pressed without typing anything on the line. In the `exit` condition, the star in `Line (*)` is used to locate the last character of the string.

The general form of the `get` statement, with its three types of input (token, character, and line-oriented) is summarized in the following syntax display. As you can see in the display, the `get` statement has an optional *fileNumber* that allows you to use this statement to read data values from computer files. You can ignore this part of the description until the last part of this chapter, which discusses files.

Exercises for Section 9.2

Self-Check

1. Explain why character-oriented input is seldom used for interactive programming.
2. Given a variable `Line` that is declared to be a string, what will be the difference in the effect of the following two statements, given that the input line is exactly the word `Mario` (followed by pressing the Return key).

   ```
   get Line : *
   get Line : 5
   ```

3. Explain how to change the program in Fig. 9.2 so it stops when the user types a line with no characters (by pressing the Return key with no previous key presses).

GET STATEMENT

Form: get [: *fileNumber,*] { *getItem,* } *getItem*

Examples: get FirstName, LastName

get : StreamNo, InputLine : *

Interpretation: A get statement contains an optional file number followed by one or more *getItems*. This statement is used to read data into the variables given in the list of comma-separated *getItems*.

A *getItem*, which is optionally followed by a formatting item, can have this form:

variable [: *formatItem*]

The variable, such as FirstName is assigned the next value in the input stream (from the keyboard or a file).

If the *formatItem* is omitted, the next value is read as follows. First, white space (blanks, tabs, etc.) are skipped. Then the value, called the *token*, is read and assigned to the variable. In the usual case, the end of the token is determined by the occurrence of more white space (or the end of file). Any white space following the token is skipped, up to the beginning of the next input line. If the token begins with a quotation mark ("), it is considered to be a character string value; the entire string value is read and assigned to the variable (with the quotation marks removed). Quoted tokens allow you to input string values, such as "Mary Martin", that contain white space.

The *formatItem* can be a star, as in InputLine : *. In this case, the variable, which must be a string, is assigned the entire (remainder of the) input line. The end-of-line character marking the end of the line is discarded.

The other possible *formatItem*, which is used less commonly, is a positive integer giving the number of characters to be read into a string variable. This form is used primarily when reading from a file, when you need to read a field that occupies particular columns (character positions) on a line. Beware that this form does not discard end-of-line characters and assigns this character as a part of the string being assigned to the variable.

A *getItem* can be the keyword skip, which causes white space (blanks, tabs, end-of-line characters, etc.) to be skipped until non-white space or the end of file is encountered.

If the optional *fileNumber* is omitted, the input comes from the keyboard (from your typing). If the *fileNumber* is present, it designates the file that is to be read. In most cases, the *fileNumber* is set by an open statement.

Note: The only types that can be input by a get statement are integers, real numbers, and strings. The format items (specifying the number of characters or the entire line) can be used only for strings.

9.3 Review of Batch Processing

Although we discussed batch processing and the use of data files in Section 2.5, all our example programs have been interactive. Interactive programs read all input data from the keyboard and display all output on the screen. This mode of operation is fine for small programs. However, as you begin to write larger programs, you will see that there are many advantages to using data files for program input and output.

You can create a data file using a text editor in the same way that you create a program file. Once the data file is entered in computer memory, you can carefully check and edit each line, and then save the final data file as a permanent disk file. When you enter data interactively, you do not always have the opportunity to examine and edit the data. Also, the data is processed as it is entered, it is not saved permanently.

After the data file is saved on disk, you can instruct your program to read data from the data file rather than from the keyboard. Recall from Chapter 2 that this mode of program execution is called batch processing. Because the program data are supplied before execution begins, prompting messages are not required in batch programs. Instead, batch programs may contain display statements that echo print data values, thereby providing a record of the data that are read and processed in a particular run.

Besides giving you the opportunity to check for errors in your data, using data files provides another advantage. A data file can be read many times. Therefore, during debugging you can rerun the program as often as you need to, without re-entering the test data each time.

You can instruct your program to write its output to a disk file rather than display it on the screen. When output is written to the screen, it disappears after it scrolls off the screen and cannot be retrieved. However, if program output is written to a disk file, you have a permanent copy of it. You can get a hard copy of a disk file by sending it to the printer, or you can use an operating system command such as the MS-DOS® command

TYPE *filename*

to list file *filename* on the screen. You can view the file using the same editor you use to edit Turing programs.

Finally, you can use the output file generated by one program as a data file for another program. For example, a payroll program may compute employee salaries and write each employee's name and salary to an output file. A second program that prints employee checks could use the output of the payroll program as its data file.

Exercises for Section 9.3

Self-Check

1. List three advantages of writing your program output to a data file, rather than simply displaying it on the computer screen.
2. a. For a computer program that handles booking of airline reservations, would batch processing of data be preferred to interactive data processing? Explain your answer.
   b. What about a program for printing student transcripts at a large university?

9.4 Text Files

Turing can process two kinds of files: text files and binary files. We will study text files in this chapter. A *text file* is a collection of characters stored under the same name in secondary memory (i.e., on a disk). It can be inspected or modified using a text editor. A text file has no fixed size. Binary files, which will not be discussed in this chapter, use the internal format of data items and cannot be inspected by a text editor. For example, Turing integers are stored in binary files as four-byte values in binary coding.

The End-of-Line Character

As you create a text file using an editor program, you press the Return key to separate the file into lines. Each time you press this key, the <eoln> character is placed in the file. This end-of-line character is also called the *new line* character.

The lines below represent a text file consisting of two lines of letters, blank characters, and the special characters . and ! .

```
This is a text file!<eoln>
It has two lines.<eoln>
```

Each line ends with the <eoln> character . For convenience in examining the file's contents, we have listed each line of the file (through <eoln>) as a separate line, although this would not be the case in the actual disk file. The disk file consists of a sequence of characters occupying consecutive storage locations on a *track* of the disk as shown next.

```
This is a text file!<eoln>It has two lines.<eoln>
```

The first character of the second line (I) would follow directly after the last character of the first line (the <eoln> character). The file would occupy 39 bytes of disk storage, including one byte for each <eoln>. In some systems, such as MS-DOS®, there will be an additional byte at the end, the End-of-File or <eof> byte, but this not present on Unix® and Macintosh systems.

The <eoln> character marks the end of a line and thus is distinct from other characters. When using token-oriented or line-oriented input, a program never reads the <eoln> character into a type string variable; however, when using character-oriented input, this special character value is read and stored in the string variable, just like any other character. The special notation "\n" is used in Turing programs to denote the <eoln> character. For example, in the following part of a program, a character is tested to see if it is the new line character:

```
var ch : string (1)
get ch : 1
if ch = "\n" then      % Test for the <eoln> character
    ... Handle the end of the line...
end if
```

The Keyboard and Screen as Text Files

In interactive programming, Turing's get and put statements use the keyboard and screen, respectively. We can consider that the keyboard and the screen are special kinds of files, sometimes called the *standard input file* (the keyboard) and *standard output file* (the screen).

Normally we enter one line of data at a time at the keyboard, pressing the Return key to indicate the end of a data line. Pressing Return inserts the <eoln> character into the standard input file. Normally in interactive programming, we use a sentinel value to indicate the end of data rather than signaling the end-of-file at the keyboard. There is no single key that represents the end-of-file character but the MS-DOS® system uses Control-Z, while Unix® and the Macintosh use Control-D.

Displaying characters on the screen is equivalent to writing characters to the standard output file. We use the put procedure to write output characters to the screen. When we use the put procedure without its optional final dot-dot (..), an <eoln> character is added after the output characters are written (or displayed), moving the cursor to the start of the next line of the screen.

Opening and Closing Files

Before a program can use a file, the file must be prepared for input or output. The file must be *opened* by Turing's open statement. This statement translates the name of a file to a number that represents this file. This is analogous to looking up a person's telephone number and then using the person's number rather than their name.

The following open statement connects the file named MYINFO.DAT to the program and returns the number of the connection in the integer variable FileNumber.

```
open : FileNumber, "MYINFO.DAT", put
```

The final keyword `put` in the statement signifies that the file is to be accessed by a `put` statement. If no file `MYINFO.DAT` has been saved on disk, a file that is initially empty (has no characters) will be created. If a file `MYINFO.DAT` is already saved on disk, its file position pointer will be set to locate the beginning of the file. Any program output will replace the old data associated with file `MYINFO.DAT` ; the old data will be lost.

Once the program is finished writing information to the file, it should disconnect from it using the `close` statement as follows.

```
close : FileNumber
```

If you wish to access a file a second time in the same program, you can do this by closing the file and then opening it a second time. For example, the program can read and echo print the output file that it has just created by closing the file and then re-opening it with this statement.

```
open : FileNumber, "MYINFO.DAT", get
```

This `open` operation prepares this file for input, and your program can then read data from that file using the `get` statement.

The *file position pointer* selects the next character to be processed in the file. After the preceding `open` statement is performed, the next character to be read will be the first character in the file. The `open` statement must be executed before any characters are read from the file. The `open` statement returns a file number of zero if file `MYINFO.DAT` was not previously saved on disk. Your program should check to see if this is the case if there is a possibility that the file has not been created before your program starts running.

OPEN STATEMENT

Form: open : *fileNumberVar, fileName, ioCapability*

Examples: open : StreamNo, "MASTER.DAT", get
          open : OutFile, "OUTFILE", put

Interpretation: An `open` statement connects the program to a file so the program can perform operations such as `get` on the file. The `open` statement translates a *fileName* such as MASTER.DAT to a file number such as 5 which is assigned to a *fileNumberVar* such as StreamNo.

The `get` statement that operates on the file uses the file number, not the file name. For example, this statement reads a line from the MASTER.DAT file:

```
get : StreamNo, LineOfInput : *
```

The *ioCapability* determines the operations that are to be performed on the file.

> **CLOSE STATEMENT**
> **Form:** `close : ` *fileNumber*
> **Examples:** `close : StreamNo`
>
> **Interpretation:** A `close` statement disconnects the program from a file. The file was, in most cases, connected to the program using the `open` statement.
>
> If the program does not close a file, the file will be automatically closed when the program finishes. There is a limit on the number of currently open files; this limit is often around 10 or 20. To avoid exceeding this limit, a program using many files one after another should close files that are no longer in use.

The End-of-File Function

Turing provides a function that enables us to determine if there are more characters that can be read by the `get` statement. The function `eof` (end-of-file) returns a value of `true` if there are no more characters, and `false` otherwise. This function has an optional parameter. If the parameter is omitted, it applies to the standard input file. It will return `true` if you have explicitly signaled end-of-file at the keyboard, for example, by typing Control-Z in MS-DOS®. The more common case of using the `eof` function is when you are reading a file from the disk and need to know if you have read the last character from the file. In that case, you must supply the number of the file as a parameter. The `eof` function is used to determine if the file contains any more information to be processed.

> **THE END-OF-FILE (EOF) FUNCTION**
> **Form:** `eof [ (`*fileNumber*`) ]`
> **Example:** `exit when eof (StreamNo)`
>
> **Interpretation:** The predefined `eof` (end-of-file) function is used to determine if a file contains more characters (bytes) that can be read. If the file pointer (the current location in the file) has reached the end of the file, this function returns `true`; otherwise it returns `false`.
>
> If `eof` is used without the optional *fileNumber*, it applies to the keyboard, and returns `true` if the person typing at the keyboard has pressed the keys corresponding to end-of-file for the particular operating system in use. Control-Z signifies end-of-file under MS-DOS®, and Control-D signifies end-of-file under Unix® and on the Macintosh.

Reading and Writing a Text File

You've learned how to open a text file to prepare it for processing. All that remains is to find out how to instruct the computer to read data from an input file or to write program results to an output file.

If NextLine is a type string variable, we know that the statement

```
get NextLine : *
```

reads the next data line typed at the keyboard into NextLine . Here is an alternate form for this statement that has exactly the same effect:

```
get : -2, NextLine : *
```

The standard input file has the file number −2. The initial optional parameter for a get or put statement is a file number. Ordinarily this number is set by an open statement. When the file number is omitted, the file is taken to be the standard input for get or the standard output for put. These standard files do not need to be opened.

The statement

```
get : InFileNumber, NextLine : *
```

reads the next line from file whose number is InFileNumber into NextLine. The computer automatically advances the file position pointer after each get operation. Remember to prepare the file for input and determine its file number using open before the first get operation.

In a similar manner, both of the statements

```
put Str
put : -1, Str
```

display the value of Str on the screen. The file number −1 locates the standard output file. The statement

```
put : OutFileNumber, Str
```

writes the value of Str to the file whose number is given by OutFileNumber. Remember to prepare the file for output and determine its file number using open before the first put operation.

EXAMPLE 9.1
For security reasons, it is a good idea to have a backup or duplicate copy of a file in case the original is lost. Even though many operating systems provide a command that will copy a file, we will write our own Turing program to do this. Program Copyfile in Fig. 9.3 copies each character in file FILE.DAT to file FILE.OUT.

FIGURE 9.3   Copying a File

```
% The "Copyfile" program
% Copy file "FILE.DAT" to file "FILE.OUT"

procedure CopyLine (InData, OutData : int)
    % Copy a line of file InData to file OutData
    % Pre : InData is opened for input and OutData for
    %       output
    % Post: Next line of InData is written to OutData

    var Line : string
    get : InData, Line : *   % Read line from input file
    put : OutData, Line      % Write line to output file
end CopyLine

var InData :int        % Input file number
var OutData : int      % Output file number

% Prepare the text files for input and output
open : InData, "FILE.DAT", get
open : OutData, "FILE.OUT", put
% Copy each line from InData to OutData
loop
    exit when eof (InData)
    CopyLine (InData, OutData)
end loop

% Display a message on the screen
put "Input file copied to output file"
```

```
Input file copied to output file
```

After FILE.DAT and FILE.OUT are opened, the loop in the Copyfile program executes. This loop calls CopyLine to copy each line of the input file to the output file until the end-of-file is reached.

Within CopyLine, the statements

```
get : InData, NextSt : *
put : OutData, NextSt
```

read the line in the file whose number is InData into Line and write that line to the file whose number is OutData.

Default File Parameters

In Fig. 9.3, the text file number InData is the parameter in the call to function eof. A common error is forgetting to use a file parameter with eof. In this case, the system uses the standard input (the keyboard) as the *default file parameter.* Similarly, if you forget to use a file parameter with `get` or `put`, the system will use the standard input or output by default. Normally no error diagnostic will be displayed so the cause of the error will not be obvious.

Reading All the Tokens in a File

It is common to want to read and process all the tokens in a file. For example, the program in Fig. 9.4 reads all the number tokens in a file. When the program detects the end-of-file, it displays the sum of the numbers it has read. The `eof` function is used to determine when there is no more input, rather than testing to see if the input number is a sentinel value. We have not set aside a special value to be the sentinel. This approach has the advantage of allowing us to have every possible number value in the file.

FIGURE 9.4

Summing the Numbers in a File

```
% The "Readsum" program
% Read numbers from a file and print their sum

var FileNumber : int
const FileName : string := "NumFile"
var Number : real       % Number read from file
var Sum : real := 0.0

open : FileNumber, FileName, get
if FileNumber = 0 then
    put "Sorry, cannot open file ", FileName
else
    loop
        exit when eof (FileNumber)
        get : FileNumber, Number
        Sum := Sum + Number
    end loop
    put "The sum of the numbers in the file is: ", Sum
end if
```

The file name in Fig. 9.4 is given by the string variable `FileName`. It is common to use a variable or a named constant as the name of a file, to allow this to be easily changed. It is possible to determine the name at run time, for example, by reading in the name of the file.

After the `open` statement is executed, the `if` statement checks to see if the file could be opened and prints out a corresponding error message if this is not the case. The test determines if the file number has been set to zero, which signifies that the open was not successful. A failure to open a file for reading (for `get`) almost always means that the file did not exist.

Given that the file was successfully opened, the loop repeatedly reads numbers until there are no more numbers to be read. Each token-oriented read skips white space following the input token up to the beginning of the next input line of the end-of-file. This implicitly skips the trailing <eoln> character at the end of the line of input. As a result, assuming there are no more lines following the line containing the last number token, the eof function will become true following the reading of the last number. This is just what is needed to make the loop in Fig. 9.4 terminate at the right time.

There are two subtleties that are illustrated by the loop in Fig. 9.4. The first is that several tokens can be placed on a single line separated by blanks, and the program will still work correctly. The second is that if there is a blank line (or lines) following the line containing the final number token, the program will not terminate correctly. The problem is that after the input of the final number, the rest of its line will be skipped, but the remaining blank line will still remain to be read. As a result, the eof function will still return a value of false, because the file still contains more characters that can be read. In the unlikely case that there can be a final blank line at the end of the file, you need to add this statement just before the exit statement.

```
get : FileNumber, skip
```

This statement skips all white space up to a non-white space character or to the end-of-file. As a result the eof function returns true exactly when there are no more tokens to be read, and the program now works even in the presence of trailing blank lines. (In older versions of Turing it was always necessary to use this statement because any <eoln> character following an input token was not skipped automatically.)

The first statement inside the loop is the exit which checks to see if there are more numbers to read. It is tempting to reverse the order of the exit and get statements on the assumption that the file should contain at least one number. If this assumption is true, reversing the order will have no effect and the program will still be correct. But the program as written is more general and thus has a better style because it also handles the special case of a file that contains no numbers at all.

Exercises for Section 9.4

Self-Check

1. Let X be type real, N type int, and S type string. Indicate the contents of each variable after each read operation is performed, assuming that the file consists of the lines below and that the file is re-opened before each lettered get statement (or pair of get statements). Indicate if an attempt will be made to read a non-numeric value into X or N or if an attempt will be made to read beyond the end-of-file.

```
123 3.145 XYZ<eoln>
35 Z<eoln>
```

a. `get : InData, N, X`
   `get : InData, S`
b. `get : InData, N, X, S`
c. `get : InData, N, X, S, S`
d. `get : InData, N`
   `get : InData, S`
e. `get : InData, X`
   `get : InData, S, N`
f. `get : InData, S, N, X`
   `get : InData, S`
g. `get : InData, S, S, S, X`
   `get : InData, N`
h. `get : InData, N, X, S, S, S, S, N`
i. `get : InData, N, X, S, S, S, S`

2. List the functions and statements that use file numbers.

Programming

1. Write a procedure that reads the characters, one at a time, from the next input line of a file, and returns a count of the number of non-blank characters.
2. Rewrite program `Copyfile` (Fig. 9.3) as a procedure with the names of the input and output files as parameters.

9.5 Using Text Files

If one program writes its output to a disk file rather than to the screen, a second program may use this output file as its own data file. In this way, the two programs communicate with each other through the disk file. This section discusses an example of a program whose output file will be used as another program's data file.

Case Study:

Preparing a Payroll File

1. Problem

Your company's accountant wants you to write two programs for processing the company's payroll. The first program will read a data file consisting of employee salary data. The data for each employee is stored on two consecutive lines: the first line is the employee's name and the second line contains that employee's hours worked and hourly rate. A sample data file follows.

```
Peter  Liacouras
40.0   500.00
Caryn  Koffman
20.0   10.00
```

The first program echoes each employee's name to an output file, followed by a line containing the employee's computed gross salary. It also computes and displays the total payroll amount. The output file corresponding to the above data file is shown next. The second line of the output file contains the product of the two values read from the second line of the data file.

```
Peter  Liacouras
20000.00
Caryn  Koffman
200.00
```

The second program will read the above file and print payroll checks based on the contents of this file. For example, the first check issued should be a check for $20,000.00 made out to Peter Liacouras.

2. Analysis

We will write the first program now and leave the second one as a programming project (see project 1 at the end of this chapter). The program must copy each employee's name to the output file. It must also compute each employee's salary, copy it to the output file, and add it to the payroll total.

DATA REQUIREMENTS
Problem Inputs (from data file INEMP)

```
NextSt  : string   % Each employee's name
Hours   : real     % Each employee's hours worked
Rate    : real     % Each employee's hourly rate
```

Problem Outputs (to output file OUTEMP)

```
NextSt  : string   % Each employee's name
Salary  : real     % Each employee's salary
```

Problem Outputs (to standard output file)

```
Payroll : real     % The payroll total
```

3. Design

The main program will prepare the files for input and output and call procedure `ProcessEmp` to process all employees and accumulate the total payroll. After `ProcessEmp` is finished, the main program will display the final payroll total.

ALGORITHM FOR MAIN PROGRAM
1. Prepare files `InEmp` and `OutEmp`
2. Process all employees and compute payroll total
3. Display the payroll total

ALGORITHM REFINEMENTS

The algorithm for `ProcessEmp` follows. Step 3 of `ProcessEmp` is performed by procedure `CopyLine` (Fig. 9.3). Figure 9.5 shows the structure chart.

ALGORITHM FOR PROCESSEMP

1. Initialize payroll total to `0.0`
   `loop`
       2. `exit` when there are no more employees
       3. Read next employee's name from `InEmp` and
             write it to `OutEmp`
       4. Read next employee's salary data
       5. Compute next employee's salary
       6. Write next employee's salary to `OutEmp` and
             add it to payroll total
   `end loop`

FIGURE 9.5   Structure Chart for Writing the Payroll File

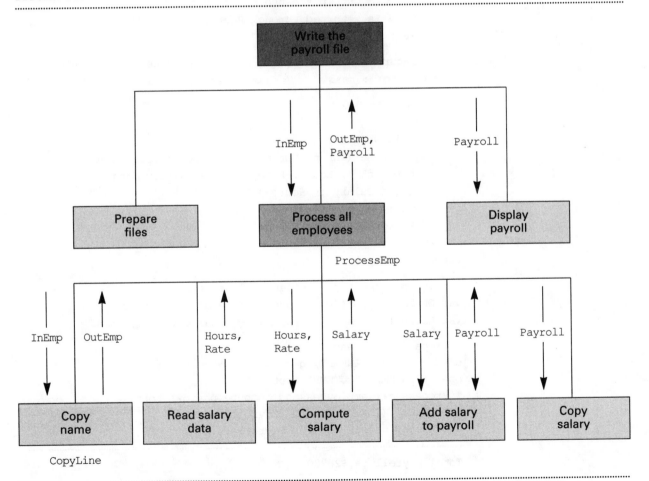

4. Implementation

Figure 9.6 shows the complete program. The program uses two text files whose stream numbers are `InEmp` and `OutEmp`. Besides `InEmp` and `OutEmp`, the only variable declared in the main program is `Payroll`. We declare variables `Hours`, `Rate`, and `Salary` in `ProcessEmp`.

FIGURE 9.6

Writing a Payroll File

```
% The "Payroll" program
% Write each employee's name and gross salary to an
% output file and compute total payroll amount

% Insert procedure CopyLine (See Figure 9.3) here

procedure ProcessEmp (InEmp, OutEmp : int,
                           var Payroll : real)
   % Process all employees and compute payroll total
   % Pre : InEmp and OutEmp are prepared for
   %          input/output
   % Post: All employee data are copied from InEmp
   %          to OutEmp and the sum of their salaries
   %          is returned through Payroll
   % Uses: CopyLine

   var Hours : real      % Input - hours worked
   var Rate  : real      % Input - hourly rate

   Payroll := 0.0
   loop
       exit when eof (InEmp)
       CopyLine (InEmp, OutEmp)      % Copy employee name
       get: InEmp, Hours, Rate       % Get salary data
       const Salary := Hours * Rate
       put: OutEmp, Salary :4:2
       Payroll := Payroll + Salary
   end loop
end ProcessEmp

var InEmp   : int      % Data file stream number
var OutEmp  : int      % Output file stream number
var Payroll : real     % Output - total payroll

% Prepare InEmp and OutEmp
open : InEmp, "INEMP", get
open : OutEmp, "OUTEMP", put
% Process all employees and compute payroll total
ProcessEmp (InEmp, OutEmp, Payroll)
put "Total payroll is $", Payroll :4:2
```

```
Total payroll is $20200.00
```

The loop in `ProcessEmp` tests whether the end of the file (`eof`) has been encountered. If not, procedure `CopyLine` copies an employee's name from its input file (`InEmp`) to its output file (`OutEmp`). `CopyLine` processes every other line of file `InEmp`, starting with the first line.

After `CopyLine` processes a line, the statement

```
get : InEmp, Hours, Rate        % Get salary data
```

reads that employee's salary data from `InEmp` and advances the file position pointer to the first letter of the next employee's name. (In older versions of Turing you would need to explicitly advance the file pointer using the keyword `skip` at the end of this `get` statement.) Next, the statement

```
put : OutEmp, Salary :4:2
```

writes the salary for the current employee to file `OutEmp`. After the current employee's salary is added to the payroll total, the next employee is processed. ✖

Advancing Past the < eoln > Character

There is a switch from line-oriented input, used in `CopyLine` (Fig. 9.3), and token-oriented input that occurs in these statements in the loop in the `ProcessEmp` procedure (Fig. 9.6):

```
CopyLine (InEmp, OutEmp)
get : InEmp, Hours, Rate
```

In `CopyLine`, the following statement reads the next entire input line:

```
get : InData, Line : *
```

For example, if the input line is

```
Peter Liacouras<eoln>
```

the value "`Peter Liacouras`" is read into `Line` (Fig. 9.3). The trailing `<eoln>` character is discarded.

The `get` statement in `ProcessEmp`, namely,

```
get : InEmp, Hours, Rate
```

reads an input line such as

```
40.0 500.00<eoln>
```

Since this is token-oriented input, any white space characters (blanks, tabs, and `<eoln>`s) preceding `40.0` and `500.00` are automatically skipped. Any white space characters following a token are also skipped up to and including the `<eoln>` character. In this case, the `<eoln>` following `500.00` is discarded and the file pointer is left locating the beginning of the next input line.

Older versions of the Turing language did not skip white space following tokens. If you run the program in Fig. 9.6 using an older version of Turing, it will not work correctly, because after reading `Rate` the file pointer will be left locating the `<eoln>` character. The successive attempt to read an entire line in `CopyLine` will immediately encounter this `<eoln>` character. As a result, a null string, rather than the intended following line, will be assigned to the variable `Line`.

Fortunately, current versions of Turing automatically skip the trailing `<eoln>`, so you do not need to worry about this problem. However, if you use character-oriented input, Turing does not automatically advance past the `<eoln>` character, and your program must explicitly deal with this character.

Exercises for Section 9.5

Self-Check

1. What would be the effect, if any, of trailing blanks at the end of data lines in the data file for the program in Fig. 9.6?
2. What would be the effect of blank lines?

Programming

1. Write a program that reads file `OutEmp` produced by program `Payroll` (Fig. 9.6) and displays a count of the number of employees processed by `Payroll` and their average salary.

9.6 Putting It All Together

Besides illustrating many of the Turing language features introduced in this chapter, the case study that follows provides a slightly different approach to problem design. As part of the problem analysis, we will design the format of the problem output and the format of each line of the data file. This is the first time that we have been concerned with these issues. Problems of this kind are often called *data processing* problems to indicate that the emphasis is on transforming data rather than performing extensive computations. Because the program solution is lengthy, we will carefully develop algorithms for the main program and all procedures before writing any code. The main point of this case study is to follow the stepwise design and development of the algorithm and to understand the modules and their interaction; a thorough understanding of the code is secondary.

❖ Case Study:

Preparing Semester Grade Reports

1. Problem   The registrar would like a program that can be used to prepare grade reports for students at the end of a semester. For each student, the program should write a table showing each course taken during the semester and the grade and credits for that course. The program should also compute the student's semester grade point average and write that on the grade report along with the number of credits earned towards graduation.

2. Analysis   This problem is different from most of the others we have studied because its main purpose is to write the student data in a particular format. We will assume that we have a great deal of freedom in designing the format of the program input and output. We can decide to have each student's data typed at the keyboard during program execution or in a previously prepared data file. To enable some editing of data beforehand, it would make more sense to prepare a data file. It would also be beneficial to write the program output to a file rather than display it on the screen. Once we have written the output file, we can send it to the printer and the grade reports will be printed so they can be mailed to each student.

The first step is to determine the format of the grade report we would like prepared for each student. Figure 9.7 shows the report form that we will use. The grade report displays the student's name, his or her performance in each course, the number of credits earned towards graduation, and his or her grade point average (GPA). The grade point average, 3.0, was computed by accumulating the total number of points earned in courses that received a grade of A through F (4 * 3 or 12 for CIS101, 3*4 or 12 for CIS210, 2 * 3 or 6 for HIS356) and dividing by the credits for those courses (10).

FIGURE 9.7   Grade Report Format

```
Spring Semester grade report for Jane Williams
Course    Grade    Credits
CIS101      A         3
CIS210      B         4
HIS356      C         3
PHI210      P         3
Graduation credits earned: 9
Semester GPA: 3.0
```

Next, we must decide the contents of the data file and its organization. We can place the data for each student in the form shown below for two students.

```
"Jane Williams" CIS101 A 3 CIS210 B 4
      HIS356 C 3 PHI210 P 3 #
"Billy Jones" PHI025 B 4 HIS120 C 3 MAT255 B 3 #
```

The student's name in quotes comes first followed by a list of course data. Each course's data consists of a character ID code, a grade, and the number of credit hours. The first two lines show that Jane Williams took four courses and received a grade of A for CIS101, a 3-credit course. She received a grade of B in CIS210 (4 credits), C in HIS356 (3 credits), and P in PHI210 (3 credits). Each student's data ends with the sentinel value #.

If we examine the grade report shown in Fig. 9.7, we see that each student's data will generate a multi-line table in the output file. Some of the information on the data line will simply be echoed (the student's name, each course ID), and some will be used in the computations (course grade and credits).

In the problem data requirements below, we list the input and output files. The variable StuCount will be used to count the students as they are processed. All other problem inputs and outputs will be declared as local variables in procedures.

DATA REQUIREMENTS
Problem Inputs
```
    StuData : int              % File number for the
                               % student data file
                               % named STUDATA
```

Problem Outputs
```
    GradeReport : int          % File number for the
                               % grade report file
                               % named REPORT
    StuCount : int             % Count of students
```

3. Design

In this subsection, we will discuss the algorithm for the main program and all procedures. We will not show any code until after we have finished discussing the procedures. The main program opens the files for input and output. It calls procedure DoOneStudent (step 5 below) to process each student's data and print that student's grade report. Figure 9.8 shows a structure chart for the program system and the main program algorithm follows.

ALGORITHM FOR MAIN PROGRAM
1. Prepare StuData for input and GradeReport for output
2. Initialize StuCount to zero
   loop
      3. exit when no more students
      4. Increment StuCount
      5. Process next student's data and
         write the student's grade report
   end loop
6. Display the count of students processed

FIGURE 9.8   Structure Chart for Student Transcript Program

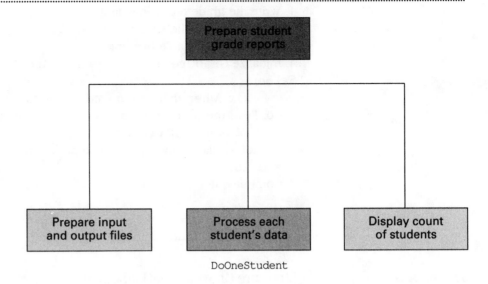

DoOneStudent

Design of Procedure DoOneStudent

The actual processing of a student's data is done by procedure DoOneStudent. DoOneStudent must write the student's name and each line of the grade report table. It must also compute and write graduation credits earned and grade point average. The inputs, outputs, and local variables for DoOneStudent follow.

DATA REQUIREMENTS FOR DOONESTUDENT

Input Parameters

```
StuData : int          % Student data file number
GradeReport : int      % Grade report file number
```

Local Variables

```
GradCredits : int      % Total graduation credits
                       % earned
GPA : real             % Grade point average
GPAPoints : int        % Total points earned
                       % towards GPA
GPACredits : int       % Total credits used to
                       % compute GPA
StudentDone : boolean  % Flag indicating handled student's
                       % last course
```

RELEVANT FORMULAS

GPA = total points earned for GPA / total credits for GPA

ALGORITHM FOR DOONESTUDENT

1. Write the grade report heading
2. Read and write the student's name
3. Write the grade table heading
4. Initialize `GradCredits`, `GPAPoints`, and `GPACredits` to zero
5. loop

     exit when there are no more courses

     6. Read the data for the next course, updating total graduation credits, GPA points, GPA credits, and `Error` if an error occurred. Write the course data on a separate line of the grade report

   end loop
7. Compute GPA

We will discuss `ProcessCourse` next. Figure 9.9 shows the relationship between `DoOneStudent` and its subordinate modules.

FIGURE 9.9   Structure Chart for DoOneStudent

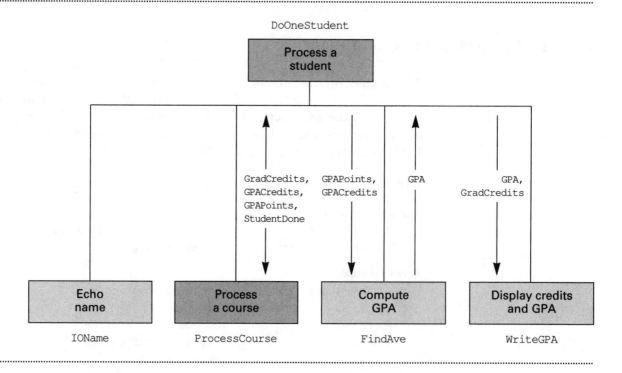

Design of ProcessCourse and Its Subordinate Modules

`ProcessCourse` reads and processes the data for a single course. Each course's data consists of a course character ID, a letter grade, and a digit character. The data requirements and algorithm for `ProcessCourse` follow.

DATA REQUIREMENTS FOR PROCESSCOURSE

Input Parameters

StuData : int	% Student data file
	% number

Input/Output Parameters

GradCredits : int	% Total graduation
	% credits earned
GPACredits : int	% Total credits used
	% to compute GPA
GPAPoints : int	% Total points earned
	% towards GPA

Output Parameters

GradeReport : int	% Grade report file
	% number
StudentDone : boolean	% Flag - True if there
	% wasn't another course

Local Variables

Grade : string	% The letter grade
Credits : int	% Number of credits

ALGORITHM FOR PROCESSCOURSE

1. Read course ID and if not sentinel, write it
   if course ID is not sentinel then
   2. Read and write the course grade
   3. Read and write the course credits
   4. Update total graduation credits, GPAPoints, and GPACredits based on the course grade and credits
   end if

IOCourse will read a course ID, write it if it is not the sentinel, and return a flag that will be tested to see if the sentinel was encountered. IOCredit will read and write the course credits. UpdateGPA will use the student's grade to determine the number of graduation and GPA credits earned as well as grade points. Figure 9.10 shows the structure chart for ProcessCourse and its subordinate modules.

4. Implementation

Figure 9.11 shows the main program for the transcript problem. The main program contains a declaration for the string constant Semester which is written to file GradeReport by procedure DoOneStudent. It also contains the declaration for the credit sentinel # which is used to mark the end of a student's data. The level-three modules (IOCourse, IOCredit, UpdateGPA) should come before ProcessCourse. The level-two modules, including `ProcessCourse`, should come before `DoOneStudent`. In the program body, the `exit` condition

    eof (StuData)

is `false` as long as there is student data left to process.

FIGURE 9.10   Structure Chart for ProcessCourse

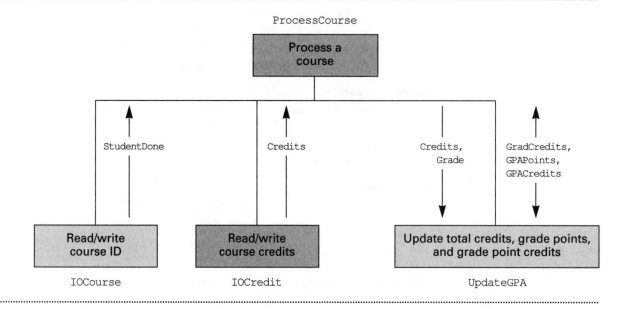

FIGURE 9.11   Main Program for Transcript Problem

```
% The "Transcr" program
% Write a semester grade report for each student

const Semester := "Spring Semester"
const CourseSentinel := "#"

% Insert level-3 modules here: IOCourse, IOCredit,
% UpdateGPA
% Insert level-2 modules here: IOName, ProcessCourse,
% FindAve, WriteGPA.
% Insert DoOneStudent here

var StuData: int          % Input - file of student data
var GradeReport : int     % Output - file of grade reports
var StuCount : int := 0   % Count of current student

% Prepare StuData for input and GradeReport for output
open: StuData, "STUDATA", get
open: GradeReport, "REPORT", put
```

```
% Process all students' data
loop
    exit when eof (StuData)
    StuCount := StuCount + 1
    DoOneStudent (StuData, GradeReport)
end loop
% Display count of students on screen
put StuCount, " students processed"
```

Figure 9.12 shows procedure DoOneStudent. The statement

```
put : GradeReport, NewPage   % Start a new page
```

causes each student's grade report to start on a new page when file GradeReport is sent to the printer. The constant NewPage has the value "\f" which is the *form feed* character. This special character causes a printer to skip to a new page. The condition in the exit statement

```
exit when StudentDone
```

is false as long as the sentinel # has not yet been reached for this student's data.

FIGURE 9.12   Procedure DoOneStudent

```
procedure DoOneStudent (StuData, GradeReport : int)
    % Process the data for one student
    % Pre : StuCount is the student being processed.
    %        The file position pointer for StuData is
    %        at the start of the student's data.
    % Post: A grade report for one student is written
    %        to the output file. The file position
    %        pointer for StuData has been advanced to
    %        the start of the next student's data.
    %        If an error occurs, the grade report is
    %        terminated and an error message is
    %        written to the screen.

    var GradCredits : int := 0   % Total graduation
                                 % credits earned
    var GPA : real               % Grade point average
    var GPAPoints: int := 0      % Total points earned
                                 % toward GPA
    var GPACredits : int := 0    % Total credits used
                                 % to compute GPA
    var StudentDone : boolean    % Flag - set to true
                                 % when student's data
                                 % has been processed
```

```
                    const NewPage := "\f"        % Formfeed character
                                                 % - starts new page

                    put : GradeReport, NewPage   % Start a new page
                    put : GradeReport, Semester, " grade report for " ..
                    % Write student name
                    IOName (StuData, GradeReport)
                    put : GradeReport, ""         % Terminate line
                    put : GradeReport, "Course    Grade    Credits"

                    % Process all course data for a student
                    loop
                        ProcessCourse (StuData, GradeReport, GradCredits,
                                        GPAPoints, GPACredits, StudentDone)
                        exit when StudentDone
                    end loop

                    % Compute GPA
                    GPA := FindAve (GPAPoints, GPACredits)
                    % Write graduation credits
                    WriteGPA (GradeReport, GradCredits, GPA)
                end DoOneStudent
```

Figure 9.13 shows the subordinate modules for `DoOneStudent` except for `ProcessCourse`, which will be discussed next, and `FindAve` (see Fig. 7.26).

FIGURE 9.13   Procedures IOName and WriteGPA

```
procedure IOName (StuData, GradeReport : int)
    % Write the student name to the output file
    % Pre : The student name must be in quotes
    % Post: The student name is copied from the input file
    %       (StuData) to the output file (GradeReport)

    var Name : string    % The student's name

    % Read and write student name
    get: StuData, Name
    put : GradeReport, Name ..
end IOName

procedure WriteGPA (GradeReport : int,
                    GradCredits : int,
                    GPA : real)
    % Write the graduation credits earned and GPA to the
    % output file
    % Pre : None
    % Post: GradCredits and GPA are written to the
    %       output file
```

```
    put: GradeReport, "Graduation credits earned: ",
        GradCredits
    put: GradeReport, "Semester GPA: ", GPA :3:1
end WriteGPA
```

Figure 9.14 shows `ProcessCourse` (at the end of the figure) and its subordinate procedures. In `ProcessCourse`, if the sentinel value # is read instead of a course ID, the flag `StudentDone` is set to `true`.

In `IOCredit`, the integer value of the student's credits is copied from the student's data to the report file and is also returned through the variable parameter `Credits`.

In `UpdateGPA`, the `if` statement increments `GradCredits` by `Credits` for a grade of A through D or P (Pass). It increments `GPACredits` by `Credits` for a grade of A through D or F (Fail). It increments `GPAPoints` by the product of `Credits` and a number between 1 (for D) and 4 (for A) for a grade of A through D. For example, the expression

```
(4 - (ord(Grade) - ord("A")))
```

evaluates to 4 − 1 or 3 when `Grade` is B.

FIGURE 9.14

ProcessCourse and Subordinate Procedures

```
procedure IOCourse (StuData, GradeReport : int,
                        var StudentDone : boolean)
    % Write the course ID to the output file
    % Pre : none
    % Post: Copy the course ID from the input file
    %       (StuData) to the output file (GradeReport)

    var CourseID : string
    get : StuData, CourseID    % Read the course ID
    if CourseID = CourseSentinel then
        StudentDone := true
    else
        StudentDone := false
        put : GradeReport, CourseID ..
    end if
end IOCourse

procedure IOCredit (StuData, GradeReport : int,
                        var Credits : int)
    % Read the number of credits and write it to the
    % output file
    % Pre : none
    % Post: Return the number of credits and copy
    %       this to the output file

    % Read and write the credits
    get: StuData, Credits
    put: GradeReport, Credits :10 ..
end IOCredit
```

```
procedure UpdateGPA (Grade : string, Credits : int,
                        var GradCredits, GPAPoints,
                        GPACredits : int)
   % Update graduation credits, GPA credits, and Credits
   % Pre : none
   % Post: If Grade is valid, return new values for
   %       GradCredits, GPAPoints, GPACredits

   if Grade = "A" or Grade = "B" or
         Grade = "C" or Grade = "D" then
      GradCredits := GradCredits + Credits
      GPACredits := GPACredits + Credits
      GPAPoints := GPAPoints + Credits *
                     (4 - (ord(Grade) - ord("A")))
   elsif Grade = "F" then
      GPACredits := GPACredits + Credits
   elsif Grade = "P" then
      GradCredits := GradCredits + Credits
   elsif Grade = "I" or Grade = "W" then
      % Do nothing
   else
      put "Error: Incorrect grade is ", Grade
   end if
end UpdateGPA

procedure ProcessCourse (StuData, GradeReport : int,
                        var GradCredits, GPAPoints,
                        GPACredits : int,
                        var StudentDone : boolean)
   % Process the data for one course
   % Pre : none
   % Post: Read all the data for one course and write
   %       it to the output file. Return the updated
   %       values of graduation credits, GPA credits,
   %       and GPA points. However, if there are no
   %       more courses, instead return with
   %       StudentDone set to true.

   var Grade : string        % Course grade
   var Credits : int         % Number of credits for
                             % the course

   IOCourse (StuData, GradeReport, StudentDone)
   if not StudentDone then
      get : StuData, Grade
```

```
                 put : GradeReport, "    ", Grade ..
                 IOCredit (StuData, GradeReport, Credits)
                 put : GradeReport, ""        % Leave a blank line
                 UpdateGPA (Grade, Credits, GradCredits,
                            GPAPoints, GPACredits)
            end if
        end ProcessCourse
```

5. Testing   When you run the transcript program with some sample student data, you should generate grade reports in the form shown earlier. Make sure that the grade point average computed and the graduation credits earned are accurate for a variety of different grades.   ✖

Exercises for Section 9.6

Self-Check

1. What would be the effect if the course sentinel # were inadvertently omitted from a student's data?
2. Explain why `GradeReport` is not a variable parameter to procedure `IOName` even though this procedure changes (writes to) the grade report file.

Programming

1. Modify the program `Transcr` so that it prints a warning message on the screen if a grade report indicates that a student has earned more than 20 graduation credits.

9.7 Common Programming Errors

File processing in any programming language tends to be difficult to master. Remember to declare a file number variable for each file your program is to use.

Remember to prepare a file for input or output using the open statement (except for standard input and output files). If you open an existing file for output (for put), the data on that file may be lost. Make sure that you do not inadvertently place the open statement in a loop. If you do, a read operation in the loop will repeatedly read the first file component; a write operation in the loop will repeatedly write the first file component.

The get statement can access a file only after the file has been opened for input (for get). Similarly, the put statement can be used only after a file has been opened for output (for put). Be sure to specify the file name as the first procedure parameter of put and get; otherwise, the standard input or output file will be assumed. An "attempt to read past end of file" error occurs if a read operation is performed after all data characters have been processed.

When using function eof to control data entry, don't forget to include the file number as the function argument.

If you press the Return key an extra time when you are finished creating a data file, you may place an extra empty line at the end of the data file. The file below contains one number per line and an empty line at the end.

```
500<eoln>
37<eoln>
<eoln>
```

Although the empty line seems perfectly harmless, if we use the exit statement

```
exit when eof (InData)
```

to control a loop that reads and processes one number at a time, the empty line will cause the loop to execute one extra time. Because there are no data to read, an "attempt to read past end of file" error will occur.

Chapter Review

In this chapter, you learned how to instruct a program to read its data from a data file rather than from the keyboard, and how to save the output generated by a program as a file on disk. Both features use files of characters, called text files. The <eoln> character breaks a text file into lines. A put statement that does not end in dot-dot places an <eoln> character in a text file. An <eoln> character is read into a type string variable only when using character-oriented input (when the explicit number of characters to be read is given by a format item).

Format items can be used in a put statement to specify the width (number of characters to output), the fractional digits (for numbers only), and the exponent digits (for numbers only). The keyword skip used in a put statement skips to the next output line.

There are three kinds of input that occur using a get statement. The first, token-oriented input, is the simplest and occurs when there is no format item. This form skips white space before the value and reads the characters until more white space is found (unless the token is a quoted string). After the token is read, any white space up to non-white space or the end of the line is skipped. The second kind of input is character-oriented and is specified by giving a width format item that determines the actual number of characters to be read. The third kind of input is line-oriented. It uses a star (*) format item to specify that the entire line is to be read into a string variable.

When processing text files, sequences of characters are transferred between main memory and disk storage. The data type of a variable used in an input list must be string or int (or a subrange of int) or real. The data type of an expression used in an output list must be string or int (or a subrange of int) or real.

The open statement moves the file-position pointer to the first character in the file. With the put option, it deletes the old contents of a file and prepares the file for writing. With the get option, it prepares an input file for reading. While reading a file, the eof function can test whether the end of the file has been reached.

New Turing Constructs in Chapter 9

The new Turing constructs introduced in this chapter are described in Table 9.1.

TABLE 9.1　　　　　Summary of New Turing Constructs

Construct	Effect
Declaring File Numbers	
var NumFile : int	NumFile, ChFile, and LineFile are the
var ChFile : int	numbers of input text files.
var LineFile : int	
var OutFile : int	OutFile is the number of an output text file.
var X : real	
var Ch : string	
var Line : string	
Opening Files	
open : NumFile, "NFILE", get	The first three files are prepared for input.
open : ChFile, "CFILE", get	
open : LineFile, "LFILE", get	The fourth file is prepared for output.
open : OutFile, "OFILE", put	
Reading and Writing Files	
get : NumFile, X	The next number is read as a token from NFILE, skipping any white space.
get : ChFile, Ch : 1	The next single character is read from CFILE.
get : LineFile, Line : *	The next line is read from LFILE.
put : OutFile, "X=", X	X is written to the OutFile. Only as many characters as needed to represent X are written.
put "X=", X:9	X is displayed on the screen right-justified in a field of width 9.
put "X=", X:9:3	X is displayed with width 9 and 3 fraction digits.

```
put "X=", X:9:3:2
```

X is displayed with width 9,
3 fraction digits and 2 exponent digits.

Closing Files

```
close : NumFile
close : ChFile
close : LineFile
close : OutFile
```

Disconnect from each file.

End-of-File Function

```
open : NumFile, "NFILE", get
open : OutFile, "OFILE", put
loop
    exit when eof (NumFile)
    get : NumFile, X
    put : OutFile, X
end loop
```

File NFILE is prepared for input and file
OFILE for output.

Each number value of file NFILE is written
to a separate line of file OFILE.

Quick-Check Exercises

1. The _____ operation prepares a file for input or output.
2. The _____ character separates a _____ file into lines.
3. What data types can be read or written to a text file?
4. How is a file passed as a parameter to a procedure?
5. Where are files stored?

Answers to Quick-Check Exercises

1. open
2. <eoln>, Text
3. Numbers (integers and real numbers) and strings
4. By passing its file number as in integer parameter
5. Secondary storage or disk

Review Questions

1. List three advantages to using files for input and output as opposed to the standard input and output you have used thus far in this course.
2. a. Explain the difference between a file name and its number.
   b. Which of these appears in a variable declaration?
   c. Which of these appears in an open statement?
   d. Which of these appears in a get statement?
3. Let X be type real, N type int, and St type string. Indicate the contents of each variable after each input operation is performed,

assuming the file consists of the lines below and that the open statement occurs before each sequence of statements.

```
23 53.2 ABC<eoln>
145 Z<eoln>
```

a. `get : InData, N, X`
   `get : InData, St`
b. `get : InData, St, N`
c. `get : InData`
   `get : InData, X, St`

4. Write a loop that reads up to 10 integer values from a data file and displays them on the screen. If there are less than 10 integers in the file, the message "`That's all folks`" should be displayed after the last number.
5. Write a procedure that copies several data lines typed at the keyboard to a text file. The copy process should be terminated when the user enters a null line.

Programming Projects

1. Write a procedure that reads the data for one employee from file `OutEmp` produced by program `Payroll` (see Section 9.5) and writes a payroll check to an output file. The format of the check should be similar to the one shown below:

```
Temple University              Check No.   12372
Philadelphia, PA               Date:       03-17-93

Pay to the
Order of:   Peter Liacouras        $ 20000.00
                                   Jane Smith
```

2. Write a program that reads the initial check number and the date from the keyboard and writes checks using the procedure from programming project 1 and a data file generated by running program `Payroll`. Write a separator line consisting of 80 underscore characters between checks.
3. Each year the state legislature rates the productivity of the faculty of each of the state-supported colleges and universities. The rating is based on reports submitted by the faculty members indicating the average number of hours worked per week during the school year. Each faculty member is rated and the university receives an overall rating.

   The faculty productivity ratings are computed as follows:
   a. Highly-Productive means over 55 hours per week reported.
   b. Satisfactory means reported hours per week are between 35 and 55.
   c. Overpaid means reported hours per week are less than 35.
   Read the following data from a data file:

Name	Hours
Herm	63
Flo	37
Jake	20
Maureen	55
Saul	72
Tony	40
Al	12

Your program should include procedures corresponding to the procedure headers shown below as part of your solution:

```
procedure PrintHeader
% Display table heading

procedure DisplayProductivity (Hours : real)
% Display productivity ranking based on value of
% Hours

procedure ProcessName (FacHours : int)
% Reads and displays one faculty name from file
% FacHours

procedure ProcessData (FacHours : int,
                         var Count : int,
                         var Sum : real)
% Read all data lines from file FacHours and
% display body of table and return number of
% faculty (Count) and the sum of their hours
% worked (Sum)

% Calls: ProcessName and DisplayProductivity
```

4. Write a program that reads several lines from a data file and prints each word of the file on a separate line of an output file followed by the number of letters in that word. Also print a count of words in the file on the screen when done. Assume that words are separated by one or more blanks (or other white space characters).

5. Compute the monthly payment and the total payment for a bank loan, given:

a. the amount of the loan
b. the duration of the loan in months
c. the interest rate for the loan

Your program should read in one loan at a time, perform the required computation, and print the values of the monthly payment and the total payment.

Test your program with at least the following data (and more if you want).

Loan	Months	Rate
16000	300	2.50
24000	360	3.50
30000	300	5.50
42000	360	4.50
22000	300	5.50
300000	240	5.25

Hints:

a. The formula for computing monthly payment is

$$monthpay = \frac{ratem \ast expm^{months} \ast loan}{expm - 1.0}$$

where

$$ratem = rate / 1200.0$$
$$expm = (1.0 + ratem)$$

b. The formula for computing the total payment is

$$total = monthpay \ast months$$

6. Use your solution to project 5, as the basis for writing a program that will write a data file containing a table of the following form:

```
                    Loan Amount: $1000
Interest        Duration        Monthly         Total
  Rate          (years)         Payment         Payment
  2.00             20           ------          ------
  2.00             25           ------          ------
  2.00             30           ------          ------
  2.25             20           ------          ------
```

The output file produced by your program should contain payment information on a $1000 loan for interest rates from 2% to 6% with increments of 0.25%. The loan durations should be 20, 25, and 30 years.

7. Monroe University offers a service to its faculty in computing grades at the end of each semester. A program will process three weighted test scores and will calculate a student's average and letter grade (an A is 90–100, a B is 80–89, etc.). Read the student data from a file and write each student's name, test score, average, and grade to an output file.

Write a program to provide this valuable service. The data will consist of the three test weights followed by three test scores and a student ID number (four digits) for each student. Calculate the weighted average for each student and the corresponding grade. This information should be printed along with the initial three test scores. The weighted average for each student is equal to:

weight1 * *score1* + *weight2* * *score2* + *weight3* * *score3*

For summary statistics, print the highest average, lowest average, average of the averages, and total number of students processed.

Sample data:

```
0.35    0.25    0.40          test weights
100    76    88    1014        test scores and id
```

8. Write a program to read in a string of characters that represent a Roman numeral and then convert it to Arabic form (an integer). The character values for Roman numerals are as follows:

M	1000
D	500
C	100
L	50
X	10
V	5
I	1

Test your program with the following data: LXXXVII (87), CCXIX (219), MCCCLIV (1354), MMDCLXXIII (2673), MCDLXXVI (1476).

Introduction to Software Engineering

Until this point in your study of programming, you have been primarily concerned with writing relatively short programs that solve particular programming problems, but that otherwise have little general use. In this chapter you will begin to consider large-scale programming, called *programming in the large*.

This chapter discusses software engineering, a term used to denote a collection of tools and techniques used by professional programmers in industry to facilitate the design and maintenance (upkeep) of large-scale programs. Our discussion will focus on some principles of software engineering that have proved useful for designing large program systems.

We will describe the different phases of a software project and elaborate on the software engineering method for problem solving and programming first discussed in Section 2.1. We will discuss how to modularize a large project so that individual pieces can be implemented by different programmers and at different times. We will discuss how to write software modules to simplify their reuse in other projects.

We will consider the question of testing a program and verifying that it works correctly. We will discuss the limitations of program testing and describe formal methods for proving that a program is correct.

Because this chapter introduces many concepts that are used by software professionals, the chapter ends with a discussion of professional behavior, ethics, and responsibilities. There are also important warnings about computer viruses and plagiarism that apply to student programmers as well as industrial programmers.

10.1 The Software Challenge

Programming in college is somewhat different from programming in the real world. In college, you are generally given the problem specification by an instructor. In many cases, the problem specification is ambiguous or incomplete, and interaction between the instructor and the class is necessary so that the students can pin down the details.

In the real world, the impetus for a software project comes from users of an existing software product or potential users of a new software product. The users see a need for improving the operation of an existing product or for computerizing an operation that is currently done manually (i.e., without the use of computers). This need is communicated to the individual(s) responsible for providing software support in the organization (normally called *systems analysts*).

Because the users are often naive as to the capabilities of a computer, the initial specification for a software product may be incomplete. The specification is clarified through extensive interaction between the users of the software and the systems analyst. Through this interaction, the systems analyst determines precisely what the users want the proposed software to do, and the users learn what to expect from the software product. This way there are no surprises in the end.

Although it may seem like common sense to proceed in this manner, very often a software product does not perform as expected. The reason is usually a communication gap between those responsible for the product's design and its eventual users; generally, both parties are at fault when the software fails to meet expectations. To avoid this possibility, it is imperative that a complete, written description of the requirements specification for a new software product be generated at the beginning of the project, and that both users and designers sign the document.

Programming Teams

Another major difference between programming in college and in industry is that it is rare for a large software project in industry to be implemented by a single programmer. Most often, a large project is assigned to a team of programmers. It is important for team members to coordinate beforehand the overall organization of the project.

Each team member is responsible for a set of procedures, some of which may be accessed by other team members. After the initial organization meeting, each team member should provide the others with a specification for each procedure that he or she is implementing. The specification will be similar to the documentation provided for each procedure in this text. It will consist of a brief statement of the purpose of the procedure, its preconditions and postconditions, and its formal parameter list. This information is all that a potential user of the procedure needs to know in order to call it correctly.

Normally one team member will act as "librarian" by assuming responsibility for determining the status of each procedure in the system. Initially, the library of procedures will consist of a stub for each procedure. As a new procedure is completed and tested, its updated version will replace the version currently in the library. The librarian will keep track of the date that each new version of a procedure was inserted in the library, and make sure that all programmers are using the latest version of any procedure.

Exercises for Section 10.1

Self-Check

1. How does the role of the systems analyst differ from that of the librarian during the development of a large software system?
2. Explain how a programming team has the potential to complete a large software project more quickly than a single programmer working independently.

10.2 The Software Life Cycle

The steps involved in the initial development and continued operation of a software system comprise the *software life cycle* (SLC) as described below.

Software Life Cycle

1. Requirements specification
   - Prepare a complete and unambiguous problem statement
2. Analysis
   - Understand the problem – determine problem outputs and required inputs
   - Evaluate alternative solutions
   - Choose the preferred solution
3. Design
   - Perform a top-down design of the system
   - For each module, identify key data elements and subordinate procedures using structure charts
4. Implementation
   - Write algorithms and pseudocode descriptions of individual procedures
   - Code the solution
   - Debug the code
5. Testing and validation
   - Test the code, validating that it is correct
6. Operation, follow-up, and maintenance
   - Run the completed system
   - Evaluate its performance
   - Remove new bugs as they are detected
   - Make required changes to keep the system up-to-date
   - Validate that changes are correct and do not adversely affect the system's operation.

The engineering and scientific method for solving problems specifies that problem analysis should always precede problem solution (synthesis). The first two stages of the SLC (requirements specification and analysis) are the analysis part and the next two stages (design and implementation) are the synthesis part. The program users take the lead in developing the requirements specification. The system developers work closely with the program users to more thoroughly understand the problem requirements and to evaluate possible alternative solutions.

The SLC is iterative. During the design phase (step 3 above), problems may arise that make it necessary to modify the requirements specification. Similarly, during implementation (step 4 above) it may become necessary to reconsider decisions made in the design phase. All changes must be approved by the systems analyst and users.

Once the system is implemented, it must be thoroughly tested before it enters its final stage (operation and maintenance). It is possible to identify necessary system changes in both these stages that require repetition of earlier stages of the SLC. These changes may come about to correct errors identified during testing or to accommodate changes required by external sources (for example, a change in the federal or state tax regulations).

There are varying estimates as to the percentage of time spent in each stage. For example, a typical system may require a year to proceed through the first four stages, three months of testing, then four or more years of operation and maintenance. Keeping these figures in mind, you can see why it is so important to design and document software in such a way that it can be easily maintained. This is especially important because the person who maintains the program may not have been involved in the original program design or implementation.

Prototyping

Before presenting an in-depth discussion of the software life cycle, we should mention that there is an alternate approach to traditional system development called prototyping. In *prototyping*, the systems analyst works closely with the system user to develop a prototype or model of the actual system. Initially the prototype will have few working features and will just mimic the input/output interaction of the user with the system. At each stage, the user and analyst decide what changes should be made and what new features should be added and these changes are incorporated into the prototype. This process continues until a complete prototype is available which performs all of the functions of the final system. The analyst and user can then decide whether to use the prototype as the final system or to use it as the basis of the design for a new system that will have the same look and feel as the prototype but will be more efficient.

Requirements Specification

Although we have illustrated most of the phases of the system life cycle in solving all prior case studies, we have not really had an opportunity to illustrate the requirements specification process. Each case study was preceded by a brief statement of the problem, and we began our solutions with the analysis phase. In the next case study, we focus on the issues that are dealt with during each stage of the SLC beginning with the requirements specification.

✖ Case Study:

Telephone Directory Program

1. Problem

Write an interactive telephone directory program that will contain a collection of names and telephone numbers. You should be able to insert new entries in the directory, retrieve an entry in the directory, change a directory entry, or delete an directory entry.

Requirements Specification

In the real world, the systems analyst works with the software users to clarify the detailed system requirements. Some of the questions that need to be answered deal with the format of the input data, the desired form of any output screens or printed forms, and the need for data validation. Often, you need to follow this process by interrogating your instructor or graduate assistant to determine the precise details of a programming assignment.

For example, assume your instructor has given you the incomplete problem specification above for the design of a telephone directory program. Some of the questions that might come to mind and require clarification are the following:

1. Is there an initial list of names and numbers to be stored in the directory beforehand or all entries inserted at the same time?
2. If there is an initial list, is it stored in a data file or will it be entered interactively?
3. If the file is a text file, what are the formatting conventions (for example, the name starts in column 1 and the phone number starts in column 20)? Are the name and number on the same data line or on separate lines?
4. Is the final directory stored in main memory or as a file in secondary memory?
5. Is it possible for there to be more than one number associated with a particular name. If so, should the first number be retrieved, the last number, or all numbers?
6. Is there a limit on the length of a name? How are the names stored (for example: *last, first* or *first, last*)?
7. Are phone numbers stored as numbers or as strings of characters? Do they contain area codes? Are there any special characters in a phone number such as hyphens and parentheses? Should we check for illegal characters in a number or for a number that is too short or too long?
8. Should the names be stored in alphabetical order or in the sequence in which they were entered into the directory?
9. Do you need a printed list of names and phone numbers for the directory and how should that list be formatted?

10. Is it possible to change a person's name as well as the person's phone number?
11. What information is needed to retrieve a directory entry?
12. When an entry is retrieved, should both the person's name and number be displayed or just the number? What form should this display take?
13. What action should be taken if a "new" entry has the same name as a person already in the directory? Should this be flagged as an error?

As you can see, there are plenty of questions left unanswered by the initial problem statement. To complete the requirements specification, you should answer these questions and more. Many of the questions deal with details of input data, handling of potential errors in input data, and formats of input data and output lists.

2. Analysis of the Problem

Once the system requirements are specified, the analysis stage begins. Before you can embark on the design of a program solution, you should make sure that you completely understand the problem. If the requirements specification has been carefully done, this will be easy. If there are any questions remaining, they should be cleared up at this time.

The next step is to evaluate different approaches to the program design. As part of this investigation, the systems analyst and users may consider whether there are commercial software packages that they can purchase to satisfy their requirements as an alternative to developing the software in-house. They must also determine the impact of the new software product on existing computer systems and what new hardware or software will be needed to develop and run the new system. They determine the feasibility of each approach by estimating its cost and anticipated benefits. The analysis stage culminates with the selection of what appears to be the best design approach.

Although your choices will be more constrained in your coursework, you will often need to determine whether to use a personal computer or a mainframe, to select a programming language for implementation, and to determine the structure and organization of internal data and also external data files. Some factors that should be considered in evaluating each design approach are the main memory requirements for the program and its data as well as the requirements for secondary storage of files.

3. Design

Once you understand the problem and have selected the overall approach to the design, it is time to develop a high-level design of the system. The top-down approach to design instructs us to start at the top level (the original problem) and divide it into subproblems. For each subproblem, we identify a subsystem with the responsibility of solving that subproblem. As we have done before, we can use a structure chart to indicate the relationship between the subproblems (and subsystems). A structure chart for our telephone directory problem is shown in Fig. 10.1.

FIGURE 10.1   Structure Chart for Telephone Directory Problem

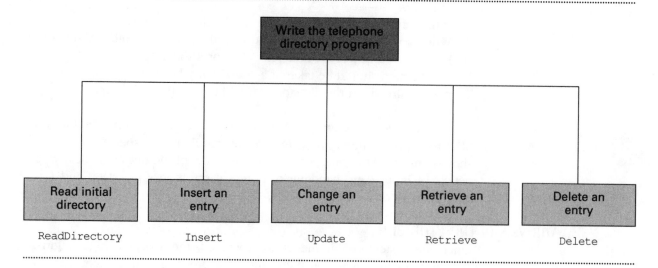

Figure 10.1 shows the two top levels of the structure chart, which includes the original problem and its major subproblems. Each major subproblem should be implemented as a separate subsystem of modules. The modules needed are determined by refining and subdividing the major subproblems into still smaller subproblems. Figure 10.2 shows that to solve the subproblem "Retrieve an entry" we must be able to "Read a name", "Find a name in the directory", and "Get entry information from the directory".

FIGURE 10.2   Structure Chart for Retrieve an Entry

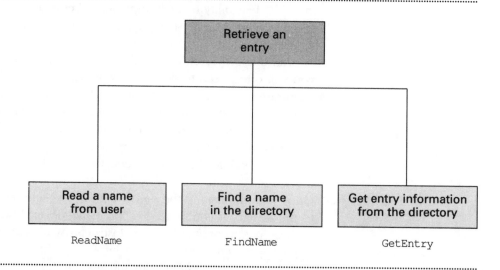

The second part of the design step of the system life cycle is to identify the major data elements and procedures for each module. We will use procedural and data abstraction to accomplish this as described next. ✖

Exercises for Section 10.2

Self-Check

1. List the six phases of the software life cycle. Which phase is the longest?
2. Draw a structure chart that shows a refinement for subproblem "Change an entry."

10.3 Procedural Abstraction Revisited

Abstraction is a powerful technique that helps programmers (or problem solvers) deal with complex issues in a piecemeal fashion. The dictionary defines *abstraction* as process of separating the inherent qualities or properties of something from the actual physical object to which they belong. One example of the use of abstraction is representing a program variable by a storage location in memory; for example, *TelNumber* is an abstraction for a storage location. We don't have to know anything about the physical structure of memory in order to use variables in programming.

So far you have practiced *procedural abstraction*, which is the philosophy that procedure development should separate the concern of *what* is to be achieved by a procedure from the details of *how* it is to be achieved. In other words, you can specify what you expect a procedure to do, then use that procedure in the design of a problem solution before you know how to implement the procedure.

As an example, we can outline a program fragment to retrieve an entry from the directory using procedural abstraction.

```
ReadName (    )     % Read the name that we are seeking
FindName (    )     % Locate the name in the directory
GetEntry (    )     % Retrieve entry from directory
```

The above fragment calls three procedures first shown in Fig. 10.2. We can fill in the parameter lists after the data flow information is added to the structure chart.

Procedure Libraries

As you progress through this course, you will write many Turing programs and procedures. You should try to keep each new procedure as general as possible so that you can reuse it in other applications. You will eventually build up a sizeable library of your own procedures. Reusing tried and tested procedures is always much more efficient than starting from scratch; each new procedure that you write will have to be thoroughly tested and debugged, requiring a lot of startup time in every case. The procedures in your personal library already will have been tested, so you will save time if you use procedures over and over again.

As an example, it would be useful to have a set of procedures available for performing some common data entry operations. Since procedure `get` cannot be used to read Boolean values, it would be useful to have our own procedure for this purpose. Procedure `GetBool` shown earlier reads a character value and returns either `true` or `false` based on the data character. `GetBool` should certainly be included in a programmer's library.

In many situations, we would like a data value to lie within a specific subrange of values. For example, we might like to read in a character that is an uppercase letter or an integer in the range −10 to +10. Procedure `EnterInt` (see Fig. 10.3) accomplishes the latter operation. You could easily write similar procedures, called `EnterString` and `EnterReal`, for the other standard data types of Turing. These procedures would also be useful additions to a programmer's library.

FIGURE 10.3 Procedure EnterInt

```
procedure EnterInt (MinN, MaxN : int, var N : int)
    % Read an integer between MinN and MaxN into N
    % Pre : MinN and MaxN are assigned values
    % Post: Return in N the first data value between
    %       MinN and MaxN if MinN <= MaxN is true;
    %       otherwise, N is not defined

    if MinN <= MaxN then % Check for non-empty range
        % Keep reading until a valid number is read
        loop
            put "Enter an integer between ",
                MinN, " and ", MaxN, "> " ..
            get N
            exit when MinN <= N and N <= MaxN
        end loop
    else
        put "Error - empty range for EnterInt"
    end if
end EnterInt
```

It would also be useful to have a function named `UpCase` (see Fig. 10.4) that returns the uppercase form of an argument that is a lowercase letter. We will use function `UpCase` later in this chapter.

FIGURE 10.4 Function UpCase

```
function UpCase (St : string) : string
    % Return the uppercase letter corresponding to St
    % Pre : St is defined
    % Post: If St is lowercase, returns the corresponding
    %       uppercase letter; otherwise, return St
```

```
        if "a" <= St and St <= "z" then
            result chr(ord(St) - ord("a") + ord("A"))
        else
            result St
        end if
    end UpCase
```

<table>
<tr><td>PROGRAM
STYLE</td><td>VALIDATING A LIBRARY PROCEDURE'S PARAMETERS
Procedure <code>EnterInt</code> begins by checking whether its user correctly entered its input parameters, <code>MinN</code> and <code>MaxN</code>. If the parameters define an empty range, an error message is displayed and the read operation is skipped. You should make sure that you carefully validate input parameters for procedures that are candidates for inclusion in a library. Since library procedures may be reused many times and by many different programmers, this extra effort can pay valuable dividends.</td></tr>
</table>

Exercises for Section 10.3

Self-Check

1. What two pieces of information must be known about a library procedure before it can be called?
2. Why is the validation of procedure parameters more critical for a library procedure than for a procedure that is only used in a single program?

Programming

1. Write procedure `EnterString` which returns a data character that lies within a specified range of characters. Your procedure should display an error message if the specified range is invalid.
2. Redo programming exercise 1 for a procedure that reads a real data value between a specified range of real numbers.

10.4 Data Abstraction

From this point on in the course we will begin to make extensive use of another type of abstraction, data abstraction. Through *data abstraction*, we specify the data objects for a problem and the operations to be performed on these data objects without being overly concerned with how they (the data objects) will be represented and stored in memory. We can describe *what* information is stored in the data object without being specific as to *how* the information is organized and represented. This is the *logical view* of the data object as opposed to its *physical view* which is the actual internal representation in memory. Once we understand the logical view, we can use the data object and its operators in our programs; however, we (or someone else) will eventually have to implement the data object and its operators before we can run any program that uses them.

One simple example of data abstraction is our use of the Turing data type `real` which is an abstraction for the set of real numbers. The computer hardware limits the range of real numbers that can be represented and not all real numbers within the specified range can be represented. Also, the results of manipulating real numbers are often approximations to the actual result. However, we can generally use the data type `real` and its Turing operators (+, −, *, /, :=, <=, <, and so on) without being concerned with these details of its implementation.

Information Hiding

One advantage of procedural abstraction and data abstraction is that they enable the designer to make implementation decisions in a piecemeal fashion. The designer can postpone making decisions regarding the actual internal representation of the data objects and the implementation of its operators. At the top levels of the design, the designer focuses on how to use a data object and its operators; at the lower levels of design, the designer works out the implementation details. In this way, the designer can control or reduce the overall complexity of the problem.

If the details of a data object's implementation are not known when a higher-level module is implemented, the higher-level module can only access the data object through its operators. From a software engineering viewpoint, this is an advantage rather than a limitation. It allows the designer to change his or her mind at a later date, and possibly choose a more efficient method of internal representation or implementation. If the higher level modules only reference a data object through its operators, the higher level module will not have to be rewritten and may not even need to be recompiled. The process of "hiding" the details of a low level module's implementation from a higher level module is called *information hiding*. We will see how this works later.

Abstract Data Types

One of the goals of software engineering is to write *reusable code* which is code that can be reused in many different applications, preferably without having to be recompiled. One way in which we can do this is to *encapsulate* or combine a data object together with its operators in a separate program module. As we discussed in the previous section, we can manipulate the data object in new programs by calling the operator procedures and functions contained in this module. We need not be concerned with details of the data object's representation in memory or with details of the operators' implementation. The combination of a data object together with its operators is called an *abstract data type* (ADT).

A primary goal of this text is to show you how to write and use abstract data types in programming. As you progress through this course, you will create a large collection of abstract data types in your own program library. Since each abstract data type in your library will already have been coded, debugged, tested, and maybe even compiled, the use of these ADTs will make it much easier for you to design and implement new applications programs.

Normally an abstract data type consists of two parts: its specification and its implementation. The *specification part* describes the structure of the data object and the capabilities of its operators. The specification part contains all the information needed by Turing to link the abstract data type with another program. It also contains the information that a potential user of the abstract data type needs to know. The *implementation part* contains the actual implementation of the operators that may be hidden from users of the abstract data type.

Although separate compilation is not supported in standard Turing, many extended versions of Turing provide the capability of separate compilation for modules that contain abstract data types. If we compile the abstract data type, then we can link its executable code with other programs that use it. If we were careful to include a fairly complete set of operator procedures in the abstract data type, the module containing the abstract data type will not have to be recompiled for each new application.

Exercises for Section 10.4

Self-Check

1. List the Turing operators and standard functions that should be considered part of the complete specifications for the built-in data types:
   a. `real`
   b. `int`
   c. `string`
   d. `boolean`
2. What is information hiding and why is it important to a software designer?

10.5 An Abstract Data Type

An abstract data type usually declares the form of a *data structure* which may be used to store an actual data object. We will see how to do this in later chapters. However, we can illustrate the fundamental concepts now by developing a simple abstract data type, `DayADT`, which declares an enumerated type `Day` whose values represent the days of the week. As part of DayADT, we provide operator procedures for reading and writing the days of the week. DayADT would be a useful addition to our library because Turing does not allow us to directly read and write enumerated-type values.

Figure 10.5 shows one possible form for abstract data type DayADT. Figure 10.5 is separated into two sections: *specification* and *implementation*. The *specification* is one long comment that should be read by a programmer who wants to use DayADT because it contains all the information the programmer needs to know.

FIGURE 10.5 Abstract Data Type DayADT

```
% Specification of DayADT

% Structure:   Day is an enumerated data type whose
%              values represent the days of the week

% Operators:   The following descriptions assume these
%              parameters:

%              ADay is type Day
%              ValidDay is type boolean.

% GetDay (var ADay, var ValidDay) : Read a string of
%   two characters and store the value represented by
%   the data in ADay. Set ValidDay to indicate whether
%   the data are valid.

% PutDay (ADay) : Display the value of ADay

%------------------------------------------------------------

% Implementation of DayADT

type Day : enum (Sunday, Monday, Tuesday, Wednesday,
                  Thursday, Friday, Saturday)

% Insert function UpCase here (see Fig. 10.4)

procedure GetDay (var ADay : Day,
                   var ValidDay : boolean)

   % Read string of two characters and store the value
   % represented by the data in ADay. Set ValidDay to
   % indicate whether the data are valid.
   % Pre : None
   % Post: ADay is assigned a value if the two
   %        characters read are SU, MO, TU, WE, TH, FR,
   %        or SA; otherwise, ADay is undefined.
   %        ValidDay is set to true if ADay
   %        is defined; otherwise, ValidDay is set to
   %        false.
   % Uses: UpCase
```

```
    var DaySt : string % Input - first two letter in day

    put "Enter first two letters of the day name> " ..
    get DaySt

    % Convert to uppercase
    DaySt := UpCase(DaySt(1)) + UpCase(DaySt(2))

    % Convert to day of week
    ValidDay := true    % Assume valid day
    if DaySt = "SU" then
        ADay := Day.Sunday
    elsif DaySt = "MO" then
        ADay := Day.Monday
    elsif DaySt = "TU" then
        ADay := Day.Tuesday
    elsif DaySt = "WE" then
        ADay := Day.Wednesday
    elsif DaySt = "TH" then
        ADay := Day.Thursday
    elsif DaySt = "FR" then
        ADay := Day.Friday
    elsif DaySt = "SA" then
        ADay := Day.Saturday
    else
        ValidDay := false        % Day is not valid
    end if
end GetDay

procedure PutDay (ADay : Day)
    % Displays the value of ADay.
    % Pre : ADay is defined.
    % Post: Displays a string corresponding to the value
    %         of ADay
    case ADay of
        label Day.Sunday : put "Sunday" ..
        label Day.Monday : put "Monday" ..
        label Day.Tuesday : put "Tuesday" ..
        label Day.Wednesday : put "Wednesday" ..
        label Day.Thursday : put "Thursday" ..
        label Day.Friday : put "Friday" ..
        label Day.Saturday : put "Saturday" ..
    end case
end PutDay
```

The specification describes the structure of the data type encapsulated in the ADT, and lists any other modules that are needed by the ADT. For each operator, there is a list of parameters and a summary of the operation performed. Variable parameters are preceded by the reserved word `var`.

The specification is followed by the implementation section which contains declarations for the encapsulated data type and its operator procedures. The procedure declarations are preceded by a comment that reminds the user of the ADT to insert function UpCase which is called by procedure GetDay.

Using the DayADT Abstract Type

The complete ADT shown in Fig. 10.5 should be saved as a file on disk. You should insert function UpCase where indicated in the implementation section before you do this. When you use DayADT in a new program, this file can be read from disk and inserted in the declaration part of the new program. The abstract data type could be inserted right after the last type declaration in the new program.

Turing compilers have *compiler directives*, which are special lines inserted in the program file that provide instructions to the compiler. There is a directive that instructs the compiler to include a previously saved file in a program that is being compiled. For example, if a disk file named dayadt contains the specification for DayADT, then the command

```
include "dayadt"
```

can be used to instruct the compiler to include the file dayadt at the point where this command appears in the program. The lines in file *dayadt* would be inserted and translated. Any syntax errors would be displayed.

Alternatively, the compiler for Object Oriented Turing allows you to compile source files that are not complete Turing programs as separate program parts. In this case, a file containing Turing code similar to that shown in Fig. 10.5 could be compiled as a separate program part, resulting in an object file that would be saved on disk. You could then write a new program that uses abstract data type DayADT without including this code in your new program, using an import command.

For our purposes, we will assume that the disk file for DayADT must be inserted directly in the source file of any new program that uses it. We will use comments such as

```
% Insert the DayADT abstract date type here
```

to remind you to do this; you should perform the insertion manually or by using the include compiler directive.

Turing has an advanced language feature that we have not yet introduced, called a module, which groups together data and subprograms that operate upon the data. These modules are especially suited for implementing abstract data types.

EXAMPLE 10.1
The program below uses the abstract data type DayADT. It reads and displays one day of the week and a message if the day read is the first day of the week.

FIGURE 10.6   Testing DayADT

```
% The "Testday" program
% Tests abstract data type DayADT
% Modules needed: Uses Day, GetDay, PutDay from DayADT
% (see Fig. 10.5)

% Insert the DayADT abstract data type here

var Today : Day % Input - day being read
var GoodDay : boolean  % Program flag for valid data

put "What day is today?"
GetDay (Today, GoodDay)
if not GoodDay then
   put "Error - no day read"
else
   put "Today is " ..
   PutDay (Today)
   put ""
   if Today = Day.Sunday then
      put "Today is the first day of the week"
   end if
end if
```

```
What day is today?
Enter first two letters of the day name> SU
Today is Sunday
Today is the first day of the week
```

The *module dependency diagram* in Fig. 10.7 summarizes the interaction between modules. It shows that program TestDay uses DayADT and that DayADT uses function UpCase. A dependency diagram resembles a system structure chart. The difference is that a system structure chart shows control flow and data flow between the procedures of a single module or program system, whereas a dependency diagram shows control flow.

FIGURE 10.7   Module Dependency Diagram

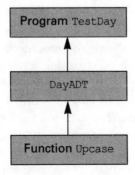

Exercises for Section 10.5

Self-Check

1. Describe the contents of the specification and implementation sections of an abstract data type.
2. Draw a structure chart for program `TestDay` showing the dataflow information between program procedures.

Programming

1. Write an abstract data type `MonthADT` containing the declaration for an enumerated type `Month`, procedures `GetMonth` and `PutMonth`, and function `MonthEquivalent`. Function `MonthEquivalent` has an integer argument 1 to 12 and returns an appropriate enumerated constant as its value.
2. Write a client program that tests your `MonthADT`.

10.6 Software Testing

It does not really matter whether a program is designed carefully and runs efficiently if it does not do what it is supposed to do. One way to show that a program is correct is through testing. However, it is difficult to determine how much testing should be done. Very often errors will appear in a software product after it is delivered, causing great inconvenience. Some notable software errors in operational programs have caused power brownouts, telephone network saturation, and space flight delays. There are also situations in which it is impossible to test a software product in advance of its use. Examples would be software that controls a missile or software that prevents a nuclear disaster in the event of a nuclear power plant malfunction.

Preparing a Test Plan Early

It is best to develop a plan for testing early in the design stage of the new system. Some aspects of a test plan include deciding how the software will be tested, when the tests will occur, and who will do the testing. Normally, testing is done by the programmer, by other members of the software team who did not code the module being tested, and by users of the software product. Some companies have special testing groups who are expert at finding bugs in other programmers' code. If the test plan is developed early in the design stage, testing can take place concurrently with the design and coding. The earlier an error is detected, the easier and less expensive it will be to correct it.

Another advantage of deciding on the test plan early is that this should encourage programmers to prepare for testing as they write their code. A good programmer will practice *defensive programming* and include code that detects unexpected or invalid data values. For example, if a procedure has the precondition

```
pre : N greater than zero
```

it would be a good idea to place the `if` statement

```
if N <= 0 then
    put "Invalid value for parameter N - ", N
end if
```

at the beginning of the procedure. This `if` statement will provide a diagnostic message in the event that the parameter passed to the procedure is invalid.

Similarly, if a data value being read from the keyboard is supposed to be between 0 and 40, a defensive programmer would use procedure `EnterInt` shown in Fig. 10.3.

```
put "Enter number of hours worked> "
EnterInt (0, 40, Hours)
```

The first and second parameters of `EnterInt` define the range of acceptable values for its third parameter.

Structured Walkthroughs

One important testing technique is called a structured walkthrough. In a *structured walkthrough*, the programmer describes or "walks through" the logic of a new module as part of a presentation to other members of the software team. The purpose of the walkthrough is for the team members to identify design errors or bugs that may have been overlooked by the programmer because he or she is too close to the problem. The goal is to detect errors in logic before they become part of the code.

Black Box versus White Box Testing

There are two basic ways to test a completed module or system: *black box* or *specification-based* testing and *white box* or *glass box* testing. In black box testing, we assume that the program tester has no idea of the code inside the module or system. The tester's job is to verify that the module does what its specification says that it should do. For a procedure, this means ensuring that the procedure's postconditions are satisfied whenever its preconditions are met. For a system or subsystem, this means ensuring that the system does indeed satisfy its original requirements specification. Because the tester cannot look inside the module or system, he or she must prepare sufficient sets of test data to ensure that the system outputs are correct for all valid system inputs. The tester should especially check the *boundaries* of the system, or particular values for the program variables where the system performance changes. For example, a boundary for a payroll program would be the value of hours worked that triggers overtime pay. Also, the module or system should not crash when presented with invalid inputs. Black box testing is most often done by a special testing team or by program users.

In glass box or white box testing, the tester has full knowledge of the code for the module or system and must ensure that each and every section of code has been thoroughly tested. For a selection statement (`if` or `case`), this means checking all possible paths through the selection statement. The tester must determine that the correct path is chosen for all possible values of the selection variable, taking special care at the boundary values where the path changes.

For a loop, the tester must make sure that the loop always performs the correct number of iterations and that the number of iterations is not off by one. Also, the tester should verify that the computations inside the loop are be correct at the boundaries – that is, for the initial and final values of the loop control variable. Finally, the tester should make sure that the module or system still meets its specification when a loop executes zero times, and that there are no circumstances under which the loop could execute forever.

Integration Testing

In Section 7.9 we discussed the differences between top-down and bottom-up testing of a single system. Another aspect of testing is called integration testing. In *integration testing*, the program tester must determine whether the individual components of the system, which have been separately tested (using either top-down, bottom-up, or some combination), can be integrated with other like components. Each phase of integration testing will deal with larger units, progressing from individual modules, through subsystems, and ending with the entire system. For example, after two subsystems are completed, integration testing must determine whether the two subsystems can work together. Once the entire system is completed, integration testing must determine whether that system is compatible with other systems in the computing environment in which it will be used.

Exercises for Section 10.6

Self-Check

1. Explain why a procedure interface error would not be discovered during white box testing.
2. Devise a set of data to test procedure `EnterInt` (Fig. 10.3) using:
   a. White box testing
   b. Black box testing

Formal Methods of Program Verification

(This material was adapted from an outline prepared by James C. Pleasant, Department of Computer and Information Sciences, Tennessee State University.)

In the last section, we described some aspects of program and system testing. We stated that testing should begin as early as possible in the design phase and continue through system implementation. Even though testing is an extremely valuable tool for providing evidence that a program is correct and meets its specification, it is very difficult to know how much testing is enough. For example, how do we know that we have tried enough different sets of test data or that all possible paths through the program have been executed?

For these reasons, computer scientists have developed a second method of demonstrating the correctness of a program. This method is called *formal verification* and it involves the application of formal rules to show that a program meets its specification. By carefully applying formal rules, we can determine that a program meets its specification just as a mathematician proves a theorem using definitions, axioms, and previously proved theorems. Although formal verification works well on small programs, there is some question as to whether this method can be used effectively on very large programs or program systems.

A thorough discussion of formal verification is beyond the scope of this book. However, we will introduce two key concepts, assertion and loop invariant, and we will use them to help document and clarify some of the modules appearing in the book.

Assertions

An important part of formal verification is to document a program using *assertions* — logical statements about the program that are "asserted" to be true. An assertion is written as a comment and it describes what is supposed to be true about the program variables at that point.

EXAMPLE 10.2
The next program fragment contains a sequence of assignment statements, each followed by an assertion.

```
A := 5          % Assert: A = 5
X := A          % Assert: X = 5
Y := X + A      % Assert: Y = 10
```

The truth of the first assertion (A = 5) follows from executing the first statement with the knowledge that 5 is a constant. The truth of the second assertion (X = 5) follows from executing X := A with the knowledge that A is 5. The truth of the third assertion (Y = 10) follows from executing

`Y := X + A` with the knowledge that `X` is 5 and `A` is 5. In the fragment above, we used assertions as comments to document the change in a program variable after each assignment statement executes.

The task of a person using formal verification is to prove that a program fragment meets its specification. For the fragment above, this means proving that the final assertion or *postcondition* (`Y = 10`) follows from the initial presumption or *precondition* (5 is a constant) after the program fragment executes. The assignment rule (described below) is critical to this process. If we know that (`A = 5`) is `true`, the assignment rule allows us to make the assertion (`X = 5`) after executing the statement `X := A`.

The Assignment Rule

```
{P(A)}
X := A
{P(X)}
```

Explanation: If `P(A)` is a logical statement (assertion) about `A`, the same statement will be `true` of `X` after the assignment statement `X := A` executes. For our purposes, it will suffice to use assertions as a documentation tool to improve our understanding of programs rather than as a means of formally proving them correct. We have already used assertions to document the effect of executing a procedure.

Preconditions and Postconditions

A procedure's precondition is a logical statement about its input parameters. A procedure's postcondition may be a logical statement about its output parameters, or it may be a logical statement that describes the change in *program state* caused by the procedure execution. Any of the following activities represents a change in program state: changing the value of a variable, writing additional program output, reading new input data.

EXAMPLE 10.3

The precondition and postcondition for procedure `EnterInt` (see Fig. 10.3) are repeated next.

```
procedure EnterInt (MinN, MaxN : int, var N : int)
    % Read an integer between MinN and MaxN into N
    % Pre : MinN and MaxN are assigned values
    % Post: Returns in N the first data value between
    %       MinN and MaxN if MinN <= MaxN is true;
    %       otherwise, N is not defined
```

The precondition tells us that input parameters `MinN` and `MaxN` are defined before the procedure begins execution. The postcondition tells us that the procedure's execution assigns the first data value between `MinN` and `MaxN` to the output parameter `N` whenever `MinN <= MaxN` is `true`.

Loop Invariant

We stated earlier that loops are a very common source of program errors. It is often difficult to determine that a loop body executes exactly the right number of times or that loop execution causes the desired change in program variables. A special type of assertion, a *loop invariant*, is used to help prove that a loop meets its specification. A loop invariant is a logical statement involving program variables that is true before the loop is entered, and after each execution of the loop body. It must, therefore, be true just after the loop is exited. It is called an invariant because it is a relationship that remains true as loop execution progresses.

As an example of a loop invariant, let's examine the loop below, which accumulates the sum of the integers 1, 2, ... , N where N is a positive integer and Sum, I, and N are type int.

```
% Accumulate the sum of integers 1 through N in Sum

% Assert: N >= 1
Sum := 0
I := 0
loop
    exit when I = N
    I := I + 1
    Sum := Sum + I
end loop
% Assert: Sum = 1 + 2 + 3 + ... + N-1 + N
```

The first assertion (N >= 1) is the precondition for the loop, and the last assertion is its postcondition.

We stated above that the loop invariant must be true before the loop begins execution and after each loop repetition. Since it traces the loop's progress, it should be a logical statement about the loop control variable I and the accumulating sum.

Figure 10.8 sketches the loop's progress for the first three iterations of the loop. At the end of the third iteration, I is 3 and Sum is 6 — the sum of all positive integers less than or equal to 4 (1 + 2 + 3). When loop repetition finishes, I will be N and Sum will contain the desired result (1 + 2 + 3 + ... + N). Therefore, we propose the invariant

```
% Invariant: I <= N and Sum = 1 + 2 + ... + I
```

In English this means that I must be less than or equal to N, and that after each loop repetition, Sum is equal to the sum of all positive integers less than or equal to I.

The loop invariant must be true before loop execution begins. At this point, I is 0 and 0 <= N is true for N >= 1 (the precondition). Also, the invariant requires that the value of Sum be equal to the summation of all positive integers less than 1. Because Sum is initialized to 0, this is also the case.

FIGURE 10.8   Sketch of Summation Loop

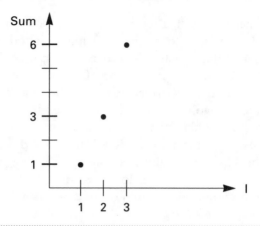

In program verification, the loop invariant is used to prove that the loop meets its specification. For our purposes, we will use the loop invariant to document what we know about the loop's behavior and we will place it just before the loop body as shown next.

```
% Accumulate the sum of integers 1 through N in Sum

% Assert: N >= 1
Sum := 0
I := 0
loop
    % Invariant: I <= N and Sum = 1 + 2 + ... + I
    exit when I = N
    I := I + 1
    Sum := Sum + I
end loop
% Assert: Sum = 1 + 2 + 3 + ... + N-1 + N
```

Loop Invariants as a Design Tool

Some computer scientists recommend writing the loop invariant as a preliminary step before coding the loop. The invariant serves as a specification for the loop, and it can be used as a guide to help determine the loop initialization, the loop repetition condition, and the loop body. For example, we can write the following loop invariant to describe a summation loop that sums N data items:

```
% Invariant: Count <= N and
% Sum is the sum of all data read so far
```

From the loop invariant, we can determine that in the initial test of the invariant, before the first iteration, Count is assumed to be one less than the initial value of 1. In this example, in the initial test, Count is assumed to be 0 so the invariant starts out with a value of true.

- The loop initialization is:

```
Sum := 0.0
Count := 0
```

- The loop exit test is:

```
Count = N
```

- The loop body is:

```
Count := Count + 1
get Next
Sum := Sum + Next
```

Given all this information, it becomes a simple task to write the summation loop (see programming exercise 2 at the end of this section).

Invariants and the For Statement

Since the loop invariant states what we know to be true about a loop after each iteration, we should be able to write an invariant for a `for` statement as well as a `loop` statement. We can place the invariant at the end of the loop body so it records the situation when the iteration with value I has completed, as illustrated here.

```
% Assert: N >= 1
Sum := 0
for I : 1 .. N
    Sum := Sum + I
    % Invariant: I <= N and Sum := 1 + 2 + ... + I
end for
% Assert: Sum = 1 + 2 + 3 + ... + N-1 + N
```

Before the first execution of this loop, counter I can be thought of as having value 0. If N = 0, the loop body will not be executed, and the invariant will be satisfied for I = 0.

More Loop Invariants

This section provides more examples of the use of assertions and loop invariants to document a loop. Studying these examples should help you understand how to write invariants.

EXAMPLE 10.4

Figure 10.9 shows a sentinel-controlled conditional loop that computes the product of a collection of data values. Loop exit occurs after reading in the sentinel value (value of `Sentinel`). The loop invariant indicates that `Product` is the product of all values read before the current one and that none of these values was the sentinel. The preconditions and postconditions for the loop are written as assertions.

FIGURE 10.9 Sentinel-Controlled Loop with Invariant

```
% Compute the product of a sequence of data values

% Assert: Sentinel is a constant
Product := 1
put "When done, enter ", Sentinel , " to stop"
loop
    put "Enter the number> " ..
    get Num
    % Invariant:
    %    Product is the product of all prior values
    %    read into Num and no prior value of Num was
    %    the sentinel
    exit when Num = Sentinel
    Product := Product * Num
end loop

% Assert: Product is the product of all numbers read
%         into Num before the sentinel
```

Exercises for Section 10.7

Self-Check

1. Write the loop invariant and the assertion following the loop for the `loop` statement in procedure `EnterInt` (Fig. 10.3).
2. If the sentinel-controlled loop in Fig. 10.9 were rewritten as a flag-controlled loop, what would the new loop invariant look like? The flag `NoZero` should remain true until a zero value is read.

Programming

1. Write a function that returns the count (N) of the number of non-zero digits in an arbitrary `int` (`Number`). Your solution should include a `loop` statement for which the following is a valid loop invariant:

   ```
   % Invariant:
   %    0 <= Count <= N and Number has been
   %    divided by 10 Count times
   ```

   and the assertion below would be valid following the loop:

   ```
   % Assert: Count = N
   ```

2. Write a program fragment that implements the loop whose invariant is described in the subsection entitled "Loop Invariants as a Design Tool."

10.8 Professional Ethics and Responsibilities

Software engineers and computer programmers are professionals and should always act that way. As part of their jobs, computer programmers may be able to access large data banks containing sensitive personnel information, information that is classified "secret" or "top secret", or financial transaction data. Programmers should always behave in a socially responsible manner and not retrieve information that they are not entitled to see. They should not use this information for their own personal gain or do anything that would be considered illegal, unethical, or harmful to others.

You may have heard stories about "computer hackers" who have broken into secure data banks by using their own computer to call (by telephone) the computer that controls access to the data bank. Some individuals have sold classified information retrieved in this way to intelligence agencies of other countries. Other hackers try to break into computers to retrieve this information for their own amusement, as a prank, or just to demonstrate that they can. Regardless of the intent, this activity is illegal, and the government will prosecute anyone who does this.

Another illegal activity sometimes practiced by hackers is the insertion of special code, called a *virus*, in a computer's disk memory. A virus will cause sporadic activities to occur which disrupt the operation of the host computer. For example, unusual messages may appear on the screen at certain times. Viruses can also cause the host computer to erase portions of its own disk memory, thereby, destroying valuable information and programs. Viruses are spread from one computer to another when data is copied from the infected disk and processed by a different computer. Certainly these kinds of activity should not be considered harmless pranks; they are illegal and should not be done under any circumstances.

A programmer who changes information in a data base containing financial records for his or her own personal gain is guilty of *computer theft* or *computer fraud*. This is a felony that can lead to fines and imprisonment.

Another example of unprofessional behavior is using someone else's program or code without permission. While it is certainly permissible to use procedures in libraries that have been developed for reuse by your own company's programmers, you cannot use another programmer's personal code or code from another company without getting permission beforehand. Doing this could lead to a lawsuit, and you or your company may have to pay damages.

Another fraudulent practice is submitting another student's code as your own. This, of course, is plagiarism, and most universities have severe penalties for plagiarism which may include failing the course and/or dismissal from the university. You should be aware that even if you modify the code slightly, or substitute your own comments or different variable names, you are still guilty of plagiarism if you are using another person's ideas and code. To avoid any question of plagiarism, find out beforehand your instructor's rules with respect to working with others on a project. If group efforts are not allowed, make sure that you work independently and submit only your own code.

Many commercial software packages are protected by copyright laws and cannot be copied or duplicated. It is illegal to make additional copies of protected software that you may be using at work in order to use this software at home on your computer or on someone else's computer. Besides the fact that this is against the law, using software copied from another computer increases the possibility that your computer will receive a virus. For all these reasons, you should act ethically and honor any copyright agreements that pertain to a particular software package.

10.9 Common Programming Errors

When using a procedure from a library, you must know the name of the library in which the procedure is found and you must have a description of the procedure interface. Specifically, you must know the number, order, and type (NOT) of the procedure's parameters. Make sure that all variable formal parameters correspond to actual parameters that are variables of the same type. Also, make sure that all preconditions for a procedure's parameters (as listed in the procedure interface) are satisfied before the procedure call statement executes.

You can use an abstract data type (ADT) in Turing. You can do this by placing the ADT in a file and using an `include` command to copy the text of the ADT into your program. There is an advanced Turing feature called the `module`, which we have not discussed, that is designed to provide the information hiding needed in ADT's. If you used Object Oriented Turing, the ADT is separately compiled and is `import`ed into your program.

Chapter Review

This chapter discussed programming in the large and the software engineering process. It introduced the software life cycle and described all phases of the software life cycle:

Software Life Cycle
1. Requirements specification
2. Analysis
3. Design
4. Implementation
5. Testing and validation
6. Operation, follow-up, and maintenance

Special emphasis was placed on discussion of two phases of the software life cycle that had not yet been covered in depth: requirements specification and testing and validation. We discussed planning for testing, selection of test teams, structured walkthroughs, black box testing, white box testing, and integration testing.

We also introduced program verification as an alternative to testing and described the use of assertions and loop invariants in this process. We will use informal logical statements about programs and loops to document our programs so that we can better understand them.

We also reviewed procedural abstraction and introduced data abstraction. We described the use of procedure libraries and special modules called abstract data types (ADTs) that encapsulate a data type together with its operators. We showed how to write in standard Turing an ADT consisting of an enumerated type together with operators that read and write values of that type.

You saw that there were many advantages to creating and using your own procedure libraries. Procedures are the building blocks of larger program systems. The use of procedures makes it easier to assign pieces of a large project to different members of a programming team. Once a procedure is completed and tested, it can be included in a library of procedures to simplify its reuse in other programs and by other programmers.

Finally, since we have geared the discussion in this chapter to techniques practised by software professionals, we have included a discussion of ethics and professional behavior. We described the special responsibilities that programmers have because of their ability to access sensitive information. We discussed computer viruses and how they are spread. We also described how using another programmer's code or ideas is plagiarism and carries severe penalties in industry as well as in the classroom.

Quick-Check Exercises

1. The six phases of the software life cycle are listed below in arbitrary order. Place them in their correct order. Testing and validation, design, requirements specification, operation and maintenance, implementation, analysis
2. In which phases are the users of a software product likely to be involved?
3. In which phases are the programmers and analysts likely to be involved?
4. Which phase lasts for the longest time period?
5. Name the two sections of an abstract data type. Where is the data type declaration found? Where are the procedure declarations found?
6. _____ testing requires the use of test data that exercises each statement in a module.
7. _____ testing focuses on testing the functional characteristics of a module.
8. Which of these may be false: loop invariant, `exit` condition, assertion?
9. The use of loop invariants is useful for which of the following: loop control, loop design, and loop verification.
10. Write a loop invariant for the code segment

```
Product := 1
Counter := 0
loop
    exit when Counter = 5
    Counter := Counter + 1
    Product := Product * Counter
end loop
```

Answers to Quick-Check Exercises

1. Requirements specification, analysis, design, implementation, testing and validation, operation and maintenance
2. Requirements specification, testing and validation, operation and maintenance
3. All phases
4. Operation and maintenance
5. Interface and implementation sections, interface, implementation
6. White box
7. Black box
8. exit condition
9. Loop design, loop verification
10. `% Invariant:`
    `% Counter <= 5 and`
    `% Product contains product of all integers <= Counter`

Review Questions

1. Explain why the principle of information hiding is important to the software designer.
2. Define the terms *procedural abstraction* and *data abstraction.*
3. Which of the following are likely to occur in a programmer's library of procedures? Explain your answers.
   a. A procedure that raises a number to a specified power.
   b. A procedure that writes the user instructions for a particular program.
   c. A procedure that displays the message HI MOM in block letters.
   d. A procedure that displays the block letter M.
4. Write an abstract data type for the positions on a baseball team (pitcher, catcher, infield, outfield) and operators to read and write these positions.
5. Write an abstract data type Money, which allows you to do basic arithmetic operations (addition, subtraction, multiplication, and division) on real numbers having exactly two digits to the right of the decimal point.
6. Which of the following statements is incorrect?
   a. Loop invariants are used in loop verification.
   b. Loop invariants are used in loop design.
   c. A loop invariant is always an assertion.
   d. An assertion is always a loop invariant.
7. Briefly describe a test plan for the telephone directory program described in Section 10.2, assuming that integration testing is used.

8. Write a procedure that computes the average number of characters found on the lines of a text file. Include loop invariants and any other assertions necessary to verify that the procedure is correct.

Programming Projects

1. Write an abstract data type that consists of data type `ColorType` and operators for reading and writing the colors (red, yellow, green, blue, black, brown, orange, purple, and white).
2. Write a set of library procedures (or functions) that may be used to determine the following information for an integer input parameter:
   a. Is it a multiple of 7, 11, or 13?
   b. Is the sum of the digits odd or even?
   c. What is the square root value?
   d. Is it a prime number?
   Write a client program that tests your library procedures using the input values: 104 3773 13 121 77 3075
3. Each month, a bank customer deposits $50 into a savings account. Assume that the interest rate is fixed (does not change) and is a problem input. The interest is calculated on a quarterly basis. For example, if the account earns 6.5 percent interest annually, it earns one-fourth of 6.5 percent every three months. Write a program to compute the total investment, total amount in the account, and the interest accrued for each of the 120 months of a 10-year period. Assume that the rate is applied to all funds in the account at the end of a quarter, regardless of when the deposits were made. Print all values accurate to two decimal places. The table printed by your program when the annual interest rate is 6.5 percent should begin as follows:

MONTH	INVESTMENT	NEW AMOUNT	INTEREST	TOTAL SAVINGS
1	50.00	50.00	0.00	50.00
2	100.00	100.00	0.00	100.00
3	150.00	150.00	2.44	152.44
4	200.00	202.44	0.00	202.44
5	250.00	252.44	0.00	252.44
6	300.00	302.44	4.91	307.35
7	350.00	357.35	0.00	57.35

4. Redo project 3, adding columns to allow comparison of interest compounded monthly (one-twelfth of annual rate every month) with continuously compounded interest. The formula for continuously compounded interest is

$$Amount = Principal * e^{Rate} * Time$$

where *Rate* is the annual interest rate and *Time* is expressed in years.

5. An employee time card is represented as one long string of characters. Write a program that processes a collection of these strings stored in a data file and writes the results to an output file.

a. Compute gross pay using the formula

gross = regular hours * rate + overtime hours * 1.5 * rate

b. Compute net pay by subtracting the following deductions

federal tax = .14 * (gross − 13 * dependents)
social insurance = 0.052 * gross
city tax = 4% of gross if employee works in the city
union dues = 6.75% of gross for union member

The data string for each employee has the form

Positions	Data
1-10	Employee last name
11-20	Employee first name
21	Contains a C for city office or S for suburban office
22	Contains a U (union) or N (nonunion)
23-26	Employee identification number
27	blank
28	blank
31-36	Hourly rate (dollars and cents)
37	blank
38-39	Number of dependents
40	blank
41-42	Number of overtime hours (a whole number)

6. Write a menu-driven program that contains options for creating a data file to be processed by the payroll program described in programming project 5 (the user should be prompted to enter several time cards from the keyboard), displaying the time cards in the file on a printer, adding new time cards to the end of an existing file, and deleting time cards from an existing file based on their ordinal position within the file (e.g., deleting the seventh time card), and quitting the program.

To add or delete lines from a text file requires copying the original data file to a *scratch* or temporary file and then back to the original file. During the copy process, time cards to be deleted are simply not copied to the scratch file. Adding new time cards to the end of the file takes place after all the time cards from the original file have been copied to the scratch file.

CHAPTER 11

Arrays

In the programs we have written so far, each variable was associated with a single memory cell. These variables are called simple variables, and their data types are simple ones. The only exceptions were file variables that were associated with a collection of characters stored on disk.

In this chapter, we begin to study *structured variables* or data structures. A structured variable represents a grouping of related data items in main memory. The items in a structured variable can be processed individually, although some operations may be performed on the structure as a whole.

Turing provides *type constructors*, which can be used to form new data types from simpler objects. The type constructor `array` is described in this chapter. The type constructors `record` and `set` will be discussed in subsequent chapters.

The *array* is a data structure in which we store a collection of data items of the same type (for example, all the exam scores for a class). By using an array, we can associate a single variable name (e.g., `Scores`) with the entire collection of data. This association enables us to save the entire collection of data in main memory (one item per memory cell) and to reference individual items easily. To process an individual item, we need to specify the array name and indicate the array element being manipulated, e.g., `Scores(3)` references the third item in the array `Scores`.

Since each score is saved in a separate cell in main memory, we can process the individual items more than once and in any order we wish. In previous programs we reused the same cell to store each exam score. Consequently, we could no longer access the third score after the fourth score was read.

11.1 The Array Data Type

This section illustrates the basic operations that can be performed on an array. We begin by showing how to allocate memory space for an array in Turing.

Array Type Declaration

Normally we first describe the structure of an array in an *array type declaration*. Then we may allocate storage for one or more arrays of that type. The `array` type `RealArray`, declared below, is followed by the declaration of array X of type `RealArray`.

```
type RealArray : array 1..8 of real
var X : RealArray
```

Turing associates eight memory cells with the name X. Each element of array X may contain a single real value. So, a total of eight real values may be stored and referenced using the array name X.

To process the data stored in an array, we must be able to reference each individual element. The *array subscript* is used to differentiate among elements of the same array. For example, if X is the array with eight elements declared above, then we may refer to the elements of array X as shown in Fig. 11.1.

The Eight Elements of the Array X

Array X

X(1)	X(2)	X(3)	X(4)	X(5)	X(6)	X(7)	X(8)
16.0	12.0	6.0	8.0	2.5	12.0	14.0	−54.5

First element   Second element   Third element   Eighth element

The *subscripted variable* X(1) (read as "X sub 1") references the first element of the array X, X(2) the second element, and X(8) the eighth element. The number enclosed in parentheses is the array subscript. Later, we will see that the subscript can be an expression of any ordinal type.

EXAMPLE 11.1
Let X be the array shown in Fig. 11.1. Some statements that manipulate this array are shown in Table 11.1.

TABLE 11.1 Statements that Manipulate Array X

Statement	Explanation
put X(1)	Display the value of X(1) or 16.0
X(4) := 25.0	Store the value 25.0 in X(4)
Sum := X(1) + X(2)	Store the sum of X(1) and X(2) or 28.0 in the variable Sum
Sum := Sum + X(3)	Add X(3) to Sum The new Sum is 34.0
X(4) := X(4) + 1.0	Add 1.0 to X(4) The new X(4) is 26.0
X(3) := X(1) + X(2)	Store the sum of X(1) and X(2) in X(3) The new X(3) is 28.0

The contents of array X are shown below after execution of these statements. Note that only X(3) and X(4) are changed.

Array X

X(1)	X(2)	X(3)	X(4)	X(5)	X(6)	X(7)	X(8)
16.0	12.0	28.0	26.0	2.5	12.0	14.0	–54.5

First element Second element Third element Eighth element

EXAMPLE 11.2

The declarations for a program for plant operations is shown below. The `type` declaration declares two simple types, `EmpRange` and `Day`, and two array types, `EmpArray` and `DayArray`. Two arrays, `Vacation` and `PlantHours`, are declared in the variable declaration section.

```
const NumEmp := 10              % Number of employees
type EmpRange : 1..NumEmp       % Subscript range
type Day : enum(Sunday, Monday, Tuesday, Wednesday,
                Thursday, Friday, Saturday)
type EmpArray : array EmpRange of boolean
type DayArray : array Day of real
var Vacation : EmpArray
var PlantHours : DayArray
```

The array `Vacation` has ten elements (subscripts 1 through `NumEmp`); each element of array `Vacation` can store a `boolean` value. The contents of this array could indicate which employees were on vacation (`Vacation(I)` is `true` if employee `I` is on vacation). If employees 1, 3, 5, 7, and 9 were on vacation, the array would have the values shown in Fig. 11.2.

FIGURE 11.2 Array Vacation

Vacation(1)	true
Vacation(2)	false
Vacation(3)	true
Vacation(4)	false
Vacation(5)	true
Vacation(6)	false
Vacation(7)	true
Vacation(8)	false
Vacation(9)	true
Vacation(10)	false

The array `PlantHours` has seven elements (subscripts `Sunday` through `Saturday`). The array element `PlantHours(Day.Sunday)` could indicate how many hours the plant was operating during `Sunday` of the past week. The array shown in Fig. 11.3 indicates that the plant was closed on the weekend, operating single shifts on `Monday` and `Thursday`, double shifts on `Tuesday` and `Friday`, and a triple shift on `Wednesday`.

FIGURE 11.3　　　Array PlantHours

`PlantHours(Day.Sunday)`	0.0
`PlantHours(Day.Monday)`	8.0
`PlantHours(Day.Tuesday)`	16.0
`PlantHours(Day.Wednesday)`	24.0
`PlantHours(Day.Thursday)`	8.0
`PlantHours(Day.Friday)`	16.0
`PlantHours(Day.Saturday)`	0.0

It would be possible to eliminate the declarations for the constant `NumEmp` and data types `EmpRange` and `EmpArray` and just declare the array `Vacation` as shown below.

```
var Vacation : array 1..10 of boolean
```

There are three advantages to the original set of declarations. First, it becomes very easy to change the declared size of array `Vacation`. By simply redefining the constant `NumEmp`, we change the array size. Second, the data types `EmpArray` and `DayArray` can be used as type identifiers elsewhere in the program. The third advantage is that the constant `NumEmp` can be referenced in the program body.

ARRAY TYPE DECLARATION

Form:　　　type *array type* : *array subscript type* of *element type*

Example:　　type `SmallArray : array 1..5 of string`

Interpretation: The identifier *array type* describes a collection of array elements; each element can store an item of type *element type*. The *subscript type* must be a subrange of the integers, a subrange of an enumerated type, or else an entire enumerated type. There is one array element for each value in the *subscript type*.

The *element type* describes the type of each element in the array. All elements of an array are the same type.

Note: The standard types `real` and `int` may not be used as a *subscript type*; however, a subrange of the integers may be a *subscript type*.

The note above states that the standard types `int` and `real` cannot be used as subscript types. These types are not allowed because the array would have an excessive number of elements.

It is important to realize that an array type declaration does not require allocation of storage space in memory. The array type describes the structure of an array only. Only variables actually store information and require storage. Storage space is not allocated until a variable of this type is declared.

Abstract Array

We can summarize what we have learned about arrays in the specification for an abstract array shown below.

> **SPECIFICATION FOR ABSTRACT ARRAY**
>
> **Structure:** An array is a collection of elements of the same data type. For each array, a subscript type is specified. There is an array element corresponding to each value in the subscript type. The types `real` and `int` may not be a subscript type; however, a subrange of type `int` may be a subscript type. An enumerated type or its subrange may be a subscript type.
>
> **Operators:** There are two basic operations that act on elements of an array: store and retrieve. The store operation inserts a value into the array. If `A` is an array and `C` is an expression that is assignable to `A`'s element type and `I` is an expression that is compatible with the subscript type, the statement
>
> ```
> A(I) := C
> ```
>
> stores the contents of `C` in element `I` of array `A`. If the element type of `A` is assignment compatible with the type of variable `D`, the statement
>
> ```
> D := A(I)
> ```
>
> retrieves element `I` of array `A` and copies its value into `D`. For both of these statements the value of subscript `I` must be in the range of the array subscript type; otherwise, a run-time error will occur.
>
> The assignment operator may also be used to copy the contents of one array to another of the same type. If arrays `A` and `B` are the same type, the statement
>
> ```
> A := B
> ```
>
> copies all values associated with array `B` to array `A`.

The display above summarizes all the information that we need to know to use an array. We do not need to know how Turing stores the elements of an array in memory or how it implements the retrieve and store operators above.

Exercises for Section 11.1

Self-Check

1. What is the difference between the expressions X3 and X(3)?
2. For the following declarations, how many memory cells are reserved for data and what type of data can be stored there? When is the memory allocated, after the type declaration or after the variable declaration?

    ```
    type AnArray : array 1..5 of string
    var Grades : AnArray
    ```

3. Which of the following arrays are valid? Write the variable and type declarations for the valid arrays.
    a. Subscript type boolean, element type real
    b. Subscript type "A" .. "F", element type int
    c. Subscript type string, element type boolean
    d. Subrange -5 to 5, element type real
    e. Subscript type string, element type real
    f. Subscript type real, element type string
    g. Subscript type Day (enumerated type), element type real

11.2 Selecting Array Elements

Using a Subscript as an Index to an Array

Each array reference includes the array name and a subscript enclosed in parentheses; the subscript determines which array element is processed. The subscript (sometimes called an *index*) used in an array reference must be an expression that is assignment-compatible with the *subscript-type* specified in the array declaration. In the most common case, the *subscript-type* is a subrange of the integers. In this case, the subscript must be an integer expression whose value is in the range specified by the *subscript-type*. For the array Vacation declared in Example 11.2, the allowable subscript values are the integers 1 through 10.

EXAMPLE 11.3
Table 11.2 shows some sample statements involving the array X shown in Fig. 11.1. I is assumed to be a type int variable with value 6. Make sure you understand each statement.

TABLE 11.2   Some Sample Statements for Array X in Fig. 11.1

Statement	Effect
put 4, X(4)	Display 4 and 8.0 (value of X(4))
put I, X(I)	Display 6 and 12.0 (value of X(6))
put X(I) + 1	Display 13.0 (value of 12.0 + 1)
put X(I) + I	Display 18.0 (value of 12.0 + 6)
put X(I+1)	Display 14.0 (value of X(7))
put X(I+I)	Illegal attempt to display X(12)
put X(2*I)	Illegal attempt to display X(12)
put X(2*I-4)	Display −54.5 (value of X(8))
put X(floor(X(5)))	Display 12.0 (value of X(2))
X(I) := X(I+1)	Assign 14.0 (value of X(7)) to X(6)
X(I-1) := X(I)	Assign 14.0 (new value of X(6)) to X(5)
X(I) - 1 := X(I-1)	Illegal assignment statement

You can see two attempts to display element X(12), which is not in the array. These attempts will result in an "out of bounds" run-time error. This means that there is no array element with the current subscript, or index, value.

The last put statement in Table 11.2 uses floor(X(5)) as a subscript expression. Since this evaluates to 2, the value of X(2) (and not X(5)) is printed. If the value of floor(X(5)) is outside the range 1 through 8, a run-time error occurs.

Two different subscripts are used in each of the three assignment statements at the bottom of the table. The first assignment statement copies the value of X(7) to X(6) (subscripts I+1 and I); the second assignment statement copies the value of X(6) to X(5) (subscripts I-1 and I). The last assignment statement causes a syntax error because there is an expression to the left of the assignment operator.

ARRAY REFERENCE

Form: *name*(*subscript*)

Example: X(3 * I - 2)

Interpretation: The *subscript* must be an expression that is assignment-compatible with the *subscript-type* specified in the declaration for array *name*. If the expression is the wrong data type, the syntax error "subscript is wrong type" will be detected. If the expression value is not in range, the run-time error "index expression out of bounds" will occur.

Using For Loops with Arrays

Frequently, we want to process the elements of an array in sequence, starting with the first—for example, entering data into the array or printing its contents. We can accomplish this sequential processing using a `for` loop whose loop control variable (I) is also the array subscript (X(I)). Increasing the value of the loop control variable by one causes the next array element to be processed.

EXAMPLE 11.4
The array `Cube` declared below stores the cubes of the first ten integers (e.g., `Cube(1)` is 1, `Cube(10)` is 1,000).

```
type IntArray : array 1..10 of int
var Cube : IntArray % Array of cubes
```

The `for` statement

```
for I := 1 .. 10
    Cube(I) := I * I * I
end for
```

initializes this array as shown below.

Array Cube

(1)	(2)	(3)	(4)	(5)	(6)	(7)	(8)	(9)	(10)
1	8	27	64	125	216	343	512	729	1000

EXAMPLE 11.5
For array `PlantHours` (see Example 11.2), the enumerated type `Day` is the declared subscript type. The assignment statements

```
PlantHours(Day.Sunday) := 0.0
PlantHours(Day.Monday) := 8.0
PlantHours(Day.Tuesday) := 16.0
PlantHours(Day.Wednesday) = 24.0
```

assign the values shown in Fig. 11.3 to the first four elements of `PlantHours`. Assuming that `Today` is type `Day`, the statements below have the same effect.

```
PlantHours(Day.Sunday) := 0.0
for Today : Day.Monday .. Day.Wednesday
    PlantHours(Today) := PlantHours(pred(Today)) + 8.0
end for
```

The assignment statement above executes for three values of Today (Monday through Wednesday). Table 11.3 shows the effect of the assignment statement for each value of Today.

TABLE 11.3 Assigning Values to Array PlantHours

Today	pred(Today)	Effect
Monday	Sunday	Assigns 8.0 to PlantHours(Day.Monday)
Tuesday	Monday	Assigns 16.0 to PlantHours(Day.Tuesday)
Wednesday	Tuesday	Assigns 24.0 to PlantHours(Day.Wednesday)

EXAMPLE 11.6

In Fig. 11.4, the declarations

```
const MaxItems := 8       % Number of data items
type IndexRange : 1 .. MaxItems
type RealArray : array IndexRange of real
var X : RealArray         % Array of data
```

allocate storage for an array X with subscripts in the range 1 .. 8. The program uses three for loops to process the array X. The loop control variable I ($1 <= I <= 8$) is also the array subscript in each loop. The first for loop

```
for I : 1 .. MaxItems
    get X(I)
end for
```

reads one data value into each array element (the first item is stored in X(1), the second item in X(2), and so on). The get statement is repeated for each value of I from 1 to 8; each repetition causes a new data value to be read and stored in X(I). The subscript I determines the array element that receives the next data value. The data line shown in the sample run causes the array to be initialized.

The second for loop accumulates (in Sum) the sum of all values stored in the array. (We will trace this loop later.) The last for loop

```
for I : 1 .. MaxItems
    put I :4, X(I) :8:1, X(I)-Average :14:1
end for
```

displays a table showing each array element, X(I), and the difference between that element and the average value, X(I) - Average.

FIGURE 11.4   Table of Differences

```
% The "Showdiff" program
% Compute the average value of an array of data and
% print the difference between each value and the
% average

const MaxItems := 8          % Number of data items
type IndexRange : 1 .. MaxItems
type RealArray : array IndexRange of real

var X : RealArray            % Array of data
var Sum : real := 0.0        % Sum of the data

% Enter the data
put "Enter ", MaxItems , " numbers> " ..
for I : 1 .. MaxItems
    get X(I)
end for

% Compute the average value
for I : 1 .. MaxItems
    Sum := Sum + X(I)        % Add each element to Sum
end for

const Average := Sum / MaxItems     % Get average value
put "Average value is ", Average :3:1, skip
% Display the difference between each item and
% the average
put "Table of differences between X(I) and ",
    "the average"
put "   I    X(I)      Difference"
for I : 1 .. MaxItems
    put I :4, X(I) :8:1, X(I)-Average :14:1
end for
```

```
Enter 8 numbers> 16.0 12.0 6.0 8.0 2.5 12.0 14.0 -54.5
Average value is 2.0

Table of differences between X(I) and the average
    I      X(I)        Difference
    1      16.0           14.0
    2      12.0           10.0
    3       6.0            4.0
    4       8.0            6.0
    5       2.5            0.5
    6      12.0           10.0
    7      14.0           12.0
    8     -54.5          -56.5
```

The program fragment

```
for I : 1 .. MaxItems
    Sum := Sum + X(I)    % Add each element to Sum
end for
```

accumulates the sum of all eight elements of array X in the variable Sum. Each time the `for` loop is repeated, the next element of array X is added to Sum. The execution of this program fragment is traced in Table 11.4 for the first three repetitions of the loop.

TABLE 11.4 Partial Trace of For Loop

Statement Part	I	X(I)	Sum	Effect
var Sum: real := 0.0			0.0	Initialize Sum
for I: 1..MaxItems		1	16.0	Set I to 1
Sum := Sum + X(I)			16.0	Add X(1) to Sum
Increment, test I	2	12.0		2 <= 8 is true
Sum := Sum + X(I)			28.0	Add X(2) to Sum
Increment, test I		3	6.0	3 <= 8 is true
Sum := Sum + X(I)			34.0	Add X(3) to Sum

In Fig. 11.4, the subscripted variable X(I) is an actual parameter for the `get` or `put` statement. You will always need to read data into an array one element at a time, as shown in this example.

It is very common to accumulate sums or differences in a loop, as was done in the case of the `for` loop in Table 11.4. Because of this, there is a shorter form of the assignment statement that indicates that the accumulating variable, such as Sum, is to be modified. In the following loop, which can replace the corresponding loop in Fig. 11.4 and Table 11.4, the += form of the assignment statement indicates that X(I) is to be added to Sum.

```
for I : 1 .. MaxItems
    Sum += X(I)          % Add A(I) to Sum
end for
```

The use of the += form makes the program somewhat shorter, and once you are used to it, makes the program somewhat clearer. We read the statement as "Increment Sum by X(I)". Turing also has the form -=, which subtracts from a variable.

INCREMENT AND DECREMENT IN ASSIGNMENT STATEMENT

Form: *variable* += *expression*

(or)

variable -= *expression*

Example:
```
Sum += X(I)
Sum -= X(I)
```

Interpretation: Expression on the right side is added to (or subtracted from) the variable. The above two statements have the same meaning as these longer statements.

```
Sum := Sum + X(I)
Sum := Sum - X(I)
```

Exercises for Section 11.2

Self-Check

1. If an array is declared to have ten elements, must the program use all ten of them?
2. The sequence of statements below changes the initial contents of array X displayed in Fig. 11.1. Describe what each statement does to the array and show the final contents of array X after all statements execute. Rewrite each `for` loop as a conditional loop that uses the += or -= form of the assignment statement to update I.

```
var J := 3
X(J) := X(J) + 10.0
X(J - 1) := X(2 * J - 1)
X(J + 1) := X(2 * J) + X(2 * J + 1)
for I : 5 .. 7
    X(I) := X(I + 1)
end for
for decreasing I : 3 .. 1
    X(I + 1) := X(I)
end for
```

3. Write program statements that will do the following to array X shown in Fig. 11.1.
   a. Replace the third element with 7.0.
   b. Copy the element in the fifth location into the first one.
   c. Subtract the first element from the fourth and store the result in the fifth one.
   d. Increase the sixth element by two.
   e. Find the sum of the first five elements.
   f. Multiply each of the first six elements by 2 and place each product in an element of the array AnswerArray.
   g. Display all even-numbered elements on one line.

11.3 Using Arrays

This section illustrates the use of an array. It demonstrates two different methods for array access: sequential access and random access. We discuss their differences after the case study.

◈ Case Study:

Home Budget Problem

1. Problem

Your parents want a program that keeps track of their monthly expenses in each of several categories. The program should read each expense amount, add it to the appropriate category total, and print the total expenditure by category. The input data consist of the category and amount of each purchase made during the past month.

2. Analysis

Your parents have selected the budget categories: entertainment, food, clothing, rent, tuition, insurance, and miscellaneous. Therefore, seven separate totals must be accumulated; each total can be associated with a different element of a seven-element array. The program must read each expenditure, determine to which category it belongs, and then add that expenditure to the appropriate array element. When done with all expenditures, the program can print a table showing each category and its accumulated total. As in all programs that accumulate a sum, each total must be initialized to zero.

DATA REQUIREMENTS

We could simply use an array with subscripts one through seven; however, the program would be more readable if we declare a data type BudgetCat and use this data type as the array subscript type.

Data Type
```
BudgetCat : enum (Entertainment, Food, Clothing,
                  Rent, Tuition, Insurance,
                  Miscellaneous)
```

Problem Inputs
Each expenditure and its category

Problem Outputs
The array of seven expenditure totals (Budget)

3. Design

INITIAL ALGORITHM
1. Initialize all category totals to zero.
2. Read each expenditure and add it to the appropriate total.
3. Print the accumulated total for each category.

REFINEMENTS AND STRUCTURE CHART

The structure chart in Fig. 11.5 shows the relationship between the three steps. The array `Budget` is manipulated by all three procedures in the program solution. Procedures `Initialize` and `Post` store information in this array; this information is displayed by procedure `Report`.

FIGURE 11.5   Structure Chart for Home Budget Problem

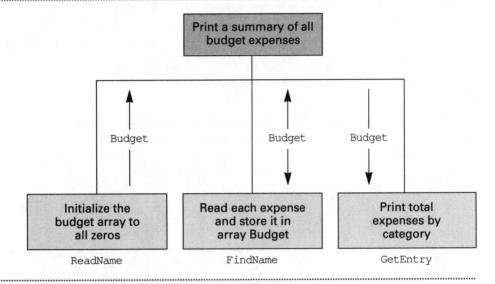

4. Implementation   ***Coding the Main Program***

Figure 11.6 shows the program. The main program contains declarations for the data type `BudgetCat` and the array `Budget`. The array `Budget` (type `BudgetArray`) appears in each parameter list and is passed between each procedure and the main program. When passing an entire array, no subscript is used. We will have more to say about the use of arrays as parameters later.

FIGURE 11.6   Home Budget Program

```
% The "Budget" program
% Print a summary of all expenses by budget category

type BudgetCat : enum (Entertainment, Food, Clothing,
                       Rent, Tuition, Insurance,Miscellaneous)
type BudgetArray : array BudgetCat of real
var Budget : BudgetArray % Output - array of totals

procedure Initialize (var Budget : BudgetArray)
    % Initialize array Budget to all zeros
    % Pre : None
    % Post: Each element of Budget is 0.0
```

```
            for NextCat : BudgetCat.Entertainment ..
                        BudgetCat.Miscellaneous
                Budget(NextCat) := 0.0
            end for
    end Initialize

    procedure Post (var Budget : BudgetArray)
        % Read each expenditure amount and add it to the
        % appropriate element of array Budget
        % Pre : Each array element Budget(I) is 0.0
        % Post: Each array element Budget(I) is the sum
        %         of expense amounts for category I

        % Stub for Post procedure
        put "Procedure Post entered"
    end Post

    procedure PrintCat (NextCat : BudgetCat)
        % Display budget category
        % Pre : NextCat is a budget category
        % Post: Display NextCat as a string

        case NextCat of
            label BudgetCat.Entertainment :
                put "Entertainment" :15 ..
            label BudgetCat.Food :
                put "Food" :15 ..
            label BudgetCat.Clothing :
                put "Clothing" :15 ..
            label BudgetCat.Rent :
                put "Rent" :15 ..
            label BudgetCat.Tuition :
                put "Tuition" :15 ..
            label BudgetCat.Insurance :
                put "Insurance" :15 ..
            label BudgetCat.Miscellaneous :
                put "Miscellaneous" :15 ..
        end case
    end PrintCat

    procedure Report (Budget : BudgetArray)
        % Print the expenditures in each budget category
        % Pre : Array Budget is defined
        % Post: Display each budget category name and amount

        put ""
        put "Category" :15, "Expenses"
        % Heading
        % Print each category name and the total
        for NextCat : BudgetCat.Entertainment ..
                    BudgetCat.Miscellaneous
```

```
            PrintCat (NextCat)
            put Budget (NextCat) :15:2
        end for
    end Report

    % Initialize array Budget to all zeros
    Initialize (Budget)

    % Read and process each expenditure
    Post (Budget)

    % Print the expenditures in each category
    Report (Budget)
```

In procedure `Initialize`, the assignment statement

```
    Budget(NextCat) := 0.0
```

is repeated once for each value of `NextCat` and sets each element of `Budget` to zero. In procedure `Report`, the statements

```
    PrintCat (NextCat)
    put Budget (NextCat) :15:2
```

use `PrintCat` to display a budget category name and `put` to display the category total.

FIGURE 11.7   Procedure Post and Subprograms for Home Budget Problem

```
const Quit := 0 % Sentinel category number
const MaxCategory := 7 % Number of budget categories

% The "helper" procedures EnterCat and ConvertCat
% are used by the Post procedure

procedure EnterCat (var Choice : int)
    % Read the budget category as an integer value
    % Pre : None
    % Post: Choice is an integer from 0 to 7

    loop
        put "1 - Entertainment"
        put "2 - Food"
        put "3 - Clothing"
        put "4 - Rent"
        put "5 - Tuition"
        put "6 - Insurance"
        put "7 - Miscellaneous"
        put "0 - Quit program"
        put "Enter the category number> " ..
        get Choice
        exit when Choice >= Quit and Choice <= MaxCategory
    end loop
end EnterCat
```

```
function ConvertCat (Choice : int) : BudgetCat
   % Convert from an integer value to a value of type
   % BudgetCat
   % Pre : Choice is between 1 and 7
   % Post: Returns a value from Entertainment to
   %        Miscellaneous
   % Stub for ConvertCat procedure
   result BudgetCat.Rent
end ConvertCat

procedure Post (var Budget : BudgetArray)
   % Read each expenditure amount and add it to the
   % appropriate element of array Budget.
   % Pre : Each array element Budget(I) is 0.0
   % Post: Each array element Budget(I) is the sum of
   %        expense amounts for category I

   const Quit := 0           % Sentinel category number
   const MaxCategory := 7    % Number of categories

   var Choice : int          % Next category
   var NextCat: BudgetCat    % Next category as type
                             % BudgetCat
   var Expense: real         % Expenditure amount

   % Read each budget category and expense and add
   % it to Budget
   loop
      EnterCat (Choice)
      % Invariant:
      %     No prior value of Choice is Quit and
      %     Budget (NextCat) is the sum of prior
      %     budget entries for category NextCat
      exit when Choice = Quit
      NextCat := ConvertCat (Choice)
                     % Convert to type BudgetCat
      put "Enter the expenditure amount $" ..
      get Expense
      put ""
      Budget (NextCat) := Budget (NextCat) + Expense
   end loop
end Post
```

Coding Procedure Post and Its Subprograms

Procedure Post must read each expenditure and add it to the appropriate array element. The total of all entertainment expenditures is accumulated in Budget(Entertainment), all food expenditures are accumulated in Budget(Food), and so forth. Procedure Post is shown in Fig. 11.7; it uses procedure EnterCat to read the budget category as an integer value and function ConvertCat (see Self-Check Exercise 2) to convert this value to type BudgetCat.

Procedure Post begins by calling EnterCat to read an int representing the category into Choice. The loop body is executed for each value of Choice that is not zero. Function ConvertCat assigns a value to NextCat (type BudgetCat) based on the value of Choice. The assignment statement

    Budget(NextCat) := Budget(NextCat) + Expense

adds the expense amount to whatever element of array Budget is selected by NextCat.

5. Testing

A sample run of the Home Budget Program is shown in Fig. 11.8. For the sake of brevity, we have displayed the list of categories just once. As indicated in this run, it is not necessary for the data to be in order by category. You should verify that all budget categories without purchases remain zero. Also, verify that out-of-range category values do not cause the program to terminate prematurely.

FIGURE 11.8   Sample Run of Home Budget Program

```
1 - Entertainment
2 - Food
3 - Clothing
4 - Rent
5 - Tuition
6 - Insurance
7 - Miscellaneous
0 - Quit program
Enter the category number> 3
Enter the expenditure amount $25.00

Enter the category number> 7
Enter the expenditure amount $25.00

Enter the category number> 3
Enter the expenditure amount $15.00

Enter the category number> 1
Enter the expenditure amount $675.00

Enter the category number> 0

Category          Expenses
Entertainment       675.00
Food                  0.00
Clothing             40.00
Rent                  0.00
Tuition               0.00
Insurance             0.00
Miscellaneous        25.00
```

Sequential Versus Random Access to Arrays

The Home Budget Program illustrates two common ways of selecting array elements for processing. Often, we need to manipulate all elements of an array in some uniform manner (for instance, we might want to initialize them all to zero). In situations like this, it makes sense to process the array elements in sequence (*sequential access*), starting with the first and ending with the last. In procedures `Initialize` and `Report`, we accomplish that by using a `for` loop whose loop control variable is also the array subscript.

In procedure `Post`, the order in which the array elements are accessed is completely dependent on the order of the data. The value assigned to `NextCat` determines the element to be incremented. This approach is called *random access* because the order is not predictable beforehand.

Enumerated and Subrange Types as Ranges of For Statements

When using enumerated types, it is common to use a `for` loop that iterates through all elements of the enumeration, as was done in the `Initialize` procedure from Fig. 11.6, copied here:

```
for NextCat : BudgetCat.Entertainment ..
              BudgetCat.Miscellaneous
    Budget(NextCat) := 0.0
end for
```

Turing provides a special form of `for` statement that allows us to write this in a shorter and clearer form. We can replace this `for` loop with the following, in which the range of values to be covered is given by simply writing the name of the enumerated type (`BudgetCat`).

```
for NextCat : BudgetCat % For all elements of BudgetCat
    Budget(NextCat) := 0.0
end for
```

We can use this form also for subranges. For example, if the subrange `1..10` has the type name `IntRange`, we can write this beginning of a `for loop`:

```
for ThisCounter : IntRange
    ...
end for
```

> **TYPES AS RANGES OF FOR STATEMENTS**
>
> **Form:**   for *counter* : *typeName*
>   ...
>   end for
>
> **Example:**   type Cards : enum (Clubs, Diamonds,
>   Hearts, Spades)
>   ...
>   for NextCard : Cards
>   ...
>   end for
>
> **Interpretation:** The for loop will be repeated with NextCard set to each of Clubs, Diamonds, Hearts, and Spades. This is equivalent to the following loop.
>
>   for NextCard : Cards.Clubs .. Cards.Spades
>   ...
>   end for

Exercises for Section 11.3

Self-Check

1. What happens if the user of the budget program enters the category –1 by mistake?
2. Write function ConvertCat. Integer values from 1 to 7 should be converted to values of type BudgetCat from Entertainment to Miscellaneous.

Programming

1. Write a procedure that copies each value stored in one array to the corresponding element of another array. (For example, if the arrays are InArray and OutArray, then copy InArray(1) to OutArray(1), next copy to OutArray(2), and so on.)
2. Write a procedure that reverses the values stored in an array. If array X has N elements, then X(1) becomes X(N), X(2) becomes X(N-1), and so forth. **Hint:** Make a local copy of the array before you start to reverse the elements.

11.4 Arrays as Operands and Parameters

The Turing operators (e.g., <, =, >, +, –) can manipulate only one array element at a time (provided the element type is an appropriate simple type). Consequently, an array name in an expression will generally be followed by its subscript.

Copying an Array

One exception to the above rule is the *array copy* operation. It is possible to copy the contents of one array to another array, provided the arrays are the same array type. Given the declarations

```
const MaxSize := 100

type Index : 1..MaxSize

type TestArray : array Index of real

var W, X, Y : TestArray
var Z : array Index of real
```

the assignment statements

```
X := Y          % Valid array copy
W := Y          % Valid array copy
```

copy each value in array Y to the corresponding element of arrays X and W (i.e., Y(1) is copied to X(1) and W(1), Y(2) to X(2) and W(2), etc.).
  The following assignments

```
Z := Y          % Valid array copy
X := Z          % Valid array copy
```

are also valid. Since array Z has the same structure as arrays W, X, and Y, the type of array Z is considered the same as the named type TestArray.

Arrays as Parameters

If several elements of an array are being manipulated by a procedure, it is generally better to pass the entire array of data instead of individual array elements. In Fig. 11.6 the procedure call statements

```
Initialize (Budget)
Post (Budget)
Report (Budget)
```

pass the entire array Budget to each procedure. Budget is declared as a variable parameter in procedures Initialize and Post and as a value parameter in procedure Report.
  In all three procedures, the formal parameter is declared as type BudgetArray. This is necessary since the formal and actual parameter must be the same array type. The procedure heading

```
procedure Initialize (var Budget : array BudgetCat of real)
```

is also valid, because the structures of the formal and actual parameter arrays are the same.

When an array is used as a variable parameter, Turing passes the address of the entire array element into the procedure data area. Since the array elements are stored in adjacent memory cells, the entire array of data may be accessed. The procedure directly manipulates the actual array.

When an array is used as a value parameter, the address of the array is again passed into the procedure area. However, in this case, you are not allowed to change the value of the formal parameter.

The next two examples illustrate the use of arrays as parameters, assuming the declarations below.

```
const MaxSize := 5
type IndexType : 1 .. MaxSize
type TestArray : array IndexType of real
var X, Y, Z : TestArray
```

EXAMPLE 11.7

Although it is possible to use a single assignment statement to copy one array to another, the assignment statement

```
Z := X + Y                    % Illegal addition of arrays
```

is invalid because the operator + cannot have an array as an operand. You might use procedure AddArray (Fig. 11.9) to add two arrays of type TestArray.

FIGURE 11.9   Procedure AddArray

```
procedure AddArray (A, B : TestArray,
                    var C : TestArray)

  % Store the sum of A(I) and B(I) in C(I)
  % Array elements with subscripts 1..MaxSize are
  % summed, element by element.
  % Pre : A(I) and B(I) (1 <= I <= MaxSize) are
  %       assigned values
  % Post: C(I) := A(I) + B(I) (1 <= I <= MaxSize)

  % Add corresponding elements of each array
  for I : 1 .. MaxSize
      C(I) := A(I) + B(I)
  end for
end AddArray
```

The parameter correspondence for arrays established by the procedure call statement

```
AddArray (X, Y, Z)
```

is shown in Fig. 11.10. The procedure results are stored directly in array Z. After execution of the procedure, Z(1) will contain the sum of X(1) and Y(1), or 3.5; Z(2) will contain 6.7; and so on. Arrays X and Y will be unchanged.

FIGURE 11.10   Parameter Correspondence for AddArray (X, Y, Z)

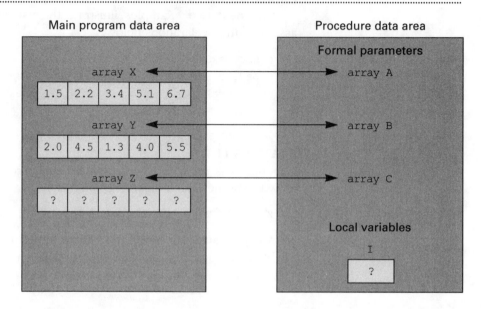

EXAMPLE 11.8

Function SameArray in Fig. 11.11 determines whether two arrays (of type TestArray) are identical. Two arrays are considered identical if the first element of one is the same as the first element of the other, the second element of one is the same as the second element of the other, and so forth.

We can determine that the arrays are not identical by finding a single pair of unequal elements. Consequently, the loop may be executed anywhere from one time (first elements unequal) to MaxSize times. Early exit from the loop occurs when a pair of unequal elements is found.

FIGURE 11.11   Function SameArray

```
function SameArray (A, B : TestArray) : boolean
    % Return a value of true if the arrays A, B are
    % identical; otherwise, return a value of false
    % Pre : A(I) and B(I) (1 <= I <= MaxSize) are
    %        assigned values
    % Post: Return true if A(I) = B(I) for all I in
    %        range 1..MaxSize; otherwise, return false
```

```
                % Test corresponding elements of arrays A and B
                for I : 1 .. MaxSize
                    if A(I) not= B(I) then
                        result false
                    end if
                end for
                result true
            end SameArray
```

If any of the pairs of elements, `A(I)` and `B(I)`, differ, the function imme-diately returns with a result of `false`. Any time a `result` statement is executed in a function, the function returns its result without further exe-cution. In this example, if `A(I)` and `B(I)` differ, the final statement (result `true`) is never reached. If all elements are equal, the `for` loop ends normally, and the final `result` statement returns `true` as the result.

As an example of how you might use function `SameArray`, the `if` statement

```
            if SameArray(X, Y) then
                Z := X
            else
                AddArray (X, Y, Z)
            end if
```

either copies array `X` to array `Z` (when `X` and `Y` are identical) or stores the sum of arrays `X` and `Y` in array `Z` (when `X` and `Y` are not identical).

Dynamic Upper Bounds for Array Parameters

The subprograms `AddArray` and `SameArray` as given in Figs. 11.9 and 11.11 work correctly for arrays with exactly `MaxSize` elements. If your program had two arrays of differing sizes, these subprograms could be used for only one of the two arrays. Turing provides a feature that allows subprograms to adjust to the sizes of their parameters. In the declaration of the formal array parameter in the subprogram, the upper bound is given as a star (*). Here is the `SameArray` parameter written to use this form of declaration. In the `for` loop in this function, the range runs up to `upper(A)`, which is the upper bound (`MaxSize`) of array A.

```
            function SameArray (A, B : array 1 .. * of real) : boolean
                % Return a value of true if the arrays A, B are
                % identical; otherwise, return a value of false
                % Pre : A(I) and B(I) (1 <= I <= MaxSize) are
                %        assigned values and they have the same
                %        number of elements
                % Post: Return true if A(I) = B(I) for all I in
                %        range 1..MaxSize; otherwise, returns false
```

```
% Test corresponding elements of arrays A and B
for I : 1 .. upper (A) % For all elements
    if A(I) not= B(I) then
        result false
    end if
end for
result true
end SameArray
```

An array parameter whose upper bound is declared using a star is called a *dynamic* array, because the size is not known until the subprogram is called. If the program has arrays of different sizes, these could all be passed to `SameArray`, with the result that the upper bound of A and B would change with each call.

DYNAMIC ARRAY PARAMETERS AND THEIR UPPER BOUNDS

Form: *identifier* :
                    array *lower bound* .. * of *element type*

Form: upper (*identifier*)

Example: var Counts : array 1 .. 10 of int
               procedure Clear (A : array 1 .. * of int)
                   for I : 1 .. upper (A)
                       A (I) := 0
                   end for
               end Clear
               Clear (Counts)

Interpretation: The array parameter, which may be a variable or a value parameter, has its upper bound declared as *, which means the upper bound is taken from the actual parameter. In this example, the upper bound, written as upper (A) is determined by the array Counts that is passed to A. All 10 elements of the Counts array are cleared to zero.

PROGRAM
STYLE

USE OF DYNAMIC ARRAY PARAMETERS
It is good practice to use dynamic array parameters when you can, because this makes your subprograms more generally useful. It allows you to re-use your subprogram for a new purpose.

PROGRAM
STYLE

EFFICIENCY OF VALUE PARAMETERS
Parameters A and B in Fig. 11.11 are declared as value parameters because their values should not be changed by `SameArray`. In Turing, all `array` parameters (whether variable or value parameters) are passed by *reference*. This is illustrated in Fig. 11.10 in which there are

double-ended arrows between X and A; Y and B; and Z and C. This is different from some languages such as Pascal that create local copies of array value parameters.

In Pascal, it is common, but unfortunate, practice to avoid these extra local copies of arrays by using variable parameters for arrays even when the subprogram does not change the value of the array. In Turing, when an array parameter is not to be changed by the subprogram, it should always be a value and not a variable parameter. This practice provides the compiler-enforced guarantee that the parameter will not be changed.

Finding the Minimum or Maximum Value in an Array

One common operation is to determine the minimum or maximum value stored in an array. In Chapter 4 we wrote a program to find the smallest of three characters. The approach taken to finding the minimum or maximum value in an array is quite similar. The algorithm for finding the maximum value follows.

Algorithm for Finding the Maximum Value in an Array

1. Assume that the first element is the largest so far and save its subscript as the subscript of the largest so far.
2. for each array element do
   3. if the current element is greater than the largest so far then
      4. Save the subscript of the current element as
         the subscript of the largest so far.
      end if
   end for

Function MaxBudget in Fig. 11.12 implements this algorithm for the array Budget displayed in Fig. 11.8. The function returns the subscript (type Category) of the largest value in array Budget.

FIGURE 11.12   Function MaxBudget

```
function MaxBudget (Budget : BudgetArray) : BudgetCat
    % Return the subscript of the largest element in
    % array Budget
    % Pre : Array Budget is defined
    % Post: Budget(MaxIndex) is the largest value in
    %       the array

    var MaxIndex : BudgetCat := BudgetCat.Entertainment
            % Index of largest element so far
```

```
        for NextIndex : BudgetCat % Each element of BudgetCat
            if Budget(NextIndex) > Budget(MaxIndex) then
                MaxIndex := NextIndex
            end if
        end for

        % Assertion:
        % All elements are examined and
        % MaxIndex is the index of the largest element
        result MaxIndex
end MaxBudget
```

It is important to realize that function `MaxBudget` returns the subscript (or *index*) of the largest value; not the largest value itself. Assuming `NextCat` is type `BudgetCat`, the statements below display the largest value.

```
NextCat := MaxBudget(Budget)
put "The largest expenditure is $",
Budget(NextCat) :4:2
```

Although it may not be as easy to read, the single statement below is equivalent; it uses the function reference as the subscript expression.

```
put "The largest expenditure is $",
        Budget(MaxBudget(Budget)) :4:2
```

Individual Array Elements as Parameters

It is acceptable practice to use a single array element as an actual parameter. For example, the expression

```
round(Budget(5))
```

rounds the value stored in the fifth element of array `Budget`, where the subscripted variable `Budget(5)` is the actual parameter passed to function `round`.

EXAMPLE 11.9
Procedure `Exchange` in Fig. 10.13 exchanges the values of its two type `real` parameters.

FIGURE 11.13   Procedure Exchange

```
procedure Exchange (var P, Q : real)
    % Exchange the values of P and Q
    % Pre : P and Q are assigned values
    % Post: P has the value passed into Q and vice-versa

    const Temp := P      % Save P's value
    P := Q
    Q := Temp
end Exchange
```

The procedure call statement Exchange (X(2), X(1)) uses this procedure to exchange the contents of the first two elements (type real) of array X. The identifier X is the name of an array in the calling program. The actual parameter X(2) corresponds to formal parameter P; the actual parameter X(1) corresponds to formal parameter Q. This correspondence is shown in Fig. 11.14 for the array X.

FIGURE 11.14 Parameter Correspondence for Exchange (X(2), X(1))

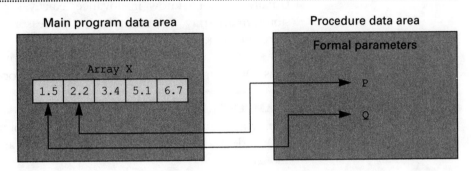

It is illegal to use a subscripted variable as a formal parameter. For example, the procedure declaration

```
procedure Exchange (var X(I), X(J) : real)
```

would cause a syntax error.

Exercises for Section 11.4

Self-Check

1. When is it better to pass an entire array of data to a procedure rather than individual elements?
2. Suppose A is a formal parameter that is an array. When are you allowed to change the values of the elements of A?
3. In function SameArray, if the two arrays are not equal, will the statement

   ```
   result true
   ```

   be executed?
4. Describe how to modify function MaxBudget to get a new function, MinBudget, that returns the smallest array element.

Programming

1. Write a procedure that assigns a value of true to element I of the output array if element I of one input array has the same value as element

I of the other input array; otherwise assign a value of `false`. If the input arrays have subscript type `IndexType`, the output array should have the type below.

```
type BoolArray : array IndexType of boolean
```

11.5 Reading Part of an Array

Usually we don't know in advance exactly how many elements will be stored in an array. For example, if a professor is processing exam scores, there might be 150 students in one class, 200 in the next, and so on. In this situation, we can declare an array that can accommodate the largest class. Only part of this array will actually be processed for a smaller class.

EXAMPLE 11.10

The array `Scores` declared below can accommodate a class of up to 250 students. Each array element can contain an integer value between 0 and 100.

```
const MaxSize := 250
const MaxScore := 100

type ClassIndex : 1 .. MaxSize
type ScoreRange : 0 .. MaxScore
type ScoreArray : array ClassIndex of ScoreRange
type ClassRange : 0 .. MaxSize

var Scores : ScoreArray
var ClassSize : ClassRange
```

Procedure `ReadScores` in Fig. 11.15 reads up to 250 exam scores and prints a warning message when the array is filled. The actual number of scores read is returned as the value of `ClassSize`. It calls `EnterInt` (see Fig. 10.3) to read each exam score.

FIGURE 11.15   Reading Part of an Array

```
procedure ReadScores (var Scores : ScoreArray,
                      var ClassSize : ClassRange)
   % Read an array of exam scores (Scores)
   % for a class of up to MaxSize students
   % Pre : None
   % Post: Data values are stored in array Scores.
   %       The number of values read is stored in
   %       ClassSize (0 <= ClassSize <= MaxSize)
   % Uses: Procedure EnterInt (see Fig. 10.3)

   const Sentinel := -1     % Sentinel value
```

```
    var TempScore : int      % Temporary storage for a score
    put "Enter next score after the prompt or enter ",
         Sentinel, " to stop."

    % Read each array element until done
    ClassSize := 0          % Initial class size
    loop
        EnterInt (Sentinel, MaxScore, TempScore)
        % Invariant: No prior value of TempScore is
        %            Sentinel and ClassSize <= MaxSize
        exit when TempScore = Sentinel or
              ClassSize = MaxSize
        ClassSize := ClassSize + 1
        Scores(ClassSize) := TempScore    % Save the score
    end loop

    % Assert: Sentinel was read or
    %         too many values for array
    if TempScore not= Sentinel then
        put "Too many values for array"
    end if
end ReadScores
```

In any subsequent processing of array `Scores`, you should use the variable `ClassSize` to limit the number of array elements processed. Only the subarray with subscripts 1 .. `ClassSize` contains meaningful data; consequently, array elements with subscripts larger than `ClassSize` should not be manipulated. `ClassSize` should be passed as a parameter to any procedure that processes the partially filled array.

Exercises for Section 11.5

Self-Check

1. In procedure `ReadScores`, what prevents the user from entering more than `MaxSize` scores?
2. What is the range of data values that can be entered? What is the range of data values that can be stored in the array?
3. In `ReadScores`, why didn't we use a `for` loop?
4. Suppose the header for `ReadScores` were changed to the following. What else should then be changed for the subprogram to adjust to the size of the `Scores` dynamic array parameter?

```
procedure ReadScores (var Scores : array 1 .. * of int,
                  var ClassSize : int)
```

11.6 More Examples of Array Processing

Many of the arrays processed so far had subscript types that were subranges of the integers. This is the usual case in Turing, but enumerated values can also be subscript types. A number of different array types are described in Table 11.5.

TABLE 11.5 Some Array Types and Applications

Array Type	Application
type NameArray : array 1..10 of string var Name : NameArray Name(1) := "Karl Weiss"	Storing up to 10 names
type Temperatures : array -10..10 of real var Fahrenheit : Temperatures Fahrenheit(0) := 32.0	Storing Fahrenheit temperatures corresponding to -10 through 10 degrees Celsius
type Counters : array ord("A")..ord("Z") of int var LetterCount : Counters LetterCount (ord("A")) := 0	Storing the number of times each uppercase letter occurs

type Flags :
    array ord("A") .. ord("Z")
        of boolean
var LetterFound : Flags
LetterFound(ord("X")) := false
	Storing a set of flags indicating which letters occurred and which did not

The array Name has 10 elements and could store ten people's names. The array Fahrenheit, with 21 elements, could store the Fahrenheit temperature corresponding to each Celsius temperature in the range -10 though +10 degrees Celsius. For example, Fahrenheit(0) would be the Fahrenheit temperature 32.0 corresponding to 0 degrees Celsius. Arrays LetterCount and LetterFound have the same subscript type (i.e., the ordinals of the uppercase letters) and will be discussed in the next section.

Arrays with Subscripts that are Character Ordinals

An array with a subscript type whose subscript range covers a sequence of character ordinals is a useful data structure as shown in the next example. For this example, we will use a special form of the get statement that allows us to read the input of a single character at a time. The following will input exactly one character and then display it.

```
var OneChar : string
put "Please type a character> " ..
get OneChar : 1 % Read next single character
put "Thank you for typing the character ", OneChar
```

In this form of the `get` statement, the input variable is followed by the format item `:1`. This item specifies that exactly one character is to be read. You can as well read other numbers of characters, for example, three characters using the format item `:3`.

There is a complication with this form of the `get` statement. The difficulty is that there is an invisible character, called a *new-line* character, at the end of each line of input. This character is explicitly read by this form of `get`. In Turing, a new-line character is written as "\n", so the following `if` statement can be used to check to see if the end of a line has been reached:

```
const NewLine := "\n"        % The new-line character
if OneChar = NewLine then     % Reached end of line?
    put "Found carriage return."
end if
```

READING ONE CHARACTER AT A TIME

Form: get *variable* : 1

Example: var OneLetter : string
               get OneLetter : 1

Interpretation: The format item `:1` indicates that the next character, whatever it may be, is input and assigned to `OneLetter`. This form will read the *new-line* character at the end of each input line into `OneLetter`. The *new-line* character is written as "\n" in Turing.

In most of our programs in this book, we read the input a word at a time, and when this is the case we do not use a format item. But in this example, it is handy to read exactly one character at a time because we are counting the occurrences of letters being typed.

EXAMPLE 11.11

The arrays `LetterCount` and `LetterFound` described in Table 11.5 have the subscript type `ord("A") .. ord("Z")`. Hence, there is an array element for each uppercase letter. The program in Fig. 11.16 displays the number of occurrences of each letter in a line of text. It uses `LetterCount(ord("A"))` to store the number of occurrences of the letter "A". If the letter A occurs, `LetterFound(ord("A"))` would be true; otherwise, `LetterFound(ord("A"))` would be `false`. Function `UpCase` (see Fig. 10.4) converts the case of each letter read into `NextString` to uppercase so that both `t` and `T` cause the count for letter `T` to be incremented.

FIGURE 11.16

Counting Letters in a Line

```
% The "Concord" program
% Find and print the number of occurrences of each letter
% The case of each letter is immaterial. Letters with
% counts of zero are not displayed

const Sentinel := "*"                  % Sentinel character
type LetterOrd : ord("A") .. ord("Z")
type CountArray : array LetterOrd of int
type FoundArray : array LetterOrd of boolean

var LetterCount : CountArray          % Output - array of counts
var LetterFound : FoundArray          % Array of flags
var NextChar : string                 % Input - each input

% Insert function UpCase (see Fig. 10.4) here

% Initialize LetterCount and LetterFound
for CharOrd : LetterOrd               % The ord of each letter
    LetterCount(CharOrd) := 0         % Initialize counts
    LetterFound(CharOrd) := false     % Initialize flags
end for

% Count the letters in a line
put "Type in a line of text ending with ", Sentinel
loop
    get NextChar : 1                   % Get next character
    NextChar := UpCase(NextChar)       % Convert to uppercase
    if "A" <= NextChar and NextChar <= "Z" then
        const NextCharOrd := ord(NextChar)
        LetterCount(NextCharOrd) += 1   % Increment count
        LetterFound(NextCharOrd) := true    % Set flag
    end if
    exit when NextChar = Sentinel
end loop

% Print counts of letters that are in the line
put skip, "Letter Occurrences"
for CharOrd : LetterOrd               % The ord of each letter
    if LetterFound(CharOrd) then
        put chr(CharOrd), LetterCount(CharOrd):8
    end if
end for
```

```
Type in a line of text ending with *
This is it!*

Letter    Occurrences
H         1
I         3
S         2
T         2
```

In the last `if` statement, the condition

```
LetterFound(CharOrd)
```

is `true` if there were one or more occurrences of the letter corresponding to `CharOrd`. This `if` statement ensures that only counts greater than zero are printed. This condition could also be written as

```
LetterCount(CharOrd) > 0
```

Doing this would be more efficient because it would allow us to eliminate the array `LetterFound`.

❈ Case Study:

Cryptogram Generator

1. Problem

Your local intelligence agency needs a program to encode messages. One approach is to use a program that generates cryptograms. A cryptogram is a coded message formed by substituting a code character for each letter of an original message. The substitution is performed uniformly throughout the original message – for instance, all `A`s might be replaced by `S`s, all `B`s by `P`s, and so forth. All punctuation (including spaces between words) remains unchanged.

2. Analysis

The program must examine each character in the message and replace each character that is a letter by its code symbol. We can store the code symbols in an array `Code` with subscript type `ord("A") .. ord("Z")` and element type `string`. The character stored in `Code(ord("A"))` will be the code symbol for the letter `"A"`. This will enable us to simply look up the code symbol for a letter by using that letter as an index to the array `Code`.

DATA REQUIREMENTS
Problem Inputs
```
Code : array ord("A") .. ord("Z") of string
       % Code symbols
```

Each message character

Problem Outputs

Each character of the cryptogram

3. Design

INITIAL ALGORITHM

1. Read in the code symbol for each letter.
2. Read each message character and display the cryptogram.

Algorithm Refinements and Structure Chart

As shown in the structure chart (see Fig. 11.17), procedure ReadCode performs step 1 and procedure Encrypt performs step 2. The data requirements and algorithms for these procedures follow the structure chart.

FIGURE 11.17   Structure Chart for Cryptogram Generator

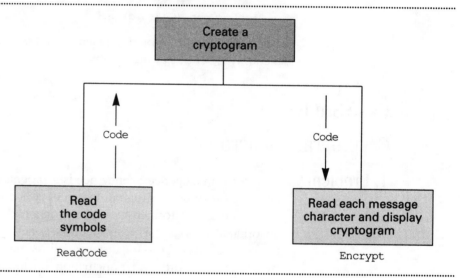

ALGORITHM FOR READCODE

1. Display the alphabet.
2. for each letter
         3. Read in the code symbol and store it in array Code.
end for

LOCAL CONSTANT FOR ENCRYPT
    Sentinel = "#"   % Message's sentinel character

LOCAL VARIABLE FOR ENCRYPT
    NextChar : string   % Each message character

ALGORITHM FOR ENCRYPT
1. loop
         2. Read the next message character.

3. Display the message character or its code symbol.
exit when the message is complete
end loop

4. Implementation

The program shown in Fig. 11.18 assumes that the uppercase letters are consecutive characters as they are in the ASCII character set. This program must be modified slightly for computers that use the EBCDIC character set. This character set contains some special characters between the letters I and J and between the letters R and S. One possibility is to use the following boolean function that determines if a character is a letter:

```
function IsLetter (Ch : string) : boolean
    result ("A" <= Ch and Ch <= "I") or
           ("J" <= Ch and Ch <= "R") or
           ("S" <= Ch and Ch <= "Z")
end IsLetter
```

This function returns true if character Ch is in the range A to I, J to R, or S to Z, and false otherwise. Using this function, the for loop in procedure ReadCode can be replaced with

```
% Read each code symbol into array Code
for CharOrd : LetterOrd
    if IsLetter (chr (CharOrd)) then
        get Code (CharOrd) : 1  % Read one code character
    end if
end for
```

The if statement causes the get statement to be skipped when CharOrd corresponds to a special character.

FIGURE 10.18

Cryptogram Generator

```
% The "Crypto" program
% Generate cryptograms corresponding to input messages

type LetterOrd : ord("A") .. ord("Z")
type CodeArray : array LetterOrd of string

var Code : CodeArray      % Input - array of code symbols

procedure ReadCode (var Code : CodeArray)
    % Read in the code symbol for each letter
    % Pre : None
    % Post: 26 data values are read into array Code.

    put "First specify the code"
    put "Enter a code symbol under each letter"
    put "ABCDEFGHIJKLMNOPQRSTUVWXYZ"
```

```
        % Read each code symbol into array Code
        for CharOrd : LetterOrd
            get Code (CharOrd) : 1  % Read one code character
        end for
        var ExtraChar : string
        get ExtraChar : 1      % Skip new-line character at
                               % the end of the line
        put ""                 % Skip a line
    end ReadCode

    procedure Encrypt (Code : CodeArray)
        % Read each character and print it or its code
        % symbol
        % Pre : Array Code is defined
        % Post: Each character is read. Either it or its code
        %        is printed. Halt when sentinel is read.
        % Uses: UpCase (see Fig. 10.4)

        const Sentinel := "#"        % Sentinel character
        var NextChar : string        % Each message character
        put "Enter your message"
        put "Terminate it with the symbol ", Sentinel
        loop
            get NextChar : 1         % Read one character
            NextChar := UpCase (NextChar)
                           % Convert to uppercase
            if NextChar >= "A" and NextChar <= "Z" then
                put Code (ord (NextChar)) .. % Print code
            else
                put NextChar ..      % Print non-letter
            end if
            exit when NextChar = Sentinel
        end loop
    end Encrypt

    % Read in the code symbol for each letter
    ReadCode (Code)
    % Read each character and print it or
    % its code symbol
    Encrypt (Code)
```

....

```
First specify the code
Enter a code symbol under each letter
ABCDEFGHIJKLMNOPQRSTUVWXYZ
BCDEFGHIJKLMNOPQRSTUVWXYZA
Enter your message
Terminate it with the symbol #
This is a short message!#
UIJT JT B TIPSU NFTTBHF!#
```

....

5. Testing   In the sample run above, the code symbol for each letter is entered directly beneath that letter and read by procedure `ReadCode`. The sample run ends with two lines: the first contains the message; the second contains its cryptogram. For one simple test, try using each letter as its own code symbol. In this case, both lines should be the same. Make sure that the program encodes lowercase letters as well as uppercase letters. Characters that are not letters should not be changed.   ✖

Exercises for Section 11.6

Self-Check

1. Describe the following array types:
   a. `array 1..20 of String`
   b. `array ord("0") .. ord("9") of boolean`
   c. `array -5 .. 5 of real`
2. Provide array type declarations for representing the following.
   a. The areas associated with each room in a group of rooms (living-room, dining-room, kitchen, etc.).
   b. The number of students in each grade of an elementary school.
   c. A letter associated with each color in a collection of colors. This letter will be the first letter of the color name.
3. Why is it that a space or a comma is not encoded in cryptogram program?
4. How do you write the new-line character in Turing?
5. How do you read a single character in Turing?

Programming

1. Make changes to the cryptogram program to encode the blank character and the punctuation symbols `, ; : ? ! . .`

11.7   Maximum Length of a String

We covered many of the basic features of the `string` type in Chapter 8. Those features include catenating (joining) strings using the + operator and taking a substring of a `string` value. We have used variables of type `string` to hold single characters as well as entire words and phrases. In this section we explain how a maximum length can be imposed on strings to save memory space.

A string variable can be assigned `string` values of differing lengths. The variable declaration

```
var Text : string
```

declares the `string` variable `Text`. The following statement assigns the null string, which is a string of zero characters, to `Text`.

```
Text := ""          % Text becomes the null string
```

After `Text` is declared, but before it is assigned a value, it is uninitialized (it does not have a value). Be sure that you understand that an uninitialized string variable is different from one whose value is the null string.

A string value can consist of many characters. In the following, the `Text` variable is set to the null string and then 100 stars are individually catenated onto it.

```
Text := ""
for I : 1 .. 100
    Text := Text + "*"
end for
```

There is a limit to the length of a string. This limit, called the string's *maximum length*, is 255 in Turing. If a program tries to create a string that is longer than this, it will be stopped with a run-time error message saying that an attempt was made to create a string that is too long. This would happen in the preceding `for` loop if the loop's range was 1 .. 300.

If your program needs to handle more than 255 characters, you should use an array of strings. In the following, the `Paragraph` array consists of 100 elements, each of which is a string.

```
var Paragraph : array 1 .. 100 of string
```

The following statements read lines of text into the `Paragraph` array until the sentinel value `###` is encountered. The format item `:*` in the `get` statement reads an entire line of text, discarding the new-line character at the end of the line (see Chapter 9).

```
const Sentinel := "###"
var LineNumber : int := 0
var Line : string
loop
    LineNumber := LineNumber + 1
    get Line : *        % Read an entire line of text
    exit when Line = Sentinel
    Paragraph (LineNumber) := Line
end loop
```

There is a potential problem with the `Paragraph` array. The problem is that it requires a great deal of memory in the computer. Each string in the array uses space for 256 characters; this is space for the maximum of 255 characters plus an extra space to mark the end of the string. Since there are 100 strings in the array, the total amount of space is 25,600 characters. Each of these characters takes up a *byte* (eight *bits*) in the computer's memory. In many modern computers this amount of space is readily available, but in personal computers this may be more space than is available for your program's data.

To conserve space, there is a special form of the `string` type that restricts the maximum length so it is less that 255. In this version of the declaration of `Paragraph` we have limited each string so that it can be at most 79 characters long.

```
var Paragraph : array 1 .. 100 of string (79)
```

Each element of type `string(79)` uses 80 bytes of memory (one byte for each character plus an extra byte to mark the end of the string). This array takes up 8,000 bytes (100 times 80 bytes per element). If we know that each line that is to be read is shorter than 79 characters, this new declaration can be used to save a great deal of memory space.

If your program uses arrays of strings, you may get a run-time error message stating that there is not enough memory to run your program. In this case, it may be necessary to place a maximum length on the strings, to avoid using too much space.

If you use a maximum length on a string, as in `string (79)`, and you want this string to be passed to a variable parameter, you must declare the procedure's formal parameter using a star (*) as the upper bound. This is very much like using a star for an upper bound of a dynamic array parameter. The following procedure accepts a string variable with any maximum length and trims any trailing blanks off the string.

```
procedure Trim (var Text : string (*) )
    const Blank := " "    % The blank character
    loop
        exit when Text = "" or Text (*) not= Blank
        Text := Text (1 .. * - 1)  % Remove a final blank
    end loop
end Trim
```

In this procedure, the last character of the string, `Text (*)`, is tested to see if it is a blank. If it is, the loop body selects the substring `Text (1 .. * - 1)`, which is the string's first through its next to last character, and sets `Text` to be this value. This is repeated until the `Text` does not end with a blank character. The first part of the test in the `exit` statement determines if `Text` is the empty string. If so, the loop is exited, thereby avoiding an illegal attempt to inspect the last character `Text (*)` when there is no last character to test.

The `Trim` procedure can be used to trim the final blanks of the end of a string variable with any maximum length. If we had declared the type of the `Text` parameter to be simply `string` instead of `string (*)`, this procedure would be able to accept only string variables declared without a maximum length.

STRING TYPE WITH MAXIMUM LENGTH

Form: string (*maximum length*)

Example: type String10 = string (10)

Interpretation: The *maximum length* must be an expression that can be evaluated at compile time to an integer value that is at least 1. In this example, space is reserved for strings of length at most 10.

PARAMETER STRING TYPE WITH DYNAMIC LENGTH

Form: string (*)

Example:
```
procedure Double ( var Msg : string (*) )
    Msg := Msg + Msg
end Double

var Greeting : string (40) := "Hi Ho "
Double (Greeting)
```

Interpretation: In a variable (var) formal string parameter, a maximum length of * specifies that the maximum length is to be that of the formal parameter. In this example, when Greeting is passed to Msg, the maximum length of Msg is 40. This means that Msg (and hence Greeting) can be assigned a string of length at most 40 in the Double procedure. In this example, Greeting ends up containing the string value "Hi Ho Hi Ho ".

Exercises for Section 11.7

Self-Check

1. If an assignment statement is used to store a string value into a string variable with a given maximum length, what must be true about the length of the string?
2. What is the difference in determining whether two arrays of real numbers are the same as opposed to determining if two string variables are the same?
3. How should you declare a variable string parameter that is to accept actual parameters of various lengths?

Programming

1. Write a procedure that stores the reverse of an input string parameter in its output parameter (for example, if the input string is "happy", the output string should be "yppah".)
2. Write a program that uses the procedure in Exercise 1 to determine whether or not a string is a palindrome. (A palindrome is a string that reads the same way from left to right as it does from right to left – for instance, "level" is a palindrome.)

11.8 Case Study: Printing a Form Letter

Now that we have a way to store character strings in memory, we can improve our capability to manipulate textual data. Suppose that, during the spring semester, you begin thinking about a summer job. One thing you might like to do is write a program that prints form letters so that you can do a mass-mailing inquiring about summer job opportunities in a variety of fields.

1. Problem

We would like a program that can help in writing job application letters. Each letter will be sent to an output file for printing.

Design Overview

Each letter consists of a heading, salutation, body, and closing. The heading, salutation, and first line of the body will be different for each letter, but the body and closing will be the same. We will first use an editor to create the letter body and closing and save it as a text file (`BodyFile`). To individualize each letter, we will want to enter data for the first part of the letter at the keyboard and then write the first part of the letter to the output file (`Letter`). Next, we can write the rest of the letter from file `BodyFile` to the output file.

An example of the data entry process for the first part of the letter follows.

```
Today's date           > July 27, 1990
Employer name          > Peter Liacouras
Company name           > Temple University
Address                > Broad and Montgomery Streets
City, state/province   > Philadelphia, PA 19122
```

This data would be inserted in the first several lines written to the output file as shown in Fig. 11.19.

FIGURE 11.19   First Lines of File Letter

```
                                          July 27, 1994

     Peter Liacouras
     Temple University
     Broad and Montgomery Streets
     Philadelphia, PA  19122

     Dear Peter Liacouras:

         I am interested in applying for a job at Temple University.
```

DATA REQUIREMENTS

Problem Inputs

```
BodyFile  : int       % File number of body of
                      % the letter
Date      : string    % Today's date
Employer  : string    % Employer's name
Company   : string    % Company name
Address   : string    % Company address
CityState : string    % City, state/province
```

Problem Outputs

```
Letter : int          % File number of the
                      % complete letter
```

INITIAL ALGORITHM

1. Read the preamble data from the keyboard and write it to `Letter`.
2. Copy the letter body to `Letter`.

ALGORITHM REFINEMENTS AND STRUCTURE CHART

From the structure chart in Fig. 11.20, we see that procedures `Preamble` and `PutBody` perform steps 1 and 2, respectively.

FIGURE 11.20   Structure Chart for Form Letter Program

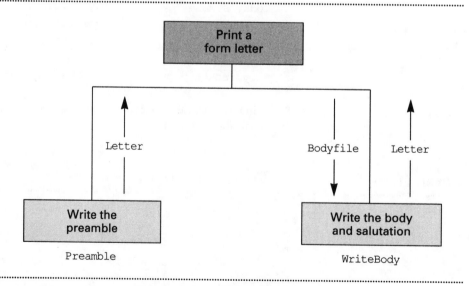

2. Implementation   The main program body shown in Fig. 11.21 opens both files and calls procedures `Preamble` and `PutBody`. The main program displays a message before data entry begins and a message after the letter is completed.

FIGURE 11.21   Form Letter Writing Program

```
% The "Formlet" program
% Write a job application letter to an output file.
% The data for the letter preamble is read
% from the keyboard.
% The letter body is copied from a data file to
% the output file.

% Insert procedures Preamble and PutBody here

var BodyFile : int     % File number of letter body
open : BodyFile, "BodyFile", get
                          % Prepare to read from file
var Letter : int       % File number of letter
open : Letter, "Letter", put
                          % Prepare to write to file

put "Writing job application letter"
Preamble (Letter)
PutBody (BodyFile, Letter)
put "Letter copied to output file"
```

Coding the Procedures

Procedure Preamble (see Fig. 11.22) reads the strings needed for the letter heading and salutation from the keyboard. After data entry, the strings read into Date, Employer, Company, Address, CityState are written to file Letter.

FIGURE 11.22   Procedure Preamble

```
procedure Preamble (Letter : int)
    % Write a preamble for a job application letter to
    % an output file whose number is in Letter
    % Pre : The output file is opened
    % Post: Write the heading, salutation, and first
    %       sentence of a job application letter using
    %       data entered at the keyboard

    const DateIndent := 30     % Start of date

    var Date      : string     % Input - data strings
    var Employer  : string
    var Company   : string
    var Address   : string
    var CityState : string
```

```
                  % Enter all data
                  put "Today's date          > " ..
                  get Date : *
                  put "Employer name         > " ..
                  get Employer : *
                  put "Company name          > " ..
                  get Company : *
                  put "Address               > " ..
                  get Address : *
                  put "City, state/province > " ..
                  get CityState : *

                  % Write letter preamble
                  put : Letter, "" : DateIndent, Date, skip
                  put : Letter, Employer
                  put : Letter, Company
                  put : Letter, Address
                  put : Letter, CityState, skip
                  put : Letter, "Dear ", Employer, ":", skip
                  put : Letter, "     I am interested in applying ",
                        "for a job at "
                  put : Letter, Company, ".", skip
              end Preamble
```

Procedure `PutBody` copies the body of the letter (not shown) from the input file to the output file. Procedure `PutBody` is shown in Fig. 11.23. The loop copies each line of the data file to the output file.

FIGURE 11.23   Procedure PutBody

```
procedure PutBody (BodyFile, Letter : int)
    % Copy the body of a job application letter from a
    % data file to an output file
    % Pre : The input file and output file are opened
    % Post: Write the letter body to the output file

    var OneLine : string            % Next data line

    % Copy each line until done
    loop
        exit when eof (BodyFile)    % End of the file?
        get : BodyFile, OneLine : *
        put : Letter, OneLine
    end loop
end PutBody
```

Testing   You should test procedure `Preamble` using a driver program before running the form letter program. Try to read strings from the keyboard giving the heading information for the letter to verify that the first part of the letter is created correctly. In running the form letter program, try using an empty file `BodyFile`.

Exercises for Section 11.8

Self-Check

1. Procedure `Preamble` displays several character strings. What would happen if the user typed nothing but a carriage return for the requested date?

Programming

1. Add a test to the `PutBody` procedure to see if a line read from the file is longer than 80 characters. If so, display the error message `"Line too long!!!"`.

11.9 Searching and Sorting an Array

In this section, we will discuss two common problems in processing arrays: *searching* an array to determine the location of a particular value and *sorting* an array to rearrange the array elements in sequence. As an example of an array search, we might wish to search the array of exam scores read in by procedure `ReadScores` (see Fig. 11.15) to determine which student, if any, got a particular score. An example of an array sort would be rearranging the array elements so that they are in increasing (or decreasing) order by score. This would be helpful if we want to display the list in order by score or if we need to locate several different scores in the array.

Array Search

We can search an array for a particular score (called the search *target*) by examining each array element, starting with the first, and testing to see whether it matches the target score. If a match occurs, we have found the target and can return its subscript as the search result. If a match does not occur, we should continue searching until we either get a match or we test all array elements without success. The data requirements and algorithm for a search function follow.

DATA REQUIREMENTS FOR SEARCH

Input Parameters
```
Scores    : ScoreArray    % The array to be searched
ClassSize : ClassRange     % The number of elements
                           % in Scores
Target    : int            % The score being searched
                           % for
```

Function Output

The subscript of the first element containing `Target` or zero if `Target` was not found

ALGORITHM FOR SEARCH

1. for Next : 1 .. ClassSize
      check Next element of the `Scores` array
      if the current element matches the target then
          Return, setting result of `Search` function to Next
      end if
    end for
2. Return, setting result to zero.

The `for` loop in step 1 executes until it finds the target in the array or it has tested all array elements without success. If it locates `Target` in the array, it returns from the function with a result which is the current subscript. Step 2 executes only if the target was not located, in which case step 2 returns a result of zero. Fig. 11.24 shows function `Search`.

FIG. 11.24   Function Search

```
function Search (Scores : ScoreArray,
                 ClassSize : ClassRange,
                 Target : int) : int
   % Search for Target in array Scores
   % Pre : 1 <= ClassSize <= MaxSize and
   %       subarray Scores(1..ClassSize) is defined
   % Post: Result is the subscript of Target if found;
   %       otherwise, result is zero

   % Compare Target with values in Scores
   for Next : 1 .. ClassSize
      if Scores (Next) = Target then
         result Next
      end if
   end for
   result 0          % Target not found
end Search
```

In the following sketch of *Scores* array

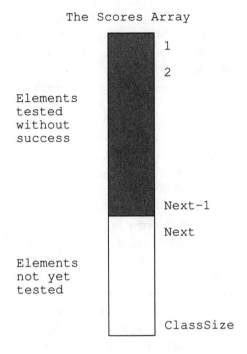

The Scores Array

at the beginning of an iteration of the `for` loop, the elements above `Next` have already been tested, and the element with subscript `Next` will be tested in the current loop iteration. If `Scores(Next)` does not match the target, the shaded portion of the array will grow by one element, and the value of `Next` will increase by one.

If the current element matches the target, the `result` statement in the loop will return the location of the target. If all array elements will have been tested without success (`Next` has effectively gone beyond the end of the `Scores` array), the loop will exit. A result of zero will be returned indicating that the search failed to locate the target.

PROGRAM
STYLE

USING RESULT STATEMENTS INSIDE LOOPS

The function `Search` uses the `result` statement inside a `for` loop. A `result` statement immediately terminates the execution of an entire function and returns as a result the value of its expression.

Stopping a `for` loop in the middle of its range, in this case before its reaches `MaxSize`, has the disadvantage that a person reading the loop may not realize that the last part of the range is not covered. Because of this difficulty, some people prefer the style of placing a `result` statement only at the end of a function. While that style does avoid some complexity, in examples such as function `Search`, it causes the program to be longer and less clear.

> The longer program would need to use a `loop` statement instead of a `for` statement and an extra local `boolean` variable to keep track of whether the target had been located. This variable would be used as the expression in the final `result` statement. To avoid this complexity, we will use a style that favors `result` statements inside loops when this makes the program shorter and clearer.

Sorting an Array

In Section 7.3, we discussed a simple sort operation involving three numbers. We performed the sort by examining pairs of numbers and exchanging them if they were out of order. There are many times when we would like to be able to sort the elements in an array, for example, to print a grade report in order by score.

This section discusses a fairly intuitive (but not very efficient) algorithm called the *selection sort*. To perform a selection sort of an array with N elements (subscripts 1 .. N), we locate the smallest element in the array, and then switch the smallest element with the element at subscript 1, thereby placing the smallest element at position 1. Then we locate the smallest element remaining in the subarray with subscripts 2 .. N, and switch it with the element at subscript 2, thereby placing the second smallest element at position 2. Then we locate the smallest element remaining in subarray 3 .. N and switch it with the element at subscript 3, and so on.

Figure 11.25 traces the operation of the selection sort algorithm. The column on the left shows the original array. Each subsequent column shows the array after the next smallest element is moved to its final position in the array. The shaded part of the array is the subarray that contains the smallest elements of the array in sorted order. In the rightmost column in Fig. 11.25, we know that the entire array has been sorted because all but the last are in order and the largest element is the final one. Note that it will require, at most, N-1 exchanges to sort an array with N elements. The algorithm follows.

ALGORITHM FOR SELECTION SORT
1. for Fill : 1 .. N - 1
    2. Find the position of the smallest element
        in subarray Fill .. N.
    3. if Fill is not the position of the smallest element then
        4. Switch the smallest element with the one at
            position Fill.
        end if
    end for

FIG. 11.25   Trace of Selection Sort

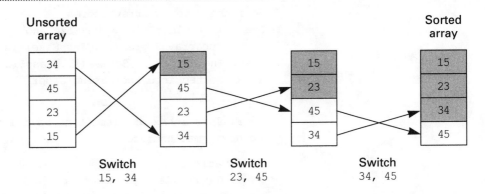

To refine step 2 of the selection sort algorithm, we need a loop that searches for the smallest element in the subarray with subscripts Fill .. N. This loop must save the index of the smallest element found so far, and compare each new element to the smallest so far. If a new element is smaller than the smallest so far, the index of the new element is saved.

Step 2 Refinement

> 2.1 Initialize the position of the smallest so far to Fill.
> 2.2 for Next : Fill+1 .. N
> > 2.3 if the element at Next < the smallest so far then
> > > 2.4 Reset the position of the smallest so
> > > > far to Next
> > > end if
> > end for

Procedure SelectSort in Fig. 11.26 implements the selection sort algorithm for the array Scores. Local variable IndexOfMin holds the location of the smallest exam score found so far in the current subarray. After each execution of the inner for loop, procedure Switch is called to exchange the elements with subscripts IndexOfMin and Fill, provided that IndexOfMin and Fill are different. After the execution of procedure SelectSort, the exam scores will be in increasing order by exam score.

FIG. 11.26   Selection Sort Procedure

```
procedure Switch (var Num1, Num2 : int)
    % Switch values of Num1 and Num2
    % Pre : none
    % Post: Num1 is old Num2, and Num2 is old Num1

    const Temp := Num1
    Num1 := Num2
    Num2 := Temp
end Switch
```

```
    procedure SelectSort (var Scores : ScoreArray,
                          ClassSize : ClassRange)
% Sort the data in array Scores
% Pre : 1 <= ClassSize <= MaxSize and
%          subarray Scores(1..ClassSize) is defined
% Post: The values in Scores(1..ClassSize) have been
%          sorted into increasing order

for Fill : 1 .. ClassSize-1
    % Fill is index of element to be filled with
    % next smallest score

    % Invariant:
    %    The smallest elements are in
    %    Scores(1..Fill-1) and are in order and
    %    Fill <= ClassSize

    % Find the position of smallest element in
    % Scores(Fill .. ClassSize)

    var IndexOfMin : ClassRange := Fill
        % IndexOfMin is index of smallest so far
    for Next : Fill+1 .. ClassSize
        % Next locates the element being compared to
        % smallest so far

        % Invariant:
        %    The element at IndexOfMin is the smallest
        %    in Scores(Fill .. Next-1)

        if Scores(Next) < Scores(IndexOfMin) then
            IndexOfMin := Next
        end if
    end for

    % Assert: Element at IndexOfMin is smallest in
    % Scores(Fill .. ClassSize)

    % Exchange elements with subscripts Fill
    % and IndexOfMin
    if IndexOfMin not= Fill then
        Switch (Scores(Fill), Scores(IndexOfMin))
    end if
end for
end SelectSort
```

The loop invariant for the outer loop

```
% Invariant:
%    The smallest elements are in
%    Scores(1..Fill-1) and are in order and
%    Fill <= ClassSize
```

summarizes the progress of selection sort. The subarray whose elements are in their proper place is shaded in the sketch below. The remaining elements are all larger than Scores(Fill-1).

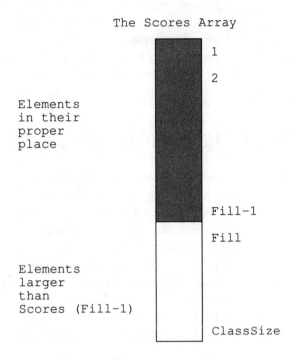

The Scores Array

Elements in their proper place

Elements larger than Scores (Fill-1)

1
2
Fill-1
Fill
ClassSize

During each pass, the shaded portion of the array grows by one element and Fill is incremented to reflect this. When the outer for loop finishes, and Fill is effectively equal to ClassSize, the first ClassSize-1 elements will be in their proper place, so Scores(ClassSize) must also be in its proper place.

Exercises for Section 11.9

Self-Check

1. Explain the loop invariant for the inner for loop and sketch its meaning.
2. Consider the Search function in Fig. 11.24. What happens if the last student score matches the target? What happens if there are several scores that match the target?
3. Trace the execution of the selection sort on the list below. Show the array after each exchange occurs. How many exchanges are required? How many comparisons? 10 55 34 56 76 5
4. How could you modify the selection sort to get the scores in descending order (largest score first)?

Programming

1. Write a procedure to count the number of students with a passing grade on the exam (60 or higher).
2. Another method of performing the selection sort is to place the largest value in position N, the next largest value in position N−1, and so on. Write this version.
3. Re-write the Search function so that it has only one result statement, located at the end of the function body.

11.10 Analysis of Algorithms: Big-O Notation (Optional)

There are many algorithms for searching and sorting arrays. Since arrays can have a very large number of elements, the time required to process all the elements of an array can become significant. Therefore, it is important to have some idea of the relative efficiency of different algorithms. It is very difficult to get a precise measure of the performance of an algorithm or program. For this reason, we normally try to approximate the effect on an algorithm of a change in the number of items, N, that it processes. In this way, we can see how an algorithm's execution time increases with N, so we can compare two algorithms by examining their growth rates.

For example, if we determine that the expression

$$2N^2 + N - 5$$

expresses the relationship between processing time and N, we say that the algorithm is an $O(N^2)$ algorithm where O is an abbreviation for Order of Magnitude. (This notation is called *Big-O Notation*.) The reason that this is an $O(N^2)$ algorithm instead of an $O(2N^2)$ algorithm or an $O(N^2 + N - 5)$ is that we are only interested in the fastest growing term (the one with the largest exponent) and we ignore constants.

To search an array of N elements for a target, we have to examine all N elements when the target is not present in the array. If the target is in the array, then we only have to search until we find it. However, it could be anywhere in the array and it is equally likely to be at the beginning of the array as at the end of the array. So on average, we have to examine $N/2$ array elements to locate a target value that is in an array. This means that an array search is an $O(N)$ process, so the growth rate is linear.

To determine the efficiency of a sorting algorithm, we normally focus on the number of array element comparisons and exchanges that it requires. To perform a selection sort on an array with N elements requires N-1 comparisons during the first pass through the array, N-2 comparisons during the second pass, and so on. Therefore, the total number of comparisons is represented by the series

$$1 + 2 + 3 + \ldots + (N - 2) + (N - 1)$$

The value of this series is expressed in closed form below.

$$\frac{N*(N-1)}{2} = N^2/2 - N/2$$

The number of comparisons performed in sorting an array of N elements using selection sort is always the same; however, the number of array element exchanges varies depending on the initial ordering of the array elements. During the search for the kth smallest element, the inner `for` loop sets `IndexOfMin` to the index of the kth smallest element in the array. If `IndexOfMin` is set to k, this means that the kth smallest element is already in its correct place, so no exchange takes place. If this never happens, there will be one exchange at the end of each iteration of the outer loop or a total of N-1 exchanges (*worst-case situation*). If the array happens to be sorted before procedure `SelectSort` is called, all its elements will be in their proper place, so there will be zero exchanges (*best-case situation*). Therefore, the number of array element exchanges for an arbitrary initial ordering is between zero and N-1 which is $O(N)$.

Because the dominant term in the expression for the number of comparisons shown earlier is $N^2/2$, selection sort is considered an $O(N^2)$ process and the growth rate is quadratic (proportional to the square of the number of elements). What difference does it make whether an algorithm is an $O(N)$ process or an $O(N^2)$ process? Table 10.6 evaluates N and N^2 for different values of N. A doubling of N causes N^2 to increase by a factor of 4. Since N^2 increases much more quickly than N, the performance of an $O(N)$ algorithm is not as adversely affected by an increase in array size as is an $O(N^2)$ algorithm. For large values of N (say 100 or more), the differences in performance for an $O(N)$ and $O(N^2)$ algorithm are significant.

TABLE 11.6

Table of Values of N and N^2

N	N^2
2	4
4	16
8	64
16	256
32	1024
64	4096
128	16384
256	65536
512	262144

There are other factors besides the number of comparisons and exchanges that affect an algorithm's performance. For example, one algorithm may take more time preparing for each exchange or comparison than another. Also, one algorithm might exchange subscripts whereas another algorithm might exchange the array elements themselves. The latter can be more time-consuming. Another measure of efficiency is the amount of memory required by an algorithm. There are many techniques for searching and sorting that are considerably more efficient than the simple ones discussed so far.

Exercises for Section 11.10

Self-Check

1. Determine how many times the `put` statement is executed in each fragment below. Indicate whether the algorithm is $O(N)$ or $O(N^2)$.

    a. ```
    for I : 1 .. N
      for J : 1 .. N
        put I, " ", J)
      end for
    end for
    ```

    b. ```
    for I : 1 .. N
      for J : 1 .. 2
        put I, " ", J)
      end for
    end for
    ```

    c. ```
    for I : 1 .. N
      for decreasing J : N .. I
        put I, " ", J)
      end for
    end for
    ```

### Programming

1. Write a program fragment that compares the values of *Y1* and *Y2* below for *N* up to 100 in increments of 10. Does the result surprise you?

    $$Y1 = 100N + 10$$
    $$Y2 = 5N^2 + 2$$

# 11.11 Common Programming Errors

A common run-time error when using arrays is an index expression out of bounds. This error occurs when the subscript value is outside the allowable range for the array being processed. Most often, this error is caused by an incorrect subscript expression, an incorrect `loop` counter, or a nonterminating `loop`. Before you spend considerable time debugging, you should carefully check all suspect subscript calculations for out-of-range errors. You can check most easily by inserting diagnostic output state-
    ```

ments in your program in order to print subscript values that might be out of range.

If an out-of-range subscript occurs inside a `loop`, you should make sure that the `loop` is terminating properly. If the `loop` control variable is not being updated as expected, the loop may be repeated more often than required.

You should also doublecheck the subscript values at the `loop` boundaries. If these values are in range, it is likely that all other subscript references in the loop will be in range as well.

As with all Turing data types, make sure that there are no type inconsistencies. The subscript type and element type used in all array references must correspond to the types specified in the array declaration. Similarly, the types of two arrays used in an array copy statement or as corresponding parameters must be the same.

You must use a star (*) as the upper bound of a variable array parameter if it is to be able to handle actual parameter arrays of various lengths. Similarly, a star should be used as the maximum length of a variable string parameter that is to handle actual parameter strings of various lengths.

Chapter Review

This chapter introduced a data structure called an array, a convenient facility for naming and referencing a collection of like items. We discussed how to declare an array type and how to reference an individual array element by placing a subscript in brackets, following the array name.

The `for` statement enables us to easily reference the elements of an array in sequence. We used `for` statements to initialize arrays, to read and print arrays, and to control the manipulation of individual array elements in sequence.

We also learned how to specify a maximum length for strings to save memory space. For variable (`var`) parameters, this length should be given as a star.

In a similar way, the upper bound of a variable array parameter must be given as a star if there are calls that pass actual arrays or various lengths to this parameter.

Two common operations involving arrays were discussed: searching an array and sorting an array. We wrote a function for searching an array and also described the selection sort procedure. Finally, we discussed how to use Big-O notation as a measure of an algorithm's efficiency.

New Turing Constructs in Chapter 11

The new Turing constructs introduced in this chapter are described in Table 11.7.

TABLE 11.7   Summary of New Turing Constructs

Construct	Effect
Array Declaration	

`type IndexRange : 1 .. 10`
`type IntArray :`
   `array 1..10 of int`
	The data type `IntArray` describes an array with 10 integer elements

`var Cube, Count : IntArray`	`Cube` and `Count` are arrays with this structure
Array References	

`for I : 1 .. 10`
   `Cube(I) := I ** 3`
`end for`
	Save I^3 in the `I`th element of array `Cube`

`if Cube(5) > 100 then`	Compare `Cube[5]` to 100
`put Cube(1), " ", Cube(2)`	Display the first two cubes
Array Copy	
`Count := Cube`	Copy contents of array `Cube` to array `Count`
Maximum Length for Strings	
`type String10 : string (10)`	The data type `String10` describes a string whose maximum length is 10
`var name : String10`	`Name` is a string whose value can be at most 10 characters long
Star Bound for Arrays	
`procedure Percent` `( var A : 1 .. * of real )`	The data type of `A` is an array whose upper bound is determined by its actual parameter
Star Maximum Length for Strings	
`procedure Nullify` `( var S : string (*))`	The data type of `S` is a string whose maximum length is determined by its actual parameter

Quick-Check Exercises

1. What is a data structure?
2. Which standard types cannot be array subscript types?
3. Can values of different types be stored in an array?
4. If an array is declared to have ten elements, must the program use all ten?

5. When can the assignment operator be used with an array as its operands? Answer the same question for the equality operator.
6. The two methods of array access are _____ and _____.
7. The _____ loop allows us to access the elements of an array in _____ order.
8. Explain when you should use a star as the upper bound of an array.
9. When is the appropriate situation to give a maximum length for a string type?

Answers to Quick-Check Exercises

1. A data structure is a grouping of related values in main memory.
2. `string`, `real` and `boolean`; all can be element types.
3. No
4. No
5. Assignment can be used when the arrays have equivalent types (the same element types and the same bounds). It is not allowed to use the equality operator with arrays.
6. Direct and sequential
7. `for`, sequential
8. In the header of a subprogram, when declaring a variable array parameter that is to be passed arrays of differing upper bounds in various calls.
9. When there is a possibility of running out of memory space.

Review Questions

1. Identify the error in the following program. When will the error be detected?

```
% The "test" program
type AnArray : array 1..8 of int
var X : AnArray
for I : 1 .. 9
    X(I) := I
end for
```

2. Declare an array of real numbers called `Week` that can be referenced by using any day of the week as a subscript, where `Sunday` is the first subscript.
3. Identify the error in the following segment of Turing program.

```
type AnArray : array string of real
var X : AnArray
var I : string
I := "A"
X(I) := 8.384
```

4. In the following Turing program, is the final statement valid?

```
type RealArray : array 1..8 of real
var X : RealArray
var I : int
I := 1
X(I) := 8.384
```

5. What are two common ways of selecting array elements for processing?
6. Write a Turing program segment to print out the index of the smallest and the largest numbers in an array X of 20 integers with values within the range 0 to 100. Assume array X already has values assigned to each element.
7. The parameters for a procedure are two arrays (type `RealArray`) and an integer representing the length of the arrays. The procedure copies the first array in the parameter list to the other array in reverse order using a loop structure. Write the procedure.

Programming Projects

1. Write a program for the following problem. You are given a collection of integer scores for the last exam in your computer course. You are to compute the average of these scores, and then assign grades to each student according to the following rule.

    If a student's score is within 10 points (above or below) of the average, assign the student a grade of `Satisfactory`. If the score is more than 10 points higher than the average, assign the student a grade of `Outstanding`. If the score is more than 10 points below the average, assign the student a grade of `Unsatisfactory`.

    The output from your program should consist of a labeled two-column list that shows each score and its corresponding grade. As a part of the solution, your program should include functions and procedures that correspond to the headers that follow.

```
const MaxSize := 40

type ArrayType : array 1 .. MaxSize of int

procedure ReadStuData (RawScores : int,
            var Score : ArrayType,
            var Count : int,
            var TooMany : boolean)
    % Read exam scores from the open file whose file
    % number is RawScores.
    % Count returns number of students read.
    % TooMany is set to true if RawScores is larger
    % than MaxSize.
```

```
procedure PutGrade (OneScore : int,
                        Average : real)
    % Display student grade after comparing OneScore
    % to Average

function Mean (Score : ArrayType,
                  Count : int) : real
    % Compute average of Count student scores

procedure PutTable (Score : ArrayType,
                        Count : int)
    % Display a table showing each student's score
    % and grade on a separate line
    % Uses: PutGrade
```

2. Redo programming project 1 assuming that each line of file
   RawScores contains a student's ID number (an integer) and an exam
   score. Modify procedure ReadStuData to read the ID number and the
   score from the Ith data line into array elements ID(I) and Score(I),
   respectively. Modify procedure PutTable to display a three-column
   table with the following headings:

   ID   Score   Grade

3. Write a program to read N data items into two arrays X and Y of size
   20. Store the product of corresponding elements of X and Y in a third
   array Z, also of size 20. Print a three-column table displaying the arrays
   X, Y, and Z. Then compute and print the square root of the sum of the
   items in Z. Make up your own data, with N less than 20.

4. Another approach to sorting an array is to create another array called
   Index, whose element values represent array subscripts. The use of
   Index allows us to access the elements of a second array in sequential
   order without rearranging the second array's element values. After sorting, the first element of the index will contain the subscript of the smallest array element; the second element of the index will contain the subscript of the second smallest element; and so on. As an example, if the
   array Scores contains the exam scores 60, 90, 50, 100, 75, the array
   ScoresIndex should contain the subscripts 3, 1, 5, 2, 4.
   ScoresIndex tells us that the third element of Scores is the smallest,
   the first element of Scores is the second smallest, and so on. Modify
   procedure SelectSort so that it creates an Index array for Scores
   without rearranging the elements in Scores.

5. The results of a true-false exam given to a Computer Science class have
   been coded for input to a program. The information available for each
   student consists of a student identification number and the students'
   answers to 10 true-false questions. The available data are as follows:

	Student	
	Identification	Answer String
	0080	FTTFTFTTFT
	0340	FTFTFTTTFF
	0341	FTTFTTTTTT
	0401	TTFFTFFTTT
	0462	TTFTTTFFTF
	0463	TTTTTTTTTT
	0464	FTFFTFFTFT
	0512	TFTFTFTFTF
	0618	TTTFFTTFTF
	0619	FFFFFFFFFF
	0687	TFTTFTTFTF
	0700	FTFFTTFFFT
	0712	FTFTFTFTFT
	0837	TFTFTTFTFT

Write a program that first reads in the answer string representing the 10 correct answers (use FTFFTFFTFT as data). Next, for each student, read the student's data and compute and store the number of correct answers for each student in one array, and store the student ID number in the corresponding element of another array. Determine the best score, Best. Then print a three-column table displaying the ID number, score, and grade for each student. The grade should be determined as follows: If the score is equal to Best or Best-1, give an A; if it is Best-2 or Best-3, give a C. Otherwise, given an F.

6. Modify the test scoring program developed for programming project 5 to allow for multiple-choice questions having answers A through E. Compute the average number of correct answers, the range of scores (that is, largest number correct to smallest number correct), and the average of the grades assigned (use the grade point equivalencies A = 4.0, C = 2.0, and F = 0.0.

7. The results of a survey of the households in your township have been made available. Each record contains data for one household, including a four-digit integer identification number, the annual income for the household, and the number of members of the household. Write a program to read the survey results into three arrays and perform the following analyses:

i)   Count the number of households included in the survey and print a three-column table displaying the data read in. (You may assume that no more than 25 households were surveyed.)

ii) Calculate the average household income, and list the identification number and income of each household that exceeds the average.

iii) Determine the percentage of households having incomes below the poverty level. The poverty level income may be computed using the formula

$$p = \$6500.00 + \$750.00 * (m - 2)$$

where m is the number of members of each household. This formula shows that the poverty level depends on the number of family members, m, and the poverty level increases as m gets larger.

Test your program on the following data.

Identification Number	Annual Income	Household Members
1041	$12,180	4
1062	13,240	3
1327	19,800	2
1483	22,458	8
1900	17,000	2
2112	18,125	7
2345	15,623	2
3210	3,200	6
3600	6,500	5
3601	11,970	2
4725	8,900	3
6217	10,000	2
9280	6,200	1

8. Assume that your computer has the very limited capability of being able to read and write only single decimal digits and to add together two integers consisting of one decimal digit each. Write a program to read in two integers of up to 30 digits each, add these numbers together, and print the result. Test your program using pairs of numbers of varying lengths.

   Hint: Store the two numbers in two arrays of size 30, one decimal digit per element . If the number is less than 30 digits in length, enter enough leading zeros (to the left of the number) to make the number 30 digits long.

   You will need a loop to add together the digits in corresponding array elements, starting with the element with subscript 30. Don't forget to handle the carry if there is one! Use a `boolean` variable `Carry` to indicate whether or not the sum of the last pair of digits is greater than 9.

9. Assume a set of sentences is to be processed. Each sentence consists of a sequence of words, separated by one or more blank spaces. Write a program that will read these sentences and count the number of words with one letter, two letters, etc., up to 10 letters.

10. Write an interactive program that plays the game of Hangman. Read the word to be guessed into string `Word`. The player must guess the letters belonging to `Word`. The program should terminate when either all letters have been guessed correctly (player wins) or a specified number of incorrect guesses have been made (computer wins).

    Hint: Use a string `Solution` to keep track of the solution so far. Initialize `Solution` to a string of symbols `"*"`. Each time a letter in `Word` is guessed, replace the corresponding `"*"` in `Solution` with that letter.

Records

The previous chapter introduced the array, a data structure fundamental to programming and included in almost every high-level programming language. In this chapter we will examine an additional data structure, the record, that is available in Turing but not in all other high-level languages. Records can make it easier to organize and represent information in Turing.

Like an array, a record is a collection of related data items. However, unlike an array, the individual components of a record can contain data of different types. We can use a record to store a variety of information about a person, such as the person's name, marital status, age, date of birth, etc. Each data item is stored in a separate record field; we can reference each data item stored in a record through its field name.

In this chapter we revisit abstract data types. This abstract data type will consist of a record type and associated operators. We develop an abstract data type and associated operators.

12.1 The Record Data Type

A *data base* is a collection of information or facts stored in a computer memory or a disk file. A data base is subdivided into records, where a record normally contains all the information that we wish to save regarding a particular data object. For example, the description of a person, place, or thing would be stored as a record.

Record Type Declaration

Before a record can be created or saved, the record format must be specified through a record type declaration.

EXAMPLE 12.1
The staff of our small software firm is growing rapidly. To keep our records more accessible and organized, we decide to store relevant data, such as the descriptive information shown below, in an employee data base.

```
ID: 1234
Name: Caryn Jackson
Gender: Female
Number of Dependents: 2
Hourly Rate: 16.00
Total wages: 640.00
```

We can declare a record type `Employee` to store this information. There must be six *fields* in the record type. We must specify the name of each field and the type of information stored in each field. The names will be chosen in the same way as all other identifiers in this book: they should describe the nature of the information represented. The content of each field is used to determine the appropriate data type. For example, the employee's name should be stored in a string field.

The record type `Employee` declared below has six distinct fields. One is a subrange, two are `string` types, one is an `int`, and two are type `real`.

```
type IDRange : 1111..9999
type NameType : string (20)
type GenderType : string(1)

type Employee :
    record
        ID : IDRange
        Name : NameType
        Gender : GenderType
        NumDepend : int
        Rate, TotWages : real
    end record
```

The `record` type is a template that describes the format of each record and the name of each individual data element. A variable declaration is required to allocate storage space for a record. The record variables `Clerk` and `Janitor` are declared next.

```
var Clerk, Janitor : Employee
```

The record variables `Clerk` and `Janitor` both have the structure specified in the declaration for record type `Employee`. Thus, the memory allocated for each consists of storage space for six distinct values. The record variable `Clerk` is pictured below assuming the values shown earlier are stored in memory.

The Record Variable Clerk

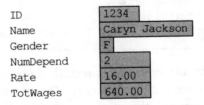

ID	1234
Name	Caryn Jackson
Gender	F
NumDepend	2
Rate	16.00
TotWages	640.00

As illustrated in the type declaration for `Employee`, each of the fields of a record can be a standard data type or a user-defined simple or structured data type. The record type definition is described in the next display.

Manipulating Individual Fields of a Record

We can reference a record field by using a *field selector* consisting of the record variable name followed by the field name. A period is used to separate the field name and record name.

RECORD TYPE DEFINITION

Form:
```
record
        id list₁ : type₁
        id list₂ : type₂
        ...
        id listₙ : typeₙ
end record
```

Example:
```
type Complex :
    record
            RealPart, ImaginaryPart : real
    end record
```

Interpretation: The identifier `Complex` is the name of the record structure being described. Each *id list*$_i$ is a list of one or more field names separated by commas. The data type of each field in *id list*$_i$ is specified by *type*$_i$.

Note: *Type*$_i$ may be any standard or user-defined data type including a structured type.

EXAMPLE 12.2

Figure 12.1 gives an example of the record variable `Clerk`. The data shown earlier could be stored in `Clerk` through the sequence of assignment statements

FIGURE 12.1   Record Variable Clerk

```
Clerk.ID := 1234
Clerk.Name := "Caryn Jackson"
Clerk.Gender := "F"
Clerk.NumDepend := 2
Clerk.Rate := 16.00
Clerk.TotWages := Clerk.TotWages + Clerk.Rate * 40.0
```

Once data are stored in a record, they can be manipulated in the same way as other data in memory. For example, the assignment statement above computes the clerk's new taxable salary by adding this week's wages to her previous total wages. The computed result is saved in the record field named `Clerk.TotWages`.

The statements

```
put "The clerk is " ..
if Clerk.Gender = "F" then
    put "Ms. " ..
else
    put "Mr. " ..
end if
put Clerk.Name
```

display the clerk's name after an appropriate title (Ms. or Mr.). The output line follows.

```
The clerk is Ms. Caryn Jackson
```

Abstract Record

We can summarize what we have learned about records in the specification for an abstract record shown below.

SPECIFICATION FOR ABSTRACT RECORD

Structure: A record is a collection of related data values of different types. Each data value is stored in a separate field of the record.

Operators: There are two basic operations that act on fields of a record: store and retrieve. The store operation inserts a value into the record field. If A is a record with a field named B and C is an expression that is assignment compatible with the type of field B, the statement

```
A.B := C
```

stores the contents of C in field B of record A. If field B of record A is assignment compatible with the type of variable C, the statement

```
C := A.B
```

retrieves the value in field B of record A and copies it into C.

The assignment operator may also be used to copy the contents of one record to another of the same type. If A and D are record variables of the same type, the statement

```
A := D
```

copies all values associated with record D to record A.

Exercises for Section 12.1

Self-Check

1. Each part in an inventory is represented by its part number, a descriptive name, the quantity on hand, and price. Define a record type Part.
2. A catalogue listing for a textbook consists of the author's name, title, publisher, and year of publication. Declare a record type CatalogueEntry and variable Book and write assignment statements that store the relevant data for this textbook in Book.

12.2   Records as Operands and Parameters

Since arithmetic and logical operations can only be performed on individual memory cells, record variables cannot be used as the operands of arithmetic and relational operators. These operators must be used with individual fields of a record as shown in the previous section. Similarly, the `get` and `put` statements can be used with the individual fields of a record, but not with an entire record. There are statements called `read` and `write`, not covered in this chapter, that can be used to transfer entire records from a variable to a disk file and from a disk file to a variable.

Record Assignment

We can copy all the fields of one record variable to another record variable of the same type using a record copy (assignment) statement. If `Clerk` and `Janitor` are both record variables of type `Employee`, the statement

```
Clerk := Janitor          % Copy Janitor to Clerk
```

copies each field of `Janitor` into the corresponding field of `Clerk`.

Records as Parameters

A record can be passed as a parameter to a function or procedure provided the actual parameter is the same type as its corresponding formal parameter. It can also be returned as the value of a function. The use of records as parameters can shorten parameter lists considerably because one parameter (the record variable) can be passed instead of several related parameters.

EXAMPLE 12.3
In a grading program, the summary statistics for an exam might consist of the average score, the highest and lowest scores, and the standard deviation. In previous problems, these data would be stored in separate variables; however, it makes sense to group them together as a record.

```
type ExamStats :
   record
      Low, High : 0..100
      Average, StandardDev : real
   end record

var Exam : ExamStats
```

A procedure that computes one of these results (e.g., `Average`) could be passed a single record field (e.g., `Exam.Average`). A procedure that manipulates more than one of these fields could be passed the entire record. An example would be procedure `PrintStat` shown in Fig. 12.2.

FIGURE 12.2

FIGURE 12.2   Procedure PrintStat

```
procedure PrintStat (Exam : ExamStats)
    % Print the exam statistics
    % Pre : The fields of record variable Exam are
    %        assigned values.
    % Post: Each field of Exam is displayed

    put "High score: ", Exam.High
    put "Low score: ", Exam.Low
    put "Average: ", Exam.Average :3:1
    put "Standard deviation: ", Exam.StandardDev : 3:1
end PrintStat
```

EXAMPLE 12.4

Before performing a potentially dangerous or costly experiment in the laboratory, we can often use a computer program to simulate the experiment. In computer simulations, we need to keep track of the time of day as the experiment progresses. Normally, the time of day is updated after a certain time period has elapsed. The record type `Time` is declared below, assuming a 24-hour clock.

```
type Time :
    record
        Hour : 0..23
        Minute, Second : 0..59
    end record
```

Procedure `ChangeTime` in Fig. 12.3 updates the time of day, `TimeOfDay` (type `Time`), after a time interval, `ElapsedTime`, expressed in seconds. Each statement that uses the `mod` operator updates a particular field of the record represented by `TimeOfDay`. The `mod` operator ensures that each updated value is within the required range; the `div` operator converts multiples of sixty seconds to minutes and multiples of sixty minutes to hours.

FIGURE 12.3   Procedure ChangeTime

```
procedure ChangeTime (ElapsedTime : int,
                        var TimeOfDay : Time)
    % Update the time of day, TimeOfDay, assuming
    % a 24-hour clock and an elapsed time of
    % ElapsedTime in seconds
    % Pre : ElapsedTime and record TimeOfDay are
    %        assigned values
    % Post: TimeOfDay is "incremented" by ElapsedTime
```

```
    const NewSec := TimeOfDay.Second + ElapsedTime
            % Total seconds
    TimeOfDay.Second := NewSec mod 60
            % Seconds mod 60
    const NewMin := TimeOfDay.Minute + (NewSec div 60)
            % Total minutes
    TimeOfDay.Minute := NewMin mod 60
            % Minutes mod 60
    const NewHour := TimeOfDay.Hour + (NewMin div 60)
            % Total hours
    TimeOfDay.Hour := NewHour mod 24
            % Hours mod 24
end ChangeTime
```

Reading a Record

Normally, we will use a procedure to read data into a record. Procedure GetEmployee in Fig. 12.4 could be used to read data into the first five fields of a record variable of type Employee. Since we are passing a record variable to GetEmployee, only one parameter is needed, not six. The procedure call statement

```
    GetEmployee (Clerk)
```

causes the data read to be stored in record variable Clerk.

FIGURE 12.4   Procedure GetEmployee

```
procedure GetEmployee (var OneClerk : Employee)
    % Read one employee record into OneClerk
    % Pre : None
    % Post: Data are read into record OneClerk

    put "ID> " ..
    get OneClerk.ID
    put "Name> " ..
    get OneClerk.Name
    put "Sex (F or M)> " ..
    get OneClerk.Gender
    put "Number of dependents> " ..
    get OneClerk.NumDepend
    put "Hourly rate> " ..
    get OneClerk.Rate
    put "Total wages to date > " ..
    get OneClerk.TotWages
end GetEmployee
```

Exercises for Section 12.2

Self-Check

1. What does the program segment below do? Provide the declarations for variables Exam1 and Exam2.

```
PrintStat (Exam1)
Exam2 := Exam1
Exam2.High := Exam2.High - 5.0
PrintStat (Exam2)
```

2. If all fields of variable Now (type Time) are initially zero, how is Now changed by the execution of these statements?

```
ChangeTime (3600, Now)
ChangeTime (7125, Now)
```

Programming

1. Write a procedure that initializes all fields of a variable of type Time to zero.
2. Write a procedure to read in the data for a record variable of type CatalogueEntry. See Exercise 2 at the end of Section 12.1.
3. Write a procedure that reads in the coordinates of a point (type Point) on the X-Y plane.

12.3 Abstract Data Types Revisited

Abstraction is an important tool in programming. Procedural abstraction enables us to focus on the operations that we want to perform without having to provide immediately the details of how each operation will be implemented.

Data abstraction is the technique of focusing on the data and the operations to be performed without being concerned about how the data are actually represented in memory. Chapter 10 shows how to implement an abstract data type consisting of a data type and its relevant operators. The abstract data type may be saved as a separate file and inserted in a Turing program as needed.

The program that uses an abstract data type is called the *client program*. A client program can declare and manipulate objects of this data type and use the data type's operators without knowing the details of the internal representation of the data type or the implementation of its operators; these details are hidden from the client program (called *information hiding* by computer scientists). In this way we separate the use of the data and operators (by the client program) from the representation and implementation (by the abstract data type).

This provides several advantages. It allows us to implement the client program and abstract data type relatively independent of each other. If we decide to change the implementation of an operator (procedure) in the abstract data type, we can do this without affecting the client program. Finally, since the internal representation of a data type is hidden from its client program, we can even change the internal representation at a later time without modifying the client.

Abstract Data Type EmpRecADT

Whenever we declare a new record type, we should determine what operators are needed to process a record variable of that type and consider encapsulating the new type and its operators in an abstract data type. At the very least, we should provide operators for reading and writing a record. We may also provide operators that set and retrieve individual field values. We may want to provide an operator that compares two record variables for equality. Figure 12.5 shows the specification for abstract data type EmpRecADT.

FIGURE 12.5 Specification for EmpRecADT

```
% Specification of EmpRecADT

% Structure: A record variable of type Employee
%       contains storage space for data items that
%       describe a single employee, such as the
%       employee's ID number, name, gender, number of
%       dependents, hourly rate, and total
%       accumulated wages.

% Operators: Here is the list of operators for
%       this ADT (EmpRecADT)

procedure CreateEmp (var Emp : Employee)
   % Initialize a new employee record by setting its ID
   % field to 9999, its name and gender fields to
   % blank, and all other fields to 0

procedure StoreID (var Emp : Employee, EmpID : IDRange)
   % Store EmpID, the employee's ID, in record Emp

procedure StoreName (var Emp : Employee, EmpName : NameType)
   % Store EmpName, the employee's name, in record Emp

procedure StoreGender (var Emp : Employee,
                       EmpGender : GenderType)
   % Store EmpGender, the employee's gender, in record Emp
```

```
procedure StoreDepend (var Emp : Employee,
                       EmpDepend : int)
   % Store EmpDepend, the number of dependents, in record
   % Emp

procedure StoreRate (var Emp : Employee, EmpRate : real)
   % Store EmpRate, the employee's hourly rate, in
   % record Emp

procedure StoreTotWages (var Emp : Employee,
                         EmpWages : real)
   % Store EmpWages, the employee's total wages, in
   % record Emp

function FetchId (Emp : Employee) : IDRange
   % Return the ID of Emp

function FetchName (Emp : Employee) : NameType
   % Return the name of Emp

function FetchGender (Emp : Employee) : GenderType
   % Return the gender of Emp

function FetchDepend (Emp : Employee) : int
   % Return the number of dependents for Emp

function FetchRate (Emp : Employee) : real
   % Return the hourly rate for Emp

function FetchTotWages (Emp : Employee) : real
   % Return the total wages for Emp

procedure GetEmp (var Emp : Employee)
   % Enter the data for Emp from the keyboard

procedure PutEmp (Emp : Employee)
   % Display employee Emp

function SameEmp (Emp1, Emp2 : Employee) : boolean
   % Return true if employee Emp1 and Emp2 are identical
   % (that is, corresponding fields are equal)
```

In the specification for EmpRecADT, operators FetchId, FetchName, and so on, that retrieve a value from an employee record are sometimes called *accessor* operators. FetchName is implemented as a function. This is allowed in Turing because functions can return string types as well as scalar types.

Using Abstract Data Type EmpRecADT

We can use abstract data type EmpRecADT to create employee records and process these records without knowing much about record type

Employee. We can use the ADT operators as building blocks to create new client programs and procedures as shown in the next examples.

EXAMPLE 12.5

The following program fragment defines the employee Clerk first shown in Example 12.1.

```
CreateEmp (Clerk)
StoreID (Clerk, 1234)
StoreName (Clerk, "Caryn Jackson")
StoreGender (Clerk, "F")
StoreDepend (Clerk, 2)
StoreRate (Clerk, 16.00)
StoreTotWages (Clerk, 640.00)
```

The first statement initializes variable Clerk. Each of the remaining statements stores the data item passed as its second parameter in Clerk. Using these procedures enables us to do this without knowing the exact structure of data type Employee or its field names.

EXAMPLE 12.6

Figure 12.6 shows procedure UpdateTotWages, which computes weekly wages earned and updates the total wages for the employee record represented by Emp. The weekly wages computation uses the hourly rate that is stored in the employee record.

FIGURE 12.6   Procedure UpdateTotWages

```
procedure UpdateTotWages (var Emp : Employee,
                               Hours : real)
   % Add the weekly wages earned to the total wages
   % for Emp
   % Pre : The hourly rate and total wages for Emp are
   %         defined
   % Post: The total wages for Emp are increased by
   %         hours worked (Hours) times the hourly rate

   const WeekWages := Hours * FetchRate(Emp)
   const NewTotal := FetchTotWages(Emp) + WeekWages
   StoreTotWages (Emp, NewTotal)
end UpdateTotWages
```

Procedure UpdateTotWages uses operators FetchRate and FetchTotWages to retrieve the employee's hourly rate and previous total wages. After the new total is computed, it uses procedure StoreTotWages to store that value in the employee record.

EXAMPLE 12.7
Boolean function `SameIDName` (see Fig. 12.7) returns `true` if the employee record passed as its first argument (type `Employee`) contains the ID and name values passed as its second and third arguments, respectively.

FIGURE 12.7   Function SameIDName

```
function SameIDName (Emp : Employee, EmpID : IDRange,
                     EmpName : NameType) : boolean
   % Determine whether the ID and name fields of Emp
   % are matched.
   % Pre : ID and Name fields of Emp are defined.
   % Post: Returns true if there is a match; otherwise,
   %        returns false

   result FetchId(Emp) = EmpID and
          FetchName(Emp) = EmpName
end SameIDName
```

The following `if` statement calls `SameIDName` to determine whether the values of `AnID` (type `IDRange` and `AName` (type `NameType`) match the ID and name of employee `Clerk`.

```
if SameIDName(Clerk, AnID, AName) then
   put "Employee ", AName, " has ",
       FetchDepend(Clerk), " dependents"
else
   put "Employee's ID and name do not match"
   put "ID is ", FetchId(Clerk)
   put "Name is ", FetchName(Clerk)
end if
```

If both fields match, the if statement displays the employee's name and number of dependents; otherwise, it displays the employee's ID and name.

PROGRAM
STYLE

INITIALIZING AN ABSTRACT DATA TYPE
In Example 12.5, we called procedure `CreateEmp` to initialize a variable of type `Employee` before storing data in that variable. We do not really need to do this; however, it is common practice to call an initialization procedure (sometimes called a *constructor* operator) before using a variable whose type declaration is encapsulated in an abstract data type.

PROGRAM
STYLE

SOFTWARE ENGINEERING: HIDING A RECORD'S INTERNAL REPRESENTATION
In the `if` statement shown earlier, we used the statements

```
put "ID is ", FetchId(Clerk)
put "Name is ", FetchName(Clerk)
```

to retrieve and display the name and ID of employee `Clerk`. If we know that `Clerk` is a record with fields called `ID` and `Name`, then we could use the following statement pair instead.

```
put "ID is ", Clerk.ID
put "Employee's name is ", Clerk.Name
```

However, this has the disadvantage that the qualified identifiers `Clerk.ID` and `Clerk.Name` depend on a particular internal representation for data type `Employee`. If we later decide to change the structure of this data type or rename its fields, the client program that contains this statement would be incorrect. However, if we always use operators `FetchID` and `FetchName` in client programs to retrieve the employee ID and name, then all client programs would still be correct. (We may, however, need to modify and recompile these operators if the internal representation of the record changes.)

Implementing the Abstract Data Type

Figure 12.8 shows the implementation part for abstract data type `EmpRecADT`. Ideally, the implementation part would be hidden from the user of the abstract data type. This would be possible using the `module` feature of Turing, but we have not introduced that feature.

The specification part, shown earlier, contains all the information that a user needs to know. Because of space limitations, we have omitted operators `StoreGender`, `StoreDepend`, `StoreRate`, and `StoreTotWages`, which are very similar to `StoreID`. We have also omitted operators `FetchGender`, `FetchDepend`, `FetchRate`, and `FetchTotWages`, which are very similar to `GetID` (see programming exercise 1 at the end of this section).

FIGURE 11.8   Implementation Part for EmpRecADT

```
% Implementation of EmpRecADT

type IDRange : 1111..9999
type NameType : string (20)
type GenderType : string(1)

type Employee :
   record
      ID : IDRange
      Name : NameType
      Gender : GenderType
      NumDepend : int
      Rate, TotWages : real
   end record
```

```
procedure CreateEmp (var Emp : Employee)
    % Initialize the ID field of a new employee record
    % to 9999, the name and gender fields to blank,
    % and all other fields to 0
    % Pre : None
    % Post: The ID of Emp is 9999, the name and gender
    %        fields are blank, and all other fields are 0.

    Emp.ID := 9999
    Emp.Name := ""
    Emp.Gender := " "
    Emp.NumDepend := 0
    Emp.Rate := 0.0
    Emp.TotWages := 0.0
end CreateEmp

procedure StoreID (var Emp : Employee, EmpID : IDRange)
    % Store EmpID as the ID of Emp
    Emp.ID := EmpID
end StoreID

procedure StoreName (var Emp : Employee,
                        EmpName : NameType)
    % Store EmpName as the name of Emp
    Emp.Name := EmpName
end StoreName

% Insert operators StoreGender, StoreDepend, StoreRate,
% StoreTotWages here

function FetchID (Emp : Employee) : IDRange
    % Return the ID of Emp
    result Emp.ID
end FetchID

function FetchName (Emp : Employee) : NameType
    % Return the name of Emp
    result Emp.Name
end FetchName

% Insert operators FetchGender, FetchDepend, FetchRate,
% FetchTotWages here

procedure GetEmp (var Emp : Employee)
    % Read one employee record into Emp
    % Pre : None
    % Post: Data are read into record Emp

    put "ID> "
    get Emp.ID
    put "Name> "
```

```
      get Emp.Name
      put "Gender (F or M)> "
      get Emp.Gender
      put "Number of dependents> "
      get Emp.NumDepend
      put "Hourly rate> "
      get Emp.Rate
      put "Total Wages > "
      get Emp.TotWages
   end GetEmp

   procedure PutEmp (Emp : Employee)
      % Display record Emp
      % Pre : Emp is defined
      % Post: Display all fields of record OneEmp along a
      %       data line

      put Emp.ID, " ", Emp.Name, " " ..
      put Emp.Gender, " ", Emp.NumDepend. " " ..
      put Emp.Rate :10:2, " ", Emp.TotWages :10:2
   end PutEmp

   function SameEmp (Emp1, Emp2 : Employee) : boolean
      % Compare records Emp1 and Emp2 for equality
      % Pre: Emp1 and Emp2 are initialized.
      % Post: Returns true if records Emp1 and Emp2 are
      %        identical

      result Emp1.ID = Emp2.ID and
             Emp1.Name = Emp2.Name and
             Emp1.Gender = Emp2.Gender and
             Emp1.NumDepend = Emp2.NumDepend and
             Emp1.Rate = Emp2.Rate and
             Emp1.TotWages = Emp2.TotWages
   end SameEmp
```

The body of function `SameEmp` contains a `boolean` expression that is `true` only when all fields of `Emp1` match their corresponding fields in `Emp2`. It returns `false` if any pair of values does not match.

Exercises for Section 12.3

Self-Check

1. What does the program segment below do? What does it display for the two records shown?

```
CreateEmp(MyEmp)
StoreID(MyEmp, 1233)
StoreName(MyEmp, "Jennie Moss")
CreateEmp(YourEmp)
StoreID(YourEmp, 1234)
StoreName(YourEmp, "Jackie Moss")
if SameEmp(MyEmp, YourEmp) then
    put "Duplicate record for employee # ",
        FetchID(MyEmp)
elsif FetchID(YourEmp) = FetchID(MyEmp) then
    put "Error - two records with same ID"
else
    put FetchName(MyEmp), "*****",
        FetchName(YourEmp)
end if
```

Programming

1. Write the following operators.
   a. `FetchGender`, `FetchDepend`, `FetchRate`, and `FetchTotWages`.
   b. `StoreGender`, `StoreDepend`, `StoreRate`, and `StoreTotWages`.
2. Write an operator `ReduceDepend` that reduces the number of dependents of its first parameter by the value of its second parameter.

12.4 Nested Records

In solving any programming problem, we must select data structures that enable us to efficiently represent in the computer a variety of different kinds of information. The selection of data structures is a very important part of the problem solving process. The data structures used can have a profound effect on the efficiency and simplicity of the completed program.

The data structuring facilities in Turing are quite powerful and general. In the previous examples, all record fields were simple types or strings. It is possible to declare a record type with fields that are other structured types. We will call a record type with one or more fields that are record types a *nested record*.

We began our study of records by introducing a record type `Employee`. In this section we will modify this record by adding new fields for storage of the employee's address and starting date and date of birth. The record type `NewEmployee` is declared in Fig. 12.9 along with two additional record types, `Date` and `Address`.

FIGURE 12.9

Declaration of a Nested Record

```
type IDRange : 1111..9999
type NameType : string (20)
type GenderType : string(1)
```

```
type Employee :
   record
        ID : IDRange
        Name : NameType
        Gender : GenderType
        NumDepend : int
        Rate, TotWages : real
   end record

type StringType : string(20)
type PostalString : string(7)

type Address :
   record
        Street, City, State : StringType
        PostalCode : PostalString
   end record

type Month : enum(January, February, March,
                  April, May, June,
                  July, August, September,
                  October, November, December)

type Date :
   record
        ThisMonth : Month
        Day : 1..31
        Year : 1900 .. 1999
   end record

type NewEmployee :
   record
        PayData : Employee
        Home : Address
        StartDate, BirthDate : Date
   end record

var Programmer : NewEmployee
```

If `Programmer` is a record variable of type `NewEmployee`, the nested structure of `Programmer` is sketched below. This is not a structure diagram in the usual sense but is used to provide a graphical display of the record form.

Figure 12.10 shows that `Programmer` is a record with fields `PayData`, `Home`, `StartDate`, and `BirthDate`. Each of these fields is itself a record (called a *subrecord* of `Programmer`). The fields of each subrecord are indicated under it.

In order to reference a field in this diagram, we must trace a complete path to it starting from the top of the diagram. For example, the field selector

```
Programmer.StartDate
```

FIGURE 12.10   Record Variable Programmer (Type NewEmployee)

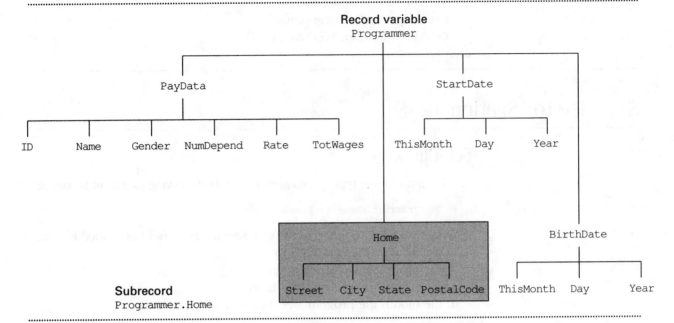

references the subrecord StartDate (type Date) of the variable Programmer. The field selector

    Programmer.StartDate.Year

references the Year field of the subrecord Programmer.StartDate. The field selector Programmer.Year is incomplete (which Year field?) and would cause a syntax error.

The record copy statement

    Programmer.StartDate := DayOfYear

is legal if DayOfYear is a record variable of type Date. This statement copies each field of DayOfYear into the corresponding field of the subrecord Programmer.StartDate.

Procedure GetNewEmp in Fig.12.11 could be used to read in a record of type NewEmployee. It calls procedures GetEmployee (see Fig. 12.4), GetAddress and GetDate (see programming exercise 1 at the end of this section).

FIGURE 12.11   Procedure GetNewEmp

```
procedure GetNewEmp (var NewEmp : NewEmployee)
    % Read a record into record variable NewEmp
    % Pre : None
    % Post: Read data into all fields of record NewEmp
    % Uses: Procedures GetEmployee (see Fig. 12.4),
    %        GetAddress, and GetDate
```

```
              GetEmployee (NewEmp.PayData)
              GetAddress (NewEmp.Home)
              GetDate (NewEmp.StartDate)
              GetDate (NewEmp.BirthDate)
       end GetNewEmp
```

Exercise for Section 12.4

Self-Check

1. What must be the type of `NewAddress` if the following statement is correct?

    ```
    Programmer.Home := NewAddress
    ```

2. Write the field selector needed to reference each field described below.
   a. the programmer's salary
   b. the programmer's street address
   c. the programmer's month of birth
   d. the month the programmer started working

Programming

1. Write procedures `GetAddress` and `GetDate`.

12.5 The Bind Declaration (Optional)

Sometimes it becomes tedious to write the complete field selector each time we reference a field of a record. The `bind` declaration, which usually occurs in a subprogram, can be used to shorten the field selector. In the following, the identifier `SDate` is bound to `Programmer.StartDate` (see Fig. 12.10). As a result, `SDate` is an abbreviation for the longer form `Programmer.StartDate`.

```
    bind SDate to Programmer.StartDate
    put "Year started: ", SDate.Year
    put "Day started: ", SDate.Day
```

These `put` statements display two fields of the subrecord `Programmer.StartDate`. Without the `bind`, the first `put` statement would have this longer form.

```
    put "Year started: ", Programmer.StartDate.Year
```

The computation for taxable salary could be written as

```
    bind var Emp to Programmer.PayData
    Emp.TotWages := Emp.Rate * 40.0 -
                    Emp.NumDepend * 14.40
```

In this case, since we are changing values in Emp we must use the keyword var (for variable) in the bind declaration. The put statement below

```
bind P to Programmer
put P.PayData.Name, " started work in ",
P.StartDate.Year
```

displays an output line of the form

```
Caryn Jackson started work in 1976
```

In this example, we have bound to a record, not to a subrecord as we did in the previous examples.

Several records can be bound to in a single declaration. This is done in the following, which displays the output line above.

```
bind Emp to Programmer.PayData,
SDate to Programmer.StartDate
put Emp.Name, " started work in ", SDate.Year
```

The order of the two parts in the bind statement is not important.

As you can see, the identifier introduced in a bind replaces the name of a record or subrecord.

BIND DECLARATION
Form: bind [var] *identifier* to *reference*,
              { [var] *identifier* to *reference* }
Example: bind var H to Programmer.Home
              if H.City = "Toronto" then
                  put "Home of Blue Jays baseball team"
              end if

Interpretation: The bind declaration creates a new name (or names) for a variable reference (or references). You are allowed to change the named item only if you specify var. The square brackets [...] around var mean that it is optional. The braces {...} indicate that more than one name (identifier) can be declared in a single bind declaration.

The scope of each identifier begins with the bind declaration and lasts to the end of the surrounding statement or subprogram. You are not allowed to use bind at the outermost level of the main program (except nested inside statements such as if).

As it states in the syntax display for bind declarations, these declarations cannot appear at the outermost level of the main program. They are usually used in a subprogram. For example, in Fig. 12.12, the subprogram GetNewEmp has been rewritten to use a bind. Although this version shortens names in the subprogram, it does not necessarily make the subprogram easier to understand, and thus is not particularly good programming style.

FIGURE 12.12   Procedure GetNewEmp Using a Bind Declaration

```
procedure GetNewEmp (var NewEmp : NewEmployee)
   % Read a record into record variable NewEmp
   % Pre : None
   % Post: Read data into all fields of record NewEmp
   % Uses: Procedures GetEmployee (see Fig. 12.4),
   %       GetAddress, and GetDate

   bind var N to NewEmp

   GetEmployee (N.PayData)
   GetAddress (N.Home)
   GetDate (N.StartDate)
   GetDate (N.BirthDate)
end GetNewEmp
```

Although our examples of binding have all involved records, there is no restriction that binds must apply to records. Later, when you learn to use arrays of records, you will see that you can use a bind to rename an element of an array of records.

PROGRAM
STYLE

> **USING A BIND DECLARATION**
> A bind declaration should be used for one primary purpose, and that is to make your program easier to understand. This will be the case when there is a long variable reference, or a set of such references, that can be shortened to a clearer form.
>
> There is a restriction in Turing (but not in Turing's extension to Object Oriented Turing) that prohibits you from using the original name (identifier) of the item during the scope of the bind. For example, in Fig. 12.12, following the bind, you are not allowed to use the identifier NewEmp.

Exercises for Section 12.5

Self-Check

1. Write the bind declaration required in the following subprogram.

```
procedure CreateNewEmpHome(var NewEmp : NewEmployee)
   % Initialize all fields of the Home subrecord of
   % NewEmp to null strings
   % Pre : None
   % Post: Set all fields of subrecord Home to ""

   % Replace this line with a bind declaration
```

```
                    H.Street := ""
                    H.City := ""
                    H.State := ""
                    H.PostalCode := ""
             end CreateNewEmpHome
```

Programming

1. Using the subprogram in the Self-Check as a model, write a procedure called GetNewEmpHome that reads values for the Home subrecord of a NewEmployee record. Use a bind declaration in your subprogram.

12.6 Variant Records (Optional)

All record variables of type NewEmployee have the same form and structure. It is possible, however, to define record-like types whose fields vary from instance to instance. These types are called *variant records* or *unions*.

For example, we might want to include additional information about an employee based on the employee's marital status. For all married employees, we might want to know the spouse's name and whether the couple files its income tax forms jointly. For all divorced employees, we might want to know the date of the divorce. For all single employees, we might want to know whether or not the employee lives alone.

This new type, Executive, is declared in Fig. 12.13. It uses data types declared in Fig. 12.9. It is just like the previously defined NewEmployee type, except it has one new field, called Family, whose type is FamilyInfo. FamilyInfo is a union type. A union type is called a *variant record*, because it defines variants that are sets of fields. Each set is essentially a record. In some languages, notably Pascal, a variant record has a syntax that is an extension of the syntax for an ordinary record, but other languages, such as C and Turing use the keyword union, and syntax that is distinct from record types.

FIGURE 12.13   Union Type FamilyInfo and Record Type Executive

```
% Use types from Fig. 12.9

type MaritalStatus : enum (Married, Divorced, Single)

type FamilyInfo:
   union MS : MaritalStatus of
      label MaritalStatus.Married :
         SpouseName : StringType
         FilingJointly : boolean
      label MaritalStatus.Divorced :
         DivorceDate : Date
      label MaritalStatus.Single :
         LivesAlone : boolean
   end union
```

```
type Executive :
    record
        PayData : Employee
        Home : Address
        StartDate, BirthDate : Date
        Family : FamilyInfo
    end record

var Boss : Executive
```

The union type `FamilyInfo` begins with the line

```
union MS : MaritalStatus of
```

This line defines a special field `MS`, of type `MaritalStatus`, that is called the *tag field*. The value of the tag field (`Married`, `Divorced`, or `Single`) indicates the form of the remainder of the union type. If the value of the tag field is `Married`, there are two additional fields, `SpouseName` (type `StringType`) and `FilingJointly` (type boolean). If it is `Divorced`, there is one additional field (`DivorceDate`), and if it is `Single`, there is a different additional field (`LivesAlone`).

Figure 12.14 shows the three variants of the `Family` field of record variable `Boss`, starting with the tag field.

For each variable or field of type `FamilyInfo`, the compiler will allocate sufficient storage space to accommodate the largest of the variants shown in Fig. 12.14. However, only one of the variants is defined at any given time; this particular variant is determined by the tag field value.

The amount of storage required for each variant depends on how many bytes are used to store integer values and enumerated-type values on a particular computer. However, the first variant above requires more than twenty bytes of storage (one byte per character of the spouse's name) and should be the largest.

FIGURE 12.14   Three Variants of the Family Field of Record Boss

Boss.Family.MS	Married
Boss.Family.SpouseName	Jim Wong
Boss.Family.FilingJointly	true
Boss.Family.MS	Divorced
Boss.Family.DivorceDate.ThisMonth	May
Boss.Family.DivorceDate.Day	20
Boss.Family.DivorceDate.Year	1989
Boss.Family.MS	Single
Boss.Family.LivesAlone	true

EXAMPLE 12.8
If the value of `Boss.Family.MS` is `Married`, only the variant fields `SpouseName` and `FilingJointly` may be correctly referenced; all other variant fields are undefined. Assuming the first variant shown in Fig. 12.14 is stored in record `Boss`, the program fragment

```
bind F to Boss.Family
put "The spouse's name is ", F.SpouseName
if F.FilingJointly then
    put "They are filing jointly"
else
    put "They are not filing jointly"
end if
```

displays the line

```
The spouse's name is Jim Wong
They are filing jointly
```

The programmer must ensure that the variant fields that are referenced are consistent with the current tag field value. For example, the reference to `F.SpouseName` is allowed only if the tag field `MS` is set to `Married`. In some languages, such as Pascal and C, the run-time system does not normally check this, but in Turing you will get a run-time error message if the tag is not consistent with the field being referenced. This check is analogous to the check that makes sure that an array subscript is in bounds.

A `case` statement is often used to process the variant part of a record. By using the tag field as the `case` selector, we can ensure that only the currently defined variant is manipulated.

EXAMPLE 12.9
The procedure in Fig. 12.15 displays the data stored in a union type `FamilyInfo`. The value of `OneFamily.MS` determines what information will be displayed.

FIGURE 12.15   Displaying the Variants of a Union Variable

```
procedure PutFamilyInfo (OneFamily : FamilyInfo)
    % Display the variant part of union OneFamily
    % Pre : OneFamily.MS and the corresponding variant
    %       is defined
    % Post: Display active variant of OneFamily on
    %       a line

    bind F to OneFamily   % Abbreviate OneFamily to F
    case F.MS of
        label MaritalStatus.Married :
            put "The spouse's name is ", F.SpouseName
```

```
                    if F.FilingJointly then
                        put "They are filing jointly"
                    else
                        put "They are not filing jointly"
                    end if
                label MaritalStatus.Divorced :
                    bind D to F.DivorceDate
                    put "Divorced on ", ord(D.ThisMonth) + 1,
                            "/", D.Day, "/", D.Year
                label MaritalStatus.Single :
                    if F.LivesAlone then
                        put "Lives alone"
                    else
                        put "Does not live alone"
                    end if
            end case
        end PutFamilyInfo
```

As you can see by comparing the `FamilyInfo` union type in Fig. 12.13 and the `case` statement for displaying its value in Fig 12.15, the syntax for `union` and `case` is analogous. The labels in a union are used to separately declare the fields in a variant. The labels in a case statement are used to separately handle each of these variants. The syntax for a `union` type is described in the following syntax display.

UNION TYPE DEFINITION

Form:
```
union tag : tag type of
    label label₁ : field list₁
    label label₂ : field list₂
    ...
    label labelₖ : field listₖ
end union
```

Example:
```
const GoneBald := 1
const HasHair := 2

type HairRange : GoneBald .. HasHair

type HairInfo :
    union HairStatus : HairRange of
        label GoneBald :
            WearsWig : boolean
        label HasHair :
            HairColor : Color
    end union
```

Interpretation: A union type (also called a variant record) is like a record in which there is a run-time choice among the accessible fields. This choice is made by the `tag` statement (see below), which deletes the current set of fields and activates a new set.

The identifier *tag* is the name of the tag field of the record; the tag field name is separated by a colon from its type (*tag type*), which must be an enumerated type or a subrange type.

The labels (*label₁*, *label₂* , ..., *labelₖ*) are lists of values of the tag field as defined by tag type. *Field list_i* declares the record fields associated with *label_i* Each element of *field list_i* is a declaration of this form:

identifier {, identifier } : type specification

In other words, each element is a sequence of identifiers separated by commas, followed by a colon (:) and then a type specification (such as `boolean`).

Note 1: All field names (across all the field lists in the union) must be unique. The tag identifier must be distinct as well.

Note 2: An empty field list (a variant with no fields) is indicated by completely omitting the field list.

Note 3: If there are no values between the keyword `label` and the colon (:) in the final variant, this variant is selected for all tag values that are not listed in any other labels.

Note 4: It is possible for a union type to have as fields other unions.

EXAMPLE 12.10
The procedure `GetFamilyInfo` in Fig. 12.16 reads the data into the unions of type `FamilyInfo`. The figure begins with a procedure (`GetBoolean`), which reads in `boolean` values (`true` as T and `false` as F). This procedure is used to read in the values for `FilingJointly` and `LivingAlone`.

FIGURE 12.16 Reading the Variants of a Union Variable

```
procedure GetBoolean (var B : boolean)
    % Read a boolean value as T or F
    % Pre : None
    % Post: Boolean reference B is set to true or false

    loop
        put "Enter T (true) or F (false)> " ..
        var Letter : string
        get Letter
        var GotBoolean : boolean := true
```

```
            if Letter = "T" or Letter = "t" then
                B := true
            elsif Letter = "F" or Letter = "f" then
                B := false
            else
                GotBoolean := false
            end if
            exit when GotBoolean
        end loop
    end GetBoolean

    procedure GetFamilyTag (var OneFamily: FamilyInfo)
        % Read tag field of OneFamily
        % Pre : None
        % Post: The tag of OneFamily is defined

        % Read a letter that represents marital status
        % and use it to set the marital status
        loop
            put "Enter marital status"
            put "Enter M (Married), D (Divorced), ",
                "or S (Single)> " ..
            var Status : string         % Input - letter
            get Status
            var GotStatus : boolean := true
            % Set tag field if input is appropriate
            if Status = "M" or Status = "m" then
                tag OneFamily, MaritalStatus.Married
            elsif Status = "D" or Status = "d" then
                tag OneFamily, MaritalStatus.Divorced
            elsif Status = "S" or Status = "s" then
            tag OneFamily, MaritalStatus.Single
            else
                GotStatus := false
            end if
            exit when GotStatus
        end loop
    end GetFamilyTag

    procedure GetFamilyInfo (var OneFamily : FamilyInfo)
        % Read tag field of OneFamily and its variant
        % Pre : None
        % Post: The tag and variant of OneFamily
        %       are defined

        bind var F to OneFamily         % Shorten OneFamily to F

        GetFamilyTag (F)                % Read the tag, which is
                                        % the marital status (MS)
        % Select the variant and read variant data
        case F.MS of
            label MaritalStatus.Married :
```

```
                    put "Enter spouse's name> " ..
                    get F.SpouseName : *      % Read entire line
                                              % including blanks
                    put "Enter T if filing jointly >"
                    GetBoolean (F.FilingJointly)
                label MaritalStatus.Divorced :
                    put "Enter divorce date> "
                    GetDate (F.DivorceDate)
                label MaritalStatus.Single :
                    put "Are you living alone> "
                    GetBoolean (F.LivesAlone)
            end case
    end GetFamilyInfo
```

In Fig. 12.16, the GetFamilyTag procedure reads in the marital status
and sets the value of OneFamily.MS. In most ways, OneFamily.MS is
like other fields in records and unions. Its value is accessed by writing
OneFamily.MS in the program. However, changing a union tag, such as
OneFamily.MS, requires a special kind of assignment statement called a
tag statement. In Fig. 12.16, in the GetFamilyTag procedure, the following statement sets the tag to MaritalStatus.Married.

```
    tag OneFamily, MaritalStatus.Married
```

This can be thought of as the following statement, which is not allowed in
Turing.

```
    OneFamily.MS := MaritalStatus.Married % Illegal!!
```

The reason that the special tag statement (not an ordinary assignment
statement) is required in Turing is because changing the tag of a union
entails destroying one variant and activating another. This action is
beyond what we expect of an assignment statement. For example, if
OneFamily, as it is passed into the GetFamilyTag procedure, has its
tag (MS) set to Divorced, changing the tag will destroy the associated
value of DivorceDate.

TAG STATEMENT

Form: tag *union reference, expression*

Example: tag OneFamily, MaritalStatus.Single

Interpretation: A tag statement is a special purpose assignment that
is used to change the tag of a union variable. A tag statement is the
only way to modify the tag field of the union (except by assigning to
the entire union variable). The tag statement destroys the current
variant and activates the new variant as determined by the *expression*.
The values in the variant are uninitialized.

When a union variable has been declared, but its tag has not yet been initialized, you are not allowed to store values into the variant part. The reason is that these parts conceptually do not exist until the tag has been set to choose one variant. Once the value of the tag field is defined by the `tag` statement, data can be read into the variant fields associated with that value.

Variant records (unions) are useful when you are dealing with values whose structure (field lists) are determined by part of the data (the tag). When using an object oriented language, such as C++, Smalltalk or Object Oriented Turing, it is common to use language features called *inheritance* and *overriding* instead of variant records. These new features encapsulate (collect together) the variants and the corresponding ADT (abstract data type) operators corresponding to the variants.

❊ Case Study:

Areas and Perimeters of Different Figures

1. Problem

We want to write a program that will determine the area and perimeter for a variety of geometric figures.

2. Analysis

To solve this problem, we will create an abstract data type that represents a geometric figure and contains operators for computing the figure's characteristics, including its perimeter and its area. Since the characteristics for each figure shape are different, we will use a union type.

DATA REQUIREMENTS

Data Types

```
const Circle := 1
const Rectangle := 2
const Square := 3

type FigKind : Circle .. Square

type Figure :
    union Shape : FigKind of
        label Circle : Radius : real
        label Rectangle : Width, Height : real
        label Square : Side : real
    end union
```

Problem Inputs

A number representing the kind of figure
The relevant characteristics for the figure selected

Problem Outputs

The figure's perimeter
The figure's area

3. Design

INITIAL ALGORITHM
1. Read in the figure's characteristics
2. Compute and display the perimeter and area of the figure

4. Implementation

Coding the Main Program

We will write procedures to perform each of the two algorithm steps above. The main program (Fig. 12.17) simply calls these two procedures (`GetFigure` and `DisplayFigure`).

FIGURE 12.17

Program Geometry

```
% The "Geometry" program
% Find perimeters and areas of various kinds of figures

const Pi := 3.14159

const Circle := 1
const Rectangle := 2
const Square := 3

type FigKind : Circle .. Square

type Figure :
    union Shape : FigKind of
        label Circle    : Radius : real
        label Rectangle : Width, Height : real
        label Square    : Side : real
    end union

var MyFig : Figure        % A figure

% Insert subprograms GetFigure, ComputePerim,
% ComputeArea, and DisplayFigure

GetFigure (MyFig)
DisplayFigure (MyFig)
```

```
Enter object's shape
Enter 1 (Circle), 2 (Rectangle), or 3 (Square)> 2
Enter width> 5.0
Enter height> 6.5
Figure shape is Rectangle
Width is 5.00
Height is 6.50
Perimeter is 23.00
Area is 32.50
```

Coding for Procedures

Procedure `GetFigure` reads in the number denoting the kind of figure and saves the corresponding value of type `FigKind` in the tag field `Shape`. `GetFigure` also reads the data required for the kind of figure indicated by the tag field. The other operator procedures are straightforward and are also shown in Fig. 12.18.

FIGURE 12.18

Operator Procedures for Data Type Figure

```
procedure GetFigure (var OneFig : Figure)
    % Read tag field of OneFig and its characteristics
    % Pre : None
    % Post: The tag and characteristics of OneFig
    %       are defined

    var FigNumber : int      % Input - data number
                             % for figure shape

    % Read a number that represents a shape
    loop
        put "Enter object's shape"
        put "Enter 1 (Circle), 2 (Rectangle), ",
            "or 3 (Square)> " ..
        get FigNumber
        exit when FigNumber >= Circle and
        FigNumber <= Square
    end loop

    tag OneFig, FigNumber    % Set the tag field

    % Select the variant and read variant data
    case OneFig.Shape of
        label Circle :
            put "Enter radius> " ..
            get OneFig.Radius
        label Rectangle :
            put "Enter width> " ..
            get OneFig.Width
            put "Enter height> " ..
            get OneFig.Height
        label Square :
            put "Enter length of side> " ..
            get OneFig.Side
    end case
end GetFigure
```

```
function ComputePerim (OneFig : Figure) : real
    % Compute perimeter of OneFig
    % Pre : The tag field and characteristics of OneFig
    %        are defined
    % Post: Return perimeter of figure

    case OneFig.Shape of
        label Circle :
            result 2.0 * Pi * OneFig.Radius
        label Rectangle :
            result 2.0 * (OneFig.Width + OneFig.Height)
        label Square :
            result 4.0 * OneFig.Side
    end case
end ComputePerim

function ComputeArea (OneFig : Figure) : real
    % Compute area of OneFig
    % Pre : The tag field and characteristics of OneFig
    %        are defined
    % Post: Return area of figure

    case OneFig.Shape of
        label Circle :
            result Pi * OneFig.Radius ** 2
        label Rectangle :
            result OneFig.Width * OneFig.Height
        label Square :
            result OneFig.Side ** 2
    end case
end ComputeArea

procedure DisplayFigure (OneFig : Figure)
    % Display the characteristics of OneFig
    % Pre : All fields of OneFig are defined
    % Post: Display each field of OneFig

    put "Figure shape is " ..
    case OneFig.Shape of
        label Circle :
            put "Circle"
            put "Radius is ", OneFig.Radius :4:2
        label Rectangle :
            put "Rectangle"
            put "Width is ", OneFig.Width :4:2
            put "Height is ", OneFig.Height :4:2
```

```
            label Square :
                put "Square"
                put "Side is ", OneFig.Side :4:2
        end case

        % Display perimeter and area
        put "Perimeter is ", ComputePerim (OneFig) :4:2
        put "Area is ", ComputeArea (OneFig) :4:2
    end DisplayFigure
```

In each procedure, a `case` statement controls the processing of the data in the variants. Procedures `ComputePerim` and `ComputeArea` return their respective results for use in `DisplayFigure`.

Exercises for Section 12.6

Self-Check

1. Write a statement that displays `Boss.Family.SpouseName`, if defined, or a message `"Not married"`.

Programming

1. Write a procedure to display a union of type `HairInfo` as declared in the syntax display for `union` type definition.
2. Add the variant

   ```
   label RightTriangle :     Base, Height : real
   ```

   to `Figure` and modify the operator procedures to include triangles. Use the formulas

   ```
   Area = 1/2 Base × Height
   Hypotenuse = sqrt(Base² + Height²)
   ```

   where `Base` and `Height` are the two sides that form the right angle.

12.7 Common Programming Errors

When programmers use records, their most common error is incorrectly specifying the record field to be manipulated. The full field selector (record variable and field name) must be used unless a `bind` declaration is used to provide an abbreviation. When reading or writing records at the terminal, each field must be processed separately.

For variant records (unions), remember that the value of the tag field determines the form of the variant part that is currently defined. Manipulating any other variant will cause a run-time error message. It is safest to manipulate a variant record in a `case` statement with the tag field used as the `case` selector, to ensure that the proper variant part is being manipulated. The tag field of a `union` variable can be changed only by a `tag` statement and not by an assignment statement.

Chapter Review

In this chapter we studied the record data structure. Records were shown to be useful for organizing a collection of related data items of different types. We were able to create some very general data structures to model our "real world" data organization through the use of nested records and variant records.

In processing records, we learned how to reference each individual component through the use of a field selector consisting of the record variable name and field name separated by a period. The `bind` declaration was introduced as a means of shortening the field selection.

Each individual component of a record must be manipulated separately in an input or output operation or in an arithmetic expression. However, it is permissible to assign one record variable to another record variable of the same type (record copy statement) or to pass a record as a parameter to a procedure or function.

Variant records (unions) are essentially records whose variant sets of fields are selected at run-time by the `tag` statement.

New Turing Constructs in Chapter 12

The new Turing constructs introduced in this chapter are described in Table 12.1.

TABLE 12.1   Summary of New Turing Constructs

Construct	Effect

Record Declaration
 	
``
type Part :
    record
        ID : 1111..9999
        Quantity : int
        Price : real
    end record
var Nuts, Bolts : Part
``
	A record type `Part` is declared with fields that can store two integers and a real number. `Nuts` and `Bolts` are record variables of type `Part`.

Construct	Effect
Record Reference	
`TotalCost := Nuts.Quantity` `            * Nuts.Price`	Multiply two fields of `Nuts`
`put Bolts.ID`	Print `ID` field of `Bolts`
Record Copy	
`Bolts := Nuts`	Copy record `Nuts` to `Bolts`
Bind Declaration	
`bind B to Bolts` `put B.ID, " ", B.Price`	Print two fields of `Bolts`
Record Variant Declaration	

`const Truck := 1`
`const Plane := 2`
`type Kind : Truck .. Plane`
 	
`type Transporter:`
`    union Which : Kind of`
`        label Truck :`
`            Wheels : int`
`        label Plane :`
`            Engines : int`
`    end union`
	A union type is declared. The variant for trucks can store an integer giving the number of wheels. The variant for planes can store an integer giving the number of engines.

`var Vehicle : Transporter`	The union variable `Vehicle` is type `Transporter`
Referencing a Record Variant	

`bind V to Vehicle`
`case V.Which of`
`    label Truck :`
`        put V.Wheels, " wheels"`
`    label Plane :`
`        put V.Engines, "engines"`
`end case`
	Use a case statement to display either the number of wheels on a truck or the number of engines on a plane.

Tag Statement	
`tag Vehicle, Truck` `Vehicle.Wheels := 4`	Set the tag of `Vehicle` to be `Truck`. Any existing variant is destroyed. The `Wheels` field is uninitialized and then has 4 assigned to it.

Quick-Check Exercises

1. What is the primary difference between a record and an array? Which would you use to store the catalogue description of a course? Which would you use to store the names of students in the course?
2. What is a field selector?
3. Why do we use a `bind` declaration?
4. When can you use the assignment operator with record operands? When can you use the equality operator?
5. For `AStudent` declared as follows, provide a statement that displays the initials of `AStudent`.

```
type Student :
    record
        First, Last : string(20)
        Age, Score : int
        Grade : string (1)
    end record
var AStudent : Student
```

6. How many fields are there in a record of type `Student`?
7. If an `int` uses four bytes of storage and a `string` $N + 1$ bytes where N is its maximum length, how many bytes of storage are occupied by `AStudent`?
8. Write a procedure that displays a variable of type `Student`.
9. When should you use a variant record?

Answers to Quick-Check Exercises

1. The values stored in an array must all be the same type; the values stored in a record do not have to be the same type. Record for catalogue item; array for list of names.
2. Used to select a particular record field for processing.
3. A `bind` declaration allows us to abbreviate field selectors. It is helpful when the reference becomes long. It is also helpful when we must reference several fields of the same record.
4. When the records are the same type. Never.
5. `put AStudent.First(1), AStudent.Last(1)`
6. 5
7. 45
8.
```
procedure WriteStudent (OneStu : Student)
    put "Student is ", OneStu.First,
        " ", OneStu.Last
    put "Age is ", OneStu.Age
    put "Score is ", OneStu.Score
    put "Grade is ", OneStu.Grade
end WriteStudent
```

9. When an object has some fields that are always the same and a small number of fields that may be different.

Review Questions

1. Declare a record called `Subscriber` that contains the fields `Name`, `StreetAddress`, `MonthlyBill` (how much the subscriber owes), and which paper the subscriber receives (`Morning`, `Evening`, or `Both`).

2. Write a Turing program to enter and then print out the data in record `Competition` declared below.

```
type StringType : string(20)
type OlympicEvent :
    record
        Event,
        Entrant,
        Country : StringType
        Place : int
    end record

var Competition: OlympicEvent
```

3. Explain the use of the `bind` declaration.

4. Identify and correct the errors in the following program.

```
% The "Report" program

type String15 : string(15)
type SummerHelp :
    record
        Name : String15
        StartDate : String15
        HoursWorked : real
    end record

var Operator : SummerHelp

SummerHelp.Name := "Stoney Viceroy"
SummerHelp.StartDate := "June 1, 1993"
SummerHelp.HoursWorked := 29.3
put Operator
```

5. Declare the proper data structure to store the following student data: `GPA`, `Major`, `Address` (consisting of `StreetAddress`, `City`, `State`, `ZipCode`) and `ClassSchedule` (consisting of up to six class records each of which has `Description`, `Time`, and `Days` fields). Use whatever data types are most appropriate for each field.

6. Write the union declaration for Supplies, which consist of either Paper, Ribbon, or Labels. For Paper, the information needed is the number of sheets per box and the size of the paper. For Ribbon, the size, color, and kind (Carbon or Cloth) are needed. For Labels, the size and number per box are needed. For each supply, the cost, number on hand, and the reorder point must also be stored. Use whatever data types are appropriate for each field.

7. Write the declaration for Vehicle. If the vehicle is a Truck, BedSize and CabSize are needed. If the vehicle is a Wagon, third seat or not is needed (boolean). If the vehicle is a Sedan, the information needed is TwoDoor or FourDoor. For all vehicles, we need to know whether the transmission is Manual or Automatic; if it has AirConditioning, PowerSteering, or PowerBrakes (all boolean); and the gas mileage. Use whatever data types are appropriate for each field.

Programming Projects

1. Implement an abstract data type consisting of the data structure described in review question 5 and procedures for reading and displaying an object of that type.

2. Implement an abstract data type consisting of the data structure described in review question 6 and procedures for reading and displaying an object of that type.

3. Implement an abstract data type consisting of the data structure described in review question 7 and procedures for reading and displaying an object of that type.

4. A number expressed in scientific notation is represented by its mantissa (a fraction) and its exponent. Write a procedure that reads two character strings that represent numbers in Turing scientific notation and stores each number in a record with two fields. Write a procedure that prints the contents of each record as a real value. Also write a procedure that computes the sum, product, difference, and quotient of the two numbers.

   Hint: The string –0.1234E20 represents a number in scientific notation. The fraction –0.1234 is the mantissa and the number 20 is the exponent.

5. At a grocery store, certain categories of food have been established and this information is to be computerized. Write a procedure to read and store information into a variant record with appropriate data types.

   The first letter read will either be a M, F, or V (indicating meat, fruit, or vegetable). The second set of information (until a blank is encountered) will be the name of the item (maximum of 20 letters). The third item read will be the unit cost. The fourth item read will be the unit (either O for ounces or P for pounds).

The last field read will be one character indicating information based on the M, F, or V read earlier. For meat, the valid input values are R for red meat, P for poultry, and F for fish. For fruit, the valid input values are T for tropical, N for non-tropical. For vegetables, the valid input values are B for beans, P for potatoes, O for other.

The procedure should check that each data item is valid before assigning a value to the record parameter. Also write a procedure to print the data stored for a food object.

Arrays with Structured Elements

So far, you have seen programs that use arrays with a number of different subscript and element types. All the arrays we have discussed to this point were subscripted by a single index and had elements that were simple types or strings. Since these arrays have a single subscript, they are called *one-dimensional arrays*. This chapter examines arrays whose elements are structured types, such as records, and which have more than one subscript (multidimensional arrays).

We will investigate arrays with more than one subscript. These are called *multidimensional arrays* and are often used to store tables of data or to represent multidimensional objects.

We will also examine arrays with elements that are records. Arrays of records are useful data structures that can be used to represent many real-world objects. For example, it is convenient to use an array of records to represent a class of students or the members of a baseball team.

Finally, we will see how to perform some common operations on arrays of records. These operations include searching for a particular record in an array and ordering the array elements according to the values in a particular field (sorting the array).

13.1 Multidimensional Arrays

Two-dimensional arrays are the most common multidimensional arrays, and they are used to store information that we normally represent in table form. Examples would be a seating plan for a room (organized by row and column) or a monthly budget (organized by category and month). We will give some examples of both two- and-three dimensional arrays in this section.

EXAMPLE 13.1

A two-dimensional object we are all familiar with is a tic-tac-toe board. The declaration

```
type BoardArray : array 1..3, 1..3 of string(1)
var TicTacToe : BoardArray
```

allocates storage for the array `TicTacToe`. This array has nine storage cells arranged in three rows and three columns. A single character value will be stored in each cell. Consequently, the variable `TicTacToe` (type `BoardArray`) is a two-dimensional array as pictured in Fig.13.1.

This array has nine elements, each of which must be referenced by specifying a row subscript (1, 2, or 3) and a column subscript (1, 2, or 3). Each array element can contain a character value. The array element `TicTacToe(2,3)` pointed to in Fig. 13.1 is in row 2, column 3 of the array; it contains the character O. The diagonal line consisting of array elements `TicTacToe(1,1)`, `TicTacToe(2,2)`, and `TicTacToe(3,3)` represents a win for player X as each cell contains the character X.

FIGURE 13.1   A Tic-Tac-Toe Board Stored as Array TicTacToe

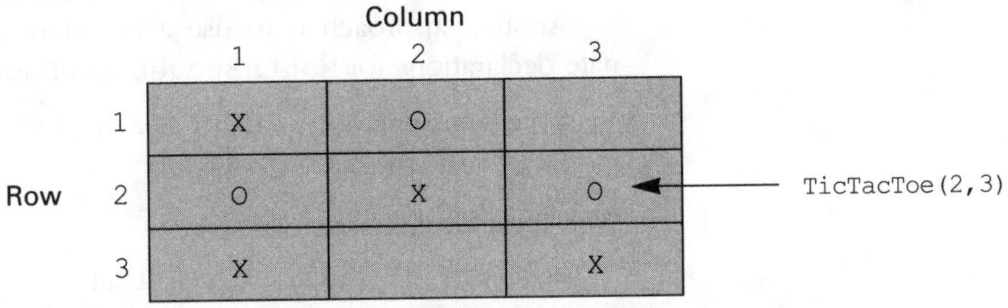

ARRAY TYPE (MULTIDIMENSIONAL)

Form: array *subscript₁, subscript₂, ..., subscriptₙ*
                                of *element type*

Example: type YearByMonth : array 1900..1999, Month
                                of real
                type Election : array Candidate,
                                Precinct of int

Interpretation: *Subscriptᵢ* represents the subscript type of dimension *i* of the array type. The subscript type may be an enumerated type or a subrange type. The *element type* may be any standard data type or a previously defined data type.

Although we will focus our discussion on arrays with two and three dimensions, there is no limit on the number of dimensions allowed in Turing. However, there may be a limit imposed by the particular implementation you are using. Be aware that the amount of memory space allocated for the storage of a multidimensional array can be quite large.

EXAMPLE 13.2

The declarations

```
type BudgetCat : enum (Entertainment, Food, Clothing,
        Rent, Tuition, Insurance, Miscellaneous)
type BudgetArray : array BudgetCat of real
type Month : enum(January, February, March, April, May,
            June, July, August, September, October,
            November, December)

type MonthBudget : array Month of BudgetArray
var Budget : MonthBudget
```

allocate storage space for an array called Budget. The array element Budget(Month.January) stores the array that contains all the budget items for January. We can further subscript this array and write

```
Budget (Month.January) (BudgetCat.Entertainment)
```

to access the amount budgeted for entertainment in the first month.

Another approach is to use a two-dimensional array and these alternate declarations for MonthBudget and Budget.

```
type MonthBudget : array Month, BudgetCat of real
var Budget : MonthBudget
```

With these declarations, we write

```
Budget (Month.January, BudgetCat.Entertainment)
```

to access the amount budgeted for entertainment in the first month. Since Budget is now a two-dimensional array, we must use two subscripts, of types Month and BudgetCat, separated by commas.

EXAMPLE 13.3

Your instructor wants you to store the seating plan (see Fig. 13.2) for your class on a computer. The declarations

```
const RowMax := 11            % Number of rows in the room
const SeatsPerRow := 9        % Number of seats in a row
const StringSize := 10        % Characters in a string

type RowRange : 1..RowMax
type SeatRange : 1..SeatsPerRow
type SeatPlan : array RowRange, SeatRange of
                    string(StringSize)

var MyClass : SeatPlan        % Seating plan for MyClass
var Row : RowRange            % Row subscript
var Seat : SeatRange          % Column subscript
```

allocate storage for a two-dimensional array of strings called MyClass. Because each string is 10 characters long, the array requires at least 990 bytes of storage (11 * 9 * 10). Array MyClass could be used to hold the names of the students seated in a classroom with 11 rows and 9 seats in each row. The statements

```
Row := RowMax div 2 + 1           % The middle row
Seat := SeatsPerRow div 2 + 1     % The middle seat
MyClass(Row, Seat) := "Marilyn"
```

place a student named Marilyn in row 6, seat 5, the center of the classroom.

EXAMPLE 13.4

The array Table declared below

```
var Table : array 1..7, 1..5, 1..6 of real
```

has three dimensions: the first subscript may take on values from 1 to 7; the second from 1 to 5; and the third from 1 to 6. A total of 7 * 5 * 6, or 210, real numbers may be stored in the array Table. All three subscripts must be specified in each reference to array Table, e.g., Table(2,3,4).

FIGURE 13.2   Seating Plan for a Class

	Seat 1	Seat 2	. . .	Seat 9
Row 1	Alice	Bill	. . .	Gerry
Row 2	Jane	Sue	. . .	Groucho
.	.	.	.	.
.	.	.	.	.
.	.	.	.	.
Row 11	Harpo	Sam	. . .	Jillian

EXAMPLE 13.5

Your job is to computerize a small office. The first step is to store the information in your boss's two file cabinets, which are labeled `Business` and `Personal`. Each file cabinet contains two drawers (labeled 1, 2) and each drawer has 26 folders labeled A through Z (See Fig. 13.3). Each folder contains a memo of up to 512 characters. The declarations below allocate storage for an array `Office` that will hold all the information in the two filing cabinets.

```
const MemoLength := 255

type CabinetType : enum (Business, Personal)
type DrawerType : 1..2
type FolderType : ord("A") .. ord("Z")
type Memo : string(MemoLength)
type FileCabinet : array CabinetType, DrawerType,
      FolderType of Memo

var Office : FileCabinet
```

FIGURE 13.3   Office Files To Be Computerized

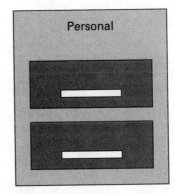

The array `Office` would occupy a large amount of storage space. Using 1K bytes to mean 1024 bytes, the array would require roughly 52K bytes of storage (2 * 2 * 26 * 512). The subscripted variable `Office` (`CabinetType.Business, 2, ord("A")` references the first folder (label A) in the middle drawer of the file cabinet labeled `Business`. The statement

```
put : MemoFile,
     Office (CabinetType.OfficeBusiness, 2, ord("A"))
```

copies the memo in this folder to output file with stream number `MemoFile`.

Storage of Multidimensional Arrays

Most implementations store multidimensional arrays in adjacent memory cells to simplify accessing the individual elements. The elements of a two-dimensional array are normally stored in order by row (i.e., first row 1, then row 2, and so on). This is called *row-major order*. To access a particular array element, the compiler computes the *offset* of that element from the first element stored. To perform this computation, the compiler must know the size of each element in bytes and the number of elements per row. Both values are available from the array type declaration.

FIGURE 13.4   Array TicTacToe in Memory

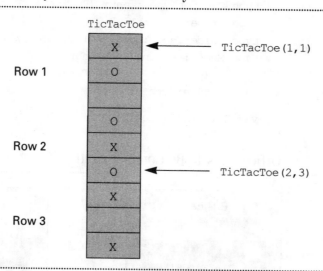

For example, the array `TicTacToe` would be stored as shown in Fig. 13.4. There are three elements per row and each element occupies one byte of storage. The offset for element `TicTacToe(i,j)` is computed from the formula

$$offset = (i-1) \times 3 + (j-1)$$

This formula gives a value of 0 as the offset for element `TicTacToe(1,1)` and a value of 5 as the offset for element `TicTacToe(2,3)`.

Exercises for Section 13.1

Self-Check

1. Declare a three-dimensional array type whose first subscript ranges from `ord("A")` to `ord("B")` inclusive, whose second subscript ranges from 1 to 10 inclusive, and whose third subscript ranges across the user-defined type `Day`. Real numbers will be stored in the array. How many elements can be stored in an array with this type?
2. Assuming the following declarations,

```
type RowRange : 1..5
type ColRange : 1..4
type MatrixType : array RowRange, ColRange of real
var Matrix : MatrixType
```

answer these questions:
   a. How many elements in array `Matrix`?
   b. Write a statement to display the elements in row 3, column 4.
   c. What is the offset for this element?
   d. What formula is used to compute the offset for `Matrix(i,j)`?

13.2 Processing of Multidimensional Arrays

We must specify a row subscript and a column subscript to reference an element of a two-dimensional array. The type of each subscript must be compatible with the corresponding subscript type specified in the array declaration.

Using the declarations in Example 13.1, this `for` loop

```
for I : 1 .. 3
    put TicTacToe(1,I) ..
end for
```

displays the first row of array `TicTacToe` (`TicTacToe(1,1)`, `TicTacToe(1,2)`, and `TicTacToe(1,3)`) on the current output line. The `for` loop

```
for I : 1 .. 3
    put TicTacToe(I,2)
end for
```

displays the second column of `TicTacToe` (`TicTacToe(1,2)`, `TicTacToe(2,2)`, and `TicTacToe(3,2)`) in a vertical line.

We can use nested loops to access all elements in a multidimensional array in a predetermined order. In the next examples, the outer loop control variable determines the row being accessed and the inner loop control variable selects each element in that row.

EXAMPLE 13.6

Procedure PrintBoard in Fig. 13.5 displays the current status of a tic-tac-toe board along with a sample output.

FIGURE 13.5   Procedure PrintBoard with Sample Output

```
procedure PrintBoard (TicTacToe : BoardArray)
    % Display the status of a tic-tac-toe board
    % Pre : Array TicTacToe is defined
    % Post: Display each element of array TicTacToe

    put "——-"
    for Row : 1 .. 3
        % Print all columns of current row
        for Column : 1 .. 3
            put "|", TicTacToe (Row, Column) ..
        end for
        put "|"
        put "——-"
    end for
end PrintBoard
```

```
 ————--
|X|O| |
 ————--
|O|X|O|
 ————--
|X| |X|
 ————--
```

EXAMPLE 13.7

Function IsFilled in Fig. 13.6 returns a value of true if a tic-tac-toe board is all filled up; it returns a value of false if there is at least one cell that contains the constant Empty. We are assuming that all cells are initialized to Empty before the game begins. To move to a particular cell, the current player replaces the constant Empty in that cell with an X or O. Function IsFilled could be called before making a move to determine whether there were any possible moves left. The if statement

```
if IsFilled(TicTacToe) then
    put "Game is a draw!"
end if
```

prints an appropriate message when there are no moves.

FIGURE 13.6   Function IsFilled

```
function IsFilled (TicTacToe : BoardArray) : boolean
   % Test whether the array TicTacToe is filled
   % Pre : All elements of array TicTacToe are
   %       assigned values
   % Post: Return false if any cell contains the
   %       constant Empty; otherwise, returns true

   const Empty := " "        % A blank character
   for Row : 1 .. 3
      for Column : 1 .. 3
         if TicTacToe(Row, Column) = Empty then
            result false    % Array is not filled
         end if
      end for
   end for
   result true              % All elements of array are filled
end IsFilled
```

EXAMPLE 13.8

Procedure EnterMove in Fig. 13.7 is used to enter a move into the array TicTacToe. EnterMove calls procedure EnterInt (see Fig. 10.3) twice to enter a pair of values into the move coordinates, MoveRow and MoveColumn. If the cell selected by these coordinates is empty, its value is reset to the character stored in Player (X or O).

FIGURE 13.7   Procedure EnterMove

```
procedure EnterMove (Player : string(1),
                     var TicTacToe : BoardArray)
   % Store an X or O (identity of Player) in the array
        % TicTacToe
   % Pre : Player is X or O and array TicTacToe has at
   %       least one empty cell
   % Post: The value of Player is stored in the empty
   %       cell of TicTacToe whose coordinates are read
   %       in; the rest of array TicTacToe is unchanged
   % Uses: Procedure EnterInt (see Fig. 10.3)

   const Empty := " "       % Contents of an empty cell
   var MoveRow, MoveColumn : int     % Coordinates of
                                     % selected cell
   loop
      put "Enter your move row and then the column"
      EnterInt (1, 3, MoveRow)
      EnterInt (1, 3, MoveColumn)
```

```
            exit when TicTacToe(MoveRow, MoveColumn) = Empty
            put "Cell is occupied - try again"
        end loop

        % Assertion: A valid move was entered
        % Define the cell
        TicTacToe(MoveRow, MoveColumn) := Player
    end EnterMove
```

EXAMPLE 13.9

A university offers 50 courses at each of five campuses. The registrar's office can conveniently store the enrollments of these courses in the array Enroll declared below.

```
const MaxCourse := 50    % Maximum number of courses
type Campus : enum (Main, Ambler, Center, Delaware, Montco)
var Enroll : array 1..MaxCourse, Campus of int
```

This array consists of 250 elements as shown in Fig. 13.8. Enroll(1, Campus.Center) represents the number of students in course 1 at Center campus.

FIGURE 13.8   Two-Dimensional Array Enroll

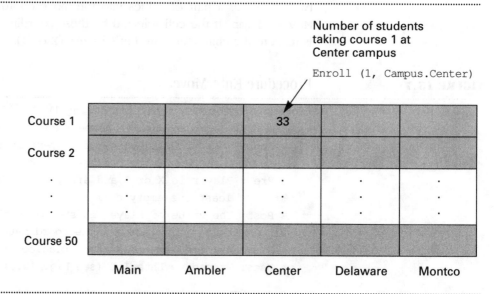

If the registrar wants to break down this enrollment information according to student rank, it would require a three-dimensional array with 1,000 elements. This array is declared below and shown in Fig. 13.9.

```
const MaxCourse := 50 % Maximum number of courses
type Campus : enum (Main, Ambler, Center, Delaware, Montco)
```

```
type Rank : enum (Freshman, Sophomore, Junior, Senior)
var ClassEnroll : array 1..MaxCourse, Campus, Rank of int

var CurCampus : Campus          % Current campus
var ClassRank : Rank            % Current rank
var Total : int                 % Student totals
```

The subscripted variable `ClassEnroll(1, Campus.Center, Rank.Senior)` represents the number of seniors taking course 1 at `Center` campus.

FIGURE 13.9   Three-Dimensional Array ClassEnroll

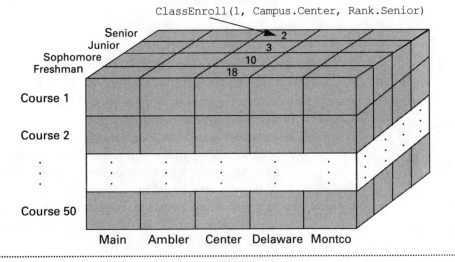

Number of seniors taking course 1 at Center campus

`ClassEnroll(1, Campus.Center, Rank.Senior)`

EXAMPLE 13.10

The program segment

```
Total := 0
for ClassRank : Rank
    Total += ClassEnroll(1, Campus.Center, ClassRank)
end for
```

computes the total number of students of all ranks in course 1 at `Center` campus.

The program segment

```
Total := 0
for CurCampus : Campus
    for ClassRank : Rank
        Total += ClassEnroll(1, CurCampus, ClassRank)
    end for
end for
```

computes the total number of students in course 1 (regardless of rank or campus).

Exercises for Section 13.2

Self-Check

1. Declare a three-dimensional array that can be used to keep track of the number of students in the math classes (Math1, Algebra, Geometry, Algebra2, Trigonometry, Calculus) at your old high school according to the grade level and sex of the students. How many elements in this array?
2. Extend row-major order to three dimensions and show how the array ClassEnroll might be stored. What would be the offset for the array element ClassEnroll(1, Campus.Center, Rank.Senior) and the general formula for ClassEnroll(i, j, k).

Programming

1. Assuming the declarations below

   ```
   type MatrixType : array 1..5, 1..4 of real
   var Matrix : MatrixType
   ```

   answer the following questions.
   a. Write a loop that computes the sum of elements in row 5.
   b. Write a loop that computes the sum of elements in column 4.
   c. Write nested loops that compute the sum of all array elements.
   d. Write nested loops that display the array elements in the following order: display column 4 as the first output line, column 3 as the second output line, column 2 as the third output line, and column 1 as the fourth output line.
2. Write a function that determines who has won a game of tic-tac-toe. The function should first check all rows to see if one player occupies all the cells in that row, then all columns, and then the two diagonals. The function should return a value from the enumerated type (NoWinner, XWins, YWins).
3. Redefine MaxCourse as 5 and write program segments that perform the following operations:
   a. Enter the enrollment data.
   b. Find the number of juniors in all classes at all campuses. Students will be counted once for each course in which they are enrolled.
   c. Find the number of sophomores on all campuses who are enrolled in course 2.
   d. Compute and print the number of students at Main campus enrolled in each course and the total number of students at Main campus in all courses. Students will be counted once for each course in which they are enrolled.
   e. Compute and print the number of upper-class students in all courses at each campus, as well as the total number of upper-class students enrolled. (Upper-class students are juniors and seniors.) Again, students will be counted once for each course in which they are enrolled.

13.3 Data Abstraction Illustrated

By this time you have learned quite a lot about Turing and programming. Your knowledge of arrays and records will enable you to write fairly sophisticated programs. This section develops a general program that might be used by a company to analyze sales figures. We will use data abstraction, focusing on the data structure and its operators, to solve this problem.

❈ Case Study:

Sales Analysis Problem

1. Problem

The HighRisk Software Company has employed us to develop a general sales analysis program that they can market to a number of different companies. This program will be used to enter monthly sales figures for a specified range of years and display these values in a variety of formats. The program will be *menu-driven*, which means that each user will be given a choice of a number of different options to perform. The menu format follows.

2. Analysis

Figure 13.10 shows a sample interaction with a program user, beginning with a display of the menu. To save space, the menu is only displayed once.

FIGURE 13.10

Sample Run for the Sales Analysis Program

```
Sales Analysis Program

Sales table initialized

Menu for Sales Analysis

0. Get help
1. Initialize the sales table
2. Enter data into the sales table
3. Display sales data as a two-dimensional table
4. Compute annual sales totals
5. Display annual sales totals
6. Display largest monthly sales amount for a year
7. Graph monthly sales data for a given year
8. Exit the program

Choose an option: Enter an integer between 0 and 8> 1
Sales table initialized

Choose an option: Enter an integer between 0 and 8> 2
First : Enter an integer between 1900 and 1999> 1991
Last : Enter an integer between 1991 and 1999> 1992
```

```
For year 1991, enter sales amount for each month or 0.0
Jan $1000.00
Feb $600.00
Mar $700.00
Apr $800.00
May $950.00
Jun $1000.00
Jul $500.00
Aug $500.00
Sep $900.00
Oct $600.00
Nov $950.50
Dec $1000.00

For year 1992, enter sales amount for each month or 0.0
Jan $500.00
Feb $400.00
Mar $400.00
Apr $900.00
May $1000.00
Jun $55.00
Jul $300.00
Aug $800.00
Sep $750.00
Oct $900.00
Nov $600.00
Dec $300.00

Choose an option: Enter an integer between 0 and 8> 3
Year        Jan        Feb        Mar        Apr        May        Jun
1991     1000.00     600.00     700.00     800.00     950.00    1000.00
1992      500.00     400.00     400.00     900.00    1000.00      55.00

Year        Jul        Aug        Sep        Oct        Nov        Dec
1991      500.00     500.00     900.00     600.00     950.50    1000.00
1992      300.00     800.00     750.00     900.00     600.00     300.00

Choose an option: Enter an integer between 0 and 8> 4
Annual sums computed

Choose an option: Enter an integer between 0 and 8> 5
Make sure you compute annual sums first!

Annual Sales Totals
Year        Sales
1991        9500.50
1992        6905.00

Choose an option: Enter an integer between 0 and 8> 6
Find largest monthly sales for a given year:
```

```
For year: Enter an integer between 1991 and 1992> 1992
The largest monthly sales amount was $1000.00 occurring in May

Choose an option: Enter an integer between 0 and 8> 7
Graph monthly sales data for a given year:
For year: Enter an integer between 1991 and 1992> 1992

Mo. |      Sales in Dollars
Jan |************************
Feb |********************
Mar |*******************
Apr |**********************************************
May |*************************************************
Jun |**
Jul |**************
Aug |***************************************
Sep |***********************************
Oct |*********************************************
Nov |****************************
Dec |**************
0.00^           ^              ^            ^              ^            ^
                                                                    $1000.00

Each point represents $20.00

Choose an option: Enter an integer between 0 and 8> 8
Exit program? Enter Y (Yes) or N (No) > Y
Sales analysis completed
```

The operations to be performed are listed in the menu and illustrated in Fig. 13.10. The main program will repeatedly display the menu and then perform each choice selected by the user.

DATA REQUIREMENTS
Problem Inputs
> The table of sales data
> Each option selected by the user

Problem Outputs
> The sales table displayed as a matrix
> The annual sales totals displayed in a table
> The largest monthly sales amount for a particular year
> A graph of the monthly sales amounts for a particular year

Abstract Data Type Specification
> We can encapsulate the sales table and its associated operators in an abstract data type. Figure 13.11 shows the specification for SalesTableADT.

FIGURE 13.11   Specification of SalesTableADT

```
% Specification of abstract data type SalesTableADT

% Structure: The sales table consists of a collection of
% real values organized by year and month; there is one
% value for each month in the range of years covered. The
% range of years covered is represented by a pair of
% integer values.

% Operators: The following are descriptions of the
% operators of this ADT.

procedure Initialize (var Sales : SalesTable)
    % Initialize all sales amounts to zero and all
    % annual totals to zero

procedure EnterSales (var Sales : SalesTable)
    % Read from the keyboard the range of years covered
    % and a sales amount for each month of the year range

function FetchSales (Sales : SalesTable, Year : int,
                        AMonth : Month) : real
    % Retrieve the sales amount for a particular year
    % and month

procedure StoreSales (var Sales : SalesTable,
                    Year : int, AMonth : Month,
                    Amount : real)
    % Store the sales amount for a particular year and
    % month

function FetchFirst (Sales : SalesTable) : int
    % Return the first year in the range of years
    % covered by the sales table

function FetchLast (Sales : SalesTable) : int
    % Return the last year in the range of years covered
    % by the sales table

procedure DisplaySales (Sales : SalesTable)
    % Display the data in the sales table

procedure ComputeAnnual (var Sales : SalesTable)
    % Compute the annual sales totals

procedure DisplayAnnual (Sales : SalesTable)
    % Display the annual sales totals

procedure LargestMonth (Sales : SalesTable, Year : int,
                        var MaxAmount : real,
                        var MaxMonth : Month)
    % Find the largest monthly sales amount (MaxAmount)
    % and its corresponding month (MaxMonth) for a
    % particular year (Year)

procedure GraphYear (Sales : SalesTable, Year : int)
    % Display the monthly sales figures in a bar graph
    % for a particular year
```

The above specification references data type Month declared in abstract data type MonthADT. We will assume that MonthADT has a new operator called PutMonthAbbreviation that displays the first three letters of a month name. For example, December is displayed as Dec. Figure 13.12 shows the module interaction for a client program of SalesTableADT.

FIGURE 13.12 Module Interaction for a Client of SalesTableADT

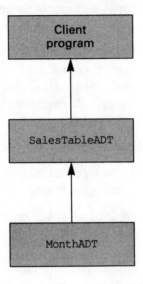

3. Design

The main program for our sales analysis solution uses the sales table and operators from SalesTableADT. The main program must first create an initially empty sales table. It then reads and processes each user request until the user is done.

ALGORITHM FOR MAIN PROGRAM
1. Create an initially empty sales table
2. loop
      3. Display the menu
      4. Read the user's choice
      5. Perform the user's choice
      exit when the user is done
   end loop

Procedure DoChoice will be used to implement step 5. DoChoice calls the sales table operators, which perform the choice selected by the user.

4. Implementation

CODING THE MAIN PROGRAM AND PROCEDURE DOCHOICE
Figure 13.13 shows the main program. Variable Sales (type SalesTable) represents the sales table.

FIGURE 13.13   Program Analysis

```
% The "Analysis" program

% Analyze data provided for a sales table organized
% by year and month. Tabulate, display, and
% graph sales data as directed by the program user

% Insert procedure EnterInt (See Fig. 10.3)

% Insert type declarations and PutMonthAbbreviation
% operator for Month (from MonthADT)

% Insert type SalesTable (from SalesTableADT) with the
% SalesTableADT operators:
% Initialize, EnterSales, DisplaySales,
% ComputeAnnual, LargestMonth, GraphYear,
% FetchFirst, FetchLast, StoreSales, FetchSales

const ExitChoice := 8    % Option for exiting program

% Insert procedures DisplayMenu, DisplayHelp,
% ShowLargest, DrawGraph, and Validate

procedure DoChoice (var Choice : int, var Sales : SalesTable)
    % Perform the option selected by Choice on sales
    % table
    % Pre : Choice is defined
    % Post: Perform option selected by Choice on Sales.
    %        Change Choice to zero if user entered
    %        ExitChoice by mistake
    % Uses: DisplayHelp, DisplayMenu, ShowLargest,
    %        DrawGraph, Validate; SalesTableADT operators;
    %        PutMonthAbbreviation from MonthADT;
    %        procedure EnterInt (see Fig. 10.3).

    case Choice of
        label 0 : DisplayHelp
        label 1 : Initialize (Sales)
        label 2 : EnterSales (Sales)
        label 3 : DisplaySales (Sales)
        label 4 : ComputeAnnual (Sales)
        label 5 : DisplayAnnual (Sales)
        label 6 : ShowLargest (Sales)
        label 7 : DrawGraph (Sales)
        label 8 : Validate (Choice)
    end case
end DoChoice

var Sales : SalesTable        % Table of sales data
var Choice : int              % Option selected
```

```
    put "Sales Analysis Program", skip
    Initialize (Sales)              % Create an empty sales table
    loop                            % Perform user's choice until done
        DisplayMenu
        EnterInt (0, ExitChoice, Choice)
        DoChoice (Choice, Sales)
        exit when Choice = ExitChoice
    end loop
```

The case statement of Fig. 13.13 calls five procedures that are not operators of SalesTableADT or MonthADT. They are procedures DisplayMenu, DisplayHelp, ShowLargest, DrawGraph, and Validate. These five are used by the main program and in turn they use SalesADT. DisplayMenu and DisplayHelp are left as programming exercises at the end of this section. We showed the menu printed by DisplayMenu earlier during the problem analysis. Procedure DisplayHelp should provide additional explanation about how to perform a particular operation and what data should be entered by the user.

Procedure ShowLargest (see Fig. 13.14) is called when Choice is 6 ("Display largest monthly sales amount in a given year"). It first reads in the desired year, calls operator LargestMonth to find the largest sales amount and month, and then displays the results returned by LargestMonth.

FIGURE 13.14   **Procedure ShowLargest**

```
procedure ShowLargest (Sales : SalesTable)

    % Display the largest monthly sales amount for a
    % given year
    % Pre : Choice is 6
    % Post: Read in a year and display the largest
    %        sales amount for that year and the month in
    %        which it was sold
    % Uses: FetchFirst, FetchLast, EnterInt,
    %        LargestMonth, PutMonthAbbreviation

    var Year : int            % Year entered by user
    var MaxAmount : real       % Largest sales amount
    var MaxMonth : Month       % Month of largest sales

    put "Find largest monthly sales for a given year:"
    put "For year: " ..
    EnterInt (FetchFirst(Sales), FetchLast(Sales), Year)
    LargestMonth (Sales, Year, MaxAmount, MaxMonth)
    put "The largest monthly sales amount was $",
            MaxAmount :4:2, " occurring in " ..
    PutMonthAbbreviation (MaxMonth)       % Display month
    put ""    % End the line
end ShowLargest
```

Procedure `DrawGraph` (see Fig. 13.15) is called when `Choice` is 7 ("Graph monthly sales amount for a given year"). It reads in the year selected by the user and then calls operator `GraphYear` to draw the graph for that year.

FIGURE 13.15   Procedure DrawGraph

```
procedure DrawGraph (var Sales : SalesTable)
    % Graph monthly sales data for a given year
    % Pre : Choice is 7
    % Post: Read in a year and graph its monthly sales
    %       figures
    % Uses: EnterInt, FetchFirst, FetchLast, GraphYear

    var Year : int            % Year entered by user

    put "Graph monthly sales data for a given year:"
    put "For year: " ..
    EnterInt (FetchFirst(Sales), FetchLast(Sales), Year)
    GraphYear (Sales, Year)
end DrawGraph
```

Procedure `Validate` (see Fig. 13.16) is the last procedure called by the main program (`Choice` is `ExitChoice`). Its purpose it to verify that the user really wants to exit the program. The style box following the figure discusses why it is desirable to do this.

FIGURE 13.16   Procedure Validate

```
procedure Validate (var Choice : int)
    % Validate the user's request to exit the program
    % Pre : Choice is ExitChoice
    % Post: Change Choice to 0 if the user does not
    %       want to exit the program

    var ExitChar : string    % Used to validate exit request

    put "Exit program? Enter Y (Yes) or N (No) > " ..
    get ExitChar
    if ExitChar = "Y" or ExitChar = "y" then
        put "Sales analysis completed"
    else
        Choice := 0            % Cancel exit request
    end if
end Validate
```

PROGRAM STYLE

VERIFYING AN EXIT REQUEST

Program users must verify that they want to exit the sales analysis program when `Choice` is `ExitChoice`. Without this verification step, all data entry and analysis performed so far may have to be repeated if the program user selects the exit option by mistake.

Choosing the Representation for SalesTable

The first step in implementing abstract data type `SalesTableADT` is to choose an internal representation for the data structure. We can use a two-dimensional array (first dimension is year, second dimension is month) of `real` values to store the sales data.

Besides the sales data, we also need to specify the first and last years of the range covered. We can store these values as separate fields in a record along with the sales data.

The last implementation decision is whether or not we should store the annual sales totals in this record. We could recompute these totals each time that we need them, or compute them once and save them in the sales table record. It makes more sense to save them rather than recompute them, so we will need an array of `real` values for storing the annual sales totals as an separate record field.

FIGURE 13.17   Record Variable Sales

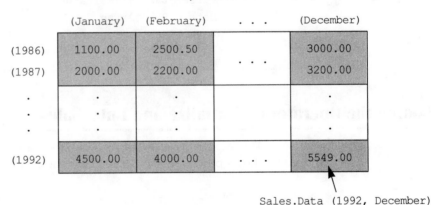

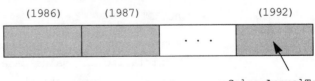

Figure 13.17 sketches record variable `Sales` (type `SalesTable`), assuming the sales data are stored in array `Sales.Data` and the annual totals are stored in array `Sales.AnnualTotal`. We have shown only the sec-

tions of these arrays that would be defined when Sales.First is 1986 and Sales.Last is 1992.

Figure 13.18 shows the type declarations for record SalesTable that would appear at the beginning of the implementation part of SalesTableADT. The specification part was shown earlier.

FIGURE 13.18   Declaration of Data Type SalesTable

```
% Implementation of SalesTableADT

% Modules needed: MonthADT and procedure EnterInt
%                 (see Fig. 10.3).

const MinYear := 1900      % Minimum year covered
const MaxYear := 1999      % Maximum year covered

% Insert declaration for Month from MonthADT

type YearRange : MinYear..MaxYear
type SalesArray : array YearRange, Month of real
type TotalArray : array YearRange of real
type SalesTable :
    record
        First, Last : YearRange      % Year range
        Data : SalesArray            % Sales data
        AnnualTotal : TotalArray     % Annual totals
    end record
```

Coding the Operators – Initialize and EnterSales

The next step is to implement the sales table operators. Figure 13.19 shows procedures Initialize and EnterSales.

FIGURE 13.19   Procedures Initialize and EnterSales

```
% Insert EnterInt and PutMonthAbbreviation from
% MonthADT

procedure Initialize (var Sales : SalesTable)
    % Initialize all sales data to zero, all sales
    % totals to zero, and the range of years covered
    % to MinYear through MaxYear
    % Pre : MinYear <= MaxYear
    % Post: All sales data and annual totals contain
    %       zero and the year range is MinYear..MaxYear
```

```
                    % Store zeros in array SalesData
                    Sales.First := MinYear
                    Sales.Last := MaxYear
                    for CurYear : MinYear .. MaxYear
                        for CurMonth : Month
                            Sales.Data(CurYear, CurMonth) := 0.0
                        end for
                    end for

                    % Store zeros in array SalesAnnualTotal
                    for CurYear : MinYear .. MaxYear
                        Sales.AnnualTotal(CurYear) := 0.0
                    end for

                    put "Sales table initialized"
                end Initialize

                procedure EnterSales (var Sales : SalesTable)
                    % Read the range of years covered and enter a sales
                    % amount for each month of the year range
                    % Pre : Record Sales has been initialized
                    % Post: The first and last years of the year range
                    %       are read in and data values are read for
                    %       each month and year in the range. MinYear <=
                    %       first year <= last year <= MaxYear
                    % Uses: EnterInt and PutMonthAbbreviation

                    var TempYear : int        % Holds data value for year

                    % Enter first and last years of year range
                    put "First: " ..
                    EnterInt (MinYear, MaxYear, TempYear)
                    Sales.First := TempYear
                    put "Last: " ..
                    EnterInt (Sales.First, MaxYear, TempYear)
                    Sales.Last := TempYear

                    % Enter sales table data
                    for CurYear : Sales.First .. Sales.Last
                        put ""
                        put "For year ", CurYear ..
                        put ", enter sales amount for each month or 0.0:"
                        for CurMonth : Month
                            PutMonthAbbreviation (CurMonth)
                            put " $" ..
                            get Sales.Data(CurYear, CurMonth)
                        end for
                    end for
                end EnterSales
```

Both procedures `Initialize` and `EnterSales` use a pair of nested `for` loops to access a block of elements in the array `Sales.Data`. `Initialize` sets all elements of arrays `Sales.Data` and `Sales.AnnualTotal` to zero.

Procedure `EnterSales` calls `EnterInt` twice to read in the range of years covered. Next, procedure `EnterSales` reads the sales data into rows `Sales.First` through `Sales.Last` of array `Sales.Data`. Procedure `EnterSales` calls `PutMonthAbbreviation` to display each month's abbreviation as a prompt.

PROGRAM STYLE

> **EXTERNAL VERSUS INTERNAL REFERENCE TO A FIELD OF AN ADT**
> Because procedure `EnterSales` is part of the abstract data type `SalesTableADT`, it is perfectly all right for `EnterSales` to use the qualified identifiers `Sales.First` and `Sales.Last`. However, functions `FetchFirst` and `FetchLast` should be used outside of `SalesTableADT` to retrieve the first and last year covered by the sales table data. For example, the procedure call statement
>
> ```
> EnterInt (FetchFirst(Sales), FetchLast(Sales), Year)
> ```
>
> is used in both `ShowLargest` and `DrawGraph` (see Figures 13.14 and 13.15) for this purpose. These functions are discussed next.

Operators FetchSales, StoreSales, FetchFirst, and FetchLast

Next, we will implement four relatively simple operators (see Fig. 13.20). `FetchSales` and `StoreSales` are used to retrieve and store sales data for a particular year and month. These operators could be used to build a client procedure that edits incorrect sales data (see programming exercise 3). `FetchFirst` and `FetchLast` are used to retrieve the first and last year of the range covered by the current sales table.

FIGURE 13.20 FetchSales, StoreSales, FetchFirst, and FetchLast

```
function FetchSales (Sales : SalesTable,
                         Year : YearRange,
                         AMonth : Month) : real
   % Retrieve the sales amount for a particular year
   % and month
   % Pre : The sales table is defined and
   %       MinYear <= Year <= MaxYear
   % Post: Return the sales entry for month AMonth and
   %       year Year
   result Sales.Data(Year, AMonth)
end FetchSales
```

```
        procedure StoreSales (var Sales : SalesTable,
                             Year : YearRange, AMonth : Month,
                             Amount : real)
        % Store the sales amount for a particular year and
        % month.
        % Pre : MinYear <= Year <= MaxYear
        % Post: The sales entry for month AMonth and year
        %       Year is Amount
        Sales.Data(Year, AMonth) := Amount
    end StoreSales

    function FetchFirst (Sales : SalesTable) : int
        % Return the first year of the range covered
        result Sales.First
    end FetchFirst

    function FetchLast (Sales : SalesTable) : int
        % Return the last year of the range covered
        result Sales.Last
    end FetchLast
```

Procedure DisplaySales

Most screens are not wide enough to display the sales data for all twelve months of a year. Consequently, DisplaySales calls ShowHalf twice: first to print the sales figures for the first six months and then to print the last six months. ShowHalf begins by displaying the six months covered as column headings. Next, a pair of nested for loops displays the sales figures for those six months of each year.

FIGURE 13.21   Procedure DisplaySales

```
    procedure ShowHalf (var Sales : SalesTable,
                       FirstMonth, LastMonth : Month)
        % Display the sales amounts by year for each of the
        % months from FirstMonth to LastMonth
        % Pre : Record Sales is defined and
        %       FirstMonth < LastMonth
        % Post: Display the sales volumes in a table whose
        %       rows are the years covered and whose columns
        %       are FirstMonth..LastMonth
        % Uses: PutMonthAbbreviation

        % Print table headings for the months displayed
        put "Year    " ..
        for CurMonth : FirstMonth .. LastMonth
            PutMonthAbbreviation (CurMonth)  % Print month
```

```
                put " " ..                        % Separate names
            end for
            put ""                                % End the heading line

        % Print sales figures for each month of each year
        for CurYear : Sales.First .. Sales.Last
        put CurYear ..
        for CurMonth : FirstMonth .. LastMonth
        put Sales.Data(CurYear, CurMonth) :8:2 ..
        end for
        put ""                % End the line of year's data
        end for
    end ShowHalf

    procedure DisplaySales (var Sales : SalesTable)
        % Display the data in the sales table
        % Pre : Record Sales is defined
        % Post: All entries of the sales table for years
        %       First through Last are displayed
        % Uses: ShowHalf
        % Display first six months and last six months of array
        % Sales

        ShowHalf (Sales, Month.January, Month.June)
        put ""
        ShowHalf (Sales, Month.July, Month.December)
        put ""
    end DisplaySales
```

Procedures ComputeAnnual and DisplayAnnual

Procedure ComputeAnnual accumulates the sum of each row of the sales table and stores it in the appropriate element of array Sales.AnnualTotal. Procedure DisplayAnnual simply displays the values stored in this array. These procedures are shown in Fig. 13.22.

FIGURE 13.22 Procedures ComputeAnnual and DisplayAnnual

```
    procedure ComputeAnnual (var Sales : SalesTable)
        % Compute and store the annual sales totals
        % Pre : Record Sales has been defined
        % Post: Annual totals for years First through Last
        %       are computed and stored in Sales

        % Find each annual total
        for CurYear : Sales.First .. Sales.Last
            % Accumulate sum for 12 months
```

```
                    var Sum : real := 0.0
                    for CurMonth : Month
                        Sum := Sum + Sales.Data(CurYear, CurMonth)
                    end for
                    Sales.AnnualTotal(CurYear) := Sum
                    % Store sales total
                end for

            put "Annual sums computed"
        end ComputeAnnual

        procedure DisplayAnnual (var Sales : SalesTable)
            % Display the annual sales totals
            % Pre : Record Sales is defined
            % Post: Each annual total is displayed
            put "Make sure you compute annual sums first!"
            put ""        % Skip a line
            put "Annual Sales Totals"
            put "Year    Sales"
            for CurYear : Sales.First .. Sales.Last
                put CurYear, Sales.AnnualTotal(CurYear) :15:2
            end for
        end DisplayAnnual
```

Procedures LargestMonth and GraphYear

Figure 13.23 shows procedures LargestMonth and GraphYear. Procedure LargestMonth returns through MaxAmount the largest value in row Year of the array SalesData. It does this by saving the largest value found so far (starting with Sales.Data(Year, January)) in parameter MaxAmount. Each time an array element containing a larger value is found, its value is stored in MaxAmount and its month subscript is stored in MaxMonth.

FIGURE 13.23   Procedures LargestMonth and GraphYear

```
        procedure LargestMonth (var Sales : SalesTable,
                                Year : YearRange,
                                var MaxAmount : real,
                                var MaxMonth : Month)
            % Find the largest monthly sales amount (MaxAmount)
            % and its month (MaxMonth) for a particular year (Year)
            % Pre : Record Sales is defined and
            %       MinYear <= Year <= MaxYear
            % Post: The largest value for year Year is returned
            %       in MaxAmount; the corresponding month is
            %       returned in MaxMonth
```

```
                    % Find the largest value in row Year of array
                    % Sales.Data

                    MaxAmount := Sales.Data(Year, Month.January)
                    MaxMonth := Month.January
                    % Assume first month was largest
                    % Examine rest of array for largest value
                    for CurMonth : Month.February .. Month.December
                        % Invariant:
                        %    MaxAmount contains largest amount so far and
                        %    Sales.Data(Year, MaxMonth) is equal to
                        %    MaxAmount
                        if Sales.Data(Year, CurMonth) > MaxAmount then
                            % Save new largest amount so far
                            MaxAmount := Sales.Data(Year, CurMonth)
                            MaxMonth := CurMonth
                        end if
                    end for
                end LargestMonth

                procedure GraphYear (var Sales : SalesTable,
                                     Year : YearRange)
                    % Display the monthly sales figures in a bar graph
                    % for a particular year
                    % Pre : Record Sales is defined and
                    %        MinYear <= Year <= MaxYear
                    % Post: Display a bar graph showing the relative
                    %        size of each monthly sales amount for a
                    %        particular year

                    const Star := "*"        % Symbol plotted
                    const PlotWidth := 50    % Longest bar length

                    var MaxAmount: real      % The largest value plotted
                    var Increment: real      % The amount represented by
                                             % each point
                    var PlotVal : real       % The amount plotted so far
                    var MaxMonth : Month     % and its month

                    % Define the scale for the horizontal axis
                    LargestMonth (Sales, Year, MaxAmount, MaxMonth)
                    Increment := round(MaxAmount / PlotWidth)
                    if Increment = 0.0 then
                        Increment := 1.0     % Prevent infinite loop
                    end if

                    % Plot the bar graph, starting with heading
                    put skip, "Mo. |     Sales in Dollars"
```

```
               % Print a bar for each month of the year
               for CurMonth : Month
                   PutMonthAbbreviation (CurMonth)  % Print month
                   put " |" ..
                   PlotVal := Increment        % Initialize sum plotted
                   loop       % Plot until value exceeds sales
                       exit when PlotVal > Sales.Data(Year, CurMonth)
                       put Star ..               % Plot a new point
                       PlotVal := PlotVal + Increment
                   end loop
                   put ""
               end for

               % Draw horizontal scale
               put 0.0 :4:2, "^          ^           ^            ^",
                       "         ^           ^"
               put "" : 45, "$", MaxAmount :4:2
               put "Each point represents $", Increment :4:2
           end GraphYear
```

Procedure `GraphYear` draws a bar chart showing the monthly sales amounts for a particular year of array `Sales.Data`. Each row of the bar graph represents a different month and each bar consists of a sequence of asterisks. To normalize the bar graph, procedure `GraphYear` first calls procedure `LargestMonth` to find the largest monthly sales amount for that year. Next, this amount is divided by the constant `PlotWidth` (value is 50) to get the value represented by each point plotted. For each month being displayed, the loop in `GraphYear` continues to plot points until the value plotted exceeds the sales amount for that month. Hence, the largest sales amount will be plotted as a bar of length `PlotWidth`; all other bars will be smaller. (The longest bar may not be exactly `PlotWidth` long. Can you explain why it may be a different length?)

5. Testing the Sales Analysis Program

A sample run of the sales analysis program was shown earlier in Fig. 13.10. To test this program, you must first implement `MonthADT` and procedure `DisplayMenu`. During testing, you should see what happens when unusual data are entered. For example, what is the effect of entering year values outside the subrange defined by `YearRange`. Also, see what happens when operators are selected in an unnatural order. For example, does the program crash or print strange values if the sales table is displayed before it is read? Does printing the annual sales totals before they are computed cause a problem? You should also provide procedure `DisplayHelp` and verify that it performs its intended operation.

Exercises for Section 13.3

Self-Check

1. Explain why the variable `TempYear` is needed in procedure `EnterSales`.
2. Why is it necessary for `DisplaySales` to call `ShowHalf` twice?

Programming

1. Write procedures `DisplayMenu` and `DisplayHelp`.
2. Write abstract data type `MonthADT` including the new operator `PutMonthAbbreviation`.
3. Develop a new procedure (not an operator) that edits an incorrect sales table entry. The user should enter the year and month (1 through 12) of the incorrect entry and the correct sales amount. Use operators `FetchSales` and `StoreSales` to display the current entry and store a revised value if needed.
4. Write a new operator that reads the sales data from an external file rather than the keyboard. The file variable should be a parameter of this procedure. Explain how the main program would have to be modified to use this operator.

13.4 Parallel Arrays and Arrays of Records

Often a data collection contains items of different types. For example, the data representing the performance of a class of students on an exam consists of the student names, exam scores, and grades assigned.

Parallel Arrays

One approach to organizing these data would be to declare separate arrays with identical subscript types for the names, scores, and grades as shown below.

```
const MaxClass := 200
const StrLength := 20

type ClassRange : 1..MaxClass
type NameArray : array ClassRange of string(StrLength)
type ScoreArray : array ClassRange of int
type GradeArray : array ClassRange of string (1)

var Names : NameArray
var Scores : ScoreArray
var Grades : GradeArray
```

These three arrays are called *parallel arrays* because all the data items with the same subscript (say, I) pertain to a particular student (the I-th student); see Fig. 13.24. The data for the first student are stored in Names(1), Scores(1), and Grades(1). A better way to organize the student data is shown in the next section.

FIGURE 13.24 **Three Parallel Arrays**

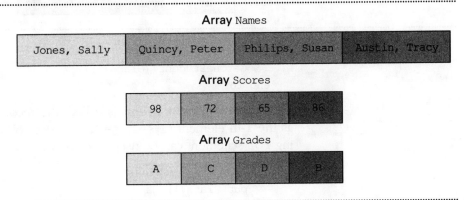

Declaring an Array of Student Records

A more natural and convenient organization of the class performance data is to group all the information pertaining to a particular student in a record. The data structure declared next represents the class data as a single array of records named Class. A sample array Class is shown in Fig. 13.25.

```
const MaxClass := 200
const StrLength := 20

type ClassRange : 1..MaxClass
type StringType : string(StrLength)
type Student :
   record
      Name : StringType
      Score : int
      Grade : string (1)
   end record
type StudentArray : array ClassRange of Student
var Class : StudentArray
```

In Fig. 13.25, the data for the first student are stored in Class(1). The individual data items are Class(1).Name, Class(1).Score, and Class(1).Grade.

If procedure GetOneStudent is available to read a single student record, the for statement below can be used to fill the entire array Class with data.

FIGURE 13.25 Array of Records

	Name	Score	Grade
Class(1)	Jones, Sally	98	A ← Class(1).Grade
Class(2)	Quincy, Peter	72	C
Class(3)	Philips, Susan	65	D
Class(4)	Austin, Tracy	86	B

```
for I : 1 .. MaxClass
   GetOneStudent (Class(I))
end for
```

Each time `GetOneStudent` is called, the record returned will be stored as the `I`-th element (`1 <= I <= MaxClass`) of array `Class`. The following `for` statement can be used to display all the names read.

```
for I : 1 .. MaxClass
   put Class(I).Name
end for
```

Using Bind Declarations with an Array of Records

Be careful when using a `bind` declaration with an array of records. For example, this `bind` declaration

```
bind C to Class(I)
```

uses the subscripted variable `Class(I)` as its record variable. The particular array element referenced depends on the value of `I`. If `I` is undefined or is out of range, a run-time error will result.

If `I` is in range but happens to be changed inside the scope of the `bind` declaration, the array element referenced will not be affected. For example, the statements below display the first student's name `MaxClass` times. Since `I` is `1` when the `bind` declaration is reached, `Class(1)` is the record referenced in the scope of the `bind` declaration. Even though the loop changes the value of `I`, `Class(1)` is still the record referenced so `Class(1).Name` will be displayed repeatedly.

```
% Incorrect attempt to display all student names
I := 1
bind C to Class(I)
loop
   put C.Name
   ...
   exit when I = MaxClass
   I := I + 1
end loop
```

The correct way to sequence these statements is shown next.

```
% Display all student names
I := 1
loop
    bind C to Class(I)
    put C.Name
    ...
    exit when I = MaxClass
    I := I + 1
end loop
```

Now all student names will be printed because I has been changed prior to each new arrival at the bind declaration. Each time the bind declaration is reached, it references a new record. Whenever a loop accesses an array of records in sequential order, the bind declaration should be nested inside the loop and not vice-versa.

Exercises for Section 13.4

Self-Check

1. For the array of records Class shown above, which of these statements are valid? What is displayed by each valid statement?

   a. put Class(3).Name(4)
   b. put Class(3).Grade(4)
   c. put Class.Grade(3)
   d. put Class(4).Name
   e. put Class(4).Name(4).Grade
   f. put Class(3).Grade
   g. put Class(3)
   h. put Class.Name(4)

2. Write a for statement that could be used to read data into the three parallel arrays declared in this section. Assume that the number of students, NumStu, is known before loop execution begins.
3. Does it require more or less memory space to store an array of records or parallel arrays?

Programming

1. Write procedure GetOneStudent. Read each student's name and score; leave the grade field undefined.

13.5 Processing an Array of Records

In the next problem, we will process the array of student records described in the previous section. This array will be part of a larger data structure that stores all the information needed to analyze student performance on an exam.

⊠ Case Study:

Grading an Exam

1. Problem   Your computer science professor wants a program that will assist her in assigning grades for an exam. This program should read and display each student's name and exam score, compute and display all exam statistics (i.e., number of students who took the exam, low score, high score, average score, median score, and standard deviation), and assign letter grades based on the class average and standard deviation.

2. Analysis   Currently your professor stores the information for her classes in a gradebook. Each gradebook page has a list of students on the left and a column for storing the exam scores and the corresponding letter grades. The exam statistics appear at the bottom of the page in the same column. A sample entry for one exam is shown in Fig. 13.26. The student names and numeric scores are provided as input data; the letter grades, number of students, and exam statistics are all initially undefined.

FIGURE 13.26   Sample Gradebook Entry for One Exam

Name	Score/Grade	
Sally Adams	87	?
Robert Baker	95	?
Jane Cohen	67	?
William Dooley	73	?
.		
.		
.		
Number of Students	?	
Lowest Score	?	
Highest Score	?	
Median Score	?	
Average Score	?	
Standard deviation	?	

Figure 13.27 shows a sample run of the grading program. The program begins by reading the name and score of three students. Next, the exam statistics are computed and displayed, grades are assigned, and the final student records are displayed.

FIGURE 13.27   Sample Run of Grading Program

```
Enter the data requested for each student
Enter a question mark for an unknown grade
Press RETURN after prompt 'Name >' when done

Name > Joe Costa
Score> 80
Grade> ?

Name > Lee Hayes
Score> 70
Grade> ?

Name > Bill Titcomb
Score> 60
Grade> ?

Name >
3 student records were read

The exam statistics follow:
   Low      High    Median    Average    Std deviation
    60       80        70        70.0          10.0
The count of students is 3

The student names, scores, and grades follow:
Joe Costa             80    A
Lee Hayes             70    C
Bill Titcomb          60    D
```

DATA REQUIREMENTS

Problem Inputs

> The name of each student taking the exam
> The score of each student taking the exam

Problem Outputs

> Each student's name, score, and letter grade
> The count of students taking the exam
> The exam statistics including the low score, high score, median score, average, and standard deviation

Specification for GradeBookADT

> We will use a single data structure to store all the information needed for one exam in the gradebook. We will encapsulate the data structure and its operators in abstract data type GradeBookADT. Figure 13.28 shows its specification.

FIGURE 13.28   Specification for GradeBookADT

```
% Specification of abstract data type GradeBookADT

% Structure:   Contains the name, score, and grade for
% each student who took the exam and a count of
% students. Also contains a collection of values
% representing the exam statistics.

% Operators:   The following are operators for this ADT.

procedure CreateBook (var Test : GradeBook)
   % Create a gradebook page that is initially empty

procedure GetBook (var Test : GradeBook)
   % Read the student names and exam scores, and count
   % the number of students who took the exam

procedure DisplayStudents (Test : GradeBook)
   % Display the name, numeric score, and letter grade
   % for each student who took the exam

procedure ComputeStats (var Test : GradeBook)
   % Compute the exam statistics

procedure DisplayStats (Test : GradeBook)
   % Display the exam statistics

procedure AssignGrades (var Test : GradeBook)
   % Assign a letter grade to each student
```

In addition to the abstract data type shown above, we will use another abstract data type, called StudentADT, which will be specified later. StudentADT will allow us to store and process a single student (data type Student). We will use operators GetStudent (read a student record) and PutStudent (write a student record). Figure 13.29 shows the interaction between modules.

FIGURE 13.29   Module Interaction for Grading Program System

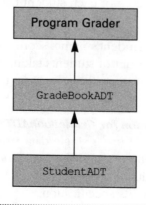

3. Design

The main program for our student grading program uses the data structure and operators described in GradeBookADT. The main program algorithm is shown next.

MAIN PROGRAM ALGORITHM
1. Read the student data.
2. Compute the exam statistics.
3. Print the exam statistics.
4. Assign letter grades to each student.
5. Print each student's final record.

4. Implementation

Coding the Main Program
Figure 13.30 shows the main program. The main program body consists of calls to the operator procedures declared in GradeBookADT.

FIGURE 13.30

Student Grading Program

```
% The "Grader" program
% Compute and display the exam statistics, assign
% letter grades, and display each student's record

% Module needed: GradeBookADT

% Insert GradeBookADT constants, type declarations,
% and operators: CreateBook, GetBook,
% DisplayStudents, AssignGrades, ComputeStats,
% DisplayStats

var Test : GradeBook        % Data for one test

CreateBook (Test)
GetBook (Test)
ComputeStats (Test)
DisplayStats (Test)
AssignGrades (Test)
DisplayStudents (Test)
```

Choosing the Representation for GradeBookADT

The first step in implementing abstract data type GradeBookADT is to choose an internal representation for the data structure. In Section 13.4, we used an array of records to store the student data for an exam. We can store all the exam statistics in a record. The student array and the statistics record could be separate fields of a composite record. Figure 13.31 sketches record variable Test (type GradeBook), assuming the student data are stored in array Test.Class and the statistics are stored in record Test.Stats. The number of students who took the exam will be stored in Test.NumStu. Figure 13.32 shows the type declarations for record GradeBook that would appear at the beginning of the implementation part of GradeBookADT.

FIGURE 13.31   Record Variable Test

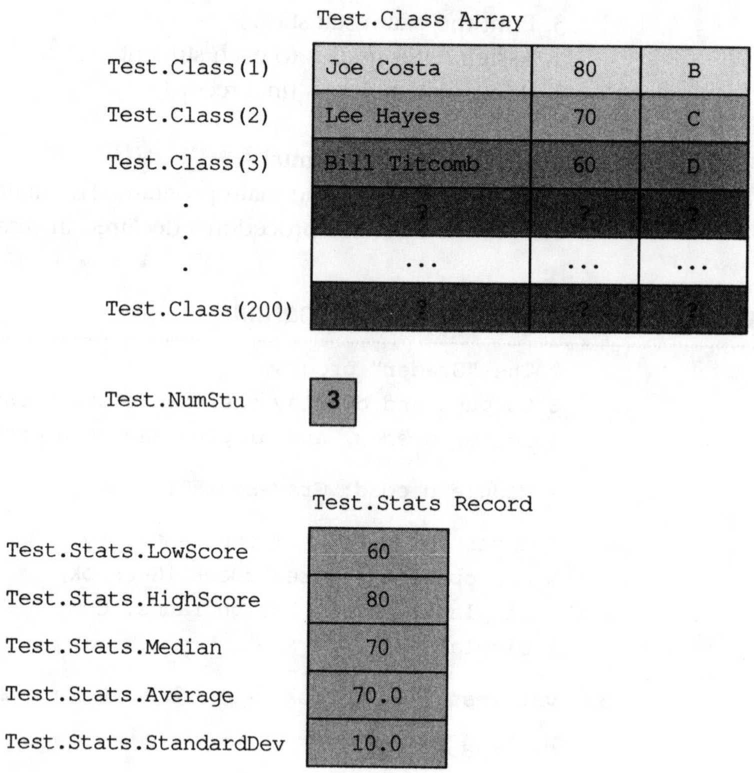

Test.Class Array

Test.Class(1)	Joe Costa	80	B
Test.Class(2)	Lee Hayes	70	C
Test.Class(3)	Bill Titcomb	60	D
.	?	?	?
.	...	...	...
Test.Class(200)	?	?	?

Test.NumStu   3

Test.Stats Record

Test.Stats.LowScore	60
Test.Stats.HighScore	80
Test.Stats.Median	70
Test.Stats.Average	70.0
Test.Stats.StandardDev	10.0

FIGURE 13.32   Declaration of Data Type GradeBook

```
% Implementation of GradeBookADT
% Module needed: StudentADT

const MaxClass := 200        % Maximum number of students

% Insert type declaration for Student from StudentADT

type ClassRange : 0..MaxClass
type StudentArray : array ClassRange of Student
                            % Array of records

type Statistics :            % Statistics record
    record
        LowScore : int
        HighScore : int
```

```
          Median : int
          Average : real
          StandardDev : real
      end record

  type GradeBook :
    record
        Class : StudentArray      % Student data
        NumStu : ClassRange       % Count of students
        Stats : Statistics        % Exam statistics
    end record
```

Coding the Operators – CreateBook and GetBook

The next step is to implement the operators described in the specification for GradeBookADT (see Fig. 13.28). Figure 13.33 shows the first two operators, CreateBook and GetBook.

FIGURE 13.33   Procedures CreateBook and GetBook

```
% Insert GetStudent and PutStudent from StudentADT

procedure CreateBook (var Test : GradeBook)
    % Initialize record Test so that it is considered empty
    % Pre : None
    % Post: Set count of students to zero

    Test.NumStu := 0
end CreateBook

procedure GetBook (var Test : GradeBook)
    % Read student names and exam scores. Also count
    % the number of students who took the exam
    % Pre : None
    % Post: Student names and exam scores are stored
    %       along with a count of students
    % Uses: Procedure GetStudent from StudentADT

    const Sentinel := ""    % Null name marks the end
    var NextStudent : Student    % Next student record

    put "Enter the data requested for each student"
    put "Enter a blank for an unknown grade"
    put "Press RETURN after prompt 'Name >' when done"
    loop
        GetStudent (NextStudent) % Read next student
        exit when NextStudent.Name = Sentinel
        if Test.NumStu = MaxClass then
            put "Sorry, too many students to handle"
            put "Ignoring this student", skip
        else
```

```
              Test.NumStu := Test.NumStu + 1
              Test.Class(Test.NumStu) := NextStudent
                      % Store student
          end if
      end loop

      % Assert: no more students or array is filled
      put Test.NumStu, " student records were read"
  end GetBook
```

Procedure `CreateBook` simply sets `Test.NumStu` to zero. Procedure `GetBook` calls procedure `GetStudent` (part of `StudentADT`) to enter the data for each student who took the exam. `GetStudent` returns the next student's data through its parameter `NextStudent`. The program user can indicate that there are no more students by pressing the Return key after the prompt for a student's name. If a non-blank name is read, the count of students processed (`Test.NumStu`) is incremented by one, and the statement

```
      Test.Class(Test.NumStu) := NextStudent
```

copies the input data into the next element of the array `Test.Class`. The final count of students is stored in `Test.NumStu` when the procedure finishes execution.

Procedure DisplayStudents

Procedure `DisplayStudents` (see Fig. 13.34) displays the count of students and also displays a table of student records. Procedure `PutStudent` (part of `StudentADT`) determines the actual form of each record displayed.

FIGURE 13.34   Procedure DisplayStudents

```
procedure DisplayStudents (Test : GradeBook)
    % Display the number of students and the name,
    % numeric score, and letter grade for each
    % student who took the exam
    % Pre : The student names and scores are defined and
    %       0 <= count of students <= MaxClass
    % Post: All student records are displayed
    % Uses: Procedure PutStudent from StudentADT

    put "The count of students is ", Test.NumStu, skip
    put "The student names, scores, and grades follow:"
    for I : 1 .. Test.NumStu
        PutStudent (Test.Class(I))
    end for
end DisplayStudents
```

Procedure AssignGrades

Procedure `AssignGrades` (see Fig. 13.35) assigns a letter grade to each student. The grade can be determined by comparing the student's score to the class average and the standard deviation. Table 13.1 describes the desired grade assignment.

FIGURE 13.35 Procedure AssignGrades

```
procedure AssignGrades (var Test : GradeBook)
    % Assigns letter grade to each student.
    % Pre : All exam scores are defined and
    %        the average and standard deviation are defined
    % Post: The grade for each student is defined

    const Avg := Test.Stats.Average
    const StdDev := Test.Stats.StandardDev

    const LowestA := Avg + 1.0 * StdDev
    const LowestB := Avg + 0.5 * StdDev
    const LowestC := Avg - 0.5 * StdDev
    const LowestD := Avg - 1.0 * StdDev

    for I : 1 .. Test.NumStu
        bind var S to Test.Class (I)
        if S.Score >= LowestA then
            S.Grade := "A"
        elsif S.Score >= LowestB then
            S.Grade := "B"
        elsif S.Score >= LowestC then
            S.Grade := "C"
        elsif S.Score >= LowestD then
            S.Grade := "D"
        else
            S.Grade := "F"
        end if
    end for
end AssignGrades
```

TABLE 13.1 Decision Table for Assigning Letter Grades

Score Range	Grade
>= Avg + 1.0 * StdDev	A
>= Avg + 0.5 * StdDev	B
>= Avg - 0.5 * StdDev	C
>= Avg - 1.0 * StdDev	D
< Avg - 1.0 * StdDev	F

The `if` statement in procedure `AssignGrades` implements the decision table above. The `for` loop causes this `if` statement to be repeated once for each student. We have used `const` declarations to shorten the names in this procedure, to make it more readable.

Procedure ComputeStats

Procedure `ComputeStats` computes the exam statistics and stores the results in the subrecord `Test.Stats`. `ComputeStats` calls a different function to compute each statistic. Function `FindAverage` returns the average score and is shown at the top of Fig. 13.36. Function `FindStandardDev` and `FindMedian` are discussed later. The rest of the statistical functions are left as exercises. Procedure `DisplayStats` displays the contents of record `Stats` and is also left as an exercise.

FIGURE 13.36   Function FindAverage and Procedure ComputeStats

```
% Insert FindLow, FindHigh, FindMedian, and
% FindStandardDev

function FindAverage (Test : GradeBook) : real
    % Define the average of the scores in array Test.Class
    % Pre : Student Scores are stored in Test.Class
    % Post: Return the average in Test.Stats.Average

    var Sum : real          % The accumulating sum of scores

    % Accumulate the sum of all scores
    Sum := 0
    for I : 1 .. Test.NumStu
        Sum := Sum + Test.Class(I).Score
    end for

    % Return the average score or 0.0
    if Test.NumStu not= 0 then
        result Sum / Test.NumStu
    else
        result 0.0
    end if
end FindAverage

procedure ComputeStats (var Test : GradeBook)
    % Compute the exam statistics
    % Pre : Array Test.Class and Test.NumStu are defined
    % Post: Each exam statistic is computed and stored

    Test.Stats.Average := FindAverage(Test)
    Test.Stats.LowScore := FindLow(Test)
    Test.Stats.HighScore := FindHigh(Test)
    Test.Stats.Median := FindMedian(Test)
    Test.Stats.StandardDev := FindStandardDev(Test)
end ComputeStats
```

Function FindStandardDev

Function `FindStandardDev` in Fig. 13.37 computes the standard deviation using these formulas:

$$sum\ of\ squares = (score_1 - average)^2 + (score_2 - average)^2 + \ldots \\ + (score_N - average)^2$$

$$standard\ deviation = \sqrt{\frac{sum\ of\ squares}{N-1}}$$

The standard deviation is a measure of the spread or dispersion of the grades around the average grade. Statistical theory states that for a bell curve, 68.34% of the grades will lie within one standard deviation of the average grade.

FIGURE 13.37   Function FindStandardDev

```
function FindStandardDev (Test : GradeBook) : real
    % Return the standard deviation of the exam scores
    % Pre : The exam scores and their average are defined
    % Post: Return the standard deviation if defined;
    %       otherwise, return zero

    var SumSquares : real := 0     % Sum of squares
    for I : 1 .. Test.NumStu
        SumSquares +=
            (Test.Class(I).Score - Test.Stats.Average)**2
    end for
    if Test.NumStu > 1 then
        result sqrt(SumSquares / (Test.NumStu - 1))
    else
        result 0.0
    end if
end FindStandardDev
```

Function FindMedian

Procedure `ComputeStats` (see Fig. 13.36) calls function `FindMedian` to compute the median score on an exam. It is relatively easy to determine the median score once the student records are in order by score. If there are an odd number of records, the median score is found in the middle element of array `Test.Class`, where the expression `(Test.NumStu div 2) + 1` computes the subscript of the middle element. For example, if there are five student records, the middle element would be the third score (`5 div 2 + 1` is 3). If there are an even number of scores, the median score is the average of the two middle scores. For example, if there are four student records, the median is the average of the second and third scores.

Function FindMedian is shown in Fig. 13.38. FindMedian first calls procedure SortStudents to sort the records in array Test.Class. Notice that record Test is declared as a value parameter in FindMedian so that only the local copy of array Test.Class will be sorted, not the actual array. SortStudents sorts the array of student records and is a modification of procedure SelectSort (see Fig. 11.26) which sorts an array of integers. In SortStudents, procedure Switch is used to switch a pair of array records instead of a pair of integer values.

FIGURE 13.38

Switch, SortStudents, and FindMedian

```
procedure Switch (var Stu1, Stu2 : Student)
    % Switch student records Stu1 and Stu2
    % Pre : none
    % Post: Stu1 is old Stu2, and Stu2 is old Stu1

    const Temp := Stu1
    Stu1 := Stu2
    Stu2 := Temp
end Switch

procedure SortStudents (var Test : GradeBook)
    % Order the student records by exam score
    % Pre : Student data are defined and the count of
    %        students is between 1 and MaxClass
    % Post: The student records are in increasing order
    %        by score

    % Sort array field Class based on exam scores

    for Fill : 1 .. Test.NumStu - 1
        % Fill locates element being filled with next
        % smallest score

        % Invariant: The elements in Class(1 .. Fill-1)
        %            are in their proper place and
        %            Fill <= Test.NumStu

        % Find index of element with smallest score in
        % Class(Fill .. Test.NumStu)

        var IndexOfMin : ClassRange := Fill
        % IndexOfMin locates the smallest so far
        for Next : Fill + 1 .. Test.NumStu
            % Next locates element being compared to
            % smallest so far
```

```
            % Invariant: IndexOfMin is the index of the
            % element with smallest score in
            % Class(Fill .. Next-1) and Next <= NumStu+1

            if Test.Class(Next).Score <
                Test.Class(IndexOfMin).Score then
                    IndexOfMin := Next
            end if
        end for

        % Assert: Element at IndexOfMin is next smallest

        % Exchange elements with subscripts Fill and
        % IndexOfMin
        if IndexOfMin not= Fill then
            Switch (Test.Class(Fill),
                Test.Class(IndexOfMin))
        end if
    end for
end SortStudents

function FindMedian (Test : GradeBook) : int
    % Return the median score for the exam
    % Pre : Student data are defined and the count of
    %        students is between 1 and MaxClass
    % Post: Return the middle score if there is an odd
    %        number of scores; otherwise, return the
    %        average of the middle two scores
    % Uses: SortStudents

    var T : GradeBook := Test      % Make local copy
                                   % so it can be sorted
    SortStudents (T)               % Sort the local array
    var Middle : ClassRange := (T.NumStu div 2) + 1
            % Index to middle element
    if T.NumStu mod 2 = 1 then     % Use middle score if odd
        result T.Class(Middle).Score
    else % Average two middle scores
        result (T.Class(Middle - 1).Score +
                T.Class(Middle).Score) div 2
    end if
end FindMedian
```

Abstract Data Type StudentADT

Before we can run the program, we must implement abstract data type StudentADT. Figure 13.39 shows the specification for abstract data type StudentADT; Figure 13.40 shows its implementation.

FIGURE 13.39

Specification of StudentADT

```
% Specification of abstract data type StudentADT

% Structure:    Student contains descriptive information % about
one student such as the student's name, exam
% score, and grade

% Operators:    The following are descriptions of the
% ADT operators

procedure GetStudent (var AStudent : AStudent)
    % Read a student record from the keyboard into
    % AStudent

procedure PutStudent (AStudent : AStudent)
    % Display student record AStudent
```

FIGURE 13.40

Implementation of StudentADT

```
% Implementation of StudentADT

const StudentNameLength := 20
type StudentName : string (StudentNameLength)

type Student :
   record
      Name : StudentName
      Score : int
      Grade : string(1)
   end record

procedure GetStudent (var AStudent : Student)
    % Read the data for one student from the keyboard
    % into AStudent
    % Pre : None
    % Post: The data read is returned through AStudent
    %        The grade field may contain a letter grade
    %        (A through F) or a blank if the grade is
    %        unknown. The score and grade are not read
    %        if the name is blank

   put ""    % Skip a line
   put "Name > " ..
   get AStudent.Name
   if length (AStudent.Name) not= 0 then
      put "Score> " ..
      get AStudent.Score
      put "Grade> " ..
      get AStudent.Grade
   end if
end GetStudent
```

```
procedure PutStudent (AStudent : Student)
    % Display student record AStudent
    % Pre : Record AStudent is defined
    % Post: The fields of AStudent are displayed across
    %       an output line

    put AStudent.Name :20, AStudent.Score :3, " ",
        AStudent.Grade :3
end PutStudent
```

5. Testing the Grading Program

A sample run of the grading program was shown in Fig. 13.27. We should verify that the program works correctly when the array `Test.Class` is empty (no student records) and when the array is completely filled (`MaxClass` students took the exam). Use a small value of `MaxClass` for the latter case.

Exercises for Section 13.5

Self-Check

1. For the sample run in Fig. 13.27, which of the following are valid statements? What is displayed by the valid statements?
   a. `put Test.Class.NumStu`
   b. `put Exam.NumStu`
   c. `bind T to Test`
      `put T.Score, T.Grade, T.Name`
   d. `put Test.NumStu`
   e. `put Class.NumStu`
   f. `put Test.Class.Name(2)`
   g. `put Test(1).Class.Name(2)`
   h. `put Test.Class(1).Name(2)`
   i. `put Test.Class(1).Name`
   j. `put Statistics.Average`
2. How could you get the scores in descending order (largest score first)? What changes would be needed to sort the array `Class` by student name instead of score?
3. Since we are ordering the array by `Score` field, we propose changing procedure `Switch` to exchange only the `Score` fields. Describe the effect of this proposal.

Programming

1. Write procedure `DisplayStats`.
2. Write procedures `FindLow` and `FindHigh`.

13.6 Common Programming Errors

When you use multidimensional arrays, make sure the subscript for each dimension is consistent with its declared type. If any subscript value is out of range, an error will be detected during run-time.

If you use nested `for` loops to process the array elements, make sure that loop control variables used as array subscripts are in the correct order. The order of the loop control variables determines the sequence in which the array elements will be processed.

When an array of records is processed, the array name and subscript must be included as part of the field selector (e.g., `Annotation (I).Key` references field `Key` of the `I`-th record). If a loop is used to process all array elements in sequence, then any `bind` declaration that references the array records must be nested inside the loop, as shown next.

```
for I : 1 .. N
    bind A to Annotation (I)
        ...
end for
```

As the loop control variable `I` changes, the next array record is processed. If the nesting order is reversed, as in

```
% Incorrect approach
I := 1
bind A to Annotation (I)
loop
    ...
    I := I + 1
end loop
```

then the same array record is processed `N` times. The record that is processed is determined by the value of `I` when the `bind` declaration is first reached. Changing the value of `I` inside the scope of the `bind` declaration has no effect.

Chapter Review

Arrays of arrays, or multidimensional arrays, were used to represent tables of information and game boards. We used nested loops to manipulate the elements of a multidimensional array in a systematic way. The correspondence between the loop-control variables and the array subscripts determines the order in which the array elements are processed.

You also saw how to manipulate arrays of records. Arrays of records can be used to represent many real-world data collections. We used the process of data abstraction to develop abstract data types that were used in the solution of two rather large applications programs.

New Turing Constructs in Chapter 13

The new Turing constructs introduced in this chapter are described in Table 13.2.

TABLE 13.2   Summary of New Turing Constructs

Construct	Effect

Declaring Multidimensional Arrays
 	
```type Day : enum(Sun, Mon, Tues,```
```   Wed, Thu, Fri, Sat)```
 	
```type Matrix :```
```   array 1..52, Day of real```
 	
```var Sales : Matrix```
	Matrix describes a two-dimensional array with 52 rows (weeks of the year) and seven columns. Sales is an array of this type and can store 364 real numbers.

Array references
```put Sales(3, Monday)```
 	
```for Week : 1 .. 52```
```   for Today : Day```
```   Sales(Week, Today) := 0.0```
```   end for```
```end for```
 	
```get Sales(1, Day.Sunday)```
	Display the element of Sales for Monday of week 3. Initialize each element of Sales to 0.
	
	Read the value for the first Sunday into Sales.

Declaring Arrays of Records
```type AElement :```
```   record```
```   Data : real```
```   Key : int```
```   end record```
```type DataArray :```
```   array 1..10 of AElement```
 	
```var MyData : DataArray```
	DataArray is an array with ten elements of type AElement (a record).
	Each element has fields named Data and Key.
	
	MyData is a variable of type DataArray.

Referencing an Array of Records
```MyData(1).Data := 3.14159```
```MyData(10).Key := 9999```
	The real value 3.14159 is stored in the first Data field of array MyData; the value 9999 is stored in the last Key field.

Quick-Check Exercises

1. How many subscripts can an array have in Turing?
2. What is the difference between row-major and column-major order? Which does Turing use?
3. What does row-major order mean when an array has more than two subscripts?
4. What control structure is used to process all the elements in a multidimensional array?
5. Write a program segment to display the sum of the values (type `real`) in each column of a two dimensional array, `Table`, with data type `array 1..5, 1..3 of real`. How many column sums will be displayed? How many elements are included in each sum?
6. Write the type declaration for an array that stores the batting averages by position (`Catcher`, `Pitcher`, `FirstBase`, etc.) for each of ten baseball teams in two leagues (`American` and `National`).
7. Write the type declaration for a data structure that stores each player's name, salary, position, batting average, fielding percentage, number of hits, runs, runs-batted-in, and errors.
8. Write the type declaration for a data structure that stores the information in question 7 for a team of twenty-five players.
9. If the array `Team` has the structure described in question 8, write a program segment that displays the first two categories of information for the first five players.

Answers to Quick-Check Exercises

1. There is no specific limit; however, the size of the array is limited by the memory space available and multidimensional arrays can require considerable memory.
2. In row-major order, the first row of the array is placed at the beginning of the memory area allocated to the array. It is followed by the second row, and so on. In column-major order, the first column is placed at the beginning of the array memory area.
3. If an array `Table` has `N` subscripts, the array elements are placed in memory in the order `Table(1, 1, ... , 1, 1)`, `Table(1, 1, ... , 1, 2)`, `Table(1, 1, ... , 1, 3)`, and so on. Then the next-to-last subscript is changed and the elements `Table(1, 1, ... , 2, 1)`, `Table(1, 1, ..., 2, 2)`, `Table(1, 1, ..., 2, 3)` ... are placed. The first subscript will be the last one that changes.
4. Nested `for` loops
5. Three column sums and five elements per sum. Here is the program segment:

```
for Column : 1 .. 3
    var ColumnSum : real := 0.0
    for Row := 1 .. 5
```

```
                    ColumnSum := ColumnSum + Table(Row, Column)
                end for
                put "Column sum for ", Column, " is ",
                    ColumnSum
            end for
```

6. Here are the declarations:

```
    type Position : enum (Pitcher, Catcher, FirstBase,
        SecondBase, ThirdBase, ShortStop, LeftField,
        CenterField, RightField)
    type League : enum (American, National)
    type BAArray : array League, 1..10, Position of real
```

7. Here are the declarations:

```
    type StringType : string(20)
    type Player :
        record
            Name : StringType
            Salary : real
            Place : Position
            BatAve, FieldPct : real
            Hits, Runs, RBIs, Errors : int
        end record
```

8. Here are the declarations:

```
    type StringType : ...
    type Player : ...
    type TeamArray : array 1..25 of Player
```

9. Here is the program segment:

```
    for I : 1 .. 5
        put Team(I).Name, Team(I).Salary
    end for
```

Review Questions

1. Define row-major order.
2. Declare an array that can be used to store each title of the Top 40 hits for each week of the year given that the `TitleLength` will be 20 characters.
3. Write the declaration of the array `YearlyHours` to store the hours of each of five employees works each day of the week, each week of the year.
4. Write the declarations for the array `CPUArray` that will hold 20 records of type `CPU`. The record `CPU` has the following fields:

IDNumber (11 characters in length), Make (five characters), Location (15 characters), and Ports (integer).

5. Use the declarations below to answer questions 5 through 9.

```
const TotalEmployees := 20

type Employee :
    record
        ID: int
        Rate : real
        Hours : real
    end record
type EmpArray : array 1..TotalEmployees of Employee

var Employees : EmpArray
```

Write the function TotalGross that will return the total gross pay given the data stored in array Employees.

6. Explain what is wrong with this fragment and fix it.

```
I := 1
bind E to Employees(I)
loop
    put E.Hours
    exit when I = TotalEmployees
    I := I + 1
end loop
```

7. Explain what is wrong with the fragment below and fix it.

```
I := 1
loop
    exit when Employees(I).ID = 999 or
            I > TotalEmployees
    I := I + 1
end loop
```

8. Write a fragment that displays the ID number of each employee who works between ten and twenty hours per week.

9. Write a fragment that displays the ID number of the employee who works the most hours.

10. How many exchanges are required to sort the list of integers below using selection sort? How many comparisons are performed?

```
20 30 40 25 60 80
```

11. Procedure SortStudents in Fig. 13.38 placed the elements of an array in order by Score field. Change the condition in the procedure so that records with the same Score value will be ordered by name (smaller name first). The field Score is called the *primary key* and the field Name is called the *secondary key*.

Programming Projects

1. Write a program that generates the `Morse` code for a sentence that ends in a period and contains only letters and blanks. After reading the `Morse` code into an array of strings, your program should read each word of the sentence and display its `Morse` equivalent on a separate line. The `Morse` code is as follows:

```
A .-, B -..., C -.-., D -.., E., F ..-., G --., H ....,
I .., J .---, K -.-, L .-.., M --, N -., O ---, P .--.,
Q --.-, R .-., S ..., T -, U ..-, V ...-, W .--, X -..-,
Y -.--, Z --..
```

Your program should include procedures corresponding to the procedure headers shown below.

```
procedure ReadCode (var CodeFile : FileNumber,
                        var Code : CodeArray)
    % Store Morse codes read from CodeFile in
    % array Code

procedure SkipBlanks (Sentence : StringType
                        var I : StringIndex)
    % If Sentence(I) is blank, advance I to next
    % non-blank in Sentence

procedure WriteCode (Code : CodeArray,
                        Letter : string(1))
    % Write Morse equivalent for a letter
```

3. Write a program that uses abstract data type `TallyADT` to store election results in an appropriate data structure. The abstract data type should contain the operators described below.

```
procedure Initialize (var Tally : TallyType)
    % Read in the number of precincts (up to 10) and
    % the letter (up to J) corresponding to the last
    % candidate. Initialize all vote totals to zero.
procedure GetTally (var Tally : TallyType)
    % Read in the votes by precinct for each candidate.
procedure PutTally (Tally : TallyType)
    % Display the election results in the form shown.
procedure CountBallot (var Tally : TallyType)
    % Determine the count of votes received by each
    % candidate and the corresponding percentage of
    % the total votes cast.
procedure FindWinner (Tally : TallyType,
                        var Cand1, var Cand2 : string,
                        var Over50 : boolean)
    % Determine the letters of the two highest scoring
```

```
% candidates (Cand1 and Cand2) and set Over50 to
% true if the highest scoring candidate receives
% more than 50 percent of the vote.
procedure DisplayWinner (Cand1, Cand2 : string,
                              Over50 : boolean)
    % Display the name of Cand1 and the message "Won
    % the election" if Over50 is true; otherwise,
    % display the message "Runoff election between two
    % highest scoring candidates", and Cand1 and Cand2.
```

Write a main program that uses this abstract data type and run the program for the data shown below and also when candidate C receives only 108 votes in precinct 4.

Candidates

Precinct	A	B	C	D
1	192	48	206	37
2	147	90	312	21
3	186	12	121	38
4	114	21	408	39
5	267	13	382	29

4. Modify project 3 to make it an interactive menu-driven program. Menu options should include initializing the vote table (prompt the user for the number of candidates, their names, and the number of precincts), displaying the vote table with row and column totals, displaying the precinct totals, displaying the candidate's names and votes received (raw numbers and expressed as a percent of the votes cast), displaying winner's name (or names in the event of a tie), and exiting the program.

5. For the sales analysis problem (See Section 13.3), provide these operators.

```
procedure GetFileData (InFileNo : int,
                           var Sales : SalesTable)
    % Read the sales data from file number InFileNo
procedure EditData (var Sales : SalesTable)
    % Prompt the user to determine the year, month, and
    % new amount for a sales entry to be changed and
    % then call StoreSales to change that entry
```

Add these options to the menu and test them.

6. For the student grading program (see Section 13.5), provide the following operators:

```
procedure GetBookFile (InFileNo : int,
                          var Test : GradeBook)
    % Read in the exam data from the data file with
    % stream number InFileNo
```

```
procedure AddStudent (var Test : GradeBook)
    % Read in a student record from the keyboard and
    % add it to the collection of student records
procedure FetchStudent (Test : GradeBook,
                            StudentName : StudentName,
                            var ExamData : Student)
    % Return through ExamData the record for the
    % student specified by StudentName
procedure StoreStudent (var Test : GradeBook,
                            StudentName : StudentName,
                            ExamData : Student)
    % Store new exam data for the student specified by
    % StudentName
procedure EditStudent (var Test : GradeBook)
    % Prompt the user for the name of a student whose
    % score and/or grade may be changed. Read in the
    % new score and grade and call PutStudent to make
    % the change.
```

Change the program to a menu-driven program and test these new operators.

7. Implement an abstract data type that represents a telephone directory for a company. The telephone directory should contain space for up to 100 names, phone numbers, and room numbers. You should have operators to create an empty directory (all names blank), read in the telephone directory, retrieve the entry corresponding to a given name, display the telephone directory, add a new entry to the directory, and edit a particular entry (that is, change the name, phone number, or room number of the entry for a particular person). You will also need an abstract data type for an individual telephone entry that contains operators to read and write a single entry.

8. Write a menu-driven program that tests the operators in programming project 7.

9. Use a three-dimensional array to represent a building (floors 1 to 3, wings A and B, and rooms 1 to 5). Each entry in the array will be a record containing a person's name and phone number. Provide operators to create an initially empty building (all names are blank), read data into the building, display the entire building, display a particular floor of the building, retrieve the entry for a particular room, and store a new entry in a particular room. To designate a particular room, the program user must enter the floor, wing, and room number as data. You will also need an abstract data type for an individual entry.

10. Many supermarkets make use of computer equipment at their checkout counters that allows the clerk to drag the item purchased across a sensor that reads the bar code on the product container. After reading the bar code, the store inventory database is examined, the item's price and product description are located, counts are reduced, and a

receipt is printed. Your task is to write a program that simulates this process.

Your program will need to read the inventory information from the data file on disk into an array of records. The data in the inventory file is written one item per line, beginning with a two-digit product code, followed by a 30-character product description, its price, and the quantity of that item in stock. Your program will need to copy the revised version of the inventory to a new data file after all purchases are processed.

Processing customers' orders involves reading a series of product codes representing each person's purchases from a second data file. A zero product code is used to mark the end of each customer order. As each product code is read, the inventory list is searched to find a matching product code. Once located, the product price and description may be printed on the receipt and the quantity on hand reduced by one. At the bottom of the receipt, you are to print the total for the goods purchased by the customer.

11. Write a program that simulates the movement of radioactive particles in a 20 by 20 two-dimensional shield around a reactor. Particles enter the shield at some random position in the shield coordinate space. Once a particle enters the shield, it can move in one of four directions. The direction for the next second of travel is determined by a random number between 1 and 4 (forward, backward, left, right). A change in direction is interpreted as a collision with another particle, which results in a dissipation of energy. Each particle can have only a limited number of collisions before it dies. A particle exits the shield if its position places it outside the shield coordinate space before K collisions occur. Determine the percentage of particles that exit the shield where K and the number of particles are input as data items. Also compute the average number of times a particle's path crosses itself during travel time within the shield.

Hint: Mark each array position occupied by a particle before it dies or exits the shield.

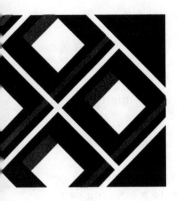

Recursion

Arecursive procedure or function is one that calls itself. This ability enables a recursive procedure to be repeated with different parameter values. You can use recursion as an alternative to iteration (looping). Generally a recursive solution is less efficient in terms of computer time than an iterative one due to the overhead for the extra procedure calls; however, in many instances the use of recursion enables us to specify a very natural, simple solution to a problem that would otherwise be very difficult to solve. For this reason, recursion is an important and powerful tool in problem solving and programming.

14.1 The Nature of Recursion

Problems that lend themselves to a recursive solution have the following characteristics:

- One or more simple cases of the problem (called *stopping cases*) have a simple, non-recursive solution.
- For the other cases, there is a process (using recursion) for substituting one or more reduced cases of the problem that are closer to a stopping case.
- Eventually the problem can be reduced to stopping cases only, all of which are relatively easy to solve.

The recursive algorithms that we write will generally consist of an `if` statement with the form shown below.

> if the stopping case is reached `then`
>   Solve it
> `else`
>   Reduce the problem using recursion
> `end if`

Figure 14.1 illustrates this approach. Let's assume that for a particular problem of size N, we can split the problem into a problem of size 1, which we can solve (a stopping case), and a problem of size $N-1$. We can split the problem of size $N-1$ into another problem of size 1 and a problem of size $N-2$, which we can split further. If we split the problem N times, we will end up with N problems of size 1, all of which we can solve.

EXAMPLE 14.1
Consider how we might solve the problem of multiplying 6 by 3, assuming that we know our addition tables but not our multiplication tables. The problem of multiplying 6 by 3 can be split into the two problems:

1. Multiply 6 by 2
2. Add 6 to the result of problem 1

FIGURE 14.1   Splitting a Problem into Smaller Problems

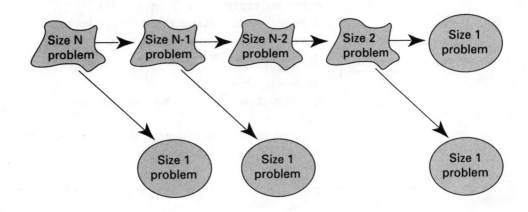

Because we don't we know our multiplication tables, we can solve problem 2 but not problem 1. However, problem 1 is simpler than the original problem. We can split it into the two problems 1.1 and 1.2 below, leaving us three problems to solve, two of which are additions.

1.1 Multiply 6 by 1
1.2 Add 6 to the result

Even though we don't know our multiplication tables, we are familiar with the simple rule that $M * 1$ is M for any M, so by solving problem 1.1 (the answer is 6) and problem 1.2, we get the solution to problem 1 (the answer is 12). Solving problem 2 gives us the final answer (18).

Figure 14.2 implements this approach to doing multiplication as the recursive Turing function Multiply which returns the product, M × N, of its two arguments. The body of function Multiply implements the general form of a recursive algorithm shown earlier. The stopping case is reached when the condition N = 1 is true. In this case, the statement

```
result M                        % Stopping case
```

executes, so the answer is M. If N is greater than 1, the statement

```
result M + Multiply(M, N-1)    % Recursive step
```

executes, splitting the original problem into the two simpler problems:

1. Multiply M by N-1
2. Add M to the result

The first of these problems is solved by calling Multiply again with N-1 as its second argument. If the new second argument is greater than 1, there will be additional calls to function Multiply.

FIGURE 14.2   Recursive Function Multiply

```
function Multiply (M, N : int) : int
    % Perform multiplication using + operator
    % Pre : M and N are defined and N > 0
    % Post: Return M * N

    if N = 1 then
        result M              % Stopping case
    else
        result M + Multiply(M, N-1)    % Recursive step
    end if
end Multiply
```

For now, you will have to take our word that function `Multiply` performs as desired. We will see how to trace the execution of a recursive function or procedure in the next section.

The next example illustrates how we might solve a difficult problem just by splitting it into smaller problems. You will solve this problem after you have more experience using recursion.

EXAMPLE 14.2

The Towers of Hanoi Problem involves moving a specified number of disks that are all different sizes from one tower (or peg) to another. Legend has it that the world will come to an end when the problem is solved for 64 disks. In the version of the problem shown in Fig. 14.3, there are five disks (numbered 1 through 5) and three towers or pegs (lettered *A*, *B*, *C*). The goal is to move the five disks from peg *A* to peg *C* subject to the following rules:

1. Only one disk may be moved at a time and this disk must be the top disk on a peg.
2. A larger disk can never be placed on top of a smaller disk.

FIGURE 14.3   Towers of Hanoi

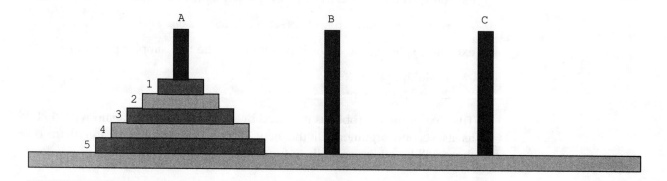

The stopping cases of the problem involve moving one disk only (e.g., "move disk 2 from peg *A* to peg *C*"). A simpler problem than the original would be to move four disks subject to the conditions above, or three disks, and so on. Therefore, we want to split the original five-disk problem into one or more problems involving fewer disks. Let's consider splitting the original problem into the three problems below.

1. Move four disks from peg *A* to peg *B*.
2. Move disk 5 from peg *A* to peg *C*.
3. Move four disks from peg *B* to peg *C*.

Step 1 moves all disks but the largest to tower *B*, an auxiliary tower that was not mentioned in the original problem. Step 2 moves the largest disk to the goal tower, tower *C*. Then, step 3 moves the remaining disks from *B* to the goal tower where they will be placed on top of the largest disk. Let's assume that we will be able to perform step 1 and step 2 (a stopping case). Figure 14.1 shows the status of the three towers after completing these steps. At this point, it should be clear that we can solve the original five-disk problem if we can complete step 3.

FIGURE 14.4   Towers of Hanoi after Steps 1 and 2

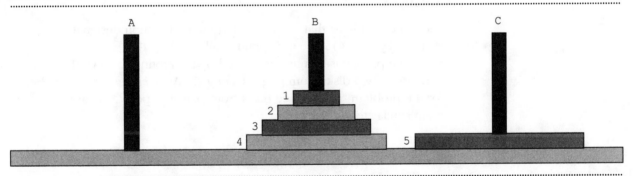

Unfortunately, we still don't know how to perform step 1 or step 3. However, both these steps involve four disks instead of five so they are easier than the original problem. We should be able to split them into simpler problems in the same way that we split the original problem. Step 3 involves moving four disks from tower *B* to tower *C*, so we can split it into two three-disk problems and a one-disk problem:

3.1 Move three disks from peg *B* to peg *A*.
3.2 Move disk 4 from peg *B* to peg *C*.
3.3 Move three disks from peg *A* to peg *C*.

Figure 14.5 shows the status of the towers after completing steps 3.1 and 3.2. We now have the two largest disks on peg *C*. Once we complete step 3.3, all five disks will be on peg *C* as required.

FIGURE 14.5   Towers of Hanoi after Steps 1, 2, 3.1, and 3.2

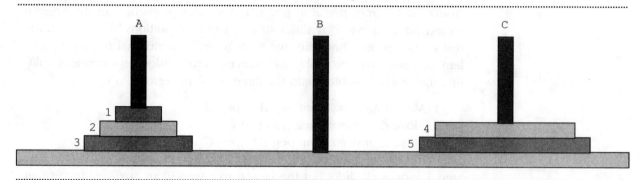

By splitting each *N*-disk problem into two problems involving *N–1* disks and a one-disk problem, we will eventually reach all cases of one disk, which we know how to solve. We will write a Turing program that solves the Towers of Hanoi problem later.

Exercises for Section 14.1

Self-Check

1. Show the problems that are generated by the function designator `Multiply(5, 4)`. Use a diagram similar to Fig. 14.1.
2. Show the problems that are generated by attempting to solve the problem "Move two disks from peg *A* to peg *C*". Answer the same question for the problem "Move three disks from peg *A* to peg *C*". Draw a diagram similar to Fig. 14.1.

14.2 Tracing a Recursive Procedure or Function

Hand-tracing an algorithm's execution provides us with valuable insight as to how that algorithm works. We can also trace the execution of a recursive procedure or function. We will illustrate how to do this by studying a recursive function and procedure next.

Tracing a Recursive Function

In the last section, we wrote the recursive function `Multiply`. We can trace the execution of the function designator `Multiply(6, 3)` by drawing an *activation frame* corresponding to each call of the function. An activation frame shows the parameter values for each call and summarizes its execution.

The three activation frames generated to solve the problem of multiplying 6 by 3 are shown in Fig. 14.6. Each new call to Multiply creates a new box (activation frame) containing its own values of M and N.

The value returned from each call is shown alongside the arrows. The return arrow from each procedure call points to the operator + because the addition is performed just after the return.

FIGURE 14.6   Trace of Function Multiply

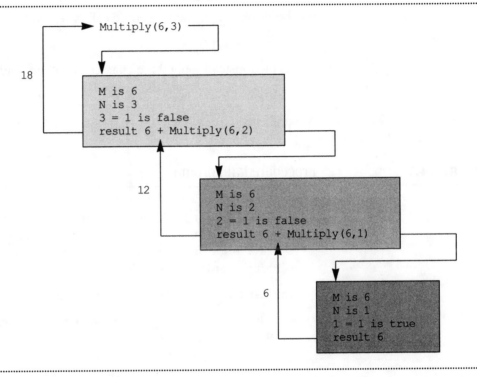

Figure 14.6 shows that there are three calls to function Multiply. Parameter M has the value 6 for all three calls; parameter N has the values 3, 2, and finally 1. Since N is 1 in the third call, the value of M(6) is returned as the result of the third and last call. After returning to the second activation frame, its value of M(6) is added to this result (6) and the sum (12) is returned as the result of the second call. After returning to the first activation frame, its value of M(6) is added to this result (12) and the sum (18) is returned as the result of the original call to function Multiply.

Tracing a Recursive Procedure

EXAMPLE 14.3

Procedure Palindrome in Fig. 14.7 is a recursive procedure that reads in a string of length N and prints it out backwards. (A palindrome is a string of characters that reads the same backwards as forwards.) If the procedure call statement

```
Palindrome (5)
```

is executed, the five characters entered at the keyboard will be printed in reverse order. If the characters abcde are entered when this procedure is called, the line

```
edcba
```

will be displayed. If the procedure call statement

```
Palindrome (3)
```

is executed instead, only three characters will be read, and

```
cba
```

will appear on the screen.

FIGURE 14.7 Procedure Palindrome

```
procedure Palindrome (N : int)
    % Input a string of length N and display it in
    % reverse order
    % Pre : N is greater than or equal to one
    % Post: Display N characters

    var Next : string(1)      % Next data character

    get Next : 1              % Read one character
    if N <= 1 then
        % Stopping case
        put ""                % Start a new line
    else
        % Recursion
        Palindrome (N-1)
    end if
    put Next ..
end Palindrome
```

Like most recursive procedures, the body of procedure Palindrome consists of an if statement that evaluates a terminating condition, N <= 1. When the terminating condition is true, the problem has reached a stopping case: a data string of length 1. When this is true, a blank line is displayed. If the terminating condition is false (N greater than 1), the recursive step (following else) is executed, and the statement

```
Palindrome (N-1)
```

calls the procedure recursively with the parameter value decreased by 1. The character just read is not displayed until later. This is because the put statement comes after the recursive procedure call; consequently, the put statement cannot be performed until after the procedure execution is completed and control is returned back to the put statement. For example, the character that is read when N is 3 is not displayed until after the procedure execution for N equal to 2 is done. Hence, this character is displayed after the characters that are read when N is 2 and N is 1.

To fully understand this it is necessary to trace the execution of the procedure call statement

```
Palindrome (3)
```

This trace is shown in Fig. 14.8, assuming the letters abc are entered as data.

FIGURE 14.8   Trace of Palindrome (3)

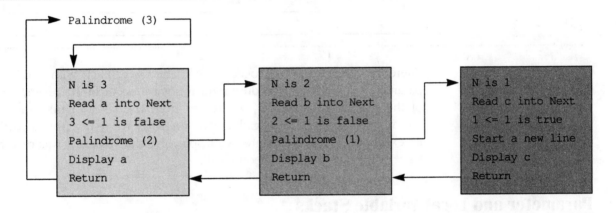

The trace shows three separate activation frames for procedure Palindrome. Each activation frame begins with a list of the initial values of N and Next for that frame. The value of N is passed into the procedure when it is called, because N is a value parameter; the value of Next is set by the get statement.

The statements that are executed for each frame are shown. Each call to Palindrome results in a new activation frame (a box). A procedure return occurs when the procedure end statement is reached. This is indicated by the word Return in Fig. 14.8 and an arrow that points to the statement in the calling frame to which the procedure returns. Tracing the arrows gives us the sequence of events listed below.

Figure 14.9 shows this action by a set of nested boxes, where each internal box corresponds to the action of one activation of the Palindrome procedure.

FIGURE 14.9 Sequence of Events for Trace of Palindrome (3)

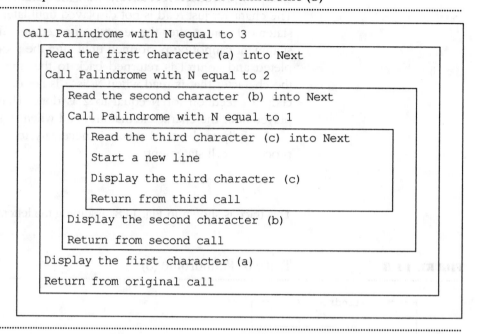

There are three calls to procedure Palindrome, each with a different parameter value. The procedure returns always occur in the reverse order of the procedure calls; i.e., we return from the last call first, then we return from the next to last call, and so on. After we return from a particular execution of the procedure, we display the character that was read into Next just prior to that procedure call.

Parameter and Local Variable Stacks

You may be wondering how Turing keeps track of the values of N and Next at any given point. Turing uses a special data structure called a *stack*, which is analogous to a stack of dishes or trays. Think of the countless times you have stood in line in a cafeteria. Recall that clean dishes are placed on top of a stack of dishes. When we need a dish, we remove the one most recently placed on the stack. This causes the next to last dish placed on the stack to move to the top of the stack.

Similarly, whenever a new procedure call occurs, the parameter value associated with that call is placed on the top of the parameter stack. Also, a new cell whose value is initially undefined is placed on top of the stack that is maintained for the local variable Next. Whenever N or Next is referenced, the value at the top of the corresponding stack is always used. When a procedure return occurs, the value currently at the top of each stack is removed, and the value just below it moves to the top.

As an example, let's look at the two stacks right after the first call to Palindrome. There is one cell on each stack, as shown below.

After first call to Palindrome

```
   N        Next
 ┌────┐   ┌────┐
 │ 3  │   │ ?  │
 └────┘   └────┘
```

The letter a is read into Next.

```
   N        Next
 ┌────┐   ┌────┐
 │ 3  │   │ a  │
 └────┘   └────┘
```

After the second call to Palindrome, the number 2 is placed on top of the stack for N, and the top of the stack for Next becomes undefined again as shown below.

After second call to Palindrome

```
   N        Next
 ┌────┐   ┌────┐
 │ 2  │   │ ?  │
 │ 3  │   │ a  │
 └────┘   └────┘
```

The letter b is read into Next.

```
   N        Next
 ┌────┐   ┌────┐
 │ 2  │   │ b  │
 │ 3  │   │ a  │
 └────┘   └────┘
```

However, Next becomes undefined again right after the third call.

After third call to Palindrome

```
   N        Next
 ┌────┐   ┌────┐
 │ 1  │   │ ?  │
 │ 2  │   │ b  │
 │ 3  │   │ a  │
 └────┘   └────┘
```

During this execution of the procedure, the letter c is read into Next. The stopping case (N <= 1) has been reached, so a new line is started and c is displayed.

```
   N        Next
 ┌────┐   ┌────┐
 │ 1  │   │ c  │
 │ 2  │   │ b  │
 │ 3  │   │ a  │
 └────┘   └────┘
```

The procedure return causes the values at the top of the stack to be removed as shown next.

After first return

```
    N          Next

    2            b
    3            a
```

Since control is returned to a put statement, the value of Next at the top of the stack (which is b) is then displayed. Another return occurs, causing the values currently at the top of the stack to be removed.

After second return

```
    N          Next

    3            a
```

Again control is returned to a put statement and the value of Next at the top of the stack (which is a) is displayed. The third and last return removes the last pair of values from the stack and there are no longer any copies of N or Next. This manipulation of stacks is all done automatically by Turing, and we can write recursive procedures without needing to worry about the stacks.

Implementation of Parameter Stacks in Turing

For illustrative purposes, we have used separate stacks for N and Next in our discussion; however, the compiler actually maintains a single stack. Each time a call to a procedure or function occurs, all its parameters and local variables are pushed onto the stack along with the memory address of the calling statement. The latter gives the computer the return point after execution of the procedure or function. Although there may be multiple copies of a procedure's parameters saved on the stack, there is only one copy of the procedure body in memory.

Exercises for Section 14.2

Self-Check

1. Why is N a value parameter (not a variable parameter) in Fig. 14.7?
2. Assume the characters *+-/ are entered for the procedure call statement

   ```
   Palindrome (4)
   ```

   What output line would appear on the screen? Show the contents of the stacks immediately after each procedure call and return.
3. Trace the execution of Multiply(5, 4) and show the stacks after each recursive call.

14.3 Recursive Mathematical Functions

Many mathematical functions are defined recursively. An example is the factorial of a number n, written as $n!$.

- 0! is 1
- $n!$ is $n \times (n-1)!$, for $n > 0$

Thus 4! is 4 * 3 * 2 * 1, or 24. It is quite easy to implement this definition as a recursive function in Turing.

EXAMPLE 14.4
Function Factor in Fig. 14.10 computes the factorial of its argument N. The recursive step

```
result N * Factor(N-1)
```

implements the second line of the factorial definition above. This means that the result of the current call (argument N) is determined by multiplying the result of the next call (argument N-1) by N.

FIGURE 14.10   Recursive Function Factor

```
function Factor (N : int) : int
   % Compute the factorial of N (N!)
   % Pre : N is defined and N >= 0
   % Post: Return N!

   if N = 0 then
      result 1
   else
      result N * Factor(N-1)
   end if
end Factor
```

A trace of

```
Fact := Factor(3)
```

is shown in Fig. 14.11. The value returned from the original call, Factor(3), is 6, and this value is assigned to Fact. Be careful when using the factorial function as its value increases very rapidly and could lead to an integer overflow error (e.g., 10! is 24320).

Although the recursive implementation of function Factor follows naturally from its definition, this function can be implemented easily using iteration. The iterative version is shown in Fig. 14.12.

FIGURE 14.11   Trace of Fact := Factor(3)

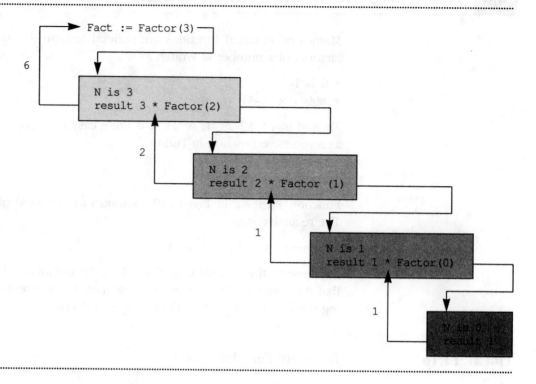

FIGURE 14.12   Iterative Function Factor

```
function Factor (N : int) : int
    % Compute the factorial of N (N!)
    % Pre : N is defined and N >= 0
    % Post: Return N!
    var Factorial : int % Storage for accumulating product

    Factorial := 1
    for I : 2 .. N
        Factorial := Factorial * I
    end for
    result Factorial      % Define result
end Factor
```

Note that the iterative version contains a loop as its major control structure whereas the recursive version contains an `if` statement. Also, a local variable, `Factorial`, is needed in the iterative version to hold the accumulating product.

EXAMPLE 14.5
The Fibonacci numbers are a sequence of numbers that have many uses. They were originally intended to model the growth of a rabbit colony. We

will not go into details of the model here, but you can see that the Fibonacci sequence 1, 1, 2, 3, 5, 8, 13, 21, 34, ... increases rapidly. The fifteenth number in the sequence is 610 (that's a lot of rabbits!). The Fibonacci sequence is defined below.

- *Fib1* is 1
- *Fib2* is 1
- *Fib$_n$* is *Fib$_{n-2}$* + *Fib$_{n-1}$*, for $n > 2$.

Verify for yourself that the sequence of numbers shown in the paragraph above is correct.

A recursive function that computes the Nth Fibonacci number is shown in Fig. 14.13. Although easy to write, the Fibonacci function is not very efficient because each recursive step generates two calls to function Fibonacci.

FIGURE 14.13   **Recursive Function Fibonacci**

```
function Fibonacci (N : int) : int
    % Compute the Nth Fibonacci number
    % Pre : N is defined and N > 0
    % Post: Return the Nth Fibonacci number

    if N = 1 or N = 2 then
        result 1
    else
        result Fibonacci(N-2) + Fibonacci(N-1)
    end if
end Fibonacci
```

EXAMPLE 14.6

Euclid's algorithm for finding the greatest common divisor of two positive integers, *GCD(M,N)*, is defined recursively below. The greatest common divisor of two integers is the largest integer that divides them both exactly.

- *GCD(M,N)* is *N* if *N* <= *M* and *N* divides *M*
- *GCD(M,N)* is *GCD(N,M)* if *M* < *N*
- *GCD(M,N)* is *GCD(N*, remainder of *M* divided by *N)* otherwise

This algorithm states that the *GCD* is *N* if *N* is the smaller number and *N* divides *M*. If *M* is the smaller number, then the *GCD* determination should be performed with the arguments transposed. If neither of the preceding apply, the answer is obtained by finding the *GCD* of *N* and the remainder of *M* divided by *N*. The declaration and use of the Turing function *GCD* is shown in Fig. 14.14.

FIGURE 14.14   Function GCD

```
% The "Findgcd" program
% Print the greatest common divisor of two integers

var M, N : int  % Two input items

function GCD (M, N : int) : int
    % Find the greatest common divisor of M and N
    % Pre : M and N are defined and both are > 0
    % Post: Return the greatest common divisor of M
    %       and N

    if N <= M and M mod N = 0 then
        result N
    elsif M < N then
        result GCD(N, M)
    else
        result GCD(N, M mod N)
    end if
end GCD

put "Enter two positive integers separated by a space: "
get M, N
put "Their greatest common divisor is ", GCD (M, N)
```

```
Enter two positive integers separated by a space:
24 84
Their greatest common divisor is 12
```

Exercises for Section 14.3

Self-Check

1. Complete the following recursive function that calculates the value of a
   number (Base) raised to a positive power (Power). Assume that
   Power is positive.

```
    function PowerRaiser (Base, Power : int) : int
        if Power = _____ then
            result _____
        else
            result _____ * _____
        end if
    end PowerRaiser
```

2. What is the output of the following program? What does function Strange compute?

```
% The "Strange" program
function Strange (N : int) : int
    if N = 1 then
        result 0
    else
        result 1 + Strange (N div 2)
    end if
end Strange

put Strange(8)
```

3. Explain what would happen if the terminating condition for function Fibonacci is just (N = 1).

Programming

1. Write a recursive function, FindSum, that calculates the sum of successive integers starting at 1 and ending at N (i.e., FindSum(N) = (1 + 2 + ... + (N-1) + N).
2. Write an iterative version of the Fibonacci function.
3. Write an iterative function for the greatest common divisor.

14.4 Recursive Procedures with Array Parameters

In this section, we will examine three familiar problems and implement recursive procedures to solve them. These problems all involve processing an array.

❈ Case Study:

Printing an Array Backwards

1. Problem Provide a recursive solution to the problem of printing the elements of an array in reverse order.

2. Analysis If the array X has elements with subscripts 1 .. N, then the element values should be printed in the sequence X(N), X(N-1), X(N-2), ..., X(2), X(1). The stopping case is printing an array with one element (N is 1); the solution is to print that element. For larger arrays, the recursive step is to print the last array element (X(N)) and then print the subarray with subscripts 1 .. N-1 backwards.

DATA REQUIREMENTS

Problem Inputs

```
X : IntArray    % An array of integer values
N : int         % The number of elements in the array
```

Problem Outputs

The array values in reverse order: $X(N)$, $X(N-1)$, ... , $X(2)$, $X(1)$

3. Design

INITIAL ALGORITHM

1. if N is 1 then
   2. Print $X(1)$
   else
   3. Print $X(N)$
   4. Print the subarray with subscripts 1 .. N–1
   end if

4. Implementation

Procedure `PrintBack` in Fig. 14.15 implements the recursive algorithm.

FIGURE 14.15

Procedure PrintBack

```
procedure PrintBack (var X : IntArray, N : int)
   % Print an array of integers (X) with subscripts 1 .. N
   % Pre : Array X and N are defined and N > 0
   % Post: Display X(N), X(N-1), ... , X(2), X(1)

   if N = 1 then
      put X(1)                    % Stopping case
   else
      % Recursive step
      put X(N)
      PrintBack (X, N-1)
   end if
end PrintBack
```

5. Testing

Given the declarations

```
type IntArray : array 1..20 of int
var Test : IntArray
```

and the procedure call statement

```
PrintBack (Test, 3)
```

three `put` statements will be executed in the order indicated below, and the elements of `Test` will be printed backwards as desired.

```
put Test(3)
put Test(2)
put Test(1)
```

To verify this we trace the execution of the procedure call statement above in Fig. 14.16. Tracing the arrows leads to the sequence of events listed below.

FIGURE 14.16   Trace of PrintBack (Test, 3)

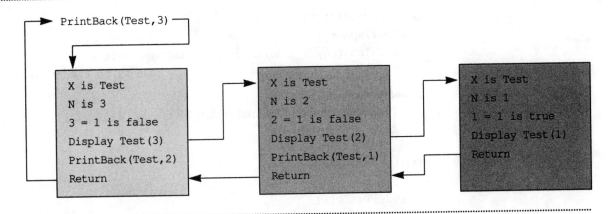

FIGURE 14.17   Sequence of Events of PrintBack (Test, 3)

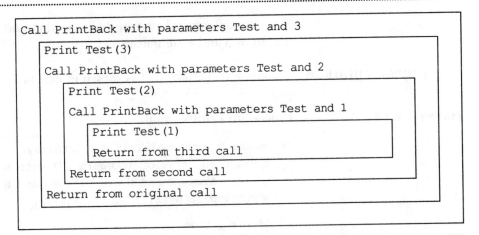

As shown there are three calls to procedure PrintBack, each with different parameters. The procedure returns always occur in the reverse order of the procedure calls; in other words, we return from the last call first, then we return from the next to last call, and so on.

✖ Case Study:

Printing an Array in Normal Order

1. Problem

Provide a recursive procedure that prints the elements of an array in normal order.

2. Analysis

We can use the approach just followed to print the elements of an array in normal order. Again the stopping case is an array with just one element.

DATA REQUIREMENTS
Problem Inputs

```
X : IntArray      % An array of integer values
N : int           % The number of elements in the array
```

Problem Outputs

The array values in normal order: X(1), X(2), ... , X(N-1), X(N)

3. Design

INITIAL ALGORITHM
1. if N is 1 then
    2. Print X(1)
    else
            3. Print the subarray with subscripts 1 .. N-1
            4. Print X(N)
    end if

The only difference between this algorithm and the one shown earlier is that Steps 3 and 4 are transposed.

4. Implementation

Procedure PrintNormal is shown in Fig. 14.18.

FIGURE 14.18 Procedure PrintNormal

```
procedure PrintNormal (var X : IntArray, N : int)
    % Print an array of integers (X) with subscripts 1 .. N
    % Pre : Array X and N are defined and N > 0
    % Post: Display X(1), ... , X(N-1), X(N)

    if N = 1 then
        put X(1)                % Stopping case
    else
        % Recursive step
        PrintNormal (X, N-1)
        put X(N)
    end if
end PrintNormal
```

5. Testing

The trace of `PrintNormal (Test, 2)` is shown in Fig. 14.19. The return arrows to each activation frame point to the display operation (`put`); therefore, the display operation is performed after the return. Following the arrows results in the sequence of events listed below. This time, there are no statements that precede the recursive calls.

FIGURE 14.19   Trace of PrintNormal (Test, 3)

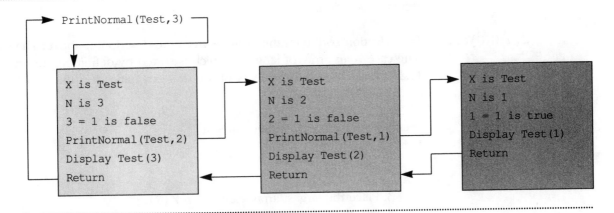

FIGURE 14.20   Sequence of Events for Trace of PrintNormal (Test, 3)

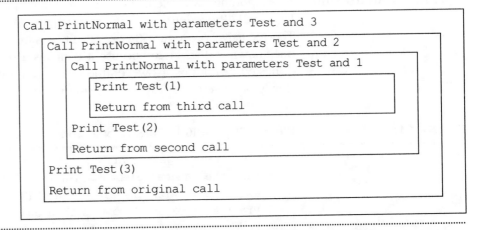

PROGRAM STYLE

USING VALUE ARRAY PARAMETERS IN RECURSIVE PROCEDURES
X is declared as a value parameter in procedures `PrintBack` and `PrintNormal` because it is used for input only. In Turing all non-scalars, such as arrays, strings, and records are passed by reference, and are not actually copied into each activation frame. This avoids a tremendous waste of time and memory space. In languages such as Pascal in which copies are made for value arrays, it would be good practice to use variable parameters to avoid all this copying.

❖ Case Study:

Recursive Selection Sort

1. Problem

We have discussed selection sort and implemented an iterative selection sort procedure (see Fig. 11.26). Because the selection sort first finds the largest element in an array and places it where it belongs, and then finds and places the next largest element and so on, it is a good candidate for a recursive solution.

2. Analysis

The selection sort algorithm follows from the description above. The stopping case is an array of length 1 which is sorted by definition. Review Fig. 11.26 to see how the elements of an array are placed in their final positions by a selection sort.

3. Design

Recursive Algorithm for Selection Sort
1. if N is 1 then
    2. The array is sorted.
  else
    3. Place the largest array element in X(N).
    4. Sort the subarray with subscripts 1 .. N-1.
  end if

4. Implementation

This algorithm is implemented as a recursive procedure at the bottom of Fig. 14.21. Procedure PlaceLargest performs step 3 of the algorithm. The recursive procedure SelectSort is simpler to understand than the one shown in Fig. 11.26 because it contains a single if statement instead of nested for loops. However, the recursive procedure will execute more slowly because of the extra overhead due to the recursive procedure calls.

FIGURE 14.21
      PlaceLargest and Recursive SelectSort

```
procedure PlaceLargest (var X : IntArray, N : int)
    % Find the largest element in array X(1)..X(N) and
    % exchange it with the element at X(N)
    % Pre : Array X and N are defined and N > 0
    % Post: X(N) contains the largest value

    var MaxIndex : int := N % Index of largest so far

    % Save subscript of largest element in MaxIndex
    for decreasing J : N-1 .. 1
        if X(J) > X(MaxIndex) then
            MaxIndex := J % X(J) is largest so far
        end if
    end for
```

```
    % Assertion: MaxIndex is subscript of largest element
    if MaxIndex not= N then
        % Exchange X(N) and X(MaxIndex)
        const Temp := X(N)
        X(N)  := X(MaxIndex)
        X(MaxIndex) := Temp
    end if
end PlaceLargest

procedure SelectSort (var X : IntArray, N : int)
    % Sort an array of integers (X) with subscripts 1..N
    % Pre : Array X and N are defined and N > 0
    % Post: The array elements are in numerical order

    if N > 1 then
        % Recursive step
        % Place largest value in X(N) and sort
        % subarray 1..N-1
        PlaceLargest (X, N)
        SelectSort (X, N-1)
    end if
end SelectSort
```

If N = 1, procedure SelectSort returns without doing anything. This behavior is correct because a one-element array is always sorted.

Exercises for Section 14.4

Self-Check

1. Trace the execution of SelectSort on an array that has the integers 5, 8, 10, 1 stored in consecutive elements.
2. For the array in exercise1 above, trace the execution of PrintNormal and PrintBack.

Programming

1. Provide an iterative procedure that is equivalent to PrintBack in Fig. 14.15.
2. Write a recursive procedure that reverses the elements in an array X(1..N). The recursive step should shift the subarray X(2.. N) down one element into the subarray X(1..N-1) (i.e., X(1) gets X(2), X(2) gets X(3), ..., X(N-1) gets X(N)), store the old X(1) in X(N), and then reverse the subarray X(1.. N-1).

14.5 Problem Solving with Recursion

The next case study is considerably more complicated than the preceding ones. It leads to a recursive procedure that solves the Towers of Hanoi Problem you encountered in Section 14.1.

❈ Case Study:

Towers of Hanoi Problem

1. Problem

Solve the Towers of Hanoi Problem for *N* disks, where *N* is a parameter.

2. Analysis

The solution to the Towers of Hanoi Problem consists of a printed list of individual disk moves. We need a recursive procedure that can be used to move any number of disks from one peg to another, using the third peg as an auxiliary.

DATA REQUIREMENTS
Problem Inputs

```
N : int                 % The number of disks to be moved
FromPeg : string(1)     % The from peg
ToPeg : string(1)       % The to peg
AuxPeg : string(1)      % The auxiliary peg
```

Problem Outputs
A list of individual disk moves

3. Design

INITIAL ALGORITHM
1. if N is 1 then
    2. Move disk 1 from the *from* peg to the *to* peg
  else
    3. Move N-1 disks from the *from* peg to the *auxiliary* peg using the *to* peg.
    4. Move disk N from the *from* peg to the *to* peg.
    5. Move N-1 disks from the *auxiliary* peg to the *to* peg using the *from* peg.
  end if

If N is 1, a stopping case is reached. If N is greater than 1, the recursive step (following else) splits the original problem into three smaller sub-problems, one of which is a stopping case. Each stopping case displays a move instruction.

4. Implementation

The implementation of this algorithm is shown as procedure `Tower` in Fig. 14.22. Procedure `Tower` has four parameters. The procedure call statement

```
Tower ("A", "C", "B", 5)
```

solves the problem posed earlier of moving five disks from tower A to tower C using B as an auxiliary.

In Fig. 14.22, the stopping case (move disk 1) is implemented as a call to procedure `put`. Each recursive step consists of two recursive calls to `Tower` with a call to `put` sandwiched between them. The first recursive call solves the problem of moving N-1 disks to the auxiliary peg. The call to `put` displays a message to move disk N to the *to* peg. The second recursive call solves the problem of moving the N-1 disks back from the auxiliary peg to the *to* peg.

FIGURE 14.22   **Recursive Procedure Tower**

```
procedure Tower (FromPeg, ToPeg, AuxPeg : string(1), N : int)
    % Move N disks from FromPeg to ToPeg using AuxPeg as
    % an auxiliary
    % Pre : FromPeg, ToPeg, AuxPeg, and N are defined.
    % Post: Display a list of move instructions that
    %        transfer the disks

    if N = 1 then
        put "Move disk 1 from peg ", FromPeg,
                       " to peg ", ToPeg
    else
        % Recursive step
        Tower (FromPeg, AuxPeg, ToPeg, N-1)
        put "Move disk ", N , " from peg ", FromPeg,
                       " to peg ", ToPeg
        Tower (AuxPeg, ToPeg, FromPeg, N-1)
    end if
end Tower
```

5. Testing

The procedure call statement

```
Tower ("A", "C", "B", 3)
```

solves the three-disk problem: Move three disks from peg A to peg C. Its execution is traced in Fig. 14.23; the output generated is shown in Figure 14.24. Verify for yourself that this list of steps does indeed solve the three-disk problem.

FIGURE 14.23 Trace of Tower ("A", "C", "B", 3)

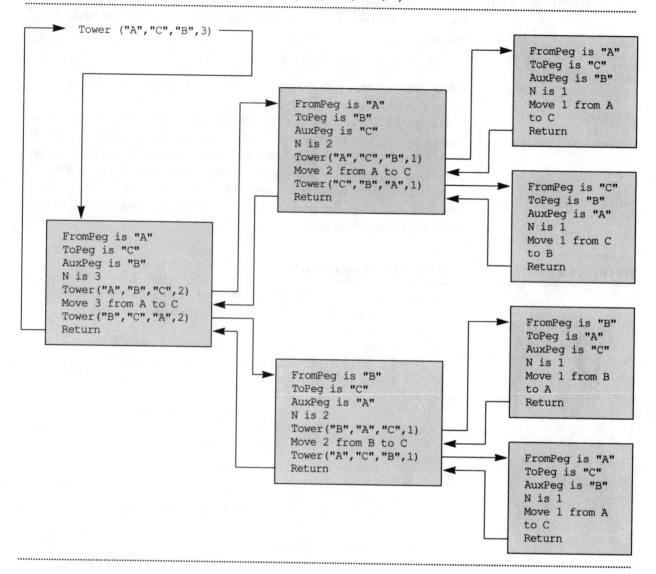

FIGURE 14.24 Output Generated by Tower("A","C","B",3)

Comparison of Iteration and Recursive Procedures

It is interesting to consider that procedure `Tower` in Fig. 14.22 will solve the Tower of Hanoi Problem for any number of disks. The three-disk problem results in a total of seven calls to procedure Tower and is solved by seven disk moves. The five-disk problem would result in a total of thirty-one calls to procedure `Tower` and is solved in thirty-one moves. In general, the number of moves required to solve the n-disk problem is $2n - 1$. Since each procedure call requires the allocation and initialization of a local data area in memory, the computer time increases exponentially with the problem size. For this reason, be careful about running this program with a value of N that is larger than ten.

The dramatic increase in processing time for larger towers is a function of this problem, not recursion. However, in general, if there are recursive and iterative solutions to the same problem, the recursive solution will require more time and space because of the extra procedure calls.

Although recursion was not really needed to solve the simpler problems in this section, it was definitely useful in formulating an algorithm for Towers of Hanoi. We will see that for certain problems, recursion leads naturally to solutions that are much easier to read and understand than their iterative counterparts. In these cases, the benefits gained from increased clarity far outweigh the extra cost (in time and memory) of running a recursive program.

Exercises for Section 14.5

Self-Check

1. How many moves are needed to solve the six-disk problem?
2. Write a main program that reads in a data value for N (the number of disks) and calls procedure `Tower` to move N disks from A to B.

14.6 Recursive Functions with Array Parameters

We can follow the process described in the previous sections to write recursive functions with array parameters. This process involves identifying the stopping cases of a problem. For the other cases, we must have a means of reducing the problem to one that is closer to a stopping case.

Case Study:
Summing the Values in an Array

1. Problem

We want to write a recursive function that finds the sum of the values in an array `X` with subscripts `1 .. N`.

2. Analysis

The stopping case occurs when `N` is `1`, that is, the sum is `X(1)`. If `N` is not `1`, then we must add `X(N)` to the sum we get when we add the values in the subarray with subscripts `1 .. N-1`.

DATA REQUIREMENTS

Problem Inputs

```
X : IntArray          % An array of integer values
N : int               % The number of elements in the array
```

Problem Outputs

The sum of the array values

3. Design

INITIAL ALGORITHM

1. `if` `N` is `1` `then`
   2. The sum is `X(1)`

   `else`

   3. Add `X(N)` to the sum of values in the subarray with subscripts `1 .. N-1`

   `end if`

4. Implementation

Function `FindSum` in Fig. 14.25 implements this algorithm. The result of calling `FindSum` for a small array (`N` is `3`) is also shown.

FIGURE 14.25 Using Recursive Function FindSum

```
% The "Testsum" program
% Test function FindSum

type IntArray : array 1..20 of int

function FindSum (X : IntArray, N : int) : int
   % Find the sum of the values in elements 1..N of
   % array X
   % Pre : Array X and N are defined and N > 0
   % Post: Returns sum of first N elements of X
   if N = 1 then
      result X(1)
   else
      result X(N) + FindSum(X, N-1)
   end if
end FindSum
```

```
var N : int := 3
var X : IntArray

X(1) := 5
X(2) := 10
X(3) := -7
put "The array sum is ", FindSum(X, 3)
```

The array sum is 8

5. Testing

Figure 14.26 shows a trace of the function call FindSum(X, 3). Each returning arrow indicates the point (the operator +) to continue after function execution. The value returned is indicated alongside the arrow. The value returned for the original call, FindSum(X, 3), is 8, and this value is printed.

FIGURE 14.26 Trace of FindSum(X, 3)

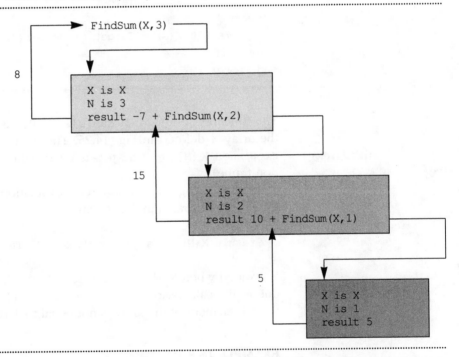

Functions that return boolean values (true or false) can also be written recursively. We will write recursive boolean functions that search an array and compare two arrays.

EXAMPLE 14.7

The boolean function Member in Fig. 14.27 returns the value true if the argument Target is in the array X with subscripts 1 .. N; otherwise it returns the value `false`. If N is 1 (the stopping case), the result is determined by comparing `X(1)` and `Target`. If N is not 1 (the recursive step), then the result is `true` if either `X(N)` is `Target` or `Target` occurs in the subarray with subscripts `1 .. N-1`. The recursive step is implemented as the assignment statement

```
result X(N) = Target or Member(X, Target, N-1)
```

in Fig. 14.27.

FIGURE 14.27   Recursive Function Member

```
function Member (X : IntArray, Target, N : int) : boolean
    % Search for Target in array X with subscripts 1..N
    % Pre : Target, N, and array X are defined and N > 0
    % Post: Return true if Target is located in array X;
    %       otherwise, returns false
    if N = 1 then
        result X(1) = Target
    else
        result X(N) = Target or Member(X, Target, N-1)
    end if
end Member
```

The function designator `Member(A, 10, 3)` is traced in Fig. 14.28 for the array X defined in Fig. 14.25. The value returned is `true` since the expression `X(N) = Target` is `true` when N is 2 (the second activation frame).

Since Turing uses short-circuit evaluation of `boolean` expressions, the further recursion in the statement

```
result X(N) = Target or Member(X, Target, N-1)
```

is avoided when `X(N) = Target` is `true`. In other words, the recursion due to the call `Member(X, Target, N-1)` actually takes place only if the Nth element of the array is not equal to `Target`.

EXAMPLE 14.8

The `boolean` function Equal returns the value `true` if two arrays, say X and Y, of N elements are the same (i.e., `X(1) = Y(1)`, `X(2) = Y(2)`, ..., `X(N) = Y(N)`). This function (see Fig. 14.29) looks similar to function Member. For the stopping case, single-element arrays, the function result depends on whether or not `X(1) = Y(1)`. For larger arrays, the result is `true` if `X(N) = Y(N)` and the subarrays with subscripts `1 .. N-1` are equal.

FIGURE 14.28   Trace of Function Member

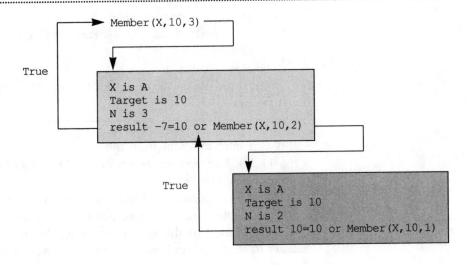

FIGURE 14.29   Recursive Function Equal

```
function Equal (X, Y : IntArray, N : int) : boolean
    % Compare arrays X and Y with elements 1..N
    % Pre : Arrays X and Y are defined and N > 0
    % Post: Return true if arrays X and Y are equal;
    %       otherwise, return false

    if N = 1 then
        result X(1) = Y(1)
    else
        result X(N) = Y(N) and Equal(X, Y, N-1)
    end if
end Equal
```

Comparison of Iterative and Recursive Functions

Consider the iterative version of the function shown in Fig. 14.30. A for loop is needed to examine each array element.

FIGURE 14.30   Iterative Function Member

```
function Member (X : IntArray, Target, N : int) : boolean
    % Compare arrays X and Y with elements 1..N
    % Pre : Arrays X and Y are defined and N > 0
    % Post: Return true if arrays X and Y are equal;
    %       otherwise, return false
```

```
            % Search array X for Target
            for I : 1 .. N
                if X(I) = Target then
                    result true        % Found Target
                end if
            end for
            result false               % Did not find Target
        end Member
```

This is a little different from the iterative array search shown earlier (see Fig. 11.24). The version shown in Fig. 14.30 would still execute faster than the recursive version.

Many programmers would argue that the recursive version is esthetically more pleasing. It is more compact (a single if statement). Once you are accustomed to thinking recursively, the recursive form is somewhat easier to read and understand than the iterative form.

Some programmers like to use recursion as a conceptual tool. Once they have written the recursive form of a function or procedure, they can always translate it into an iterative version if run-time efficiency is a major concern.

Exercises for Section 14.6

Self-Check

1. Trace the execution of recursive function Equal (Fig. 14.29) for the three-element arrays X (element values 1, 15, 10) and Y (element values 1, 15, 7). Write out completely in one equivalent boolean expression the values that function Equal is assigned through all three recursive calls. Spell out all the values that are being compared.
2. What does the following recursive function do? Trace its execution on array X above.

```
        function Mystery (X : IntArray; N : int) : int
            if N = 1 then
                result X(1)
            else
                const Temp := Mystery(X, N-1)
                if X(N) > Temp then
                    result X(N)
                else
                    result Temp
                end if
            end if
        end Mystery
```

Programming

1. Write a recursive function that finds the product of the elements in an array X of N elements.
2. Write a recursive function that finds the index of the smallest element in an array.

14.7 Picture Processing with Recursion

✖ Case Study:

Counting Cells in a Blob

This problem illustrates of the power of recursion. Its solution is relatively easy to write recursively; however, the problem would be much more difficult without using recursion.

1. Problem

We have a two-dimensional grid of cells, each of which may be empty or filled. The filled cells that are connected form a blob. There may be several blobs on the grid. We would like a function that accepts as input the coordinates of a particular cell and returns the size of the blob containing the cell.

There are three blobs in the sample grid below. If the function parameters represent the X and Y coordinates of a cell, the result of BlobCount(3, 4) is 5; the result of BlobCount(1, 2) is 2; the result of BlobCount(5, 5) is 0; the result of BlobCount(5, 1) is 4.

FIGURE 14.31　　　　　Grid with Three Blobs

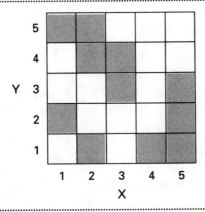

2. Design

Function BlobCount must test the cell specified by its arguments to see whether it is filled. There are two stopping cases: the cell (X, Y) is not on the grid or the cell (X, Y) is empty; in either case, the value returned by BlobCount is 0. If the cell is on the grid and filled, then the value returned is 1 plus the size of the blobs containing each of its eight neighbors. To avoid counting a filled cell more than once, we will mark it as empty once we have visited it.

DATA REQUIREMENTS

Problem Inputs

```
Grid : BlobArray    % The grid
X, Y : int          % The X and Y coordinates of
                    % the point being visited
```

Problem Outputs

The number of the cells in the blob containing point X, Y

3. Design

INITIAL ALGORITHM

1. if cell (X, Y) is not in the array then
    2. Return a count of 0
   elsif cell (X, Y) is empty then
    3. Return a count of 0
   else
    4. Mark cell (X, Y) as empty
    5. Add 1 and see whether the blob contains any of
       the eight neighbors of cell (X, Y)
   end if

4. Implementation

Function BlobCount is shown in Fig. 14.32, assuming the declarations below. The array type BlobArray has element values Filled or Empty. The constants MaxX and MaxY represent the largest X and Y coordinate, respectively.

```
const MaxX := 100
const MaxY := 100

type RowIndex : 1..MaxX
type ColIndex : 1..MaxY
type Fullness : enum (Filled, Empty)
type BlobArray : array RowIndex, ColIndex of Fullness
```

FIGURE 14.32   Functions BlobCount and StartBlob

```
function BlobCount (var Grid : BlobArray,
                    X, Y : int) : int
% Perform counting operation for StartBlob
% Pre : Array Grid and point (X, Y) are defined
% Post: Return the size of the blob containing the
%       point (X, Y). Reset the status of each
%       cell in the blob to Empty
```

```
       if X < 1 or X > MaxX or Y < 1 or Y > MaxY then
           result 0                 % Cell not in grid
       elsif Grid(X, Y) = Fullness.Empty then
           result 0                 % Cell is empty
       else                         % Cell is filled
           % Recursive step
           Grid(X, Y) := Fullness.Empty
           result 1  + BlobCount(Grid, X-1, Y+1)
                     + BlobCount(Grid, X,   Y+1)
                     + BlobCount(Grid, X+1, Y+1)
                     + BlobCount(Grid, X+1, Y)
                     + BlobCount(Grid, X+1, Y-1)
                     + BlobCount(Grid, X,   Y-1)
                     + BlobCount(Grid, X-1, Y-1)
                     + BlobCount(Grid, X-1, Y)
       end if
   end BlobCount

   function StartBlob (Grid : BlobArray,
                       X, Y : int) : int
       % Count the number of filled cells in the blob
       % containing point (X, Y)
       % Pre : Array Grid and point (X, Y) are defined
       % Post: Return the size of the blob containing the
       %       point (X, Y)
       % Uses: BlobCount to perform the counting operation
       % Call BlobCount and return its result
       var LocalGrid : BlobArray := Grid
       result BlobCount(LocalGrid, X, Y)
   end StartBlob
```

Function `StartBlob` in Fig. 14.32 calls the recursive function `BlobCount`, and returns the count computed by function `BlobCount` as its own result. The reason we used two functions instead of one was to protect the actual array from being modified when filled cells are reset to empty by function `BlobCount`. We will come back to this point shortly.

If the cell being visited is off the grid or is empty, a value of zero will be returned immediately. Otherwise, the recursive step executes, causing function `BlobCount` to call itself eight times; each time a different neighbor of the current cell is visited. The cells are visited in a clockwise manner, starting with the neighbor above and to the left. The function result is defined as the sum of all values returned from these recursive calls plus 1 (for the current cell).

The sequence of operations performed in function `BlobCount` is very important. The `if` statement tests whether the cell (X, Y) is on the grid before testing whether (X, Y) is empty. If the order were reversed, the run-time error "out of bounds" would occur whenever (X, Y) was off the grid.

Also, the recursive step resets Grid(X, Y) to Empty before visiting the neighbors of point (X, Y). If this were not done first, then cell (X, Y) would be counted more than once since it is a neighbor of all its neighbors. A worse problem is that the recursion would not terminate. When each neighbor of the current cell is visited, BlobCount is called again with the coordinates of the current cell as arguments. If the current cell is Empty, an immediate return occurs. If the current cell is still Filled, then the recursive step would be executed erroneously. Eventually the program will run out of time or memory space; the latter is often indicated by a "stack overflow" message.

A side-effect of the execution of function BlobCount is that all cells that are part of the blob being processed are reset to Empty. To avoid changing the original grid, we make a local copy (LocalGrid) in StartBlob, so all the changes occur only in the copy.

Exercise for Section 14.7

Self-Check

1. Trace the execution of function BlobCount for the coordinate pairs (1, 1) and (1, 2) in the sample grid.
2. Is the order of the two tests performed in function BlobCount critical? What happens if we reverse them or combine them into a single condition?

Programming

1. Write the recursive function FindMin that finds the smallest value in an integer array X with subscripts 1 .. N.

14.8 Common Programming Errors

The most common problem with a recursive procedure is that it may not terminate properly. For example, if the terminating condition is not correct or incomplete, then the procedure may call itself indefinitely or until all available memory is used up. Normally, a "stack overflow" run-time error is an indicator that a recursive procedure is not terminating. Make sure that you identify all stopping cases and provide a terminating condition for each one. Also be sure that each recursive step leads to a situation that is closer to a stopping case and that repeated recursive calls will eventually lead to stopping cases only.

Sometimes it is difficult to observe the result of a recursive procedure execution. If each recursive call generates a large number of output lines and there are many recursive calls, the output will scroll down the screen more quickly than it can be read. On most systems, it is possible to stop the screen temporarily by pressing a control character sequence (e.g., Control S). If this cannot be done, it is still possible to cause your output to stop temporarily by printing a prompting message followed by a `get NextChar` operation. Your program will resume execution when you enter a data character.

Chapter Review

Many examples of recursive procedures and functions were provided in this chapter. Hopefully, studying them has given you some appreciation of the power of recursion as a problem solving and programming tool and has provided you with valuable insight regarding its use. It may take some time to feel comfortable thinking in this new way about programming, but it is worth the effort.

Quick-Check Exercises

1. Explain the use of a stack in recursion.
2. Which is generally more efficient, recursion or iteration?
3. Which control statement do you almost always find in a recursive procedure or function?
4. Why would a programmer conceptualize the problem solution using recursion and implement it using iteration?
5. Explain the problem with value array parameters in recursion.
6. In a recursive problem involving N items, why must N be a value parameter?
7. What causes a stack overflow error?
8. What can you say about a recursive algorithm that has the following form?

```
if condition then
Perform recursive step
end if
```

Answers to Quick-Check Exercises
1. The stack is used to hold all parameter and local variable values and the return point for each execution of a recursive procedure.
2. Iteration is generally more efficient than recursion.
3. `if` statement
4. When its solution is much easier to conceptualize using recursion but its implementation would be too inefficient.

5. In Turing, each value array parameter has its address, not its value, saved on the stack. As a result, it is not possible to retain a different value for each call.
6. Too many recursive calls.
7. Nothing is done when the stopping case is reached.

Review Questions

1. Explain the nature of a recursive problem.
2. Discuss the efficiency of recursive procedures.
3. Differentiate between stopping cases and a terminating condition.
4. Write a Turing procedure that prints the accumulating sum of ordinal values corresponding to each character in a string. For example, if the string is "a boy", the first value printed would be the ordinal number of a, then the sum of ordinals for a and the space character, then the sum of ordinals for a, space, b, and so on.
5. Write a Turing function that returns the sum of ordinal values in a string; exclude any space characters from the sum.
6. Convert the program below from an iterative process to a recursive function that calculates an approximate value for e, the base of the natural logarithms, by summing the series $1 + 1/1! + 1/2! + ... 1/N!$ until additional terms do not affect the approximation.

```
% The "elog" program
var ENL, Delta, Fact : real := 1.0
var N : int := 1

loop
    ENL := ENL + Delta
    N := N + 1
    Fact := Fact * N
    Delta := 1.0 / Fact
    exit when ENL = ENL + Delta
end loop
put "The value of e is ", E :18:15
```

Programming Projects

1. Write a procedure that reads each row of an array as a string and converts it to a row of Grid (see Fig. 14.31). The first character of row 1 corresponds to Grid(1,1), the second character to Grid(1,2), etc. Set the element value to Empty if the character is blank; otherwise, set it to Filled. The number of rows in the array should be read first. Use this procedure in a program that reads in cell coordinates and prints the number of cells in the blob containing each coordinate pair.

2. The expression for computing $c(n,r)$, the number of combinations of n items taken r at a time is

$$c(n,r) = \frac{n!}{r!(n-r)!}$$

Write and test a function for computing $c(n,r)$ given that n! is the factorial of n.

3. A palindrome consists of a word that is spelled exactly the same when the letters are reversed, for example, such words as `level`, `deed`, and `mom`. Write a recursive function that returns the `boolean` value `true` if a word, passed as a parameter, is a palindrome.

4. Write a recursive function that returns the value of the following recursive definition:

```
F(X,Y) = X - Y              if X or Y < 0
F(X,Y) = F(X-1,Y) + F(X,Y-1)    otherwise
```

5. Write a recursive procedure that lists all of the pairs of subsets for a given set of letters. For example:

```
("A", "C", "E", "G") =>   ("A", "C"), ("A", "E"),
                          ("A", "G"), ("C", "E"),
                          ("C", "G"), ("E", "G")
```

6. Write a procedure that accepts an 8 by 8 array of characters that represents a `Maze`. Each position can contain either an `"X"` or a blank. Starting at position $(1,1)$, list any path through the maze to get to location $(8,8)$. Only horizontal and vertical moves are allowed (no diagonal moves). If no path exists, write a message indicating this. Moves can only be made to locations that contain a blank. If an `"X"` is encountered, that path is blocked and another must be chosen. Use recursion.

7. Programming project 6 in Chapter 8 described the bisection method, which finds an approximate root for the equation `f(X)=0` on the interval `XLeft` to `XRight`, inclusive (assuming the function is continuous on this interval). The interval endpoints (`XLeft` and `XRight`) and the tolerance for the approximation (`Epsilon`) are input by the user.

One stopping criterion for the bisection method is the identification of an interval (`XLeft`, `XRight`) that is less than `Epsilon` in length over which `f(X)` changes sign (from positive to negative or vice versa). The midpoint (`XMid = (XLeft + XRight) / 2.0`) of the interval will be an approximation to the root of the equation when `f(XMid)` is very close to zero. Of course, if you find a value of `XMid` such that `f(XMid)=0`, you have found a very good approximation of the root, and the algorithm should also stop.

To perform the recursive step, replace either `XLeft` or `XRight` with `XMid`, depending on which one has the same sign as `XMid`. Write a program that uses the bisection method to determine an approximation to the equation

$$5x^3 - 2x^2 + 3 = 0$$

over the interval (-1, 1) using `Epsilon = 0.0001`.

8. The Eight Queens problem is a famous chess problem that has as its goal the placement of eight queens on a single chessboard so that no queen will be able to attack any other queen. A queen may move any number of squares vertically, horizontally, or diagonally. A chessboard can be represented by a two-dimensional array with eight rows and eight columns. Write a program that contains a recursive routine that solves the Eight Queens problem.

Hint: Arbitrarily choose a location for the first queen, then attempt to place a second queen in the next available open row. This process continues as long as it is possible to place queens. If a dead end is reached, the last-placed queen is removed from the board and repositioned. To do this, the algorithm would need to backtrack to a previous activation of the recursive routine and attempt to place the queen in a different location.

Summary of Turing Constructs

Variable, Constants, and Declarations (See Chapter 2)

Constant Declaration

```
const Tax := 25.00
const Star := "*"
```

Associates the constant `Tax` with the real value `25.00` and the constant `Star` with the type string value `"*"`.

Variable Declaration

```
var X, Y, Z : real
var Me, It : int
```

Allocates memory cells named `X`, `Y`, and `Z` for storage of real numbers and `Me` and `It` for storage of integers.

Assignment Statement

```
Area := Width * Height
```

Assigns the product of `Width` and `Height` as the value of `Area`.

Get Statement

```
get Hours, Rate
```

Enters data into the variables `Hours` and `Rate`.

Put Statement

```
put X, Y
```
Displays the values of X and Y and advances the cursor to the next line.

Put Statement with Dot-Dot

```
put "X = ", X :4:2 ..
```
Displays the string "X = " followed by the value of X printed in a field of four or more columns and rounded to two decimal places.

Subprograms Without Parameters (See Chapter 3)

Procedure Declaration

```
% Print 3 lines
procedure Display
    const Star := "*"
    put Star
    put Star
    put Star
end Display
```
Procedure Display is declared and may be called to print three lines of asterisks.
The local constant Star is defined only when Display is executing.

Procedure Call Statement

```
Display
```
Calls procedure Display and causes it to begin execution.

Function Designator

```
sqrt (X + Y)
```
Calls function sqrt to compute the square root of expression X + Y.

Statements: IF And Case (See Chapter 4)

If Statement: One Alternative

```
if X not= 0.0 then
    Product := Product * X
end if
```
Multiplies Product by X only if X is nonzero.

If Statement: Two Alternatives

```
if X >= 0.0 then
    put X :12:2, " is pos"
else
    put X :12:2, " is neg"
end if
```
If X is greater than or equal to zero, display " is pos" otherwise display " is neg".

If Statement: Several Alternatives

```
if X < 0.0 then
    put "negative"
    AbsX := -X
elsif X = 0.0 then
    put "zero"
    AbsX := 0.0
else
    put "positive"
    AbsX := X
end if
```

One of three messages is printed depending on whether X is negative positive, or zero. AbsX is set to represent the absolute value or magnitude of X.

Case Statement

```
case Ranking of
    label 10 :
        put "Excellent"
    label 8, 9 :
        put "Good"
    label 6, 7 :
        put "O.K."
    label :
        put "Poor, student is"
        put "on probation"
end case
```

Prints one of four messages based on the value of Ranking (type int). If Ranking is anything other than 6, 7, 8, 9 or 10, the student is put on probation.

Statements: Loop, Exit, And For (See Chapter 5)

Loop and Exit Statements

```
Sum := 0
loop
    exit when Sum > MaxSum
    put "Next integer> " ..
    get Next
    Sum := Sum + Next
end loop
```

A collection of input data items is read and their sum is accumulated in Sum. This process stops when the accumulated sum exceeds MaxSum.

For Statement

```
for CurMonth : 3 .. 9
    get MonthSales
    YearSales := YearSales +
        MonthSales
end for
```

The loop body is repeated for each value of CurMonth from 3 to 9, inclusive. For each month, the value of MonthSales is read and added to YearSales.

Graphics (See Chapter 6)

Character Graphics

maxrow	Number of rows on screen.
maxcol	Number of rows on screen.
maxcolor	Largest color number.
locate (Row, Column)	Next output goes in the row and column.
color (ColorNumber)	Sets color used by put statement.
cls	Clear the screen.
delay (Ms)	Delays for Ms milliseconds.
length (Str)	Number of characters in string Str.
repeat (Str, N)	Makes a string consisting of N copies of the string Str.

Pixel Graphics

maxx	Maximum x (horizontal pixels).
maxy	Maximum y (vertical pixels).
setscreen ("graphics:vga")	Sets PC to VGA with 16 colors.
setscreen ("noecho")	Do not echo keystrokes.
setscreen ("nocursor")	Do not the cursor.
hasch	Sees if character can be read.
getch	Reads one character immediately.
string (1)	Type that holds only one character; used by getch.
locatexy (x, y)	Next output goes near (x,y).
drawdot (x, y, c)	Set pixel (x,y) to color c.
drawline (x1, y1, x2, y2, c)	Draws line from (x1,y1) to (x2,y2) in color c.
drawbox (x1, y1, x2, y2, c)	Draws box with corners at (x1,y1) and (x2,y2) in color c.
drawoval (x1, y1, XRadius, YRadius, c)	Draws oval with center at (x1,y1) with x radius and y radius in color c.
drawarc (x1, y1, XRadius, YRadius, InitialAngle, FinalAngle, c)	Like drawoval, but draws just an arc, from initial to final angle in color c.
drawfillbox (...)	Like drawbox, but fills the box.
drawfilloval (...)	Like drawoval, but fills the oval.
drawfillarc (...)	Like drawarc, but fills the arc.
whatdotcolor (x, y)	Returns the color number of the pixel.

Subprograms with Parameters (See Chapter 7)

Function Declaration

```
function Sign (X : real)
              : string
   if X > 0.0 then
      result "+"
   else
      result "-"
   end if
end Sign
```

Returns a string value that indicates the sign ("+" or "-") of its type real argument X.

Procedure Declaration

```
procedure DoIt (X : real,
         Op : string,
         var Y : real ,
         var Sign : string)
   if Op = "+" then
      Y := X + X
   elsif Op = "*" then
      Y := X * X
   end if
   if X > 0.0 then
      Sign := "+"
   else
      Sign := "-"
   end if
end DoIt
```

If Op is "+", return X + X through Y; if Op is "*", returns X * X through Y. Returns a string value that indicates the sign "+" or "-" of X through Sign.

Procedure Call Statement

```
DoIt (-5.0, "*", Y, MySign)
```

Calls procedure DoIt. -5.0 is passed into X, "*" into Op, 25.0 is returned to Y, and "-" is returned to MySign.

Strings, Subranges, and Enumerations (See Chapter 8)

Subrange Declaration

```
type Digit : 0 .. 9
```

A subrange of the integers is declared. This subrange (named Digit) consists of the numbers 0 through 9.

Enumerated Type Declaration

```
type BColor : enum (Blue,
      Black, Brown)
```

An enumerated type BColor is declared with values Blue, Black, and Brown.

String Comparisons

`"Angela" < "Beth"`	The string `Angela` comes before the string `Beth` because A comes before B.
`"21.0" not= "21"`	These two strings cannot be equal because their lengths differ.

String Catenation

`"dist" + "rust" = "distrust"`	The strings `"dist"` and `"rust"` are catenated to form the string `"distrust"`.

Substrings

```
const Language := "Turing"
Language (1) = "T"
Language (*) = "g"
Language (3 .. *) = "ring"
```

`Language` is a constant string. Its first character is extracted by writing `Language (1)`. Its last character is extracted by `Language (*)`. Its third through last characters are extracted by `Language (3 .. *)`.

Files (See Chapter 9)

Declaring File Numbers

```
var NumFile : int
var ChFile : int
var LineFile : int
var OutFile : int
var X : real
var Ch : string
var Line : string
```

`NumFile`, `ChFile`, and `LineFile` are the numbers of input text files. `OutFile` is the number of an output text file.

Opening Files

```
open :NumFile, "NFILE", get
open :ChFile, "CFILE", get
open :LineFile, "LFILE", get
open :OutFile, "OFILE", put
```

The first three files are prepared for input.
The fourth file is prepared for output.

Reading and Writing Files

```
get : NumFile, X

get : ChFile, Ch : 1
get : LineFile, Line : *
```

The next number is read as a token from `NFILE`, skipping any white space.
The next single character is read from `CFILE`.
The next line is read from `LFILE`.

```
put : OutFile, "X=", X
```
X is written to `OFile`. Only as many characters as needed to represent X are written.

```
put "X=", X:9
```
X is displayed on the screen right-justified in a field of width 9.

```
put "X=", X:9:3
put "X=", X:9:3:2
```
X is displayed with width 9 and 3 fraction digits.
X is displayed with width 9, 3 fraction digits and 2 exponent digits.

Closing Files

```
close : NumFile
close : ChFile
close : LineFile
close : OutFile
```
Disconnects from each file.

End-of-File Function

```
open : NumFile, "NFILE", get
open : OutFile, "OFILE", put
loop
    exit when eof (NumFile)
    get : NumFile, X
    put : OutFile, X
end loop
```
File `NFILE` is prepared for input and file `OFILE` for output.
Each number value of file `NFILE` is written to a separate line of file `OFILE`.

Arrays: One-Dimensional (See Chapter 11)

Array Declaration

```
type IndexRange : 1 .. 10
type IntArray :
    array 1..10 of int
```
The data type `IntArray` describes an array with 10 integer elements.

```
var Cube, Count : IntArray
```
`Cube` and `Count` are arrays with this structure.

Array References

```
for I : 1 .. 10
    Cube(I) := I ** 3
end for
```
Saves I^3 in the `I`th element of array `Cube`.

```
if Cube(5) > 100 then
```
Compares `Cube[5]` to 100.

```
put Cube(1), " ", Cube(2)
```
Displays the first two entries of `Cube`.

Array Copy

```
Count := Cube
```
Copies contents of array `Cube` to array `Count`.

Maximum Length for Strings

```
type String10 : string (10)

var Name : String10
```
The data type `String10` describes a string whose maximum length is `10`.
`Name` is a string whose value can be at most 10 characters long.

Star Bound for Arrays

```
procedure Percent
    (var A : 1 .. * of real)
```
The data type of `A` is an array whose upper bound is determined by its actual parameter.

Star Maximum Length for Strings

```
procedure Nullify
    (var S : string (*))
```
The data type of `S` is a string whose maximum length is determined by its actual parameter.

Records (See Chapter 12)

Record Declaration

```
type Part :
    record
        ID : 1111..9999
        Quantity : int
        Price : real
    end record
var Nuts, Bolts : Part
```
A record type `Part` is declared with fields that can store two integers and a real number. `Nuts` and `Bolts` are record variables of type `Part`.

Record Reference

```
TotalCost := Nuts.Quantity
         * Nuts.Price
```
Multiplies two fields of `Nuts`.

```
put Bolts.ID
```
Prints `ID` field of `Bolts`.

Record Copy

```
Bolts := Nuts
```
Copies record `Nuts` to `Bolts`.

Bind Declaration

```
bind B to Bolts
put B.ID, " ", B.Price
```

B becomes a synonym for `Bolts`.
Prints two fields of `Bolts`.

Record Variant Declaration

```
const Truck := 1
const Plane := 2
type Kind : Truck .. Plane

type Transporter:
    union Which : Kind of
        label Truck :
            Whl : int
        label Plane :
            Eng : int
    end union

var Vehicle : Transporter
```

A union type is declared. The variant for `Trucks` can store an integer giving the number of wheels.
The variant for `Planes` can store an integer giving the number of engines.

The union variable `Vehicle` has type `Transporter`.

Referencing a Record Variant

```
bind V to Vehicle
case V.Which of
    label Truck :
        put V.Whl, " wheels"
    label Plane :
        put V.Eng, "engines"
end case
```

Uses a case statement to display either the number of wheels on a `Truck` or the number of engines on a `Plane`.

Tag Statement

```
tag Vehicle, Truck
Vehicle.Whl := 4
```

Set the tag of `Vehicle` to be `Truck`. Any existing variant is destroyed. The `Whl` field is uninitialized and then has 4 assigned to it.

Arrays: Multidimensional (See Chapter 13)

Declaring Multidimensional Arrays

```
type Day : enum(Sun, Mon,
    Tues, Wed, Thu, Fri, Sat)

type Matrix :
    array 1..52, Day of real

var Sales : Matrix
```

`Matrix` describes a two-dimensional array with 52 rows (weeks of the year) and seven columns.

Sales is an array of this type and can store 364 real numbers.

Array References

```
put Sales(3, Monday)
```
Display the element of Sales for Monday of week 3.

```
for Week : 1 .. 52
    for Today : Day
        Sales(Week, Today)
            := 0.0
    end for
end for
```
Initialize each element of Sales to 0.

```
get Sales(1, Day.Sunday)
```
Read the value for the first Sunday into Sales.

Declaring Arrays of Records

```
type AElement :
    record
        Data : real
        Key : int
    end record
type DataArray :
    array 1..10 of AElement

var MyData : DataArray
```
DataArray is an array with ten elements of type AElement (a record). Each element has fields named Data and Key.

MyData is a variable of type DataArray.

Referencing an Array of Records

```
MyData(1).Data := 3.14159
MyData(10).Key := 9999
```
The real value 3.14159 is stored in the first Data field of array MyData. The value 9999 is stored in the last Key field.

Answers to Selected Self-Check Exercises

CHAPTER 1

SECTION 1.2

1. Contents: -27.2, 75.62
Memory cells: 998, 2

SECTION 1.5

1. Add A, B, and C. Store result in X.
Divide Y by Z. Store result in X.
Subtract B from C and then add A. Store result in D.
Add 1 to X. Store result back in X.

3. Machine language

SECTION 1.6

1. A compiler attempts to translate a source file into machine language. If there are syntax errors, the compiler generates error messages. If there are no errors, it creates an object file. Syntax errors occur when statements do not follow exactly the syntax rules of a language. Syntax errors are found in the source file.

CHAPTER 2

SECTION 2.1

1. Requirements specification, analysis, design, implementation, testing

SECTION 2.2

1. It is not a good idea to use a standard identifier as the name of a memory cell because the identifier then cannot be used for its intended purpose. The compiler does not allow the use of reserved words as memory cell names.

SECTION 2.3

1. Because the value of Pi will not change during program execution

3. Reserved words: put, const
  Standard identifiers:
  Valid identifiers: Bill, Rate, Start, XYZ123, ThisIsALongOne
  Invalid identifiers: Sue's, 123XYZ, Y=Z, Prog#2, "MaxScores"

SECTION 2.4

1. Enter two integers:
  M = 10   N = 21

3. My name is: Doe, Jane
  I live in Waterloo, Ontario and my postal code is N2L 3G1

SECTION 2.5

1. Missing close of comment (*/). The second example has an embedded comment, which is not allowed in Turing.

3.
```
var X, Y, Z : real

Y : = 15.0
Z : = -Y + 3.5
X : = Y + Z
put X, Y, Z
```

The reserved word var indicates the start of the variable declarations. The first line declares and reserves space in memory for three variables (X, Y, Z) of type real. The first assignment statement sets the variable Y to the value 15.0. The next statement sets the variable Z to minus the value of Y plus 3.5, which is -11.5. The next statement sets the variable X to the sum of Y and Z, which is 3.5. The next statement prints the values of X, Y, and Z (3.5, 15.0, and -11.5, respectively).

SECTION 2.6

1. 15, int   "XYZ", string   "*", string
  $, invalid   25.123, real   15., real
  -999, int   .123, real   "x", string
  'x', invalid   "9", string   "-5", string
  true, Boolean   "true", string

3. a. 3
  b. -3
  c. invalid – real operand used with mod
  d. -3.14159
  e. invalid – assignment of real expression to int variable
  f. 0.75
  g. invalid – real operand used with mod
  h. invalid – division by 0
  i. 3
  j. 3
  k. -3.0
  l. invalid assignment of real expression to int variable
  m. -3
  n. 0
  o. 1
  p. invalid – division by 0
  q. 3

5. a. 1
  b. −2
  d. 66.28318
  f. 2.5
  i. 5
  j. 2
  k. 2.5
  m. 16
  n. 2
  o. 0
  q. 5

7. a. X := 4.0 * A * C
  b. A := A * C
  c. I := Z − J
  d. K := 3 * (I + J)
  e. X := (5 * A) / (B * C)
  f. I := 5 * J * 3

SECTION 2.7

1. #−99#Bottles
  #−99##−99.00

3. −15.5640
  #−15.564
  ##−15.56
  ###−15.6
  ####−16
  #−15.564

SECTION 2.8

1. Put statements used to display prompts are placed before the get statements and are used in interactive programs. Put statements that echo data are placed after the get statements and are used in batch programs.

CHAPTER 3

SECTION 3.1

1. Inputs : Hours : real % Number of hours worked
            Rate : real % Hourly rate of pay
  Output : Gross : real % Gross salary
  Algorithm:
  1. Read hours worked and rate of pay.
  2. Compute gross salary.
  3. Print the gross salary.

SECTION 3.2

1. The algorithm needs to read separately the number of hours to be payed at the normal hourly rate (RegHours) and hours to be paid at overtime rate (OTHours); the formula used to compute the gross salary would also need to be modified.

SECTION 3.3

1. To allow one or more algorithm steps to be executed several times during a single run of the program

SECTION 3.4

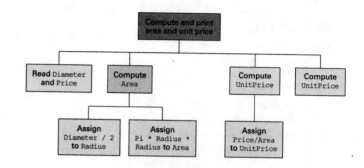

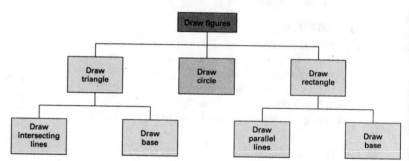

SECTION 3.5

1. Executing this program would display the message HI MOM vertically with three blank lines between words (first H, then I, and so on)

SECTION 3.7

1. Procedure parameters are used to pass information between the separate modules of a program and between the main program and its modules. Parameters make it easier for a procedure to be used by many different calling procedures, or other programs. Procedures with parameters are building blocks for constructing larger programs.

SECTION 3.8

1. a. sqrt (U + V) * (W ** 2)
  b. ln (X ** Y)
  c. sqrt ((X − Y) ** 2)
  d. abs ((X * Y) − (W / Z))

CHAPTER 4

SECTION 4.1

1. true, false, true, true

3.

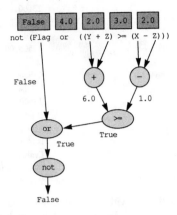

SECTION 4.2

1. a. Always   **b.** O.K.

SECTION 4.3

1. R245, A23B, A1c

SECTION 4.4

1. if X > Y then
        X : = X + 10.0
        put "X Bigger"
    else
        put "X Smaller"
        put "Y is ", Y
    end if

3. Y would always be printed.

5. The if statement, expression, simple expression, term, factor, variable, statement, and assignment syntax diagrams would be used to validate this if statement.

SECTION 4.5

1.

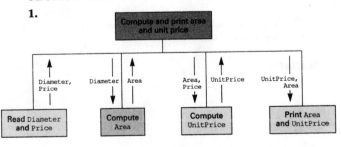

Area is not used by subproblem "Read Diameter and Price," Area is produced as an output from "Compute Area," and Area is used as an input by subproblems "Compute UnitPrice" and "Print Area and UnitPrice."

SECTION 4.6

1.

a. Case 1 (Both conditions are true. Data: MUD)

Program Statement	Ch1	Ch2	Ch3	AlphaFirst	Effect
	?	?	?	?	
put "Enter three..."					Prints prompt.
get Ch1, Ch2, Ch3	M	U	D		Reads data.
if Ch1 < Ch2 then					Is "M" < "U"? Value is true.
AlphaFirst := Ch1				M	"M" is first so far
if Ch3 < AlphaFirst then					Is "D" < "M"? Value is true.
AlphaFirst := Ch3				D	"D" is first.
put AlphaFirst ...					Prints D is the first letter...

b. Case 2 (First condition is true, second is false, Data: COT)

Program Statement	Ch1	Ch2	Ch3	AlphaFirst	Effect
	?	?	?	?	
put "Enter three..."					Prints prompt.
get Ch1, Ch2, Ch3	C	O	T		Reads data.
if Ch1 < Ch2 then					Is "C" < "O"? Value is true.
AlphaFirst := Ch1				C	"C" is first so far.
if Ch3 < AlphaFirst then					Is "T" < "C"? Value is false.
put AlphaFirst ...					Prints C is the first letter...

c. Case 3 (Both conditions are false. Data: TOP)

Program Statement	Ch1	Ch2	Ch3	AlphaFirst	Effect
	?	?	?	?	
put "Enter three. . ."					Prints prompt.
get Ch1, Ch2, Ch3	T	O	P		Reads data.
if Ch1 < Ch2 then					Is "T" < "O"? Value is false.
AlphaFirst := Ch2				O	"O" is first so far.
if Ch3 < AlphaFirst then					Is "P" < "O"? Value is false.
put AlphaFirst. . .					Prints O is the first letter...

Both conditions evaluate to false if all three letters are the same.

3. a. (Hours = 30.0, Rate = 5.00)

Program Statement	Hours ?	Rate ?	Gross ?	Net ?	Effect
put "This program..."					Print
put "An amount..."					instructions.
put "Hours worked"					Print prompt.
get Hours	30.0				Read Hours.
put "Hourly rate"					Print prompt.
get Rate		5.00			Read Rate.
Gross := Hours * Rate			150.0		Gross is 150.
if Gross > TaxBracket					Is 150 > 100?
then					Value is true.
Net := Gross - Tax				125.0	Net is 125.
put "Gross salary..."					Print 150.00.
put "Net salary..."					Print 125.00.

b. Hours = 20.0, Rate = 4.00)

Program Statement	Hours ?	Rate ?	Gross ?	Net ?	Effect
put "This program..."					Print
put "An amount..."					instructions.
put "Hours worked"					Print prompt.
read Hours	20.0				Read Hours.
put "Hourly rate"					Print prompt.
get Rate		4.00			Read Rate.
Gross := Hours * Rate			80.0		Gross is 80.
if Gross > TaxBracket					Is 80 > 100?
then					Value is false.
Net := Gross				80.0	Net is 80.
put "Gross salary..."					Print 80.00.
put "Net salary..."					Print 80.00.

SECTION 4.7

1.

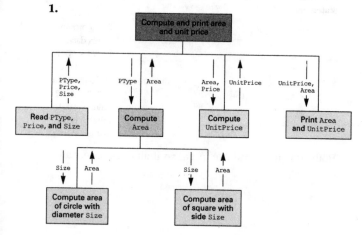

SECTION 4.8

1.

Statement Part	Salary 13500.00	Tax ?	Effect
if Salary < 0.0			13500.00 < 0.00 is false.
elsif Salary < 1500.00			13500.00 < 1500.00 is false.
elsif Salary < 3000.00			13500.00 < 3000.00 is false.
elsif Salary < 5000.00			13500.00 < 5000.00 is false.
elsif Salary < 8000.00			13500.00 < 8000.00 is false.
elsif Salary <= 15000.00			13500.00 <= 15000.00 is true.
Tax := (Salary - 8000.00)			Evaluates to 5500.00.
* 0.25			Evaluates to 1375.00.
+ 1425.00		2800.00	Tax is 2800.00.

3. a. True with and without short-circuit evaluation.
b. True with short-circuit evaluation—a division by zero error results without short-circuit evaluation.

SECTION 4.9

1.
```
if X = 0 then
    put "X is zero"
elseif X = 1 then
    put "X is one"
elsif X = 2 then
    put "X is two"
end if
```

3. Standard Pascal requires that every possible value of the selector variable must appear as a case label.

CHAPTER 5

SECTION 5.1

1. The loop will be executed three times.
Output:
```
        9
        81
        6561
```

3. The loop will execute forever if the last statement in the loop body is omitted.

SECTION 5.2

1. 5
25
125
625

SECTION 5.3

1. 0

3. a. Output with data value of 9.45:

```
Enter initial distance
between worm and apple in inches> 9.45
The distance is 9.45
The distance is 5.95

The last distance before the worm enters
the apple is 2.45
```

b. Output with data value of 9.45 and the order of statements in the loop body reversed;

```
Enter initial distance
between worm and apple in inches> 9.45
The distance is 5.95
The distance is 2.45

The last distance before the worm enters
the apple is 2.45
```

SECTION 5.4

1. This problem is similar to the example in the text. Because the first power of N that is to be displayed is for Power = 0, the initial value of Power should be 1.

SECTION 5.5

1. a.

Program Statement	I ?	J ?	Effect
J := 10		10	Set J to 10.
for I : 1 .. 5	1		Initialize I and 1.
put I, " ",J			Display 1 and 10.
J := J - 2		8	Assign 10 - 2 to J.
increment and test I	2		2 <= 5 is true.
put I, " ", J			Display 2 and 8
J := J - 2		6	Assign 8 - 2 to J.
increment and test I	3		3 <= 5 is true.
put I, " ", J			Display 3 and 6.
J := J - 2		4	Assign 6 - 2 to J.
increment and test I	4		4 <= 5 is true.
put I, " ", J			Display 4 and 4.
J := J - 2		2	Assign 4 - 2 to J.
increment and test I	5		5 <= 5 is true.
put I, " ", J			Display 5 and 2.
J := J - 2		0	Assign 2 - 2 to J.
increment and test I	?		Exit loop.

b.
```
J := 10
for I : 0 .. 4
    put I + I, " ", J
    J := J - 2
end for
```

3. a. for Celsius : -10 .. 10
b. for decreasing Celsius : 100 .. 1
c. for Celsius : 15 .. 50
d. for decreasing Celsius : 50 .. -75

SECTION 5.6

1. Output: 10
20
30
40
50
60
70
80
90

```
% Done as a for statement
Num := 10;
for Count : 1 .. 9
    put Num
    Num := Num + 10
end for
```

3. A loop statement would be used instead of a for statement when you do not know in advance the exact number of times the loop will be executed.

SECTION 5.7

1. a.
```
*
**
***
****
*****
```
b.
```
***
***
***
***
***
```

SECTION 5.8

1.
```
Count := 0;
loop
    exit when Count > N
    put "Count = ", Count :1
    Sum := Sum + Count
    Count := Count + 1
    put "Sum = ", Sum :1
end loop
```

CHAPTER 6

SECTION 6.1

1. Without the dot-dot, each `put` will blank out the right part of the line, so generally there will be few stars to the right.

3. Use the `rand` function.
Use the `rand` function and multiply the results by 20.0.
Use the `rand` function, multiply the results by 20.0, then add 20.0.

SECTION 6.2

1. Add in a loop around the call to `RandomStars` as follows:

```
loop
    RandomStars

    delay (3000)
    cls
end loop
```

3. `locate (maxrow div 2, maxcol div 2)`
`put "X"`

5. Insert the lines:

```
varC : int
randint (C, 1, maxcolor)
color (C)
put "*" ..
```

SECTION 6.3

1. Instead of:
`put Ball ..`

Use your name, for example:
`put "Chrysanne" ..`

Then instead of replacing the ball with a dot, "erase" the name with blanks:
`put "          " ..`

SECTION 6.4

1. `get` always waits until Return is pressed.
`getch` reads a single character without waiting for Return to be pressed.

3. Add in the following declarations:
```
const UpLeftKey := "7"
const UpRightKey := "9"
const DownLeftKey := "1"
const DownRightKey := "3"
```

Add to top of `if` statement new statements like the following:
```
if KeyStroke = UpLeftKey and
        Row > 1 and Col > 1 then
    RowMove := -1 % Bat upward
    ColMove := -1 % Bat to left

elsif [...]
```

SECTION 6.5

1. `drawdot (2, maxx, green)`

3.
```
const C := 1
var X, Y : int
randint (X, 0, maxx)
randint (Y, 0, maxy)

drawline (X, Y, X+100, Y, C)
drawline (X, Y, X+50, Y+100, C)
drawline (X+100, Y, X+50, Y+100, C)
```

SECTION 6.6

1. This is a trick question! The `"0"` on the horizontal axis was overwritten by the `"0.0"` on the graph.

3. The vertical lines are drawn by:
`drawline (X, 0, X, Y, LineColor)`.

The `Y` part causes the lines to stop at the curve. Therefore, to make the lines go to the top of the screen, use:

`drawline (X, 0, X, maxy, LineColor)`

To go nearly to the top, but leave room for the titles, do something like:

```
const RoomForTitles := 15
[...]
drawline (X, 0, maxy-RoomForTitles,
    LineColor)
```

SECTION 6.7

1.
```
const X := maxx div 2
const Y := maxy div 2

const Radius := 50
const Thickness := 50

% Draw the donut
drawfilloval (X, Y, Radius+Thickness,
    Radius+Thickness, brown)

% Draw the hole
drawfilloval (X, Y, Radius, Radius, 0)
```

3.
```
drawbox (X1, Y1, X2, Y2, C)
drawbox (X1+1, Y1+1, X2-1, Y2-1, C)
drawbox (X1+2, Y1+2, X2-2, Y2-2, C)

drawfillbox (X1, Y1, X2, Y2, C)
drawfillbox (X1+3, Y1+3, X2-3, Y2-3, 0)
```

SECTION 6.8

1. The ball would go partially off the screen before it bounces back.

CHAPTER 7

SECTION 7.1

1. Parameters allow information to be exchanged between a procedure and its caller.

3. a. Pre : N contains some initial integer value.
Post : The value of N cubed is displayed.

  b. Pre : X and Y contain initial values.
Post : Displays absolute value of the difference of X and Y.

SECTION 7.2

1. The new if statement would not allow FindTax to be written as a function because it contains put statements.

3. Pre : X and Y contain some initial real values.
Post : Returns the square root of the sum of the square of X and the square of Y.

SECTION 7.3

1.

Program Statement	ChangeDenom	ChangeNeeded	NumUnits	Effect
	5.0	5.56	?	
NumUnits := floor(ChangeNeeded/ChangeDenom)			1	Set NumUnits to 1.
ChangeNeeded := ChangeNeeded - (NumUnits * ChangeDenom)		0.56		Set ChangeNeeded to 0.56

3. a. Case 1 (Num1 = 8.0, Num2 = 0.0, Num3 = 6.0)

Program Statement	X	Y	Temp	Effect
	?	?	?	
Order (Num3, Num2) if X > Y then	6.0	10.0	?	Call Order. Is 6.0 > 10.0? Value is false.
Order (Num3, Num1) if X > Y then	6.0	8.0	?	Call Order. Is 6.0 > 8.0? Value is false.
Order (Num2, Num1) if X > Y then	10.0	8.0	?	Call Order. Is 10.0 > 8.0?
Temp := X			10.0	Set Temp to 10.0.
X := Y	8.0			Set X(Num2) to 8.0.
Y := Temp		10.0		Set Y(Num1) to 10.0.

  b. Effect of this sequence of calls is arrange the values stored in Num1, Num2, and Num3 from largest to smallest.

SECTION 7.4

1.

Actual Parameter	Formal Parameter	Description
M	A	int, value
MaxInt	B	int, value
Y	C	real, variable
X	D	real, variable
Next	E	string, variable
35	A	int, value
M * 10	B	int, value
Y	C	real, variable
X	D	real, variable
Next	E	string, variable

3. a. Type real of Z does not correspond to type int of formal parameter X.

  b. Procedure call is correct.

  c. Procedure call is correct.

  d. Type int of M does not correspond to type real of formal parameter A.

  e. 25.0 and 15.0 cannot correspond to variable parameters.

  f. Procedure call is correct.

  g. Parameter names A and B have not been declared in the main program.

  h. Procedure call is correct.

  i. Expression (X + Y) and (Y - Z) may not correspond to a variable parameter.

  j. Type real of actual parameter X does not correspond with type int of formal parameter X.

  k. Four actual parameters are one too many for three formal parameters.

  l. Procedure call is correct.

SECTION 7.5

1. FindSum contains calls to get and put

3.

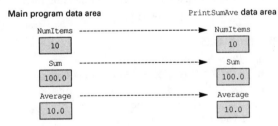

SECTION 7.6

1. The declaration of an identifier can be moved within the local scope, such as a loop statement, within which the identifier applies, so that the identifier will not be accidentally used when it is not valid.

SECTION 7.7

1. Variable `Temp` is a local declaration in procedure `Order`.

3. `Z` is not declared in the main program.

SECTION 7.8

1. Data requirements for `DisplayTran`:

Input Parameters

```
TranType : string   % Transaction type
Amount : real       % Amount of transaction
CurBal : real       % Current balance
```

Algorithm
```
if TranType is
"C" : display Amount of check and CurBal;
                check for overdraft.
"D" : display Amount of deposit and CurBal.
"O" : do nothing.
end if
```

SECTION 7.10

1. `Mystery(4, 3) = 4 * (4 * Mystery(4, 1))`
`Mystery` computes the value of M^N.

CHAPTER 8

SECTION 8.1

1. Valid constants: `MinInt, MaxLetter`
`MaxSize, MinSize`

SECTION 8.2

1. A cancellation error might occur when a very large number is added to a very small number and the resulting sum contains more significant digits than the computer can store. Representational errors result when the computer cannot represent a number exactly (e.g., the decimal fraction 0.1 is a repeating fraction using base 2 representation).

SECTION 8.3

1. a. `(X > Y) or (X = 15)`
  b. `((X > Y) or (X = 15)) and (Z not= 7.5)`
  c. `(X = 15) and ((Z not= 7.5) or (X > Y))`
  d. `not Flag and (X not= 15.7)`
  e. `Flag or (X > 8)`

SECTION 8.4

1. a. 3
  b. 3
  c. Invalid
  d. C
  e. c

  f. 1
  g. 9
  h. Invalid
  i. F

3. a. true
  b. false
  c. false
  d. true
  e. true

SECTION 8.5

1. a. Legal
  b. Illegal
  c. Legal
  d. Illegal
  e. Legal
  f. Illegal
  g. Legal
  h. Illegal
  i. Illegal
  j. Legal

SECTION 8.6

1. a. K has not been declared.
  b. Legal
  c. Legal
  d. Legal
  e. I/J must be in the range 0 .. 10. J must not be 0.
  f. Legal
  g. K has not been declared.

SECTION 8.7

1. a. 1
  b. 4
  c. false
  d. `Day.Thursday`
  e. `Day.Thursday` (i.e., Today)
  f. `Day.Friday`
  g. `Day.Wednesday`
  h. true
  i. Undefined
  j. 6

SECTION 8.9

1. Output with Epsilon = 0.00001:

Initial guess for a root> 0.0
The approximate root is 9.9999237061E-01
The function value is 5.8207660913E-11
18 guesses made

CHAPTER 9

SECTION 9.1

1. The put causes one blank line. The skip causes another.

SECTION 9.2

1. We usually want to read in a whole line of text in interactive programming and are not interested in just a few characters of it.
3. Exit the loop when length (Line) is 0.

SECTION 9.3

1. You get a permanent copy of the data.
You can display the data on the screen or on a printer. The data file can now be used as input to another program.

SECTION 9.4

a. N is 123. X is 3.145. S is XYZ.
b. N is 123. X is 3.145. S is XYZ.
c. N is 123. X is 3.145. S is 35.
d. N is 123. S is 3.145 X is uninitialized.
e. X is 123. S is 3.145. N will cause an attempt to read a non-numeric.
f. S is 123. N will cause an attempt to read a real value into an int variable.
g. S is XYZ. X is 35. N will cause an attempt to read a non-numeric.
h. N is 123. X is 3.145. S is Z. Attempt to read past end-of-file.
i. N is 123. X is 3.145. S is Z. Attempt to read past end-of-file.

SECTION 9.5

1. None.

SECTION 9.6

1. The program would attempt to read past the end of the data.

CHAPTER 10

SECTION 10.1

1. The systems analyst interacts with program users to determine the specifications for software that will meet the users' needs. The librarian interacts with the members of the programming team to monitor the status and the location of each module during the software development process.

SECTION 10.2

1. The six phases of the software life-cycle are (1) requirements specifications, (2) analysis, (3) design, (4) implementation, (5) testing and validation, and (6) operation and maintenance.

The last phase, operations and maintenance, lasts the longest.

SECTION 10.3

1. The procedure's physical location in the computing system must be known, along with a precise description of its interface.

SECTION 10.4

1. a. real: prefix -, +, -, *, /, div, mod, rem, **, <, >, =, <=, >=, not= ceil, floor, round, abs, arctan, arctand, cos, cosd, exp, ln, sin, sind, sqrt, rand
   b. int: prefix -, +, -, *, /, div, mod, rem, **, <, >, =, <=, >=, not= abs, randint,
   c. string: +, index, length, repeat
   d. boolean: not, and, or

SECTION 10.5

1. An ADT specification section might be a long comment that contains a description of the structure of the data type and its operator interfaces. The ADT implementation section would consist of the type and the procedure declarations that must be imported by a client program using the ADT.

SECTION 10.6

1. Test data used during white box testing are designed to exercise every logic path within the given code segment or procedure. A procedure interface error would not be discovered until after the procedure has become part of a larger module or complete program and has been called at least once.

SECTION 10.7

1. a.
```
% Invariant:
% No N has been read satisfying the condition:
% MinN <= N <= MaxN.
```

Use the following assertion after the loop:

```
% Assert:
% MinN <= N <= MaxN or
% MinN > MaxN and N is not defined
```

CHAPTER 11

SECTION 11.1

1. X3 is a simple variable, whereas X(3) refers to the third element of the array named X.

3. a. Invalid array
   b. Invalid array
   c. Invalid array
   d. `var RealArray: array -5..5 of real`
   e. Invalid array
   f. Invalid array
   g. `var DayArray : array Day of real`

SECTION 11.2

1. No

3. a. `X(3) := 7.0`
   b. `X(1) := X(5)`
   c. `X(5) := X(4) - X(1)`
   d. `X(6) := X(6) + 2`
   e.
```
Sum := 0
for I : 1 .. 5
    Sum := Sum + X(I)
end for
```
   f.
```
for I : 1 .. 6
    AnswerArray(I) := X(I) * 2
end for
```
   g.
```
I := 2
loop
    exit when I > 8
    put X(I) : 8 ..
    I := I + 2
end loop
```

SECTION 11.3

1. The user will be continually prompted to choose a category until a valid one is entered.

SECTION 11.4

1. It is better to pass the entire array of data rather than individual elements if several elements of the array are being manipulated by a procedure.

3. No.

SECTION 11.5

1. The loop that calls `EnterInt` is exited when `MaxSize` is passed.

3. We don't know in advance how many data items will be read in.

SECTION 11.6

1. a. An array of strings with subscripts of 1 to 20.
   b. An array of Boolean type values with 10 elements and subscripts of the integers 48 through 57.
   c. An array of real numbers with 11 elements and subscripts of the integers –5 to 5.

3. Program Cryptogram checks to see that a letter is in the set `"A" .. "Z"` before encoding it. Because commas and blanks are not members of this set, they are not encoded.

5. Use the `getch` function.

SECTION 11.7

1. The length of the string must be less than or equal to the maximum length specified.

3. `var MyString : string`

SECTION 11.8

1. Date would be the empty string.

SECTION 11.9

1. The inner for-loop invariant says that `IndexOfMin` contains the subscript of the smallest array element found so far in the unsorted portion of the array.

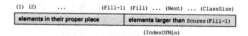

3.

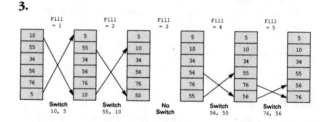

Fifteen comparisons and four exchanges were made.

SECTION 11.10

1. a. put executes N * N times; $O(N^2)$
   b. put executes N * 2 times $O(N)$
   c. put executes $(N + (N – 1) + (N – 2) + ... + 2 + 1)$ times; $O(N^2)$

CHAPTER 12

SECTION 12.1

1. ```
const StrLength := 20

type StringType : array 1.. StrLength of string
type Part : record
                PartNum : int
                Name : StringType
                Quantity : int
                Price : real
            end record
```

## SECTION 12.2

1. ```
type ExamStats : record
                Low, High : 1..100
                Average, StandardDev : real
            end record

var Exam1, Exam2, : ExamStats
```

This program segment prints the statistics for Exam1, copies Exam1 into Exam2, modifies the High field of Exam2, and finally prints new statistics for Exam2.

SECTION 12.3

1. The program segment initializes two employee records (MyEmp and YourEmp); stores values for ID and Name in each; checks for duplicate Name and ID; checks for different names with same ID; and stores the Name fields from the two records in string variables if the records are unique. For the two records shown, the output would be

```
Jennie Moss        ***** Jackie Moss
```

MyEmp and YourEmp must be of type Employee; Name1 and Name2 must be of type StringType.

SECTION 12.4

1. NewAddress must be type Address.

SECTION 12.5

1. bind var H to NewEmp.Home

SECTION 12.6

1. ```
bind F to Boss.Family
case F.MS of
    label MaritalStatus.Married:
        put Boss.Family.SpouseName
    label:
        put "Not married"
end case
```

# CHAPTER 13

## SECTION 13.1

1. ```
type ThreeDimArray : array ord("A") ..
                           ord("B"),
                           1 .. 10,
                           Day of real
```

An array of this type can hold 140 elements (2 * 10 * 7).

SECTION 13.2

1. ```
const Math1 := 1
const Algebra := 2
const Geometry := 3
const Algebra2 := 4
const Trigonometry := 5
const Calculus := 6
type MathSubject : Math1 .. Calculus
type GradeLevel : 10 .. 12
const Male := 0
const Female := 1
type Sex : Male .. Female

type MathClassArray : array Sex of int,
MathSubject, GradeLevel
```

This array would have 36 elements (6 * 3 * 2).

## SECTION 13.3

1. TempYear is needed in EnterSales to enable use of procedure EnterInt. This is because EnterInt has an int as its formal variable argument and Sales.First is type YearRange. A complication error would result from trying to read Sales.First directly.

## SECTION 13.4

1. **a.** 1
   **d.** Austin, Tracy
   **f.** D

3. It takes the same amount of space to store an array of records as it does to store parallel arrays.

## SECTION 13.5

1. **c.** 80AJoe Costa
   **d.** 3
   **h.** c
   **i.** Joe Costa

3. The scores will no longer be matched with the correct names.
```

CHAPTER 14

SECTION 14.1

1.

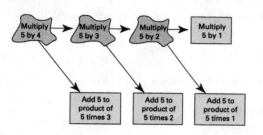

SECTION 14.2

1. The actual parameter in the recursive call `Palindrome(N-1)` is an expression and must, therefore, correspond to a formal parameter that is a value parameter.

3.

					Result
Multiply (5, 4)	M	5	N	4	?
Multiply (5, 3)	M	5,5	N	4,3	?
Multiply (5, 2)	M	5,5,5	N	4,3,2	?
Multiply (5, 1)	M	5,5,5,5	N	4,3,2,1	?
return from (5, 1)	M	5,5,5	N	4,3,2	5
return from (5, 2)	M	5,5	N	4,3	10
return from (5, 3)	M	5	N	4	15
return from (5, 4)	M		N		20

SECTION 14.3

1.
```
function PowerRaiser (Base, Power : int) : int
  if Power = 1 then
    result Base
  else
    result Power * PowerRaiser(Base, Power-1)
  end PowerRaiser
```

3. The recursion would go on forever when N is 2, a recursive call to `Fibonacci(0)` results. This causes calls to `Fibonacci(-1)`, `Fibonacci(-2)`, and so on.

SECTION 14.4

1.

X is 5, 8, 10, 1.	X is 5, 8, 1, 10.	X is 5, 1, 8, 10.
N is 4.	N is 3	N is 2.
X becomes 5, 8, 1, 10.	X becomes 5, 1, 8, 10.	X becomes 1, 5, 8, 10.
SelectSort (X, 3)	SelectSort (X, 2)	SelectSort (X, 1)

For the last frame (not shown) N is 1, so an immediate return occurs.

SECTION 14.5

1. $2^6 - 1$, or 63

SECTION 14.6

1.

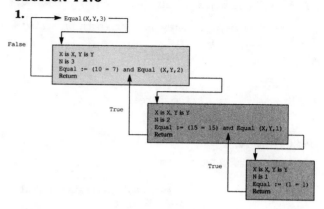

$Equal := (X(3) = Y(3)$ and $(X(2) = Y(2)$ and $(X(1) = Y(1)$

SECTION 14.7

1. `BlobCount (1,1) Grid (X, Y)` is empty, so 0 is returned.

`BlobCount (1,2)` has the value of the expression:

```
1 + BlobCount (0,3) + BlobCount (1,3) +
  BlobCount (2,3) + BlobCount (2,2) +
  BlobCount (2,1) + BlobCount (1,1) +
  BlobCount (0,1) ) BlobCount (0,2)
```

An immediate return occurs with a value of 0 for all function designators except `BlobCount (2,1)`.

Index

int, 48. *See also* Integer
Integer, 33, 48. *See also* Data types
  division, 49, 359
    format, 358
    remainder, 49
Integrated circuits, 4
Integrated programming, 211
Integration testing, 464
Interactive graphics, 242
Interactive mode, 65
Invariant mode, 65
Invariant of loop, 468
Iteration, 87, 663, 667
Iterative approximations, 389

K

Keyboard, 9, 19, 39, 414
Keywords, 31, 33. *See also*
  Reserved words

L

Labels, 160, 566
Language standard, 26
Leading blanks, 64
Left associative, 54
Librarian, 447
Library, 144, 146
  function, 290
  procedural, 453
Life-cycle, 448
Line oriented, 409
Listing compiler, 70
Lists, parameter, 284
Literal, 40, 48
Load file, 18
Loader, 18
Local identifier, 102
Local variable stacks, 646
locate statement, 224, 225, 252
locatexy statement, 252, 253
log on, 20. *See also* Boot
Logarithm, 107
Logical complement, 119
Logical view, 455

Loop
  body, 172, 206
  boundaries, 213-214
  condition, 173, 182, 206
  control variable, 174
  counter-controlled, 182
  counting, 182, 206
  design, 185-186
  exit, 173, 180
  flag-controlled, 193
  generalizing, 179
  infinite, 175, 215
  initialization, 189
  invariant of, 467
  nested, 208, 588
  sentinel-controlled, 193
Lowercase, 32

M

Macintosh, 18, 66
Machine language, 14-16
Main memory, 6, 7, 10
Main program, 92, 95. *See also*
  Program body
Mainframes, 4, 6
Maintenance, 87, 449
Mantissa, 358
Mathematical formulas, 57
maxcol, 226
maxint, 48. *See also* Integer
maxrow, 226
maxx, 249, 250
maxy, 249, 250
Memory cells, 7, 8, 32. *See also*
  Variables
Memory cell address, 15
Menu-driven, 204, 593
Microcomputers, 4, 9
Minicomputers, 4
mod, 49, 50, 236, 359
Module, 329
Module dependency diagram, 461
Monitor, 9. *See also* Screen
Mouse, 9
MS-DOS, 20, 66

Multidimensional arrays, 582-591
Multiple-alternative decisions,
  149
Multiple declarations, 324, 330
Multiple operators, 54
Multiple statements, 130. *See also*
  if statement
Mutually exclusive conditions,
  153

N

Negation, 199
Nested
  if statement, 149
  loops, 208, 588
New-line character, 509. *See also*
  End-of-line character
Newton's method, 391
not, 118. *See also* Boolean
  operator
Numeric data types, 357-358
  inaccuracies, 360
  literal, 359
Numerical analysis, 389

O

Object file, 18
Off-by-one error, 213
Offset, 586
Operating systems, 19, 20
Operator precedence, 54, 199.
  See also Boolean operators
or, 124. *See also* Boolean opera-
  tors
ord, 369, 372. *See also* Ordinal
  function
Order of conditions, 152
Ordinal function, 369
Otherwise clause, 162
Output
  cursor, 225
  devices, 7, 9
  operations, 38
  parameters, 101, 304